T0321943

ARTIFICIAL INTELLIGENCE
From Beginning to Date

ARTIFICIAL INTELLIGENCE

From Beginning to Date

Zixing Cai

Central South University and Hunan ZIXING AI Academy, China

Lijue Liu

Central South University and Hunan ZIXING AI Academy, China

Baifan Chen

Central South University and Hunan ZIXING AI Academy, China

Yong Wang

Central South University, China

清華大学出版社
TSINGHUA UNIVERSITY PRESS

World Scientific

Published by

World Scientific Publishing Co. Pte. Ltd.

5 Toh Tuck Link, Singapore 596224

USA office: 27 Warren Street, Suite 401-402, Hackensack, NJ 07601

UK office: 57 Shelton Street, Covent Garden, London WC2H 9HE

Library of Congress Cataloging-in-Publication Data
Names: Cai, Zixing, 1938– author. | Liu, Lijue, author. | Chen, Baifan, author. |
  Wang, Yong, 1980, author.
Title: Artificial intelligence : from beginning to date / Zixing Cai, Lijue Liu, Baifan Chen,
  Yong Wang, Central South University, China.
Other titles: Ren gong zhi neng ji qi ying yong. English
Description: [Beijing] : Tsinghua University Press ; Singapore ; Hackensack :
  World Scientific, [2021] | English edition developed and updated from the Chinese work
  Artificial intelligence and its applications (Ren gong zhi neng ji qi ying yong). |
  Includes bibliographical references and index.
Identifiers: LCCN 2020034704 | ISBN 9789811223716 (hardcover) |
  ISBN 9789811223723 (ebook for institutions) | ISBN 9789811223730 (ebook for individuals)
Subjects: LCSH: Artificial intelligence--History.
Classification: LCC Q334 .C3518 2021 | DDC 006.309--dc23
LC record available at https://lccn.loc.gov/2020034704

British Library Cataloguing-in-Publication Data
A catalogue record for this book is available from the British Library.

Artificial Intelligence: From Beginning to Date

Copyright © 2021 by World Scientific Publishing Co. Pte. Ltd. Under exclusive license by
Tsinghua University Press Limited.
The print edition is not for sale within the Mainland of China.

All rights reserved.

For photocopying of material in this volume, please pay a copying fee through the Copyright Clearance
Center, Inc., 222 Rosewood Drive, Danvers, MA 01923, USA. In this case permission to photocopy
is not required from the publisher.

For any available supplementary material, please visit
https://www.worldscientific.com/worldscibooks/10.1142/11921#t=suppl

Typeset by Stallion Press
Email: enquiries@stallionpress.com

Printed in Singapore

To my family Huan, Jingfeng, Qingbo, Yufeng, Xiaoxue
Tianyun, Andrew Tianyu, Grace Tianjiao, and Tianle

Zixing Cai

To my family Mengheng, Quqing, Yue, Yuliu

Lijue Liu

To my family Mars, Xunhao, and Xunzhi

Baifan Chen

To my family Yang, Qingche, and Qingtian

Yong Wang

Foreword

In May 1983, I went to Purdue University in the United States to study artificial intelligence under the direction of Professor K.S. Fu, a member of the National Academy of Engineering Sciences, an international pioneer in artificial intelligence, and the father of international pattern recognition. Under the advice and guidance of Academician K.S. Fu, Guangyou Xu, and I edited and wrote a book, *Artificial Intelligence and Its Applications*. It was published by Tsinghua University Press in 1987 and became the first published artificial intelligence book with independent intellectual property rights in China. This book has played a major role in promoting the spread and development of artificial intelligence in China in the past 35 years. I deeply miss and thank Professor Fu, Professor Wenjun Wu and Professor Tong Chang, and deeply thank to Dr. Jian Song and Professor Yanda Li.

As a frontier and interdisciplinary subject, artificial intelligence has been advancing with the times along with the progress of world society and the development of science and technology. It has made great progress in the past 60 years. In recent years, a new round of artificial intelligence research and entrepreneurial climax has emerged, pushing the development of artificial intelligence into a new era. New artificial intelligence algorithms represented by deep learning promote the widespread application of artificial intelligence, and the industrialization of artificial intelligence has also risen to new heights.

At present, there is a lack of monographs at home and abroad that fully reflect the latest developments in artificial intelligence. People hope to have such a book available. The book should not only have a novel system architecture, fully reflect the scientific and technological connotation of artificial intelligence, but also highlight the innovative development of artificial intelligence and guide its application. WSPC advised us to publish a new monograph on artificial intelligence at the right time. After reviewing and discussing our *Publication Proposal*, on the recommendation of AI experts such as Dr. A. Ng and Dr. J.H. Zheng, as well as the recommendation of IEEE Fellow Dr. YC Jin and IEEE Fellow Dr. L.C. Jiao, the publishers agreed to compile and publish a new artificial intelligence monograph named *Artificial Intelligence: From Beginning to Date*, and proposed a new architecture and related content.

This book covers a wide range of topics in artificial intelligence and has three characteristics. First, this book is a systematic and comprehensive book covering the core technologies of artificial intelligence, including the basic theories and techniques of "traditional" artificial intelligence, and the basic principles and methods of computational intelligence. Secondly, this book pays attention to innovation, focusing on the introduction of machine learning, especially deep learning technology and other artificial intelligence learning methods that have been widely used in recent years. Third, the theory and practice of this book are highly integrated. There are theories, techniques, methods, and many examples of deep learning applications that can help readers understand the theory of artificial intelligence and its application development.

This book is divided into three parts, following the introductory Chapter 1, which describes the definition, classification, origin, and development of artificial intelligence, introduces the research objectives and main contents of artificial intelligence, and lists the research and application fields of artificial intelligence. The first part is knowledge-based artificial intelligence, including Chapters 2 to 4; Chapters 2 and 3 study the knowledge representation method and search inference technology of artificial intelligence, and Chapter 4 discusses knowledge-based machine learning. Part 2 is data-based artificial intelligence, including Chapters 5 to 7; Chapters 5 and 6 introduce neural computing and evolutionary computing, respectively, and Chapter 7 discusses data-based machine learning. Part 3 contains application examples of artificial intelligence, including Chapters 8 to 11, elaborating on the important application areas of artificial intelligence in each of the following: expert system, intelligent planning, intelligent perception (including pattern recognition and speech recognition), and natural language processing, etc., with special attention being paid to introduce the application of deep learning in various related fields. The last chapter, Chapter 12, is the prospect of artificial intelligence, involving the impact of artificial intelligence on humans, the deep integration of artificial intelligence technology, and the industrialization of artificial intelligence. This book is a practical guide for artificial intelligence research and development personnel, and a valuable reference book for undergraduate and graduate students to learn artificial intelligence.

In the process of writing this book, we have referred to hundreds of references, citing some of their materials, so that this book can draw on the strengths of each family, more comprehensively reflecting the latest developments in various fields of artificial intelligence. In Part III, each chapter focuses on X.A. Bao, Siyu Guo, J. Johnson, Fei-Fei Li, L.J. Li, J.D. Lu, A.Y. Ng, D. Wu, as well as Z.H. Zhou, etc. in deep learning application research examples. Their works or discussions with them have provided rich nutrition for this book, which has greatly benefited us. We express our heartfelt thanks to them. We also wish to sincerely thank Dr. A. Ng and Dr. JH Zheng and other experts for their important suggestions on the content organization of this book, as well as IEEE Fellow Dr. Y.C Jin and IEEE Fellow Dr. L.C. Jiao, who strongly recommend the topic selection of this book. Special thanks to Dr. J.F. Cai for his strong support and help in the work of this book.

We sincerely thank the relevant leaders, experts, and editors from Central South University, Hunan ZIXING Academy of Artificial Intelligence, Tsinghua University Press, and WSPC. Without their support and encouragement, wisdom and talent, hard work and vigorous cooperation, this book could not have been made available to the readers as quickly.

The writing of this book is presided over and drafted by Zixing Cai. The division of tasks for each chapter is as follows: Chapter 1–5, Chapter 8–9, and Chapter 11–12 by Zixing Cai, Chapter 6 by Yong Wang, Chapter 7 by Lijue Liu, and Chapter 10 by Baifan Chen. For a long time, the three young authors, Dr. Wang, Dr. Liu, and Dr. Chen, were all core members of my research team, and they have emerged in the field of artificial intelligence research and education. Due to our limited knowledge and the rapid development of artificial intelligence in recent years, we are not familiar enough with the latest developments in some areas of artificial intelligence; therefore, shortcomings are inevitable. We sincerely hope that experts and readers will not hesitate to provide valuable feedback.

Zixing Cai
Deyi Garden, E'yang Mountain, Changsha, China
March 21, 2021

Contents

Part 3:   Application Examples of Artificial Intelligence   301

Chapter 8.   Expert System   303

List of Tables

List of Figures

About the Authors

Zixing Cai, IEEE Fellow and IEEE Life Fellow, Fellow of the International Academy of Navigation and Motion Control, CAAI Fellow, United Nations Expert (UNIDO), Professor and Doctoral Supervisor of the School of Information Science and Engineering, Central South University, Chief Scientist of Hunan ZIXING Academy of Artificial Intelligence. He has served as the Vice President of the Chinese Association for Artificial Intelligence (CAAI) and Founding Director of the Intelligent Robotics Professional Committee of CAAI, Honorary Chairman of Hunan Society of Artificial Intelligence, Director of Chinese Association of Automation (CAA) and member of Intelligent Automation Professional Committee of CAA, Member of the Artificial Intelligence and Pattern Recognition Professional Committee of Chinese Computer Federation (CCF), Member of the Evaluation Committee of the IEEE Computational Intelligence Society (CIS), and Member of the IEEE CIS Evolutionary Computing Technology Committee. Prof Cai also served as an Adjunct Professor at Rensselaer Polytechnic Institute (RPI), St. Petersburg Technical University, Technical University of Denmark, Peking University, National University of Defense Technology, Beijing University of Aeronautics and Astronautics, Beijing University of Posts and Telecommunications, etc., and also served as a Visiting Researcher at the Institute of Automation, Chinese Academy of Sciences, St. Petersburg Automation and Informatics Institute, Russian Academy of Sciences and so on. Prof Cai is one of the academic leaders in the fields of artificial intelligence, intelligent control and robotics in China. He is known as "the first person in artificial intelligence education in China", "founder of the Chinese intelligent robotics discipline" and "founder of Chinese intelligent control". He has written and published more than 50 monographs/textbooks, and published more than 1,000 papers, which have been cited tens of thousands of times. He has presided over eight national quality engineering projects of the Ministry of Education, China, including national quality courses, quality resource sharing courses, and national teaching teams.

Lijue Liu, Associate Professor, Department of Artificial Intelligence, School of Automation, Central South University. She obtained a doctorate degree in computer application technology from Central South University in 2016. She has participated in five books including *Artificial Intelligence and Its Applications (5th and 6th Edition)*, and has written and participated in more than ten research projects. She has authored more than 20 papers and holds five patents. Her current research involves intelligent processing of medical data, artificial intelligence, computational intelligence, and machine learning. She is the deputy dean of the Hunan ZIXING Academy of Artificial Intelligence, the executive director of the Guangxi Association for Artificial Intelligence, a member of the Chinese Association for Artificial Intelligence, a lecturer of the national-level excellent course "Artificial Intelligence" and a national-level video open class "Artificial Intelligence PK Human Intelligence" and member of the national teaching team of the National Intelligent Basic Series Courses.

Baifan Chen, Associate Professor, Department of Artificial Intelligence, School of Automation, Central South University, Deputy Dean of Hunan ZIXING Academy of Artificial Intelligence, Deputy Secretary-General of Hunan Association for Artificial Intelligence, IEEE Member and CAAI Member. She received a master's degree in pattern recognition and intelligent systems and a doctorate in computer application technology from Central South University in 2004 and 2009, respectively. In 2015, she served as a visiting scholar in the NetBot laboratory of Texas A & M University. She is a member of the national teaching team of the "Basic Series Course of Intelligent Science", the lecturer of the "Artificial Intelligence" boutique course of the Ministry of Education, and the national "Twelfth Five-Year" planning textbook *Artificial Intelligence and Its Application*. Her current research interests include artificial intelligence, mobile robots, and computer vision.

Yong Wang received a Ph.D. degree in control science and engineering from the Central South University, Changsha, China, in 2011. He is a Professor with the School of Automation, Central South University, Changsha, China. His current research interests include intelligent optimization and learning and its applications. He has been the principal investigator of four National Natural Science Foundation of China (NSFC) projects, and has published 47 international journal papers including 30 IEEE Transactions papers. In addition, he was a recipient of the Cheung Kong Young Scholar by Ministry of Education in 2018, and a Highly Cited Researcher in computer science by Clarivate Analytics in 2017 and 2018. He is currently serving as an Associate Editor for *the IEEE Transactions on Evolutionary Computation* and *Swarm and Evolutionary Computation*.

Introduction

Sitting at my computer in the study, I started writing a new book on artificial intelligence. The study faces the Goose-Sheep Mountain, a well-known hill. Legend has it that the mountain used to be deserted thousands of years ago and that it was uninhabited. One day, several immortals traveled together to this point, and they started to value the blessings of the mountain and live there. They opened new channels for water diversion, paved roads along the slopes, planted the arable land, harvested melons and fruits, raised geese and sheep, refined elixir, and were happy living there. Year after year, heaven rewards the diligent; the barren mountains here have become green mountains, melons and fruits, and the mountains are full of geese and sheep. Many people have migrated and settled around the mountain from other places and have become residents of this mountain, living a stable farming life. People call the mountain the Goose-Sheep (E'yang) Mountain. Later, the E'yang Mountain became famous all over the country and became one of China's 72 blessed places. The canals, roads, and medicines mentioned in the story belong to the category "artificial products" according to the modern viewpoint, i.e., artificial rivers, artificial roads, and artificial medicines.

Since ancient times, human beings have had the concept and practice of "artifacts". The canals dug by humans are artificial rivers called canals and are different from natural rivers; in comparison with natural satellites, humans have manufactured and launched countless artificial satellites; in comparison with natural fibers, humans have invented artificial fibers such as velvet and polyester fleece; in comparison with natural hearts, natural babies and natural limbs, humans have created artificial artifacts such as artificial hearts, test-tube babies, and artificial limbs. Now, different from natural intelligence (such as human intelligence), a new kind of "artifact" has emerged — Artificial Intelligence (AI).

What exactly is artificial intelligence, how to understand artificial intelligence, what is artificial intelligence studying, what is the theoretical basis of artificial intelligence, what magical powers does artificial intelligence have, in which fields can it benefit human beings, how does artificial intelligence affect human beings, etc.? All of these questions are researched and answered by artificial intelligence disciplines. This book intends to discuss these issues one by one.

This chapter focuses on the definition and development of artificial intelligence, the classification of artificial intelligence systems, the research goals and content of artificial intelligence, the research methods and technologies, and the research areas and application areas of artificial intelligence. It then introduces the main contents and layout of this book.

1.1   Definition and Development of Artificial Intelligence

Since 1936, A. M. Turing and others have proposed some ideas and concepts of artificial intelligence [42]. From its birth in 1956, the subject of artificial intelligence has made great progress for more than 60 years. It has attracted unprecedented attention from scholars of many disciplines and different professional backgrounds, as well as the governments and entrepreneurs of various countries, and has become a cutting-edge science with an increasingly perfect theoretical basis, an increasingly large range of applications and a wide cross-section. With the progress of international society and the development of science and technology, artificial intelligence keeps pace with the times and makes new progress. In recent years, a new wave of development and application of artificial intelligence has emerged. In the past decade, the development of modern information technology, especially computer technology, big data, and network technology, has greatly improved the capacity, speed, and quality of information processing. It is capable of processing massive data, performing rapid information processing, and implementing software functions and hardware that have made tremendous progress, because of which artificial intelligence became more widely used [21, 22]. The participation of up-to-date network, intelligent robotization and big data have promoted the rapid development of artificial intelligence core technology and the deep integration of various essential factors, and pushed artificial intelligence to enter even more fields of technology, economy and livelihood, and led to the new generation of artificial intelligence industrialization. The sustainable development of technology and artificial intelligence has a huge driving effect. Although artificial intelligence still faces many difficulties and challenges in the development process, these challenges always coexist with opportunities, and these difficulties will eventually be resolved. It is foreseeable that the research results on artificial intelligence will be able to create increasingly advanced artificial intelligence products, and to a certain extent surpass human intelligence in more and more fields; artificial intelligence will promote technological development, industrial transformation, and economic upgrading, social progress and human life.

1.1.1 *Definition of artificial intelligence*

The artificial intelligence we want to discuss is also called machine intelligence or computer intelligence. No matter which name it takes, it is noteworthy that the "intelligence" it contains is a kind of intelligence that is only artificially created or expressed by machines and computers and this distinguishes AI from natural intelligence, especially human intelligence. It can be seen that artificial intelligence is fundamentally different from natural intelligence. It is an artificial intelligence imitated and created by artificial means; at least it can be understood in the visible future.

Like many emerging disciplines, there is no unified definition of artificial intelligence, and it is difficult to give an accurate definition of artificial intelligence [14, 33, 36, 37]. Human natural intelligence (human intelligence) is always present with human activities. Many human activities, such as chess, competitions, solving problems, guessing riddles, discussing, planning, and writing computer programs, and even driving cars and cycling, all require "intelligence". If a machine can perform such a task, it can be considered that the machine already has some kind of "artificial intelligence". Scholars with different scientific or disciplinary backgrounds have different understandings of artificial intelligence and put forward different viewpoints. People call these viewpoints Symbolism, Connectionism, Actionism, or Logicism, Bionicsism, and Cyberneticsism [7, 20, 32, 34].

Below we define artificial intelligence based on our own understanding [1, 2].

Definition 1.1. Intelligence: Intelligence is the ability to understand and learn things, or in other words, intelligence is the ability to think and understand, not the ability to do things instinctively.

Definition 1.2. Intelligent machine: An intelligent machine is a machine capable of showing human intelligent behavior. This intelligent behavior is similar to how humans use the brain to think about problems or create ideas.

Definition 1.3. Artificial intelligence (discipline): Artificial intelligence (discipline) is the science of researching, designing, and applying intelligent machines. Its main goal in the near future is to study the use of machines to mimic and perform certain intellectual functions of the human brain, and to develop related theories, technologies and applications.

Definition 1.4. Artificial intelligence (ability): Artificial intelligence (ability) is the intelligent behavior usually performed by intelligent machines that is related to human intelligence. These intelligent behaviors involve learning, perception, thinking, understanding, recognition, judgment, reasoning, proof, communication, design, planning, action, and problem-solving and other activities [2].

The famous experiment designed and conducted by Turing in 1950 (later known as the Turing Test), which raised and partially answered the question of "whether the machine can think", is also a good comment on artificial intelligence [42].

Two newly provided definitions are given below.

Definition 1.5. Artificial intelligence is the theory and development of computer systems capable of performing tasks that normally require human intelligence, such as visual perception, speech recognition, decision-making, and language translation [19].

Simply put, artificial intelligence refers to the use of computers to do things that normally require human intelligence.

Definition 1.6. Artificial intelligence is a software or computer program with a learning mechanism that uses knowledge to make decisions in new situations just like humans make decisions. The researchers who built this software try to write code to read and learn from images, text, video, or audio. Once machines can learn, their knowledge can be used elsewhere [17].

In other words, artificial intelligence is the ability of a machine to apply algorithms to learn from data and use what it learns to make decisions just like humans do.

1.1.2 *Origin and development of artificial intelligence*

It may be useful to explain the development process of international artificial intelligence by period, although this period division method is sometimes difficult to follow rigorously, because there are many events that may span different periods, and there are other events that may be closely related although they are far apart in time.

(1) Pregnancy period (before 1956)

We do not intend to list the thousands of imaginations, practices, and achievements of humans in the pursuit of intelligent machines and artificial intelligence for more than 3,000 years, but to cross the 3,000 years to the 20th century. The trend of the times directly helped scientists to study certain phenomena. For the development of artificial intelligence, two of the most important things appeared in the intelligent world from 1910 to 1950: mathematical logic and new ideas about computing. In 1913, Wiener, who was only 19 years old, simplified the mathematical relationship theory into a class theory in his dissertation, contributed to the development of mathematical logic, and took a step towards machine logic [45]. It coincided with the logical machine proposed by Turing later. Studies by Frege, Whitehead, Russell, Tarski, and others have shown that certain aspects of reasoning can be formalized with simpler structures. Mathematical logic is still an active area of artificial intelligence research, in part because some logic-deduction systems have been implemented on computers. However, even before the advent of computers, the mathematical formula of logical reasoning established the concept of the relationship between calculation and intelligence for people.

The ideas of the Church, Turing, and others on the nature of computing provided the link between the concept of formal reasoning and the computer yet to be invented. Important work in this area was related to theoretical concepts of computation and symbol processing. In 1936, Turing, who was only 26 years old, founded the theory of automata (later known as Turing Machines), and proposed a theoretical computer model to lay the foundation for the design of electronic computers and promote the study of artificial intelligence, especially thinking machines. The first digital computers did not seem to contain any real intelligence; long before these machines were designed, Church and Turing had discovered that numbers were not the main aspect of computing, but were just a way to explain the internal state of the machine. Turing, known as the father of artificial intelligence, published a paper "Computing Machinery and Artificial Intelligence" in the British philosophy journal *Mind* in 1950 and a recorded speech "Can Digital Computers Think?" on the British BBC in 1951; both of them were significant contributions to the foundation of artificial intelligence [42]. Not only did he create a simple, general, non-numerical computing model, but also he directly proved that computers may work in a way that is understood to be intelligent.

The "brain-like machine" proposed by McCulloch and Pitts in 1943 was the world's first neural network model (called the MP model), which pioneered the structural study of the human brain. The connection mechanism of neural networks later developed into a representative of the connectionism school of artificial intelligence [29].

It is worth mentioning the influence of cybernetics thought on the early research in artificial intelligence. As Allen Newell and Herbert Simon have pointed out in their "historical supplements" to their excellent book *Human Problem Solving*, the founders of artificial intelligence in the mid-20th century have initiated several powerful trends in artificial intelligence research. The concepts of cybernetics and self-organizing systems, proposed by Wiener, McCulloch, and others, focus on the macro characteristics of "partially simple" systems. It is particularly important that the work "Cybernetics, or control and communication in the animal and the machine" published by Wiener in 1948 pioneered not only modern cybernetics, but also the cybernetics school of artificial intelligence (i.e. the behaviorist school) has set a new milestone [45]. Cybernetics affects many fields, because the concept of cybernetics spans many fields and connects the working principle of the nervous system with information theory, control theory, logic, and computing. These ideas of cybernetics are part of the ideological trend of the times, and in many cases have influenced many early and recent artificial intelligence workers (behavioral school) as their guiding ideology.

From the above, it can be seen that the creative contributions of artificial intelligence pioneers in mathematical logic, computational nature, cybernetics, information theory, automata theory, neural network models, and electronic computers laid the theoretical foundation for the development of artificial intelligence, and gave birth to the fetus of artificial intelligence. People will soon hear the baby crying and see the cute figure of this baby of AI coming to the earth!

(2) Formation period (1956–1970)

By the 1950s, artificial intelligence was agitated as the mother of human science and technology society, and was about to give birth. In the summer of 1956, the young American mathematician and computer expert McCarthy, the mathematician and neurologist Minsky, the director of IBM Corporation Information Center, Lochester, and a mathematician at Bell Labs Information Department co-sponsored with information scientist Shannon, inviting IBM's More and Samuel, MIT's Selfridge and Solomonff, and RAND with CMU's Newell and Simon, a total of 10 people, held a seminar for more than two months at Dartmouth College in the United States, and seriously and enthusiastically discussed the question of using machines to simulate humans intelligence. At the meeting, the term "artificial intelligence" was formally put forward by McCarthy. This is the first artificial intelligence seminar in human history, marking the birth of the artificial intelligence discipline, which has very important scientific and historical significance. Most of these outstanding young scholars engaged in research in mathematics, psychology, information theory, computer science and neurology, and later most of them became well-known artificial intelligence experts, making a significant contribution to the development of international artificial intelligence.

What ultimately connected these different ideas was the computer itself, developed by Babbage, Turing, Von Neumman, and others. Soon after the application of the machine became feasible, people began to try to write programs to solve intelligence test puzzles, automatic proofs of mathematical theorems and other propositions, play chess, and translate text from one language to another. This is the first artificial intelligence program. Many of the computing concepts related to artificial intelligence that appeared in early designs include the concepts of memory and processors, the concepts of systems and controls, and the concept of the program level of languages. For computers, what's driving artificial intelligence? The only characteristic of the new machines that has caused the emergence of new disciplines is the complexity of these machines, which has facilitated new and more direct studies of methods that describe complex processes, using complex data structures and having hundreds of thousands of different process steps to describe these methods.

In 1965, a research group led by Feigenbaum, known as the "father of expert systems and knowledge engineering", began to study expert systems, and in 1968 successfully researched the first expert system DENDRAL for mass spectrometry to analyze the molecular structure of organic compounds. Later, other expert systems were developed to make groundbreaking contributions to the research on the application of artificial intelligence.

Known as the "Father of International Pattern Recognition", K.S. Fu, in addition to his pioneering contributions in syntactic pattern recognition, applied the heuristic inference rules of artificial intelligence to learning control systems in 1965. With the connection between artificial intelligence and automatic control, it has made a foundational contribution to intelligent control and has become an internationally recognized founder of intelligent control [15, 16].

The first International Joint Conference on AI (IJCAI) was held in 1969, marking the arrival of artificial intelligence on the international academic stage as an independent discipline. Since then, IJCAI has been held every two years. In 1970, the *International Journal of AI* was founded. These events have played a positive role in conducting international academic activities and exchanges in artificial intelligence, and promoting the research and development of artificial intelligence.

The above events show that artificial intelligence has experienced an enthusiastic period from birth to growth and has formed an independent discipline, which has initially established a relatively good environment for artificial intelligence and laid an important foundation for further development. Although artificial intelligence will still face many difficulties and challenges in the way forward, with this foundation, we can meet the challenges, seize the opportunities, and promote the continuous development of artificial intelligence.

(3) The gloomy period (1966–1974)

Between the formation period and the subsequent knowledge application period, there was a bleak period for artificial intelligence. While achieving "enthusiastic" development, artificial intelligence encountered some difficulties and problems.

On the one hand, because some AI researchers were blinded by victory and were blindly optimistic, they made too optimistic predictions about the future development and results of artificial intelligence, and the failure of these predictions caused significant damage to the reputation of artificial intelligence. At the same time, many artificial intelligence theories and methods had not been universalized and popularized, and expert systems were not widely developed. Therefore, people did not see the value of artificial intelligence. Artificial intelligence was even regarded as "pseudoscience"

[52]. Digging deeper, it can be seen that artificial intelligence in this period mainly had the following three limitations:

(i) Limitations of knowledge. Earlier developed artificial intelligence programs involved too little or no subject knowledge, and only simple syntax processing. For example, for natural language understanding or machine translation, if there is insufficient professional knowledge and common sense, language cannot be processed correctly, and even nonsense translations can occur.

(ii) Limitations of solution. Many problems that artificial intelligence tries to solve are unsolved due to the limitations of its solution methods and steps. These make the designed program in fact unable to find the answer to the problem, or it can only get the answer to a simple problem, and this simple problem does not require the participation of artificial intelligence.

(iii) Limitations of structure. Artificial intelligence systems or programs used to generate intelligent behavior have a basic structure. Some serious limitations, such as the failure to consider bad structures and the inability to deal with combinatorial explosions, can only be used to solve relatively simple problems, affecting the promotion and application.

On the other hand, the development of science and technology places new requirements or even challenges on artificial intelligence. For example, cognitive physiology research found that the human brain contains more than 10^{11} neurons, and artificial intelligence systems or intelligent machines could not structurally simulate the function of the brain under existing technical conditions [20, 26]. In addition, various academic circles of philosophy, psychology, cognitive physiology, and computer science held a critical and skeptical attitude to the nature, theory, and application of artificial intelligence, which put artificial intelligence in crisis. In 1971, James, a mathematician at the University of Cambridge in the United Kingdom, published a comprehensive report on artificial intelligence in accordance with the British government's will, claiming that "artificial intelligence is not a scam, but it is also a mediocre self-interference". Under the influence of this report, the British government cut funding for artificial intelligence research and dismissed artificial intelligence research institutions. In the United States, the birthplace of artificial intelligence disciplines, even IBM, which has a great influence on artificial intelligence research, was forced to cancel all the company's artificial intelligence research. It can be seen from this that artificial intelligence research was in trouble and at a low point.

Nothing can be smooth-sailing. Spring will come after winter. By summing up experience and lessons, and carrying out more extensive, in-depth and targeted research, artificial intelligence came out of the trough and ushered in a new development period.

(4) Knowledge application period (1970–1988)

The Feigenbaum research team began to study the expert system in 1965, and after the first expert system DENDRAL was successfully researched in 1968, they developed the MYCIN medical expert system for antibiotic drug treatment from 1972 to 1976. Since then, many well-known expert systems, such as the PROSPECTOR geological exploration expert system developed by Duda at the Stanford International Center for Artificial Intelligence Research, CASNET Glaucoma Diagnosis and Treatment Expert System at Rutgers University, MACSYMA Symbolic Integral and Mathematical Expert System at MIT, as well as the R1 computer structure design expert system, the ELAS drilling data analysis expert system, and the ACE telephone cable maintenance expert system, have been successively developed, providing powerful tools for industrial and mining data analysis and processing, medical diagnosis, computer design, symbolic operations, and so on. At the Fifth International Conference on Artificial Intelligence held in 1977, Feigenbaum formally proposed the concept of knowledge engineering and predicted that the 1980s would be a booming era of expert systems.

This was indeed the case. Throughout the 1980s, expert systems and knowledge engineering developed rapidly throughout the world. Expert systems provided huge economic benefits for users such as enterprises. For example, the first successful commercial expert system, R1, began operating in the United States Digital Equipment Group Corporation (DEC) in 1982 for the structural design of new computer systems. By 1986, R1 had saved the company $4 million annually. By 1988, the artificial intelligence team at DEC had developed 40 expert systems. What's more, the company had used 100 expert systems and developed 500 expert systems. Almost every major American company had its own artificial intelligence team and applied expert systems or invested in expert system technology. In the 1980s, Japan and Western Europe also scrambled to invest in the development of intelligent computer systems for expert systems and their application in the industrial sector. An example is the "Fifth Generation Intelligent Computer Project" released by Japan in 1981. In the process of developing expert systems, many researchers have reached a consensus that artificial intelligence systems are a knowledge processing system, and knowledge acquisition, knowledge representation, and knowledge utilization have become the three basic issues of artificial intelligence systems.

(5) Integrated development period (1980–2010)

By the late 1980s, the intelligent computer research projects that countries strived for had encountered severe challenges and difficulties, and were unable to achieve their expected goals. This prompted AI researchers to reflect on existing AI and expert system ideas and methods. Existing expert systems have problems such as lack of common sense knowledge, narrow application fields, difficult knowledge acquisition, a single reasoning mechanism, and failure to process in a distributed manner. They found that the difficulties reflected some fundamental problems of artificial intelligence and knowledge engineering, such as interaction problems, expansion problems, and system problems, which were not well solved. The discussion of existing problems and the debate on basic ideas will help artificial intelligence to find new technological routes and methods, get rid of the predicament, and usher in new development opportunities [8].

Artificial intelligence application technology should take knowledge processing as the core to realize the intelligence of software. Knowledge processing requires an in-depth understanding of application fields and problem-solving tasks and is rooted in mainstream computing environments. Only in this way can the research and application of artificial intelligence be put on a path of continuous development.

Since the late 1980s, research on machine learning, computational intelligence, artificial neural networks, and behaviorism has been intensively carried out, which has culminated from time to time. The connection mechanism which is different from symbolism and behaviorism has also taken the lead and gained new development. The debate between different schools of artificial intelligence has promoted the further development of artificial intelligence research and applications. Symbolism based on mathematical logic, from propositional logic to predicate logic to multivalued logic, including fuzzy logic and rough set theory, has made historical contributions to the formation and development of artificial intelligence, and has exceeded the scope of traditional symbolic operations. It shows that symbolism is constantly looking for new theories, methods and ways to achieve its development. The mathematical calculation system of traditional artificial intelligence (we call it AI) is still not strict and complete.

In addition to fuzzy computing, many computational methods (such as neural computing, evolutionary computing, natural computing, immune computing, and swarm computing) that mimic human brain thinking, natural characteristics, and biological behavior have made important research progress during this period, and have been introduced into the artificial intelligence discipline. We call these intelligent computing theories and methods different from traditional artificial intelligence such as computational intelligence (CI). Computational intelligence makes up for the lack of mathematical theories and calculations of traditional AI, updates and enriches the theoretical framework of artificial intelligence, and enables artificial intelligence to enter a new period of development. The integration of different perspectives, methods and technologies of artificial intelligence is necessary for the development of artificial intelligence, and it is also inevitable for the development of artificial intelligence.

It is particularly worth mentioning the revival of neural networks and the emergence of intelligent agents in this period.

Hopfield proposed a discrete neural network model in 1982, and a continuous neural network model in 1984, which promoted the revival of artificial neural networks (ANN) research. The back-propagation (BP) algorithm proposed by Bryson and Ho and the parallel distributed processing (PDP) theory proposed by Rumelhart and McClelland in 1986 had been the real impetus for the revival of neural network research, and artificial neural network research became booming again. The first International Conference on Neural Networks was held in the United States in 1987, and the International Society for Neural Networks (INNS) was launched. Thus neural networks were placed in the forest of international information technology and became an important sub-discipline of artificial intelligence. The research results of multilayer neural networks provided a theoretical basis for deep neural networks and deep learning. Intelligent agents emerged in the 1990s with the development of network technology, especially computer network communication technology, and developed into another new research hotspot for artificial intelligence. The goal of artificial intelligence is to build an agent that can show a certain intelligent behavior. Therefore, the agent should be a core problem of artificial intelligence. In the process of artificial intelligence research, people have gradually realized that the essence of human intelligence is a kind of social intelligence; the solution of social problems, especially complex problems, needs to be completed by all parties. The solution of artificial intelligence, especially the more complicated artificial intelligence problems, also requires the negotiation, collaboration and coordination of all relevant individuals. The "person" or the basic individual in human society corresponds to the basic component agent in the artificial intelligence system, and the artificial intelligence "multi-agent system" corresponding to the social system became a new research object in the field of artificial intelligence.

The above-mentioned emerging artificial intelligence theories, methods, and technologies, including the three artificial intelligence schools, namely symbolism, connectionism, and behaviorism, were no longer a single path but a full vitality road of co-operation, comprehensive integration, complementary advantage, and common development. Gone were the intense debates in the field of artificial intelligence.

(6) New era of fusion development (2005–present)

After mankind entered the 21st century, a new era of the second machine revolution and artificial intelligence was ushered in. Unlike each development period in the history of artificial intelligence, it is necessary to realize the high integration of various core technologies of artificial intelligence and the deep integration of artificial intelligence and the real economy. Knowledge (such as original knowledge, macro knowledge and common sense), algorithms (such as deep learning algorithms and evolutionary algorithms), big data (such as massive data and live data), networks (Internet, Internet of Things, and 5G), cloud computing, computing power (such as ultra-large-scale integration of central processing unit (CPU) and graphics processing unit (GPU)), their rapid development and mutual penetration have promoted artificial intelligence into a new era of fusion development and pushed the new generation of artificial intelligence technology and industry to flourish like never before.

The above-mentioned artificial intelligence fusion development process was gradually formed. The emergence of computational intelligence closely integrated artificial intelligence and data; intelligent computing has realized the fusion of "knowledge + algorithm + data"; big data has created conditions for the fusion of "knowledge + big data + algorithm"; the upgrade of the network has made "knowledge + big data". "Data + algorithm + network" artificial intelligence fusion becomes possible [21].

The breakthrough advance of algorithm research injected new vitality into artificial intelligence, especially the deep learning algorithm. In the past decade, the research on deep learning and deep reinforcement learning has gradually deepened and been widely used in the fields of natural language processing and image processing. These research results have activated the academic atmosphere and promoted the application and development of machine learning and artificial intelligence [24, 41].

In 2006, Geoffrey Hinton of the University of Toronto in Canada proposed the following: (1) The artificial neural network with multiple hidden layers has very outstanding feature learning capabilities, and the obtained feature data can describe the data's essential characteristics in a deeper and more effective manner. (2) The difficulty of deep neural network training can be effectively overcome by "layer-wise pre-training". These ideas started the upsurge of research and application of deep learning in academia and industry.

Artificial intelligence has been used more and more widely, penetrated deeply into other disciplines and scientific and technological fields, made an indispensable contribution to the development of these disciplines and fields, and provided new ideas and references for the study of artificial intelligence theory and applications. This is the case, for example, in bioinformatics, biological robotics, and genomic research.

With the upgrading of the economy and industry, the need for social development and serving people's livelihood, and the promotion of the artificial intelligence industry, a wave of artificial intelligence industrialization is surging around the world and sweeping the globe. We have reason to believe that in the new era of artificial intelligence development, artificial intelligence will definitely create more, better, and greater new results, and create a new era of fusion development of artificial intelligence [5,11,35,36].

1.2 Classification of Artificial Intelligence Systems

Taxonomy and subject science study the classification of science and technology as a very rigorous science, but it is difficult to classify some new disciplines. There is no unified classification method for artificial intelligence systems. It can be divided into the following systems according to their working principles [2, 30]:

(1) Expert system

The expert system is one of the most active and extensive fields of application research in artificial intelligence. Since the first expert system DENDRAL came out at Stanford University in 1965 after 20 years of research and development to the mid-1980s, various expert systems have spread across different professional fields and achieved great success.

Expert systems are now more widely used and further used in application development [23].

The expert system is an organic combination of expert system technology and methods, especially the feedback mechanism of engineering cybernetics. Expert systems have been widely used in fault diagnosis, industrial design and process control. Expert systems generally consist of a knowledge base, an inference engine, a control rule set, and algorithms. The problems studied by expert systems are generally uncertain and based on imitating human intelligence [4, 27].

(2) Fuzzy logic system

The fuzzy set theory proposed by L. Zadeh in 1965 became a method for dealing with various objects in the real world, which meant the birth of fuzzy logic technology. Since then, the theoretical research and practical application of fuzzy sets and fuzzy control have been widely developed. From 1965 to 1975, Zadeh studied a number of important concepts, including fuzzy multilevel decision-making, fuzzy approximations, fuzzy constraints, and linguistic boundaries [49, 50]. In the following 10 years, many mathematical structures were fuzzified with the help of fuzzy sets. These mathematical structures involve logic, relationships, functions, graphics, classification, grammar, language, algorithms, and programs.

A fuzzy logic system is a kind of intelligent system applying fuzzy set theory. It proposes a new mechanism for implementing knowledge (rules) and semantic description-based representation, reasoning and operation rules, and proposes an easier design method for nonlinear systems.

(3) Neural network system

The pioneers of artificial neural network research McCulloch and Pitts proposed an interconnection model based on the characteristics of biological neurons in 1943 [29]. In the 1970s, Grossberg and Kohonen proposed several nonlinear dynamic system structures and self-organizing mapping models based on biological and psychological evidence. Werbos developed a back-propagation algorithm in the 1970s. Hopfield introduced a recurrent neural network based on neuron interactions. In the mid-1980s, as a feedforward neural network learning algorithm, Parker and Rumelhart rediscovered the back-propagation algorithm [13, 48]. In the past decade, neural networks, especially layered neural networks (such as deep learning networks), have found application in a wide range of fields ranging from household appliances to industrial objects. The main applications include speech recognition, image processing, automatic control, robotics, signal processing, management, and commercial, medical and military fields.

(4) Machine learning system

Learning is a very common term. People and computers both learn and gain knowledge and improve technology and skills. People with different backgrounds have different views and definitions of "learning".

Learning is one of the main intelligences of human beings; it has played a great role in human evolution. Since the beginning of the 21st century, much progress has been made in the study of machine learning. In particular, some new learning methods, such as deep learning algorithms and big data-driven knowledge learning, have injected new blood into the learning system and will definitely promote the further development of learning system research [32].

(5) Bionic evolution system

Scientists and engineers apply mathematics and science to mimic nature, including the natural intelligence of humans and organisms. Natural intelligence has inspired advanced computing and learning methods and technologies. Bionic intelligent systems are intelligent systems that mimic and simulate human and biological behavior. Attempts to imitate human intelligence through artificial methods have a long history. Biology adapts to the natural environment through individual selection, crossing, and mutation. Individuals in the population are selected or eliminated by Nature based on their ability to adapt to the environment [2, 3, 12]. The result of the evolutionary process is reflected in the structure of the individual. Its chromosome contains several genes. The corresponding phenotype and genotype relationship reflects the logical relationship between the individual's external characteristics and internal mechanisms. Using evolutionary computing, especially genetic algorithm mechanisms, for artificial systems and processes, a new type of intelligent system, namely bionic intelligent system, can be realized [31].

(6) Swarm intelligence system

A swarm can be defined as a structural collection of interacting organizations or agents. In the research on swarm intelligence computing, the swarm's individual organization includes ants, termites, bees, wasps, fish swarms and bird swarms. In these swarms, individuals are structurally simple, but their collective behavior can become quite complex. The global swarm behavior of social organizations is realized in a nonlinear manner by the individual behaviors within the swarm. Therefore, there is a close relationship between individual behaviors and the global swarm behavior. The collective behavior of these individuals constitutes and governs the swarm behavior. On the other hand, swarm behavior determines the conditions under which individuals perform their roles. The social network structure of the swarm forms a setting for the swarm existence, which provides a communication channel for exchanging experience and knowledge between individuals. Swarm computing modeling has found many successful applications, and different applications have been obtained from different swarm studies [2, 13].

(7) Distributed intelligent system

The emergence and development of computer technology, artificial intelligence, and network technology has overcome the limitations of centralized systems. Parallel computing and distributed processing technologies (including distributed artificial intelligence) and multiple agent systems (MAS) have been generated. Think of the agent as anything that can perceive its environment through sensors and act on its environment with the help of actuators. Multi-agent systems have many characteristics of distributed systems, such as interactivity, sociality, collaboration, adaptability, and distribution [2, 37]. Multi-agent systems include key technologies such as mobile distributed systems, distributed intelligence, computer networks, communications, mobile models and computing, programming languages, security, fault tolerance, and management. Multi-agent systems are used in robot coordination, process control, remote communication, flexible manufacturing, network communication, traffic control, e-commerce, distance education and telemedicine.

(8) Integrated intelligent system

The intelligent systems introduced earlier each have their inherent advantages and disadvantages. For example, fuzzy logic is good at dealing with uncertainty, neural networks are mainly used for learning, and evolutionary computing is a master of optimization. In the real world, not only different knowledge, but also different intelligent technologies are required. This demand has led to the emergence of hybrid intelligent systems. Integrated intelligent systems have become a trend in the research and development of intelligent systems since a long time ago, and various integrated intelligent solutions have emerged just like bamboo shoots. The success of the integration depends not only on the inherent characteristics of the parties before the integration and the effect of "reinforcing the shortcomings" or "complementing the advantages" after the integration, but also needs to be tested in practical applications [28, 43].

(9) Autonomous intelligent system

"Autonomy" means the ability to manage itself. An autonomous intelligent system is a type of artificial system that can be operated by artificial intelligence technology without human intervention. The autonomous intelligent system is also a complex system composed of a variety of technologies such as machinery, control, computer, communication, and materials. Autonomy and intelligence are the two most important characteristics of autonomous intelligent systems. The use of artificial intelligence's image recognition, human–computer interaction, intelligent decision-making, reasoning and learning technologies is the most effective way to achieve and continuously improve the above two characteristics of autonomous intelligent systems. The autonomous intelligent system is one of the important applications of artificial intelligence, and its development can greatly promote the innovation of artificial intelligence technology. Various types of autonomous intelligent systems, including unmanned vehicles, drones, service robots, space robots, marine robots, and unmanned workshops/smart factories as well as intelligent manufacturing, will have a significant impact on human life and society [9, 10, 51, 52].

(10) Man–machine collaborative intelligent system

The human–computer collaborative intelligent system realizes the organic combination of human intelligence and artificial intelligence through human–computer interaction. Human–computer collaborative intelligence is an advanced application of hybrid intelligence and human brain mechanism research, and it is also an inevitable trend in the development of hybrid intelligence research. Human–computer collaborative intelligence means that the human brain and the machine are integrated into one, solving key technical problems such as signal acquisition, signal analysis, information intercommunication, information fusion, and intelligent decision-making, so that the human brain and the machine truly become a complete system. In the research method of man–computer collaborative intelligence, the expression of human intelligence is different. Some studies are expressed in the form of data, and the goal of man–machine collaboration is achieved by training machine intelligence models using data formed by human intelligence. This collaborative method usually uses offline fusion; that is, human intelligence cannot guide and supervise machine intelligence in real time [43,44]. Intelligent systems can be classified according to application fields, such as intelligent robot systems, intelligent decision systems, intelligent manufacturing systems, intelligent control systems, intelligent planning systems, intelligent transportation systems, intelligent management systems, intelligent smart home appliances systems, automatic theorem proving systems and automatic programming systems, and so on [46].

1.3 Research Objectives and Contents of Artificial Intelligence

This section explores the research goals and the main research content of artificial intelligence.

1.3.1 *Research objectives of artificial intelligence*

In defining the disciplines and capabilities of artificial intelligence, we pointed out that in recent years the goal of research on artificial intelligence is to "study the use of machines to mimic and perform certain intellectual functions of the human brain and develop related theories and technologies. It involves activities such as learning, perception, thinking, understanding, identification, judgment, reasoning, proof, communication, design, planning, action, and problem solving". Below we discuss the research goals of artificial intelligence.

The general research goals of artificial intelligence are the following:

(1) To gain a better understanding of human intelligence. Imitate and test theories about human intelligence by programming.
(2) To create useful smart programs that can perform tasks that normally require human experts.

Generally speaking, the research goals of artificial intelligence can be divided into two types: short-term research goals and long-term research goals.

The short-term research goal of artificial intelligence is the following: to build intelligent computers to replace certain human intelligence activities; in layman's terms, it is to make the existing computer smarter and more useful, so that it not only performs general numerical calculations and non-numerical information processing, but also uses knowledge, computational intelligence, and virtual computing to simulate some of the human intelligence functions and solve problems that traditional methods cannot handle. In order to achieve this short-term goal, it is necessary to research and develop relevant theories, technologies, and methods that can mimic these intellectual activities of human beings, and establish corresponding artificial intelligence systems.

The long-term goal of artificial intelligence is to use artificial machines to mimic human thinking activities and intellectual functions. In other words, it is to build an intelligent system that can realize human thinking activities and intellectual functions. There is still a long way to go to achieve this ambitious goal. This is not only because the current artificial intelligence technology has not yet reached the level it should, but also because human beings have a deeper understanding of their own thinking process and various intellectual behavior mechanisms. The nature and mechanisms of many problems that need to be imitated by machines are still unknown.

The short-term and long-term goals of artificial intelligence research have an inseparable relationship. On the one hand, the realization of short-term goals makes theoretical and technical preparations for long-term goals research, lays down the necessary foundation, and enhances people's confidence in achieving long-term goals. On the other hand, the long-term goals indicate the direction of the short-term goals and strengthen the strategic position of the short-term research goals.

As for the research goals of artificial intelligence, in addition to the above understanding, there are some more specific formulations. For example, Leeait and Feigenbaum proposed nine "final goals" of artificial intelligence research, including a deep understanding of the human cognition process, realizing effective intelligent automation, effective intelligent extension, constructing superman programs, realizing general problem-solving, realizing natural language understanding, performing tasks autonomously, self-learning and self-programming, and large-scale text data storage and processing technology. As another example, Sloman proposed three main research goals of artificial intelligence, namely, effective theoretical analysis of intelligent behavior, interpretation of human intelligence, and construction of artificial artifacts.

1.3.2 *Research and application fields of artificial intelligence*

The subject of artificial intelligence has very wide and extremely rich research connotation. Different artificial intelligence researchers classify the research content of artificial intelligence from different perspectives, such as based on brain function simulation, based on different cognitive perspectives, based on the application domain and application system, and based on the system structure and supporting environment. Therefore, a comprehensive and systematic introduction to the research content of artificial intelligence is difficult, and may not be necessary. The following is a comprehensive introduction to the basic content of that artificial intelligence research that has been recognized by many scholars and has universal significance.

(1) Cognitive modeling

Human cognitive processes are very complex. As a discipline that studies the information processing process of human perception and thinking, cognitive science (or thinking science) aims to explain how humans process information in the cognitive process. Cognitive science is an important theoretical basis for artificial intelligence and involves a very wide range of research topics. In addition to the related activities of perception, memory, thinking, learning, language, imagination, creation, attention and problem-solving proposed by Houston, it is also affected by environmental, social and cultural backgrounds. The cognitive thinking of artificial intelligence must not only study logical thinking, but also deeply study image thinking and inspirational thinking, so that artificial intelligence has a more solid theoretical foundation and provides new ideas and new approaches for the development of intelligent systems [31, 41].

(2) Knowledge representation

Knowledge representation, knowledge reasoning, and knowledge application are the three core research contents of traditional artificial intelligence. Among them, knowledge representation is the basis, knowledge reasoning is used to solve problems, and knowledge application is the purpose. Knowledge representation is the conceptualization, formalization, or modeling of human knowledge. In general, symbolic knowledge, algorithms, and state diagrams are used to describe the problem to be solved. The proposed knowledge representation methods mainly include two types: symbolic representation and neural network representation. Knowledge representation includes state space method, problem reduction method, predicate calculus, semantic network method, knowledge base, knowledge graph, frame representation, ontology representation, process representation, and neural network representation.

(3) Knowledge reasoning

Reasoning is the basic function of the human brain. Almost all areas of artificial intelligence are inseparable from reasoning. In order for a machine to implement artificial intelligence, we must give the machine reasoning capabilities and perform Machine Reasoning. The so-called reasoning is the thought process of deriving a new judgment or conclusion from some known judgments or premises. Reasoning in formal logic is divided into deductive reasoning, inductive reasoning, and analogical reasoning. Knowledge reasoning, including uncertainty reasoning and non-classical reasoning, seems to be an eternal research topic in the field of artificial intelligence, and there are still many undiscovered and unresolved issues worthy of research.

(4) Computational intelligence

The intersection, penetration and mutual promotion of information science and life sciences is a prominent feature of the development of modern science and technology. Computational intelligence is a convincing example of this. Computational intelligence includes the fields of neural computing, fuzzy computing, evolutionary computing, swarm computing, ant colony algorithm, natural computing, immune computing, and artificial life. Research and development of computationary intelligence reflect the important development trend of the interdisciplinary nature and integration of contemporary science and technology [13, 48, 50].

Almost all human inventions have their natural counterparts. Scientific and technological personnel apply mathematics and science to imitate nature, expand nature, and develop computing theory, methods, and technologies for computational intelligence.

(5) Knowledge application

Examining whether artificial intelligence can be widely used is an important tool to measure its vitality and test its viability. In the 1970s, it was the widespread application of expert systems that made artificial intelligence come out of the trough and achieve rapid development. Subsequent machine learning and recent research in applied natural language understanding have made significant progress, especially major advances in deep learning applied basic research, and have promoted the further development of artificial intelligence. Of course, the development of the application fields is inseparable from the progress of basic theories and technologies, such as knowledge representation and knowledge reasoning.

(6) Machine perception

Machine perception aims to make machines have human-like sensations, including vision, hearing, force, touch, smell, pain, proximity, and speed. Among them, the most important and widely used ones are machine vision and machine hearing. Machine vision can recognize and understand the identity of text, images, scenes, and even people; machine hearing can recognize and understand sounds and languages. Machine perception is the basic way for machines to obtain external information. To make the machine perceptive, it is necessary to equip it with various sensors.

(7) Machine thinking

Machine thinking is the purposeful processing of sensory information and working information inside the machine. In order for machines to realize thinking, they need to comprehensively apply research results in knowledge representation, knowledge reasoning, cognitive modeling, and machine perception, develop knowledge representation (especially the representation of various uncertain and incomplete knowledge), knowledge organization (including knowledge accumulation and management technology), knowledge reasoning (including uncertainty reasoning, inductive reasoning, non-classical reasoning), various heuristic search and control strategies, human brain structure, and the working mechanism of neural networks [20, 24, 26, 39, 51].

(8) Machine learning

Machine learning is another important research area of artificial intelligence applications after expert systems, and it is also one of the core research topics of artificial intelligence and neural computing. Learning is an important intelligent behavior of human beings. Machine learning is the ability of machines (computers) to learn new knowledge and new technologies, and to continuously improve and perfect themselves in practice. Machine learning enables machines to learn from books and other literature and to talk with people or observe the environment to automatically acquire knowledge [25, 33, 48].

(9) Machine behavior

Machine behavior refers to the expression and action capabilities of intelligent systems (computers, robots, etc.), such as dialogue, description, characterization, and movement, walking, operation, and grasping of objects. Studying the anthropomorphic behavior of machines is a difficult task for artificial intelligence. Machine behavior is closely related to machine thinking and machine emotion. Machine thinking is the basis of machine behavior, and machine emotion is an advanced embodiment of machine behavior.

(10) Intelligent system construction

The realization of the various above-mentioned artificial intelligence research areas is inseparable from the intelligent computer system or intelligent system, and the hardware and software support of the new theory, new technology and new method, and the system. Research is needed on models, system architecture and analysis techniques, system development environments and construction tools, and artificial intelligent programming languages. Some special programs that can simplify deduction, robot operation and cognitive models, as well as the development of computer distributed systems, parallel processing systems, multi-computer collaboration systems, and various computer networks, will directly promote the development of artificial intelligence technology [3, 30].

(11) The application fields of artificial intelligence

The application fields of artificial intelligence include natural language processing, automatic theorem proof, automatic programming, intelligent retrieval, intelligent scheduling and command, robotics, expert system, intelligent control, pattern recognition, machine vision, neural network, machine game, distribution intelligent agent, artificial life, artificial intelligence programming language, etc. Over the past 60 years, many computer systems with artificial intelligence have been established, e.g., those capable of solving differential equations, playing chess, designing and analyzing integrated circuits, synthesizing human natural languages, retrieving information, diagnosing diseases, and controlling space, and computer systems with different degrees of artificial intelligence for aircrafts, ground mobile robots and underwater robots. These application areas are not just for application and research; each of their fields is also a research area. For example, robotics, expert systems, intelligent control and automation, pattern recognition, machine vision, and neural networks have all been developed as independent disciplines, each with its own theory and application system [11, 18, 40, 47].

1.4 Core Elements of Artificial Intelligence

What are the core elements of artificial intelligence? There are different opinions in the field of artificial intelligence (see Figure 1.1). After studying and researching, we believe that from the perspective of the development of artificial intelligence disciplines, artificial intelligence should contain four elements, namely knowledge, data, algorithm, and computing power [2, 6].

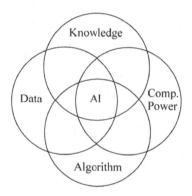

Figure 1.1 Core elements of AI.

(1) Knowledge

Knowledge is the objective regularity of the world that people recognize through experience, learning or association. **Knowledge is the source of artificial intelligence**, and artificial intelligence originates from and relies on knowledge; knowledge systems, such as expert systems and fuzzy computing, are developed on the basis of knowledge. The research on artificial intelligence aims to study the problems of knowledge representation, knowledge reasoning, knowledge application, and knowledge acquisition that are the bottleneck of knowledge engineering [2].

The pathway of knowledge development is as follows: the development of knowledge representation from surface knowledge representation to deep knowledge representation, from language (graph) representation to semantic representation, from explicit representation to implicit representation, and from simple knowledge representation to knowledge + data representation. As for knowledge reasoning, it involves the development from deterministic reasoning to uncertainty reasoning and from classic reasoning to nonclassical reasoning. As for knowledge application, it has developed from traditional knowledge engineering to comprehensive integration of knowledge and data, such as knowledge base, knowledge graph, knowledge mining, and knowledge discovery.

(2) Data

Data is the result of facts or observations and a general term for all kinds of media such as numbers, letters, symbols, image signals, and analog quantities that can be input to a computer and processed by a program. **Data is the foundation of artificial intelligence** and promotes AI development. Computational intelligence depends on data rather than knowledge; computational intelligence techniques, such as neural computing, and evolutionary computing, are developed based on data. The data has undergone rapid development from the computational intelligent data of neural networks to the massive data brought by the Internet.

Data development pathways include the following: from classic data to big data, from big data to live data, from the Internet to the Internet of Things and the integration of the two networks to bring about massive data, from supervised and semi-supervised learning to unsupervised and enhanced learning, and to data obtained through the new computing architecture (GPU and its parallel computing, programmable gate array, cloud computing, quantum computing, professional artificial intelligence chips, etc.). The 5G networks enable faster data transmission, less delay, and wider and more effective applications. The new generation of data will make greater contributions to the development of artificial intelligence.

(3) Algorithm

An algorithm is an accurate and complete description of a problem-solving scheme. It is a series of clear instructions for solving a problem. In short, algorithms are instruction descriptions for problem-solving. **The algorithm is the soul of artificial intelligence** and the core of its soft power. Intelligent algorithms such as deep learning algorithms and genetic algorithms are examples of algorithms. Existing algorithms, such as deep learning algorithms, have solved many practical problems, but the research on algorithms in the cognitive layer has made little progress and needs to make progress.

Approaches to algorithm development include the following: data + knowledge, deep learning combined with knowledge atlas, logical reasoning, symbol learning, unsupervised learning from unstructured or unlabeled data, development of cognitive computing, cognitive decision-level algorithms, and brain-like computing, development of universal computing (ubiquitous computing) and universal algorithms, as well as evolutionary computing and evolutionary algorithms based on the iterative evolution of swarm.

(4) Computing power

Computing power refers to computing ability, and the machine's mathematical induction and transformation ability is the ability to convert abstract and complex mathematical expressions or numbers into understandable mathematical formulas through mathematical methods. **Computing power is the power of artificial intelligence**, and it is also the key guarantee for the hard power of artificial intelligence.

The development pathway of computing power is as follows: create new computing architecture, including the research and development of new chips, such as GPU, FPGA professional artificial intelligence chips and neural network chips; develop new computing techniques, such as cloud computing systems and quantum computers. In addition, parallel computing speeds up data calculations and improves data processing capabilities. The continuous enhancement of computing power and the increase of computing speed have greatly promoted the development of artificial intelligence, especially the vigorous development of artificial intelligence industrialization.

Each of the above artificial intelligence core elements is gradually embracing the path of deep integration development, but this integration development requires a process. With the rapid development and deep integration of these core and key technologies, artificial intelligence and its industrialization are very promising, and will definitely bring better and more satisfactory services to human beings.

1.5 Outline of the Book

This book introduces the theory, methods, and technologies of artificial intelligence and their applications. It covers a very wide range of topics in artificial intelligence. In addition to discussing basic principles and methods that are still useful and effective, it highlights some new and interesting artificial intelligence methods and technologies, especially those methods and technologies developed in recent years. In addition, the application of artificial intelligence is discussed in a relatively large space, including new applied research. Specifically, this book includes the following:

(1) Briefly introduces the origin and development of artificial intelligence, and discusses the definition and classification of artificial intelligence, artificial intelligence research goals, research content, core elements, as well as research and application areas.

(2) Discusses knowledge-based artificial intelligence, including knowledge representation, knowledge search and reasoning, and knowledge-based machine learning. The state space method, problem reduction method, predicate logic method, and structured representation method (semantic network method, frame and ontology) of knowledge representation are introduced. The graph search strategy, resolution principle, rule deduction system, and uncertainty reasoning are discussed; non-monotonic reasoning, subjective Bayesian reasoning, credibility methods, and evidence theory and other search principles and inference solving techniques are explored. The knowledge-based machine learning, methods, such as inductive learning, explanation-based learning, example learning, concept learning, analog learning, and reinforcement learning, are expounded.

(3) Discusses data-based artificial intelligence, introduces evolutionary computing and neural computing, and focuses on data-based machine learning, including linear regression, decision trees, clustering, support vector machines, KNN algorithms, comprehensive learning, neural-based network learning, and deep learning.

(4) Analyzes in more detail the main application areas of artificial intelligence, including expert systems, automatic planning systems, intelligent perception, and natural language understanding.

(5) Summarizes the huge benefits and security issues of artificial intelligence, studies the integration trend of knowledge-based artificial intelligence and data-based artificial intelligence, and explores the history, current situation and development trend of artificial intelligence industrialization, and looks forward to the development of artificial intelligence.

This book has three distinct features. First, the book is systematic and comprehensive, covering the core technologies of artificial intelligence, including both the basic theories and technologies of "traditional" artificial intelligence and the basic principles and methods of computational intelligence. Secondly, the book focuses on innovation of machine learning and deep learning technologies that have been widely used in recent years, as well as other advanced research methods of artificial intelligence. Thirdly, the book's theory and practice are both highly integrated. It not only elaborates the theory, technology, and methods, but also introduces many application examples, which will help readers to deepen their understanding of artificial intelligence theory and methods and their application development. This book is a comprehensive manual and practical guide for artificial intelligence research and development personnel in them conducting research on artificial intelligence-related projects. It can also be used as a valuable reference for university undergraduates and graduate students to study artificial intelligence.

References

1. Cai, Z.X. and Chen, A.B. (2008). *Dictionary of Artificial Intelligence* (Chemical Industry Press, Beijing, in Chinese).
2. Cai, Z.X., Liu, L.J., Cai, J.F. and Chen, B.F. (2020). *Artificial Intelligence and Its Applications*, 6th Edition (Tsinghua University Press, in Chinese)
3. Cai, Z.X. and Wang, Y. (2015). *Intelligent Systems: Principles, Algorithms and Applications* (Mechanical Industry Press, Beijing, in Chinese).
4. Cai, Z.X., Durkin, J. and Gong, T. (2014). *Advanced Expert System: Principle, Design and Application*, 2nd Edition (Science Press, Beijing, in Chinese).
5. Cai, Z.X. (2016). 40 years of artificial intelligence in China, *Science and Technology Herald*, *15*: 13–22 (in Chinese).
6. Cai, Z.X. (2020). Artificial intelligence helps digital transformation of new infrastructure. *Guangming Daily*, April 2: 16 (in Chinese).
7. Cai, Z.X. (1995). Artificial intelligence schools and their viewpoints on theory and method, *High-tech Communication*, *5*: 55–57 (in Chinese).
8. Cai, Z.X. (2003). Intelligence science: disciplinary frame and general features. *Proc. of the 2003 IEEE International Conference on Robotics, Intelligent Systems and Signal Processing* (IEEE RISSP), Changsha, China-October 8-13, 2003, 393–398.
9. Cai, Z.X. (1997). *Intelligent Control: Principles, Techniques and Applications* (World Scientific Publishers, Singapore).
10. Cai, Z.X. (2019). *Intelligent Control: Principles and Applications*, 3rd Edition (Tsinghua University Press, Beijing, in Chinese).
11. Daron, A. and Pascual, R. (2018). Artificial intelligence, automation and work. In Ajay Agrawal, Joshua Gans and Avi Goldfarb (eds.), *The Economics of Artificial Intelligence: An Agenda*, 197-236 (NBER Books, National Bureau of Economic Research).
    University of Chicago Press. 2018: 197–236.
12. Darwin, C. (1859). *The Origin of Species* (John Murray, London).
13. Engelbrecht, A.P. (2002). *Computational Intelligence. An Introduction* (John Wiley & Sons).
14. Fu, K.S., Cai, Z.X. and Xu, G.Y. (1987). *Artificial Intelligence and Its Application* (Tsinghua University Press, Beijing, in Chinese).

15. Fu, K.S., *et al.* (1965). A heuristic approach to reinforcement learning control system, *IEEE Transactions on Automatic Control*, AC-10: 390–398.
16. Fu, K.S. (1971). Learning control systems and intelligent control systems: an intersection of artificial intelligence and automatic control, *IEEE Transactions on Automatic Control*, AC-16: 70–72.
17. Gershgorn, D. (2017). The Quartz guide to artificial intelligence: What is it, why is it, important, and should we be afraid? *Quarts*, September, 10, https://qz.com/1046350/the-quarta-guide-to-artificial-intelligence-what-is-it-why-is-it-important-and-should-we-be-afraid.
18. China Association for Science and Technology. 2016 Global Artificial Intelligence Technology Conference held in Beijing, (Chinese), http://news.sciencenet.cn/htmlnews/2016/4/344452.shtm.
19. Google (2017). www.google.com.
20. Gu, F.H. (2014). Recent developments in the EU and US brain research programs, *Science, 66*(5): 16–21.
21. Khaled, S., Rehman, M.H. Ur., Nishara, N. and Ala, Al-Fuqaha. (2019). Blockchain for AI: Review and open research challenges. *IEEE Access, 7*: 10127–10149.
22. Koch, M. (2018). Artificial intelligence is becoming natural, *Cell, 3*: 531–533.
23. Leondes, C.T. ed. (2002). *Expert Systems, the Technology of Knowledge Management and Decision Making for the 21st Century* (Academic Press, San Diego).
24. Li, D., Yu, D. and Xie, L., translated. (2016). *Deep Learning Methods and Applications* (Mechanical Industry Press, Beijing, in Chinese).
25. Li, Y. (1999). *Life and Intelligence* (Shenyang Publishing House, China).
26. Lu, H., Li, Y., Chen, M., Kim, H. and Serikawa, S. (2018). Brain intelligence: Go beyond artificial intelligence, *Mobile Netw. Appl.*, 2018, *23*(2): 368–375.
27. Lu, Y. Ed. (2001). *Knowledge Engineering and Knowledge Science at the Turn of the Century* (Tsinghua University Press, Beijing, in Chinese).
28. Luger, G.F. (2002). *Artificial Intelligence: Structures and Strategies for Complex Problem Solving*, 4th Edition (Pearson Education Ltd).
29. McCulloch, W. and Pitts, W. (1943). A logical calculus of the ideals immanent in nervous activity, *Bulletin of Mathematical Biology, 4*: 115–133.
30. Meystel, A.M. and Albus, J.S. (2002). *Intelligent Systems: Architecture, Design and Control* (John Wiley & Sons, New York).
31. Minsky, M. (1991). Logical versus analogical or symbolic versus connectionist or neat versus scruffy, *AI Magazine, 2*: 34–51.
32. Mitchell, T.M. (1997). *Machine Learning* (McGraw-Hill, New York).
33. Nilsson, N.J. (1998). *Artificial Intelligence: A New Synthesis* (Morgan Kaufmann).
34. Qian, X.S. and Song, J. (1980). *Engineering Cybernetics*, Revised Edition (Science Press, Beijing).
35. Rouhiainen, L. (2019). *Artificial Intelligence: 101 Things You Must Know Today about Our Future* (San Bernardino, CA, USA).

36. Russell, S.J. and Norvig, P. (2016). *Artificial Intelligence: A Modern Approach* (Pearson Education Limited).
37. Shi, Z.Z. and Wang, W.J. (2007). *Artificial Intelligence* (National Defense Industry Press, Beijing, in Chinese).
38. Simon, H.A., Jing, Q.C. and Zhang, H.Y., translated. (1986). *Human Cognition: Information Processing Theory of Thinking* (Science Press, Beijing).
39. Song, J. (1999). Intelligent control — A goal exceeding the century. *Chinese Journal of Engineering*, 1: 1–5; *IFAC 14th World Congress Report*, July 5, 1999, Beijing.
40. Song, J. (2003). The most wonderful achievements of frontier disciplines. See *AI and Its Application* written by Cai Zixing and Xu Guangyou (3rd Edition, in Chinese), Preface (Tsinghua University Press, Beijing).
41. Tan, B.Z. (2017). Artificial intelligence 2017 — AI has beaten human players in almost all game areas, *Technology Network*, 2017-12-29, https://baijiahao. baidu.com/s?id=1588090853019844023 (in Chinese).
42. Turing, A.A. (1950). Computing machinery and intelligence, *Mind, 59*: 433–460.
43. What is human–machine collaborative intelligent system, *Information Quick View,* 2019-01-06. https://baijiahao.baidu.com/s?id=1621920800449537851.
44. Verghese, A., Shah, N.H. and Harrington, R.A. (2018). What this computer needs is a physician: humanism and artificial intelligence, *JAMA, 1*: 19–20.
45. Wiener, N. (1948). Cybernetics, or control and communication in the animal and the machine (MIT Press, Cambridge, MA, USA).
46. Wu, W.J. (2004). The mechanization of brain labor and the modernization of science and technology in the computer age. See *Artificial Intelligence and Its Applications* (3rd Edition) written by Cai Zixing and Xu Guangyou, Preface (Tsinghua University Press).
47. Yang, K.C., Onur, V., Clayton, A.D., Emilio, F., Alessandro, F. and Filippo, M. (2019). Arming the public with artificial intelligence to counter social bots, *Human Behavior and Emerging Technologies*, 1(1): 48–61.
48. Yann, L., Yoshua, B. and Geoffrey, H. (2015). Deep learning, *Nature, 521.7553*: 436–444.
49. Zadeh, A. (2001). A new direction in AI: toward a computational theory of perceptions, *AI Magazine*, Spring 2001: 73–84.
50. Zadeh, A. (1984). Making computers think like people, *IEEE Spectrum*, August, 1984.
51. Tao, L.Q., *et al.* (2018). The development trend of intelligent unmanned autonomous systems, *Haiying Information*, 2018-07-19. http://wemedia.ifeng. com/69925435/wemedia.shtml
52. Zong, H. (2016). Artificial intelligence was once regarded as "pseudoscience", *Cultural History Exploration, 5*: 40.

PART 1
Knowledge-based Artificial Intelligence

Knowledge — The Source of AI

Knowledge Representation

2

"Knowledge" is an abstract term used to describe a person's understanding of a particular object. Plato defines "knowledge" in *Theaetetus* as true belief and justification. Later, Western philosophers such as Aristotle, Descartes, and Kant also studied epistemology. Epistemology has long gone beyond the realm of philosophy and has become one of the cornerstones of Western civilization [5, 7].

Knowledge is the source of artificial intelligence. In the process of artificial intelligence generation and development, most of the early research studies were based on knowledge, established knowledge-based artificial intelligence systems, solved knowledge-based problems, and developed knowledge-based artificial intelligence applications.

In artificial intelligence systems, knowledge is usually domain-specific. In order for an artificial intelligence system to understand knowledge, to process knowledge, and to complete knowledge-based tasks, it is first necessary to construct a model of knowledge, i.e., the representation of knowledge. Although knowledge representation is the most basic concept in artificial intelligence, there is rarely a direct answer to the question "What is knowledge representation?". Davis attempts to answer this question through the role of knowledge in various tasks.

With different tasks and types of knowledge, different knowledge representation methods will appear. The commonly used knowledge representation methods include state space, knowledge base, framework, ontology, semantic network, knowledge graph, and predicate logic.

For traditional artificial intelligence problems, any more complex solution technology cannot be separated from two aspects: representation and search. There can be multiple different representations of the same problem; these representations have different representation spaces. The pros and cons of the problem representation have a great impact on the result and efficiency of the solution [12, 19].

In order to solve actual complex problems, many different representation methods are usually used. This is because each representation has its advantages and disadvantages, and no single method has the many different functions required.

2.1 State Space Representation

Problem solving is a large subject which involves core concepts such as reduction, inference, decision-making, planning, common sense reasoning, theorem proof, and related processes. After analyzing the problem-solving methods used in artificial intelligence research, it will be found that many problem-solving methods use heuristic search methods. That is, these methods solve the problem by finding a solution in a possible solution space. This type of problem representation and solution method is based on solution space and called the state space method, which represents and solves problems by using state and operator [6, 13].

The state space problem representation and solution method is one of the most traditional methods, and very typical. It is universal; some other methods are developed from the state space method. Therefore, it is necessary to briefly introduce state space representation and search methods.

2.1.1 *Problem state space description*

First define the state and state space.

Definition 2.1. A state is an ordered set of minimum variables $q_0, q_1, \ldots, q_n$ introduced to describe the difference between different types of things. The vector form is as follows:

$$Q = [q_0, q_1, \ldots, q_n] \tag{2.1}$$

Each element $q_i (i = 0, 1, \ldots, n)$ in the equation is a component of the set, called a state variable. Given a set of values for each component, a specific state can be obtained, such as

$$Q_k = [q_{0k}, q_{1k}, \ldots, q_{nk}]^T \tag{2.2}$$

The means of changing a problem from one state to another is called an operator. Operators can be walks, procedures, rules, mathematical operators, arithmetic symbols, or logical symbols.

The state space of a problem is a graph representing all possible states of the problem and their relationships. It contains a set of three descriptions, namely all possible problem initial state sets S, operator sets F, and goal state sets G. Therefore, the state space can be recorded as a ternary state (S, F, G).

The concept of state space representation is illustrated by a 15 puzzle problem. The puzzle consists of 15 walkable pieces numbered 1–15 and placed on a 4×4 checkerboard. There is always a space on the board that is empty, so that the pieces around the empty space can enter the empty space, which can also be understood as moving spaces. The 15 puzzle is shown in Figure 2.1. The figure depicts two types of games, the initial game and the target game, which correspond to the initial state and target state of the problem.

How to transform the initial chess game into the target chess game? The answer to this problem is a suitable sequence of chess moves, such as "Move chess piece 12 to the left, move chess piece 15 down, move chess piece 4 to the right ..." and so on.

The most direct solution to the 15 puzzle is to try various moves until you obtain the target chess by chance. This attempt essentially involves some kind of heuristic search. Starting from the initial game, test each new game obtained by each legal move, and then calculate the next set of games obtained by taking another step. This continues until the target game is reached. Imagine the space composed of the states that can be reached in the initial state as a graph composed of nodes corresponding to various states. Such diagrams are called state diagrams or state space diagrams. For the initial game shown in Figure 2.1(a), first apply the applicable operator to the initial state to generate new states; then, apply other applicable operators to these new states; this continues until the goal state is generated.

(a) Initial state   (b) Target state

Figure 2.1   The 15 digital puzzle.

The term "state space method" is generally used to indicate the following methods: starting from an initial state, adding an operator each time, and incrementally establishing a test sequence of operators until the goal state is reached.

The entire process of finding the state space includes generating new state descriptions from the old state descriptions, and thereafter examining these new state descriptions to see if they describe the goal state. This test is often just to see if a certain state matches a given goal state description. However, sometimes more complex goal tests are performed. For some optimization problems, it is not enough to just find any path to the goal. You must also find a path that achieves optimization according to a certain criterion (e.g., the least moves in chess).

From the above discussion, we know that to complete the state description of a problem, three things must be determined: (1) the state description mode, especially the initial state description; (2) the operator set and its effect on the state description; (3) the characteristics of the goal state description.

2.1.2 Graph theory terminology and graphic method

In order to have a deeper understanding of state space diagrams, here are some terms in graph theory and formal representation of diagrams.

A graph consists of a collection of nodes (not necessarily finite nodes). A pair of nodes is connected by arcs, from one node to another. Such a graph is called a directed graph. If an arc points from node n_i to node n_j, node n_j is called the successor or descendant of node n_i, and node n_i is called the parent node or ancestor of node n_j. A node generally has only a limited number of successor nodes. A pair of nodes may be descendants of each other, in which case the pair of directed arcs is replaced by a ridge line. When a graph is used to represent a certain state space, each node in the graph is marked with a corresponding state description, and an operator is marked next to the directed arc.

In a sequence of nodes $(n_{i1}, n_{i2}, \ldots, n_{ik})$ when $j = 2, 3, \ldots, k$, if $n_{i,j-1}$ has a successor node n_{ij}, then this node sequence is called a path with length k from node n_{i1} to node n_{ik}. If there is a path from node n_i to node n_j, then the node n_j is called a node reachable from the node n_i, or the node n_j is a descendant of the node n_i, and n_i is called the ancestor of the node n_j. It can be found that the problem of finding a sequence of operators from one state to another state is equivalent to finding a certain path problem with a graph.

A cost is assigned to each arc to represent the cost added to the corresponding operator. Let $c(n_i, n_j)$ represent the cost of the arc from node n_i to node n_j. The cost of a path between two nodes is equal to the sum of all arc costs connecting the nodes on the path. For optimization problems, find the path with the least cost between the two nodes.

For the simplest type of problem, a path (possibly with the least cost) between a specified node s (representing the initial state) and another node t (representing the goal state) is required.

A graph can be either explicitly stated or implicitly stated. For an explicit explanation, each node and its arc with a cost are explicitly given by a table. This table may list the cost of each node in the graph, its successor nodes, and the connecting arc. Obviously, the explicit description is impractical for large graphs but impossible for graphs with an infinite set of nodes.

For an implicit description, an infinite set of nodes $\{s_i\}$ is known as the starting node. Furthermore, it is convenient to introduce the concept of subsequent node operators. The operator of successor node Γ is also known, and it can act on any node to generate the cost of all successor nodes and the connecting arcs of the node. Applying the successor operator to the members of $\{s_i\}$ and their successor nodes and the successor nodes of these successors, proceeding indefinitely, and finally making the implicit graph specified by Γ and $\{s_i\}$ into an explicit graph. The process of applying a successor to a node is the process of extending a node. Thus, the process of searching for a state space to find a solution to a sequence of operators corresponds to the process of changing a large enough portion of the implicit graph into an explicit graph to include the goal node. Such a search graph is the main basis for solving state space problems.

The representation of the problem has a great impact on the workload of the solution. It is clear that there is a desire for a smaller state space representation. Many seemingly difficult problems may have a small and simple state space when indicated as appropriate.

Selecting various representations based on problem state, operators, and goal conditions is required for efficient problem solving. First, the problem needs to be expressed, and then the proposed representation improved. In the problem solving process, experience will be gained constantly to get simplified representations. For example, find symmetry or merge into a valid sequence such as a macro rule. For the initial state representation of the 15 digital puzzle, $15 \times 4 = 60$ rules can be specified, i.e., move the chess piece 1 to the left, move the chess piece 1 to the right, move the chess piece 1 upward, move the chess piece 1 downward, move the chess piece 2, ..., move down the chess pieces 15, and so on. It will soon be found that as long as the space is moved up and down, four rules can be used instead of the above 60 rules. It can be seen that moving spaces is a good representation.

Various problems can be represented by the state space and solved by the state space search method.

2.1.3 *Problem reduction representation*

Problem reduction is another method for describing and solving problems based on state space. The description of the known problem turns this problem into a set of primitive problems through a series of transformations; solutions to these primitive problems can be obtained directly, thereby solving the initial problem.

The problem reduction representation can be composed of the following three parts:

(1) An initial problem description;
(2) A set of operators that transform the problem into sub-problems;
(3) A set of primitive problem descriptions.

Starting from the objective (problem to be solved), reverse reasoning is executed, sub-problems and sub-problems of the sub-problems are established, and finally the initial problem is reduced to an ordinary set of primitive problems. This is the essence of problem reduction.

(1) Problem reduction description

In order to prove how to solve the problem using the problem reduction method, consider a kind of puzzle — the Tower of Vatican Puzzle.

There are three columns (1, 2, and 3) and three discs (A, B, and C) of different sizes. There is a hole in the center of each disc so that the discs can be stacked on posts. Initially, all three discs were stacked on pillar 1: the largest disc C was at the bottom and the smallest disc A was at the top. It is required to move all the discs to the pillar 3, only one disc at a time, and only the disc at the top of the pillar can be moved first, and the larger discs cannot be stacked on the smaller discs. The initial configuration and target configuration for this problem are shown in Figure 2.2.

If the state space method is used to solve this problem, the state space graph contains 27 nodes, and each node represents a proper configuration of the disc on the column.

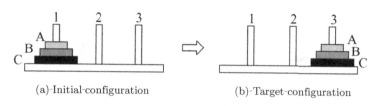

(a) Initial-configuration   (b) Target-configuration

Figure 2.2   Tower of Vatican puzzle.

This problem can also be solved using problem reduction. By reverse reasoning from the goal to the original problem shown in Figure 2.2, the process is as follows:

(i) To move all discs to pillar 3, disc C must first be moved to pillar 3; and before disc C is moved to pillar 3, pillar 3 must be empty.

(ii) Only move disc C after removing discs A and B; and discs A and B should not be moved to column 3, otherwise disc C cannot be moved to column 3. Therefore, discs A and B should be first moved to pillar 2.

(iii) Only then a critical step can be taken to move disc C from pillar 1 to pillar 3 and continue to solve the rest of the puzzle.

The above argument allows the original puzzle to be reduced into the following three sub-problems:

(i) A two-disc puzzle moves discs A and B to pillar 2.

(ii) Move disc C to the single disc puzzle of pillar 3.

(iii) Move the two-disc puzzle of discs A and B to pillar 3.

Since each of the three simplified (reduced) puzzles is smaller, it is easier to solve than the original puzzle. Sub-problem 2 can be considered as the original problem, because its solution contains only a one-step movement. Using a series of similar inferences, sub-problems 1 and 3 can also be reduced to primitive problems, as shown in Figure 2.3. This kind of schema structure is called the AND/OR graph. It can effectively explain how to get the answer to the problem by the problem reduction method.

Problem reduction methods apply operators to transform problem descriptions into sub-problem descriptions. Problem descriptions can have a variety of data structure forms. Table columns, trees, strings, vectors, arrays, and other forms have been used. For the Tower of Vatican puzzle, its sub-problems can be described by a table containing two sequences.

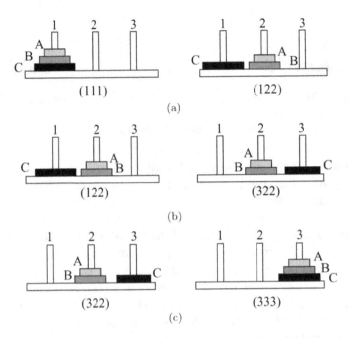

Figure 2.3   Reduction map of the Tower of Vatican Puzzle. (a) Move discs A and B to pillar 2; (b) Middle: Move disc C to pillar 3; (c) Move discs A and B to pillar 3.

Therefore, the problem description [(113), (333)] means "Transform configuration (113) into configuration (333)". Among them, the items in the number series indicate that the three discs are arranged from left to right according to size, and the numerical value of each item indicates the number of the column in which the disc is located.

The ternary combination (S, F, G) represented by the state space can be used to specify and describe the problem. A sub-problem can be described as a problem of finding a path between two states. The Tower of Vatican puzzle is reduced to sub-problems [(111) $\Rightarrow$ (122)], [(122) $\Rightarrow$ (322)] and [(322) $\Rightarrow$ (333)], and the key intermediate states of the problem (122) and (322) can be seen.

The purpose of reducing all questions is to ultimately produce primitive questions with obvious answers. These problems may be problems that can be solved by taking a step in the state space search, or they may be other more complex problems with known answers. In addition to the obvious role of the primitive problem in terminating the search process, it is sometimes used to limit the replacement set that generates subsequent problems in the reduction process. This limitation occurs when one or more successor problems belong to a specified subset of a primitive problem.

(2) AND/OR Graph Representation

It is convenient to use a graph-like structure to represent the replacement set of problem reduction to subsequent problems, and draw a reduction problem graph. For example, imagine that problem A can be solved either by solving problems B and C, by solving problems D, E, and F, or by solving problem H alone. This relationship can be represented by the structure shown in Figure 2.4, where nodes represent problems.

Problems B and C constitute a set of successor problems; problems D, E, and F constitute another set of successor problems; and problem H is a third set. The nodes corresponding to a given set are indicated by a special marker of the arc connecting them.

Some additional nodes are usually introduced into this structure graph so that sets containing more than one successor problem can be aggregated under their respective parent nodes. According to this convention, the structure of Figure 2.4 becomes the structure shown in Figure 2.5. Among them, the additional nodes labeled N and M are, respectively, the sole

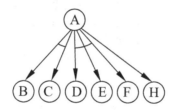

Figure 2.4   Sub-question replacement set structure.

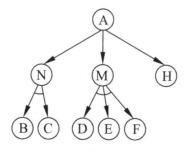

Figure 2.5   The AND/OR graph.

parent nodes of the sets {B, C} and {D, E, F}. If N and M are understood to have the role of problem description, then it can be seen that problem A is reduced to a single replacement sub-problem N, M, and H. Therefore, nodes N, M, and H are called OR nodes. However, the problem N is reduced to a single set of sub-problems B and C, and all sub-problems must be solved for the solution N. Therefore, nodes B and C are called AND nodes. In the same way, nodes D, E, and F are also called AND nodes. Each node is marked with a small arc that spans the arcs of their successor nodes. This structure diagram is called an AND/OR graph.

In the AND/OR graph, if a node has any successor nodes, then these successor nodes can be either all OR nodes or all AND nodes (when a node only contains a single successor node, this successor node can of course be seen as an OR node or an AND node).

Normal graphs applied in state space searches do not appear with AND nodes. Since the AND nodes appear in the AND/OR graph, the structure is quite different from that of the ordinary graph. The AND/OR graph needs to have its own unique search technology, and the existence of AND nodes has become the main basis for distinguishing between the two problem solving methods.

To describe the AND/OR graph, terms such as the parent node, the successor node, and the arc connecting the two nodes will continue to be used to give them a clear meaning. The starting node in the AND/OR graph corresponds to the original problem description. The node corresponding to the primitive problem is called the terminal leaf node. Through an AND/OR graph, a single problem reduction operator is specifically applied to a problem description, and an intermediate OR node and its descendant AND nodes are generated in turn.

In the above graph, each node represents an obvious problem or problem set. Except for the starting node, each node has only one parent node. So, in fact, these graphs are AND/OR trees.

2.2   Knowledge Base

In order to discuss the knowledge base, you first need to know what a database is.

Definition 2.2. A database is a warehouse built on a computer storage device to organize, store, and manage data in accordance with the data structure.

Generally speaking, a database can be regarded as an electronic file cabinet — a place where electronic files are stored, and users can access, add, delete, intercept, and update data in the files.

Definition 2.3. A database is an organized and shareable data collection stored in a computer for a long time. Its data is organized, described, and stored together in a certain data model. It has as little redundancy as possible, high data independence, is easily expandable and can be shared by multiple users within a certain range.

2.2.1 *Definition and characteristics of knowledge base*

Knowledge base is also known as intelligent database. The organic combination of artificial intelligence's knowledge engineering and traditional databases has contributed to the generation and development of knowledge bases and their systems [10, 15, 17].

(1) Definitions of a knowledge base

Definition 2.4. A knowledge base is a structured, easy-to-operate, easy-to-use, comprehensively organized collection of knowledge in knowledge engineering. It is used to solve the problem in one or some fields, and it is stored, organized, managed, and used in a computer using a certain (or several) knowledge representation, an interconnected and ordered collection of knowledge pieces.

These knowledge pieces include theoretical knowledge and factual data related to the domain, heuristic knowledge obtained from expert experience (such as related definitions, theorems, and algorithms in a domain), and common sense.

Definition 2.5. A knowledge base is used to store the expertise of expert systems in a certain field, including facts, feasible operations, and rules. In order to build a knowledge base, we must solve the problems of knowledge acquisition and knowledge representation. Knowledge acquisition involves the question of how a knowledge engineer obtains expertise from an expert; knowledge representation deals with how to express and store knowledge in a form that a computer can understand.

The knowledge base renders knowledge-based systems (or expert systems) intelligent. Not all intelligent programs have a knowledge base; only a knowledge-based system has a knowledge base. Generally, the application program encodes the problem-solving knowledge implicitly in the program, and the knowledge-based system explicitly expresses the problem-solving knowledge of the application domain and forms a relatively independent program entity separately.

(2) Characteristics of a knowledge base

A knowledge base has the following characteristics:

(i) **Modularity of knowledge pieces:** The knowledge in the knowledge base constitutes an easy-to-use and structured organizational form according to their application domain characteristics, background characteristics, usage characteristics, and attribute characteristics.

(ii) **Knowledge:** In the knowledge base the lowest level is "fact knowledge"; the middle level is used to control the "fact" knowledge (usually expressed by rules, processes, etc.); the highest level is "strategy", which uses the middle level knowledge as the control object. Therefore, the basic structure of the knowledge base is a hierarchical structure, which is determined by the characteristics of the knowledge itself. In the knowledge base, there is usually an interdependent relationship between knowledge pieces. Rules are the most typical and commonly used kind of knowledge pieces.

(iii) **No uncertainty measure:** The knowledge base can have a special form of knowledge that belongs to more than one level (or exists at any level). All data processing in the database is "deterministic".

(iv) **A library of typical methods exists:** If the solution to certain problems is affirmative and inevitable, it can be directly stored in a typical method library as part of a fairly certain problem-solving solution. In using this part, machine reasoning will be limited to the selection of a layer body part of a typical method library.

2.2.2 *Design and application of knowledge base*

(1) Design steps of knowledge base

The general steps to establish a knowledge base are as follows [15]:

(i) **Design the initial knowledge base:** The design of the knowledge base is the most important and arduous task in building an expert system.

The initial knowledge base design includes the following:

(a) Becoming knowledgeable of the problem, i.e., to identify the essence of the problem under study, such as the task to be solved, how it is defined, whether it can be broken down into sub-problems and sub-tasks, what typical data it contains, etc.

(b) The conceptualization of the knowledge, which summarizes the key concepts and relationships required for knowledge representation, such as data types, known conditions (states) and goals (states), proposed assumptions, and control strategies.

(c) The conceptualization of the knowledge, which summarizes the key concepts and relationships needed for knowledge representation, such as data types, known conditions (states) and goals (states), proposed assumptions, and control strategies.

(d) The formalization of the concepts, i.e., determining the form of data structures used to organize knowledge, and applying various knowledge representation methods in artificial intelligence to transform key concepts, sub-problems, and information flow characteristics related to the conceptualization process into more formal expressions. It includes hypothesis space, process models, and data characteristics.

(e) The regularization of the forms, which is the process of formulating rules, transforming formalized knowledge into computer-executable statements and programs represented by programming languages.

(f) The legalization of the rules, i.e., the confirmation of the rationality of the knowledge and the validity of the rules.

(ii) **Improvement and induction of the knowledge base:** After repeated experiments on the initial knowledge base, it is necessary to repeatedly improve the knowledge base and reasoning rules to derive more perfect results. After a considerable amount of effort, the system reaches the level of human experts within a certain range.

The knowledge base design and knowledge acquisition steps are shown in Figure 2.6.

(2) Application of knowledge base

Knowledge bases and knowledge base systems have been widely used in the development of related software systems, including Internet-based architecture, rapid analysis of corporate knowledge structure, classified storage of knowledge data, shared knowledge applications, improvement

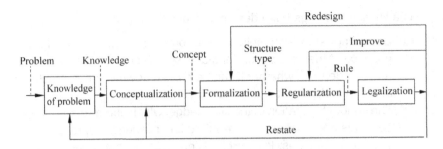

Figure 2.6   Steps of knowledge base design and knowledge acquisition.

of corporate management efficiency, value-added corporate knowledge assets, and core competitiveness software development.

The knowledge base is one of the key components of the expert system. Together with the inference engine, it constitutes the core part of the expert system. It is also the basis for the successful development and application of the expert system.

Various structured knowledge bases are also an integral part of the knowledge graph. For example, open-link knowledge bases such as Freebase, Wikidata, DBpedia, and YAGO and industry knowledge bases such as IMDB, MusicBrainz, and ConceptNet are representatives of the library of all large-scale knowledge bases with high visibility.

The knowledge base is also a core part of a machine learning system and an important factor influencing the design of a machine learning system. Every learning system needs some knowledge to understand the information provided by the environment, analyze and compare, make hypotheses, and test and modify these hypotheses. Machine learning systems are extensions and improvements to existing knowledge.

2.3 Ontology

This section discusses the basic concepts, composition, and classification of ontology and briefly introduces the modeling methods of ontology.

2.3.1 *Concept and definition of ontology*

Gruber pointed out in 1993 the following: "Ontology is an explicit specification or representation of conceptualization". In order to clarify the understanding of ontology, Guarino and Giaretta conducted an in-depth analysis of the seven different conceptual interpretations of ontology. In

1995, the following definition was given: "Ontology is an explicit specification or representation of certain conceptualization aspects". Borst gave a similar definition in 1997: "The ontology can be defined as a formal specification of the sharing conceptualization".

These three definitions have become frequently cited definitions, all of which emphasize formal interpretations and specification of "conceptualization". At the same time, it shows that the knowledge described by ontology is shared.

Grinot gave a more reasonable explanation of "conceptualization" in the above definition, and further explained the relationship between conceptualization and ontology. The following paragraphs briefly explain his interpretation of "conceptualization".

Definition 2.6. Domain space: The domain space is defined as $\langle D, W \rangle$, where D represents the domain and W represents the set of the largest states of the event in the domain (also known as the possible world).

Definition 2.7. Conceptual relationship: The n-element concept relation on $\langle D, W \rangle$ is defined as $\rho^n: W \to 2^{D^n}$, which represents the full function of all n-element relation sets of the set W in the domain D.

For the conceptual relation ρ, the set $E_\rho = \{\rho(w) \mid w \in W\}$ contains all the extensions that ρ can accept.

Definition 2.8. Conceptualization: The conceptualization of D in the domain space $\langle D, W \rangle$ is defined as an ordered triplet $C = \langle D, W, \acute{R} \rangle$, where $\langle D, W \rangle$ is the domain space, and $\acute{R}$ is a set of conceptual relationships.

As can be seen from the above definition, conceptualization is a collection of all conceptual relationships defined in a domain space.

Definition 2.9. Intended structure: $(\forall w) \in W$, S_{wC} is the intention structure of the possible world w with respect to C, $S_{wC} = \langle D, R_{wC} \rangle$, where $R_{wC} = \{\rho(w) \mid \rho \in \acute{R}\}$, which means an extended set of w for the concept relationship in $\acute{R}$.

The symbol S_C represents all intentional world structures of conceptual C, $S_C = \{S_{wC} \mid w \in\}$.

Definition 2.10. Model: Assume that the logical language L has a vocabulary V, and the vocabulary V consists of a set of constant symbols and a set of predicate symbols. The model of the logical language L is defined as the structure $\langle S, I \rangle$, where $S = \langle D, R \rangle$ represents a world structure; I: $V \rightarrow D \cup R$ represents an interpretation function, mapping the constant symbols in V to D, an element that maps a predicate symbol in V to an element in R.

As can be seen from the above definition, a model determines the specific extended interpretation of a language. Similarly, through conceptualization, the connotation interpretation $\langle C, 3 \rangle$ can be determined as a structure $\langle C, 3 \rangle$ through conceptualization, where $C = \langle D, W, \acute{R} \rangle$ is a conceptualization, $3 : V \rightarrow D \cup \acute{R}$ denotes an interpretation function, the constant symbols in V are mapped to elements in D, and the predicate symbols in V are mapped to elements in $\acute{R}$.

Definition 2.11. Ontological commitment: An ontological commitment $\langle K = C, 3 \rangle$, of the logical language L is defined as an intrinsic interpretation model of L, where $C = \langle D, W, \acute{R} \rangle$, 3, $V \rightarrow D \cup \acute{R}$ represents a connotative interpretation function that maps the constant symbols in V to elements in D and maps the predicate symbols in V to elements in $\acute{R}$.

If $K = \langle C, 3 \rangle$ is the ontological commitment of the logical language L, then the logical language L promises to conceptualize C by the ontology commitment K, and at the same time, C is the basic conceptualization of K.

Knowing the logical language L and its vocabulary V, $K = \langle C, 3 \rangle$ are the ontological promises of the logical language, then the model $\langle S, I \rangle$ and K compatibility need to meet the following conditions:

$$S \in S_C.$$

For each constant c, $I(c) = 3(c)$;

There is a possible world w, for each predicate symbol p, satisfying I to map the predicate p to the extension allowed by $3(p)$. That is, there is a conceptual relationship ρ that satisfies $3(p) = \rho \wedge \rho(w) = I(p)$.

Definition 2.12. Intended model: All the K-compatible models $M(L)$ of the logical language L form a set, called the intentional model of L with respect to K, denoted $I_K(L)$, see Figure 2.7.

Given a logical language L and its ontology commitment $K = \langle C, 3 \rangle$, the ontology of L is an axiom set designed in such a way that the set of models of the ontology is closest to the set of connotative models of L with respect to K.

Definition 2.13. Ontology is a logical theory that explains the connotation of formal vocabulary, i.e., a specific conceptualization of the vocabulary world. The connotation model of the logical language L using the vocabulary is subject to the ontology commitment K.

If there is an ontology commitment $K = \langle C, 3 \rangle$ that causes the ontology O to contain a connotation model of L with respect to K, then the ontology O of the language L is said to be similar to the conceptual C.

If the design of the ontology O is to describe the features of the conceptual C, while the ontology O is similar to the conceptual C, then the ontology is committed to C. If the logical language L is committed to a conceptual C, and the ontology O is committed to conceptualizing C, then the logical language L is committed to the ontology O.

Figure 2.7 shows a schematic diagram of the relationship between language L, ontology O, and conceptual C. Ontology O is a logical theory used to explain the meaning of formal vocabulary connotations. The connotative model of logical language L using this vocabulary is bound by ontology commitment K. The ontology indirectly reflects these ontology commitments by approaching these intrinsic models. The ontology O is language-dependent, while the conceptual C is language-independent.

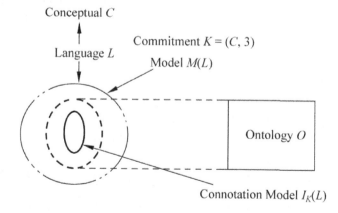

Figure 2.7   Conceptualization, language, and ontology diagram.

2.3.2 *Composition and classification of ontology*

(1) Composition of the ontology

In the field of knowledge engineering, ontology is an engineering artifact that consists of a specific set of terms used to describe a certain real-world situation, plus an explicit hypothetical set of meanings about the connotation of the term. In the simplest case, the ontology only describes the hierarchical structure of the concept; in complex cases, the ontology can add a set of appropriate relationships, axioms, and rules to represent other relationships between concepts based on the conceptual classification hierarchy, and the connotation of the concept of constraints.

In a nutshell, a complete ontology should consist of five basic elements: concept, relationship, functions, axiom, and instance.

The concepts are concepts in a broad sense. In addition to concepts in the general sense, they can also be tasks, functions, behaviors, strategies, reasoning processes, and so on. These concepts in ontology usually form a hierarchy of classifications.

Relationships represent a type of association between concepts. A typical binary association, such as an inheritance relationship, forms the hierarchical structure of the concept.

A function is a special relationship in which the nth element is uniquely determined for the first $n - 1$ elements. In general, the functions are represented by $F: C_1...C_{n-1} C_n$.

Axioms are used to describe some immortal. More specifically, axioms are assertions that are established under any conditions in the field.

An instance is a concrete instance of a concept, and all instances of a particular domain constitute the referential domain of the domain concept class.

(2) Classification of Ontology

From different perspectives, there are a variety of classification criteria for ontology. According to the theme of the ontology, the current common ontology can be divided into the following five types:

(i) Knowledge representation ontology: it includes the essential features and basic attributes of knowledge.
(ii) Common sense ontology: it includes common knowledge engineering and common sense knowledge base.

(iii) Domain ontology: it provides a concept that can be reused in a specific domain, the attributes of a concept, the relationship between concepts, and the constraints on the attributes and relationships, or the main theories and basic principles of the domain.

(iv) Ontology of linguistics: it refers to the ontology of language and vocabulary, etc.

(v) Task ontology: it mainly involves dynamic knowledge, not static knowledge.

In addition, ontology has many other classifications. Just like the concept of ontology, the academic community currently has many different views on the classification of ontology. Some commonly used concepts have a guiding role in the classification of ontology and will also help to build ontology.

2.3.3 *Ontology modeling*

Constructing a domain of ontology can greatly improve the information processing capability of the computer in the field and improve its information sharing effect in the field. At present, ontology has become the core of research areas such as knowledge acquisition and representation, planning, process management, database framework integration, natural language processing, and enterprise simulation.

(1) Method of ontology modeling

The process of establishing an ontology model can be divided into an informal phase and a formal phase. In the informal phase, the ontology model is described by natural languages and graphs, such as using conceptual diagrams to represent ontology and forming ontology prototypes. In the formal phase, the ontology model is encoded by knowledge representation languages (such as RDF, DAML+OIL, OWL, etc.) to form an ontology that is convenient for people to communicate and is unambiguous and can be directly interpreted by software or agents.

Since ontology engineering is still in a relatively immature stage, each project has its own independent method. For example, the "skeleton" method of Uschold and King, the "evaluation method" (TOVE) of Gruninger Fox, and the KACTUS project of Berneras, the Methontology method of the University of Madrid, the SENSUS method, and the five-stage method of Gandon.

The NUDT5 ontology established by Gan and Tang's five-stage method describes the status of an information system and management laboratory, which can be used for the information system and knowledge management of each laboratory. The five phases of the ontology modeling process are the following:

Phase 1: Data collection and analysis: Relevant concepts are extracted from the organization's documents and reports.

Phase 2: Build a dictionary: Get definitions of these concepts.

Phase 3: Refine the dictionary and build a richer table: Categorize concepts, establish more detailed tables, and draw a hierarchical structure diagram of the ontology concepts.

Phase 4: Describe the above tables in RDFS language: Describe the top-level concept, middle-level concept, extension-level concept, top-level relationship, middle-level relationship, and extension-level relationship by the use of RDFS.

Ontology is divided into three layers: top-level concepts and relationships, middle-level concepts and relationships, and extension-level concepts and relationships. The top-level ontology is the most abstract one, and it can be reused for all problems and domains. The middle-level ontology can be reused for similar domains. The extension-level ontology is only available in this field. For other fields, this part of the ontology needs to be re-established.

Phase 5: Define the algebraic properties of the relationship and define the rules of reasoning for knowledge.

(2) Ontology modeling language

The original design of the Internet was to provide a distributed shared information space to support human information query and information communication through hyperlinks. However, such information representation and organization methods are not structured, and the machine program cannot understand the content of the information and perform automatic processing. Semantic web technology, which has emerged in recent years, aims to establish a "Web that talks to computers" so that computers can make full use of the resources of the Web to provide better services to human beings. Semantic web technology goes beyond the limitations of the traditional Internet. It uses a structured and logically linked representation to encode information so that the information on the Web has computer-understandable semantics that satisfy the agent's effectiveness in access, search, and reasoning heterogeneous and distributed information on the Web. W3C is the main creator of Web standards and the main advocate of new technologies. The organization has set up a research group on semantic Web named WorkGroup, and used the XML protocol family as one of the foundations for implementing semantic Web.

One of the core concepts of semantic Web is ontology, which defines the basic terms and relationships that make up the subject domain vocabulary, as well as the rules for combining terms and relationships to define lexical extensions. This section uses ontology to acquire knowledge in a certain domain and ontology to describe concepts in the domain and the relationships between these concepts. After the ontology is established, the ontology should be described and stored according to a certain standard format. The language used to describe the ontology is called the ontology description language. The ontology description language enables users to write clear and formal concept descriptions for the domain models, so it should meet the following requirements:

(1) well-defined grammar;
(2) well-defined semantics;
(3) effective reasoning support;
(4) sufficient ability to express;
(5) easy to express.

Many researchers are working on ontology description languages, so many ontology description languages have emerged, each with its own merits, including RDF and RDF-S, OIL, DAML, DAML+OIL, OWL, XML, KIF, SHOE, XOL, OCML, Ontolingua, CycL, Loom, etc. Among them, related to the specific system (basically only used in related projects) are Ontolingua, CycL, Loom, and so on. Related to the Web are RDF and RDF-S, OIL, DAML, DAML+OIL, OWL, SHOE, XOL, etc. Among them, RDF has a close relationship with RDF-S, OIL, DAML, OWL, and XOL. It is a different level in W3C's ontology language standard, and it is also based on XML. SHOE is based on HTML and is an extension of HTML.

Realizing the semantic representation and automatic processing of Web data is a long-term goal of the future development of Internet technology. At present, DARPA, W3C, Standford, MIT, Harvard, TC&C, and many other research institutions are working hard to achieve the vision of the semantic web and explore solutions to this problem from different aspects.

The intelligent processing model represented by Agent technology is considered to be a model with good application prospects in widely distributed, heterogeneous and uncertain information environments, and multi-agents need to use ontology when running on the semantic Web. Therefore, ontology technology has become a research hotspot of current semantic Web technology.

The application of ontology in the field of information systems has become increasingly important and widespread. Its main applications include knowledge engineering, database design and integration, information system inter-operation, simulation, information retrieval and extraction, semantic Web, and knowledge management, knowledge graph, intelligent information processing and other fields.

2.4 Semantic Network Representation

The semantic network is a structured graphical representation of knowledge that is different from state-space graphics.

2.4.1 *Composition and characteristics of the semantic network*

The semantic network consists of nodes and arcs or chains. Nodes are used to represent entities, concepts, and situations, and arcs are used to represent the relationships between nodes. The semantic network representation consists of the following four related parts:

(1) Lexical part: Determines which symbols are allowed in the vocabulary, involving various nodes and arcs.
(2) Structure part: Describes the constraints of symbol arrangement and specifies the pairs of nodes to which each arc is connected.
(3) Process part: Explains the access process, which can be used to create and correct descriptions, and to answer related questions.
(4) Semantic part: Determine the arrangement of related nodes, their possessions and corresponding arcs.

The semantic network has the following characteristics:

(1) The structure and attributes of entities and the causal relationship between entities can be expressed explicitly and concisely. Facts, characteristics, and relationships related to entities can be deduced through

corresponding node arcs, which facilitates the realization of associations in an associative manner, which facilitates the interpretation of the system in an associative manner.

(2) Because the attributes and connections related to the concept are organized in a corresponding node, the concept is easy to access and learn.

(3) Performance issues are more intuitive and easier to understand, and are suitable for knowledge engineers to communicate with domain experts. The inheritance style in the semantic network also conforms to human thinking habits.

(4) The semantic interpretation of the semantic network structure depends on the reasoning process of the structure without a structural convention, so the resulting reasoning cannot guarantee the validity of the predicate logic method.

(5) The connections between nodes may be linear, tree-like, network-like, or even recursive structures, so that the corresponding knowledge storage and retrieval may require more complicated processes.

2.4.2 *Representation of a binary semantic network*

First, use the semantic network to represent some simple facts. For example, all swallows are birds. Create two nodes, SWALLOW and BIRD, which represent swallows and birds, respectively. The two nodes are connected by an "is one" (ISA) chain, as shown in Figure 2.8(a). For example, XIAOYAN is a swallow. Then, only one node (XIAOYAN) and one ISA chain need to be added to the semantic network, as shown in Figure 2.8(b). In addition to classifying objects by taxonomy, people often need to represent knowledge about the properties of the objects. For example, to represent the fact that birds have wings with a semantic network, you can build a semantic network as shown in Figure 2.8(c).

Suppose you want to represent the fact that Xiaoyan has a nest, so that the ownership chain OWNS can be connected to the node nest-1 (NEST-1), which is Xiaoyan's nest, as shown in Figure 2.9. Nest-1 is one of the nests, i.e., the NEST node represents the type of object, and NEST-1 represents an example of such an object. If you want to add Xiaoyan's information of occupying a nest from spring to fall to a semantic network, the existing semantic network cannot achieve this. Because the relationship of possession is represented as a chain in the semantic network, it can only represent binary relationships. If a predicate calculus is used to represent the example in question, a quaternary predicate calculus is used. What is needed

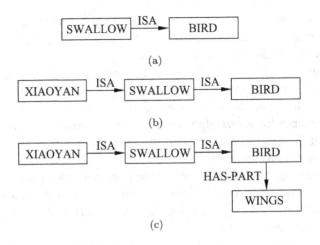

Figure 2.8   Example 1 of a semantic network.

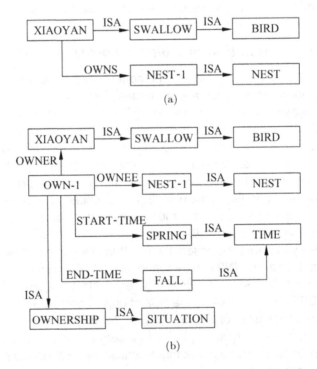

Figure 2.9   Example 2 of semantic network.

now is a semantic network that is equivalent to such a quaternary predicate calculus and can represent the start time, end time, possessor, and possession of the possessive relationship.

The methods proposed by Simmons and Slocum allow nodes to represent either an object or a group of objects, as well as situations and actions. Each case node can have a set of outward arcs (case arcs) called a case box to illustrate the various variables associated with the instance. For example, the semantic network of the fact that the situation node with the case arc indicates that "Xiaoyan has a nest from spring to autumn" is shown in Figure 2.9(b). The "Occupy-1" (OWN-1) node is set up in the figure, indicating that Xiaoyan has its own nest. Of course, Xiaoyan can also have other things. Therefore, possession-1 is only an instance of ownership. Possession is just a specific "situation". Xiaoyan is a specific "owner" of "Occupy-1", while NEST-1 is a specific "OWNEE" of OWN-1. In Xiaoyan's possession of "OWN-1" from spring to fall, spring and fall is again defined as an example of time.

When selecting a node, you must first understand whether the node is used to represent basic objects or concepts, or used for multiple purposes. Otherwise, if the semantic network is only used to represent a specific object or concept, then more semantic networks are needed when there are more instances. Knowledge about an object or concept, or a group of related objects or concepts, is usually represented by a semantic network. Otherwise, it will cause too much network and complicate the problem. Related to this is the problem of finding basic concepts and some basic arcs. This is called the "choose semantic primitive" problem. Choosing a semantic primitive is an attempt to represent knowledge with a set of primitives. These primitives describe the basics and are interconnected in a graphical representation. In this way, simple knowledge can be used to express more complex knowledge.

2.4.3 *Representation of a multi-element semantic network*

The semantic network is a network structure. Nodes are connected by chains. Essentially, the connections between nodes are binary relationships. If the knowledge to be represented is a unitary relationship, for example, to indicate that Li Ming is a person, this can be expressed as MAN (LI MING) in the predicate logic. With a semantic network, this can be expressed as LI MING ISA MAN. The relationship equivalent to such a representation is expressed as ISA (LIMING, MAN) in the predicate logic. This shows that the semantic network can represent the unary relationship without difficulty.

If the facts to be represented are multi-relations, for example, to express the score of a basketball team of Peking University (PKU) and Tsinghua University (TU) at Peking University as 85 to 89. If the predicate logic is used, it can be expressed as SCORE (BU, TU, (85–89)). This expression contains three items, and the semantic network can only represent binary relations in essence. One way to solve this contradiction is to transform this multivariate relationship into a set of binary relations or a conjunction of binary relations. Specifically, the multivariate relationship $R(X_1, X_2, \ldots, X_n)$ can always be converted into $R_1 (X_{11}, X_{12}) \wedge R_2 (X_{21}, X_{22}) \wedge \ldots \wedge R_n (X_{n1}, X_{n2})$. For example, three lines a, b, c constitutes a triangle. This can be expressed as TRIANGLE (a, b, c). This ternary relationship can be converted into a conjunction of a set of binary relations, i.e.

$$\text{CAT } (a, b) \wedge \text{CAT } (b, c) \wedge \text{CAT } (c, a)$$

where CAT represents a serial connection.

To make this conversion in the semantic network, the introduction of additional nodes is required. For the above game, you can create a G25 node to represent this particular game. Then, link the game information to the game. This process is shown in Figure 2.10.

Semantic networks can be used to represent various conjunctions and quantifications in predicate logic.

2.4.4 *Inference process of a semantic network*

In the knowledge representation method of a semantic network, there is no formal semantics; that is to say, unlike the predicate logic, there is no uniform representation of what semantics is for a given expression structure. The

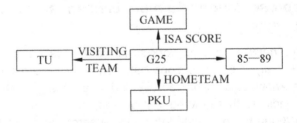

Figure 2.10   Multivariate relationships representation of a semantic network.

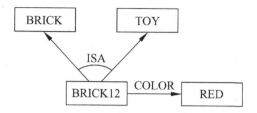

Figure 2.11 Slots and values of the semantic network.

meaning assigned to the network structure is entirely determined by the nature of the process of managing the network. A variety of network-based systems have been designed so that each employs a completely different process of reasoning.

In order to facilitate the following description, the symbols used are further defined. Distinguish between the head of the chain and the node at the end of the chain, and refer to the node at the end of the chain as a value node. In addition, it is also stipulated that the slot of the node is equivalent to the chain, but takes a different name. In Figure 2.11, the brick 12 (BRICK 12) has three chains that form two slots. One slot has only one value and the other slot has two values. The color slot (COLOR) is filled in red (RED), and the ISA slot is filled with bricks (BRICK) and toys (TOY).

There are two main reasoning processes in the semantic network: one is inheritance and the other is matching.

Inheritance is the transfer of descriptions of things from concept nodes or class nodes to instance nodes. There are three types of inheritance: value inheritance, "if needed" inheritance, and "default" inheritance. Matching refers to the need to find the connection between nodes (such as parts) that satisfies the corresponding relationship when solving a thing composed of several parts, i.e., to find related connections to achieve the matching of the corresponding parts of the thing.

2.5 Knowledge Graph

Since the advent of computer networks, Web technology has continued to undergo rapid development. It has experienced the "Web 1.0" era featuring document interconnection and the "Web 2.0" era featuring data interconnection, and is developing to the "Web 3.0" era based on knowledge interconnection. The goal of Web 3.0 is to build a World Wide Web that people and machines understand together, reveal the integrity and relevance of human cognition at a deeper level, and realize network intelligence. The knowledge graph, with its strong semantic processing capabilities and open interconnection capabilities, lays a solid foundation for knowledge interconnection, making the "knowledge network" concept proposed by Web 3.0 possible [1, 14].

Google formally proposed the knowledge map on May 17, 2012. Its original wish was to improve the search capabilities of the engine, improve the search quality of the users, and enhance the search experience.

2.5.1 *Definition and architecture of knowledge graph*

(1) Definition of knowledge graph

Definition 2.14. According to Wikipedia entries, the Knowledge Graph is a knowledge base that Google uses to enhance its search engine capabilities. Knowledge graph is essentially a semantic network representing the relationship between entities, which can formally describe real-world things and their relationships [23].

From the above definitions, the knowledge graph is a kind of knowledge base and a kind of semantic network; it illustrates the close relationship between the knowledge graph, the knowledge base, and the semantic network. The current knowledge graph is often used to refer to various large-scale knowledge bases.

The general representation of the knowledge graph is a triplet, i.e., $G = (E, R, S)$, where

$E = \{e1, e2, e \mid E|\}$ is a set of entities in the knowledge base, which contains $|E|$ E different entities;

$R = \{r1, r2, r \mid E|\}$ is a set of relationships in the knowledge base, which contains $|R|$ R different relationships;

$S \subseteq E \times R \times E$ represents the set of triples in the knowledge base.

The basic form of triples mainly includes entity 1, relationship, entity 2 and concepts, attributes, attribute values, etc. Entities are the most basic elements of the knowledge graph, and different entities have different relationships. Concepts mainly refer to collections, categories, types of objects, types of things, such as plants and animals, countries, etc. Attributes mainly refer to the attributes, characteristics, and parameters that an object may have, such as weight, place of birth, etc. Attribute values mainly refer to object designation. Examples of the values of the attributes are Egypt,

2020-01-16, 65 kg, 26 years, etc. Each entity (concept extension) can be identified by a globally unique ID. Each attribute–value pair is used to describe the intrinsic characteristics of the entity, and the relationship can be used to connect two entities and describe their association.

According to the scope of application, knowledge graphs can be divided into general knowledge graphs and industry knowledge graphs. The general knowledge graph is mainly used in intelligent search and other fields. It pays attention to breadth and emphasizes the integration of more entities. Its accuracy is lower than that of the industry knowledge graph, and it is susceptible to the scope of the concept. It is difficult to use the ontology library's ability to support axioms, rules, and constraints to regulate its entities, their relationships, and attributes. The industry knowledge graph generally needs to be constructed based on the data of a specific industry, which has specific industry significance. In the industry knowledge graph, the attributes and data models of entities are often rich, and different business scenarios and users need to be considered.

(2) The structure of the knowledge graph

The structure of the knowledge graph is shown in Figure 2.12. The dashed box in the figure indicates the construction process of the knowledge graph, and it is also the process of updating the knowledge graph, including information acquisition, knowledge fusion, and knowledge processing. The data acquisition part on the left involves data acquisition of structured data, semistructured, and unstructured data; on the right is a large-scale database — knowledge graph that can be used for knowledge search [3,11].

The technical architecture of the knowledge graph is further explained below.

The three input data structures to the left of the dashed box are structured data, semi-structured data, and unstructured data; they can come from anywhere as long as they are needed to build this knowledge graph.

The dotted box indicates the construction process of the entire knowledge graph. It includes the following three stages: information acquisition, knowledge fusion, and knowledge processing.

On the far right is the generated knowledge graph, and this technical architecture is a process of cyclical and iterative updating. The knowledge graph is not generated at one time, but a process of gradual accumulation. Information acquisition is to extract entities, attributes, and relationships between entities from various types of data sources, and form an ontological knowledge representation based on this; knowledge fusion is the

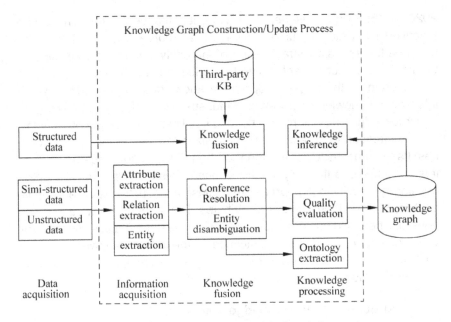

Figure 2.12   Technical architecture of the knowledge graph.

integration of acquired new knowledge to eliminate possible occurrences of contradictions and ambiguities, such as an entity may have multiple representations, some specific titles may correspond to multiple different entities, etc.; knowledge processing is to evaluate the quality of new knowledge that has been fused (some require manual participation in screening), and then only qualified new knowledge can be added to the knowledge graph to ensure the quality of the knowledge graph in the knowledge base.

2.5.2 *Key technologies of knowledge graph*

The information acquisition, knowledge fusion, and knowledge processing of the knowledge graph are the key technologies for constructing the knowledge graph. Each of the three processes of the knowledge graph has its own difficulties. The problems and difficulties encountered in the three modules are described below [2, 8].

(1) Information acquisition

Information acquisition is the first step in constructing a knowledge graph. The key issue is how to automatically extract information from heterogeneous data sources to obtain candidate indication units. Information acquisition is a technology that automatically extracts structured information such as entities, relationships, and entity attributes from semi-structured and unstructured data. It involves key technologies such as entity extraction, relationship extraction, and attributes extraction [20].

(i) Entity Extraction

Entity extraction, also known as named entity recognition (NER), refers to the automatic identification of named entities from a text data set. The quality (accuracy and recall) of entity extraction has a great impact on the efficiency and quality of subsequent knowledge acquisition and is the most basic and critical part of information acquisition.

In 2012, Ling *et al.* summarized 112 types of entities, based on the conditional random field (CRF) for entity boundary recognition and used an adaptive perceptron algorithm to achieve automatic classification of entities and achieved good results.

With the dynamic changes of Internet content, the use of artificially defined entity classification systems has been unable to meet new requirements, and research on entity recognition and classification for open domains has emerged as the times require. Such entity recognition and classification research does not need (and is not possible) to establish a separate corpus as a training set for each domain or each entity category. Therefore, the main challenge in this field is how to automatically discover discriminative models from a given small number of entity instances. One idea is to perform feature modeling based on known entity instances, then use this model to process massive data sets to obtain a new named entity list, and then model the new entity to iteratively generate an entity tagging corpus. Another idea is to use the server log of the search engine, without giving the entity classification and other information in advance, but based on the semantic characteristics of the entity to identify named entities from the search log and then use a clustering algorithm to identify the identified entity objects classification.

(ii) Relation Extraction

The text corpus is extracted by entities, and a series of discrete named entities are obtained. In order to obtain semantic information, it is also necessary to extract the association relationship between entities from related corpora, and to associate entities (concepts) through association relationships to form a network knowledge structure. The purpose of researching relation extraction technology is to solve the basic problem of how to extract the relations between entities from text corpora.

Relation extraction methods include pattern matching methods (artificially constructed grammar and semantic rules), statistical machine learning methods, supervised learning methods based on feature vectors or kernel functions, semi-supervised and unsupervised learning methods, open domain-oriented information extraction methods, and an open domain-oriented information extraction method combined with a closed domain-oriented traditional method.

(iii) Attribute Extraction

The goal of attribute extraction is to collect attribute information of specific entities from different information sources. Attribute extraction technology can aggregate this information from multiple data sources to achieve a complete picture of entity attributes.

The methods of attribute extraction include the following: transforming the attribute extraction task into a relation extraction task (considering the attribute of the entity as a nominal relationship between the entity and the attribute value); based on rules and heuristic algorithms (extracting structured data); based on the method for extracting semi-structured data from encyclopedia websites (generating a training corpus by automatically extracting semi-structured data for training entity attribute labeling models and then applying it to entity attribute extraction of unstructured data); data mining methods (mining the relationship pattern between entity attributes and attribute values directly from the text, the positioning of attribute names and attribute values in the text is achieved accordingly).

(2) Knowledge fusion

Through information extraction, entities, relationships, and entity attribute information are obtained from the original unstructured and semi-structured data.

If the next process is likened to a jigsaw, then the extracted information is jigsaw pieces, cluttered, and the wrong pieces running from other jigsaw pieces to interfere with the extracted jigsaw.

The relationship between puzzle pieces (information) is flat, lacking hierarchy and logic; there are also a lot of redundant and incorrect puzzle pieces (information) in the puzzle (knowledge). How to solve this problem is what the knowledge fusion needs to determine.

Knowledge fusion includes two elements: entity linking and knowledge merging.

(i) Entity linking:

Entity linking refers to the operation of linking the entity objects extracted from the text to the corresponding correct entity objects in the knowledge base. The basic idea is the following: first, according to a given entity reference item, a set of candidate entity objects is selected from the knowledge base, and then the referral necklace is connected to the correct entity object through similarity calculation.

The process of entity linking is as follows: entity references are extracted from the text through entities. Perform entity disambiguation and co-reference resolution to determine whether entities with the same name in the knowledge base have different meanings and whether other named entities in the knowledge base have the same meaning. After confirming the corresponding correct entity object in the knowledge base, the entity reference necklace is connected to the corresponding entity in the knowledge base.

Entity disambiguation: It is a technique used to resolve ambiguity issues with entities of the same name. Through entity disambiguation, entity linking can be accurately established based on the current context. Entity disambiguation adopts the clustering method, which can also be regarded as a context-based classification problem, similar to part-of-speech disambiguation and word-sense disambiguation.

Co-reference resolution: It is mainly used to solve the problem that multiple references correspond to the same physical object. In one session, multiple references may point to the same physical object. Co-finger resolution techniques can be used to associate (merge) these references with the correct physical object. There are other names for co-reference resolution, such as object alignment, entity synonymy, and entity matching.

(ii) Knowledge merger:

When building a knowledge graph, knowledge input can be obtained from third-party knowledge base products or existing structured data. There are two common knowledge merger requirements. One is to merge external knowledge bases, and the other is to merge relational databases.

Fusion of an external knowledge base to a local knowledge base needs to deal with two layers of issues: data layer fusion and mode layer fusion. Data layer fusion includes entity references, attributes, relationships, and categories. The main problem is how to avoid conflicts between instances and relationships, causing unnecessary redundancy. The fusion of the pattern layer integrates the newly obtained ontology into the existing ontology library. Then it has to merge relational databases. In the process of knowledge graph construction, an important source of high-quality knowledge is the relational database of an enterprise or an institution. In order to incorporate these structured historical data into the knowledge graph, a resource description framework (RDF) can be used as the data model. The industry and academia refer to this data conversion process as RDB2RDF. Its essence is to replace the data of the relational database with the triples of RDF.

(3) Knowledge processing

Information elements such as entities, relationships, and attributes were previously extracted from the original corpus through information acquisition, and after knowledge fusion, the ambiguity between entity references and entity objects was eliminated, and a series of basic facts were obtained. However, facts are not the same as knowledge. In order to finally obtain a structured and networked knowledge system, a process of knowledge processing is required. Knowledge processing mainly includes four aspects: (i) ontology construction, (ii) knowledge reasoning, (iii) quality assessment, and (iv) knowledge update [2, 16].

(i) Ontology construction:

Ontology refers to the formal expression of certain concepts and their relationships in specific fields, such as "people", "things", "objects", etc. The ontology can be constructed manually by means of manual editing (by means of ontology editing software), or it can be constructed by data-driven automation. Because the manual method has a huge workload and it is difficult to find experts who meet the requirements, the current mainstream global ontology library products are based on existing ontology libraries that are oriented to specific fields and are gradually expanded by using automatic construction technology.

The process of building an automated ontology includes three phases: similarity calculation of entity parallel relationships, extraction of upper and lower entity relationships, and generation of ontology.

(ii) Knowledge reasoning:

After the construction of the ontology is completed, a prototype of the knowledge graph has been established. Most of the relationships between the knowledge graphs may be incomplete, and the missing values are very serious. Knowledge discovery techniques can be used to complete further knowledge discovery.

It can be found that if A is the spouse of B, B is the boss of C, and C is located in D, then we can think that A lives in the city of D.

According to this rule, you can discover whether there are other paths in the graph that meet this condition, and you can associate A and D. In addition, you can also think that there is a link in the series where B is the boss of C. Then B is the CEO of C or B is the CTO of C. Can it also be used as part of this reasoning strategy?

Of course, the object of knowledge reasoning is not limited to the relationship between entities, but can also be the attribute value of the entity and the conceptual hierarchical relationship of the ontology.

Reasoning attribute value: Given the birthday attribute of an entity, the age attribute of the entity can be obtained by inference.

Reasoning concepts: Known (Tiger, family, feline) and (Feline, order, carnivorous) can be introduced (tiger, order, carnivorous).

Knowledge reasoning algorithms can be divided into three categories: logic-based reasoning, graph-based reasoning, and deep learning-based reasoning.

(iii) Quality assessment:

Quality assessment is also an important part of the knowledge base construction technology. It can quantify the credibility of the knowledge and guarantee the quality of the knowledge base by discarding knowledge with lower confidence.

(iv) Knowledge update:

The update of the knowledge base includes the update of the concept layer and the update of the data layer. Concept layer update means that new concepts are obtained after new data is added, and new concepts need to be automatically added to the concept layer of the knowledge base. The data layer update is mainly to add or update entities, relationships, and attribute values. To update the data layer, you need to consider reliable data sources such as the reliability of the data source and the consistency of the data. Properties are added to the knowledge base.

There are two ways to update the content of the knowledge graph: a comprehensive update takes all the updated data as input and builds a knowledge graph from scratch. This method is relatively simple, but it consumes a lot of resources and requires a lot of human resources for system maintenance. Incremental update takes newly added data as input and adds new knowledge to the existing knowledge graph. This method consumes less resource, but requires a lot of manual intervention (defining rules, etc.), so it is difficult to implement [4, 22].

2.6 Frame Representation

The results of psychological research show that in the daily thinking and understanding activities of human beings, when analyzing and explaining new situations, we must use the accumulated knowledge of past experience. This knowledge is huge and retained in people's memory in a well-organized form. For example, when walking into a restaurant that one has never been to, based on past experience, it is expected that menus, tables, waiters, etc. will be seen in the restaurant. When entering the classroom, you can foresee chairs, blackboards, etc. in the classroom. People try to use their past experience to analyze and explain the current situation, but they cannot save the past experience in their minds, and can only store the past experience in the form of a general data structure. Such a data structure is called a frame. The frame provides a structure, or an organization. In this structure or organization, new information can be analyzed and explained with concepts derived from experience. Therefore, a frame is also a structured representation.

Generally, the frame uses nodes, slots, and values in the semantic network to represent the structure. So the frame can also be defined as a set of nodes and slots in the semantic network. This set of nodes and slots can describe things, actions, and events in a fixed format. The semantic network can be viewed as a collection of nodes and arcs, or a collection of frames.

2.6.1 *Frame composition*

A frame usually consists of slots that describe various aspects of things, each slot can have several sides, and each side can have several values.

These contents can be selected according to the specific needs of specific problems. The general structure of a framework is as follows:

<Frame name>
  <Slot 1> <Side 11> <Value 111> ...
 <Side 12> <Value 121> ...

   ...

  <Slot 2> <Side 21> <Value 211> ...

   ...

   ...

  <Slot n> <Side n1> <value n11> ...

   ...

   <Side nm> <Value nm1> ...

The simpler scenario is to use frames to represent things such as people and houses. For example, a person can be described by his occupation, height, and weight, and so these items can be used to form a frame slot. When describing a specific person, fill in the corresponding slots with the specific values of these items. Table 2.1 gives a framework for describing John.

For most problems, it cannot be expressed in such a simple frame. Many frames must be used in a frame system at the same time.

Figure 2.13 shows a frame representing a view of a cube. In the figure, the top-level frame uses the ISA slot to indicate that it is a cube, and the region slot indicates the three visible faces A, B, and E that it has. A, B, and E are described in detail using three frames. The slots "must be" indicate that they must be parallelograms.

Table 2.1 Example of a simple framework

JOHN		
Isa	:	PERSON
Profession	:	PROGRAMMER
Height	:	1.8 m
Weight	:	76 kg

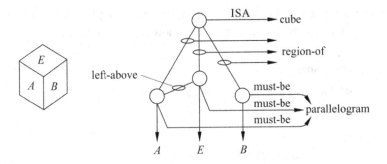

Figure 2.13   Frame representation of a perspective view.

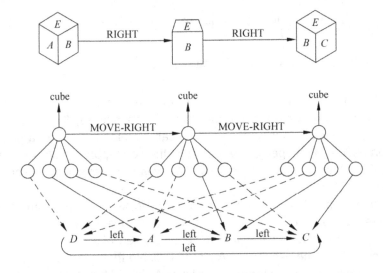

Figure 2.14   Frame system representing cube.

In order to be able to describe objects from different angles, frames can be established for different angles of view, and then they can be linked to form a frame system. Figure 2.14 shows an example of studying a cube from three different perspectives. For the sake of simplicity, some details are omitted in the figure. In the slot representing the surface of the cube, a solid line is connected to the visible surface, and a dotted line is connected to the invisible surface.

It can be seen from the figure that one frame structure can be the slot value of another frame, and the same frame structure can be used as the slot value of several different frames. In this way, some of the same information need not be stored repeatedly, saving storage space. An important feature of the frame is its inheritance. For this reason, a frame system is often represented as a tree structure. Each node of the tree is a frame structure. The child nodes and the parent nodes are connected by ISA or AKO slots. The so-called frame inheritance is that when some slot values or side values of a child node are not directly recorded, these values can be inherited from its parent node. For example, a chair usually has four legs. If a specific chair does not indicate how many legs it has, you can conclude that it also has four legs based on the characteristics of a general chair.

Frame is a general form of knowledge expression. There is no unified form for how to use a frame system, and it is often determined by the different needs of various problems.

The frame system has a tree structure. Each node of the tree structure frame system has the following frame structure form:

Frame name
AKO VALUE <value> .
PROP DEFAULT <Table 2.1>
SF IF-NEEDED <Arithmetic Expression>
CONFLICT ADD <Table 2.2>

The frame name is represented by the class name. AKO is a slot, and VALUE is its side. By filling in the content of <value>, it indicates which category the frame belongs to. The PROP slot is used to record the characteristics of the node. The DEFAULT on the side indicates that the contents of the slot can be inherited by default. That is, when <Table 1> is non-NIL, the PROP slot value is <Table 1>. When it is NIL, the PROP slot value is replaced by the PROP slot value of the parent node.

2.6.2 *Frame reasoning*

As mentioned earlier, a frame is a complex structured semantic network. Therefore, matching and feature inheritance in semantic network reasoning can also be implemented in the frame system. In addition, because frames are used to describe things, actions, and events in a fixed format, new situations can be used to infer unobserved facts. The frame uses several approaches to help achieve this:

(1) A frame contains multiple aspects of the situation or object it describes. This information can be cited as if it had been directly observed. For example, when a program accesses a ROOM frame, it can be inferred

that there is at least one door in the room, whether or not there is evidence that there are doors in the room.

(2) The frame contains the attributes that the object must have. These attributes are used when filling the slots of the frame. Establishing a description of a situation requires a description of all aspects of the situation.

(3) Frames describe typical examples of the concepts they represent. If a situation matches a frame in many ways, only a few parts differ from each other. These differences are likely to correspond to important aspects of the current situation, and perhaps they should be answered.

Of course, before applying the frame in some way, you must first confirm that the frame is applicable to the situation being studied. At this time, a certain amount of evidence can be used to initially select the candidate frame. These candidate frames are materialized to create an instance that describes the current situation. Such a frame will contain several slots that must be filled with padding values. The program then attempts to find a suitable padding value by examining the current situation. If you can find padding values that meet the requirements, fill them into the corresponding slots in this specific frame. If you cannot find a suitable padding value, you must choose a new frame. If a suitable value is found, the frame is considered suitable for describing the current situation. Of course, the current situation may change. Then, information about what has changed (for example, you can walk around the house clockwise) can be used to help choose a frame that describes this new situation.

The process of using a frame to embody a specific situation is often not smooth. But when this process encounters obstacles, it is often not necessary to give up the original effort to start from scratch, but there are many ways to think:

(1) Select the frame fragment corresponding to the current situation, and match this frame fragment with the candidate frame. Choose the best match. If the current frame is almost acceptable, much of the work already done on building substructures to fill this framework will be preserved.

(2) Although there is a mismatch between the current frame and the situation to be described, the frame can still be applied. For example, the chair under study has only three legs. It could be a broken chair or another object in front of the chair blocking one leg. A part of the frame

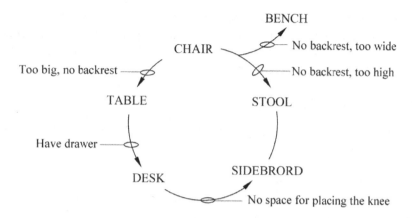

Figure 2.15   Similar networks.

contains information about which features are allowed to mismatch. Similarly, there are general heuristic principles, such as a frame that misses a desired characteristic (possibly due to obstruction of view) being more suitable for the current situation than another frame that has an undesired characteristic.

(3) Query the specially saved chain between the frames to come up with a suggestion on which direction to explore. An example of such a chain is similar to the network shown in Figure 2.15. For example, if you match the CHAIR frame and find that there is no backrest and it is too wide, then it is recommended to use a BENCH frame; if it is too high and there is no backrest, it is recommended to use a STOOL frame.

(4) Move up the hierarchy arranged along the frame system (i.e., from dog frame → mammal frame → animal frame) until you find a frame that is universal enough and does not contradict existing facts. If the frame is sufficiently specific to provide the required knowledge, then adopt the frame. Or create a new frame that matches the next layer.

2.7   Predicate Logic Representation

Although propositional logic can represent various facts of the objective world as logical propositions, it has greater limitations and is not suitable for expressing more complex problems. Predicate logic allows to express things that cannot be expressed with propositional logic. Logical statements, more specifically, first-order predicate calculus, is a formal language whose fundamental purpose is to symbolize logical arguments in mathematics. If you can use mathematical deduction to prove that a new sentence is derived from those that are known to be correct, then you can also conclude that the new sentence is also correct [9, 10, 21].

2.7.1 *Predicate calculus*

The following paragraphs briefly introduce the language and methods of predicate logic.

(1) Syntax and semantics

The basic components of predicate logic are predicate symbols, variable symbols, function symbols, and constant symbols. They are separated by parentheses, square brackets, curly brackets, and commas to represent relationships within the universe [18]. For example, to indicate "ROBOT is in room 1 (ROOM1)", a simple atomic formula can be applied:

$$INROOM \ (ROBOT, r1)$$

In the formula: ROBOT and r1 are constant symbols, and INROOM is a predicate symbol. Generally, atomic formulas consist of predicate symbols and terms. The constant symbol is the simplest term used to represent objects or entities in the universe. It can be actual objects and people, or it can be a concept or anything with a name. Variable symbols are also terms and do not have to explicitly refer to which entity. Function symbols represent functions within the universe. For example, the function symbol mother can be used to represent a mapping between someone and his (or her) mother. The relationship "Li's mother marries his father" is expressed by the following atomic formula:

$$MARRIED \ [father \ (LI), mother \ (LI)]$$

For an atomic formula with a certain definition already defined, it has the value T (true) only when its corresponding statement is true in the domain; and when its corresponding statement is false in the domain, the atomic formula only has the value F (false). Therefore, INROOM (ROBOT, r1) has the value T, and INROOM (ROBOT, r2) has the value F.

When an atomic formula contains a variable symbol, there may be several settings for variables of entities in the domain. For some set variables, the atomic formula takes the value T; for other set variables, the atomic formula takes the value F.

(2) Conjunctions and quantifiers

The atomic formula is the basic building block of predicate calculus. Atomic formulas can form a more complex formula by using the connectives $\wedge$ (AND), $\vee$ (OR), and $\Rightarrow$ (implication) (in some studies in the literature, also by using "$\rightarrow$" to represent implicit relationships), which can combine multiple atomic formulas to form more complex well-formed formulas (WFF).

The connective $\wedge$ is used to denote a compound sentence. For example, the sentence "I love music and painting" can be written as

$$\text{LIKE (I, MUSIC)} \wedge \text{LIKE (I, PAINTING)}$$

In addition, some simpler sentences can also be written in a composite form. For example, "Li lives in a yellow house", that can be indicated as

$$\text{LIVES (LI, HOUSE-1)} \wedge \text{COLOR (HOUSE-1, YELLOW)}$$

where the predicate LIVES represents the relationship between the person and the object (house), while the predicate COLOR represents the relationship between the object and its color. A formula formed by concatenating several formulas with a connective $\wedge$ is called a conjunction, and each component of the conjunction is called a conjunction item. Any conjunction of some WFFs is also a WFF.

The connective $\vee$ is used to mean an OR that can be combined. For example, the sentence "Li Ming plays basketball or plays football" can be expressed as

$$\text{PLAYS (LIMING, BASKETBALL)} \vee \text{PLAYS (LIMING, FOOTBALL)}$$

The formula formed by concatenating several formulas with a conjunction $\vee$ is called disjunction, and each component of the disjunction is called a disjunction item. Any disjunction made up of some suitable formulas is also a WFF.

The true value of the conjunction and disjunction is determined by the true value of its components. If each of the conjunctions takes the value T, the conjunction value is T, otherwise the conjunction value is F. If at least one of the disjunctions takes a T value, the disjunction value is T, otherwise the disjunction value F is taken.

The connective $\Rightarrow$ is used to mean "if-then". For example, "If the book is Heping's book, then it is blue (cover)" can be expressed as

$$\text{OWNS (HEPING, BOOK-1)} \Rightarrow \text{COLOR (BOOK-1, BLUE)}$$

Another example is "If Liuhua runs the fastest, then he wins the championship", which can be expressed as

RUNS (LIUHUA, FASTEST) $\Rightarrow$ WINS (LIUHUA, CHAMPION)

The formula formed with two formulas concatenating by the connective $\Rightarrow$ is called implication. The left form of implication is called the former term, and the right form is called the latter term. If both the front and the back terms are WFFs, then implication is also a WFF. If the latter term takes the value T (regardless of the value of the preceding term), or the value of the previous term F (regardless of the true value of the latter term), the implication takes the value T; otherwise, the implication takes the value F.

The symbol $\sim$ (non) is used to negate the true value of a formula, i.e., to change the value of a WFF from T to F, or from F to T. For example, the clause "Robot is not in room 2" can be expressed as

$\sim$ INROOM (ROBOT, r2)

The formula with the symbol "$\sim$" in front is called negation. A negation of a WFF is also a WFF.

Sometimes an atomic formula such as $P(x)$ has a value of T for all possible variables x. This property can be represented by adding a universal quantifier $(\forall x)$ in front of $P(x)$. If at least one value of x can cause $P(x)$ to have a value of T, then this property can be represented by adding the existential quantifier $(\exists x)$ in front of $P(x)$. For example, the sentence "All robots are gray" can be expressed as

$(\forall x)[\text{ROBOT}(x) \Rightarrow \text{COLOR } (x, \text{GRAY})]$

The sentence "There is an object in room 1" can be expressed as

$(\exists x)\text{INROOM } (x, \text{r1})$

Here, x is a quantized variable, i.e., x is quantized. An expression obtained by quantifying a variable in a WFF is also a WFF. If a variable in a WFF is quantized, this variable is called a constraint variable; otherwise it is called a free variable. In the WFF, the main interest is that all variables are constrained. Such a WFF is called a sentence.

It is worth pointing out that the predicate calculus used in this book is a first-order predicate calculus, and it is not possible to quantify the predicate symbols or functional symbols. For example, in the first-order predicate calculus, formulas such as $(\forall P) P(A)$ are not well-formed formulas.

2.7.2 *Predicate formula*

(1) Definition of predicate formula

The predicate formula is defined as follows:

Definition 2.15. Let $P(x_1, x_2, \ldots, x_n)$ represent an n-variate predicate formula, where P is an n-variate predicate, and $x_1, x_2, \ldots, x_n$ are object variables or arguments. Usually, $P(x_1, x_2, \ldots, x_n)$ is called the atomic formula of the predicate calculus or the atomic predicate formula. You can use a conjunction to form an atomic predicate formula into a compound predicate formula and call it a molecular predicate formula. For this reason, the definition of the predicate formula is given by induction. The recursive definition of WFF in predicate calculus is as follows:

(i) The atomic predicate formula is a WFF.
(ii) If A is a well-formed formula, then $\sim A$ is also a WFF.
(iii) If both A and B are WFFs, then $(A \wedge B)$, $(A \vee B)$, $(A \Rightarrow B)$ and $(A \longleftrightarrow B)$ are also WFFs.
(iv) If A is a WFF and x is a free argument in A, then $(\forall x)A$ and $(\exists x)A$ are WFFs.
(v) Only those formulas that are obtained according to rules (i)–(iv) are WFFs.

(2) The nature of the WFF

If P and Q are two WFFs, the compound expression consisting of these two WFFs can be given by Table 2.2.

If two WFFs, no matter how they are interpreted, have the same truth tables, then the two WFFs are equivalent. Applying the truth table above,

Table 2.2   Truth table.

P	Q	$P \vee Q$	$P \wedge Q$	$P \Rightarrow Q$	$\sim P$
T	T	T	T	T	F
F	T	T	F	T	T
T	F	T	F	F	F
F	F	F	F	T	T

the following equivalence relationships can be established:

   (i) Negation of negation

      $\sim(\sim P)$ is equivalent to P

  (ii) $P \vee Q$ is equivalent to $\sim P \Rightarrow Q$

 (iii) De Morgan Law

      $\sim(P \vee Q)$ is equivalent to $\sim P \wedge \sim Q$

      $\sim(P \wedge Q)$ is equivalent to $\sim P \vee \sim Q$

 (iv) Distribution law

      $P \wedge (Q \vee R)$ is equivalent to $(P \wedge Q) \vee (P \wedge R)$

      $P \vee (Q \wedge R)$ is equivalent to $(P \vee Q) \wedge (P \vee R)$

  (v) Exchange law

      $P \wedge Q$ is equivalent to $Q \wedge P$

      $P \vee Q$ is equivalent to $Q \vee P$

 (vi) Combination law

      $(P \wedge Q) \wedge R$ is equivalent to $P \wedge (Q \wedge R)$

      $(P \vee Q) \vee R$ is equivalent to $P \vee (Q \vee R)$

(vii) Inverse law

      $P \Rightarrow Q$ is equivalent to $\sim Q \Rightarrow \sim P$

      In addition, the following equivalence relationships can be established:

(viii) $\sim(\exists x)P(x)$ is equivalent to $(\forall x)\,(\sim P(x))$

      $\sim(\forall x)P(x)$ is equivalent to $(\exists x)\,(\sim P(x))$

 (ix) $(\forall x)\,(P(x) \wedge Q(x))$ is equivalent to $(\forall x)P(x) \wedge (\forall x)Q(x)$

      $(\exists x)(P(x) \vee Q(x))$ is equivalent to $(\exists x)P(x) \vee (\forall x)Q(x)$

  (x) $(\forall x)P(x)$ is equivalent to $(\forall y)P(y)$

      $(\exists x)P(x)$ is equivalent to $(\exists y)P(y)$

    The last two equivalence relationships described above indicate that a constraint variable in a quantified expression is a type of virtual element that can be replaced with any other variable symbol that does not appear in the expression.

    If the two truth formulas are the same, no matter how to interpret them, then they are said to be equivalent. By applying the above truth table, it is possible to establish equivalence relations such as negation of predicate calculus, De Morgan's law, distribution law, exchange law, combination law, inverse negation law, and equivalent relations of predicate calculus containing variables and quantification.

    Here is an example of an English sentence represented by a predicate calculus:

For every set x, there is a set y, such that the cardinality of y is greater than the cardinality of x.

This English sentence can be expressed as a predicate calculus as

$$(\forall x)(\text{SET}(x) \Rightarrow (\exists y)(\exists u)(\exists v))$$

$$(\text{SET}(y) \wedge \text{CARD}(x, u) \wedge \text{CARD}(y, v) \wedge G(v, u))$$

2.8 Summary

The problem of knowledge representation discussed in this chapter is one of the core issues of artificial intelligence research. There are many ways to represent knowledge. This chapter introduces seven of them, including graphic and formula methods, structured methods, and declarative representations.

The state space method is a method of problem representation and solution based on solution space. It is based on states and operators. When using the state space diagram to represent, starting from an initial state, one operator is added at a time, and the test sequence of the operators is incrementally established until the goal state is reached. Because the state space method needs to expand too many nodes, it is prone to "combination explosion", so it is only suitable for simpler expression problems.

The problem reduction method starts from the goal (the problem to be solved), reverses the reasoning, and transforms the initial problem into a set of sub-problems and a set of sub-problems through a series of transformations, until it is reduced to a trivial set of primitive problems. The solutions to these primitive problems can be directly obtained to solve the initial problem, and the AND/OR graph is used to effectively explain the solution method of the problem reduction method.

The knowledge base is used to store the expertise of expert systems in a certain field, including facts, feasible operations, and rules. The general steps of knowledge base design include the design of the initial knowledge base, and the improvement and induction of the knowledge base, which are gradually improved. Knowledge bases and knowledge base systems have been widely used in the development of related software systems.

Ontology is an explicit specification or representation of a concept. Ontology can be defined as a formal specification of the shared conceptualization. After discussing the basic concepts of ontology, this section discusses the composition, classification, and modeling of ontology. Ontology is a more efficient representation than a framework.

The semantic network is a structured representation method that consists of nodes and arcs or chains. Nodes are used to represent objects, concepts, and states, and arcs are used to represent the relationships between nodes. The solution of the semantic network is a new semantic network with clear results obtained through inference and matching. Semantic networks can be used to represent multivariate relationships, which can be extended to represent more complex problems.

Knowledge graph is a kind of knowledge base used by Google to enhance the function of search engines. It can formally describe things in the real world and their relationships. The process of knowledge graph construction and update includes information acquisition, knowledge fusion, and knowledge processing. Information acquisition, knowledge fusion, and knowledge processing are the key technologies for constructing a knowledge graph.

A frame is a structured representation. The frame usually consists of slots that specify various aspects of things, each slot has several sides, and each side can have several values. Most practical systems must use many frames at the same time and link them into a frame system. Frame representation is widely used, but not all problems can be represented by frames.

The predicate logic method uses a predicate WFF and a first-order predicate calculus to turn the problem to be solved into a problem to be proved, and then uses the resolution principle and resolution refutation to prove that a new sentence is derived from a known correct sentence, thereby proving that this new statement is also correct. Predicate logic is a formal language that symbolizes logical arguments in mathematics. The predicate logic method can be often mixed with other representation methods, so that allows for more flexible and convenient uses and can express more complex problems.

When representing and solving more complex problems, a single knowledge representation method is not enough. Often, multiple methods must be used to represent it. For example, the comprehensive use of the process representation methods (two or more), such as framework, ontology, semantic network, and predicate logic, can solve the problem studied more effectively.

In addition, when selecting knowledge representation methods, the functions and features provided by the programming language used should also be considered in order to better describe these representation methods.

References

1. AMIT, S. (2012). Introducing the knowledge graph, America: Official Blog of Google, 2012-05. Google.
2. A comprehensive understanding of knowledge graph. (2019) 2019-03-08 09:36:59, https://blog.csdn.net/u010626937/article/details/88106081.
3. (2018). Analysis of knowledge graph construction. Blog garden (in Chinese), 2018-12-02, https://www.cnblogs.com/small-k/p/10054479.html.
4. Bonatti, P. A., *et al.* (2019). Knowledge graphs: new directions for knowledge representation on the semantic web, Dagstuhl Seminar 18371. In: Dagstuhl Reports 8.9, 29–111.
5. Cai, Z.X. and Chen, A.B. (Ed.) (2008). *Dictionary of Artificial Intelligence*, (Chemical Industry Press, Beijing, in Chinese).
6. Cai, Z.X., Liu, L.J., Cai, J.F. and Chen. B.F. (2020). *Artificial Intelligence and Its Applications*, Sixth Edition, (Tsinghua University Press, Beijing, in Chinese).
7. Davis, R., Shrobe, H. and Szolovits, P. (1993). What is a Knowledge Representation? *AI Magazine, 1*: 17–33.
8. (2018). Easy to understand knowledge graph. Blog garden (in Chinese), 2018-11-30, https://www.cnblogs.com/huangyc/p/10043749.html.
9. Ernst, G.W. and Newll, A. (1969). *GPS, A Case Study in Generality and Problem Solving*, (Academic Press, New York).
10. Fu, J.S., Cai, Z.X. and Xu, G.Y. (1987). *Artificial Intelligence and Its Application*, (Tsinghua University Press, Beijing, in Chinese).
11. Hua, M. (2018). Bottom-up: Preliminary study on knowledge graph construction technology (in Chinese), 2018-07-03, https://developer.aliyun.com/article/603347.
12. Lieto, A., Lebiere, C. and Oltramari, A. (2018). The knowledge level in cognitive architectures: Current limitations and possible developments, *Cognitive Systems Research, 2018, 48*: 39–55.
13. Nilsson, N.J. (1998). *Artificial Intelligence: A New Synthesis*, (Morgan Kaufmann).
14. (2019). Overview and understanding of knowledge graph, (in Chinese), 2019-12-13 14:54:29, https://blog.csdn.net/u012325865/article/details/102771063.
15. Russell, S. and Norvig, P. (2003). *Artificial Intelligence: A Modern Approach*, (Prentice-Hall, Englewood Cliffs, NJ).
16. Simon, H.A., translated by Jing, Q.C. and Zhang, H.Y. (1986). *Human Cognition: Information Processing Theory of Thinking*, (Science Press, Beijing).
17. (2020). Sogou Encyclopedia. Knowledge Base, (in Chinese), 2020-07-10, https://baike.sogou.com/v454142.htm?FromTitle=%E7%9F%A5%E8%AF%86%E5%BA%93.
18. Tenorth, M. and Beetz, M. (2017). Representations for robot knowledge in the KnowRob framework, *Artificial Intelligence, 2017, 247*: 151–169.
19. Vassev, E. and Hinchey, M. (2018). Toward artificial intelligence through knowledge representation for awareness, software technology: 10 years of innovation, in *IEEE Computer*, edited by Mike Hinchey (John Wiley & Sons).

20. (2016). Wikipedia. Knowledge graph, 2016-05-09. https://en.wikipedia.org/wiki/ Knowledge_Graph.
21. Winston, P.H. (1992). *Artificial Intelligence*, Third Edition, (Addison Wesley, Boston, MA).
22. Xie, R.B., Liu, Z.Y., Jia, J., Luan, H.B. and Sun, M.S. (2016). Representation learning of knowledge graphs with entity descriptions, *Proc. 30th AAAI Conference on Artificial Intelligence* (AAAI-16), 2659–2665.
23. Xu, Z.L., Sheng, Y.P., He, L.R. and Wang, Y.F. (2016). Review on knowledge graph technique, *Journal of University of Electronic Science and Technology of China, 4*: 589–606.

Knowledge Search and Reasoning

3

The knowledge representation method studied in the previous chapter is necessary for problem solving. The representation of a problem is for further resolution of the problem. From problem representation to problem solving, there is a problem-solving process, which is the search process. In the search process, appropriate search techniques, including various rules, processes, and algorithms, are used to reason about the problems and try to find answers to the questions. This chapter first discusses some search principles used to solve simple problems, and then studies some reasoning techniques that can solve more complex problems, including uncertain reasoning and probabilistic reasoning [1, 7].

3.1 Graph Search Strategy

The state space method uses a graph structure to describe all possible states of the problem, and the problem-solving process is transformed into finding a path from the initial node to the goal node in the state space graph. How to search for a path through graph search and then solve the problem? First, the general strategy of graph search is studied, then the general steps of the graph search process are given, and the difference between no formation search and heuristic search can be seen from it [23].

Think of the graph search control strategy as a way to find paths in the graph. The initial node and the goal node represent the initial database and the goal database that meet the termination conditions, respectively. The problem of finding a sequence of rules that transforms one database into another is equivalent to finding a path problem in the graph. In addition to the graph itself, the data structure involved in the graph search process also requires two auxiliary data structures, namely, the accessed but not expanded node (called the OPEN table) and the expanded node (called the CLOSED table). The process of searching is actually the process of continuously generating the displayed search graph and search tree from the implicit state space graph and finally finding the path. In order to achieve this process, in addition to storing its own state information, each node in the graph also needs to store information such as who the parent node is, what operations the parent node can use to reach the node, what is the depth of the node in the search tree, and what is the path cost from the initial node to the goal node.

The general process of GRAPHSEARCH is as follows:

(1) Create a search graph G containing only the initial node S and put S in the OPEN table.
(2) Initialize the CLOSED table as an empty table.
(3) LOOP: If the OPEN table is an empty table, it will fail to exit.
(4) Select the first node on the OPEN table, remove it from the OPEN table and put it in the CLOSED table. This node is called node n.
(5) If n is a goal node, there is a solution and there will be a successful exit. This solution is obtained by following the path from n to S in the tracking graph G (the pointer will be set in step 7).
(6) Expand node n to generate a successor node set, M.
(7) For those M members that have not appeared in G (neither on the OPEN table nor on the CLOSED table), set their parent node pointer to n and join the OPEN table. Determine whether you need to change its original parent into n for each M member that has already appeared in the OPEN or CLOSED table. For each M member already on the CLOSED table, if its parent node is modified, the node is removed from the CLOSED table and rejoined into the OPEN table.
(8) Rearrange the OPEN table in any arbitrary way or according to a certain test value.
(9) GO LOOP.

The above search process is represented by the block diagram of Figure 3.1.

This process generally includes a variety of specific graph search algorithms. This process generates a displayed graph G (called a search graph) and a subset T of G (called a search tree), and each node on the tree T is also in graph G. The search tree is determined by the pointer set in step 7. During each search process, it is determined whether to modify the pointer of the current node to its parent node, as each node in the G that has been expanded (except S) has only one parent node. That is, a tree is formed,

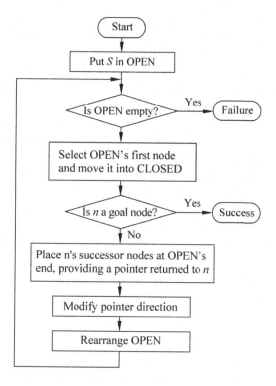

Figure 3.1   Block diagram of the graph search process.

namely, the search tree T. Since there is only one path between any two points in the tree structure, the unique path to any node can be found from T. The OPEN table used in the search process stores the leaf nodes of the current search tree, so it is also called as the front table, or the leading edge table. More specifically, in the third step of the process, the nodes on the OPEN table are those nodes that are not extended on the search tree. The nodes on the CLOSED table are either several leaf nodes that have been expanded but no successor nodes are generated in the search tree, or non-leaf nodes of the search tree.

Step 8 of the process sorts the nodes on the OPEN table so that a "best" node can be selected as the fourth step extension. This sorting can be arbitrary or blind (belonging to blind search) or it can be based on various heuristics or other criteria to be discussed later (belonging to heuristic search). This process is declared successful each time the node selected as the extension is the goal node. At this time, the successful path from the initial node to the goal node can be reproduced by returning the trace from the goal node to the *S* by the pointer. When the search tree no longer has leaf nodes that are not extended, the process ends in failure (some nodes may end up with no successor nodes, so the OPEN table may eventually become an empty table). In the case of a failure termination, the goal node must not be reached from the initial node.

The GRAPHSEARCH algorithm simultaneously generates all subsequent nodes of a node. To illustrate some of the general nature of the graph search process, algorithms that generate all subsequent nodes at the same time will continue to be used instead of the modified algorithm. In the correction algorithm, only one successor node is generated at a time.

It can be seen from the graph search process whether the OPEN table is rearranged, i.e., whether the unexpanded nodes are reordered according to a certain heuristic value (or criterion, heuristic information, etc.) will determine whether the graph search process is non-informed search or heuristic search. Sections 3.2 and 3.3 will discuss the non-informed search (i.e., blind search) and heuristic search strategies in turn.

3.2 Blind Search

The search that does not require rearranging the OPEN table is called a non-information search or a blind search, and it includes breadth-first search, depth-first search, and equal-cost search. Blind search is only suitable for solving simple problems [3].

3.2.1 *Breadth-first search*

A search that sequentially expands nodes to a degree close to the starting node is called breadth-first search. This search is performed layer by layer; before searching any node in the next layer, all nodes in this layer must be searched [2].

The breadth-first search algorithm is as follows:

(1) Put the start node into the OPEN table (if the start node is a goal node, find an answer).
(2) If OPEN is an empty table, there is no solution, fail to exit; otherwise continue.
(3) Remove the first node (node *n*) out of the OPEN table and place it in the CLOSED extended node table.
(4) Expand node *n*. If there is no successor node, then go to step (2) above.

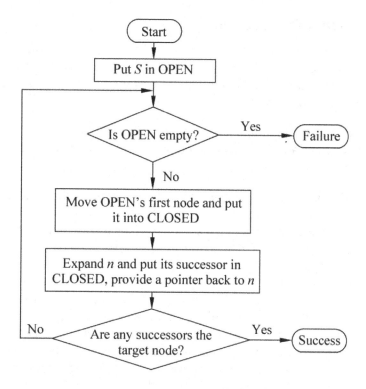

Figure 3.2   Breadth first algorithm block diagram.

(5) Put all subsequent nodes of n at the end of the OPEN table and provide pointers from these successor nodes back to n.

(6) If any of the successor nodes of n is a goal node, find a solution and exit successfully; otherwise, go to step (2).

The above breadth priority algorithm is shown in Figure 3.2.

This algorithm assumes that the start node itself is not the goal node. To verify the possibility that the start node is the goal node, as long as at the end of step (1), adding a sentence "If the start node is a goal node, then find a solution" can be done, just as the first step (1) written in the brackets.

Obviously, the breadth-first search method can ensure that a shortest path to the goal node is found in the search tree under the assumption that the cost of each operation is equal. In the breadth-first search, the order of the nodes entering and leaving the OPEN table is first-in, first-out. Therefore, its OPEN table is a queue structure.

3.2.2 *Depth-first search*

Another type of blind (no information) search is called depth-first search. In depth-first search, the newly generated (i.e., the deepest) node is first expanded. Nodes of equal depth can be arranged arbitrarily. Define the depth of the nodes as follows:

(1) The depth of the starting node (i.e., the root node) is 0.
(2) The depth of any other node is equal to the depth of its parent node plus 1.

First, the result of extending the deepest node causes the search to go down the start node along a single path in the state space; it only considers another alternative path when the search reaches a state without descendants. The alternative path differs from the previously tried path only in that the last n steps are changed, and n is kept as small as possible.

For many problems, the depth of the state space search tree may be infinitely deep or it may be at least deeper than the known depth limit of an acceptable solution sequence. In order to avoid considering too long paths (to prevent the search process from expanding along unhelpful paths), it is often given the maximum depth of a node extension — the depth limit. Any node that reaches the depth limit will treat them as no successor. It is worth noting that even if the depth limit is applied, the solution path obtained is not necessarily the shortest path.

The depth-first search algorithm with depth limits is as follows:

(1) Put the start node S into the unexpanded node OPEN table. If this node is a goal node, then one solution is obtained.
(2) If OPEN is an empty table, it fails to exit.
(3) Move the first node (node n) from the OPEN table to the CLOSED table.
(4) If the depth of node n is equal to the maximum depth, turn to step (2).
(5) Extend node n, generate all its descendants, and put them in front of the OPEN table. If there is no descendant, turn to step (2).
(6) If any of the successor nodes is the goal node, a solution is found and exits successfully; otherwise, turn to step (2).

3.2.3 *Uniform cost search*

In breadth-first search, assuming that the cost of each operation is the same, it can find the shortest path. This path is actually a solution containing the minimum number of operations or application operators. However, for many problems, the solution with the least operator sequence is often not the desired solution, nor is it the same as the optimal solution. Usually, people want to find a solution with certain characteristics, especially the least cost solution. The relevant cost on each connected arc in the search tree and the solution path with the obtained lowest cost are consistent with many such generalized criteria. Breadth-first search can be generalized to solve the problem of finding the path with the least cost from the initial state to the goal state. This generalized breadth-first search algorithm is called the equal-cost search algorithm. If all connected arcs have equal cost, the equal-cost algorithm is simplified to a breadth-first search algorithm. In the equal-cost search algorithm, instead of describing the expansion along the equal-length path, it describes the expansion along the equal-cost path.

In the equal-cost search algorithm, record the cost of the arc of the connection from node i to its successor node j as $c(i, j)$, and the path cost from the starting node S to any node i as $g(i)$. In the search tree, it is assumed that $g(i)$ is also the cost on the least cost path from the starting node S to the node i, because it is the only path. The equal-cost search method expands its nodes in increasing order of $g(i)$, and its algorithm is as follows:

(1) Place the starting node S in the unexpanded node table OPEN. If the starting node is a target node, a solution is obtained. Otherwise, let g $(S) = 0$.
(2) If OPEN is an empty list, it exits without a solution.
(3) Select a node i from the OPEN table so that $g(i)$ is the smallest. If several nodes are qualified, then a goal node is selected as the node i (if there is a goal node); otherwise, one is selected as the node i. Move node i from the OPEN table to the extended node table CLOSED.
(4) If node i is the target node, find a solution.
(5) Expand node i. If there are no successor nodes, go to step (2).
(6) For each successor node j of node i, calculate $g(j) = g(i) + c(i,j)$, and put all successor nodes j into the OPEN table. Provide a pointer back to node i.
(7) Go to step (2).

3.3 Heuristic Search

Blind search is inefficient and consumes too much computing space and time. If you can find a way to arrange the order of the nodes to be expanded, i.e., to select the most promising nodes to expand, then the search efficiency will be greatly improved. In many cases, a reasonable order can be determined by inspection. The search methods described in this section are prioritized for this type of detection. This type of search is called a heuristic search or an informative search [5, 6].

3.3.1 *Heuristic search strategy and valuation function*

To find a solution in a blind search, the number of nodes that need to be expanded may be large. The expansion order of these nodes is completely arbitrary, and does not take advantage of any features of the solved problem. Therefore, in addition to the simplest problems, it usually takes up a lot of time and/or space. This result is a manifestation of combo explosion [18].

Information about specific problem areas can often be used to simplify searches. Assume that the definitions of the initial state, the operator, and the goal state have been completely determined, and then determine a search space. So the question is how to efficiently search this given space. Techniques for conducting this search generally require some information about the characteristics of a particular problem area. Such information has been called heuristic information, and a search method using heuristic information has been called a heuristic search method.

Use heuristic information to decide which node to expand next. This search always selects the "most promising" node as the next expanded node. This type of search is called ordered search, also known as best-first search [17].

Generally, for the search problem of graphs, it is always hoped that the cost of solving a path and some of the comprehensive indicators of the search cost required to obtain this path should be minimized. A more flexible (but costly) method of using heuristic information is to apply some guidelines to rearrange the order of all nodes in the OPEN table at each step. The search may then expand outwards along the edge segment that is considered the most promising. Applying this sorting process requires some measure of the "hope" of the estimation node. This measure is called an evolution function. The smaller the value of the evaluation function, the greater the "hope" of the node on the optimal solution path, and the optimal path finally found, i.e., the path with the smallest average comprehensive index.

The evaluation function can provide a way to evaluate candidate extended nodes in order to determine which node is most likely to be on the best path to the goal. Heuristic information can be used in step 8 of GRAPHSEARCH to rearrange the nodes on the OPEN table so that the search expands along those segments that are considered most promising. An important way to measure the "hope" of a node is to use a real-valued function of the evaluation function for each node. There are many ways to define the evaluation function, e.g.: trying to determine the probability of a node on the best path; proposing the distance or difference between any node and the goal set; or in chessboard games and puzzles based on the game, certain characteristics of the game determine the number of points scored. These characteristics are considered to be related to the degree of hope of moving forward to the goal node.

The evaluation function is labeled with the symbol f, and the evaluation function value of node n is represented by $f(n)$. Let f be an arbitrary function for the time being, and it will be proposed later that f is an estimated cost on the minimum cost path from the initial node to the goal node through node n with constraint. Use the function f to arrange the nodes on the OPEN table in step 8 of GRAPHSEARCH. According to the convention, the nodes on the OPEN table are arranged in increasing order of their f-function values. It is speculated that a node with a low valuation is more likely to be on the best path.

3.3.2 *Ordered search*

An algorithm (such as an equal-cost algorithm) is used to select the node with the smallest f value on the OPEN table as the next node to be expanded. This search method is called ordered search or best-first search, and its algorithm is called ordered search algorithm or best-first algorithm. Ordered search always selects the most promising node as the next node to be expanded.

The ordered state space search algorithm is as follows:

(1) Put the start node S into the OPEN table, calculate $f(S)$ and associate its value with node S.
(2) If OPEN is an empty table, it will fail to exit without any solution.
(3) Select a node i with the smallest f value from the OPEN table. As a result, several nodes are qualified. When one of them is the goal node, the goal node is selected, otherwise one of the nodes is selected as the node i.
(4) Move node i from the OPEN table and place it in the extended node table of CLOSED.

(5) If *i* is a goal node, it exits successfully and finds a solution.
(6) Extend node *i* to generate all its successors. For each successor node *j* of *i*:

    (a) Calculate $f(j)$.
    (b) If *j* is neither in the OPEN table nor in the CLOSED table, then it is added to the OPEN table using the evaluation function *f*. Add a pointer from *j* to its parent node *i* to remember a solution path once the goal node is found.
    (c) If *j* is already on the OPEN table or on the CLOSED table, compare the *f*-value that was just calculated for *j* with the *f*-value of the node that was previously calculated in the table. If the new *f* value is small, then perform the following steps:

        (i) Replace the old value with this new value.
        (ii) Point to *i* from *j* instead of pointing to its parent.
        (iii) If node *j* is in the CLOSED table, move it back to the OPEN table.

(7) Turn to step (2).

Step (6.c) is required for a general search graph, which may have more than one parent node. The node with the smallest evaluation function value $f(j)$ is selected as the parent node. However, for a tree search, it has at most one parent node, so step (6.c) can be omitted. It is worth pointing out that even if the search space is a general search graph, its explicit sub-search graph is always a tree, because node *j* has never recorded more than one parent node at the same time.

The ordered search algorithm block diagram is shown in Figure 3.3.

Breadth-first search, equal-cost search, and depth-first search are all special cases of ordered search technology. For breadth-first search, $f(i)$ is selected as the depth of node *i*. For equal-cost search, $f(i)$ is the cost of the path from the starting node to node *i*.

Of course, compared to the blind search method, the purpose of the ordered search is to reduce the number of nodes being expanded. The effectiveness of an ordered search depends directly on the choice of *f*, which will sharply identify promising nodes and undesired nodes. However, if this distinction is inaccurate, then an ordered search may lose a best solution or even a full solution. If there is no accurate measure of interest, then the choice of *f* will involve two aspects: on the one hand, a compromise

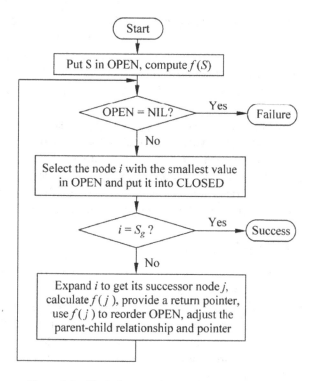

Figure 3.3   Block diagram of ordered search algorithm.

between time and space; on the other hand, guaranteeing an optimal solution or arbitrary solution.

The degree of hope for the node and the appropriateness of a particular evaluation function depend on the problem at hand. According to the type of answer required, the problem can be divided into the following three cases:

The first case assumes that the state space contains several solution paths of different costs, the problem being the optimal (i.e., minimum cost) solution. A representative example of this is Algorithm A*.

The second case is similar to the first case, but with one additional condition: such problems are more difficult. If processed in the first case, the search process is likely to exceed the time and space boundaries before finding the solution. The key issues in this case are the following: (a) how to find a good (but not optimal) solution through appropriate search experiments; (b) how to limit the scope of the search experiment and the degree of difference between the resulting solutions and optimal solutions.

The third case is that the optimization of the solution is not considered; perhaps there is only one solution, or any one solution is as good as other solutions. At this point, the question is how to minimize the number of search trials, rather than trying to minimize the composite of certain search trials and answers as in the second case. An example of this type of problem is the traveling salesman problem (TSP).

Proper selection of the evaluation function is decisive for determining the search results. Using an evaluation function that does not recognize the true hopes of some nodes will result in a non-minimum cost path; and using an evaluation function that overestimates the hope of all nodes will expand too much node. In fact, different evaluation function definitions directly lead to search algorithms with completely different performances.

3.3.3 *Algorithm A*

Let the evaluation function f make the function value $f(n)$ at any node estimate the sum of the cost of the least cost path from node S to node n and the cost of the least cost path from node n to a goal node; that is, $f(n)$ is an estimate of the cost of constraining a minimum cost path through node n. Therefore, the node with the smallest value f on the OPEN table is the estimated node with the least strict constraint, and it is appropriate to extend this node in the next step.

Before discussing the Algorithm A* formally, let us introduce several useful tokens. Let $k(n_i, n_j)$ denote the actual cost of the least cost path between any two nodes n_i and n_j. Thus, from node n to a specific goal node t_i, the cost of a certain minimum cost path can be given by $k(n, t_i)$. Let $h^*(n)$ denote the smallest of all $k(n, t_i)$ on the entire goal node set $\{t_i\}$, so $h^*(n)$ is the cost of the minimum cost path from n to the goal node, and from n to any path whose cost of the goal node is $h^*(n)$ is an optimal path from n to a goal node.

It is usually interesting to know the cost $k(S, n)$ of an optimal path from the known start node S to an arbitrary node n. To do this, a new function g^* is introduced, which will give the token some simplification. For all paths that can reach n from S, the function g^* is defined as

$$g^*(n) = k(S, n)$$

Second, define the function f^* such that its function value $f^*(n)$ on any node n is the actual cost of an optimal path from node S to node n plus an optimal path from node n to a goal node. The sum of the costs, i.e.,

$$f^*(n) = g^*(n) + h^*(n)$$

Thus, the $f^*(n)$ value is the cost of constraining an optimal path through node n from S, and $f^*(S) = h^*(S)$ is the most optimal path coat of the path unconstrained from S to a goal node.

The evaluation function f is an estimate of f^*, which can be given by the following:

$$f(n) = g(n) + h(n)$$

where g is an estimate of g^*; h is an estimate of h^*. For $g(n)$, an obvious choice is to search the cost of the path from S to n in the tree. This cost can be used to find the pointer from n to S, and the costs of each arc encountered are added up to give (this path is the least cost path from S to n found by the search algorithm so far). This definition contains $g(n) \geq g^*(n)$. The estimate $h(n)$ of $h^*(n)$ depends on the heuristic information about the domain of the problem. This information may be similar to the one used for the function $W(n)$ in the eight digital puzzle. Call h the heuristic function.

The Algorithm A* is an ordered search algorithm characterized by the definition of the evaluation function. For a general ordered search, the node with the smallest f-value is always selected as the extended node. Therefore, f is the point of estimating the node based on the need to find a minimum cost path. It can be considered that the evaluation function value of each node n has two components: the cost from the start node to the node n and the cost from the node n to the goal node.

Before discussing the Algorithm A*, make the following definitions:

Definition 3.1. In the GRAPHSEARCH process, if the rearranged OPEN table in step 8 is performed according to $f(x) = g(x) + h(x)$, then the process is called the Algorithm A.

Definition 3.2. In the Algorithm A, if $h(x) \leq h^*(x)$ exists for all x, then $h(x)$ is called the lower bound of $h^*(x)$, which represents a somewhat conservative estimate.

Definition 3.3. Algorithm A which uses the lower bound $h(x)$ of $h^*(x)$ as the heuristic function is called the Algorithm A*. When $h = 0$, the Algorithm A* becomes a uniform cost search algorithm.

Algorithm A*

(1) Put S into the OPEN table, note $f = h$, and make CLOSED an empty table.

(2) Repeat the following procedure until the goal node is found. If OPEN is an empty table, then it will fail.

(3) Select the node with the smallest f value that is not set in the OPEN table as the best node BESTNODE and move it into the CLOSED table.

(4) If BESTNODE is a goal node, then a solution is successfully obtained.

(5) If BESTNODE is not the goal node, then it is expanded to generate the successor node SUCCSSOR.

(6) Perform the following process for each SUCCSSOR:

 (a) Establish a pointer to return to BESTNODE from SUCCSSOR.

 (b) Calculate $g(SUC) = g(BES) + g(BES, SUC)$.

 (c) If SUCCSSOR $\in$ OPEN, then this node is called OLD and is added to the successor node table of BESTNODE.

 (d) Compare the old and new path costs. If $g(SUC) < g(OLD)$, then re-determine that the parent node of OLD is BESTNODE, note the smaller cost $g(OLD)$, and modify the value of $f(OLD)$.

 (e) If the cost to the OLD node is lower or the same, then stop expanding the node.

 (f) If SUCCSSOR is not in the CLOSE table, then see if it is in the CLOSED table.

 (g) If SUCCSSOR is in the CLOSE table, compare the costs of old path and new path. If $g(SUC) < g(OLD)$, then redetermine the parent node of OLD as BESTNODE, note the smaller cost $g(OLD)$, and correct the value of $f(OLD)$, then move OLD from the CLOSED table into OPEN table.

 (h) If SUCCSSOR is neither in the OPEN table nor in the CLOSED table, then put it in the OPEN table and add it to the BESTNODE descendant table, and turn to step (7).

(7) Calculate the value of f.

(8) GO LOOP

The reference block diagram of Algorithm A* can be found in [8].

As mentioned earlier, the definition of the evaluation function in the Algorithm A* is very important, especially the heuristic function $h(n)$, since the heuristic information is embodied by $h(n)$ in the algorithm; if the definition of the evaluation function is just let $h(n) = h^*(n)$, then it can be seen that the search tree will only extend the best path, which is the most ideal situation, but in general it must satisfy $h(n)$ not to exceed $h^*(n)$ so that the algorithm can guarantee finding the optimal solution. The property of $h(n)$ is called the admissibility, i.e., the definition of $h(n)$ must satisfy the sufficiency to ensure the optimality of the algorithm.

3.4 Resolution Principles

The predicate formula, some inference rules, and the concept of substitution and unification are discussed in some references [16,18,25]. On this basis, the resolution principle can be further studied. Some experts call it the resolution principle.

Resolution is an important inference rule that can be applied to certain clause formulas. A clause is defined as a formula consisting of the disjunction of literals (an atomic formula and the negation of atomic formulas are both called literals). When the resolution is available, the resolution process is applied to the parent clause pair to produce a derived clause. For example, if there is some axiom $E_1 \vee E_2$ and another axiom $\sim E_2 \vee E_3$, then $E_1 \vee E_3$ is logically true. This is the resolution, and $E_1 \vee E_3$ is called the resultant of $E_1 \vee E_2$ and $\sim E_2 \vee E_3$.

3.4.1 *Extraction of the clause set*

Before explaining the resolution process, firstly, any predicate calculus formula can be turned into a clause set. The transformation process consists of the following steps:

(1) Eliminate implication symbols

Apply only symbols $\vee$ and $\sim$, and replace $A \rightarrow B$ with $\sim A \vee B$.

(2) Reduce the scope of negative symbols

Each negative symbol "$\sim$" uses only one predicate symbol and repeatedly applies the DeMorgan law. For example,

$$\text{Replace } \sim(A \wedge B) \text{ with } \sim A \vee \sim B$$

$$\text{Replace } \sim(A \vee B) \text{ with } \sim A \wedge \sim B$$

$$\text{Replace } (\sim A) \text{ with } A$$

$$\text{Replace } \sim(\forall x)A \text{ with } (\exists x)(\sim A)$$

$$\text{Replace } \sim(\exists x)A \text{ with } (\forall x)(\sim A)$$

(3) Standardization of variables

In any quantifier domain, the variable bound by the quantifier is a dummy variable (virtual variable), which can be uniformly replaced by another variable that has not appeared in the jurisdiction without changing the true value of the formula. The standardization of variables in a suitable formula means that the dummy is renamed to ensure that each quantifier has its own unique dummy. For example, put

$$(\forall x)(P(x) \wedge (\exists x)Q(x))$$

Standardized:

$$(\forall x)(P(x) \wedge (\exists y)Q(y))$$

(4) Eliminate the existential quantifiers

In the formula $(\forall y)((\exists x)P(x, y))$, the quantifier is in the jurisdiction of the universal quantifier, and allow the existence of x to depend on the value of y. Let this dependency be explicitly defined by the function $g(y)$, which maps each y value to the x that exists.

This function is called the Skolem function. If you replace the existing x with a Skolem function, all existing quantifiers can be eliminated and written as follows:

$$(\forall y)P(g(y), y)$$

The general rule for eliminating an existing quantifier from a formula is to replace the quantified variable of each existing quantifier with a Skolem function, and the variable of the Skolem function is the quantified variable of the universal quantifier constrained by those universal quantifiers. The domain includes the jurisdiction of the quantifier that is to be eliminated. The function symbols used by the Skolem function must be new; that is, they are not allowed to be function symbols that have already appeared in the formula. For example,

$$\forall(y)(\exists x)P(x, y) \text{ is replaced by } ((\forall y)P(g(y), y)),$$

where $g(y)$ is a Skolem function.

If the existential quantifier to be eliminated is not within the jurisdiction of any universal quantifier, then the Skolem function without the variable is used as the constant. For example, $(\exists x)P(x)$ is transformed into $P(A)$, where constant symbol A is used to represent a presence entity that is known to people. A must be a new constant symbol that has never been used elsewhere in the formula.

(5) Convert into a prenex form

At this point, there are no existing quantifiers, and each universal quantifier has its own variables. Move all the universal quantifiers to the left of the formula, and make the domain of each quantifier include the entire part of the formula behind the quantifier. The resulting formula is called the prenex form. The prenex form consists of a prefix and a matrix, the prefix consists of a universal quantifier string, and the matrix consists of a formula without a quantifier, i.e.,

$$\text{Prenex form} = (\text{prefix})(\text{matrix})$$

where the prefix consists of a string of universal quantifiers, and the matrix is a formula without any quantifiers.

(6) Convert the matrix into a conjunctive normal form

Any matrix can be written as a conjunction consisting of a set of the disjunction of some predicate formulas and/or the negation of predicate formulas. This type of matrix is called the conjunctive normal form. The distribution law can be applied repeatedly. Convert any matrix into a conjunctive normal form. For example,

Turn $A \vee (B \wedge C)$ into

$$(A \vee B) \wedge (A \vee C)$$

(7) Eliminate the universal quantifier

At this point, all the remaining quantifiers have been quantified by the universal quantifier. At the same time, the order of the universal quantifiers is not important. Therefore, the prefix can be eliminated; that is, the apparently universal quantifier is eliminated.

(8) Eliminate the conjunction symbol $\wedge$

Replace $(A \wedge B)$ with (A, B) to eliminate the obvious sign $\wedge$. As a result of repeated substitutions, we finally get a finite set, where each formula is a disjunction of literals. Any suitable formula consisting of only the disjunction of literals is called a clause.

(9) Replace the variable name

The name of the variable symbol can be changed so that a variable symbol does not appear in more than one clause.

Not all of the problem's predicate formulas are formulated into clause sets that require the above nine steps. For some problems, some of these steps may not be needed.

It must be pointed out that the clause in a sentence can contain variables, but these variables are always understood as the variables quantified by the universal quantifier. If a variable in an expression is replaced by a term without a variable, you get a result called a literal instance. For example, $Q(A, f(g(B)))$ is a base instance of $Q(x, y)$. In the theorem-proving system, when resolution is used as an inference rule, in order to prove a certain theorem from a formula set, we must first set the formula into a clause set. It can be proved that if the formula X logically follows the formula set S, then X logically also follows the clause set transformed from the formula of S. Therefore, a clause is a perfect general form of a formula.

3.4.2 *Rules of resolution reasoning*

Let L_1 be any atomic formula and L_2 be another atomic formula; L_1 and L_2 have the same predicate symbol, but generally have different variables. Two clauses $L_1 \vee \alpha$ and $\sim L_2 \vee \beta$ are known. If L_1 and L_2 have the most general unification σ, then a new clause $(\alpha \vee \beta)\sigma$ can be derived from the two parent clauses by resolution. This new clause is called a resultant. It is obtained by taking the disjunction of these two clauses and then eliminating the complementary pairs [26].

The rules for the resolution of base clauses can be extended to clauses containing variables. In order to apply a resolution rule to a clause containing a variable, a substitution must be found that acts on the parent clause to include a complementary literal.

The base clauses and the clauses containing variables are resolved. The parent clauses and the resultant are shown in Table 3.1. These examples show some common rules for resolution reasoning.

3.4.3 *Solving process of resolution refutation*

The problem to be solved can be used as a proposition to prove. Resolution produces evidence through refutation. That is to say, to prove a

Table 3.1　Clauses and resultant.

Father clause	Resultant
P and $\sim P \vee Q$, (i.e., $P \to Q$)	Q
$P \vee Q$ and $\sim P \vee Q$	Q
$P \vee Q$ and $\sim P \vee \sim Q$	$Q \vee \sim Q$ and $P \vee \sim P$
$\sim P$ and P	NIL
$\sim P \vee Q$ (i.e., $P \to Q$) and $\sim Q \vee R$ (i.e., $Q \to R$)	$\sim P \vee R$ (i.e., $P \to R$)
$B(x)$ and $\sim B(x) \vee C(x)$	$C(x)$
$P(x) \vee Q(x)$ and $\sim Q(f(y))$	$P(f(y))$, $\sigma = \{f(y)/x\}$
$P(x, f(y)) \vee Q(x) \vee R(f(a), y)$ and $\sim P(f(f(a)), z) \vee R(z, w)$	$Q(f(f(a))) \vee R(f(a), y) \vee R(f(y), w)$ $\sigma = \{f(f(a))/x, f(y)/z\}$

certain proposition, its goal formula is negated and transformed into a sub-sentence, and then added to the propositional formula set, the resolution refutation system is applied to the joint set, and an empty clause (NIL) is derived, resulting in a contradiction, so that the theorem is proved.

The proof of the resolution refutation is very similar to the idea of counter-evidence in mathematics.

(1) Resolution refutation

Give a formula set S and a goal wff L, and verify the goal formula L by means of counter-inversion or refutation. The proof steps are as follows:

(i) negate L to get $\sim L$;
(ii) add $\sim L$ to S;
(iii) convert the newly generated set $\{\sim L, S\}$ into a clause set;
(iv) apply the resolution principle, and try to derive an empty clause that represents a contradiction.

Let us briefly discuss the correctness of the process of using refutation proof. Let formula L logically follow formula set S, then each interpretation that satisfies S by definition also satisfies L. There is never an explanation that can simultaneously satisfy S and $\sim L$, so there is no explanation that can satisfy the union $S \cup \{\sim L\}$. If a formula set cannot be satisfied by any interpretation, then this formula is unsatisfactory. Therefore, if L logically follows S, then $S \cup \{\sim L\}$ is unsatisfiable. It can be proved that if the resolution refutation is repeatedly applied to the unsatisfiable clause set, then the empty clause NIL will eventually be generated. Therefore, if L logically follows S, then the clause obtained by the union of $S \cup \{\sim L\}$ will eventually produce an empty clause; otherwise, it can be proved that if an empty clause is resolved from the clause of $S \cup \{\sim L\}$, then L logically follows S.

(2) Refutation solving process

Finding the answer to a problem from the refutation tree is as follows:

(i) Add each clause resulting from the negation of the goal formula to the negation clause of the goal formula negation.
(ii) According to the refutation tree, perform the same refutation as before until a certain clause is obtained at the root.
(iii) Use the clause of the root as an answer.

The answer is to transform a refutation tree with a NIL at the root into a proof tree with a statement at the root that can be used as an answer. Since the transformation relationship involves transforming each clause generated by the negation of the goal formula into a tautology, the transformed proof tree is a proof tree of the refutation, and the statement at the root logically follows the axiom plus tautology and thus also axioms. Therefore, the transformed proof tree itself proves that the obtaining method is correct.

3.5 Rule Deduction System

For many formulas, a clause form is a low-efficiency expression because some important information may be lost in the process of finding a clause. This section will study the use of easy-to-report if-then rules to solve problems.

The rule-based problem-solving system uses the following rules to establish:

$$\text{If} \rightarrow \text{Then} \tag{3.1}$$

which is

$$\text{If} \quad \text{if 1} \quad \text{if 2}$$
$$\vdots$$
$$\text{Then then 1} \tag{3.2}$$
$$\text{then 2}$$
$$\vdots$$

Among them, the If part may consist of several If's, and the Then part may consist of one or more Then.

In all rule-based systems, each If may match one or more assertions in an assertion set. This assertion set is sometimes referred to as working memory. In many rule-based systems, the Then part is used to specify new assertions placed into working memory. This rule-based system is called the rule-based deduction system. In such a system, each If part is usually called an antecedent, and each Then part is called a consequent.

Sometimes the Then part is used to specify the action; in this case, the rule-based system is called a reaction system or a production system.

3.5.1 *Rule forward deduction system*

In rule-based systems, there are two ways of reasoning, namely forward chaining and backward chaining. The process of reasoning from the If part to the Then part is called forward reasoning. Forward reasoning operates from facts or situations to goals or actions. Conversely, the process of reasoning from Then to If is called reverse reasoning. Reverse reasoning operates from a goal or action to a fact or situation.

(1) Forward reasoning

Forward reasoning starts from a set of predicates or propositions that represent facts, and uses a set of production rules to prove whether the predicate formula or proposition is true. The following rule sets R1–R3 are provided:

$$R1 : P_1 \rightarrow P_2$$
$$R2 : P_2 \rightarrow P_3$$
$$R3 : P_3 \rightarrow P_4$$

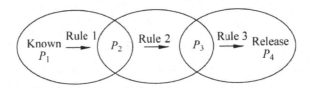

Figure 3.4   Forward reasoning process.

Among them, P_1, P_2, P_3, and P_4 are predicate formulas or propositions. Assuming that P1 already exists in the general database, rules R1, R2, and R3 are applied for forward reasoning. The process is shown in Figure 3.4.

The general strategy for achieving forward reasoning is to provide a batch of facts (data) to the general database first. The system uses these facts to match the premise of the rules, triggers the rules that match successfully, and adds its conclusions to the general database as new facts. Continue the above process, use all the facts of the updated general database to match another rule in the rule base, and use its conclusions to modify the content of the general database again until there are no new rules that can be matched, and no new facts will be added to the general database. When the left and right parts of the production system are represented by predicates, matching the premise of the global rule with the facts in the general database means uniformly replacing the variables appearing in the left predicate, so that the replaced left predicate becomes an instance of a predicate in the general database, making the left predicate instance the same as a fact in the general database. Performing the right part means that when the left part is successfully matched, the same variables used in the left part match are used, and the right predicate is replaced in the same way, and the replacement result (i.e., the right predicate instance) is added to the general database.

(2) AND/OR form transformation of fact expressions

In a rule-based forward deductive system, the facts are represented as non-implied forms of the AND/OR form as the general database of the system. Instead of turning these facts into clause forms, they are represented as predicate calculus formulas, and these formulas are transformed into non-implied forms called AND/OR form. See the previous section for a step to formulate the AND/OR form.

For example, there are fact expressions

$$(\exists u)(\forall v)(Q(v, u) \wedge {\sim}((R(v) \vee P(v)) \wedge S(u, v)))$$

Turn them into

$$Q(v, A) \wedge ((\sim R(v) \wedge \sim P(v)) \vee \sim S(A, v))$$

The renaming variable is standardized so that the same variable does not appear in different main conjunctions of the fact expression. After the name is changed, the expression is

$$Q(w, A) \wedge ((\sim R(v) \wedge \sim P(v)) \vee \sim S(A, v))$$

It must be noted that the variable v in $Q(v, A)$ can be replaced by the new variable w, but the variable v in the conjunction $(\sim R(v) \wedge \sim P(v))$ cannot be renamed because the latter also appears in the disjunction $\sim S(A, v)$. The AND/OR form expression is composed of sub-expressions of some characters connected by the symbols $\wedge$ and $\vee$. An expression with AND/OR form is not a clause, but is close to the original expression, especially if its sub-expression is not compounded.

(3) AND/OR graph representation of fact expressions

The fact expressions with AND/OR form are represented by AND/OR graphs. The AND/OR tree of Figure 3.5 represents the fact expression of AND/OR form in the above example. In the figure, each node represents a sub-expression of the fact expression. The sub-expressions of the disjunction relation $(E_1 \vee \cdots \vee E_k)$ of a fact expression $E_1, \ldots, E_k$ are represented by successor nodes and are connected to the parent node by a k-line connector. Each of the conjunction sub-expressions $(E_1 \wedge \cdots \wedge E_n)$ of a factual expression $E_1, \ldots, E_n$ is represented by a single successor node and is connected to the parent contact by a single-line connector. In fact expressions,

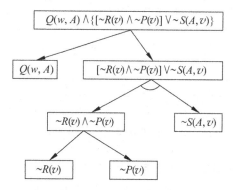

Figure 3.5   AND–OR tree representation of a fact expression.

it is probably surprising to use the k-line connector (a conjunction token) to resolve the expression. In the discussion that follows, the reasons for adopting this convention will be understood [16].

The leaf nodes of an AND graph representing a certain fact expression are marked by the literals in the expression. The node labeled with the entire fact expression in the graph and called the root node has no ancestors in the graph.

An interesting property of the AND/OR graph representation of a formula is that the set of clauses obtained by transforming the formula can be read as a set of solutions of the sum AND/OR graph (terminating at the terminal node); that is, each clause obtained is the disjunction of the literal on each leaf node of the solution graph. So, the expression

$$Q(w, A) \wedge ((\sim R(v) \wedge \sim P(v)) \vee \sim S(A, v))$$

has the resulting clause

$$Q(w, A)$$

$$\sim S(A, v) \vee \sim R(v)$$

$$\sim S(A, v) \vee \sim P(v)$$

Each of the above clauses is the disjunction of the literals on the leaf node of one of the solution graphs in Figure 3.10. Therefore, the AND/OR graph can be thought of as a concise representation of the clause set. However, in fact, the AND/OR of the expression indicates that the expression of this clause set is slightly less versatile, because not combining the common sub-expressions will hinder the renaming of some variables that may be done in the clause form. For example, in the last clause above, the variables v can all be changed to u, but they cannot be represented in the AND/OR graph, thus losing versatility and possibly causing some difficulties.

Generally, the representation of the AND/OR graph of the fact expression are reversed drawing; that is, the terminal node is drawn at the bottom and the subsequent node is drawn upward. The AND/OR graph representation of Figure 3.10 is drawn in the usual way, i.e., the goal is on top.

(4) F rule transformation of the AND graph

These rules are based on the implication formula of ordinary declarative knowledge in a problem domain. Limit the types of formulas that are allowed to be used as rules to the following forms:

$$L \to W \qquad (3.3)$$

where L is a single literal; W is the only formula of the AND/OR form. It is also assumed that any variable that appears in the implication has a universal quantifier that acts on the entire implication. Some of these facts and rules are separated and standardized so that no single variable appears in more than one rule, and the rule variable is made different from the fact variable.

Any implication of the antecedent of a single literal, regardless of its situation of quantification, can be turned into an entire implication form in some quantitative domain. This transformation process firstly exchanges the quantifiers of these variables locally to the antecedent, and then Skolemize all the existing quantifiers. An example is as follows. Consider the equation

$$(\forall x)(((\exists y)(\forall z)P(x, y, z)) \to (\forall u)Q(x, u))$$

It can be transformed using the following steps:

(i) Temporarily eliminate the implication symbol

$$(\forall x)(\sim((\exists y)(\forall z)P(x, y, z)) \vee (\forall u)Q(x, u))$$

(ii) Move the negation symbol into the first disjunction and exchange the quantifier of the variable

$$(\forall x)((\forall y)(\exists z)(\sim P(x, y, z)) \vee (\forall u)Q(x, u))$$

(iii) Performing Skolemization

$$(\forall x)((\forall y)(\sim P(x, y, f(x, y))) \vee (\forall u)Q(x, u))$$

(iv) Move all the universal quantifiers to the front and then eliminate them

$$\sim P(x, y, f(x, y)) \vee Q(x, u)$$

(v) Restore implication

$$P(x, y, f(x, y)) \to Q(x, u)$$

Use a propositional calculus with free variable to illustrate how to apply such rules to an AND/OR graph. Applying a rule of the form $L \to W$ to any AND/OR graph with a leaf node n and marked by the letter L, a new AND/OR graph can be obtained. In the new graph, node n is connected to the successor node (also marked with L) by a single-line connector, which is the leaf node of an AND/OR graph structure represented as W.

To make the AND/OR graph obtained by applying a rule continue to represent the fact expression and the derived expression, this can be achieved by using nodes with the same mark on both sides of the matching arc. After applying a rule to a node, the node is no longer the leaf node of the graph. However, it is still marked by a single literal and can continue to have some rules applied to it. Any node marked with a single literal in the graph is referred to as a literal node, and the set of clauses represented by an AND/OR graph corresponds to the graph solution set terminated by the literal node in the figure.

(5) Goal formula as the termination condition

The purpose of applying F rules is to prove a certain goal WFF from a certain fact formula and a certain rule set. In the forward reasoning system, this goal expression is limited to provable expressions, especially the provable goal expression formula for literal disjunction. Use the literal set to represent this goal formula, and set the elements of the set to be the disjunction relationship. (The reverse chaining system and the bidirectional chaining system to be discussed in the following sections do not impose this limitation on the goal expression.) The goal literal and rules can be used to add successor nodes to the AND/OR graph when a goal literal is on the literal node n in the graph. When a literal matches, the new descendant of the node n is added to the graph and marked as the matching goal literal. This descendant is called the goal node, and the goal nodes are each connected to their parent node with matching arcs. When an AND/OR graph is generated and contains a solution that terminates on the goal node, the system ends successfully. At this point, a clause equivalent to a part of the goal clause has actually been introduced.

When the forward deduction system generates a solution with the goal node as the termination, the system terminates successfully.

For a forward production system with expressions containing variables, consider applying a rule of the form $(L \rightarrow W)$ to the AND/OR graph process, where L is the literal, W is a formula of the AND/OR form, and all expressions can contain variables. If this AND/OR graph contains a literal node L' that unifies with L, then this rule is applicable. Let the most common unifier be u, then this graph can be extended by using this rule. To this end, a directed matching arc is established, starting from the node labeled L' in the AND/OR graph to reach a new successor node labeled L.

This successor node is the terminal node represented by the AND/OR graph, and the matching arc is marked with mgu or abbreviated as *u*.

3.5.2 *Rule reverse deduction system*

As to the rule-based reverse deductive system, its operation process is contrary to the forward deductive system; that is, the operation process is from the goal to the fact, and the reasoning process from the Then to the If.

(1) Reverse reasoning

Reverse reasoning starts from a predicate or proposition that represents the goal, and uses a set of production rules to prove that the fact predicate or proposition is true; that is, first propose a set of hypothetical goals, and then verify these hypotheses one by one. If the above three rules R1–R3 are used, the reverse reasoning process is shown in Figure 3.6.

First assume that the goal P_4 is established, and the rule R3 ($P_3 \rightarrow P_4$) must first verify that P_3 is established to prove that P_4 is established. However, the fact P_3 does not exist in the general database, so it can only be assumed that the sub-object P_3 is established. From rule R2 ($P_2 \rightarrow P_3$), P_2 should be verified; also because of the fact that P_2 does not exist in the general database, it is assumed that sub-objective P_2 is established. Then by rule R1 ($P_1 \rightarrow P_2$), to verify that P_2 is established, P_1 must be verified first. Since there is no P_1 in the general database, it is assumed that the sub-object P_1 is established, and finally the conclusion that P_4 is present is obtained.

To achieve reverse reasoning, the strategy is as follows: first, a possible goal is assumed, and then the production system tries to prove whether the

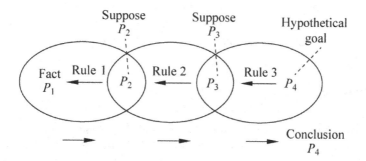

Figure 3.6　Reverse reasoning process.

hypothetical goal is in the general database. If it is in the general database, the hypothetical goal is established; otherwise, if the hypothesis is a terminal (evidence) node, then the user is queried. If not, then assume another goal; that is, look for those rules that contain the hypothesis in the conclusion, and use their premise as a new hypothesis, and try to prove that it is true. This is repeated until all goals have been proven or all paths have been tested.

From the above discussion, it can be seen that forward reasoning and reverse reasoning each have their own characteristics and applicable occasions. Forward reasoning is driven by facts (data) to derive conclusions from a set of facts. The advantage is that the algorithm is simple and easy to implement, allowing the user to store the relevant fact data into the database from the beginning, and the system can quickly obtain the data during the execution process without having to wait for the user to ask when the system needs the data. Its main disadvantage is blind search, which may solve many sub-objectives that are not related to the overall goal. When the general database content is updated, the entire rule base must be traversed, and the reasoning efficiency is low. Therefore, the forward reasoning strategy is mainly used for the known initial data, but cannot provide the inference goal, or have a large solution space for problems such as monitoring, prediction, planning and design.

Reverse reasoning is driven by the goal, starting from a set of assumptions to verify the conclusion. The advantage is that the search purpose is strong and the reasoning efficiency is high. The disadvantage is that the choice of the goal is blind and may solve many false goals; when the number of possible conclusions is large, i.e., the goal space is large, the reasoning efficiency is not high; when the right part of the rule is to perform some action (such as opening the valve) rather than the conclusion, reverse reasoning is inconvenient to use. Therefore, reverse reasoning is mainly used to conclude a single or known goal conclusion, and for the problem solving of required verification systems, such as selection, classification, and fault diagnosis.

(2) The AND/OR form of the goal expression

The reverse deductive system can handle any form of goal expression. First, the same process as transforming the fact expression is used to formulate the goal formula into an AND/OR form, i.e., to eliminate the implication symbol $\rightarrow$, to move the negation symbol into the parentheses, to Skolemize the whole quantifier and to delete the existential quantifier.

Variables left in the goal expression AND/OR are assumed to have quantified quantifiers.

The goal formula of AND/OR form can also be expressed as an AND graph. However, unlike the AND/OR graph of the fact expression, for the goal expression, the k-line connector in the AND/OR graph is used to separate the sub-expressions of the conjunction. The goal clauses are conjunctions of literals, and the disjunction of these clauses is the clause form of the goal formula.

(3) B-rule transformation of the AND/OR graph

Now apply the B rule, the inverse inference rule, to transform the AND/OR graph structure of the reverse deductive system. This B rule is based on the determined implication, just like the F rule of the forward system. However, now limit these B rules to the formal expression

$$W \rightarrow L$$

where W is any AND/OR formula, L is a literal, and the quantifier domain of any variable in the implication is the entire implication form. Second, limiting B rules to this form of implication form can also simplify matching so that it does not cause significant practical difficulties. In addition, an implication form such as $W \rightarrow (L_1 \wedge L_2)$ can be reduced into two rules: $W \rightarrow L_1$ and $W \rightarrow L_2$.

(4) Consistent resolution graph of fact nodes as termination conditions

The fact expressions in the reverse system are limited to literal conjunctions, which can be represented as a set of literals. When a fact literal matches the literal marked on the graph's literal node, the corresponding descendant fact node can be added to the AND/OR graph. This fact node is connected to the matching sub-goal literal node by a matching arc labeled mgu. The same fact literal can be reused multiple times (using different variables each time) to create multiple fact nodes.

The successful termination condition of the reverse system is that the AND/OR graph contains a consistent solution that terminates at the fact node [21].

Let's discuss a simple example to see how a rule-based reverse deductive system works. The facts, application rules, and problems of this example are shown below:

Fact:

F1: DOG (FIDO); the name of the dog is Fido

F2: ~BARKS (FIDO); Fido is not barked

F3: WAGS-TAIL (FIDO); Fido wags the tail

F4: MEOWS (MYRTLE); the name of the cat is Myrtle

Rule:

R1: (WAGS-TAIL($x1$) $\land$ DOG($x1$)) $\rightarrow$ FRIENDLY($x1$); the dog that wags its tail is a docile dog

R2: (FRIENDLY($x2$)$\land \sim$ BARKS($x2$)) $\rightarrow\sim$ AFRAID($y2, x2$); docile and not barking is not worth the fear

R3: DOG($x3$) $\rightarrow$ ANIMAL($x3$); dogs are animals

R4: CAT($x4$) $\rightarrow$ ANIMAL($x4$); cats are animals

R5: MEOWS($x5$) $\rightarrow$ CAT($x5$); MEOWS is a cat

Question: Is there such a cat and a dog that makes this cat not afraid of this dog?

Use the goal expression to represent this problem as

$$(\exists x)(\exists y)(CAT(x) \land DOG(y) \land \sim AFRAID(x, y))$$

Figure 3.7 shows a consistent solution graph to this problem. In the figure, the fact nodes are represented by double-line boxes, and the applied rules are marked with rule numbers R1, R2, and R5. There are eight matching arcs in this solution graph, and each matching arc has a substitution. These substitutions are $\{x/x5\}$, $\{MYRTLE/x\}$, $\{FIDO/y\}$, $\{x/y2, y/x2\}$, and ($\{FIDO/y\}$ is reused four times. As can be seen from Figure 3.7, the substitutions terminated in the fact node are $\{MYRTLE/x\}$ and $\{FIDO/y\}$. Apply it to the goal expression and get the answer to the question as follows:

$$(CAT(MYRTLE) \land DOG(FIDO) \land \sim AFRAID(MYRTLE, FIDO)$$

3.5.3 *Rule bidirectional deduction system*

(1) Bidirectional reasoning

Bidirectional reasoning, also known as forward–reverse hybrid reasoning, combines the advantages of forward and reverse reasoning and overcomes the shortcomings of both. The reasoning strategy of bidirectional reasoning is to simultaneously infer from the goal to the fact and from the fact to the goal, and at some step in the reasoning process, to achieve the match

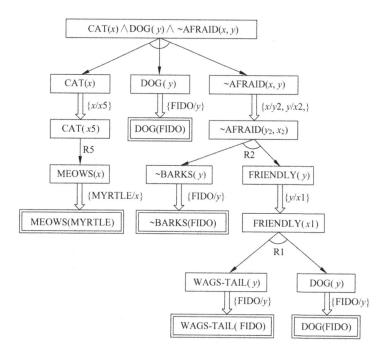

Figure 3.7 A consistent solution diagram of a reverse system.

between the fact and the goal. There are many specific reasoning strategies. For example, data are driven to help select a goal, i.e., forward reasoning from the initial evidence (facts), while the goal is driven to solve the problem that is solved by using alternately forward and inverse mixed reasoning. The control strategy of bidirectional reasoning is more complicated than the former two methods. KAS, a rule-based expert system tool developed by the Artificial Intelligence Center of the Stanford Research Institute in the United States, is a typical example of a production system using forward–reverse hybrid reasoning.

Figure 3.8 shows a schematic diagram of the bidirectional hybrid inference process.

(2) Deduction system

Both the rule-based forward deductive system and the reverse deductive system discussed in Subsections 3.5.2 and 3.5.3 have limitations. The forward deductive system can handle any form of If expression, but is limited to

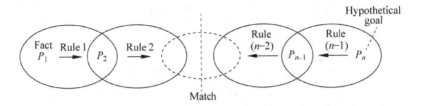

Figure 3.8　Bidirectional hybrid reasoning process.

the Then expression as some expression consisting of literal disjunctions. The inverse deductive system can handle any form of the Then expression, but is limited to some expressions in which the If expression is a combination of literals. It is desirable to be able to construct a combined system that has the advantages of both forward and reverse systems in order to overcome their respective shortcomings (limitations). This system is the bidirectional (forward and reverse) combined deductive system to be studied in this subsection.

The forward and reverse combined system is based on a combination of two systems. The general database of this combined system consists of two AND/OR graph structures that represent the goal and the facts. These AND/OR graph structures were originally used to represent some expression set of the given facts and goals, now the form of these expressions are unconstrained. These AND/OR graph structures are corrected by the F rule of the forward system and the B rule of the reverse system, respectively. The designer must decide which rules are used to process the fact graph and which rules are used to process the goal graph. Although the new system actually only proceeds in one direction when modifying a two-part database, these rules are still referred to as F rules and B rules, respectively. Continue to restrict the F rule to a single-literal antecedent and the B rule to a single-literal consequent.

The main complication of the combined deductive system is its termination condition, which terminates the appropriate junction between the two graph structures. These structures can be connected by matching ridge lines on nodes labeled with a corresponding mgu. For the initial graph, the matching ridge lines between the fact graph and the goal graph must be between the leaf nodes. When the graph is extended with the F rule and the B rule, the match can appear on any literal node.

After completing all possible matches between the two graphs, the question of whether the expression on the root node in the goal graph has been proven according to the expressions and rules on the root node in the fact graph still needs to be determined. Only when such a proof is obtained can the proof process be successfully terminated. Of course, the process ends in failure when it can be concluded that the proof cannot be found within the limits of a given method.

We apply F rules and B rules to extend AND/OR search graphs, so the substitution is related to the application of each rule. All substitutions in the solution graph, including the mgu obtained in the rule matching and the mgu obtained between the matching fact and the goal literal, must be consistent.

3.6 Reasoning with Uncertainty

The reasoning methods such as resolution refutation reasoning, resolution deduction reasoning and rule deduction reasoning discussed above are all deterministic reasoning [4]. They are based on classical logic and use deterministic knowledge for precise reasoning. It is also a monotonic reasoning. The problems encountered in the real world and the relationships between things are often more complex. The randomness, ambiguity, incompleteness, and inaccuracy of existence of objective things often lead to a certain degree of uncertainty in people's understanding. At this time, if the classical precise reasoning method is still used for processing, it will inevitably reflect the authenticity of things. To this end, it is necessary to use uncertain knowledge for reasoning in incomplete and uncertain situations, i.e., to make uncertainty reasoning [10, 25].

Reasoning with uncertainty, also called inexact reasoning, is an uncertainty-based reasoning established on non-classical logic. It starts from the initial evidence of uncertainty and uses uncertainty knowledge, and releases reasonable or near-reasonable conclusions with a certain degree of uncertainty [15].

The knowledge and evidence used in uncertainty reasoning have a certain degree of uncertainty, which increases the complexity and difficulty of the design and implementation of the inference engine. In addition to basic problems such as reasoning direction, reasoning method, and control strategies, it is generally necessary to solve important problems such as uncertainty representation and measurement, uncertainty matching, uncertainty transfer algorithm, and uncertainty synthesis [8].

3.6.1 *Representation and measurement of uncertainty*

(1) Representation of uncertainty

There are three kinds of uncertainties in uncertainty reasoning, namely, uncertainty about knowledge, uncertainty about evidence, and uncertainty about conclusions. They all have corresponding representations and metrics.

(i) Representation of knowledge uncertainty

The representation of knowledge is closely related to reasoning. Different methods of reasoning require corresponding knowledge representation patterns to correspond with them. In uncertainty reasoning, because knowledge is uncertain, appropriate methods must be used to express the uncertainty of knowledge and the degree of uncertainty.

When establishing the representation of uncertainty, there are two directly related factors that need to be considered: First, it is necessary to accurately describe the uncertainty based on the characteristics of the domain problem to meet the needs of problem solving. The second factor is to facilitate the calculation of uncertainty in the process of reasoning. It is only practical to combine the two factors to form a comprehensive representation.

(ii) Representation of evidence uncertainty

The facts learned when observing things often have some uncertainty. For example, when observing the color of an animal, it may be said that the animal's color is white or gray. That is to say, this observation has some degree of uncertainty. Uncertainties arising from such observations can lead to uncertainty in the evidence. In reasoning, there are two sources of evidence: one is the initial evidence provided by the user when solving the problem, such as the patient's symptoms, test results, and so on. The other is to use the previously proposed conclusions in reasoning as evidence of current reasoning. In the former case, since this kind of evidence is mostly derived from observation, there is often uncertainty, so the conclusion that is introduced is, of course, also uncertain, when it is used as evidence for later reasoning, it is also an evidence of uncertainty.

(iii) Representation of conclusion uncertainty

The above-mentioned uncertainties due to the use of knowledge and evidence make the conclusions uncertain. The uncertainty of this conclusion is also called the uncertainty of the rule, which represents the degree of uncertainty that produces some conclusion when the condition of the rule is fully satisfied.

(2) Measurement of uncertainty

Different data and methods are needed to measure the degree of certainty. First, you must determine the range of values for the data. For example, in expert systems such as MYCIN, credibility is used to represent the uncertainty of knowledge and evidence, with a value range of $[-1, +1]$. The value between 0 and 1 can also be used to indicate the uncertainty of certain problems.

When determining the metric method and its range, note the following:

(i) The degree of measurement should be able to fully express the uncertainty of the corresponding knowledge and evidence.
(ii) The measurement range should be specified to facilitate the estimation of uncertainty by domain experts and users.
(iii) The measurement should be easy to calculate the transmission of uncertainty, and the uncertainty measure calculated from the conclusion cannot exceed the range specified by the measurement.
(iv) The determination of the measurement should be intuitive and have a corresponding theoretical basis.

3.6.2 *Algorithm of uncertainty*

(1) Uncertainty matching algorithm

Reasoning is a process of continuous use of knowledge. In order to find the required knowledge, it is necessary to use the preconditions of knowledge to match the known evidence in this process, and only the knowledge that is successfully matched can be applied [22].

In deterministic reasoning, it is easy to determine whether the knowledge matches successfully. However, in uncertainty reasoning, because knowledge and evidence are uncertain, and the degree of uncertainty required by knowledge is different from the degree of uncertainty actually existing in evidence, there is a problem such as "How to match successfully". For this problem, the current common solution is to design an algorithm to calculate the similarity between the matching parties, and then specify a similar limit to measure whether the degree of similarity between the matching parties falls within the specified limits. If they fall within the specified limits, they are said to be matchable, and the corresponding knowledge can be applied. Otherwise, they are said to be unmatchable, and the corresponding knowledge cannot be applied. The above algorithm for calculating the degree of similarity between the matching parties is called an uncertainty matching algorithm, and the similarity limit is called a threshold.

(2) Uncertainty update algorithm

The fundamental purpose of uncertainty reasoning is to use the initial evidence provided by the user (this evidence is often uncertain), and finally use the uncertainty knowledge to introduce the conclusion of uncertainty and to derive the degree of certainty of the conclusion. Therefore, in addition to solving the problems raised above, uncertainty reasoning needs to solve the problem of updating the uncertainty, i.e., how to consider the dynamic accumulation and transmission of knowledge uncertainty in the reasoning process. The update algorithm for uncertainty generally includes the following algorithms:

(i) Uncertainty algorithm for hypothesis. Know the uncertainty $C(E)$ of the rule premise, i.e., the evidence E and the rule strength $f(H, E)$, in which H indicates the hypothesis, solve the uncertainty $C(H)$ of H. Define the algorithm g_1 so that

$$C(H) = g_1[C(E), f(H, E)]$$

(ii) Parallel rule algorithm. According to the independent evidences E_1 and E_2, the uncertainty $C_1(H)$ and $C_2(H)$ of the hypothesis H is obtained separately. Finding the combination of evidences E_1 and E_2 and resulting uncertainty $C(H)$ of the conclusion H, i.e., defining the algorithm g_2, makes

$$C(H) = g_2[C_1(H), C_2(H)]$$

(iii) Uncertainty algorithm for evidence conjunction. According to the uncertainty $C(E_1)$ and $C(E_2)$ of the two evidences E_1 and E_2, the uncertainty of the conjunction of the evidences E_1 and E_2 is determined, i.e., defining algorithm g_3, so that

$$C(E_1 \text{ AND } E_2) = g_3[C(E_1), C(E_2)]$$

(iv) Uncertainty algorithm for evidence disjunction. According to the uncertainty $C(E_1)$ and $C(E_2)$ of the two evidences E_1 and E_2, the uncertainty of the disjunction of the evidences E_1 and E_2 is determined, i.e., defining the algorithm g_4, so that

$$C(E_1 OR E_2) = g_4[C(E_1), C(E_2)]$$

The uncertainty algorithm of evidence conjunction and evidence disjunction is collectively called the uncertainty algorithm of combined evidence. In fact, the premise of the rule can be a composite condition in which multiple conditions are joined by AND and OR. At present, a variety of methods have been proposed for the calculation of the uncertainty of combined evidence, and the following are most commonly used.

(a) MINIMAX method

$$C(E_1 \text{ AND } E_2) = \min\{C(E_1), C(E_2)\}$$
$$C(E_1 \text{ OR } E_2) = \max\{C(E_1), C(E_2)\} \qquad (3.4)$$

(b) Probability method

$$C(E_1 \text{ AND } E_2) = C(E_1)C(E_2) \qquad (3.5)$$
$$C(E_1 \text{ OR } E_2) = C(E_1) + C(E_2) - C(E_1)C(E_2)$$

(c) Bounded method

$$C(E_1 \text{ AND } E_2) = \max\{0, C(E_1) + C(E_2) - 1\} \qquad (3.6)$$
$$C(E_1 \text{ OR } E_2) = \min\{1, C(E_1) + C(E_2)\}$$

Each of the above equations has a corresponding scope of application and conditions of use, such as the following: probabilistic methods can only be used when the events are completely independent.

3.7 Probabilistic Reasoning

Some of the main issues to be solved by uncertainty reasoning have been discussed above. However, not all uncertain reasoning models must include the above, and in different uncertainty reasoning models, the solutions to these problems are different. At present, more inexact reasoning models are used in probabilistic reasoning, credibility methods, evidence theory,

Bayesian inference, and fuzzy inference. They will be introduced separately in this section [9, 19].

3.7.1 Basic properties and computing formulas of probability

Under certain conditions, the test results that may or may not occur are called random events, simplified as events. There are two special cases of random events, namely, inevitable events and impossible events. An inevitable event is an event that must occur in each test under certain conditions; an impossible event is an event that must not occur in each test under certain conditions. Probability theory is the science of studying the laws of quantity in random phenomena [11, 20].

Irrespective of whether or not a random event occurs in a test is an accidental phenomenon that cannot be confirmed in advance, when a variety of repeated tests are performed, the statistical regularity of the probability of its occurrence can be found. This statistical regularity indicates that the probability of an event occurring is an objective attribute inherent to the event itself. The probability size that such an event occurs is called the probability of the event. Let A indicate an event, and its probability is recorded as $P(A)$. Probability has the following basic properties:

(1) For any event A, there is

$$0 \leq P(A) \leq 1$$

(2) The probability of an inevitable event D is $P(D) = 1$, and the probability of an impossible event Φ is $P(\Phi) = 0$.
(3) If A, B are two events, then

$$P(A \cup B) = P(A) + P(B) - P(A \cap B) \tag{3.7}$$

(4) If events $A_1, A_2, \ldots, A_k$ are incompatible with each other (or mutually exclusive), i.e.,

$$A_i \cap A_j = \emptyset, \quad i \neq j$$

then

$$P\left(\bigcup_{i=1}^{k} A_i\right) = P(A_1) + P(A_2) + \cdots + P(A_k) \tag{3.8}$$

If the event is mutually exclusive, then

$$P(A \cup B) = P(A) + P(B) \qquad (3.9)$$

(5) If A, B are two events, and $A \supset B$ (indicating that the occurrence of the event B necessarily leads to the occurrence of the event A), then

$$P(A \backslash B) = P(A) - P(B) \qquad (3.10)$$

Among them, the event $A \backslash B$ indicates that the event A occurred and the event B did not occur.

(6) For any event A, there is

$$P(\overline{A}) = 1 - P(A) \qquad (3.11)$$

where $\overline{A}$ represents the inverse of an event A, that is, out of events A and event $\overline{A}$ only has one occurred.

The partial formula for the probability is calculated as follows:

(1) Conditional probability and multiplication formula

Under the condition that the event B occurs, the probability of occurrence of the event A is called the conditional probability of the event A under the condition that the event B has occurred, and is recorded as $P(A|B)$. As $P(B) > 0$, provide

$$P(A|B) = \frac{P(A \cap B)}{P(B)}$$

As $P(B) = 0$, provide $P(A|B) = 0$; at that time, the multiplication formula was derived:

$$P(A \cap B) - P(B)P(A|B) - P(A)P(B|A)$$

$$P(A_1 A_2 \cdots A_n) = P(A_1)P(A_2|A_1)P(A_3|A_1 A_2) \cdots$$

$$P(A_n|A_1 A_2 \cdots A_{n-1}), \quad (P(A_1 A_2 \cdots A_{n-1}) > 0) \qquad (3.12)$$

(2) Independence formula

If the events A and B met $P(A|B) = P(A)$, then the event A is said to be independent of the event B. Independence is the nature of each other, i.e., A about B independence, and also B about A independence, or called A and B independence from each other.

The necessary and sufficient conditions for *A* and *B* independence from each other are the following:

$$P(A \cap B) = P(A)P(B) \qquad (3.13)$$

(3) Full probability formula

If the events B_1 and B_2 meet

$$B_i \cap B_j = \emptyset, \quad (i \neq j)$$

$$P\left(\bigcup_{i=1}^{\infty} Bi\right) = 1, \quad P(B_i) > 0, \quad i = 1, 2, \ldots$$

Then for any event *A*, there is

$$P(A) = \sum_{i=1}^{\infty} P(A|B_i)P(B_i) \qquad (3.14)$$

If B_i has only *n* items, then this formula is also true, and only the *n* items are added at the right end.

(4) Bayes formula

If events $B_1, B_2, \ldots, B_i$ meet the full probability formula condition, then for any event *A*, $(P(A) > 0)$, there is

$$P(B_i|A) = \frac{P(B_i)P(A|B_i)}{\sum_{i=1}^{\infty} P(B_i)P(A|B_i)} \qquad (3.15)$$

If B_i has only *n* items, then this formula is also true, and only the *n* items are added at the right end.

3.7.2 *Method of probabilistic reasoning*

There are production rules as follows:

$$\text{IF } E \text{ THEN } H$$

Then the probability of uncertainty in the evidence (or precondition) *E* is $P(P/E)$; the purpose of the inexact reasoning of the probabilistic method is to find the probability $P(E|H)$ of the conclusion *H* occurring under the evidence *E*.

One of the original conditions for applying the Bayesian method to inexact reasoning is the probability $P(E)$ of the known premise E and the prior probability $P(H)$ of the conclusion H, and the conditional probability $P(E|H)$ of E that occurs when H is established. If only one rule is used for further reasoning, then the posterior probability $P(H|E)$ of H can be derived from the prior probability $P(H)$ of H using the simplest form of Bayesian formula

$$P(H|E) = \frac{P(E|H)P(H)}{P(E)} \qquad (3.16)$$

If an evidence E supports multiple hypotheses $H_1, H_2, \ldots, H_n$, i.e.,

$$\text{IF } E \text{ THEN } H_i \quad (i = 1, 2, \ldots, n)$$

Then you can get the following Bayesian formula:

$$\frac{P(H_i)P(E|H_i)}{\sum_{j=1}^{n} P(H_j)P(E|H_j)}, \quad (i = 1, 2, \ldots, n) \qquad (3.17)$$

If there are multiple evidences $E_1, E_2, \ldots E_m$ and multiple conclusions $H_1, H_2, \ldots, H_n$, and each evidence supports the conclusion to a certain extent, then

$$P(H_i|E_1 E_2 \cdots E_m) = \frac{P(E_1|H_i)P(E_2|H_i) \cdots P(E_m|H_i)P(H_i)}{\sum_{j=1}^{n} P(E_1|H_j)P(E_2|H_j) \cdots P(E_m|H_j)P(H_j)} \qquad (3.18)$$

At this time, as long as the known prior probability $P(H_i)$ of H_i and the condition probability $P(E_1|H_i), P(E_2|H_i), \ldots, P(E_m|H_i)$ of H_i hold, the conditional probability $P(H_i|E_1 E_2 \cdots E_m)$ of H_i can be used to calculate in the presence of $E_1, E_2, \ldots, E_m$.

Example. Let H_1, H_2, and H_3 be three conclusions, and E is an evidence supporting these conclusions and is known:

$$P(H_1) = 0.3, \qquad P(H_2) = 0.4, \qquad P(H_3) = 0.5$$

$$P(E|H_1) = 0.5, \quad P(E|H_2) = 0.3, \quad P(E|H_3) = 0.4$$

Find out the values of $P(H_1|E)$, $P(H_2|E)$, and $P(H_3|E)$.

Solution: According to Eq. (4.14) you have the following:

$$P(H_1|E) = \frac{P(H_1) \times P(E|H_1)}{P(H_1) \times P(E|H_1) + P(H_2) \times P(E|H_2) + P(H_3) \times P(E|H3)}$$

$$= \frac{0.15}{0.15 + 0.12 + 0.2}$$

$$= 0.32$$

According to the same equation, you can find the following:

$$P(H_2|E) = 0.26$$

$$P(H_3|E) = 0.43$$

The calculation results show that due to the emergence of evidence E, the possibility that H_1 is established is slightly increased, and the possibility that H_2 and H_3 are established has declined to different degrees.

The probabilistic reasoning method has a strong theoretical basis and a good mathematical description. When the evidence and conclusions are independent of each other, the calculations are not very complicated. However, the application of this method requires the prior probability $P(H_i)$ of the conclusion H_i and the conditional probability $P(E_i|H_i)$ of the evidence E_i, but it is quite difficult to obtain these probability data. In addition, the application conditions of the Bayesian formula are quite strict; that is, the events are required to be independent of each other. If there is a dependency relationship between the evidences, then this method cannot be directly adopted [14, 24].

3.8 Subjective Bayesian Method

To directly use the Bayesian formula to find the probability $P(H_i|E)$ of the existence of evidence E, it is necessary to give the prior probability $P(H_i)$ of the conclusion H_i and the conditional probability $P(H_i|E)$ of the evidence E. For practical applications, this is not easy to achieve. On the basis of the Bayesian formula, Duda and Hart proposed the subjective Bayesian method in 1976, established the inexact reasoning model, and successfully applied it to the expert system PROSPECTOR [12–14].

3.8.1 *Representation about knowledge uncertainty*

In the subjective Bayesian method, knowledge is represented using the following production rules:

$$\text{IF } E \text{ THEN } (LS, LN)H \tag{3.19}$$

In the formula, (LS, LN) is the static strength of the knowledge, where LS is the sufficiency factor of Eq. (3.19), and LN is the necessary factor for the establishment of Eq. (3.19), which respectively measure the degree of support of the evidence (premise) E to conclusion H and the degree of support of $\sim E$ to conclusion H. Define

$$LS = \frac{P(E|H)}{P(E|\sim H)} \tag{3.20}$$

$$LN = \frac{P(\sim E|H)}{P(\sim E|\sim H)} = \frac{1 - P(E|H)}{1 - P(E|\sim H)} \tag{3.21}$$

The range of values of LS and LN is $[0, +\infty)$, and their specific value is determined by the domain experts.

The inexact reasoning process of the subjective Bayesian method is based on the probability $P(E)$ of the premise E, using LS and LN of the rules, and updating the prior probability $P(H)$ of the conclusion H into the posterior probability $P(H|E)$.

It can be seen from Eq. (4.13) that

$$P(H|E) = \frac{P(E|H)P(H)}{P(E)}$$

$$P(\sim H|E) = \frac{P(E|\sim H)P(\sim H)}{P(E)}$$

Divided by the above two equations, you can get

$$\frac{P(H|E)}{P(\sim H|E)} = \frac{P(E|H)}{P(E|\sim H)} \cdot \frac{P(H)}{P(\sim H)} \tag{3.22}$$

Then redefine the probability function as

$$O(X) = \frac{P(X)}{1 - P(X)} \quad \text{or} \quad O(X) = \frac{P(X)}{P(\sim X)} \tag{3.23}$$

That is, the probability function of $X(t)$ is equal to the ratio of the probability of X appearing to the probability of X not appearing. It can be seen from Eq. (3.23) that as the number of $P(X)$ increases, $O(X)$ increases too, and there is

$$O(X) = \begin{cases} 0, & \text{if } P(X) = 0 \\ +\infty, & \text{if } P(X) = 1 \end{cases} \qquad (3.24)$$

In this way, the value $[0,1]$ of $P(X)$ can be amplified to a value $[0, +\infty)$ of $O(X)$.

Substitute Eq. (3.23) into the relational Eq. (3.22), and there is available the following:

$$O(H|E) = \frac{P(E|H)}{P(E|{\sim}H)} \cdot O(H)$$

Then substitute Eq. (3.20) into the above equation and get

$$O(H|E) = LS \cdot O(H) \qquad (3.25)$$

For the same reason, we have

$$O(H|{\sim}E) = LN \cdot O(H) \qquad (3.26)$$

Equations (3.25) and (3.26) are modified Bayesian formulas. It can be known from the two equations that when E is true, the prior probability $O(H)$ of H can be updated to its posterior probability $O(H|E)$ by using LS; when E is false, the prior probability $O(H)$ of H can be updated to its posterior probability $O(H|{\sim}E)$ by using LN.

It can be seen from the above three equations that the larger the LS, the larger $O(H|E)$ and the larger the $P(H|E)$, which indicates that the stronger is the support of E to H. When $LS \to \infty$, $O(H|E) \to \infty$, $P(H|E) \to 1$, which indicates that the existence of E resulting in H is true. Therefore, E is sufficient for H, and LS is called a sufficient factor. Similarly, it can be seen that LN reflects the degree of support for H in the presence of $\sim H$. When $LN = 0$, $O(H|{\sim}E) = 0$ will be made, which means that the absence of E causes H to be false. Therefore, E is necessary for H, and LN is called a necessary factor.

3.8.2 *Representation about evidence uncertainty*

The uncertainty of evidence in the subjective Bayesian method is also expressed by probability. For example, for initial evidence E, the user gives $P(E|S)$ based on an observation S; it is equivalent to the dynamic strength. Because it is difficult to give $P(E|S)$, appropriate workarounds are often used in specific application systems. For example, the concept of credibility is introduced in PROSPECTOR, allowing users to select a number based on the actual situation among 11 integers between −5 and 5, and to select one integer as the credibility of the initial evidence, indicating the extent to which the evidence provided can be trusted. The correspondence between credibility $C(E|S)$ and probability $P(E|S)$ is as follows:

$C(E|S)$ = −5, indicating that the evidence E does not exist under observation S, i.e., $P(E|S)$ = 0.
$C(E|S)$ = 0, indicating that E is not related to S, i.e., $P(E|S)$ = $P(E)$.
$C(E|S)$ = 5, indicating that the evidence E does exist under observation S, i.e., $P(E|S)$ = 1.
$C(E|S)$ is another number, and the relationship between $C(E|S)$ and $P(E|S)$ can be obtained by segmentation linear interpolation of the above three points, as shown in Figure 3.9.

It can be obtained from Figure 3.9 that:

$$
P(E|S) = \begin{cases} \dfrac{C(E|S) + P(E) \times (5 - C(E|S))}{5}, & \text{if } 0 \le C(E|S) \le 5 \\[3mm] \dfrac{P(E) \times (C(E|S) + 5)}{5}, & \text{if } -5 \le C(E|S) \le 0 \end{cases}
$$

$$(3.27)$$

$$
C(E|S) = \begin{cases} 5 \times \dfrac{P(E|S) - P(E)}{1 - P(E)}, & \text{if } P(E) \le P(E|S) \le 1 \\[3mm] 5 \times \dfrac{P(E|S) - P(E)}{P(E)}, & \text{if } 0 \le P(E|S) \le P(E) \end{cases}
$$

$$(3.28)$$

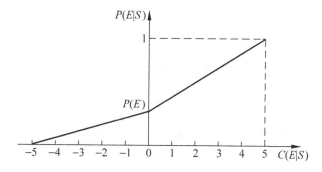

Figure 3.9 The corresponding relationship between $C(E|S)$ and $P(E|S)$.

As can be seen from the above two equations, as long as the user gives the corresponding credibility $C(E|S)$ to the initial evidence, the system converts it into $P(E|S)$, which is equivalent to the probability $P(E|S)$ of giving evidence E.

When the evidence is uncertain, the posterior probability is calculated using the following equation certified by Duda *et al.*:

$$P(H|S) = P(H|E)P(E|S) + P(H|\sim E)P(\sim E|S) \qquad (3.29)$$

When $P(E|S) = 1$, $P(\sim E|S) = 0$, $P(H|S) = P(H|E)$
When $P(E|S) = 0$, $P(\sim E|S) = 1$, $P(H|S) = P(H|\sim E)$
When

$$P(E|S) = P(E), P(H|S) = P(H|E)P(E|S) + P(H|\sim E)P(\sim E|S)$$
$$= P(H|E)P(E) + P(H|\sim E)P(\sim E)$$
$$= P(H)$$

When $P(E|S)$ is another value, the equations for calculation of $P(E|S)$ can be obtained by segmentation linear interpolation, as shown in Figure 3.10. The analytical form of the function is the following:

$$P(H|S) = \begin{cases} P(H|\sim E) + \dfrac{P(H) - P(H|\sim E)}{P(E)} \times P(E|S), & \text{if } 0 \leq P(E|S) < P(E) \\[3mm] P(H) + \dfrac{P(H|E) - P(H)}{1 - P(E)} \times [P(E|S) - P(E)], & \text{if } P(E) \leq P(E|S) \leq 1 \end{cases} \qquad (3.30)$$

which is called the EH formula.

Substituting Eq. (3.24) into Eq. (3.27), you can get the following:

$$P(H|S) = \begin{cases} P(H|\sim E) + [P(H) - P(H|\sim E)] \times \left[\dfrac{1}{5}C(E|S) + 1\right], & \text{if } C(E|S) \leq 0 \\[3mm] P(H) + [P(H|E) - P(H)] \times \dfrac{1}{5}C(E|S), & \text{if } C(E|S) > 0 \end{cases} \qquad (3.31)$$

which is called the CP formula.

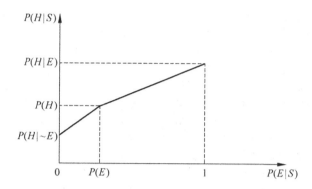

Figure 3.10   Interpolation calculation chart of the EH formula.

3.8.3 Reasoning procedure of the subjective Bayesian method

When the initial evidence is used for reasoning, $C(E|S)$ can be obtained by asking the user and $P(H|S)$ can be obtained using the CP formula. When the intermediate conclusion obtained in the reasoning process is used as evidence for reasoning, $P(H|S)$ can be obtained by the EH formula.

If there are n pieces of knowledge that support the same conclusion H, and the premises of each piece of knowledge are independent evidences, and the antecedents of each piece of knowledge are n evidences $E_1, E_2, \ldots, E_n$ independent of each other, and these evidences correspond to observations $S_1, S_2, \ldots, S_n$. At this time, first determine the posterior probability $O(H|S)$ of H for each piece of knowledge, and then determine the posterior probability of all observed H according to the following equation:

$$O(H|S_1, S_2, \ldots, S_n) = \frac{O(H|S_1)}{O(H)} \times \frac{O(H|S_2)}{O(H)} \times \cdots \frac{O(H|S_n)}{O(H)} \times O(H) \quad (3.32)$$

The subjective Bayesian method has the following advantages:

(1) The calculation formulas of the subjective Bayesian method are mostly derived on the basis of probability theory and have a relatively solid theoretical basis.
(2) The rules *LS* and *LN* are given by domain experts based on practical experience, avoiding a lot of data statistics work. In addition, it not only indicates the degree of support of the evidence E to the conclusion H by using *LS*, but also indicates the degree of necessity of the evidence E to the conclusion H by using *LN*. It comprehensively reflects the

causal relationship between the evidence and the conclusion, which is consistent with the actual situation in certain areas of the real world. The conclusion has a relatively accurate certainty.

(3) The subjective Bayesian method not only gives the method of updating the prior probability of H to the posterior probability in the case of evidence determination, but also gives the method for updating the prior probability to the posterior probability when the evidence is uncertain. It can also be seen from the reasoning process that the stepwise transfer of uncertainty is implemented. Therefore, it can be said that the subjective Bayesian method is a more practical and flexible method of uncertainty reasoning, which has been successfully applied in expert systems.

The subjective Bayesian approach also has some drawbacks:

(1) It requires domain experts to give prior probabilities $P(H)$ of H while giving rules, which is more difficult.
(2) The requirement for independence between events in Bayes' theorem limits the application of the subjective Bayesian method.

3.9 Summary

The search and reasoning of knowledge discussed in this chapter is another core issue of artificial intelligence research. Research on this issue has been very active, and there are still many high-level research topics. Just like knowledge representation, there are many methods for knowledge search and reasoning. The same problem may use different search strategies, and some of them are more effective and some are not suitable for specific problems.

In the process of applying blind search to solve, it is generally "blind" exhaustion; that is, no special information is used. Blind search includes breadth-first search, depth-first search, and equal-cost search. Among them, bounded depth-first search is heuristic to some extent. In terms of search efficiency, generally speaking, bounded depth-first search is better, breadth-first search is second, and depth-first search is worse. However, if there are solutions, then breadth-first search and depth-first search will definitely find the solution, no matter how much it costs; and bounded depth-first search may lose some solutions.

Heuristic search mainly discusses ordered search (or best-first search) and optimal search Algorithm A*. Unlike blind search, heuristic search uses heuristic information and references certain criteria or experiences to rearrange the order of the nodes in the OPEN table so that the search expands along some of the most promising frontier segments. Proper selection of the evaluation function is critical to find the least-cost path or solution tree. Heuristic search is much more effective than blind search, so it is used more commonly.

In solving the problem, the problem can be expressed as a problem or theorem to be proved, and then proved by the principle of resolution and the process of resolution refutation. In the proof, a forward search is performed using inference rules, hoping that the problem (theorem) will eventually be proved. Another strategy is to use a refutation method to prove that the negation of a certain theorem is not valid. To this end, first assume that the negation of the theorem is correct, and then prove that the set consisting of the axioms and the negation of the assumed theorem is invalid; that is, it leads to a contradictory conclusion — the negation of the theorem is invalid, thus proving that the theorem must be true. This method of proof that the negation of the theorem cannot be established is called refutation proof.

Some problems can be searched using both forward and reverse search, or you can search from both search directions, i.e., bidirectional search. When the search boundaries of the two directions meet in some form, the search ends in success.

The rule deduction system uses if-then rules to solve the problem. Among them, IF is the preceding item or premise, and THEN is the latter item or conclusion. According to the different reasoning methods, the rule deduction system can be divided into three types, namely the forward rule deduction system, the reverse rule deduction system and the bidirectional rule deduction system. The forward rule deduction system operates from facts to goals, namely, from the condition to the action to reason, i.e., from the IF to THEN direction. This reasoning rule is called the forward reasoning rule or the F rule. Apply the F rule to the structure of the AND/OR graph, and change the structure of the AND/OR graph until the goal is obtained. At this time, the resulting AND/OR graph contains a termination goal node, and the solving process ends successfully after obtaining the goal solution graph, and the goal node is equivalent to the goal clause.

The reverse rule deduction system is inferred from THEN to IF, i.e., inferred from the goal or action to the fact or condition. This reasoning rule is called the reverse reasoning rule or the B rule. Apply the B rule to the AND/OR graph structure, and change it until it finds a consistent solution graph that ends in the fact node and ends successfully. The inverse rule deduction system can handle any form of goal expression, so it is widely used.

Both forward rule deduction systems and reverse rule deduction systems have limitations. The former can handle any form of fact expression, but only applies to goal expressions consisting of disjunction of literals. The latter can handle arbitrary forms of goal expressions, but only applies to factual expressions consisting of conjunctions of literals. The bidirectional rule deduction system combines the advantages of both forward and reverse rule deduction systems, overcomes their respective shortcomings, and has higher search and solution efficiency. The bidirectional combined system is based on the combination of forward and reverse systems. Its general database is composed of two AND/OR graphs that represent goals and facts. Use F rules and B rules to expand and modify the AND/OR structure. When a match occurs between two AND/OR graph structures at a suitable junction, the solution is successful and the system stops searching.

Deterministic reasoning methods often cannot solve the real-world problems faced in many cases, and therefore need to apply advanced knowledge reasoning methods such as uncertainty reasoning, including non-monotonic reasoning, time series reasoning and uncertainty reasoning. They all belong to non-classical reasoning.

Uncertainty reasoning is a kind of reasoning based on uncertainty knowledge based on non-classical logic. It starts from the initial evidence of uncertainty and applies uncertainty knowledge to introduce a degree of uncertainty or an almost reasonable conclusion.

Probabilistic reasoning is based on applying the basic properties of probabilistic theory and calculation methods. It has a strong theoretical basis and good numerical descriptions. Probabilistic reasoning is mainly calculated using Bayes' formula.

For many practical problems, it is difficult to directly use Bayesian formulas to calculate various related probabilities. Based on the Bayesian formula, a subjective Bayesian method was proposed, and an inexact reasoning model was established. The subjective Bayesian method can be used to represent the uncertainty of knowledge and the uncertainty of evidence. The CP formula is used to reason with the initial evidence, and the EH formula is used to reason with the intermediate conclusion of the reasoning as evidence, and an analytical function of probability can be found. The subjective Bayesian method has been successfully used in some expert systems (such as PROSPECTOR).

In addition, there are methods such as credibility method, non-monotonic reasoning, evidence theory, possibility theory, and fuzzy reasoning. Due to space limitations, some methods will not be introduced, while others (such as fuzzy reasoning) will be described in subsequent chapters of this book.

References

1. Baral, C. and Giacomo, G.D. (2015). Knowledge representation and reasoning: what's hot, *Proc. of the 29th AAAI Conference on Artificial Intelligence*, 4316–4317.
2. Barley, M.W., Riddle, P.J., Linares, L.C., Dobson, S. and Pohl, I. (2018). GBFHS: a generalized breadth-first heuristic search algorithm, *SoCS*, 28–36.
3. Barr, A. and Feigenbaum, E.A. (1981). *Handbook of Artificial Intelligence*, Vol. 1 & 2, (William Kaufmann Inc., Los Altos, CA).
4. Bobrow, D.G. (1984). Qualitative reasoning about physical systems: an introduction, *Artificial Intelligence*, 24(1–3): 1–5.
5. Burke, E.K., Hyde, M.R., Kendall, G. and Ochoa, G.A. (2019). Classification of hyper-heuristic approaches: revisited In *Handbook of Metaheuristics*, (Springer), 453–477.
6. Cai, Z.X. and Chen, A.B. (2008). *Dictionary of Artificial Intelligence*, (Chemical Industry Press, Beijing, in Chinese).
7. Cai, Z.X. (1997). *Intelligent Control: Principles, Techniques and Applications*, (World Scientific Publishers, Singapore).
8. Cai, Z.X., Liu, L.J., Cai, J.F. and Chen, B.F. (2020). *Artificial Intelligence and Its Applications*, Sixth Edition, (Tsinghua University Press, Beijing, in Chinese).
9. Cerutti, F. and Thimm, M. (2018). A general approach to reasoning with probabilities (extended abstract), *Proceedings of the 16th International Conference on Principles of Knowledge Representation and Reasoning (KR'18)*.
10. Cohen, P.R. (1985) *Heuristic Reasoning about Uncertainty: An Artificial Intelligence Approach*, (Pitman Advanced Publishing Program).
11. Dechter, R. (2019). Reasoning with probabilistic and deterministic graphical models: Exact algorithms. *Synthesis Lectures on Artificial Intelligence and Machine Learning*, Second Edition, (Morgan & Claypool Publishers).
12. Jun, S. (2018). Bayesian count data modeling for finding technological sustainability, *Sustainability*, 10(9): 3220.
13. Kaplan, L. and Ivanovska, M. (2018). Efficient belief propagation in second-order Bayesian networks for singly-connected graphs, *International Journal of Approximate Reasoning*, 93: 132–152.
14. Kim, J., Jun, S., Jang, D. and Park, S. (2018). Sustainable technology analysis of artificial intelligence using Bayesian and social network models, *Sustainability*, 10(1): 115.
15. Li, D.Y. and Du, Y. (2005). *Uncertainty Artificial Intelligence*, (National Defense Industry Press, Beijing, in Chinese).

16. Luckman, D.C. and Nilsson, N.J. (1971). Extracting information from resolution proof trees, *Artificial Intelligent*, *2*(1): 27–54.
17. Luger, G.F. (2002). *Artificial Intelligence: Structures and Strategies for Complex Problem Solving*, Fourth Edition, (Pearson Education Ltd.)
18. Nilsson, N.J. (1998). *Artificial Intelligence: A New Synthesis*, (Morgan Kaufmann).
19. Potyka, N. and Thimm, M. (2015). Probabilistic reasoning with inconsistent beliefs using inconsistency measures, *Proc. IJCAI'15*, 3156–3163.
20. Raedt, L.D., Kersting, K., Natarajan, S. and Poole, D. (2016). Statistical relational artificial intelligence: logic, probability, and computation, *Synthesis Lectures on Artificial Intelligence and Machine Learning*, *10*(2): 1–189.
21. Rich, E. (1983). *Artificial Intelligence*, (McGraw-Hill Book Company, New York).
22. Steen, A., Wisniewski, M. and Benzmuller, C. (2016). Tutorial on reasoning in expressive non-classical logics with Isabelle/HOL. In Benzuller, C., Rojas, R., Sutcliffe, G. (eds.) *GCAI 2016 EPiC, Series in Computing*, *41*: 1–10.
23. Vassev, E. and Hinchey, M. (2018). Toward Artificial Intelligence through Knowledge Representation for Awareness, Software Technology: 10 Years of Innovation. In Mike Hinchey (ed.) *Software Technology: 10 Years of Innovation in IEEE Computer*, Chapter 7 (John Wiley & Sons).
24. Wang, W.S. (2016). *Principles and Applications of Artificial Intelligence*, Third Edition, (Electronic Industry Press, Beijing, in Chinese).
25. Xiao, X.M. and Cai, Z.X. (1997). Quantification of uncertainty and training of fuzzy logic systems, *IEEE Int. Conference on Intelligent Processing Systems*, 321–326.
26. Yang, X.F., Gao, J. and Ni, Y.D. (2018). Resolution principle in uncertain random environment, *IEEE Transactions on Fuzzy Systems*, *26*(3): 1578–1588.

Knowledge-Based Machine Learning

4

From the development trend of artificial intelligence, machine learning is another important research field of artificial intelligence application after expert systems, and it is also one of the core research topics of artificial intelligence and neural computing. With the victory of AlphaGo, the emergence of driverless cars and breakthroughs in speech recognition and image recognition, machine learning as an important field of artificial intelligence has achieved rapid development and has attracted much attention. This chapter will first introduce the definition, meaning and brief history of machine learning, then discuss the main strategies and basic structure of machine learning, and lastly study various methods and techniques of machine learning one by one, including inductive learning, analog learning, explanation-based learning, and reinforcement learning. Data-based machine learning is discussed in Chapter 7. The discussion on machine learning and the progress of research on machine learning will inevitably promote the further development of artificial intelligence and the entire field of science and technology [19].

4.1 Definition and Development of Machine Learning

What is machine learning? What is the development process of machine learning? This section will introduce these issues.

4.1.1 Definition of machine learning

Learning is an important intelligent behavior that human beings have, but its exact definition has been subject to debate for a long time. Sociologists, logicians, and psychologists all have their own different opinions on it. According to the artificial intelligence master Herbert Simon, learning is the enhancement or improvement of the system's own ability in repeated work, so that when the system performs the same or similar tasks next time, it will do better or be more efficient.

The different definitions of learning, learning systems, and machine learning are given below.

N. Wiener gave a more general definition of learning in 1965:

Definition 4.1. A viable animal can be transformed by the environment that it is subjected to throughout its lifetime. An animal capable of breeding off-spring can produce at least animals similar to itself (offspring), even though this similarity may change over time. If the change is self-inheritable, then there is a chance that can be influenced by natural selection. If the change occurs in a behavioral pattern and assuming that the behavior is harmless, then the change will be passed down from generation to generation. This type of change from one generation to the next is called racial learning or system growth learning, and such a behavioral change or behavioral learning that occurs on a particular individual is called individual development learning or individual growth learning.

C. Shannon defined more restrictions on learning in 1953:

Definition 4.2. Assume that the following: (1) an organism or a machine is under or is associated with a certain type of environment; (2) there is a "successful" measure or "adaptive" measure to the environment; (3) such a measure is more local in time; that is, one can test this measure of success with a shorter time than the life of the organism. For the environment under consideration, if this global measure of success can improve over time, then we can say that for the chosen measure of success, the organism or machine is learning to adapt to such an environment.

Tsypkin has a more general definition of learning and self-learning:

Definition 4.3. Learning is a process in which the system responds specifically to a particular input by repeatedly inputting various signals to the system and correcting the system from the outside. Self-learning is learning without external correction, i.e., learning without rewards and punishments. It does not give any additional information as to whether the system responds correctly or not.

H. Simon gives a more accurate definition of learning:

Definition 4.4. Learning is an adaptive change in the system that enables the system to perform the same tasks performed by the same population more effectively than the previous one.

T. M. Mitchell gave a broad definition of learning that included the definition that any computer program uses experience to improve the performance of a task:

Definition 4.5. For a certain type of task T and performance measure P, if a computer program's performance measured by P on T improves with experience E, then the computer program is said to learn from experience E.

Definition 4.6. A learning system is a system that can learn unknown information about a process and uses the learned information as an experience for further decision-making or control, thereby gradually improving its own performance.

Definition 4.7. If a system can learn the inherent information of unknown characteristics of a process or environment, and uses the experience to estimate, classify, decide or control, and improve the quality of the system, then the system is called a learning system.

Definition 4.8. The learning system is an intelligent system that can gradually obtain unpredictable information from the process and environment during its operation, accumulate experience, and evaluate, classify, make decisions, and continuously improve system quality under certain evaluation criteria.

In human society, no matter how much knowledge and skill a person has, if he is not good at learning, then he will not be valued. Because his ability always stays at a fixed level, he will not create novelty. However, if a person has a strong ability to learn, he should wait and see. Although his current ability is not very strong, but as the saying goes "Don't wait for three days, and treat each other with admiration" he may acquire many new skills in a few days; it is not the original situation at all.

A machine has the ability to learn, similar to humans. In 1959, A. Samuel of the United States designed a chess software program that had the ability to learn and improve its game in constant gameplay. Four years later, this program defeated the designer himself. After another three years, this program defeated the undefeated champion of the United States, which record has remained for 8 years. This program demonstrates the power of machine learning and presents many thought-provoking social and philosophical questions.

Whether or not the ability of a machine can exceed that of people, one of the main arguments of many negative opinions is that a machine is man-made, and its performance and movement are completely stipulated by the designer, so its ability will not comprehensively exceed the designer himself anyway. This kind of opinion is true for machines without learning ability, but less so for a machine with learning ability, because the ability of such a machine is constantly improving in the application. After a period of time, the designer himself may also be ignorant of the level of the machine's capabilities.

The self-learning capabilities of Google Brain and the Go games AlphaGo and DeepMind, which have appeared in recent years, are even more amazing. Their study time is measured in days or even minutes.

What is machine learning? As of now, there is no unified definition of "machine learning", and it is difficult to give a recognized and accurate definition. In order to facilitate discussion and to estimate the progress of the discipline, it is necessary to give a definition of machine learning, even if this definition is incomplete and inadequate.

Definition 4.9. As the name implies, machine learning is a discipline that studies how to use machines to simulate human learning activities.

Definition 4.10. Machine learning is a study of those machines that acquire new knowledge and new skills and identify existing knowledge.

Combining the above two definitions, the following definitions can be given:

Definition 4.11. Machine learning is a discipline that studies the theory and methods of simulating human learning activities and acquiring knowledge and skills to improve system performance.

The term "machine" as used herein refers to a computer; now it is an electronic computer, but may be a neutron computer, a quantum computer, a photon computer, or a neural computer in the future.

4.1.2 Development history of machine learning

Machine learning is a very important branch of artificial intelligence application research, and its development process can be roughly divided into four periods.

(1) The enthusiastic period of machine learning

The first stage was from the mid-1950s to the mid-1960s and was a period of enthusiasm. In this period, the objective was "no knowledge" learning, i.e., "ignorance" learning; research objectives were various self-organizing and adaptive systems; the main research method was to constantly modify the system's control parameters to improve the system's execution ability, but did not involve knowledge related to specific tasks. The theoretical basis for guiding this phase of research was the neural network model that began research in the early 1940s. With the emergence and development of electronic computers, the realization of machine learning became possible. This phase of research led to the birth of a new science of pattern recognition, and at the same time emerged two important methods of machine learning, namely the discriminant function method and evolutionary learning. A. L. Samuel's chess software program is a typical example of using the discriminant function method. However, this knowledge-free learning system that is separated from knowledge has numerous limitations. Whether it is a neural model, an evolutionary learning or a discriminant function method, the learning results obtained are very limited, far from meeting people's expectations of machine learning systems.

(2) The calm period of machine learning

The second phase, from the mid-1960s to mid-1970s, was called the cool period of machine learning. The research object in this stage was to simulate the conceptual learning process of human beings and adopt a logical structure or graph structure as the internal description of the machine. Machines can use symbols to describe concepts (symbolic concept acquisition) and propose various assumptions about learning concepts. Representative works in this stage include the structure or example learning system of P. H. Winston, the concept learning system of E. B. Hunt, and the logic-based inductive learning system such as Hayes-Roth and R. S. Michalski.

It is worth mentioning K.-S. Fu's "enthusiastic" contribution to machine learning, especially learning control, during this "calm" period. In 1965, he applied the heuristic reasoning learning mechanism to the learning control system; in 1971, he discussed the connection between the learning control system and the automatic control system to promote the development of artificial intelligence and machine learning.

Although such learning systems have achieved great success, they can only learn a single concept and fail to put it into practical use. In addition, the neural network learning machine fell into disuse due to theoretical defects so that it failed to achieve expected results.

Some experts refer to the above two stages collectively as the "inference period" of machine learning, because during this period, researchers simply gave reasoning capabilities to the machine learning systems without providing knowledge. At the same time, people call machine learning thereafter the "knowledge period".

(3) The revival period of machine learning

The third phase, from the mid-1970s to the mid-1980s, was called the revival period. During this period, people expanded from learning a single concept to learning multiple concepts, exploring different learning strategies and various learning methods. The learning process of the machine was generally built on a large-scale knowledge base to achieve knowledge-enhanced learning. It was particularly encouraging that this phase began to integrate learning systems with a variety of applications and achieved great success in promoting the development of machine learning. After the emergence of the first expert learning system, the example reduction learning system became the mainstream of research, and automatic knowledge acquisition became the application research goal of machine learning. In 1980, the first International Symposium on Machine Learning was held at Carnegie Mellon University (CMU) in the United States, marking the rise of machine learning research around the world. Thereafter, the machine inductively learned to enter the application. In 1986, the international magazine "Machine Learning" was launched, which ushered in a new era of machine learning.

In 1979, S. Tangwongsan and K. S. Fu applied analog learning to robot planning. After the emergence of the first expert learning system, the example reduction learning system became the mainstream of research, and automatic knowledge acquisition became the applied research target of machine learning. In 1983, R.S. Michalski, J.G. Carbonell, and T.M. Mitchell edited and published *Machine Learning: An Artificial Intelligence Approach*, a comprehensive summary of the machine learning research work and its results. During this period, machine learning was divided into machine learning, example learning, observation learning, analog learning, and inductive learning. Inductive learning entered applications.

Unlike the first and the second period's machine learning methods which focused on "reasoning" and "knowledge", the statistical learning method represented by neural networks was a "data" driven learning method. It focused on studying the learning mechanism to obtain effective information from a large amount of data. During this period, artificial neural network research was active. In 1982, John Hopfield discovered a special type of recurrent neural network, the Hopfield Network. In 1984, Fukushima proposed a neural cognitive machine based on the concept of receptive fields, which was the first implementation of a convolutional neural network. In 1986, David Rumelhart proposed a backward error propagation algorithm, which systematically solved the hidden layer connection weight learning problem of multi-layer neural networks.

(4) The integrated development period of machine learning

The latest phase of machine learning began in 1986 when the international magazine *Machine Learning* was launched, ushering in a new era of booming machine learning.

On the one hand, due to the re-emergence of neural network research, the research on the connection mechanism (connectionism) learning method grew. The research on machine learning has emerged in the world, and the research on the basic theory and comprehensive system of machine learning has been strengthened and developed. On the other hand, experimental research and applied research have received unprecedented attention. With the rapid development of artificial intelligence technology and computer technology, new and more powerful research methods and environments have been provided for machine learning. Specifically, during this period, symbolic learning shifted from "ignorance" learning to growth-oriented learning with specialized domain knowledge, and thus there was an analytical learning with a certain knowledge background. Due to the progress of hidden nodes and back-propagation algorithms, neural networks made the connection mechanism learn again and challenged traditional symbol learning.

Evolutionary learning systems and genetic algorithms based on the theory of biological developmental evolution have received attention because of the advantages of inductive learning and connection mechanisms. The behaviorism-based reinforcement learning system showed new vitality by developing new algorithms and applying connection mechanisms to learn new achievements of genetic algorithms. In 1989, C. Watkins proposed Q-learning, which promoted in-depth research on enhanced learning. In the same year, the international magazine *Artificial Intelligence* published the "Machine Learning" album, which showed that machine learning research had reached a new level.

Knowledge discovery was first proposed in August 1989. In 1997, the international professional magazine "Knowledge Discovery and Data Mining" came out. The rapid development of knowledge discovery and data mining research provided a new method for extracting useful information and knowledge from computer databases and computer networks (including the Internet). Knowledge discovery and data mining have become an important research topic in machine learning in the 21st century, and many valuable research and application results have been obtained. The core of knowledge discovery is data-driven. From the large amount of data used to find useful information, many statistical methods are applied. Since the mid-1990s, statistical learning has gradually become the mainstream technology of machine learning. During this period, Boser, Guyon and Vapnik proposed an effective Support Vector Machine (SVM) algorithm, and its superior performance was first revealed in the study of text classification. Neural Network and Support Vector Machines are representative methods of statistical learning.

In summary, it is not difficult for us to infer that the interaction and combination of "reasoning" and knowledge appeared during this period, showing the coordinated development of symbolism, connectionism, and behaviorism, creating excellent research and development for machine learning in the new era surroundings.

Since the beginning of the 21st century, connection-based learning methods, especially deep learning methods, have been unprecedentedly developed and widely used. By 2011, there have been scientific research results showing that deep learning algorithms have almost the same or comparable levels as humans on some recognition tasks.

In 2012, the Google Brain project co-hosted by Andrew Ng and Jeff Dean used a parallel computing platform composed of 16,000 CPU cores to train a Deep Neural Network. The new model enables the system to automatically learn from the data, thereby "recognizing" many features of things and achieving great success in applications, such as speech recognition and image recognition.

The strong performance of machine learning in Go is another illustration of the deep learning ability of deep learning algorithms. In March 2016,

AlphaGo and the world's top professional Go player Li Shishi won a 4:1 man–machine match. From December 29, 2016 to January 4, 2017 in the man–machine New Year's Eve, the Master program created by DeepMind once again showed its absolute advantage over human players in the fast chess game. The Master played 60 games against 60 world and domestic champions and played the next fast chess game every 30 seconds to win a full victory of 60:0. In the early morning of October 19, 2017, in a research paper published in the international academic journal *Nature*, the new version of the program AlphaGo Zero developed by Google's subsidiary Deepmind started from a blank state and in the absence of any human input. Under the conditions, it was able to quickly learn Go by itself and defeat the "predecessors" with a record of 100:0. The key is to adopt and develop new reinforcement learning algorithms. AlphaGo Zero had only four TPUs and zero human experience. Its self-training time was only 3 days, and the number of self-playing chess games was 4.9 million. AlphaGo Zero defeated the previous version of AlphaGo, which had previously defeated Li Shishi, with a record of 100:0. After 40 days of self-training, AlphaGo Zero defeated the AlphaGo Master version.

Now, machine learning has entered a new stage, and its important aspects are as follows:

(i) As artificial intelligence enters a new era, machine learning has become a new subject of great concern worldwide and an important course in colleges and universities. It integrates applied psychology, biology, and neurophysiology, as well as mathematics, automation, and computer science to form the theoretical foundation of machine learning.

(ii) Combining various learning methods, research on various forms of integrated learning systems that complement each other is emerging. In particular, the coupling of connected learning and symbol learning can better address the problem of acquisition and refinement of knowledge and skills in continuous signal processing.

(iii) A unified view of various basic issues of machine learning and artificial intelligence is taking shape. For example, the combination of learning and problem solving, and knowledge representation for learning, led to block learning of the general intelligent system SOAR. The case-based approach combining analog learning with problem solving has become an important direction of empirical learning.

(iv) The application scope of various learning methods are constantly expanding, and some have formed commodities. The knowledge acquisition tools for inductive learning have been widely used in diagnostic classification expert systems. Connected learning is dominant in acoustic image recognition. Analytical learning has been used to design integrated expert systems. Genetic algorithm and reinforcement learning have good application prospects in engineering control. Neural network connection learning coupled with the symbol system will play a role in intelligent enterprise management and intelligent robot motion planning.

(v) Research on data mining and knowledge discovery, especially the study of deep learning, has formed a boom and been successfully applied in biomedical, financial management, commercial sales and other fields, injecting new vitality into machine learning.

(vi) Academic activities related to machine learning are unprecedentedly active. In addition to the annual machine learning seminars, there are international conferences on computer learning theory and genetic algorithm. In recent years, machine learning and artificial intelligence have become hot topics in various large forums, and the awareness and affinity of society and the public for machine learning and artificial intelligence have been rapidly improved.

Today, the application of machine learning has spread to various branches of artificial intelligence, such as expert systems, automatic reasoning, natural language understanding, pattern recognition, computer vision, and intelligent robots, etc.

4.2 Main Strategies and Basic Structure of Machine Learning

4.2.1 *Main strategies of machine learning*

Learning is a complex intelligent activity. From the 1950s to the early 1970s, artificial intelligence research was in the "inference period". People thought that as long as the machine was given a logical reasoning ability, the machine could be intelligent. In the famous "Artificial Intelligence Handbook", Feigenbaum divided machine learning techniques into four categories according to the amount of reasoning used in learning — rote learning, learning by teaching, analog learning, and example learning [5, 12]. The more the reasoning in learning, the stronger the system's ability.

Rote learning is memory and the simplest learning strategy. This learning strategy does not require any reasoning process. The representation of external input knowledge is exactly the same as the internal representation of the system, and no processing or conversion is required. Although rote learning seems simple in terms of method, because the storage capacity of a computer is quite large, the retrieval speed is quite fast, and the memory is accurate and has no error, it can also produce unpredictable effects. A. Samuel's chess software program uses this rote memory strategy. In order to evaluate the pros and cons of the game, he scored every game. The scores favorable to him were high, and the unfavorable scores low. When he played, he tried to choose a game with a high score. This program can remember more than 53,000 games and their scores, and can constantly modify these scores in the game to improve their level, which cannot be done for people anyway.

A more complicated learning than rote learning is the learning by teaching strategy. For a system using learning by teaching strategies, the expression of external input knowledge is not completely consistent with internal expression. The system needs a little reasoning, translation, and transformation work when accepting external knowledge. Expert systems such as MYCIN and DENDRAL used this learning strategy in acquiring knowledge.

The analog learning system can obtain only relevant knowledge to complete similar tasks. Therefore, the learning system must be able to discover the similarities between the current task and the known tasks, in order to formulate a solution for completing the current task. It needs more reasoning than the above two learning strategies.

Computer systems that use the example learning strategy do not have any regular information for completing the tasks in advance, and only some specific work examples and work experiences are obtained. The system needs to analyze, summarize, and generalize these examples and experiences, obtain the general rules for completing the tasks, and verify or modify these rules in further work, so more reasoning is needed [3, 11].

In addition, from the perspective of statistical learning, machine learning can be divided into supervised learning, unsupervised learning, semi-supervised learning, and reinforcement learning.

Supervised learning learns a function from a given set of training data, and when new data arrives, it can predict the result based on this function. The training set requirements for supervised learning include input and output, and can also be said to be features and goals. The goal of the training set is marked by people. Common supervised learning algorithms include regression analysis and statistical classification.

Unsupervised learning has no artificially labeled results as compared to supervised learning. Common unsupervised learning algorithms have clusters.

Semi-supervised learning lies between supervised and unsupervised learning.

Reinforcement learning uses observation to learn how to do an action. Each action has an impact on the environment, and the learning object makes a judgment based on feedback from the observed surrounding environment [15, 17].

Deep learning is a type of machine learning algorithm based on biology to further understand the human brain. The working principle of the nerve center brain is designed as a process of continuous iteration and abstraction in order to obtain the optimal data feature representation. The signal starts with low-level abstraction first, and then iterates gradually to high-level abstraction, thus forming the basic framework of deep learning algorithms [20].

4.2.2 *Basic structure of the machine learning system*

Starting from Simon's learning definition, a simple learning model can be established for the machine learning system of the "inference period", and some general principles that the design learning system should pay attention to are summarized [23, 25].

Figure 4.1 shows the basic structure of the learning system. The environment provides certain information to the learning part of the system. The learning part uses this information to modify the knowledge base to improve the performance of the system execution part of the task. The execution part completes the task according to the knowledge base, and feeds the obtained information back to the learning part. In the specific application,

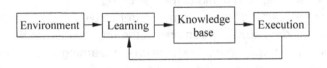

Figure 4.1   Basic structure of the learning system.

the environment, knowledge base, and execution part determine the specific work content, and the problems to be solved in the learning part are completely determined by these three parts. The effects of these three parts on the design learning system are described below.

The most important factor affecting the design of a learning system is the information or the quality of the information that the environment provides to the system. The knowledge base stores general principles that guide some actions in the execution part, but the information provided by the environment to the learning system is varied. If the quality of the information is relatively high and the difference from the general principle is small, the learning part is easier to handle. If the learning system is provided with specific information that guides the execution of specific actions, the learning system needs to delete unnecessary details, summarize and promote, and form the general principle for guiding actions into the knowledge base after obtaining sufficient data. The task of the learning part is more cumbersome and difficult to design.

Because the information obtained by the learning system is often incomplete, the reasoning of the learning system is not completely reliable, and the rules it concludes may or may not be correct. This is checked by the effect of the execution. The correct rules can improve the performance of the system and should be retained; incorrect rules should be modified or removed from the database.

The knowledge base is the second factor that affects the design of learning systems. The representation of knowledge can take many forms, such as feature vectors, state space, first-order logic statements, production rules, semantic networks, and frameworks. Each of these representations has its own characteristics. When choosing a representation, the following four aspects must be taken into account:

(1) Strong expression ability. An important issue in the study of artificial intelligence systems is that the chosen representation can easily express relevant knowledge. For example, if you are studying some isolated wooden blocks, you can choose a feature vector representation.

(2) Easy to reason. On the basis of strong expressive ability, in order to make the computational cost of the learning system relatively low, it is hoped that the knowledge representation method can make the reasoning easier. For example, in the reasoning process, the need to judge whether two representations are equivalent is often encountered.

(3) Easy to modify the knowledge base. The essence of the learning system requires that it continually modify its own knowledge base, and when it is generalized to the general execution rules, it is added to the knowledge base. Delete some rules when they are found to be inapplicable. Therefore, the knowledge representation of the learning system generally adopts a clear and unified way, such as feature vectors, production rules, etc., to facilitate the modification of the knowledge base.

(4) Easy to expand the knowledge representation. As the system's learning ability increases, a single knowledge representation can no longer meet the needs; a system sometimes uses several knowledge representations at the same time. Not only that, sometimes the system itself can construct a new representation to adapt to the changing needs of outside information. The system is therefore required to contain a meta-level description of how the representation is constructed.

One of the last questions that need to be explained in the knowledge base is that the learning system cannot acquire certain knowledge to understand the information provided by the environment, and cannot analyze and compare the information, make hypotheses, test and modify these hypotheses. Therefore, more precisely, the learning system is an extension and improvement of existing knowledge.

Unlike the early machine learning methods focusing on "inference" and "knowledge", the statistical learning method represented by neural networks and support vector machines is a data-driven learning method. This type of learning method focuses on "learning" and studies learning mechanisms that obtain effective information from large amounts of data. The system built on this basis contains two parts of training and prediction [16]. The basic structure is shown in Figure 4.2.

There is no "knowledge base" displayed in this structure, but only one learning model. This model can be a neural network, a support vector

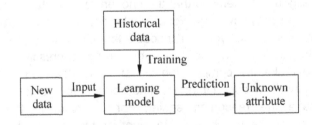

Figure 4.2   Basic structure of statistical learning system.

machine, or a decision tree. These models learn from historical data according to different learning algorithms. By establishing the objective function, i.e., the structured risk, the model parameters that minimize risk are found so that the calculation result of the model output is consistent with the training data, and has a good generalization ability to acquire predictive power for new data [4, 6].

4.3 Inductive Learning

From this section onward, we will discuss several commonly used learning methods one by one. This section first studies the methods of inductive learning [10].

Induction is an important method for humans to develop their cognitive abilities. It is a kind of reasoning behavior from the individual to the general, from part to the whole. Inductive reasoning is the application of inductive methods, summarizing general knowledge from enough concrete cases, extracting the general law of things. When conducting induction, it is generally impossible to examine all relevant cases, and the conclusions drawn cannot be guaranteed to be absolutely correct, and can be believed to be true to some extent. This is an important feature of inductive reasoning. For example, some known facts such as "The sparrow can fly", "The pigeon can fly", "The swallow can fly", etc. It is possible to conclude that "Winged animals can fly", "Long feathered animals can fly", etc., in conclusion. These conclusions are generally correct, but when it is found that the ostrich has feathers and wings but does not fly, it shakes the conclusions summarized above. This shows that the conclusions summarized above are not absolutely true and can only be believed to be true to some extent.

Induction learning is a method of applying inductive reasoning to learn. According to the inductive study, there is no teacher guidance, which can be divided into sample learning and observation and discovery learning. The former belongs to supervised learning, and the latter belongs to unsupervised learning.

4.3.1 *Modes and rules of inductive learning*

In addition to finite induction and mathematical induction, the general inductive reasoning conclusion is only false; that is, if the premise of the induction basis is wrong, then the conclusion is wrong, but the conclusion is not necessarily correct when the premise is correct. From the same set of examples, different theories can be proposed to explain it, and the best one should be selected as the learning result according to a certain criterion.

It can be said that the growth of human knowledge is mainly due to the inductive learning method. Although the inductive new knowledge is not as reliable as the deductive reasoning conclusion, it has strong falsifiability and is of great inspiration for the development and improvement of cognition.

(1) Inductive learning mode

The general mode of inductive learning is the following:

Given the following: (i) observation statement (fact) F to indicate specific knowledge about certain objects, states, processes, etc.; (ii) assumed initial induction assertions (possibly empty); (iii) background knowledge, used to define knowledge, assumptions, and constraints on observational statements, candidate induction assertions, and any related problem areas, including prioritization criteria that characterize the nature of the inductive assertions sought.

Seek: Inductive assertion (hypothesis) H can reproduce implication or weak implication observation statements, and satisfy background knowledge.

Suppose that H is the true implication of the fact F, indicating that F is a logical reasoning of H, then:

$$H| > F \text{ (read as } H \text{ specialized to } F)$$

$$\text{Or } F| < H \text{ (read as } F \text{ generalized or resolved to } H)$$

Here, deriving F from H is deductive reasoning and therefore fidelity; deriving H from the fact F is inductive reasoning, and it is not fidelity, but is fake.

The model of the inductive learning system is shown in Figure 4.3. The experimental planning process completes the instance selection by searching the instance space and submits the selected active instances to the

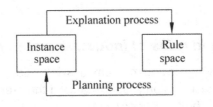

Figure 4.3   Inductive learning system model.

interpretation process. The interpretation process transforms the instance appropriately, transforming the active instance into a specific concept in the rule space to guide the search for the rule space.

(2) Inductive generalization rules

In the process of inductive reasoning, some inductive rules need to be quoted. These rules are divided into two categories: selective generalization rules and constructive generalization rules. Let D_1 and D_2 be the knowledge descriptions before and after induction, respectively, and the induction is $D_1 \Rightarrow D_2$. If all the basic units described in D_2 (such as the predicate of the predicate clause) are in D_1, but only the basic unit in D_1 has a trade-off, or change in the connection relationship, then it is a selective generalization. If there is a new description of the basic unit in D_2 (such as a new unit reflecting a certain relationship between the units of D_1), then it is called a constructive generalization. The main difference between these two generalization rules is that the latter can construct new descriptors or attributes. Let CTX, CTX_1, and CTX_2 represent arbitrary descriptions, and K represent the conclusion, then there are several commonly used selective generalization rules:

(i) Cancel some conditions

$$CTX \wedge S \to K \Rightarrow CTX \to K \qquad (4.1)$$

Among them, S is a restriction on the case. This restriction may be unnecessary, but it is related to some irrelevant characteristics of specific things, so it can be removed. For example, in medical diagnosis, when examining a patient's body, the patient's clothing is not related to the problem, so the description of the clothing should be removed from the description of the patient. This is a common induction rule. Here, $\Rightarrow$ is understood as "equivalent to".

(ii) Relax conditions

$$CTX_1 \to K \Rightarrow (CTX_1 \vee CTX_2) \to K \qquad (4.2)$$

There may be more than one reason for an instance. When new reasons arise, then new reasons should be included. A special use of this rule is to extend the range of values that CTX_1 can take. For example, expand a description unit item $0 \le t \le 20$ to $0 \le t \le 30$.

(iii) Trace up the concept tree

$$\left. \begin{array}{l} \text{CTX} \wedge [L = a] \to K \\ \text{CTX} \wedge [L = b] \to K \\ \quad \cdots \\ \text{CTX} \wedge [L = i] \to K \end{array} \right| \Rightarrow \text{CTX} \wedge [L = S] \to K \qquad (4.3)$$

where L is a structural description item and S represents the closest common ancestor of the L values under all conditions on the conceptual hierarchical tree. This is a method of deducing the population from the individual.

For example, people are very smart, monkeys are smarter, and orangutans are also smarter. People, monkeys, and orangutans are primates in the animal classification. Therefore, using this induction method can lead to the conclusion that primate animals are very smart.

(iv) Form a closed area

$$\left. \begin{array}{l} \text{CTX} \wedge [L = a] \to K \\ \text{CTX} \wedge [L = b] \to K \end{array} \right| \Rightarrow \text{CTX} \wedge [L = S] \to K \qquad (4.4)$$

where L is a description item with a linear relationship, and a and b are its special values. This rule is actually a method of selecting extreme situations and then summarizing them according to the characteristics of extreme situations.

For example, when the temperature is $8°C$, water does not freeze and is in a liquid state; when the temperature is $80°C$, water does not freeze and is in a liquid state. It can be derived that when the temperature is between $8°C$ and $80°C$, water does not freeze and is in a liquid state.

(v) Convert constants into variables

$$F(A, Z) \wedge F(B, Z) \wedge \cdots \wedge F(I, Z) \Rightarrow F(a, x) \wedge F(b, x) \wedge \cdots \wedge F(i, x) \to K$$
$$(4.5)$$

where $Z, A, B, \dots, I$ are constants, and $x, a, b, \dots, i$ are variables.

This rule is a method that only extracts some interrelationship between individual description items and ignores other relationship information. This relationship appears in the same relationship in the rules; that is, Z in $F(A, Z)$ and Z in $F(B, Z)$ are the same thing.

4.3.2 *Example-based learning*

(1) Introduction to example learning

Learning from examples, also known as sample learning or case-based learning, is a learning method that generalizes concepts through a number of examples related to a concept in the environment. In this learning method, the external environment (teacher) provides a set of examples (positive and counterexamples), which are a special set of knowledge, each of which expresses knowledge that applies only to that example. Example learning is to generalize the general knowledge applicable to a wider range from these special knowledges to cover all positive cases and exclude all counterexamples [22]. For example, assume that a batch of animals is used as an example and the learning system is told which animal is a "horse", which animal is not. When there are enough examples, the learning system can generalize the conceptual model of the "horse" so that it can identify the horse and distinguish the horse from other animals.

Example 4.1. Table 4.1 shows some cases of pneumonia and tuberculosis. Each case contains five symptoms: fever (no, low, high), cough (slight, moderate, intense), shadows seen by X-rays (points, cords, flaky, hollow), erythrocyte sedimentation (normal, fast), and auscultation (normal, dry sound, blisters).

Through the example study, the following diagnostic rules can be summarized from the case:

(i) ESR = normal sputum $\land$ (auscultation = dry sound $\lor$ bubble sound) $\rightarrow$ diagnosis = pneumonia
(ii) ESR = fast $\rightarrow$ diagnosis = tuberculosis

Table 4.1   Examples of lung diseases.

Symptom / Case No.		Fever	Cough	X-ray image	ESR	Auscultation
Lung Inflammation	1	high	severe	flake	normal	blisters
	2	moderate	severe	flake	normal	blisters
	3	low	Slight	point	normal	dry sound
	4	high	moderate	flake	normal	blisters
	5	moderate	slightly	flake	normal	blisters
Lung Knot Nuclear	1	none	slight	cable	fast	normal
	2	high	severe	empty	fast	dry sound
	3	low	slight	cable	fast	normal
	4	none	slight	point	fast	dry sound
	5	low	moderate	flake	fast	normal

(2) Compatible heuristics support case characteristics

Definition 4.12. Compatible heuristics

Whenever you want to guess the characteristics of something, you have no knowledge about other things except a set of reference things. By measuring the known characteristics of other things, you can find the most similar case. As a guess, the unknown characteristics sought are the same as the known characteristics of the most similar case.

When using case-based learning methods, the consistency heuristic method can be applied at any time to assign the characteristics of a previously observed thing to another new thing never seen.

The following discusses the use of compatible heuristics to identify the types of problems; by recording cases, these problems can be solved in the application.

Consider the nine blocks shown in Figure 4.4. The color, width, and height of each block are known, but there is a new No. 1 block (denoted as U) with a width and height of 1 × 4 cm, and the color is unknown. If you want to guess its color, you must guess that: this color should be the same as the other blocks (such as width and height) that are most similar to this one. In this guess, compatible heuristics will be used.

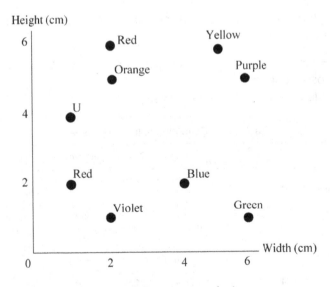

Figure 4.4 Feature space of color.

With the feature space map of each building block as shown in Figure 4.4, the compatible heuristic method can be easily used to guess colors without the need to imagine reasoning. As can be seen from Figure 4.4, the width and height of the unknown color blocks are the closest to the orange blocks, so we can make the following assumptions: the orange blocks are a valid example, and the U blocks are guessed to be orange.

4.3.3 *Learning from observation and discovery*

Learning from observation and discovery is also called descriptive generalization. Its goal is to determine a general description of a law or theory, characterize observation sets, and specify the properties of certain types of objects. Observation learning can be divided into observation learning and machine discovery. The former is used to cluster cases to form a conceptual description; the latter is used to discover laws and generate laws or rules [2].

(1) Concept clustering

The basic idea of concept clustering is to group cases in a certain way and criteria, such as dividing into different classes or different levels, so that different groups represent different concepts, and feature generalization of each group to get a semantic symbol description of a concept. For example, consider the following:

magpies, sparrows, cuckoos, crows, chickens, ducks, geese ...

They can be divided into the following two categories according to whether they are domesticated:

Bird = {Magpie, Sparrow, Cuckoo, Crow ...}

Poultry = {chicken, duck, goose ...}

Here, "bird" and "poultry" are new concepts derived from classification, and can be known according to the characteristics of the corresponding animals:

"Birds have feathers, wings, fly, call, wild"

"Poultry has feathers, wings, no flying, bark, domestic"

If their common characteristics are extracted, the concept of "birds" can be further formed.

(2) Machine discovery

Machine discovery is a learning method that summarizes rules or rules from observations or empirical data. It is also the most difficult and creative learning method. It can be divided into two types: empirical discovery and knowledge discovery. Empirical discovery refers to the discovery of laws and laws from empirical data. Knowledge discovery refers to the discovery of new knowledge from observed cases. Machine discovery is a data-based machine learning method that is not discussed in this chapter [8].

4.4   Learning by Explanation

Explanation-based learning, which can be referred to as interpretation learning, is a machine learning method that began to emerge in the mid-1980s. Interpretation learning analyzes and solves the current instance according to the domain knowledge of the task and the conceptual knowledge being learned, and obtains a causal explanation tree that characterizes the solution process to acquire new knowledge. In the process of acquiring new knowledge, new knowledge is learned by interpreting attributes, characterization phenomena, and internal relationships [14, 23, 29].

4.4.1 *Process and algorithm of explanatory learning*

Interpretation learning generally includes the following three steps:

(1) Analyze and interpret the training examples using an explanation-based approach to illustrate that it is an example of a target concept.
(2) Explain the structure of the example in general and establish an explanatory structure of the training example to satisfy the definition of the learned concept; the leaf nodes of the explanatory structure should conform to the operability criterion and should make this interpretation better than the original example, and can be applied to a larger class of examples.
(3) Identify the characteristics of the training examples from the explanatory structure, and obtain a general description of a larger class of examples to obtain general control knowledge.

Explanatory learning is the transformation of existing unusable or impractical knowledge into usable forms, so an initial description of the goal concept must be understood. In 1986, Mitchell *et al.* proposed a unified

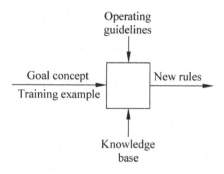

Figure 4.5   EBG problem.

algorithm EBG for interpretation-based learning. This algorithm established a generalization process based on interpretation and solved the problem by using logical representation and deductive reasoning. The EBG problem can be represented by Figure 4.5, and the process of problem solving can be described as follows:

Given:

(i) The objective concept (concept to learn) TC;
(ii) Training example (an example of a goal concept) TE;
(iii) Domain knowledge (a knowledge base composed of a set of rules and facts for explaining training examples) DT;
(iv) Operational criteria (indicating the formal predicate formula that the concept description should have) OC.

Solving:

A generalized generalization of the training examples has to satisfy the following:

(i) Full description of the goal concept description TC;
(ii) The operating guidelines OC.

Among them, the domain knowledge DT is the facts and rules in the related field. It is used as background knowledge in the learning system to prove why the training instance TE can be used as an example of the target concept, thus forming a corresponding explanation. The training example TE is an example provided for the learning system and plays an important role in the learning process. It should fully explain the target concept TC.

The operational criteria OC is used to guide the learning system to make a trade-off between the target concepts, so that the general description of the target concept TC generated by the learning becomes available general knowledge.

As can be seen from the above description, in explanation learning, in order to learn a certain target concept and obtain corresponding knowledge, it is necessary to provide a complete domain knowledge and a training example for explaining the target concept for the learning system. When the system is learning, first use the domain knowledge DT to find out why the training instance TE is a proof (i.e., an explanation) of the instance of the target concept TC, and then generalize the proof according to the operating criterion OC, thereby obtaining a general description about the target concept TC, and a general knowledge of a formal representation for later use.

The EBG algorithm can be divided into two steps:

(i) Interpretation: An interpretation based on domain knowledge to demon-strate how the training examples meet the target concept definition. The initial description of the target concept is usually not operational.

(ii) Generalization: The proof tree of step 1 is processed, and the target concept is regressed, including the use of variables instead of con-stants, and the necessary new item synthesized, to obtain the desired concept description.

It can be seen from the above that the explanation work separates the related attributes of the example from the irrelevant attributes; the general-ization work analyzes the interpretation results.

4.4.2 *Example of explanatory learning*

The following is an example of the working process of explanatory learning.

Example 4.2. Learn from the concept of obtaining an object (x) that can be safely placed on another object (y).

It is known that the target concept is a pair of objects (x, y), so that safe-to-stack(x, y) has the following:

$$\text{safe-to-stack}(x, y) \rightarrow \sim \text{fragile}(y)$$

The training example is the following facts describing two objects:

on(*a*, *b*)

isa(*a*, brick)

isa(*b*, endtable)

volume(*a*, 1)

density(*a*, 1)

weight(brick, 5)

times(1, 1, 1)

less(1, 5)

...

Domain knowledge in the knowledge base is a safety criterion for placing an object on another object:

lighter(X, Y) → safe-to-stack(X, Y)

weight(P_1, W_1)∧ weight(P_2, W_2)∧ less(W_1, W_2) → lighter(P_1, P_2)

volume(P, V)∧ density(P, D)∧ times(V, D, W) → weight(P, W)

isa(P, endtable) ∧ weight(B, S) → weight(P, S)

Its proof tree is shown in Figure 4.6.

Generalizing constants into variables in the proof tree, you can get the following general rules:

volume(X, V)∧ density(X, D)∧ times(V, D, W_1)∧ isa(Y, endtable) ∧ weight(B, W_2)∧ less(W_1, 5) → safe-to-stack(X, Y)

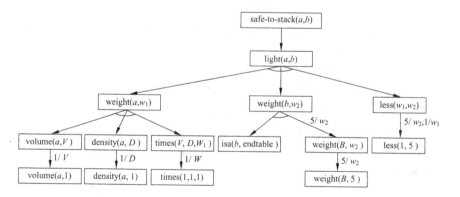

Figure 4.6   Proof tree explained by safe-to-stack.

4.5 Learning by Analogy

Analogy is a useful and effective method of reasoning. It can clearly and succinctly describe the similarity between objects. It is also an important method for human beings to understand the world. Learning by analogy is a kind of learning through analogy, i.e., by comparing similar things. When people encounter a new problem that needs to be dealt with but do not have the knowledge to deal with it, they always think back at similar problems that have been solved before, and seek and find an existing method that is closest to the current situation to deal with the current problem. For example, when a teacher wants to teach a new concept that is difficult to understand, the teacher always uses some examples that the student has mastered and that has many similarities with the new concept as a metaphor to enable students to deepen their understanding of the new concept through analogy. Learning like this by comparing similar things is called analogy. Analogy learning plays an important role in the development of science and technology. Many inventions and discoveries are obtained through analogy. For example, Rutherford compared the atomic structure with the solar system and found the atomic structure; the water pressure calculation formula in the water pipe is similar to the voltage calculation formula in the circuit and so on [21, 24].

This section first introduces analogy reasoning, then discusses the forms and learning steps of analogy learning, and lastly studies the process and type of analogy learning.

4.5.1 *Analogy inference and form of analogy learning*

Analogy inference is based on the similarities between new and known situations in some respects to derive their similarities in other related aspects. Obviously, analogy inference is carried out between two similar domains: one is the already recognized domain, which includes problems and related knowledge that have been solved in the past and are similar to the current problem, called the source domain, denoted as S; another is a domain that is not yet fully understood; it is a new problem to be solved and is called the target domain and is recorded as T. The purpose of analogy inference is to select the problem closest to the current problem from S and its solving method to solve the current problem, or to establish the connection between existing propositions in the target domain to form new knowledge.

Let S_1 and T_1 denote a certain situation in S and T, respectively, and S_1 is similar to T_1; and if S_2 is related to S_1, then T_2 in T can be derived by analogy inference, and T_2 is similar to S_2. The reasoning process is as follows:

(1) Memories and associations:

When some new situations or new problems are encountered, first find out the situation that is similar to the current situation in S by memory and association. These situations have been dealt with in the past, and there are ready-made solutions and related knowledge. There may be more than one similar situation, which can be sorted according to their similarity from high to low.

(2) Selection:

Select the situation most similar to the current situation and its related knowledge from the similar situations found. When selecting, the higher the similarity, the better the similar case, that is helpful for improving the reasoning reliability.

(3) Establish a correspondence:

Correspondence between similar elements is established between similar cases of S and T, and corresponding mappings are established.

(4) Conversion:

Under the mapping established in the previous step, the relevant knowledge in S is introduced into T to establish a method for solving the current problem or to learn new knowledge about T.

There are some specific issues that need to be addressed in each of the above steps.

The following describes the form of analogy learning.

Assume that there are two domains of the same or similar nature: the source domain S and the target domain T; the elements a in the known S and the elements b in the T have similar properties P, i.e. $P(a) \cong P(b)$ (here the symbol $\cong$ indicates similarity), a also has the property Q, i.e., $Q(a)$. According to analogy inference, b also has the property Q, i.e.,

$$P(a) \wedge Q(a), P(a) \cong P(b) \vdash Q(b)Q(a) \tag{4.9}$$

Among them, the symbol $\vdash$ indicates analogy inference.

Analogy learning uses analogy inference. The general steps are as follows:

(1) Find the similarity property P between the source domain and the target domain, and find the relationship between another property Q and the property P in the source domain to the element a: $P(a) \to Q(a)$.
(2) Generalize the relationship between P and Q in the source domain as a general relationship, that is, for all variables x, there is: $P(x) \to Q(x)$.
(3) Mapping the relationship between the source domain and the target domain to obtain the new property of the target domain, that is, for all variables x of the target domain, there is: $P(x) \to Q(x)$.
(4) Using modus ponens: $P(b)$, $P(x) \to Q(x) \vdash Q(b)$, we finally conclude that b has the property Q.

As can be seen from the above steps, analogy learning is actually a combination of deductive learning and inductive learning. Step (2) is an inductive process, i.e., to infer the general law from individual phenomena; and step (4) is a deductive process, i.e., to find individual phenomena from general laws.

4.5.2　*Process and research type of analogy learning*

Analogy learning mainly includes the following four processes:

(1) Enter a set of known conditions (resolved issues) and a set of conditions that are not fully defined (new questions).
(2) For the two sets of conditions entered, according to their description, find the correspondence between the two analogies according to the definition of similarity.
(3) According to the similar transformation method, map the concepts, characteristics, methods, relationships, etc. of existing problems to new problems, and obtain the new knowledge needed to solve new problems.
(4) Verify the knowledge of new problems derived from analogy. Verify that the correct knowledge is stored in the knowledge base, and that the knowledge that cannot be verified for the time being can only be used as reference knowledge in the database.

The key to analogy learning is the definition of similarity and the method of similar transformation. The object on which the similarity definition is based varies with the purpose of analogy learning. If the purpose of learning is to obtain a certain attribute of a new thing, then the definition of similarity should be based on similar correspondence between other attributes of new and old things. If the purpose of learning is to obtain a solution to a new problem, then the analogy should be based on the relationship between the various states of the new problem and the various states of the old problem. Similar transformations are generally determined by a similar analogy between the new and old things.

The study of analogy learning can be divided into two categories:

(1) Problem-solving analogy learning: The basic idea is that when solving a new problem, always recollect whether a similar problem has been solved before, and whether the new problem can be solved based on this, namely by modifying the previous solution process in order to make it satisfy the solution to the new problem.

(2) Predictive presumptive analogy learning: It can be divided into two types. One type is traditional analogy, which is used to infer other attributes that an incompletely determined thing may have. Let X and Y be two things, and P_i be an attribute $(i = 1, 2, \ldots, n)$, then we have the following relationship:

$$P_1(x) \wedge \cdots \wedge P_n(x) \wedge P_1(y) \wedge \cdots \wedge P_{n-1}(y) \wedge P_n(y) \qquad (4.10)$$

The other type is the analogy of causality. The basic problem is that for the known causal relationship $S_1: A \to B$, given that things A' are similar to A, there may be things B' similar to B that satisfy the causal relationship $S_2: A' \to B'$.

The key to making an analogy is the similarity of judgment, and the premise is matching. The combination of the two is a match. There are many ways to achieve matching, and the following are commonly used:

(1) Equivalent matching: requires two identical matching objects to have identical characteristic data.

(2) Select matching: Select important features in the matching object to match.

(3) Rule matching: If the conclusions of the two rules match, and the premise parts also match, the two rules match.

(4) Heuristic matching: According to certain background knowledge, the features of the object are extracted, and then the generalization operation makes the two objects the same at a higher and more abstract level.

4.6   Reinforcement Learning

Reinforcement learning (some people call it "intensive learning") has attracted interest from many researchers and has become one of the main ways of machine learning, owing to the versatility of its methods, less requirement for learning background knowledge, and the application to complex and dynamic environments [20, 26].

In reinforcement learning, the learning system adjusts the parameters of the system based on the state of the feedback signal (reward/penalty) from the environment. This kind of learning is generally difficult, mainly because the learning system does not know which action is correct, and does not know which rewards and punishments are assigned to which action [9, 18]. In the computer field, the first problem of reinforcement learning is to use rewards and punishments to learn the maze strategy. In the mid-to-late 1980s, reinforcement learning gradually led to extensive research. The simplest way of reinforcement learning is to use learning automata. In recent years, based on the state of the feedback signal, reinforcement learning methods such as Q-learning and jet-lag (time difference) learning have been proposed.

4.6.1   *Overview of reinforcement learning*

(1) Learning automata

Learning automata is the most common way to use reinforcement learning. The learning mechanism of this system consists of two modules: learning automata and environment. The learning process begins with the stimulation generated by the environment. The automata respond to the environment based on the received stimuli, and the environment receives its response to evaluate it, and provides new stimuli to the automata. The learning system automatically adjusts its parameters based on the last reaction of the automata and the current input [30]. The learning automata can be represented as shown in Figure 4.7. Here the delay module is used to ensure that the last reaction and the current stimulus enter the learning system at the same time.

Many practical problems can apply the basic ideas of learning automata, such as NIM games. In NIM games, there are three piles of coins on the desktop, as shown in Figure 4.8. There are two people involved in the game. Each player must take at least one coin at a time, but only in the same line. Whoever took the last coin would be considered the loser.

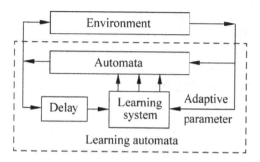

Figure 4.7   Learning mode of learning automata.

Figure 4.8   NIM game.

Original state Goal state	135	134	133	...	...	125	...
135	#	#	#	#	#	#	...
134	1/9	#	#	...	...	#	...
133	1/9	1/8	#	...	...	#	...
132	1/9	1/8	1/7	#	...	#	...
124	#	1/8	#	#	...	1/8	...

Figure 4.9   Partial state transition diagram in NIM games.

Note: The symbol # indicates an invalid status.

It is assumed that both sides of the game are computers and people, and the computer keeps a record of the number of coins that it takes each time during the game. This can be represented by a matrix, as shown in Figure 4.9, where the (i, j)th element represents the probability of success for the computer from the jth state to the ith state. It is obvious that the sum of the elements of each column of the above matrix is 1.

A reward and punishment mechanism can be added to the system to facilitate systematic learning. After completing a game, the computer adjusts the elements in the matrix. If the computer wins, all the choices corresponding to the computer are increased by one amount, and the other elements in the corresponding column are reduced by one amount to maintain the sum of the elements of each column as 1. If the computer fails, on the contrary, all the choices of the computer are reduced by one amount, and the other elements in each column are increased by one amount, and the sum of the elements of each column is also maintained as 1. After a large number of experiments, the amount in the matrix is basically stable, when it is the computer's turn to choose, it can choose the element that maximizes the probability of winning from the matrix.

(2) Adaptive dynamic programming

Reinforcement learning assumes that the system receives responses from the environment, but only when its behavior is over (i.e., terminated) its status can be determined (reward or punishment). And assume that the initial state of the system is S_0 and after the action (assumed to be a_0) is performed, the system arrives at the state S_1, i.e.,

$$S_0 \xrightarrow{a0} S_1$$

Rewards to the system can be represented by a utility function. In reinforcement learning, the system can be active or passive. Passive learning refers to the system trying to learn its utility function through its own feelings in different environments. Active learning means that the system can derive a utility function in an unknown environment based on the knowledge it has learned.

Regarding the calculation of the utility function, it can be considered as follows: Assume that if the system reaches the goal state, the utility value should be the highest, assuming that it is 1, and for other states, the static utility function can be calculated by the following simple method. Assume that the system passes the state S_2 and reaches the goal state S_7 from the initial state S_1 (see Table 4.2). Now repeat the test and count the number of times S_2 was accessed. Assuming that in 60 trials, S_2 were accessed 5 times, then the utility function of the state S_2 can be defined as $5/100 = 0.05$. It is now assumed that the system transitions from a state to its adjacency state in an equal probability (no oblique movement is allowed), for example, the system can move from S_1 with a probability of

Table 4.2   Simple random environment.

S_3	S_4	S_7 (target)
S_2	S_5	S_8
S_1	S_6	S_9

0.5 to S_2 or S_6, if the system is present in S_5, it can move with a probability of 0.25 to S_2, S_4, S_6, and S_8.

For the utility function, it can be considered that "the utility of a sequence is the sum of rewards accumulated in the state of the sequence". Static utility function values are more difficult to obtain because they require a lot of experimentation. The key to reinforcement learning is to update the effect values given a training sequence.

In adaptive dynamic programming, the effect value $U(i)$ of state i can be calculated using the following equation:

$$U(i) = R(i) + \sum_{\forall j} M_{ij} U(j)$$ (4.15)

where $R(i)$ is the reward of the state i, and M_{ij} is the probability of moving from the state i to the state j.

For a small stochastic system, $U(i)$ can be calculated by solving the effective equations in all states like the above equation. But when the state space is large, it is not very convenient to solve.

To avoid solving an equation similar to the above equation, you can calculate $U(i)$ by using the following equation:

$$U(i) \leftarrow U(i) + \alpha[R(i) + (U(j) - U(i)]$$ (4.16)

where α ($0 < \alpha < 1$) is learning effectiveness, which gradually become smaller as the learning process progresses.

Since Eq. (4.16) takes into account the time difference of the utility function, this learning is called time difference learning.

In addition, for passive learning, M is generally a constant matrix. But for active learning, it is variable. Therefore, Eq. (4.16) can be redefined as

$$U(i) = R(i) + Max_a \sum_{\forall j} M_{ij}^a U(j)$$ (4.17)

Here, Max_{ij}^a represents the probability that in the state i the action a reaches the state j. In this way, the system will choose the biggest action, which will make Max_{ij}^a the biggest.

4.6.2 Q-learning

Q-learning is reinforcement learning based on Time Difference (TD) strategy. It is a utility function that is specified after a certain action is executed in a given state. The function is an action-value function [7,28]. In Q-learning, the action-value function is expressed as $Q(a, i)$, it represents the value of action a in state i, also known as Q-learning, using Q-value instead of utility value, and the relationship between the utility value and the Q-value is as follows:

$$U(i) = Max_a Q(a, i)$$

In reinforcement learning, Q-values play a very important role. First, similar to condition-action rules, they can make decisions without using a model. Second, unlike condition-action, Q-values can be learned directly from feedback from the environment.

Like the utility function, for the Q-value you can have the following equation:

$$U(a, j) = R(i) + \sum_{\forall j} M_{ij}^a \max_a Q(a', j) \tag{4.18}$$

The corresponding time difference equation is the following:

$$Q(a, j) \leftarrow Q(q, j) + \alpha[R(i) + Max_a Q(a', j) - Q(a, j)] \tag{4.19}$$

As a method of machine learning, the reinforcement learning method has achieved many applications in practice, such as machine game and robot control.

In addition, in the Internet information search method, the search engine must be able to automatically adapt to the user's requirements. This type of problem is the advantage of the back-groundless model, but it also has some problems.

(1) **General issues.** Typical reinforcement learning methods, such as Q-learning, assume that the state space is finite and allow the state action to record its Q-value. Many practical problems often have a large

state space, and even the state is continuous; or the state space is not very large, but there are many actions. On the other hand, for some problems, different states may have some commonality, so the optimal action corresponding to these states is the same. Thus, it is meaningful to study state-action representations in reinforcement learning, which can use the traditional generalization learning, such as case learning, neural network learning, and so on.

(2) **Dynamic and uncertain environments.** Reinforcement learning through exploratory interaction with the environment, obtaining environmental state information, and enhanced signals for learning, which make it possible to accurately observe the state information, has become the key to affect the system learning performance. However, the environment of many practical problems often contains a lot of noise, and it is impossible to accurately obtain the state information of the environment, and the reinforcement learning algorithm may not be able to converge, such as the Q-value swing.

(3) When the state space is large, the number of experiments may require a lot before the algorithm converges.

(4) Multi-objective learning. Most of the reinforcement learning models are aimed at the decision-making strategies of single-objective learning problems. It is difficult to adapt to multi-objective learning and the learning requirements of being multi-objective and multi-strategy [13].

(5) Many problems are faced with a dynamic environment, and the problem solving target itself may also change. Once the target changes, the learned strategy may become useless, and the entire learning process begins from scratch.

4.7 Summary

This chapter provides an introduction to machine learning.

Machine learning has made great progress over the past 20 years, and more and more researchers have joined the ranks of machine learning research. Many machine learning theories and techniques have been established. In this chapter, inductive learning, example learning, concept learning, explanation-based learning, analogy learning, and reinforcement learning have been introduced. The machine learning methods introduced in this chapter are knowledge-based learning; data-based machine learning methods are discussed in Chapter 7 of this book. As one of the core technologies of artificial intelligence, machine learning will play an increasing role.

Induction learning is a method of applying inductive reasoning to learning. Inductive learning can be divided into example learning, concept learning, and observation learning with or without teacher guidance. Example learning and concept learning belong to unsupervised learning, and observations show that learning belongs to supervised learning.

Explanation-based learning analyzes and solves the current instance according to the domain knowledge of the task and the concept knowledge being learned, and obtains a causal explanation tree representing the solution process to acquire new knowledge.

Learning by analogy is learning by using analogy, i.e., the learning is carried out by comparing similar things.

In reinforcement learning, the learning system adjusts the parameters of the system based on the state (reward/penalty) of the feedback signal from the environment. Reinforcement learning has become one of the main ways of machine learning. The simplest reinforcement learning technique uses a learning automaton. In recent years, Q-learning and jet-lag learning have been proposed.

With the continuous development of machine learning research and the advancement of computer technology, many machine learning systems with excellent performance have been designed and put into practical use. These application areas involve computer vision, image processing, pattern recognition, robot dynamics and control, automatic control, natural language understanding, speech recognition, signal processing, and expert systems. At the same time, various improved learning algorithms were developed, which has significantly improved the performance of machine learning networks and systems.

The development trend of machine learning has shown that machine learning is considered as a new application field of artificial intelligence, and its technical level and application field may exceed expert system, which will make outstanding contribution to the development of artificial intelligence [28].

In the future, machine learning researchers will carry out new research in theoretical concepts, computing mechanism, comprehensive technology, and their popularization and application. Among them, the development of structural models, computational theories, algorithms, and hybrid learning is particularly important. In these areas, there are many things to be done and many new problems that people need to solve.

References

1. Alpaydin, E. (2004). *Introduction to Machine Learning*, (MIT Press, Cambridge, MA).
2. Atilim, G.B., Barak, A.P. and Alexey, A.R. (2018). Automatic differentiation in machine learning: a survey, *Journal of Machine Learning Research, 18*: 1–43.
3. Baldi, P. and Brunak, S. (1998). *Bioinformatics: The Machine Learning Approach*, (MIT Press, Cambridge, MA).
4. Baltrusaitis, T., Ahuja, C. and Morency, L.P. (2018). Multimodal machine learning: a survey and taxonomy, *IEEE Transactions on Pattern Analysis and Machine Intelligence, 2*: 423–443.
5. Barr, A. and Feigenbaum, E.A. (1981). *Handbook of Artificial Intelligence*, Vol. 1 & 2, (William Kaufmann Inc.)
6. Biamonte, J., Wittek, P., Pancotti, N., Rebentrost, P., Wiebe, N. and Lloyd, S. (2017). Quantum machine learning, *Nature, 549*: 195–202.
7. Blog Park. Reinforcement learning: Q-learning algorithm. https://www.cnblogs.com/USTC-ZCC/p/11088009.htm.
8. Boris, K. (2018). *Visual Knowledge Discovery and Machine Learning*, From *Series of Intelligent Systems Reference Library*, Volume 144, Series editor: Janusz Kacprzyk, Lakhmi C. Jain, (Springer).
9. Cade, M. (2019). Turing award won by 3 pioneers in artificial intelligence, *The New York Times*, https://www.nytimes.com/2019/03/27/technology/turing-award-hinton-lecun-bengio.html.
10. Campero, A., Pareja, A., Klinger, T., Tenenbaum, J. and Riedel, S. (2018). Logical rule induction and theory learning using neural theorem proving, ArXiv e-prints.
11. Carrie, J., Jonas, J. and Jess, H. (2019). The effects of example-based explanations in a machine learning interface, *Proceedings of the 24th International Conference on Intelligent User Interfaces*. ACM' 2019, 258–262.
12. Cohen, P.R. and Feigenbaum, E.A. (1982). *Handbook of Artificial Intelligence*, Vol. 3, (William Kaufmann, Inc.).
13. CSDN software development network. Q learning and deep Q learning (DQN) paper notes, 2019-01-02, https://blog.csdn.net/geter_CS/article/details/85618242.
14. Doshi-Velez, F. and Kim, B. (2017). Towards a rigorous science of interpretable machine learning, arXiv:1702.08608.
15. Fu, K.S. and Walts, M.A. (1965). Heuristic approach to reinforcement learning control systems, *IEEE Transactions on Automatic Control, 10*(4): 390–398.
16. Ghahramani, Z. (2015). Probabilistic machine learning and artificial intelligence, *Nature, 521*: 452–459.
17. Guo, X. and Fang, Y. (2018). An introduction to reinforcement learning principles CSDN software development network, Q learning and deep Q learning (DQN) paper notes, PDF. https://pan.baidu.com/s/10eQYLaMxl9u7shNWlseD6Q.
18. Henderson, P.I., Islam, R., Bachman, P., Pineau, J., Precup, D. and Meger, D. (2018). Deep reinforcement learning that matters, *Proceedings of the Thirty-Second AAAI Conference on Artificial Intelligence*, 3207–3214.

19. Jordan, M.I. and Mitchell, T.M. (2015). Machine learning: trends, perspectives, and prospects, *Science, 349*(6245): 255–260.
20. Li, Y.X. (2018). Deep reinforcement learning: an overview, arXiv:1701.07274v6.
21. Michalski, R.S., Carbonell, J.G. and Mitchell, T.M. (eds) (1983). *Machine Learning: An Artificial Intelligence Approach*, Vol. 1, (Morgan Kaufmann, San Mateo, CA).
22. Michalski, R.S. and Chilausky, R.L. (1980). Learning by being told and learning from examples, *International Journal of Policy Analysis and Information Systems, 4*: 125–161.
23. Miller, T. (2019). Explanation in artificial intelligence: insights from the social sciences, *Artificial Intelligence, 267*: 1–38.
24. Mitchell, T.M. (1997). *Machine Learning*, (McGraw-Hill, New York).
25. Shi, Z.Z. (1992). *Principles of Machine Learning*, (International Academic Publishers, Beijing, in Chinese).
26. Sutton, R. and Barto, A. (1998). *Reinforcement Learning: An Introduction*, (MIT Press, Cambridge, MA).
27. Trinity, L. (2019). *Machine Learning: Beginner's Guide to Machine Learning, Data Mining, Big Data, Artificial Intelligence and Neural Networks*, (Amazon Digital Services LLC).
28. Watkins, C.J. and Dayan, P. (1992). *Q-learning for Reinforcement Learning*, (Springer, Berlin).
29. Winston, P.H. (1970). Learning structural descriptions from examples, Technical Report AI-TR-231, AI Lab, MIT, Cambridge, MA.
30. Xu, X. (2002). Reinforcement learning and its application and research in robot navigation and control, PhD dissertation, National University of Defense Technology (in Chinese).
31. Zhou, Z.H. (2016). *Machine Learning*, (Tsinghua University Press, Beijing, China, in Chinese).

PART 2
Data-based
Artificial Intelligence

Data — The Foundation of AI

Neural Computation

5

A distinctive feature of the development of modern science and technology is the mutual intersection, mutual penetration, and mutual promotion of information science and life science. Bioinformatics is a new interdisciplinary subject that combines information science and life science. Computational intelligence is another convincing example and involves neural computation, fuzzy computation, evolutionary computation, swarm computation, ant colony algorithm, natural computation, immune computation, and artificial life. Its research and development reflect the important development trend of multidisciplinary intersection and integration of contemporary science and technology [13, 17, 32, 37].

Creation, invention, and discovery are the common characteristics and eternal pursuits of thousands of technology pioneers. Scientists, including Newton, Einstein, Turing, and Wiener, were committed to seeking and discovering the technology and order of creation. Almost all human inventions have their natural counterparts. The peaceful use and military application of atomic energy corresponds to the thermonuclear explosion that appears on the planet; various electronic impulse systems are similar to the pulse modulation of the human nervous system; the vocalization of bats and dolphins serves as a mysterious phone, and inspired humans to invent sonar sensors and radars; the flight behavior of birds inspired the dream of human flying, inventing aircraft, and spacecraft to achieve air and space flight. Scientists and engineers apply mathematics and science to imitate nature and expand nature. Human intelligence has spurred advanced computing, learning methods, and technology. There is no doubt that intelligence is accessible, and the evidence is in front of our eyes and happening all around us in our daily work and life [4, 9, 20].

5.1 Overview of Computational Intelligence

Trying to imitate human intelligence through manual methods has a long history. From the aerodynamic animal device invented by the hero of the first century AD, Alexandria, to von Neumann's first machine with regenerative behavior and methods, to Wiener's Cybernetics, that is, the study of control and communication in animals and machines, these are all typical examples of human imitating intelligence [43]. The field of modern artificial intelligence (AI) seeks to capture the essence of intelligence.

Artificial neural network (ANN) research has seen a few waves since 1943. In the 1980s, the renaissance of artificial neural networks was mainly promoted by training multi-layer perceptrons through the promotion and back propagation networks of the Hopfield network. It may not be appropriate to classify a neural network (NN) as AI, and a classification of computational intelligence (CI) is more illustrative of the nature of the problem. Some of the topics of evolutionary computation, artificial life, and fuzzy logic systems are also classified in computational intelligence.

What is CI and how does it differ from traditional AI?

The first definition of CI was proposed by Bezdek in 1992. He believes that, in a strict sense, CI depends on the numerical data provided by the manufacturers, and does not depend on knowledge; on the other hand, AI applies knowledge tidbits. He believes that artificial neural networks should be called computational neural networks (CNN) [2].

Although the boundaries between CI and AI are not very obvious, it is useful to discuss their differences and relationships. Marks mentioned the difference between CI and AI in 1993 [30], while Bezdek is concerned with the relationships among pattern recognition (PR) and biological neural networks (BNN), artificial neural networks and CNN, as well as the relationship between pattern recognition and other intelligence [2,7]. Neglecting the difference between ANN and CNN may lead to confusion, misunderstanding and misuse of NN models in pattern recognition.

Bezdek gives certain symbols and brief descriptions or definitions of these related terms. First, he gives an interesting ABC:

A — Artificial, meaning artificial (non-biological), that is, man-made
B — Biological, which means physical + chemical + something others
    = biological
C — Computational, representing mathematics + computer

Figure 5.1 shows ABC and its relationship to NN, PR, and intelligence (I). It was proposed by Bezdek in 1994 [3]. The middle part of Figure 5.1 has

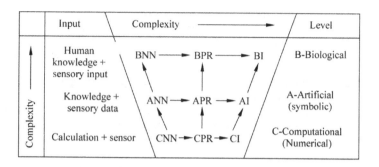

Figure 5.1 ABC interaction diagram.

9 nodes representing 9 research areas or disciplines. A, B, and C correspond to three different levels of system complexities, and their complexity increases gradually from left to right and from bottom to top. The distance between nodes measures the difference between the fields. For example, the difference between CNN and CPR is much smaller than the difference between BNN and BPR. The difference between CI and AI is much smaller than the difference between AI and BI. In the figure, the symbol $\rightarrow$ means "appropriate subset". For example, for the middle layer: ANN$\subset$ APR$\subset$ AI, for the right column: CI$\subset$AI$\subset$BI, etc. When defined, any computing system is an artificial system, but the inverse proposition cannot be established.

Table 5.1 defines the various sub-areas in Figure 5.1. According to Table 5.1, CI is a low-level cognition of intelligence. The difference between CI and AI is that the cognitive hierarchy falls from the middle level to the lower level. The middle system contains knowledge and the low level system does not.

When a system involves only numerical (lower) data, it contains pattern recognition, does not apply knowledge in the sense of AI, and can present: (1) computational adaptability; (2) computational fault tolerance; (3) proximity to humans speed; (4) if the error rate is close to people, then the system is a computing intelligent system.

When an intelligent computing system adds knowledge (boutique) values in a non-numerical manner, it becomes an AI system.

This chapter will first introduce the origin, characteristics, structure, models, and algorithms of artificial neural networks; then explore the characteristics and models of deep neural networks (DNNs) and deep learning, and finally discuss the representation and reasoning of neural networks. These are the basics of neural networks. Neural computing is based on neural networks.

Table 5.1   Definitions of ABC and its related fields.

BNN	Human intelligent hardware: Brain	Processing of human sensing inputs
ANN	Mid-level model: CNN + knowledge boutique	Mid-level processing in the brain mode
CNN	Low-level, bio-stimulus mode	Sensory data processing in the brain mode
BPR	Search for human sensory data structure	Structure recognition of perception environment
APR	Mid-level model: CPR + knowledge boutique	Middle-level numerical/grammatical processing
CPR	Search for sensor data structures	CNN + fuzzy, statistical/deterministic models
BI	Human intelligence software: Intelligence	Human cognition, memory and function
AI	Mid-level model: CI + knowledge boutique	Middle-level cognition in the brain mode
CI	Low-level algorithm for computational inference	Low-level cognition in the brain mode

5.2   Research Advances in Artificial Neural Networks

As a new and interesting tool for dynamic system identification, modeling and control, artificial neural networks have been researched and made significant progress over the past 25 years. Magazines and conference papers involving ANNs have exploded: monographs, textbooks, conference proceedings, and albums on ANN have been published. Among them, some albums play an important role in promoting this trend of thought [7, 8, 35].

The pioneers of ANN research, McCulloch and Pitts, proposed in 1943 a concept called "mindlike machine", which can be made by an interconnected model based on biological neuron properties; this is the concept of a neuroscience network [31]. They constructed a neuron model that represents the basic components of the brain and showed versatility to the logical operating system. With the development of brain and computer researches, the research goal has changed from "brain-like machine" to "learning machine". For this reason, Hebb, who has been concerned with the nervous system adaptation law, proposed a learning model. Rosenblatt named the perceptron and designed a striking structure. By the early 1960s, the special design methods for learning systems were Adaline (adaptive linear elements) proposed by Widrow *et al.* and learning matrices proposed by Steinbuch *et al.* Because the concept of the perceptron is simple, people had great hopes for it at the beginning of the introduction. However, not long after Minsky and Papert mathematically proved that the perceptron could not implement complex logic functions.

In the 1970s, Grossberg and Kohonen made important contributions to NN research. Based on biological and psychological evidence, Grossberg proposed several nonlinear dynamic system structures with novel properties. The network dynamics of the system is modeled by first-order differential equations, and the network structure is a self-organizing neural implementation of the pattern aggregation algorithm. Based on the idea that neurons organize themselves to adjust various modes, Cohorn developed his research work on self-organizing mapping. Werbos developed a backpropagation algorithm in the 1970s. Hopfield introduced a recursive NN based on neuronal interactions, a well-known Hopfield network. In the mid-1980s, as a learning algorithm for feedforward neural networks, Parker and Rumelhart rediscovered the backpropagation algorithm. For more than a decade, the layered neural networks have received much attention, in particular, various DNNs have shown extraordinary computing power in applications. The main applications of ANN include pattern recognition, image processing, automatic control, robotics, signal processing, management, commerce, medical and military, and other fields.

The following characteristics of ANNs are critical [6, 18]:

(1) Parallel distributed processing:

Neural networks have a high degree of parallel structure and parallel implementation capability, and thus can have better fault tolerance and faster overall processing capability. This is especially suitable for real-time and dynamic processing.

(2) Nonlinear mapping:

Neural networks have inherent nonlinear characteristics, which stem from their ability to approximate arbitrary nonlinear mapping. This feature brings new hope to dealing with nonlinear problems.

(3) Learning through training:

Neural networks are trained through past data records of the research system. A properly trained NN has the ability to summarize all data. Therefore, neural networks can solve problems that are difficult to deal with by mathematical models or description rules.

(4) Adaptation and integration:

The neural network can adapt to online operation and can perform quantitative and qualitative operations at the same time. The strong adaptation and information fusion capabilities of the neural network enable it to simultaneously input a large number of different control signals, solve the problem of complementary and redundancy between input information, and realize information integration and fusion processing. These features are especially suited for complex, large-scale, and multivariable systems.

(5) Hardware implementation:

The neural network can realize parallel processing not only through software but also by hardware. In recent years, some VLSI implementation hardware and GPU have been introduced and is commercially available. This allows the neural network to have a network with fast and large-scale processing capabilities.

It is clear that neural networks have the potential for intelligent systems due to their ability to learn and adapt, self-organization, function approximation, and parallely process massively.

The application of neural networks in pattern recognition, signal processing, system identification, and optimization has been extensively studied. In the field of control, many efforts have been made to use neural networks for control systems, to deal with the nonlinearity and uncertainty of control systems, and to approach the identification functions of systems.

Now, neural networks have found their use in a wide range of fields from home appliances to industrial objects, such as management, business, medical, and military fields, and are gaining wider and wider application [10, 23, 27, 28, 36, 40].

5.3 Basic Structure of Artificial Neural Network

The structure of the neural network is determined by the basic processing unit and its interconnection method [12, 14, 22].

5.3.1 *Neuron and its characteristics*

The basic processing unit of the connection mechanism structure and neurophysiological analogy are often referred to as neurons. Each neuron model that constructs the network simulates a biological neuron, as shown in Figure 5.2. The neuron unit consists of a plurality of inputs x_i, $i = 1, 2, \ldots, n$ and an output y. The intermediate state is represented by the weight sum of the input signals, and the output is:

$$y_j(t) = f\left(\sum_{i=1}^{n} w_{ji} x_i - \theta_j\right) \tag{5.1}$$

where, θ_j is the bias (threshold) of the neuron unit, w_{ji} is the connection weight coefficient (for the excited state, w_{ji} take a positive value, for the suppression state, w_{ji} take a negative value), n is the number of input signals, y is the neuron output, t is the time, $f(\_)$ is the output transformation function, sometimes called the excitation function, often using 0 and 1 binary function or sigmoid function, see in Figure 5.3, these three functions are continuous and nonlinear. A binary function can be represented by the following formula:

$$f(x) = \begin{cases} 1, & x \geq x_0 \\ 0, & x < x_0 \end{cases} \tag{5.2}$$

As shown in Figure 5.3(a). A conventional sigmoid function is shown in Figure 5.3(b), which can be expressed by:

$$f(x) = \frac{1}{1 + e^{-ax}}, \quad 0 < f(x) < 1 \tag{5.3}$$

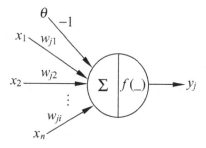

Figure 5.2 Neuron model.

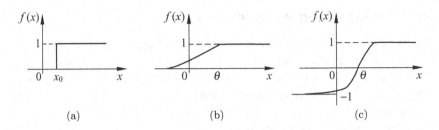

Figure 5.3   Some transformation (excitation) functions in neurons.

The hyperbolic tangent function (see Figure 5.3(c)) is commonly used to replace the conventional sigmoid function because the output of the sigmoid function is positive and the output value of the hyperbolic tangent function can be positive or negative. The hyperbolic tangent function is as follows:

$$f(x) = \frac{1 - e^{-ax}}{1 + e^{-ax}}, \quad -1 < f(x) < 1 \tag{5.4}$$

5.3.2 *Basic characteristics and structure of ANN*

The human brain contains extremely large neurons (some estimated to be about 100 billion), which are interconnected to form neural networks and perform advanced problem solving intelligent activities [12–14].

The ANN consists of a neuron model, and the information processing network composed of many neurons has a parallel distribution structure. Each neuron has a single output and can be connected to other neurons; there are many (multiple) output connection methods, each connection method corresponds to a connection weight coefficient. Strictly speaking, an ANN is a directed graph with the following characteristics:

(1) There is one state variable x_i for each node i;
(2) From node i to node j, there is a coefficient w_{ij} of connection wight;
(3) For each node i, there is a threshold w_{ij};
(4) For each node i, define a transformation function $f_i(x_i, w_{ji}, \theta_i)$, $i \neq j$; for the most general case, this function takes the form $f_i(\sum_j w_{ji} x_j - \theta_i)$.

The structure of artificial neural networks is basically divided into two categories, namely, recursive (feedback) networks and multilayer (feedforward) networks, described as follows.

(1) Recursive network:

In a recursive network, multiple neurons are interconnected to form an interconnected NN, as shown in Figure 5.4. The output of some neurons is fed back to the neurons in the same or anterior layers. Therefore, the signal can flow from the forward and reverse directions. The Hopfield network, the Elmman network, and the Jordan network are representative examples of recursive networks. A recursive network is also called a feedback network.

In Figure 5.4, V_i is the state of the node, x_i is shown as the input (initial) value of the node, x_i' is the output value after convergence, $i = 1, 2, ..., n$.

(2) Feedforward network:

The feedforward network has a hierarchical structure consisting of layers that do not have interconnections between neurons in the same layer [5, 17]. The signal from the input layer to the output layer flows through a one-way connection; the neurons are connected from one layer to the next, and there is no connection between the neurons in the same layer, as shown in Figure 5.5. In the figure, the solid line indicates the actual signal flow and the broken line indicates the back propagation. Examples of feedforward networks are multilayer perceptron (MLP), learning vector quantization (LVQ) networks, cerebellar model connection control (CMAC) networks, and group method of data handling (GMDH) networks.

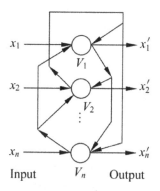

Figure 5.4   Recursive (feedback) network.

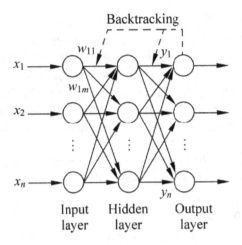

Figure 5.5　Feedforward (multilayer) network.

5.3.3 *Main learning algorithms of ANN*

The neural network is mainly trained through two learning algorithms, namely, a supervised (with teacher) learning algorithm and an unsupervised (without teacher) learning algorithm. In addition, there is a third kind of learning algorithm, namely, the reinforcement learning algorithm; it can be regarded as a special case of supervised learning.

(1) Supervised learning:

A supervised learning algorithm can adjust the strength or weight of connections between neurons based on the difference between the desired (corresponding to a given input) and actual network output. Therefore, a supervised learning needs to have a teacher or tutor to provide a desired or target output signal. Examples of supervised learning algorithms include Δ rules, generalized Δ rules or backpropagation algorithms, and LVQ algorithms.

(2) Unsupervised learning:

The unsupervised learning algorithm does not need to know the expected output. During the training process, as long as the input mode is provided to the neural network, the neural network can automatically adapt to the connection weight to gather the input patterns into groups according to similar features. Examples of unsupervised learning algorithms include the Kohonen algorithm and the Carpenter–Grossberg Adaptive Resonance Theory (ART).

(3) Reinforcement learning:

As mentioned earlier, reinforcement (enhanced) learning is a special case of supervised learning. It does not require the teacher to give the target output. The Reinforcement learning algorithm uses a "reviewer" to evaluate the goodness (quality factor) of the neural network output corresponding to a given input. An example of a reinforcement learning algorithm is the genetic algorithm (GA).

5.4 Deep Neural Networks

This section introduces the basic principles of DNNs, discusses the relationship between deep learning and the distributed representation of AI and traditional ANN models, expounds the common models of DNNs and CNNs, and looks deep into various common models of DNN and analyzes the hierarchical structure of CNNs [19, 33].

5.4.1 *Brief introduction to DNNs*

Deep neural networks can be understood as neural networks with many hidden layers. The idea stems from the simulation and reconstruction of the human brain nervous system. It is the basis of deep learning and is also called deep feedforward network (DFN) and Multi-Layer Perceptron (MLP). The feedforward (multilayer) network and the learning vector quantization network discussed earlier are both neural networks with hidden layers.

According to the position of different layers, the NN layer inside DNN can be divided into input layer, hidden layer, and output layer. Generally, the first layer is the input layer, the last layer is the output layer, and the middle layers are all hidden layers, as shown in Figure 5.6; where, the hidden layer is like a black box. The hidden layer can have many layers, such as 3 layers, 7 layers, 21 layers, and so on. The number of hidden layers is designed according to application needs. The layers are fully connected, that is, any neuron in layer i must be connected to any neuron in layer $i + 1$.

The feedforward (multilayer) network and the learning vector quantization network discussed earlier are both neural networks with hidden layers.

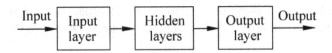

Figure 5.6   Schematic diagram of DNN structure.

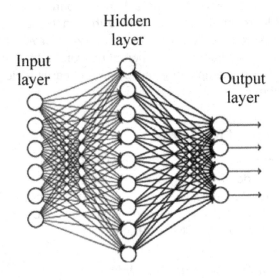

Figure 5.7   Basic structure of a simple neural network.

The basis of DNNs is simple neural networks. First, simple neural networks are introduced.

(1) Simple neural network:

When combining multiple single "neurons" together, the output of some neurons is used as the input of other neurons, thus forming a single-layer neural network, as shown in Figure 5.7.

The layer that receives input data is called the input layer, and the layer that outputs results is called the output layer. The middle neuron forms the middle layer (or hidden layer). In most cases, when designing a NN, the input layer and output layer are fixed, while the number of layers and nodes in the middle hidden layer can be freely changed. When the output of each layer of nodes will be sent to all nodes in the next layer as input, it is called a fully connected network.

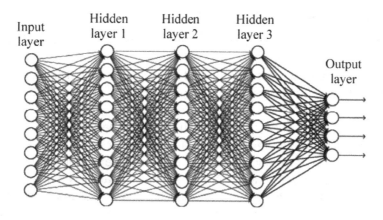

Figure 5.8   Basic structure of DNN.

(2) Deep neural network:

When the hidden layer in a simple single-layer neural network is expanded into multiple layers, a DNN is obtained.

Like the simple neural network, the neural network layer inside the DNN can be divided into: input layer, hidden layer, and output layer. The layers are fully connected, that is, any neuron in layer i must be connected to any neuron in layer $i + 1$. The basic structure of DNN is shown in Figure 5.8.

5.4.2   *Common models of deep neural network*

In practical applications, the hierarchical structure used for deep learning usually consists of an ANN and a complex set of conceptual formulas. In some cases, some implicit variable methods are also available for the depth generation mode. For example, deep belief networks, deep Boltzmann machines, etc. A variety of deep learning frameworks have been available to date, such as DNNs, CNNs, and deep concept networks.

A DNN is a NN with at least one hidden layer. Similar to shallow neural networks, DNNs can also provide modeling for complex nonlinear systems, but the extra levels provide a higher level of abstraction for the model, thus improving the model's capabilities. In addition, DNNs are usually feedforward neural networks. Common deep learning models include the following categories.

(1) Convolutional neural networks:

The Convolutional Neural Network (CNN) is essentially an input-to-output mapping. In 1984, Japanese scholar Fukushima proposed a neural cognition machine based on the concept of receptive field. This is the first realization network of convolutional neural network, and it is also the first application of the ANN in the receptive field. Inspired by the structure of the visual system, when a neuron with the same parameters applies different positions of the previous layer, a transform invariant feature can be obtained. Based on this idea, LeCun *et al.* designed and trained CNN using the direction propagation algorithm. CNN is a special DNN model. Its particularity is mainly reflected in two aspects. One is that the connections between its neurons are not fully connected; the other is that the connections between neurons in the same layer use weight sharing [8,11,24]. The learning process is shown in Figure 5.9. Among them, input to C_1, S_4 to C_5, C_5 to output are fully connected, C_1 to S_2, C_3 to S_4 are in one-to-one correspondence, S_2 to C_3 in order to eliminate network symmetry, remove some of the connections, can make feature mapping with more diversity. It should be noted that the size of the C_5 convolution kernel is the same as the output of S_4. Only in this way the output can be a one-dimensional vector.

The basic structure of the CNN includes two layers, a feature extraction layer and a feature mapping layer. In the feature extraction layer C, the input of each neuron is connected to the local accepted domain of the previous layer and the local features are extracted. Once the local feature is extracted, the positional relationship between it and other features is also determined; each feature extraction layer is followed by a calculation layer, and is used to calculate the weighted average of local features and secondary extraction. The unique two feature extraction structure makes

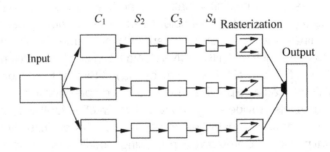

Figure 5.9 Principle of convolutional neural network.

the network highly invariant to translation, scaling, tilting, or other forms of deformation. The computing layer in the network is composed of multiple feature maps. Each feature map is a plane. The weight sharing technique is adopted on the plane, which greatly reduces the training parameters of the network and makes the structure of the NN simpler and more adaptable. In addition, the image can be directly used as the input of the network, so it requires very little preprocessing, avoiding the complex feature extraction and data reconstruction process in the traditional recognition algorithm [18]. The feature mapping structure uses a small sigmoid function that affects the function kernel as the activation function of the convolutional network, so that the feature map has displacement invariance [26, 41].

Based on this, CNN is widely used in face detection, document recognition, handwritten font recognition, voice detection, and other fields [25, 27].

CNN also has some shortcomings. For example, due to the large number of parameters of the network, the training speed is slow and the calculation cost is high.

(2) Recurrent neural networks:

Recurrent Neural Networks (RNNs) are commonly used models in deep networks. Their inputs are sequence data. The connections between nodes in the network form a directed graph along time series, enabling them to display temporal dynamic behavior [1, 39]. In 1982, John Hopfield discovered a special type of RNN, the Hopfield network. As RNN with external memory, all nodes in the Hopfiled network are connected to each other and learn using energy functions. In 1986, David Rumelhart proposed Error Back Propagation Training (BP), which solved the problem of multilayer neural network implicit layer connection weight learning. On this basis, in the same year, Jordan established a new circular neural network, the Jordan network. Since then, in 1990, Jeffrey Elman proposed the first fully connected recurrent neural network, the Elman network. Both networks are RNNs for sequence data.

The basic recurrent neural network is shown in Figure 5.10, which is a network of neuron-like nodes in a continuous layer. Each neuron node in a given layer is oriented to connect with every other neuron node in the next successive layer, each neuron node has a real-valued activation function that changes over time, while each connection has modifiable real value weight. The input set of the RNNs input unit is $\{x_0, x_1, \ldots, x_{t+1}, \ldots\}$, and the output set of the output unit is $\{o_0, o_1, \ldots, o_{t+1}, \ldots\}$, the state set of the hidden unit is $\{h_0, h_1, \ldots, h_{t+1}, \ldots\}$, and can capture sequence information.

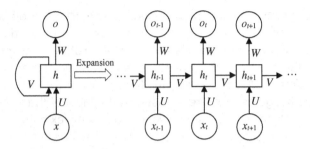

Figure 5.10   Structure of a basic recurrent neural network.

The hidden layers are connected and the input of the hidden layer includes not only the input of the input layer but also the output of the hidden layer at the previous moment, and the neurons of the hidden layer can be self-connected or interconnected. The h_t is the state of the hidden layer at time t, and is also the memory unit of RNNs, and its calculation formula is $h_t = f(U_*x_t + V_*h_{t-1})$, where f is a general nonlinear activation function, such as the Tanh function. The parameters in the traditional NN are not shared. In RNNs, each layer shares the parameters U, V, W, i.e., the U matrix between x_t and h_t and the U between x_{t-1} and h_{t-1} are the same, the same for V, W. Weight sharing greatly reduces the parameters that need to be learned in the network and reinforcement network complexity [34].

RNNs use time series information to process input and output data of any length. Unlike feedback neural networks, RNNs can use their internal memory to process arbitrary input sequences, making it widely used in handwriting recognition, natural language processing, and speech recognition tasks. However, RNNs have problems such as "gradient disappearance", "gradient explosion", and long-term dependence.

(3) Restricted Boltzmann Machine:

The Restricted Boltzmann Machine (RBM) is a kind of stochastic generated neural network that can learn the probability distribution through the input dataset. It is a variant of the Boltzmann machine, but the qualified model must be a bipartite graph. As shown in Figure 5.11, the model includes: The visual layer corresponds to the input parameters and is used to represent the observed data. The hidden layer can be regarded as a set of feature extractors, and corresponds to the training results, to find the high-order data correlation shown in the visual layer. Each edge must connect to a

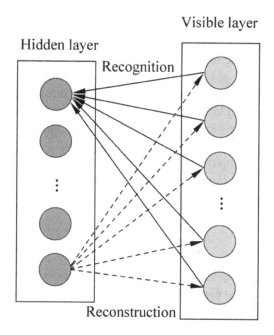

Figure 5.11   Restricted Boltzmann Machine.

visible unit and a hidden unit respectively, and is the connection weight between the two layers. Restricted Boltzmann Machines are widely used in dimensionality reduction, classification, collaborative filtering, feature learning, and topic modeling. Depending on the task, the RBM can be trained using supervised learning or unsupervised learning.

The purpose of training RBM is to obtain an optimal weight matrix. The most common method was originally proposed by Geoffrey Hinton in training "expert product", called Contrast Divergence (CD) algorithm. Contrast divergence provides a maximum likelihood approximation that is ideally used to learn the weight training of RBM. The algorithm uses Gibbs sampling to update the weights during the gradient descent process, similar to the use of backpropagation algorithms in training feedforward neural networks.

The Deep Boltzmann Machine (DBM) increases the number of layers in the hidden layer and can be viewed as multiple RBM stacks and can be optimized using gradient descent and backpropagation algorithms.

(4) Auto Encoder (AE):

The AE is a NN that reproduces the input signal as much as possible. It is another deep learning algorithm model proposed by Hinton *et al.* after the deep belief network based on the layer-by-layer greedy unsupervised training algorithm. The basic unit of the AE has an encoder and a decoder; the encoder is a mapping function that maps the input to the hidden layer, and the decoder maps the hidden layer representation back to a reconstruction of the input [15,38].

Set a training sample $x = \{x_1, \ldots, x_t\}$ of the auto encoder network, and the coding activation function and the decoding activation function are S_f and S_g, respectively.

$$f_\theta(x) = S_f(b + Wx)$$

$$g_\theta(h) = S_g(d + W^T h)$$

The training mechanism is to obtain the parameter θ by minimizing the reconstruction error of the training sample D_n, that is, to minimize the objective function.

$$J_{AE}(\theta) = \sum_{x \in D_n} L(x^t, g(f(x^t)))$$

where $\theta = \{W, b, W^T, d\}$; b and d are the offset vectors of the encoder and the decoder, respectively; W and W^T are the weight matrix of the encoder and decoder; and S is the Sigmoid function. For a nonlinear auto encoder network with multiple hidden layers, if the initial weight selection is good, the gradient descent method can achieve good training results. Based on this, Hinton and Salakhutdinov proposed to use the RBM network to obtain the initial weight of the self-encoding network. But as mentioned earlier, an RBM network contains only one hidden layer, and its modeling of continuous data is not ideal. Multiple RBM networks are introduced to form a continuous random regeneration model. The network structure of the auto encoding system is shown in Figure 5.12. The pretraining phase is to learn these RBM networks layer by layer. After pretraining, these RBM networks are "opened" to form a deep auto-encoding network. Then use the backpropagation algorithm to fine tune to get the final weight matrix.

In fact, the self-encoding network can also be regarded as consisting of an encoding part and a decoding part. The encoding part reduces the dimension of the input, that is, the original high-dimensional continuous data are reduced to a low-dimensional structure with a certain dimension;

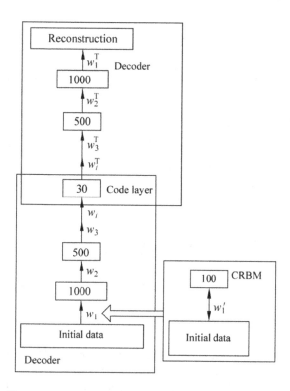

Figure 5.12 Network structure of the self-encoding system.

the decoding part is restore points on low dimensions to high dimensional continuous data. The intersection between the coding part and the decoding part is the core of the entire continuous auto-encoding network, which can reflect the essential laws of the high-dimensional continuous dataset with nested structure and determine the essential dimension of the high-dimensional continuous dataset.

As a typical nonlinear dimensionality reduction method, the Auto Encoder is widely used in the fields of image reconstruction and recovery of loss data.

(5) Deep Belief Network:

Deep Belief Networks (DBNs) is a Bayesian probability generation model consisting of multiple layers of random hidden variables [15, 16, 29]. The structure is shown in Figure 5.13. The upper two layers have an undirected symmetrical connection, the lower layer receives a top-down directional

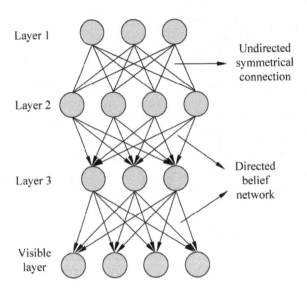

Figure 5.13   Deep belief network structure.

connection from the upper layer, and the lowermost unit forms a visible layer. It can also be understood that the DBN uses a Bayesian belief network (i.e., a directed graph model) in the part close to the visible layer, and a composite structure using a RBM in the portion farthest from the visible layer. It is also often seen as a composite model that combines multiple layers of simple learning models.

The DBN can be used as a pretraining part of the DNN and provides initial weight to the network, and then use back-propagation or other judgment algorithms as a means of tuning [34]. This is valuable when the training data are lacking, because improper initialization weights can significantly affect the performance of the final model, and the weights obtained by the pre-training are closer to the optimal weights in the weight space than the random weights. This not only improves the performance of the model, but also speeds up the convergence of the tuning phase.

The inner layers in the deep belief network are all typical RBMs that can be trained using efficient unsupervised layer-by-layer training methods. After the single-layer RBM is trained, another layer of RBM can be stacked on the RBM that has been trained to form a multilayer model. At each stack, the original multilayer network input layer is initialized as a training sample, the weight is the weight obtained by the previous training, the output of the network is used as the input of the subsequent RBM, and the new RBM repeats the previous single-layer training process, the whole process can continue until a desired termination condition is reached.

(6) Hybrid convolutional neural network:

Convolutional neural networks were originally designed for supervised learning problems, but they also developed unsupervised learning paradigms, including Convolutional AutoEncoders (CAE), Convolutional Restricted Boltzmann Machines (CRBMs), Convolutional Deep Belief Networks (CDBN), Deep Convolutional Generative Adversarial Networks (DCGAN), etc. These algorithms can also be regarded as a hybrid algorithm constructed by introducing convolutional neural networks in the original version of the unsupervised learning algorithm [42].

(i) The construction logic of the **CAE** is similar to the traditional AE. First, the convolutional layer and the pooling layer are used to establish a conventional CNN as the encoder, and then the deconvolution and the up-pooling as a decoder, learning from the errors before and after encoding of the samples, and outputting the encoding results of the encoder to achieve dimentionality reduction and clustering of the samples. In the image recognition problem, the CNN with the same structure of CAE and its encoder performs well in large samples, but it has better recognition effect in small sample problems [38].

(ii) The **CRBM** is a RBM with a convolutional layer as the hidden layer. On the basis of traditional RBMs, the hidden layer is divided into multiple "groups". Each group contains a convolution kernel, and the convolution kernel parameters are shared by all binary nodes corresponding to the group. CDBN is a hierarchical generation model obtained by stacking CRBM as a structure. In order to extract high-order features in the structure, CDBN adds a probabilistic max-pooling layer and its corresponding energy function. CRBMs and CDBMs use greedy layer-wise training to learn, and can use sparsity regularization technology.

(iii) Generative Adversarial Networks (GAN) can be used for unsupervised learning of convolutional neural networks. **Deep Convolutional Generation Adversarial Networks** (DCGAN) are randomly sampled from a set of probability distributions, namely, latent space, and the signal is input to a group of generators composed entirely of transposed convolution kernels; after the generator generates an image, a discriminant model composed of a CNN is input, and the discriminant model judges whether the generated image is a real learning sample. When the generation model cannot judge the difference between the generated image and the learning sample, the learning ends. Research shows that DCGAN can extract high-level representations of input images in image processing problems and classify images with high accuracy.

5.4.3 *Structure analysis of convolutional neural network*

The hidden layer of CNN usually includes three types: convolutional layer, pooling layer, and fully connected layer. The convolution kernel in the convolutional layer contains weight coefficients, while the pooling layer does not contain weight coefficients [21, 32, 37]. Taking LeNet-5 as an example, the order of the three common layers in the hidden layer is usually: input–convolutional layer–pooling layer–fully connected layer–output.

(1) Convolutional layer:

Convolution is an operation in mathematics. Since the image is a two-dimensional structure, two-dimensional convolution is often used in image processing. The result obtained by the image after the convolution operation is called a feature map. The two-dimensional convolution operation is as follows:

$$S(i, j) = (I * K)(i, j) = \Sigma_m \Sigma_n I(i + m, j + n) K(m, n) \qquad (5.5)$$

Figure 5.14 is an example of convolution operation:

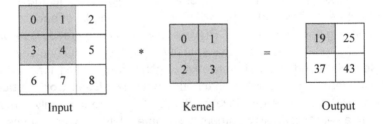

Figure 5.14   Example of convolution operation.

The input is a 3 * 3 two-dimensional array, and after a 2 * 2 size convolution kernel (also called a filter) operation, a 2 * 2 size output is obtained. The convolution kernel starts from the upper left of the input array and slides in order from left to right and from top to bottom. Each time you slide to a position, the input sub-array in the window and the convolution kernel are multiplied and summed by the corresponding elements to get the elements at the corresponding positions in the output array. For example, the calculation process of the first element in the output data is: $0*0+1*1+3*2+4*3 = 19$.

The parameters of the convolution layer include the size of the convolution kernel, the step size, and the padding. The three together determine the size of the output feature map of the convolution layer, which is the hyper-parameter of the CNN. The size of the convolution kernel can be specified as any value smaller than the size of the input image. The larger the convolution kernel, the more complex the input features that can be extracted. The convolution step (striding) defines the distance between the positions of the convolution kernel when sweeping the feature map twice. When the convolution step is 1, the convolution kernel will sweep through the elements of the feature map one by one, when the stride is n, will skip $n - 1$ pixels in the next scan. Padding refers to the padding elements at the edge of the input array, usually filled with 0 elements, which can increase the size of the output. The step size refers to the amplitude of each sliding of the convolution kernel on the input array, which can reduce the size of the output. By default, the padding is 0 and the step size is 1. The calculation formula of the output image size of the convolution layer is as follows:

$$O = (I - K + 2P)/S + 1 \qquad (5.6)$$

In the formula, O is the size of the output image, I is the size of the input image, K is the kernel size of the convolution layer, S is the moving step size, and P is the number of padding.

(2) Pooling layer:

In addition to convolutional layers, CNNs also commonly use pooling layers to reduce the size of the model and increase the calculation speed and the robustness of the extracted features. Generally there are maximum pooling and average pooling, maximum pooling and average pooling, and

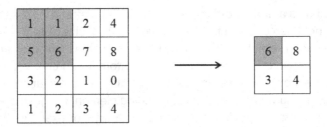

Figure 5.15   2 * 2 maximum pooling operation example.

the pooling layer is generally placed behind the convolution layer. So what the pooling layer wants to pool is the output of the convolutional layer.

Maximum pooling: Taking Figure 5.15 as an example, the pooling layer sampling window is 2 * 2, and the step size is 2. When sliding on the input data, the maximum number in the pooling window is taken out.

Average pooling: Similar to the maximum pooling, the arithmetic average of the data in the pooling window is taken each time.

(3) Fully connected layer:

The fully connected layer in the CNN is equivalent to the hidden layer in the traditional feedforward neural network. The fully connected layer is located in the last part of the hidden layer of the CNN, and only transmits signals to other fully connected layers. The feature graph loses the spatial topology in the fully connected layer and is expanded into a vector by the excitation function.

According to the representation learning perspective, the convolutional layer and the pooling layer in the CNN can extract the input data, and the role of the fully connected layer is to nonlinearly combine the extracted features to obtain the output, that is, the fully connected layer does not have the ability to extract features, but tries to use existing higher-order features to complete the learning goal.

(4) Output layer:

The upstream of the output layer in the CNN is usually a fully connected layer, so its structure and working principle are the same as the output layer in the traditional feedforward neural network. For image classification problems, the output layer uses logical functions or normalized exponential functions to output classification labels. In the object recognition problem, the output layer can be designed to output the center coordinates, size, and classification of objects. In image semantic segmentation, the output layer directly outputs the classification result of each pixel.

(5) Training of convolutional neural networks:

There are many options for the loss function of convolutional neural networks, common ones include Softmax loss function, hinge loss function, triple loss function, and so on. In the training of convolutional neural networks, the gradient descent method is still used to optimize the loss function [25]. Stochastic Gradient Descent (SGD) and its variants, such as the Adam algorithm (Adaptive moment estimation), are usually used in the BP framework. SGD randomly selects sample calculation gradient in each iteration, which is conducive to information screening when the number of learning samples is sufficient. It can quickly converge at the early stage of the iteration when the calculation complexity is smaller.

Similar to other neural network algorithms, since the gradient descent algorithm is used for learning, the input features of the CNN need to be standardized. Specifically, before inputting the learning data into the convolutional neural network, the input data need to be normalized in the channel or time/frequency dimension. If the input data are pixels, the original pixel values distributed in [0, 255] can be normalized to the interval [0,1]. The standardization of input features is conducive to improving the learning efficiency and performance of CNNs.

Convolutional neural networks have been widely used in image recognition and target detection. Typical CNN models include LeNet-5, AlexNet, Inception network, ResNet, Faster R-CNN, and SSD (Single Shot MultiBox Detector), etc. [23, 24, 26, 28].

5.5 Summary

This chapter discusses neurocomputing issues. Section 5.1 outlines the basic concepts of computational intelligence, and uses neural computing, fuzzy computing, evolutionary computing, artificial life, and swarm optimization as the main research areas of computational intelligence. These research areas reflect the close integration of life sciences and information sciences, and are also important advances in general AI's efforts to study and imitate human and animal intelligence (mainly human thinking processes and intellectual behavior). CI is understood as the low-level cognition of intelligence, which mainly depends on data and does not depend on knowledge. AI is the middle-level cognition of intelligence produced by introducing knowledge on the basis of computational intelligence. Biological intelligence, especially human intelligence, is the highest level of intelligence. That is, both neural network-based neural computing and fuzzy logic-based fuzzy computing are based on numerical calculations. They are an important part of CI.

Section 5.2 introduces the progress of ANN research. Artificial neural networks have the characteristics of parallel distributed processing, nonlinear mapping, learning through training, adaptation and integration, and hardware implementation. That is, they have the ability to learn and adapt, self-organize, function approximation, and large-scale parallel processing, so it has the potential for intelligent systems, and has been widely used in pattern recognition, signal processing, system identification, and optimization.

Section 5.3 discusses the primitive neurons of neural networks, which have multiple inputs and one output. There are weighted directed connections between neurons. The input signal is gotten output with the help of an excitation function. Artificial neural networks can be divided into two basic structures: recursive (feedback) networks and multilayer (feedforward) networks. In terms of learning algorithms, ANNs can use both supervised learning and unsupervised learning. Think of reinforcement learning as a special case of supervised learning.

Section 5.4 summarizes the basic principles of DNNs, discusses the common models of DNNs and CNNs, introduces CNNs, RNNs, RBMs, AE, DBNs, and other common models of DNN, and analyzes the hierarchical structure of convolutional neural networks.

Through the study in this chapter, the reader can understand the basics of neural computing. Readers who need to dig deeper into neural computing may see related references.

References

1. Ashraf, S.M. Gupta, A., Choudhary, D.K. and Chakrabarti, S. (2017). Voltage stability monitoring of power systems using reduced network and artificial neural network, *International Journal of Electrical Power & Energy Systems, 87*: 43–51.

2. Bezdek, J.C. (1992). On the relationship between neural networks, pattern recognition and intelligence, *The Int. J. of Approximate Reasoning, 6*(2): 85–107.

3. Bezdek, J.C. (1994). What is computational intelligence? In: Zurada J.M. *et al.* (eds): *Computational Intelligence Imitating Life* , pp.1–12, (IEEE Press, New York).

4. Cai, Z.X., Liu, L.J., Cai, J.F. and Chen, B.F. (2020). *Artificial Intelligence and Its Applications*, 6th Edition, (Tsinghua University Press, Beijing, in Chinese).

5. Cai, Z.X. and Xu, G.Y. (2004). *Artificial Intelligence and Its Applications*, 3rd Edition, Graduate Book, (Tsinghua University Press, Beijing, in Chinese).

6. Cai, Z.X. (1997). *Intelligent Control: Principles, Techniques and Applications*, Chapter 7 (World Scientific Publishers, Singapore).

7. Ciresan, D., Meier, U. and Schmidhuber, J. (2012). Multi-column deep neural networks for image classification, *Proc. 2012 IEEE Conference on Computer Vision and Pattern Recognition* (CVPR), pp. 3642–3649.

8. Ciresan, D.C., Meier, U. and Masci, J., *et al.* (2011). Flexible, high performance convolutional neural networks for image classification, *IJCAI Proceedings-International Joint Conference on Artificial Intelligence, 22*: 1237.

9. Engelbrecht, A.P. (2002). *Computational Intelligence, An Introduction*, (John Wiley & Sons).

10. Faizollahzadeh, A.S., Najafi, B. and Shamshirband, S., *et al.* (2018). Computational intelligence approach for modeling hydrogen production: A review, *Engineering Applications of Computational Fluid Mechanics, 12*: 438–458.

11. Gu, J., Wang, Z. and Kuen, J., *et al.* (2015). Recent advances in convolutional neural networks. arXiv preprint arXiv:1512.07108.

12. Haykin, S. and Ye, S. Translated by Shi, Z.Z. (2004). *Principles of Neural Networks*. (Mechanical Industry Press, Beijing).

13. Hecht, N.R. (1990). *Neurocomputing*. (Addison-Wesley, Reading, MA, 1990) and (Addison-Wesley, New York, 1990).

14. Hertz, J., Krogh, A. and Palmer, R.G. (1991). *Introduction to the Theory of Neural Computation*, Santa Fe Institute Studies in the Sciences of Complexity lecture notes. (Addison Wesley Longman Publ. Co., Inc., Reading, MA).

15. Hinton, G.E., Osindero, S. and The, Y.-W. (2006). A fast learning algorithm for deep belief nets, *Neural Computation, 18*(7): 1527–1554.

16. Hinton, G.E. (2009). Deep belief networks, *Scholarpedia, 4*(5): 5947.

17. Hopfield, J.J. (1988). Artificial neural networks, *IEEE Circuit and Devices Magazine, 4*(5): 3–10.

18. Huang, F.J., Boureau, Y.L. and LeCun, Y. (2007). Unsupervised learning of invariant feature hierarchies with applications to object recognition, *IEEE Conference on Computer Vision and Pattern Recognition*, CVPR'07, 1–8.

19. Sergey, I. and Christian, S. (2015). Batch normalization: Accelerating deep network training by reducing internal covariate shift, *International Conference on Machine Learning* (ICML), 448–456.

20. Iqbal, R., Doctor, F., More, B., Mahmud, S. and Yousuf, U. (2018). Big data analytics: Computational intelligence techniques and application areas, *Technological Forecasting and Social Change*, Elsevier, vol. *153*(C): 119253.

21. Jeff, H. (2014). *Artificial Intelligence for Human.*, Volume 2: Nature-Inspired Algorithms. (Heaton Research, Inc., St. Louis, MO, USA).

22. Jiao, L.C. (1990). *Neural Network System Theory.* (Xi'an: Xidian University Press, China, in Chinese).

23. Johnson, J., Karpathy, A. and Li, F-F. (2016). DenseCap: Fully convolutional localization networks for dense captioning, *Proc. CVPR, 2016.*

24. Krizhevsky, A., Sutskever, I. and Hinton. G. (2012). ImageNet classification with deep convolutional neural networks// NIPS. (Curran Associates Inc.)

25. Lawrence, S., Giles, C.L., Tsoi, A.C. and Back, A.D. (1997). Face recognition: A convolutional neural-network approach, *IEEE Transactions on Neural Networks.*, *8*(1): 98–113.

26. LeCun, Y. and Bengio, Y. (1995). Convolutional networks for images, speech, and time series, *The Handbook of Brain Theory and Neural Networks*, *3361*(10).

27. LeCun, Y., Boser, B. and Denker, J.S., *et al.* (1989). Backpropagation applied to handwritten zip code recognition, *Neural Computation*, *1*(4): 541–551.

28. LeCun, Y., Kavukcuoglu, K. and Farabet, C. (2010). Convolutional networks and applications in vision, *ISCAS, 2010*: 253–256.

29. Lee, H., Grosse, R., Ranganath, R. and Ng, A.Y. (2009). Convolutional deep belief networks for scalable unsupervised learning of hierarchical representations, *Proceedings of the 26th annual international conference on machine Learning*, ACM, 609–616.

30. Marks, R. (1993). Intelligence: Computational versus artificial, *IEEE Transactions on Neural Networks*, *4*(5): 737–739.

31. McCulloch, W.S. and Pitts, W. (1943). A logical calculus of the ideas immanent in nervous activity, *Bulletin of Mathematical Biophysics*, *5*: 115–133.

32. Ng, A., Kian, K. and Younes, B. (2018). Convolutional Neural Networks, Deep learning [NetC], *Coursera and deeplearning.ai.*

33. Radford, A., Metz, L. and Chintala, S. (2015). Unsupervised representation learning with deep convolutional generative adversarial networks. arXiv preprint arXiv:1511.06434.

34. Rumelhart, D.E., Hinton, G.E. and Williams, R.J. (1986). Learning representations by back-propagating errors, *Nature*, *323*(6088): 533.

35. Schwefel, H.-P., Wegener, I. and Weinert, K. (eds). (2003). Advances in computational intelligence: *Theory and Practice*, (Springer-Verlag).

36. Simard, P.Y., Steinkraus, D. and Platt, J.C. (2003). Best practices for convolutional neural networks applied to visual document analysis, *Proc. Seventh International Conference on Document Analysis and Recognition*, p. 958.

37. Szegedy, C., Liu, W. and Jia, Y., *et al.* (2014). Going deeper with convolutions. arXiv:1409.4842[cs.CV].

38. Turchenko, V., Chalmers, E. and Luczak, A. (2017). A deep convolutional auto-encoder with pooling-unpooling layers in Caffe. arXiv preprint arXiv:1701.04949.

39. Wen, D.W. and Cai, Z.X. (2003). Fuzzy random learning algorithm of recurrent neural network, *High Technology Communication*, *12*(1): 54–57.
40. Lina, X. (2003). *Neural Network Control*, (Electronic Industry Press, Beijing).
41. Yang, X.J. and Zheng, J.L. (2003). *Artificial Neural Networks and Blind Signal Processing*, (Tsinghua University Press, Beijing, in Chinese).
42. Zadeh, L.A. (2001). A new direction in AI: toward a computational theory of perceptions, *AI Magazine*, 73–84, (Spring).
43. Zurada, J.M., Marks II, R.J. and Robinson, C.J. (eds). (1994). *Computational Intelligence Imitating Life*, (IEEE Press, New York).

Evolutionary Computation

6

Darwin put forward the theory of natural selection in his scientific masterpiece "The Origin of Species" in 1859, pointing out that species are constantly evolving, and it is an evolutionary process from low to high, from simple to complex. In many science and engineering disciplines, it is common to face a large number of optimization problems, such as constrained and multi-objective optimization problems. In order to solve optimization problems, many optimization methods have been proposed, which can be briefly grouped into two classes: deterministic methods and randomized methods. In general, deterministic methods are gradient-based search methods. This kind of methods will face great difficulties when handling complex optimization problems, since complex optimization problems may usually lack explicit mathematical formulations and have discrete definition domains. Randomized methods mainly include simulated annealing algorithms [1], tabu search [2], etc. Simulated annealing algorithms are inspired by the principle of solid annealing. At each step, simulated annealing algorithms consider some neighboring state s' of the current state s, and probabilistically decide between moving the system to state s' and staying in state s. These probabilities ultimately lead the system to move to states of lower energy [1]. In addition, tabu search uses memory structures that describe the visited solutions or user-provided sets of rules. If a potential solution has been previously visited within a certain short-term period or if it has violated a rule, it is marked as "taboo" so that the algorithm does not consider that possibility repeatedly [2].

Evolutionary algorithms (EAs) are a kind of population-based intelligent randomized method, which have a different structure from other optimization methods. Compared with deterministic methods, EAs exhibit the following advantages: (1) using from a population (i.e., many individuals) rather than one point to search for the global optimal solution, (2) selecting the individuals based on their fitness, without the need for gradient information,

207

(3) using the probabilistic transition rule rather than the deterministic transition rule, and (4) ease of parallel computing. In addition, with respect to other randomized methods (such as simulated annealing algorithms and tabu search), EAs have more powerful search performance and greater robustness.

This chapter will first introduce the basic idea of EAs, and then introduce how to solve constrained and multi-objective optimization problems using EAs. Finally, a practical application of EAs is introduced.

6.1 Evolutionary Algorithms (EAs)

6.1.1 *The basic idea of EAs*

EAs take their inspiration from natural selection and survival of the fittest in the biological world [3, 4]. They simulate the learning process of the population consisting of some individuals. In EAs, each individual represents one point in the search space. Beginning with the initial population, EAs update the population through an iterative way, and finally reach the global optimal solution or some satisfactory solutions. Needless to say, the above population iteration-based evolution provides a novel idea for problem solving. Figure 6.1 illustrates the general framework of EAs.

In this framework, an initial population, which is composed of some randomly selected individuals from the search space, should be generated first. Thereafter, some excellent individuals are chosen from the population by the selection operator to form the parent set. Subsequently, the individuals in the parent set will be used to produce some new solutions by making use of the recombination operator (i.e., crossover operator and mutation operator). Finally, the population of the next generation can be obtained through applying the replacement operator to the parent population and

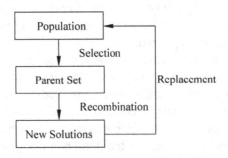

Figure 6.1   The general framework of EAs.

the new solutions. During the evolution, the aim of the recombination operator is to find some promising solutions, and the replacement operator aims at determining the evolution directions for the next population.

6.1.2 *The research areas and paradigms of EAs*

(1) The research areas of EAs

Currently, the research on EAs mainly concentrates on three aspects: design, analysis, and applications. In terms of the EA design, how to balance exploration and exploitation abilities is deemed a key factor to the performance. Exploration means that an algorithm should have the capability to probe a more extensive search region, and has a better robustness. Exploitation, on the other hand, makes the search concentrate on neighborhoods of the current solutions, which has a direct impact on convergence speed. In addition, as far as theoretic analysis is concerned, global convergence properties and time complexity of EAs have been actively researched [5]. Moreover, EAs have been broadly applied to various fields, such as project scheduling, control system design, task assignment, antenna array optimization, and power system optimization.

(2) The paradigms of EAs

The paradigms of EAs date back to the early 1950s. At that time, researchers realized that Darwinian evolution can be used to solve complex optimization problems. Inspired by Darwinian evolution, Holland [6] proposed the genetic algorithm (GA) in the 1960s. De Jong [7] first utilized GA for numerical optimization. In the mid-1960s, Fogel *et al.* [8] introduced evolutionary programming (EP). Almost in the same period, Rechenberg and Schwefel [9, 10] initiated research on the evolution strategy (ES). In the early 1990s, genetic programming (GP) was introduced by Koza [11] as a new paradigm of EAs. Traditionally, GA, EP, ES, and GP are the four classic paradigms of EAs and have gained much attention from researchers and practitioners in various fields.

Actually, more and more EA paradigms have been proposed over the past two decades. For example, Dorigo [12] introduced ant colony optimization (ACO) in 1992, Robert [13] proposed the cultural algorithm (CA) in 1994, Kennedy and Eberhart [14] presented particle swarm optimization (PSO) in 1995, and Storn and Price [15,16] introduced differential evolution (DE) in the same year. Besides these, artificial immune system (AIS) [17], hormone-based algorithm (HBA) [18], harmony search (HS) [19], bacterial foraging optimization (BFO) [20], memetic algorithm (MA) [21], honeybee algorithm (HA) [22], biogeography-based optimization (BBO) [23], and group search optimizer (GSO) [24] have also been proposed successively. The above EA paradigms have greatly advanced the development of the field of evolutionary computation.

(3) Differential Evolution (DE)

Next, a very popular EA paradigm, i.e., differential evolution (DE) [15, 16], was introduced. Similar to other EAs, DE is a population-based optimization algorithm. In DE, each individual in the population is called a target vector. DE produces a mutant vector by making use of the mutation operator, which perturbs a target vector using the difference vector of other individuals in the population. Afterwards, the crossover operator is applied to the target vector and the mutant vector to generate a trial vector. Finally, the trial vector competes with its target vector for survival according to their objective function values. Owing to some advantages, e.g., a simple structure, ease of implementation, and a fast convergence speed, DE has been widely applied in diverse fields.

During the evolution, DE maintains a population of NP individual members, where NP is the population size, and each member is a point in the search space S. DE improves its population generation by generation. It extracts distance and direction information from the current population for generating new solutions for the next generation. Almost all the DE variants adopt the following algorithmic framework:

Step 1: Set the current generation number $G = 0$.

Step 2: Sample NP points $\vec{x}_{i,G}, \ldots, \vec{x}_{NP,G}$ from S to form an initial population.

Step 3: For $i = 1, \ldots, NP$ do the following:

> **Step 3.1: Mutation:** Generate a mutant vector $\vec{v}_{i,G}$ by using a DE mutation operator;
>
> **Step 3.2: Repair:** If $\vec{v}_{i,G}$ is not feasible (i.e., not in S), use a repair operator to make $\vec{v}_{i,G}$ feasible;
>
> **Step 3.3: Crossover:** Mix $\vec{x}_{i,G}$ and $\vec{v}_{i,G}$ to generate a trial vector $\vec{u}_{i,G}$ by using a DE crossover operator;

Step 3.4: Replacement: If $f(\vec{u}_{i,G}) \leq f(\vec{x}_{i,G})$, set $\vec{x}_{i,G+1} = \vec{u}_{i,G}$, otherwise set $\vec{x}_{i,G+1} = \vec{x}_{i,G}$.

Step 4: If a preset stopping condition is not met, set $G = G + 1$ and go to Step 3.

In the ith pass of the loop in Step 3, $\vec{x}_{i,G}$ is called a target vector, $\vec{v}_{i,G}$ is its mutant vector, and $\vec{u}_{i,G}$ is its trial vector. $\vec{u}_{i,G}$ inherits some parameter values from $\vec{x}_{i,G}$ in Step 3.3 and enters the next generation if its objective function value is better than or equal to the objective function value of $\vec{x}_{i,G}$.

The characteristic feature of DE is its mutation operators. Five commonly used mutation operators are the following:

- **DE/rand/1:**

$$\vec{v}_{i,G} = \vec{x}_{r1,G} + F \cdot (\vec{x}_{r2,G} - \vec{x}_{r3,G}) \qquad (6.1)$$

- **DE/rand/2:**

$$\vec{v}_{i,G} = \vec{x}_{r1,G} + F \cdot (\vec{x}_{r2,G} - \vec{x}_{r3,G}) + F \cdot (\vec{x}_{r4,G} - \vec{x}_{r5,G}) \qquad (6.2)$$

- **DE/best/1:**

$$\vec{v}_{i,G} = \vec{x}_{best,G} + F \cdot (\vec{x}_{r1,G} - \vec{x}_{r2,G}) \qquad (6.3)$$

- **DE/best/2:**

$$\vec{v}_{i,G} = \vec{x}_{best,G} + F \cdot (\vec{x}_{r1,G} - \vec{x}_{r2,G}) + F \cdot (\vec{x}_{r3,G} - \vec{x}_{r4,G}) \qquad (6.4)$$

- **DE/current-to-best/1:**

$$\vec{v}_{i,G} = \vec{x}_{i,G} + F \cdot (\vec{x}_{best,G} - \vec{x}_{i,G}) + F \cdot (\vec{x}_{r1,G} - \vec{x}_{r2,G}) \qquad (6.5)$$

where $r1$, $r2$, $r3$, $r4$, and $r5$ are different indexes uniformly randomly selected from $\{1, \dots, NP\} \backslash \{i\}$, F is the scaling factor, and $\vec{x}_{best,G}$ is the best individual in the current population.

DE performs a crossover operator on $\vec{x}_{i,G}$ and $\vec{v}_{i,G}$ to generate the trial vector $\vec{u}_{i,G}$. The following two crossover operators are widely used in the DE implementations.

- **Binomial crossover:** The trial vector $\vec{u}_{i,G} = (u_{i,1,G}, u_{i,2,G}, \ldots, u_{i,D,G})$ is generated in the following way:

$$u_{i,j,G} = \begin{cases} v_{i,j,G} & \text{if } rand_j \ (0,1) \leq CR \quad \text{or} \quad j = j_{rand} \\ x_{i,j,G} & \text{otherwise} \end{cases} \tag{6.6}$$

where j_{rand} is a randomly chosen integer in the range $[1, D]$, $rand_j(0,1)$ is a uniform random number in $(0,1)$, and $CR \in (0,1]$ is the crossover control parameter. Due to the use of j_{rand}, $\vec{u}_{i,G}$ is always different from $\vec{x}_{i,G}$.

- **Exponential crossover:** The trial vector $\vec{u}_{i,G} = (u_{i,1,G}, u_{i,2,G}, \ldots, u_{i,D,G})$ is created as follows:

$$u_{i,j,G} = \begin{cases} v_{i,j,G} & \text{for, } j = \langle l \rangle_D, \langle l + 1 \rangle_D, \ldots, \langle l + L - 1 \rangle_D \\ x_{i,j,G} & \text{otherwise} \end{cases} \tag{6.7}$$

where $i = 1, 2, \ldots, NP, j = 1, 2, \ldots, D$, and $\langle \ \rangle_D$ denotes the modulo function with modulus D. The starting index l is a randomly chosen integer in the range of $[1, D]$. The integer L is also drawn from the range $[1, D]$ with probability $P_r(L \geq v) = CR^{v-1}$, $v > 0$. The l and L are re-generated for each trial vector $\vec{u}_{i,G}$.

- **Repair operator:** A simple and popular repair operator works as follows: if the jth element $v_{i,j,G}$ of $\vec{v}_{i,G} = (v_{i,1,G}, v_{i,2,G}, \ldots, v_{i,D,G})$ is out of the search region $[L_j, U_j]$, then $v_{i,j,G}$ is reset as follows:

$$v_{i,j,G} = \begin{cases} \min\{U_j, 2L_j - v_{i,j,G}\} & \text{if } v_{i,j,G} < L_j \\ \max\{L_j, 2U_j - v_{i,j,G}\} & \text{if } v_{i,j,G} > U_j \end{cases} \tag{6.8}$$

Different DE variants can be obtained by combining different mutation operators with different crossover operators. For example, DE/rand/1/bin can be obtained by combining DE/rand/1 with the binomial crossover, and DE/rand/1/exp can be obtained by combining DE/rand/1 with the exponential crossover. In general, DE/rand/1/bin is the most classic variant of DE.

The illustration of DE/rand/1/bin in the two-dimensional search space has been given in Figure 6.2, where the triangle points represent the trial vectors. From Figure 6.2, it is evident that the trial vector is a vertex of the hyper-rectangle defined by the mutant and target vectors, regardless of the binomial crossover and the exponential crossover.

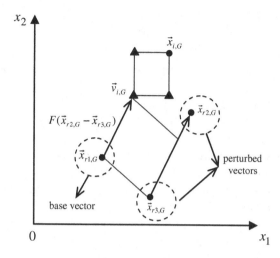

Figure 6.2   Illustration of DE/rand/1/bin.

6.2 Solving Constrained Optimization Problems by Evolutionary Algorithms

6.2.1 *Constrained optimization problems (COPs) and constraint-handling techniques*

Constrained optimization problems (COPs) are a kind of mathematical programming problem. Solving COPs is also an important area in the optimization field. This chapter considers the following general COPs:

$$
\begin{cases}
\min f(\vec{x}), & \vec{x} = (x_1, x_2, \dots, x_D) \in \Re^D \\
g_j(\vec{x}) \le 0, & j = 1, \dots, l \\
h_j(\vec{x}) = 0, & j = l + 1, \dots, p \\
L_i \le x_i \le U_i & 1 \le i \le D
\end{cases}
\tag{6.9}
$$

where $(x_1, x_2, \dots, x_D)$ are the D decision variables; $f(\vec{x})$ is the objective function; $g_j(\vec{x})$ is the jth inequality constraint; $h_j(\vec{x})$ is the jth equality constraint; L_i and U_i are the lower and upper bounds of the ith decision variable x_i.

The search space S is a D-dimensional rectangular space in $\Re^D$ defined by the parametric constraints:

$$
L_i \le x_i \le U_i, \quad 1 \le i \le D.
\tag{6.10}
$$

The feasible region $\Omega \subseteq S$ is defined as follows:

$$\Omega = \{\vec{x} | g_j(\vec{x}) \le 0, \ j = 1, \ldots, l; \ h_j(\vec{x}) = 0, \ j = l + 1, \ldots, p; \ \vec{x} \in S\} \quad (6.11)$$

Any point $\vec{x} \in \Omega$ is called a feasible solution; otherwise $\vec{x}$ is an infeasible solution.

If an inequality constraint satisfies $g_j(\vec{x}) = 0$ ($j \in \{1, \ldots, l\}$) at any point $\vec{x} \in \Omega$, it is *active* at $\vec{x}$. All equality constraints $h_j(\vec{x})(j = l + 1, \ldots, p)$ are considered *active* at all points of Ω.

In general, COPs are intractable, especially when the landscape of the objective function is very complex and the feasible region is concave and covers a very small part of the whole search space. In the past two decades, EAs have gained increasing attention for solving COPs owing to their flexibility and adaptability to the task at hand. As a result, a large number of constrained optimization EAs have been proposed [25–27].

It is noteworthy that EAs are unconstrained search methods and lack an explicit mechanism to bias the search in constrained search space. This has motivated the development of different constraint-handling techniques to cope with constraints. In the constraint-handling techniques targeted at EAs, equality constraints are always transformed into inequality constraints as follows:

$$|h_j(\vec{x})| - \delta \le 0 \quad (6.12)$$

where $j = l + 1, \ldots, p$ and δ is a positive tolerance value. Usually, the degree of constraint violation of individual $\vec{x}$ on the jth constraint is calculated as follows:

$$G_j(\vec{x}) = \begin{cases} \max\{0, g_j(\vec{x})\}, & 1 \le j \le l \\ \max\{0, |h_j(\vec{x})| - \delta\}, & l + 1 \le j \le p \end{cases} \quad (6.13)$$

Then

$$G(\vec{x}) = \sum_{j=1}^{p} G_j(\vec{x}) \quad (6.14)$$

reflects the degree of constraint violation of the individual $\vec{x}$.

Michalewicz and Schoenauer [25] and Coello Coello [26] provided an extensive survey of constraint-handling techniques suitable for EAs. The current popular constraint-handling techniques can be briefly classified into three categories: methods based on penalty functions [28], methods based on the preference of feasible solutions over infeasible solutions [29,30], and methods based on multi-objective optimization [31]. Actually, after producing an offspring population for the parent population by EAs, the purpose of constraint-handling techniques is to determine a criterion to compare individuals in the parent and offspring populations. The methods based on penalty functions first construct a fitness function by adding a penalty term proportional to the constraint violation into the objective function and then using this fitness function to compare individuals. In the methods based on the preference of feasible solutions over infeasible solutions, the comparison of individuals is based on either the degree of constraint violation or the objective function. Moreover, feasible solutions are always considered to be better than infeasible ones to a certain degree. In addition, the methods based on multi-objective optimization transform a COP into a multi-objective optimization problem (MOP) with two objectives (i.e., $F_1(\vec{x}) = (f(\vec{x}), G(\vec{x}))$ or a MOP with $(p+1)$ objectives (i.e., $F_2(\vec{x}) = (f(\vec{x}), G_1(\vec{x}), \dots, G_p(\vec{x}))$). After the above transformation, Pareto dominance is usually employed to compare individuals.

6.2.2 *Further analysis of the methods based on multi-objective optimization techniques*

As pointed out in Section 6.2.1, there are two kinds of transformation from COPs to MOPs, i.e., $F_1(\vec{x})$ and $F_2(\vec{x})$. Actually, some researchers have suggested that multi-objective optimization techniques are not suitable for solving COPs [32, 33]. They claim that multi-objective optimization does not appear to be any easier than constrained optimization since one has to balance different objectives in optimization. This is unsurprising since some previous papers use multi-objective EAs to solve COPs directly. Moreover, the results of these papers ignore the essential characteristics of COPs.

Next, $F_1(\vec{x})$ will be considered as an example to explain the essential difference between the solution of the converted COPs and that of the general MOPs. The graph representation of $F_1(\vec{x})$ [34] has been shown in Figure 6.3, where the Pareto set is mapped to the Pareto front, the feasible region Ω is mapped to the solid segment, the global optimum $\vec{x}^*$ is mapped to the intersection of the Pareto front and the solid segment, and the search space S is mapped to points on and above the Pareto front.

With respect to COPs, the aim of the solution of $F_1(\vec{x})$ is to find the global optimal solution in the feasible region (i.e., the global optimum in Figure 6.3). However, the global optimal solutions (also called the Pareto optimal solutions) of the general MOPs constitute a curve or a surface and,

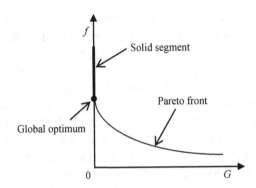

Figure 6.3   Graph representation of $F_1(\vec{x})$.

therefore, there are usually infinite global optimal solutions for the general MOPs. More importantly, the goal of the solution of the general MOPs is to obtain a final population with a diversity of nondominated individuals, i.e., the image of the population in the objective space should be distributed as uniformly as possible in the Pareto front (i.e., the Pareto front in Figure 6.3). Therefore, the solution of $F_1(\vec{x})$ is not equivalent to that of the general MOPs. Moreover, it is unnecessary to uniformly distribute the nondominated individuals found during the evolution when solving $F_1(\vec{x})$.

The above illustration clarifies the misunderstanding of some researchers on the methods based on multi-objective optimization techniques.

Due to the fact that COPs may contain many constraints, if COPs are converted into $F_2(\vec{x})$, it is evident that $F_2(\vec{x})$ may also contain many objective functions accordingly. Although the solution of $F_2(\vec{x})$ has an essential difference with that of the general MOPs, the large number of objective functions may inevitably cause significant side effects on the solution of $F_2(\vec{x})$. Therefore, it is more suitable to convert COPs into $F_1(\vec{x})$, when the methods based on multi-objective optimization techniques are applied.

6.2.3   *A multi-objective optimization-based EA for COPs*

Next, a classic multi-objective optimization-based EA (called CW) for COPs was introduced [35], in which a COP is converted into $F_1(\vec{x})$. The CW only exploits Pareto dominance that is often used in multi-objective optimization to compare the individuals in the population.

(1) The procedure of CW

Initially, population P_t is randomly produced in the search space defined by $[L_i, U_i]$, $1 \leq i \leq D$, where t is the generation number. Subsequently, μ individuals (set Q) are randomly chosen from P_t to yield λ offspring (set C) and are deleted from P_t. Thereafter, the nondominated individuals (set R) are identified from C and one randomly selected nondominated individual (denoted as $\vec{y}$) from R is used to replace one dominated individual (if it exists) in Q according to the following criteria: (1) if condition 2 does not hold, the above replacement is based on Pareto dominance, otherwise (2) the replacement is based on the feasibility-based rule [30]. As a result, Q is updated. After combining the updated Q with P_t, the update of P_t is also achieved. Additionally, if neither condition 1 nor condition 2 holds, and if R contains only infeasible solutions which means that C is also entirely composed of infeasible solutions, then the infeasible solution with the lowest degree of constraint violation in R is stored into archive A. Every k generations, *num* infeasible individuals randomly chosen from A are used to replace the same number of individuals in P_t. The above procedure is repeated until the maximum number of function evaluations (FES) is reached. Conditions 1 and 2 in the above procedure are explained as follows.

Condition 1: The absolute difference in the original objective function values (i.e., $f(\vec{x})$) between the best and worst feasible solutions in P_t is less than θ_1, where θ_1 is a user-defined parameter with a very small positive value.

Condition 2: P_t consists entirely of infeasible individuals and $| \max\{f(\vec{x}_i)|1 \leq i \leq NP\} - \min\{f(\vec{x}_j)|1 \leq j \leq NP\}| < \theta_2$, where θ_2 is a user-defined parameter with a very small positive value and NP is the population size.

Clearly, Condition 1 means that the difference among feasible solutions in a population is very slight, and Condition 2 indicates that the difference among infeasible individuals in an infeasible population is extremely tiny. The detailed features of CW are the following.

(2) The importance of nondominated individuals

In CW, one nondominated individual in set R is used to replace one individual in set Q according to some criteria, with the aim of updating set Q.

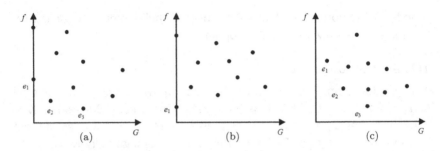

Figure 6.4　Nondominated individuals in a population.

Figure 6.4 shows an example for illustrating the importance of nondominated individuals. As shown in Figure 6.4(a), there are three nondominated individuals denoted as "e_1", "e_2", and "e_3" in a population. It can be found that "e_1" denotes the best feasible solution, "e_2" denotes the infeasible solution with the lowest degree of constraint violation, and "e_3" denotes the infeasible solution with the minimum objective function value, therefore the most important information of a population is clearly represented by nondominated individuals. Figures 6.4(b) and 6.4(c) also verify the above phenomenon. As shown in Figure 6.4, nondominated individuals in a population may consist of one feasible solution (Figure 6.4(b)), infeasible solutions (Figure 6.4(c)), or a combination of feasible and infeasible solutions (Figure 6.4(a)).

(3) Infeasible solution archiving and replacement

In CW, the comparison of individuals is based on Pareto dominance. If the feasible region occupies a very small part of the whole search space, in the early stage the population may often contain infeasible solutions only. Under this condition, the offspring may be infeasible. Thus, the nondominated individual $\vec{y}$ in set R may be frequently nondominated with or dominated by the individuals in set Q and, as a result, the replacement seldom occurs. An illustrative example is shown in Figure 6.5. In Figure 6.5, the parent $\vec{x}$ is an infeasible solution since $G(\vec{x}) > 0$; the corresponding offspring can Pareto dominate $\vec{x}$ only when its image in the objective and constraint spaces is located in the region $ABCDA$. As a result, the offspring might be always nondominated with or dominated by $\vec{x}$ and, consequently, the replacement seldom occurs. The above phenomenon will lead us to the conclusion that the population cannot quickly approach the feasible region and may stagnate in the infeasible region.

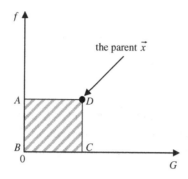

Figure 6.5   A schematic diagram to illustrate the Pareto dominance relationship.

To address this, provided the current offspring population is composed of only infeasible individuals, the best of the infeasible individuals in the current offspring population, which has the lowest degree of constraint violation, is stored into a predefined archive A. Then, after a fixed interval of generations, *num* randomly selected individuals of population P_t are replaced by the same number of randomly selected infeasible individuals in archive A. This process is called infeasible solutions archiving and replacement, the main aim of which is to motivate the population toward the feasible region from different directions quickly.

(4) Experimental study

The performance of CW is evaluated on 13 test functions. These test cases include various types (linear, nonlinear, and quadratic) of objective functions with different numbers of decision variables (D) and a range of types (linear inequalities, nonlinear equalities, and nonlinear inequalities) and a number of constraints.

For each test case, 50 independent trials are executed. About the parameter settings, $\mu = D + 1$, $\lambda = 10$, $k = 10$, *num* $= 2$, and $\theta_1 = 1\text{E} - 10$. Also, θ_2 is set to $10\theta_3 + \log_{10}^{abs(current\_min\_objective)}$, where $\theta_3 = -12$, and "*current_min_objective*" denotes the minimum original objective function value in the current population. The number of FES is 350,000 for all the test cases. To ensure that each individual in the population has enough lifespan to contribute its valuable information, each individual should carry out the crossover operation about once before being replaced. According to this analysis, for the sake of convenience, the population size of each test case is set as follows:

$$NP = \begin{cases} 50, & 0 < D < 5 \\ 100, & 5 \leq D \leq 15 \\ 150, & 15 < D \leq 20 \end{cases} \qquad (6.15)$$

CW is compared with some other representative approaches using two metrics, i.e., solution qualities and computation effort. The other approaches in the comparison include self-adaptive fitness formulation (SAFF) [28], simple multimembered evolution strategy (SMES) [36], and stochastic ranking (SR) [29]. The experiment results are listed in Table 6.1, where "Best", "Mean", "Worst", and "Std Dev" denote the best, mean, worst objective function values, and the standard deviations after 50 independent runs, respectively.

From Table 6.1, CW performs pretty well in that it consistently finds the global optima of all test cases for all 50 runs, except for problem g02. Furthermore, for problem g02, the resulting objective function values are less than -0.803619 for 48 out of the 50 runs. In addition, it is apparent that the standard deviations provided in Table 6.1 are very small, which shows that CW is capable of performing a robust and stable search.

One can conclude that CW can consistently produce the best performance for all the test functions, as opposed to SAFF, SMES, and SR, which only manage to achieve the best performance for certain test functions. Moreover, SAFF, SMES, and SR seem to have a great tendency to converge to a local optimum, especially for those complicated functions, e.g., g02, g05, g07, g09, g10, and g13. For the large feasible problem g02, they are unable to reach the true optimum. Although the best objective function value of -0.803601 found by SMES is very close to the optimum, the resulting objective function values of CW are less than those for 48 out of 50 trials. In terms of the highly constrained problem g10, the best objective function values of SAFF, SMES, and SR are still far from the true optimum. Moreover, for problems g10, SAFF and SR have trouble finding feasible solutions. More specifically, SAFF finds 17 feasible solutions from 20 runs, and SR finds only six from 30 runs. However, CW consistently finds the feasible optimum for this problem.

On the other hand, because of the transformation from an equality constraint into an inequality constraint (Eq. (6.12)) and the use of the

Table 6.1   Comparison of CW with three algorithms.

Prob./ Optimal	Status	Methods			
		SAFF	SMES	SR	CW
g01/ −15.000	Best	−15.000	−15.000	−15.000	−15.000
	Mean	−15.000	−15.000	−15.000	−15.000
	Worst	−15.000	−15.000	−15.000	−15.000
	Std Dev	0	0	0.0E+00	1.3E-14
g02/ −0.803619	Best	−0.80297	−0.803601	−0.803515	−0.803619
	Mean	−0.79010	−0.785238	−0.781975	−0.803220
	Worst	−0.76043	−0.751322	−0.726288	−0.792608
	Std Dev	1.2E-02	1.7E-02	2.0E-02	2.0E-03
g03/ −1.000	Best	−1.000	−1.000	−1.000	−1.000
	Mean	−1.000	−1.000	−1.000	−1.000
	Worst	−1.000	−1.000	−1.000	−1.000
	Std Dev	7.5E-05	2.1E-04	1.9E-04	2.8E-16
g04/ −30665.539	Best	−30665.50	−30665.539	−30665.539	−30665.539
	Mean	−30665.20	−30665.539	−30665.539	−30665.539
	Worst	−30663.30	−30665.539	−30665.539	−30665.539
	Std Dev	4.9E-01	0	2.0E-05	8.0E-12
g05/ 5126.498	Best	5126.989	5126.599	5126.497	5126.4981
	Mean	5432.080	5174.492	5128.881	5126.4981
	Worst	6089.430	5304.167	5142.472	5126.4981
	Std Dev	3.9E+03	5.0E+01	3.5E+00	1.5E-12
g06/ −6961.814	Best	−6961.800	−6961.814	−6961.814	−6961.814
	Mean	−6961.800	−6961.284	−6875.940	−6961.814
	Worst	−6961.800	−6952.482	−6350.262	−6961.814
	Std Dev	0	1.9E+00	1.6E+02	1.8E-12
g07/ 24.306	Best	24.48	24.327	24.307	24.306
	Mean	26.58	24.475	24.374	24.306
	Worst	28.40	24.843	24.642	24.306
	Std Dev	1.1E+00	1.3E-01	6.6E-02	5.7E-12
g08/ −0.095825	Best	−0.095825	−0.095825	−0.095825	−0.095825
	Mean	−0.095825	−0.095825	−0.095825	−0.095825
	Worst	−0.095825	−0.095825	−0.095825	−0.095825
	Std Dev	0	0	2.6E-17	3.2E-17

(*Continued*)

Table 6.1 (*Continued*)

Prob./ Optimal	Status	Methods			
		SAFF	SMES	SR	CW
g09/	Best	680.64	680.632	680.630	680.630
680.630	Mean	680.72	680.643	680.656	680.630
	Worst	680.87	680.719	680.763	680.630
	Std Dev	5.9E-02	1.6E-02	3.4E-02	4.7E-13
g10/	Best	7061.34	7051.903	7054.316	7049.248
7049.248	Mean	7627.89	7253.047	7559.192	7049.248
	Worst	8288.79	7638.366	8835.655	7049.248
	Std Dev	3.7E+02	1.4E+02	5.3E+02	4.0E-09
g11/	Best	0.750	0.75	0.750	0.750
0.75	Mean	0.750	0.75	0.750	0.750
	Worst	0.750	0.75	0.750	0.750
	Std Dev	0	1.5E-04	8.0E-05	0.0E+00
g12/	Best	−1.000	−1.000	−1.000	−1.000
−1.000	Mean	−1.000	−1.000	−1.000	−1.000
	Worst	−1.000	−1.000	−1.000	−1.000
	Std Dev	0	0	0.0E+00	0.0E+00
g13/	Best	*NA*	0.053986	0.053957	0.0539498
0.0539498	Mean	*NA*	0.166385	0.067543	0.0539498
	Worst	*NA*	0.468294	0.216915	0.0539498
	Std Dev	*NA*	1.8E-01	3.1E-02	6.5E-17

Note: *NA* = not available.

parameter δ, some results provided by SAFF, SMES, and SR are better than the "known" optimum. For instance, for problems g03, g04, g06, and g11, the best results provided by SMES, and for problem g05, the best result provided by SR are better than the "known" optima, respectively. But the such behaviors do not mean that the "new" optima are really found by them.

As far as computational cost (the number of FES) is concerned, SMES has minimum computational cost for most test functions, while SAFF has considerable computational cost for all test functions (1,400,000 FES). In general, the cost required by CW (350,000 FES) is moderate in comparison with the other approaches.

6.3 Solving Multi-objective Optimization Problems by Evolutionary Algorithms

6.3.1 *Multi-objective optimization problems (MOPs) and the related definitions*

Without loss of generality, multi-objective optimization problems (MOPs) with D decision variables and m objective functions have the following form:

$$\text{minimize} \quad \vec{y} = \vec{f}(\vec{x}) = (f_1(\vec{x}), f_2(\vec{x}), \ldots, f_m(\vec{x})) \tag{6.16}$$

where $\vec{x} = (x_1, x_2, \ldots, x_D) \in X \subseteq \Re^D$ is the decision vector, X is the search space, $\vec{y} \in Y \subseteq \Re^m$ is the objective vector, and Y is the objective space.

Definition 1 (Pareto dominance):
    A decision vector $\vec{x}_u \in X$ is said to Pareto dominate another decision vector $\vec{x}_v \in X$, denoted as $\vec{x}_u \prec \vec{x}_v$, if

(1) $\forall i \in \{1, \ldots, m\}$, $f_i(\vec{x}_u) \leq f_i(\vec{x}_v)$;
(2) $\exists j \in \{1, \ldots, m\}$, $f_j(\vec{x}_u) < f_j(\vec{x}_v)$.

    In this case, $\vec{x}_v$ is Pareto dominated by $\vec{x}_u$. Note that if Pareto dominance does not hold between $\vec{x}_u$ and $\vec{x}_v$, then they are considered nondominated with each other.

Definition 2 (Pareto optimality):
    A decision vector $\vec{x}_u \in X$ is called a Pareto optimal solution if there does not exist another decision vector $\vec{x}_v \in X$ such that $\vec{x}_v \prec \vec{x}_u$.

Definition 3 (Pareto set):
    For a given MOP $\vec{f}(\vec{x})$, the Pareto set, denoted as *PS*, is defined as

$$PS = \{\vec{x}_u \in X \mid \neg \exists \vec{x}_v \in X, \vec{x}_v \prec \vec{x}_u\}. \tag{6.17}$$

The vectors included in the Pareto set are called nondominated individuals.

Definition 4 (Pareto front):
    For a given MOP $\vec{f}(\vec{x})$, according to the Pareto set, the Pareto front, denoted as *PF*, is defined as

$$PF = \{\vec{f}(\vec{x}_u) \mid \vec{x}_u \in PS\}. \tag{6.18}$$

Clearly, the Pareto front is the image of the Pareto set in the objective space.

6.3.2 *A regularity model-based multi-objective estimation of distribution algorithm (RM-MEDA)*

EAs have been widely used to solve MOPs, and the resultant algorithms are called multi-objective EAs (MOEAs). MOEAs can approximate the Pareto front with a population in a single run. After decades of development, a number of MOEAs have emerged in the field of evolutionary multi-objective optimization. According to their characteristics, MOEAs can be generally grouped into three different classes: (1) Pareto dominance-based methods, such as the nondominated sorting genetic algorithm II [37] and strength Pareto EA 2 [38], (2) indicator-based methods, such as the indicator-based EA [39], and (3) decomposition-based methods, such as MOEA based on decomposition (MOEA/D) [40].

Next, a classic regularity model-based multi-objective estimation of distribution algorithm, referred to as RM-MEDA, was introduced.

It can be inferred from the Karush–Kuhn–Tucker condition that the *PS* of a MOP is an $(m - 1)$-dimensional piecewise continuous manifold in the search space, where m is the number of objectives. Based on the above regularity, Zhang *et al.* [41] proposed RM-MEDA. As a kind of estimation of distribution algorithms, RM-MEDA employs the $(m - 1)$-dimensional local principal component analysis (referred to as $(m - 1)$-D local PCA) to build a model of the *PS* in the search space. In RM-MEDA, firstly, the $(m - 1)$-D local PCA divides the population into K (K is a constant integer) disjoint clusters and computes the central point and principal component of each cluster. Afterwards, one model is built based on the corresponding central point and principal component for each cluster. The primary aim of modeling in RM-MEDA is to approximate one of the pieces of the *PS* by making use of the solutions in one cluster. Ideally, if the number of clusters K is equal to the number of the pieces of the *PS*, each piece of the *PS* can be approximated by one cluster. In this case, a precise model may be built and the performance of RM-MEDA may be excellent.

(1) Framework

During the evolution, RM-MEDA maintains the following:

- a population P_G of NP individuals: $P_G = \{\vec{x}_1, \ldots, \vec{x}_{NP}\}$, where G is the generation number;
- their $\vec{f}$ values: $\vec{f}(\vec{x}_1), \ldots, \vec{f}(\vec{x}_{NP})$.

RM-MEDA is implemented as follows:

Step 1: **Initialization:** Generate an initial population P_0 by randomly sampling NP individuals from the search space S and compute the $\vec{f}$ values of these individuals.

Step 2: **Modeling:** According to P_G, build the probability model by using the $(m-1)$-D local PCA.

Step 3: **Sampling:** Generate an offspring population Q_G by sampling from the probability model established in Step 2 and compute the $\vec{f}$ value of each individual in Q_G.

Step 4: **Selection:** Select NP individuals from P_G and Q_G to construct the population P_{G+1} for the next generation.

Step 5: **Stopping criterion:** If the stopping criterion is satisfied, stop and output the $\vec{f}$ values of the nondominated individuals in the final population, otherwise set $G = G+1$ and go to Step 2.

(2) Modeling

RM-MEDA exploits the distribution information of the current population in the search space to build the model. Thereafter, new solutions will be obtained by sampling from the model. Hopefully, the individuals in the population will be uniformly scattered around the *PS* in the search space as the search goes on. RM-MEDA envisages the individuals in the population as independent observations of a random vector $\vec{\xi}$, which can be formulated as follows:

$$\vec{\xi} = \vec{\varsigma} + \vec{\varepsilon} \tag{6.19}$$

where $\vec{\varsigma}$ is uniformly distributed over a piecewise continuous $(m-1)$-dimensional manifold, and $\vec{\varepsilon}$ is an n-dimensional zero-mean noise vector.

One of the aims of modeling is to find the principal curve or surface of the population. For the sake of simplicity, suppose that the centroid of $\vec{\xi}$ consists of K manifolds: $\psi_1, \dots, \psi_K$, each of which is an $(m-1)$-dimensional hyper-rectangle. That is to say, $\vec{\varsigma}$ is uniformly distributed over these manifolds. An illustration is given in Figure 6.6. Suppose that $\vec{\varsigma}$ is uniformly randomly sampled from $\psi_i (i = 1, \dots, K)$ and $\vec{\varepsilon} \sim N(0, \sigma_i I)$, where I is the $D \times D$ identity matrix and $\sigma_i > 0 (i = 1, \dots, K)$. By doing so, the task of modeling is transformed to estimate ψ_i and σ_i.

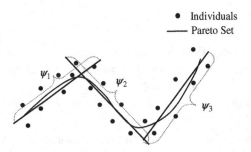

Figure 6.6   The manifolds of the PS for a biobjective optimization problem.

RM-MEDA first splits P_G into K subpopulations: $C_1, \ldots, C_K$. Then, C_i is utilized to estimate ψ_i and σ_i ($i \in \{1, \ldots, K\}$). RM-MEDA uses the following procedure to achieve the above purpose:

Step 1: Randomly initialize L_i^{m-1}, $i = 1, \ldots, K$, to be an affine $(m-1)$-dimensional principal subspace containing an individual randomly chosen from P_G.

Step 2: Partition the individuals of P_G into K clusters $C_1, \ldots, C_K$:

$$C_i = \{\vec{x} | \vec{x} \in P_G, dist(\vec{x}, L_i^{m-1}) \leq dist(\vec{x}, L_k^{m-1}), \forall k \neq i\} \quad (6.20)$$

where $dist(x, L_i^{m-1})$ means the Euclidean distance between $\vec{x}$ and its projection in L_i^{m-1}.

Step 3: Update L_i^{m-1}, $i = 1, \ldots, K$.

Step 4: Repeat Steps 2 and 3 until no change in partition is made.

In the above procedure, L_i^{m-1} is the affine $(m-1)$-dimensional principal subspace of the individuals in C_i. In Step 3, L_i^{m-1} can be updated by the mean and the covariance matrix of the individuals in C_i. The mean of C_i is

$$\bar{x}_i = \frac{1}{|C_i|} \sum_{\vec{x} \in C_i} \vec{x} \quad (6.21)$$

and the covariance matrix is

$$Cov = \frac{1}{|C_j| - 1} \sum_{\vec{x} \in C_j} (\vec{x} - \bar{x}_j)(\vec{x} - \bar{x}_j)^T \quad (6.22)$$

In addition, the jth principal component $\vec{U}_i^j$ is a unity eigenvector associated with the jth largest eigenvalue of the covariance matrix Cov. Then, L_i^{m-1} is updated as follows:

$$\left\{ \vec{x} \in R^D | \vec{x} = \bar{x}_i + \sum_{j=1}^{m-1} \alpha_j \vec{U}_i^j, \alpha_j \in R, j = 1, \dots, m-1 \right\} \quad (6.23)$$

Next, RM-MEDA uses the above clustering results to build the model. RM-MEDA calculates the range of projections of the individuals of C_i in the first $(m-1)$ principal components:

$$l_i^j = \min_{\vec{x} \in C_i} \{ (\vec{x} - \bar{x}_i)^T \vec{U}_i^j \} \quad (6.24)$$

and

$$u_i^j = \max_{\vec{x} \in C_i} \{ (\vec{x} - \bar{x}_i)^T \vec{U}_i^j \} \quad (6.25)$$

where $\bar{x}_i$ is the mean, $\vec{U}_i^j$ is the jth principal component of the covariance matrix Cov of C_i, and $j \in \{1, \dots, m-1\}$.

Then, each $(m-1)$-D manifold ψ_i is constructed as follows:

$$\psi_i = \left\{ \vec{x} \in R^D | \vec{x} = \bar{x}_i + \sum_{j=1}^{m-1} \beta_j \vec{U}_i^j, \ l_i^j - 0.25(u_i^j - l_i^j) \le \beta_j \le u_i^j + 0.25(u_i^j - l_i^j), \right.$$

$$\left. j = 1, \dots, m-1 \right\} \quad (6.26)$$

It is necessary to note that in order to make a better approximation of the PS, RM-MEDA enlarges the range of projections in each direction $\vec{U}_i^j (j = 1, \dots, m-1)$ by 50%.

In addition, σ_i is set as follows:

$$\sigma_i = \frac{1}{n - m + 1} \sum_{j=m}^{n} \lambda_i^j \quad (6.27)$$

where λ_i^j is the jth largest eigenvalue of the covariance matrix Cov of C_i.

6.3.3 *The drawback of modeling in RM-MEDA*

According to the introduction in Sec. 6.3.2, modeling is a very important process in RM-MEDA. Moreover, more promising solutions may be generated by sampling from a more precise model. Since the PS of the continuous MOPs is a piecewise continuous $(m-1)$-dimensional manifold, RM-MEDA firstly partitions the population P_G into K clusters $C_1, \dots, C_K$ by making use of the $(m-1)$-D local PCA, with the aim of estimating one manifold ψ_i with

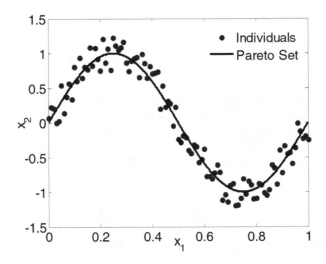

Figure 6.7   The *PS* is a piecewise continuous sine curve.

one cluster C_i. However, a question which naturally arises is: How to determine the value of K? In RM-MEDA, K is set to a constant integer (i.e., 5). However, needless to say, different shapes of the *PS* may require different number of clusters, and thus, require different values of K.

Suppose that the *PS* of a MOP is shown in Figure 6.6. Clearly, in this case if K is set to 3, the ψ_i obtained by modeling can approximate one of the pieces of the *PS* effectively. However, if K is not equal to 3, what will be the corresponding result then? Next, the influence of the value of K on the performance is discussed.

As shown in Figure 6.7, the *PS* is a piecewise continuous sine curve:

$$x_i = \sin(2\pi x_1), \quad i = 2, 3, \ldots, D, \quad 0 \le x_1 \le 1 \qquad (6.28)$$

where D is the dimension of the search space. For simplicity, D is equal to 2. In Figure 6.7, the dots denote the individuals which uniformly scatter around the *PS*.

Clearly, in this case, three manifolds $\psi_i(i = 1, 2, \text{and } 3)$ can approximate the sine curve effectively. That is, 3 is a suitable value for the number of clusters K. Figure 6.8(a) shows the result of clustering by the $(m - 1)$-D local PCA with $K = 3$ and Figure 6.8(b) exhibits the $\psi_i(i = 1, 2, \text{and } 3)$ computed by Eq. (6.25). From Figure 6.8, the *PS* can be approximated by $\psi_i(i = 1, 2, \text{and } 3)$ very well.

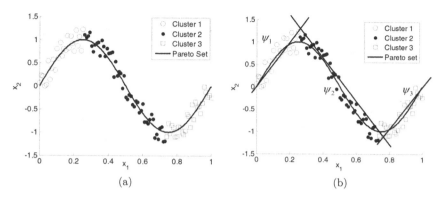

Figure 6.8 (a) The results of clustering with $K = 3$; (b) the manifolds $\psi_i(i = 1, 2,$ and 3) built from the clusters.

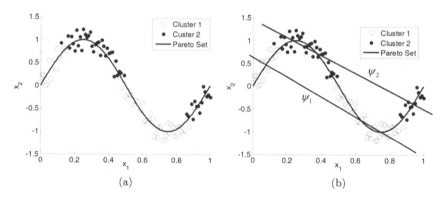

Figure 6.9 (a) The results of clustering with $K = 2$; (b) the manifolds $\psi_i(i = 1$ and 2) built from the clusters.

When K is set to 2 that is less than what is actually required, a typical clustering result is shown in Figure 6.9. From Figure 6.9, the estimated manifolds $\psi_i(i = 1$ and 2) cannot approximate the *PS* very well. In particular, few better solutions could be sampled from the model built for each cluster. Hence, in this case the performance of the algorithm will significantly degrade. More importantly, perhaps the algorithm could not converge to the *PS* because of incorrect approximation.

Remark 1: If the number of clusters is less than what is required, the model built will be incorrect, and thus, causes a side effect on the performance of the algorithm.

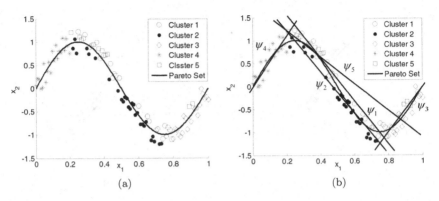

Figure 6.10   (a) The results of clustering with $K = 5$; (b) the models $\psi_i(i = 1, \dots, 5)$ built from the clusters.

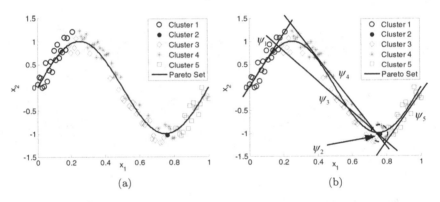

Figure 6.11   (a) The results of clustering with $K = 5$; (b) the models $\psi_i(i = 1, \dots, 5)$ built from the clusters.

On the other hand, how about the number of clusters being more than required? Figures 6.10–6.11 show three typical clustering results with $K = 5$.

As shown in the two figures, among all the manifolds, three manifolds can be used to estimate the distribution of the *PS* while there are two redundant manifolds. For example, from Figure 6.10 it is clear that ψ_1, ψ_2, and ψ_5 approximate the same part of the *PS* and, consequently, they can be reduced to just one. As shown in Figure 6.11, the second cluster only includes one point. Indeed, it is not an effective cluster and the occurrence of this phenomenon is due to the inappropriate clustering number.

Remark 2: If the number of clusters is more than what is required, although the *PS* can be approximated by the model built, there exist some redundant and incorrect manifolds, which have a side effect on the convergence speed and the convergence quality of the algorithm.

6.3.4 *An improved RM-MEDA (IRM-MEDA)*

In order to overcome the above drawback of RM-MEDA, a reducing redundant cluster operator (RRCO) was introduced [42]. By combining RRCO with RM-MEDA, an improved version of RM-MEDA, referred as IRM-MEDA, was obtained [42].

(1) RRCO

According to the discussion in Section 6.3.3, if there exist some redundant clusters, two particular phenomena may occur as follows: (1) the cluster only has one point (as shown in Figure 6.11); and (2) some overlapped manifolds approximate the same part of the *PS*; see, e.g., ψ_1, ψ_2, and ψ_5 in Figure 6.10, and ψ_3 and ψ_4 in Figure 6.11.

RRCO is designed to address the above two particular phenomena. After implementing the local PCA, K clusters $C_1, \ldots, C_K$ and K manifolds $\psi_1, \ldots, \psi_K$ are obtained. Then, RRCO works as follows:

Step 1) Set $A = \{\psi_i, \ldots, \psi_K\}$;

Step 2) For $i = 1:K$

Step 3)   If C_i only contains one individual, then $A = A \backslash \psi_i$;

Step 4) End For

Step 5) $L = 0$;

Step 6) While $|A| > 0$

Step 7)   Choose the first manifold from A, denoted as ψ' and $A = A \backslash \psi'$;

Step 8)   **For** $i = 1:|A|$

Step 9)   If both condition 1 and condition 2 are satisfied for the ith manifold in A and ψ', store this manifold to B;

Step 10) End For

Step 11) $A = A \backslash B$;

Step 12) $L = L + 1$;

Step 13) End While

Step 14) $K = L$.

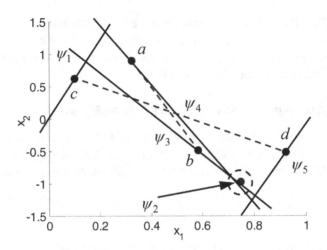

Figure 6.12   The overlapped manifolds and the parallel manifolds.

During the evolution, K is adjusted by RRCO at each generation and the updated K is used as the new number of clusters for the next generation.

In RRCO, the included angle of two manifolds is used to identify the overlapped manifolds. When a MOP has m objectives, the included angle is computed between $(m-1)$-D hyper-rectangles. In general, if the included angle of two manifolds is less than a predefined value θ, these two manifolds overlap with each other. Note, however, that the included angle between parallel manifolds is also very small. As shown in Figure 6.12 (this Figure is obtained from Figure 6.11(b) by eliminating the sine curve and the dots), the included angle between the manifolds ψ_3 and ψ_4 which overlap with each other is small, while the included angle between the manifolds ψ_1 and ψ_5 which are parallel to each other is also very small. Therefore, if only the included angle of two manifolds is used to judge whether these two manifolds overlap with each other, some errors may arise.

Next, Figure 6.12 is employed as an example to explain how to identify the overlapped manifolds and the parallel manifolds. In Figure 6.12, points a, b, c, and d are the central points of the fourth, third, first, and fifth clusters, respectively. The included angle between line segment $\overline{ab}$ and the manifold ψ_3 or the manifold ψ_4 is relatively small, so ψ_3 and ψ_4 are overlapped manifolds. However, the included angle between line segment $\overline{cd}$ and ψ_1 or ψ_5 is relatively large, so ψ_1 and ψ_5 are parallel manifolds. Based on the above analysis, the following conditions are used to distinguish the overlapped manifolds and the parallel manifolds:

Condition 1: $\langle \psi_i, \psi_j \rangle < \theta$

Condition 2: $\min(\langle \overline{CP_{ij}}, \psi_i \rangle, \langle \overline{CP_{ij}}, \psi_j \rangle) < \langle \psi_i, \psi_j \rangle$, where $\overline{CP_{ij}}$ denotes the line segment between CP_i and CP_j, and CP_i and CP_j are the central points of the clusters C_i and C_j, respectively.

In the above two conditions, $\langle \psi_i, \psi_j \rangle$ denotes the included angle between ψ_i and ψ_j, $\langle \overline{CP_{ij}}, \psi_i \rangle$ denotes the included angle between $\overline{CP_{ij}}$ and ψ_i, and $\langle \overline{CP_{ij}}, \psi_j \rangle$ denotes the included angle between $\overline{CP_{ij}}$ and ψ_j. θ is a threshold value and is set to $\frac{3}{180}\pi$. If both Conditions 1 and 2 are satisfied, ψ_i and ψ_j are considered overlapped, while if Condition 1 is satisfied and Condition 2 is unsatisfied, ψ_i and ψ_j are considered parallel.

(2) IRM-MEDA

The framework of IRM-MEDA is the same as that of RM-MEDA except that IRM-MEDA uses RRCO to update K. In RM-MEDA, K is fixed during the evolution, whereas IRM-MEDA dynamically adjusts K by extracting some information from the result of clustering at each generation.

IRM-MEDA performs as follows:

Step 1: Initialization: Randomly generate an initial population $P_0 = \{\vec{x}_1, \vec{x}_2, \dots, \vec{x}_{NP}\}$ and initialize K (i.e., the number of clusters).

Step 2: Modeling: Use the $(m-1)$-D local PCA to build the model.

Step 3: Modify the value of K by RRCO.

Step 4: Sampling: Generate the offspring population Q_G by sampling from the model built.

Step 5: Selection: Select NP individuals from P_G and Q_G to construct the next population P_{G+1}.

Step 6: Stopping criterion: If the stopping criterion is satisfied, stop and output the $\vec{f}$ values of the nondominated individuals of the final population, otherwise go to Step 2.

6.3.5 *Experimental study*

(1) Test instances

Nine test instances (F1–F9) are used to verify the effectiveness of IRM-MEDA. The main information of them is summarized in Table 6.2. Test instances F1–F5 are taken from [41]. Since the primary purpose of RM-MEDA is to approximate the *PS* of complex MOPs by taking advantage of the $(m-1)$-D local PCA, four additional test instances (i.e., F6–F9) with various *PS* structures are constructed to further compare RM-MEDA

Table 6.2   The main information of test instances.

Variables	Objectives	Characteristics
F1 $[0,1]^D$	$f_1(\vec{x}) = x_1$ $f_2(\vec{x}) = g(\vec{x})[1 - \sqrt{f_1(\vec{x})/g(\vec{x})}]$ $g(\vec{x}) = 1 + 9 \left(\sum_{i=2}^{D} (x_i - x_1)^2 \right) /(D-1)$	convex *PF* linear linkage $D = 50$ the *PS* is a line segment: $x_D = \cdots = x_2 = x_1,\ 0 \le x_1 \le 1$
F2 $[0,1]^D$	$f_1(\vec{x}) = x_1$ $f_2(\vec{x}) = g(\vec{x})[1 - (f_1(\vec{x})/g(\vec{x}))^2]$ $g(\vec{x}) = 1 + 9 \left(\sum_{i=2}^{D} (x_i - x_1)^2 \right) /(D-1)$	concave *PF* linear linkage $D = 50$ the *PS* is a line segment: $x_D = \cdots = x_2 = x_1,\ 0 \le x_1 \le 1$
F3 $[0,1]^D$	$f_1(\vec{x}) = \cos\left(\frac{\pi}{2}x_1\right) \cos\left(\frac{\pi}{2}x_2\right)(1 + g(\vec{x}))$ $f_2(\vec{x}) = \cos\left(\frac{\pi}{2}x_1\right) \sin\left(\frac{\pi}{2}x_2\right)(1 + g(\vec{x}))$ $f_3(\vec{x}) = \sin\left(\frac{\pi}{2}x_1\right)(1 + g(\vec{x}))$ $g(\vec{x}) = \sum_{i=3}^{D} (x_i - x_1)^2$	concave *PF* linear linkage 3 objectives $D = 30$ the *PS* is a 2-D rectangle: $x_D = \cdots = x_3 = x_1,\ 0 \le x_1, x_2 \le 1$
F4 $[0,1]^D$	$f_1(\vec{x}) = x_1$ $f_2(\vec{x}) = g(\vec{x})[1 - \sqrt{f_1(\vec{x})/g(\vec{x})}]$ $g(\vec{x}) = 1 + 9 \left(\sum_{i=2}^{D} (x_i^2 - x_1)^2 \right) /(D-1)$	convex *PF* nonlinear linkage $D = 50$ the *PS* is a bounded continuous conic: $x_D = \cdots = x_2 = \sqrt{x_1},\ 0 \le x_1 \le 1$
F5 $[0,1]^D$	$f_1(\vec{x}) = x_1$ $f_2(\vec{x}) = g(\vec{x})[1 - (f_1(\vec{x})/g(\vec{x}))^2]$ $g(\vec{x}) = 1 + 9 \left(\sum_{i=2}^{D} (x_i^2 - x_1)^2 \right) /(D-1)$	concave *PF* nonlinear linkage $D = 50$ the *PS* is a bounded continuous conic: $x_D = \cdots = x_2 = \sqrt{x_1},\ 0 \le x_1 \le 1$

Table 6.2 (*Continued*)

Variables	Objectives	Characteristics
F6 $[0,1] \times [-1,1]^{D-1}$	$f_1(\vec{x}) = x_1$ $f_2(\vec{x}) = g(\vec{x})\left[1 - \sqrt{f_1(\vec{x})/g(\vec{x})}\right]$ $g(\vec{x}) = 1 + 9\left(\sum_{i=2}^{D}(x_i - \sin(2\pi x_1))^2\right)/(D-1)$	convex *PF* nonlinear linkage $D = 30$ the *PS* is a period continuous sine curve: $x_D = \cdots = x_2 = \sin(2\pi x_1),\ 0 \le x_1 \le 1$
F7 $[0,1] \times [-1,1]^{D-1}$	$f_1(\vec{x}) = x_1$ $f_2(\vec{x}) = g(\vec{x})[1 - \sqrt{f_1(\vec{x})/g(\vec{x})}]$ $g(\vec{x}) = 1 + 9\left(\sum_{i=2}^{D}(x_i - \cos(2\pi x_1))^2\right)/(D-1)$	convex *PF* nonlinear linkage $D = 30$ the *PS* is a period continuous cosine curve: $x_D = \cdots = x_2 = \cos(2\pi x_1),\ 0 \le x_1 \le 1$
F8 $[0,1] \times [-1,1]^{D-1}$	$f_1(\vec{x}) = x_1 + \frac{2}{|J_1|}\sum_{j\in J_1}(x_j - \sin(2\pi x_1))^2$ $f_2(\vec{x}) = 1 - \sqrt{x_1} + \frac{2}{|J_2|}\sum_{j\in J_2}(x_j - \sin(2\pi x_1))^2$ *where* $J_1 = \{j \mid j \text{ is odd and } 2 \le j \le D\}$ *and* $J_2 = \{j \mid j \text{ is even and } 2 \le j \le D\}$	convex *PF* nonlinear linkage $D = 30$ the *PS* is a period continuous sine curve: $x_D = \cdots = x_2 = \sin(2\pi x_1),\ 0 \le x_1 \le 1$
F9 $[0,1] \times [-1,1]^{D-1}$	$f_1(x) = x_1 + \frac{2}{|J_1|}\sum_{j\in J_1}(x_j - \cos(2\pi x_1))^2$ $f_2(x) = 1 - x_1^2 + \frac{2}{|J_2|}\sum_{j\in J_2}(x_j - \cos(2\pi x_1))^2$ *where* $J_1 = \{j \mid j \text{ is odd and } 2 \le j \le D\}$ *and* $J_2 = \{j \mid j \text{ is even and } 2 \le j \le D\}$	concave *PF* nonlinear linkage $D = 30$ the *PS* is a period continuous cosine curve: $x_D = \cdots = x_2 = \cos(2\pi x_1),\ 0 \le x_1 \le 1$

with IRM-MEDA. It is necessary to note that the *PS* structures of F6–F9 are more complex than those of the other five test instances and, therefore, F6–F9 pose a great challenge for both RM-MEDA and IRM-MEDA. The *PS* of these nine test instances is introduced in Table 6.2. In terms of the nature of variable linkages, they can be divided into two categories: test instances with linear variable linkages (i.e., F1–F3) and test instances with nonlinear variable linkages (i.e., F4–F9).

(2) Performance indicators

Two performance indicators are adopted to compare RM-MEDA and IRM-MEDA.

The first performance indicator measures the convergence speed of an algorithm. The hypervolume (HV) value [43] is calculated for this purpose. Let P^* be a set of points uniformly distributed on the true *PF*, and P a set of points which are the image of the nondominated individuals of the population in the objective space. In the experiments, the size of P^* is set to 300 and 800 for the biobjective optimization problems and for the triobjective optimization problems, respectively. The approach introduced by Nebro *et al.* [44] is used to determine the stopping condition. In [44], once the HV value of P attains or surpasses 98% of the HV value of P^*, i.e.,

$$\frac{HV(P)}{HV(P^*)} \geq 98\% \qquad (6.29)$$

the algorithm terminates and the number of function evaluations (FES) is recorded. In Eq. (6.29), $HV(P)$ denotes the hypervolume surrounded by P and a fixed reference point, and $HV(P^*)$ denotes the hypervolume surrounded by P^* and a fixed reference point. The mean and standard derivation of FES among 20 independent runs are used as the first performance indicator to measure the convergence speed of an algorithm on each test instance.

The second performance indicator measures the convergence quality of an algorithm. The inverted generational distance (IGD) is employed for this purpose, which is one of the most commonly used performance indicators in MOEAs and can be described as follows [41]:

$$D(P^*, P) = \frac{\sum_{v \in P^*} d(v, P)}{|P^*|} \qquad (6.30)$$

where $d(v, P)$ denotes the minimum Euclidean distance between v and the points in P. The IGD indicator computes the average distance from all members in the true *PF* to their nearest points in P. This performance indicator can measure both the diversity and the convergence of the population. $D(P^*, P) = 0$ indicates that all the points in P are on the true PF and cover the true PF uniformly.

(3) Experimental results

(i) *Convergence speed:* Firstly, the convergence speed of IRM-MEDA and RM-MEDA is compared in terms of the first performance indicator. The maximal number of FES is set to 30,000 for F1, F2, F4, F5, and F7, 50,000 for F6, F8, and F9, and 80,000 for F3. For test instances with two objectives, the population size is set to 100, and for test instances with three objectives, the population size is set to 200. A total of 20 independent runs have been performed for each test instance, and the average and standard deviation ("Mean FES" and "Std Dev") of the number of FES to satisfy Eq. (6.29) in each run have been recorded. Table 6.3 summarizes the results. Wilcoxon's rank sum test at a 0.05 significance level is conducted between IRM-MEDA and RM-MEDA. "+", "−", and "≈" denote that the performance of IRM-MEDA is better than, worse than, and similar to that of RM-MEDA, respectively. In addition, the *acceleration rate* (*AR*) is used to compare the convergence speed, which is defined as follows:

$$AR = \frac{AVE_{RM-MEDA} - AVE_{IRM-MEDA}}{AVE_{RM-MEDA}} \qquad (6.31)$$

Table 6.3 Results of IRM-MEDA and RM-MEDA in terms of the convergence speed.

Instance	IRM-MEDA Mean FES ± Std Dev $(\times 10^3)$	RM-MEDA Mean FES ± Std Dev $(\times 10^3)$	AR
F1	7.9833 ± 1.0371+	11.047 ± 1.0743	27.73%
F2	10.103 ± 1.3720+	17.788 ± 3.5596	43.20%
F3	24.613 ± 2.9569+	41.367 ± 12.291	40.50%
F4	13.152 ± 2.6990+	19.589 ± 4.2625	32.86%
F5	18.607 ± 2.9081+	28.677 ± 3.3935	35.12%
F6	26.297 ± 3.7591+	34.450 ± 3.3414	23.67%
F7	15.870 ± 2.7343+	21.117 ± 2.4598	24.85%
F8	27.613 ± 4.3017+	40.597 ± 6.0242	31.98%
F9	26.093 ± 4.4161+	36.893 ± 5.5490	29.27%
+	10		
−	0	Mean	31.67%
≈	0		

where $AVE_{RM-MEDA}$ and $AVE_{IRM-MEDA}$ denote the average number of FES provided by RM-MEDA and IRM-MEDA in Table 6.3, respectively.

As shown in Table 6.3, IRM-MEDA performs significantly better than RM-MEDA on all the test instances according to Wilcoxon's rank sum test. Furthermore, IRM-MEDA saves 20–50% FES compared with RM-MEDA, and the mean AR is 31.67%. The above discussion demonstrates that RRCO has the capability to significantly accelerate the convergence of RM-MEDA.

(ii) *Convergence quality:* As mentioned above, the IGD indicator is applied to measure both the convergence and diversity of the population. For each test instance, the same number of FES has been performed for both IRM-MEDA and RM-MEDA. Based on the results in Table 6.3, the maximal number of FES for each test instance is set to the mean number of FES required by IRM-MEDA to achieve 98% of the HV value of the true *PF*. A total of 20 independent runs are performed for IRM-MEDA and RM-MEDA, and the mean and standard deviation ("Mean Error" and "Std Dev") of the IGD indicator are obtained as shown in Table 6.4. In order to ensure the results with statistical confidence, Wilcoxon's rank sum test at a 0.05 significance level has also been performed.

Table 6.4 demonstrates that IRM-MEDA provides evidently lower IGD values than RM-MEDA in all the test instances. Moreover, the statistical test indicates that IRM-MEDA outperforms RM-MEDA in all the test instances.

Table 6.4   Results of IRM-MEDA and RM-MEDA in terms of the IGD indicator.

Instance	The number of FES	IRM-MEDA Mean Error ± Std Dev ($\times 10^{-3}$)	RM-MEDA Mean Error ± Std Dev ($\times 10^{-3}$)
F1	10000	5.8516 ± 1.3174+	10.790 ± 3.0714
F2	10000	7.7836 ± 3.4711+	17.583 ± 10.817
F3	25000	47.910 ± 2.4211+	51.048 ± 1.8803
F4	15000	12.578 ± 6.7505+	24.630 ± 14.534
F5	20000	8.0418 ± 1.5723+	28.764 ± 17.663
F6	30000	10.698 ± 5.7848+	24.848 ± 11.772
F7	18000	8.1101 ± 3.7198+	33.083 ± 21.231
F8	30000	12.772 ± 8.7324+	28.554 ± 16.414
F9	25000	7.7968 ± 2.7730+	28.982 ± 18.337
+	10		
−	0		
≈	0		

Therefore, RRCO is able to significantly improve the convergence quality of RM-MEDA.

6.4 An Application of EA for Descriptor Selection in Quantitative Structure–Activity/Property Relationship (QSAR/QSPR)

6.4.1 *Background*

Quantitative structure–activity/property relationship (QSAR/QSPR), an important area in the chemical and biomedical sciences, searches the relationship between compounds and corresponding biological activities or chemical properties [45]. In order to obtain this relationship, a variety of statistical learning methods have been proposed in QSAR/QSPR. In QSAR/QSPR studies, the chemical structure of compounds is represented by several descriptors, such as molecular constitutional, topological, shape, autocorrelation, and charge descriptors. In general, the number of descriptors is relatively larger than the number of involved biological activities. Some redundant, noisy, and irrelevant descriptors have a side effect on the QSAR/QSPR model development. Meanwhile, too many descriptors may result in either overfitting or a low correlation between structures and activities. Therefore, it is necessary to perform descriptor selection before the QSAR/QSPR model development. Actually, descriptor selection in QSAR/QSPR has the following advantages [46]: (1) increasing the prediction accuracy of the model, (2) facilitating the interpretability of the relationship between descriptors and activities, (3) balancing the effective number of degrees of freedom for calculating reliable estimates of the model's parameters, and (4) decreasing the time complexity of model development.

As the selection of informative descriptors has become one of the key steps for QSAR/QSPR model development, many descriptor selection methods have been presented. These methods can be briefly divided into two categories [47]: filtering methods and wrapper methods. Filtering methods assess the relevance of descriptors by only using the intrinsic properties of the data. In most cases, a descriptor relevance score is calculated and low scoring descriptors are removed. Afterwards, the resulting subset of descriptors is presented as the input of the modeling algorithm. The common disadvantages of filtering approaches are threefold: (1) they ignore the interaction with the algorithms, i.e., the search in the descriptor subset space is separated from the search in the hypothesis space, (2) most proposed methods are univariate, and (3) in these approaches, each descriptor is considered separately, thereby ignoring descriptor dependencies. The above disadvantages lead to worse prediction performance of the filtering approaches when compared to other types of descriptor selection methods. On the other hand, the wrapper methods consist of two components: the objective function and the optimization algorithm. The latter is used to select the optimal descriptor subset for the former. The advantages of wrapper approaches include the interaction between descriptor subset search and model selection, and the ability to take into account descriptor dependencies. The current popular optimization algorithms include simulated annealing algorithms and EAs. Among these optimization algorithms, EAs have become more and more popular to deal with the large space of descriptor subsets. Note, however, that most EAs do not exploit the model information to guide the evolution. As a result, it is still an open issue to incorporate the model information or prior information into EAs to search for the optimal descriptor subset quickly.

The above issue can be addressed by considering the interaction information between the model and EAs. Particle swarm optimization (PSO), one of the most representative paradigms of EAs, has been widely applied to select descriptors in QSAR/QSPR studies. Taking PSO-PLS [48] as an example, weighted sampling PSO-PLS (referred to as WS-PSO-PLS) has been developed to select the optimal descriptors subset in QSAR/QSPR model development [49].

6.4.2 *Weighted sampling PSO-PLS (WS-PSO-PLS)*

(1) The main idea of WS-PSO-PLS

PSO simulates the social behavior of organisms, such as bird flocking and fish schooling. In PSO, every particle in the swarm is a potential solution to an optimization problem. All particles "fly" through a D-dimension search space by learning their own experiences and the experiences of the entire swarm. PSO is initialized with a group of random particles, and each particle (also called an individual) has a velocity, a position, and a corresponding fitness evaluated by the fitness function. The velocity and the position of the ith particle are represented as $\vec{v}_i = (v_{i,1}, v_{i,2}, \ldots, v_{i,D})$ and $\vec{x}_i = (x_{i,1}, x_{i,2}, \ldots, x_{i,D})$, respectively. In addition, the best previous position of the ith particle is called the personal best and represented as $\vec{p}_i = (p_{i,1}, p_{i,2}, \ldots, p_{i,D})$, and the best previous position of all the particles in the swarm is called the global best and represented as $\vec{p}_g = (p_{g,1}, p_{g,2}, ..., p_{g,D})$. At each generation, the velocity of each particle is updated by making use of $\vec{p}_i$ and $\vec{p}_g$. Afterwards, it is necessary to update the position of each particle.

For a discrete optimization problem expressed in a binary notation, a particle moves in the search space, each dimension of which is restricted to "0" or "1". Under this condition, the jth dimension of the position of the ith particle (i.e., $x_{i,j}$) should be in either state "1" or state "0", and the corresponding velocity (i.e., $v_{i,j}$) represents the probability of $x_{i,j}$ being equal to "1". For descriptor selection in QSAR/QSPR, if there are D descriptors in the model development, then an individual in PSO will have D bits (i.e., D dimensions) correspondingly. If a bit of an individual is equal to "1", then the corresponding descriptor will be selected, otherwise the corresponding descriptor will not be selected. In WS-PSO-PLS, the discrete PSO developed in [48], which is proposed to select descriptors in MLR and PLS modeling for QSAR/QSPR, has been adopted. Just as in [48], the jth dimension of the velocity of the ith particle (i.e., $v_{i,j}$) is a random number between 0 and 1, and $x_{i,j}$ is updated by the following rules:

$$\text{if } (0 < v_{i,j} \leq a) \text{, then } x_{i,j}^{G+1} = x_{i,j}^{G} \tag{6.32}$$

$$\text{if } \left(a < v_{i,j} \leq \frac{1+a}{2}\right) \text{, then } x_{i,j}^{G+1} = p_{i,j}^{G} \tag{6.33}$$

$$\text{if } \left(\frac{1+a}{2} < v_{i,j} \leq 1\right) \text{, then } x_{i,j}^{G+1} = p_{g,j}^{G} \tag{6.34}$$

where a is a constant between 0 and 1, and G denotes the generation number.

In WS-PSO-PLS, the PLS model information is incorporated into the discrete PSO developed in [48] to guide the search of the optimal descriptor subset. Firstly, the PLS model is built with all the descriptors and the coefficients corresponding to each descriptor are normalized. Note that the importance of a descriptor can be determined by its normalized coefficient in the PLS model, i.e., the larger the normalized coefficient, the more important the descriptor in model development. Afterwards, *subsize* individuals (denoted as set A, $A = \{\vec{s}_i, i = 1, ..., subsize\}$) are produced via weighted sampling with the normalized coefficients. During the weighted sampling, the value of the normalized coefficient is regarded as the probability of a bit of an individual being "1", and as a result, the more important a descriptor, the higher probability it will be selected. Subsequently, the population is sorted according to the fitness in ascending order and *subsize* individuals (denoted as set B, $B = \{\vec{x}_i, i = 1, \dots, subsize\}$) with the worst quality are selected at each generation. Next, each dimension of an individual $\vec{s}_i$ in set A is utilized to replace the corresponding dimension of an individual $\vec{x}_i$ in set B by the following equation:

$$\text{if } rand > b, \text{ then } x_{i,j}^{G+1} = s_{i,j}^{G+1}, \quad i = 1, \dots, subsize, \ j = 1, \dots, D \quad (6.35)$$

where b is a constant between 0 and 1. By using Eq. (6.35), the quality of the individuals in set B could be improved by exploiting the information of some important descriptors. Moreover, how much the model information will be incorporated into the inferior individuals in the population is controlled through tuning the value of b. In WS-PSO-PLS, *subsize* is set to $\alpha * popsize$, where α is a constant in $(0,1)$ and *popsize* is the number of individuals in the population. It is necessary to point out that in the initial population, *subsize* individuals are generated based on the weighted sampling and the remaining individuals are generated randomly.

Next, an example is used to illustrate the weighted sampling. Suppose that there are four descriptors in QSAR/QSPR model development, which implies that an individual in PSO includes four bits (i.e., four dimensions) correspondingly. Suppose also that the vector of the normalized coefficients, which are obtained by building the PLS model with all the four descriptors, is equal to $p = [0.1, 0.5, 0.25, 0.15]$. Under this condition, the probability that the first bit of an individual is equal to "1" and that the first descriptor is selected is 0.1, the probability that the second bit of the individual is equal to "1" and that the second descriptor is selected is 0.5, and so on. Compared with the random sampling, in which each descriptor is selected with the same probability (i.e., 0.25), in the weighted sampling the important descriptors, which have relatively larger normalized coefficients, are more likely to be selected. As a result, high-quality individuals can be generated by weighted sampling, which is beneficial to improve the overall quality of the whole population. Such information is incorporated into each generation of PSO to improve the quality of individuals, thus guiding the evolution process.

According to the above introduction, it is clear that the PLS model coefficients can be utilized to improve the quality of the population in PSO. Consequently, WS-PLS-PSO has the capability to find the optimal descriptor subset promptly.

In WS-PSO-PLS, a mutation strategy has been proposed, the purpose of which is to prevent the population from getting trapped into a local optimum. The mutation strategy is implemented as follows. Firstly, $\lceil c * popsize \rceil$ individuals are chosen from the population randomly, where c is the mutation probability between 0 and 1. Then, a randomly selected bit of each individual is flipped from "1" to "0" or from "0" to "1".

(2) The fitness function

In order to evaluate the performance of each individual, the predictive Q^2 value [50] is used as the fitness function, which is defined as follows:

$$Q^2 = 1 - \frac{\sum_{i=1}^{n} (y_i - y_{pred})^2}{\sum_{i=1}^{n} (y_i - \bar{y})^2} \qquad (6.36)$$

where $y_i (i = 1, 2, 3, \ldots, n)$ is the observed values of activities, n is total number of compounds, $\bar{y}$ is the average of y_i, and y_{pred} is the value predicted by the PLS model via the five-fold cross-validation procedure. In the five-fold cross-validation procedure, the original dataset is randomly partitioned into five subsets with equal size. Afterwards, four of these five subsets are used as training data, and the remaining one is used as the validation data for testing the model. By doing so, a predicted result of the validation data is obtained. Subsequently, the other four subsets are used as training data, and the remaining one is used as the validation data for testing the model. Similarly, another predicted result is obtained. The above cross-validation procedure is repeated five times (i.e., five folds) and y_{pred} is the set of the five predicted results.

(3) The implementation of WS-PLS-PSO

The detailed steps of WS-PLS-PSO can be summarized as follows:

Step 1: Define the parameters (all the parameters are listed in Table 6.5), set the generation number $G = 1$, obtain the coefficients by establishing the PLS model with all the descriptors and normalize the above coefficients.

Step 2: Initialize the population (i.e., $\vec{x}_i$, $i = 1, \ldots, popsize$): $\alpha * popsize$ individuals are generated based on weighted sampling (sampling part), and the remaining individuals are generated randomly (random part). Next, initialize $\vec{p}_i$: $\vec{p}_i = \vec{x}_i$, $i = 1, \ldots, popsize$.

Step 3: Evaluate the population: for each individual $\vec{x}_i$, the bits, one of which is equal to "1", are chosen. Then, the corresponding descriptors constitute a subset. Subsequently, the PLS regression is applied to the subset to calculate the fitness Q^2. Clearly, the larger the value of Q^2, the better the individual. Afterwards, initialize $\vec{p}_g$: $\vec{p}_g$ is equal to the individual with the maximum Q^2.

Step 4: Update each individual according to Eqs. (6.32)–(6.34), perform the mutation strategy, and evaluate the population. Then, find *subsize* individuals with the worst quality in the population, update these individuals according to Eq. (6.35), and evaluate these *subsize* updated individuals.

Step 5: Update $\vec{p}_i$ and $\vec{p}_g$ according to the following rules:

$$\text{If } Q^2\left(\vec{x}_i^{G+1}\right) > Q^2\left(\vec{p}_i^{G}\right), \text{ then } \vec{p}_i^{G+1} = \vec{x}_i^{G+1} \qquad (6.37)$$

$$\text{If } Q^2\left(\vec{x}_i^{G+1}\right) > Q^2\left(\vec{p}_g^{G}\right), \text{ then } \vec{p}_s^{G+1} = \vec{x}_i^{G+1} \qquad (6.38)$$

Step 6: If the stopping criterion is satisfied, then stop and output $\vec{p}_g$, otherwise let $G = G+1$ and go to **Step 4**.

6.4.3 *Experimental study*

(1) QSAR/QSPR datasets

Three QSAR/QSPR datasets are used to demonstrate the effectiveness of WS-PLS-PSO. The first is the artemisinin dataset which consists of 211 artemisinin analogues [51]. Due to the fact that this dataset has many enantiomeric pairs of activities, the element in each enantiomeric pair with the smaller logarithm of the relative activity is used as the output variable (referred to as log RA), and the other element is removed [52]. Therefore, the artemisinin dataset used has 178 compounds. As pointed out in [53], several structurally diverse compounds have the same log RA (i.e., −4.0), which makes the model development more difficult. For each compound, two-dimensional (2D) descriptors are calculated using the ChemoPy software package [53]. Note that before further descriptor selection by WS-PSO-PLS, two descriptor pre-selection steps are performed to eliminate some uninformative descriptors: (i) remove the descriptors, the variance of which is near zero or zero, and (ii) if the correlation of the two descriptors is larger than 0.95, then remove one of them. Finally, 89 molecular descriptors are obtained for representing compounds in the artemisinin dataset, and these molecular descriptors are used as inputs for QSAR/QSPR model development.

The second is the BZR dataset. In the BZR dataset, benzodiazepines are a class of psychoactive drugs which are used to treat anxiety, insomnia, and a range of other circumstances. At the same time, benzodiazepines exhibit sedative, hypnotic, anti-anxiety, anticonvulsant, and muscle relaxant properties, and act via the benzodiazepine receptors (BZR), which have been extensively researched in QSAR/QSPR. The BZR dataset is presented in [54]. It contains 163 compounds and 75 2.5D descriptors consisting of S_ sCH3, S_ dssC, CHI-0, etc.

The third is the Selwood dataset [55], which has become a benchmark to evaluate the performance of different methods and has been well studied in QSAR/QSPR. It consists of 29 compounds, 53 descriptors, and a set of corresponding antifilarial antimycin activities expressed as $-\log(IC50)$. The molecular descriptors in the Selwood dataset include partial atomic charges for atoms 1–10 (ATCH1–ATCH10), dipole vector (DIPV_ X, DIPV_ Y, and DIPV_ Z), dipole moment (DIPMOM), etc.

(2) Results and discussion

WS-PSO-PLS includes two main features: (i) the mutation strategy, and (ii) introducing the PLS model coefficients into PSO, including the first generation and the subsequent evolution process. In order to demonstrate the effectiveness of WS-PSO-PLS, five different methods are employed for comparison on the three datasets. These methods include: (i) PLS, (ii) PSO-PLS [48], (iii) PSO-PLS-1, which is formed by combining the original PSO-PLS with the mutation strategy, (iv) WS-PSO-PLS-1, the difference between it and PSO-PLS-1 lies in the fact that WS-PSO-PLS-1 only incorporates the PLS model information into the population at the first generation, and (v) WS-PSO-PLS-2, the difference between it and PSO-PLS-1 lies in the fact that WS-PSO-PLS-2 incorporates the PLS model information into the population throughout the search process except for the first generation.

For comparing the performance of the involved methods, three performance metrics have been chosen: Q^2, the root mean square error from five-fold cross-validation (denoted as *RMSECV*), and the number of selected descriptors (denoted as *NSD*). All the data were firstly auto-scaled to have zero mean and unit variance before modeling. Note that in PLS, all descriptors were directly used for the model development. The maximum number

Artificial Intelligence: From Beginning to Date

Table 6.5   The parameter values.

Parameters / Methods	PSO-PLS	PSO-PLS-1	WS-PSO-PLS-1	WS-PSO-PLS-2	WS-PSO-PLS
Population size: 50	✓	✓	✓	✓	✓
Total function evaluations: 10000	✓	✓	✓	✓	✓
Learning rate a: 0.5	✓	✓	✓	✓	✓
Mutation probability c: 0.05		✓	✓	✓	✓
Proportion of weighted sampling: 0.5			✓	✓	✓
Learning rate b: 0.8				✓	✓

of latent components was set to 20 and the optimal number of latent components was determined by five-fold cross-validation. Owing to the randomness of PSO, the results may be different for different experiments. Thus, all the methods were implemented 100 times to obtain the statistical results. Moreover, Wilcoxon's rank sum test at a 0.05 significance level was used to check the statistical significance between two methods. The parameter settings for all the involved methods have been listed in Table 6.5, and the results have been presented in Table 6.6.

The first observation from Table 6.6 is that when using all the descriptors in PLS, the mean Q^2 is 0.60, 0.40, and 0.24 and the mean *RMSECV* is 0.99, 0.85, and 0.65 for the artemisinin, BZR, and selwood datasets, respectively. In contrast, the average number of the selected descriptors in PSO-PLS is drastically decreased. However, under this condition the mean Q^2 is 0.7476, 0.5396, and 0.8685 and the mean *RMSECV* is 0.7875, 0.7451, and 0.2668 for the artemisinin, BZR, and selwood datasets, respectively. The above results suggest that PSO-PLS with a lower number of descriptors is significantly better than PLS, which verifies the need to perform descriptor selection before the QSAR/QSPR model development.

From Table 6.6, it can be seen that PSO-PLS-1 performs better than PSO-PLS in terms of all the performance metrics on the three datasets. For example, with respect to the artemisinin dataset, the mean Q^2 is 0.7545 versus 0.7476, the mean *RMSECV* is 0.7716 versus 0.7875, and the mean *NSD* is 35.05 versus 39.04. As pointed out previously, PSO-PLS-1 is a combination of PSO-PLS with the mutation strategy. Therefore, the mutation strategy can be adopted to enhance the performance of PSO-PLS based on the results.

Table 6.6   Results on the three datasets.

Dataset	Methods	Mean $Q^2 \pm$ Standard Deviation	Mean $RMSECV \pm$ Standard Deviation	Mean $NSD \pm$ Standard Deviation
Artemisinin	PLS	0.60	0.99	89
	PSO-PLS[a]	0.7476 ± 0.0093	0.7875 ± 0.0145	39.04 ± 4.40
	PSO-PLS-1	0.7545 ± 0.0107	0.7716 ± 0.0168	35.05 ± 4.19
	WS-PSO-PLS-1	0.7601 ± 0.0090	0.7686 ± 0.0130	34.45 ± 4.17
	WS-PSO-PLS-2	0.7622 ± 0.0075	0.7646 ± 0.0119	34.34 ± 3.98
	WS-PSO-PLS[b]	0.7744 ± 0.0067	0.7447 ± 0.0110	32.24 ± 3.55
BZR	PLS	0.4	0.85	75
	PSO-PLS[a]	0.5396 ± 0.0092	0.7451 ± 0.0075	32.35 ± 4.02
	PSO-PLS-1	0.5489 ± 0.0131	0.7330 ± 0.0099	29.14 ± 3.68
	WS-PSO-PLS-1	0.5585 ± 0.0096	0.7296 ± 0.0079	27.42 ± 3.14
	WS-PSO-PLS-2	0.5588 ± 0.0095	0.7298 ± 0.0084	28.34 ± 2.93
	WS-PSO-PLS[b]	0.5632 ± 0.0073	0.7258 ± 0.0061	26.96 ± 2.74
Selwood	PLS	0.24	0.65	53
	PSO-PLS[a]	0.8685 ± 0.0337	0.2668 ± 0.0331	20.43 ± 2.79
	PSO-PLS-1	0.8917 ± 0.0334	0.2416 ± 0.0340	18.74 ± 3.07
	WS-PSO-PLS-1	0.8986 ± 0.0228	0.2347 ± 0.0259	17.89 ± 3.01
	WS-PSO-PLS-2	0.9153 ± 0.0122	0.2125 ± 0.0152	17.34 ± 2.34
	WS-PSO-PLS[b]	0.9200 ± 0.0130	0.2090 ± 0.0170	16.44 ± 2.79

The results of Wilcoxon's rank sum test at a 0.05 significance level between "a" and "b" in terms of the mean Q^2 are $p = 4.46 \times 10^{-33}$, 1.11×10^{-30}, and 9.90×10^{-29} on the artemisinin, BZR, and Selwood datasets, respectively.

The PLS model information has been incorporated into WS-PSO-PLS-1 only at the first generation, and PSO-PLS-1 does not use such model information. Compared with PSO-PLS-1, the mean Q^2 of WS-PSO-PLS-1 increases by 0.74%, 1.75%, and 0.77%, the mean $RMSECV$ of WS-PSO-PLS-1 decreases by 0.39%, 0.46%, and 2.86%, and the mean NSD of WS-PSO-PLS-1 decreases by 1.71%, 5.90%, and 4.54% for the artemisinin, BZR, and selwood datasets, respectively, as shown in Table 6.6. Thus, the incorporation of the PLS model information at the first generation does improve the performance of PSO-PLS-1. In order to further compare WS-PSO-PLS-1 with PSO-PLS-1, Figure 6.13(a) shows the mean Q^2 of all individuals at the first generation for these two methods on the artemisinin dataset. From Figure 6.13(a), WS-PSO-PLS-1 outperforms PSO-PLS-1 for the first half of the population, while the performance of WS-PSO-PLS-1 and PSO-PLS-1 is nearly the same for the remaining half of the population at the first generation. Note that the first 50% individuals in the population

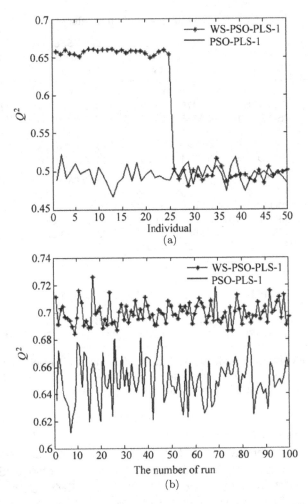

Figure 6.13   (a) The mean Q^2 of the population at the first generation for the artemisinin dataset. (b) The initial Q^2 of PSO-PLS-1 and WS-PSO-PLS-1 for the artemisinin dataset.

of WS-PSO-PLS-1 are generated by weighted sampling while the remaining 50% individuals are generated randomly. The above phenomenon verifies that the model information can be exploited to enhance the quality of the population even in the initialization. Moreover, the superiority of WS-PSO-PLS-1 can also be demonstrated by the initial Q^2 in each run for the artemisinin dataset (see Figure 6.13(b)). It is not difficult to understand since the initial individuals are of higher quality by weighted sampling.

As shown in Table 6.6, WS-PSO-PLS-2 is better than PSO-PLS-1 in terms of all the performance metrics on the three datasets. As mentioned earlier, the difference between them lies in the fact that WS-PSO-PLS-2 incorporates the PLS model information into the population after the first generation. As a result, WS-PSO-PLS-2 benefits from the PLS model information during the evolution.

Based on the above experiments, WS-PSO-PLS with a lower number of selected descriptors can achieve the best performance.

6.5 Summary

This chapter first introduces the basic idea, research areas, and paradigms of evolutionary algorithms (EAs). Moreover, one of the most popular EA paradigms, i.e., differential evolution (DE), is introduced in detail. Subsequently, this chapter introduces how to solve constrained optimization problems (COPs) by EAs. After a thorough analysis of the methods based on multi-objective optimization techniques, a classic multi-objective optimization-based EA (called CW) is introduced. This chapter also introduces how to solve multi-objective optimization problems (MOPs) by EAs. A classic regularity model-based multi-objective estimation of distribution algorithm, referred to as RM-MEDA, is introduced. After analyzing the drawback of the clustering process in the modeling suggested by RM-MEDA, an improved RM-MEDA, which incorporates a reducing redundant cluster operator (RRCO) to dynamically modify the number of clusters during the evolution, is introduced. Finally, this chapter introduces an application of EA for descriptor selection in quantitative structure–activity/property relationship (QSAR/QSPR), which is an important research area in the chemical and biomedical sciences.

References

1. Kirkpatrick, S., Gelatt, C. and Vecchi, M. (1983). Optimization by simulated annealing, *Science*, 22, 671–680.
2. Battiti, R. and Tecchiolli, G. (1994). The reactive tabu search, *ORSA J. Comput.*, 6, 126–140.
3. Bäck, T., Fogel, D.B. and Michalewicz, Z. (1997). *Handbook of Evolutionary Computation*, (Oxford University Press).
4. De Jong, K.A. (2006). *Evolutionary Computation: A Unified Approach*, (MIT Press, Cambridge, MA).

5. He, J. and Yao, X. (2002). From an individual to a population: an analysis of the first hitting time of population-based evolutionary algorithms, *IEEE Trans. Evol. Comput.*, *6*, 495–511.

6. Holland, J. (1975). *Adaptation in Natural and Artificial Systems*, (University of Michigan Press, Ann Arbor, MI).

7. De Jong, K. (1975). An analysis of the behavior of a class of genetic adaptive systems, Doctoral Dissertation, (University of Michigan, Ann Arbor, MI).

8. Fogel, L.J., Owens, A.J. and Walsh, M.J. (1966). *Artificial Intelligence through Simulated Evolution*, (John Wiley & Sons, New York).

9. Rechenberg, I. (1971). Evolutions strategie — Optimierung Technischer Systeme nach Prinzipien der Biologischen Evolution, PhD Thesis, (Technical University of Berlin).

10. Schwefel, H.P. (1981). *Numerical Optimization of Computer Models*, (Wiley, Chichester, UK).

11. Koza, J.R. (1992). *Genetic Programming: On the Programming of Computers by Means of Natural Evolution*, (MIT Press, Cambridge, MA).

12. Dorigo, M. (1992). *Apprendimento automatico, ed algoritmi basati su metafora naturale*, (Politecnico di Milano).

13. Robert, R.G. (1994). An introduction to cultural algorithms, *Proceedings of the 3rd Annual Conference on Evolutionary Programming*, World Scientific Publishing, pp. 131–136.

14. Kennedy, J. and Eberhart, R. (1995). Particle swarm optimization, *Proceedings of the 4th IEEE International Conference on Neural Networks*, IEEE Service Center, pp. 1942–1948.

15. Storn, R. and Price, K. (1995). Differential evolution — A simple and efficient adaptive scheme for global optimization over continuous spaces, *Berkeley, CA, Tech. Rep.* TR-95-012.

16. Storn, R. and Price, K. (1995). Differential evolution — A simple and efficient heuristic for global optimization over continuous spaces, *Journal of Global Optimization*, *11*, 341–359.

17. De Castro, L.N. and Timmis, J. (1996). *Artificial Immune Systems: A New Computational Intelligence Approach*, (Springer-Verlag).

18. Shen, W.M., Lu, Y. and Will, P. (2000). Hormone-based control for self-reconfigurable robots, *Proceedings of International Conference on Autonomous Agents*, Barcelona, Spain, pp. 1–8.

19. Geem, Z.W., Kim, J.H. and Loganathan, G.V. (2001). A new heuristic optimization algorithm: harmony search, *Simulation*, *76*, 60–68.

20. Passino, K.M. (2002). Biomimicry of bacterial foraging for distributed optimization and control, *IEEE Control Systems Magazine*, *22*, 52–67.

21. Ong, Y.S. and Keane, A.J. (2004). Meta-Lamarckian learning in memetic algorithm, *IEEE Transactions on Evolutionary Computation*, *8*, 99–110.

22. Loengarov, A. and Tereshko, V. (2008). Phase transitions and bistability in honeybee foraging dynamics, *Artificial Life*, *14*, 111–120.

23. Simon, D. (2008). Biogeography-based optimization, *IEEE Transactions on Evolutionary Computation*, *12*, 702–713.

24. He, S., Wu, Q.H. and Saunders, J.R. (2009). Group search optimizer — an optimization algorithm inspired by animal searching behaviour, *IEEE Trans. Evol. Comput.*, *13*, 973–990.

25. Michalewicz, Z. and Schoenauer, M. (1996). Evolutionary algorithm for constrained parameter optimization problems, *Evolutionary Computation*, *4*, 1–23.

26. Coello Coello, C.A. (2002). Theoretical and numerical constraint-handling techniques used with evolutionary algorithms: A survey of the state of the art, *Computer Methods in Applied Mechanics And Engineering*, *191*, 1245–1287.

27. Wang, Y., Cai, Z., Zhou, Y. and Xiao, C. (2009). Constrained optimization evolutionary algorithms, *Journal of Software.*, *20*, 11–29. (in Chinese with English abstract)

28. Farmani, R. and Wright, J.A. (2003). Self-Adaptive fitness formulation for constrained optimization, *IEEE Transactions on Evolutionary Computation*, *7*, 445–455.

29. Runarsson, T.P. and Yao, X. (2000). Stochastic ranking for constrained evolutionary optimization, *IEEE Transactions on Evolutionary Computation*, *4*, 284–294.

30. Deb, K. (2000). An efficient constraint handling method for genetic algorithms, *Computer Methods in Applied Mechanics And Engineering*, *86*, 311–338.

31. Mezura-Montes, E. and Coello Coello, C.A. (2003). A numerical comparison of some multiobjective-based techniques to handle constraints in genetic algorithms, *Technical Report*, EVOCINV-01.

32. Mezura-Montes, E. and Coello Coello, C.A. (2003). Multiobjective-based concepts to handle constraints in evolutionary algorithms, *Proceedings of the 4th Mexican International Conference on Computer Science (ENC'2003)*, IEEE Press, pp. 192–199.

33. Runarsson, T.P. and Yao, X. (2005). Search biases in constrained evolutionary optimization, *IEEE Transactions on Systems, Man, and Cybernetics: Systems, Part C*, 35, pp. 233–243.

34. Deb, K. (2001). *Multiobjective Optimization Using Evolutionary Algorithms*, (Wiley, Chichester).

35. Cai, Z. and Wang, Y. (2006). A multiobjective optimization-based evolutionary algorithm for constrained optimization, *IEEE Transactions on Evolutionary Computation*, *10*, 658–675.

36. Mezura-Montes, E. and Coello Coello, C.A. (2005). A simple multimembered evolution strategy to solve constrained optimization problems, *IEEE Transactions on Evolutionary Computation*, *9*, 1–17.

37. Deb, K., Pratab, A., Agrawal, S. and Meyarivan, T. (2002). A fast and elitist nondominated sorting genetic algorithm for multi-objective optimization: NSGA-II, *IEEE Transactions on Evolutionary Computation*, *6*, 182–197.

38. Zitzler, E., Laumanns, M. and Thiele, L. (2001). SPEA2: Improving the strength Pareto evolutionary algorithm for multiobjective optimization, *Proceedings of the EUROGEN 2001 — Evolutionary Methods for Design, Optimization and Control with Applications to Industrial Problem*, pp. 95–100.

39. Zitzler, E., Brockhoff, D. and Thiele, L. (2007). The hypervolume indicator revisited: on the design of Pareto-compliant indicators via weighted integration, *Proceedings of the Conference on Evolutionary Multi-Criterion Optimization*, Berlin, pp. 862–876.

40. Zhang, Q. and Li, H. (2007). MOEA/D: A multi-objective evolutionary algorithm based on decomposition, *IEEE Transactions on Evolutionary Computation*, *11*, 712–731.

41. Zhang, Q., Zhou, A. and Jin, Y. (2008). RM-MEDA: A regularity model based multiobjective estimation of distribution algorithm, *IEEE Transactions on Evolutionary Computation*, *12*, 41–63.

42. Wang, Y., Xiang, J. and Cai, Z. (2012). A regularity model-based multiobjective estimation of distribution algorithm with reducing redundant cluster operator, *Applied Soft Computing*, *12*, 3526–3538.

43. Zitzler, E. and Thiele, L. (1999). Multiobjective evolutionary algorithms: a comparative case study and the strength Pareto approach, *IEEE Transactions on Evolutionary Computation*, *3*, 257–271.

44. Nebro, A.J., Durillo, J.J., Coello Coello, C.A., Luna, F. and Alba, E. (2008). Design issues in a study of convergence speed in multi-objective metaheuristics, *Proceedings of the Conference on Parallel Problem Solving from Nature, PPSN X*, pp. 763–772.

45. Nantasenamat, C., Isarankura-Na-Ayudhya, C., Naenna, T. and Prachayasittikul, V. (2009). A practical overview of quantitative structure–activity relationship, *EXCLI Journal*, *8*, 1611–2156.

46. Shahlaei, M. (2013). Descriptor selection methods in quantitative structure–activity relationship studies: A review study, *Chemical Reviews*, *113*, 8093–8103.

47. Dutta, D., Guha, R., Wild, D. and Chen, T. (2007). Ensemble feature selection: consistent descriptor subsets for multiple QSAR models, *Journal of Chemical Information and Modeling*, 47, 989–997.

48. Shen, Q., Jiang, J., Jiao, C., Shen, G. and Yu, R. (2004). Modified particle swarm optimization algorithm for variable selection in MLR and PLS modeling: QSAR studies of antagonism of angiotensin II antagonists, *European Journal of Pharmaceutical Sciences*, *22*, 145–152.

49. Wang, Y., Huang, J., Zhou, N., Cao, D., Dong, J. and Li, H. (2015). Incorporating PLS model information into particle swarm optimization for descriptor selection in QSAR/QSPR, *Journal of Chemometrics*, *29*, 627–636.

50. Cao, D., Liu, S., Fan, L. and Liang, Y. (2014). QSAR analysis of the effects of OATP1B1 transporter by structurally diverse natural products using a particle swarm optimization-combined multiple linear regression approach, *Chemometrics and Intelligent Laboratory Systems*, *130*, 84–90.

51. Litina, D.H. and Hansch, C. (1994). Quantitative structure–activity relationships of the benzodiazepines. A review and reevaluation, *Chemical Reviews*, *6*, 1483–1505.

52. Lu, A., Liu, B., Liu, H. and Zhou, J. (2004). 3D-QSAR study of benzodiazepines at five recombinant GABAA/benzodiazepine receptor subtypes, *Acta Physico-Chimica Sinica*, *20*, 488–493.

53. Cao, D., Xu, Q., Hu, Q. and Liang, Y. (2013). ChemoPy: freely available python package for computational biology and chemoinformatics, *Bioinformatics*, *29*, 1092–1094.

54. Haefely, W., Kyburz, E., Gerecke, M. and Mohler, H. (1985). Recent advances in the molecular pharmacology of benzodiazepine receptors and in the structure–activity relationships of their agonists and antagonists, *Advances in Drug Research*, *14*, 165–322.

55. Selwood, D.L., Livingstone, D.J., Comley, J.C., O'Dowd, A.B., Hudson, A.T., Jackson, P., Jandu, K.S., Rose, V.S. and Stables, J.N. (1990). Structure-activity relationships of antifilarial antimycin analogues: a multivariate pattern recognition study, *Journal of Medicinal Chemistry*, *33*, 136–142.

Data-based Machine Learning

7

The core of big data is to use the value of data, and machine learning is a key technology to use the value of data. The prosperity of machine learning is also inseparable from the help of big data. Big data and machine learning are mutually reinforcing and interdependent.

This chapter mainly introduces data-based machine learning. In the practical sense, machine learning is a method that uses data to train a model and then uses the model to predict. This chapter mainly describes some basic concepts of data-based machine learning methods, including linear regression, decision trees, support vector machines (SVMs), integrated learning (including Adaboost and random forest), k-means clustering, and deep learning.

7.1 Linear Regression

Definition 7.1 (Linear regression). Linear regression is a regression analysis method. Regression analysis uses equations to express the relationship between the variable of interest (the dependent variable) and a series of related variables (independent variables). Its purpose is to estimate the approximate functional relationship between the independent variables and the dependent variable. If the function is a linear function, it is called linear regression.

(1) Basic form of a linear model

The simplest linear regression model is a linear combination of input variables. For an input containing n dimensions, the linear model is

$$f(x) = w_1 x_1 + w_2 x_2 + \cdots + w_n x_n + b \tag{7.1}$$

The general vector form is the following:

$$f(x) = w^T x + b \tag{7.2}$$

In this formula, $w = (w_1, w_2, \ldots, w_n)$, $x = (x_1 x_2, \ldots, x_n)$, is an example given by n attributes, where x_i is x in the i-th value of each attribute.

After learning the w and b, the model can be determined. Among them, w intuitively expressed the importance of each attribute in the prediction, so the linear model has a good interpretability.

(2) Linear regression measures

Given a dataset

$$D = \{(x_1, y_1), (x_2, y_2), \ldots, (x_m, y_m)\}, x_i = (x_{i1}; x_{i2}; \ldots; x_{in})$$

where $y_i \in R$. Linear regression will learn a linear model to predict the real output value, $f(x_i) = w^T x_i + b$, as accurately as possible, and make $f(x_i)$ as close to y_i as possible.

For unary linear regression, the key to learning w and b is to measure the difference between $f(x_i)$ and y_i. In the regression task, the mean square error is commonly used as a performance metric:

$$E(f; D) = \frac{1}{m} \sum_{i=1}^{m} (f(x_i) - y_i)^2 \tag{7.3}$$

Definition 7.2 (Least squares). The method of solving the model based on the minimization of the mean square error is called the least square method [14]. In linear regression, the least square method tries to find a straight line so that the sum of the Euclidean distances from all samples to the straight line is minimized.

Determining w and b is the process of minimizing

$$E_{(w,b)} = \sum_{i=1}^{m} (f(x_i) - y_i)^2 = \sum_{i=1}^{m} (y_i - wx_i - b)^2$$

which is called the least square parameter estimation of linear regression.

In order to minimize $E_{(w,b)}$, first derive w and b, respectively:

$$\frac{\partial E_{(w,b)}}{\partial w} = 2 \left(w \sum_{i=1}^{m} x_i^2 - \sum_{i=1}^{m} (y_i - b) x_i \right) \tag{7.4}$$

$$\frac{\partial E_{(w,b)}}{\partial b} = 2 \left(mb - \sum_{i=1}^{m} (y_i - w x_i) \right) \tag{7.5}$$

Let $\frac{\partial E_{(w,b)}}{\partial w} = 0$ and $\frac{\partial E_{(w,b)}}{\partial b} = 0$, and be solved to get w and b:

$$w = \frac{\sum_{i=1}^{m} y_i (x_i - \bar{x})}{\sum_{i=1}^{m} x_i^2 - \frac{1}{m} \left(\sum_{i=1}^{m} x_i \right)^2} \tag{7.6}$$

$$b = \frac{1}{m} \sum_{i=1}^{m} (y_i - w x_i) \tag{7.7}$$

where $\bar{x} = \frac{1}{m} \sum_{i=1}^{m} x_i$ is the mean value of x.

For multiple linear regression, each sample is described by n attributes. Similarly, the least squares method can be used to estimate the parameters of w and b. To facilitate the derivation, write w and b in a vector form $\hat{w} = (w; b)$. Correspondingly, the dataset D is a matrix X of size $m \times (n + 1)$, i.e.,

$$X = \begin{pmatrix} x_{11} & \cdots & x_{1n} & 1 \\ \vdots & \ddots & \vdots & 1 \\ x_{m1} & \cdots & x_{mn} & 1 \end{pmatrix} = \begin{pmatrix} x_1^T & 1 \\ \vdots & \vdots \\ x_m^T & 1 \end{pmatrix} \tag{7.8}$$

The label is also written in vector form $y = (y_1; y_2; \ldots; y_m)$. If you want to determine w and b to determine the linear model, you must minimize the mean square error; that is, you should minimize $E_{\hat{w}} = (y - X\hat{w})^T (y - X\hat{w})$.

Similarly, by derivation of $\hat{w}$, we get the following:

$$\frac{\partial E_{\hat{w}}}{\partial \hat{w}} = 2X^T (X\hat{w} - y) \tag{7.9}$$

Let $\frac{\partial E_{\hat{w}}}{\partial \hat{w}} = 0$, $\hat{w}$ can be solved. At this time, you need to consider whether $X^T X$ is a full rank. When $X^T X$ is a full rank matrix or a positive definite matrix, let $\frac{\partial E_{\hat{w}}}{\partial \hat{w}} = 0$, then you can get

$$\hat{w} = (X^T X)^{-1} X^T y \qquad (7.10)$$

where $(X^T X)^{-1}$ is the inverse matrix of $(X^T X)$; let $\hat{x}_i = (x_i, 1)$, then the final multiple linear regression model is

$$f(\hat{x}_i) = \hat{x}_i^T (X^T X)^{-1} X^T y \qquad (7.11)$$

However, in actual calculations, $X^T X$ is usually not a full rank matrix. For example, when the number of independent variables is greater than the number of samples, it will cause the number of columns in the matrix X to be greater than the number of rows, and thus $X^T X$ is not full rank. At this time, multiple solutions $\hat{w}$ can be obtained, all of which can minimize the mean square error. As to which solution will be selected in the end, it will be determined by the preference of the learning algorithm.

The application of linear regression is divided into the following two categories [9]: (1) If the goal is prediction, linear regression can fit a prediction model. After completing such a model, for a new value, you can use the model to predict a corresponding value; (2) given a variable y and variables $x_1, x_2, \ldots, x_n$, these variables may be related to y, linear regression can be used to quantify the strength of the correlation between y and x_j, and to evaluate x_j that is not related to y. Linear regression is simpler and more convenient when analyzing multi-factor models. It can accurately measure the degree of correlation between various factors and the degree of regression fitting to improve the prediction effect.

7.2 Decision Tree

7.2.1 *Decision tree model and learning*

(1) Decision tree model

Decision tree is a basic classification method. In learning, the training data sample set is used to establish a decision tree model according to the principle of minimizing the loss function. When predicting new data samples, as long as the learned decision tree model is used, it can be classified [28]. Decision tree learning mainly includes three steps: feature selection, tree generation, and pruning of the tree.

A decision tree is a tree structure in which each internal node represents a judgment on an attribute, each branch represents the output of a judgment result, and finally each leaf node represents a classification result.

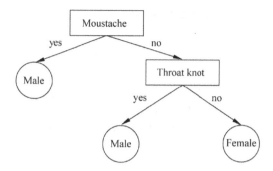

Figure 7.1   Decision tree model.

Figure 7.1 is a schematic diagram of a decision tree, where the boxes represent internal nodes and the circles represent leaf nodes.

(2) Decision tree learning

Decision tree learning algorithm is the process of recursively selecting the optimal feature, then dividing the training dataset based on that feature, and finally getting a good classification result for the sub-dataset. The resulting decision tree may be a good classification of the training dataset, but it may not be a good classification of the new test data, so the generated decision tree needs to be pruned to allow for a better generalization. So far, we have seen that the decision tree learning algorithm includes feature selection, decision tree generation and the pruning process.

7.2.2 *Feature selection*

Feature selection is the process of selecting the features that have a good classification effect on the training dataset in order to improve the efficiency of decision tree learning. The general feature selection criterion is information gain or information gain ratio.

(1) Definition of information gain

First, the definitions of entropy and conditional entropy are given below:

Definition 7.3 (Entropy). Entropy represents a measure of the uncertainty of random variables. Let X be a discrete random variable with a finite number of values, and its probability distribution is

$$P(X = x_i) = p_i, i = 1, 2, \ldots, n \tag{7.12}$$

Then the entropy of the random variable X is defined as

$$H(X) = -\sum_{i=1}^{n} p_i \log p_i \qquad (7.13)$$

Conditional entropy $H(Y|X)$ represents the uncertainty of a random variable Y under the condition that the random variable X is known. There is a random variable (X, Y) whose joint probability distribution is

$$P(X = x_i, Y = y_j) = p_{ij}, i = 1, 2, \ldots, n; j = 1, 2, \ldots, m \qquad (7.14)$$

Definition 7.4 (Conditional entropy). Conditional entropy is defined as the mathematical expectation of the entropy of the conditional probability distribution of Y under given conditions X.

$$H(Y|X) = \sum_{i=1}^{n} p_i H(Y|X = x_i) \qquad (7.15)$$

Among them, $p_i = P(X = x_i), i = 1, 2, \ldots, n$.

When the probabilities in entropy and conditional entropy are obtained from data estimation (especially maximum likelihood estimation), the corresponding entropy and conditional entropy are called empirical entropy and empirical conditional entropy, respectively.

Definition 7.5 (Information gain). Information gain is the degree to which the uncertainty of the category Y is reduced when the feature information A is known. The information gain $g(D, A)$ of the feature A on the training dataset D is defined as the difference between the experience entropy $H(D)$ of the set D and the experience conditional entropy $H(D|A)$ under the given conditions D, of the feature A, namely

$$g(D, A) = H(D) - H(D|A) \qquad (7.16)$$

The difference between entropy $H(Y)$ and conditional entropy $H(Y|X)$ is called mutual information, and the information gain learned by the decision tree is mutual information. In general, features with large information gain have stronger classification capabilities. Therefore, the method of using information gain for feature selection is to calculate the information gain of each feature for the training dataset or subset D, and then select the feature with the largest information gain by comparison.

(2) Calculation of information gain

Let D be the training dataset and $|D|$ represents the number of samples. There are K classes $C_k, k = 1, 2, \ldots, K$, $\{C_k\}$ is the number of samples belonging to the class C_k, there is $\sum_{k=1}^{K} |C_k| = |D|$. Suppose the feature A has n values $\{a_1, a_2, \ldots, a_n\}$; according to the value, D will be divided into $D_1, D_2, \ldots, D_n$, and $|D_i|$ is the number of samples D_i; there are $\sum_{i=1}^{n} |D_i| = |D|$. The sample set belonging to the class C_k in the subset D_i is D_{ik}, i.e., $D_{ik} = D_i \cap C_k$, and $|D_{ik}|$ is the number of samples of D_{ik}. Then the information gain is calculated as follows:

First calculate the empirical entropy $H(D)$ of the dataset D

$$H(D) = -\sum_{k=1}^{K} \frac{|C_k|}{|D|} \log_2 \frac{|C_k|}{|D|} \tag{7.17}$$

Then, calculate the empirical conditional entropy $H(D|A)$ of the feature A to the dataset D

$$H(D|A) = \sum_{i=1}^{n} \frac{|D_i|}{|D|} H(D_i) = -\sum_{i=1}^{n} \frac{|D_i|}{|D|} \sum_{k=1}^{K} \frac{|D_{ik}|}{|D_i|} \log_2 \frac{|D_{ik}|}{|D_i|} \tag{7.18}$$

Finally, calculate the information gain

$$g(D, A) = H(D) - H(D|A) \tag{7.19}$$

When the empirical entropy of the training dataset is large, the value of the information gain will be too large, otherwise the value of the information gain will be too small, resulting in the problem of difficulty in classification. In order to correct this problem, the information gain ratio can be used as another criterion.

Definition 7.6 (Information gain ratio). The information gain ratio of feature A to training dataset D, i.e., $g_R(D, A)$, to the training dataset is defined as the ratio of the information gain $g(D, A)$ to the empirical entropy $H(D)$ of the training dataset D:

$$g_R(D, A) = \frac{g(D, A)}{H(D)} \tag{7.20}$$

An example is now used to illustrate how to use the principle of information gain to select features.

Table 7.1   Sample data table of software user loss.

ID	Gender	Activity	Category
1	Male	High	No
2	Female	Medium	No
3	Male	Low	Yes
4	Female	High	No
5	Male	High	No
6	Male	Medium	No
7	Male	Medium	Yes
8	Female	Medium	No
9	Female	Low	Yes
10	Female	Medium	No
11	Female	High	No
12	Male	Low	Yes
13	Female	Low	Yes
14	Male	High	No
15	Male	High	No

Example 1. Table 7.1 is a software user churn training dataset composed of 15 samples; the data includes two characteristics of software users: gender (there are two possible values: male and female); activity (there are three possible values: high, medium, and low). The last column of the table is category, i.e., whether the user is lost (there are two values: yes and no).

For the training dataset D given in Table 7.1, select features according to the information gain criterion. First calculate the empirical entropy $H(D)$:

$$H(D) = -\frac{5}{15} \log_2 \left(\frac{5}{15}\right) - \frac{10}{15} \log_2 \left(\frac{10}{15}\right) = 0.9182$$

Then, calculate the information gain of each feature on the dataset D, and represent the two features of gender and activity by A_1, and A_2, respectively; then,

$$g(D, A_1) = H(D) - \left[\frac{8}{15} H(D_1) + \frac{7}{15} H(D_2)\right]$$

$$= 0.9182 - \left[\frac{8}{15} \left(-\frac{3}{8} \log_2 \left(\frac{3}{8}\right) - \frac{5}{8} \log_2 \left(\frac{5}{8}\right)\right)\right.$$

$$\left. + \frac{7}{15} \left(-\frac{2}{7} \log_2 \left(\frac{2}{7}\right) - \frac{5}{7} \log_2(7)\right)\right]$$

$$= 0.0064$$

Among them, D_1 and D_2 are the sample subsets where the value of A_1 (gender) in D is male and female respectively. In the same way

$$g(D, A_2) = H(D) - \left[\frac{6}{15}H(D_1) + \frac{5}{15}H(D_2) + \frac{4}{15}H(D_3)\right] = 0.6776$$

Among them, D_1, D_2, and D_3 are the sample subsets where the value of A_2 (activeness) in D is high, medium, and low respectively.

Finally, the information gain of each feature is compared. The information gain of Activity is greater than that of Gender; that is, the effect of Activity on user churn is greater than that of Gender. Therefore, the feature A_2 is selected as the optimal feature.

7.2.3 Generation algorithm of decision trees

Regarding the generation algorithm of the decision tree, here we introduce the basic algorithm of the decision tree, ID3 algorithm, and C4.5 algorithm.

Basic algorithm for decision tree learning: The basic algorithm flow follows a simple and intuitive "divide and conquer" strategy, as shown in Figure 7.2.

ID3 Algorithm: Starting from the root node, calculate the information gain of all features, then select the feature with the largest information gain as the node feature, get each sub-node according to the different values of the feature, and then recursively for each sub-node. The same method is used to generate a decision tree until the information gain of all features is very small or no features can be selected, which generates a decision tree.

C4.5 Algorithm: The C4.5 algorithm is similar to the ID3 algorithm. The C4.5 algorithm has improved the ID3 algorithm. In the C4.5 algorithm, the information gain ratio is used to select feature [19,29].

7.2.4 Pruning of decision trees

Since the generated decision tree has the problem of overfitting, it is necessary to prune the generated decision tree to simplify the decision tree.

Definition 7.7 (Decision tree pruning). Decision tree pruning is the process of cutting off some leaf nodes or sub-trees above the leaf tree from

Input: training set $D = \{(x_1, y_1), (x_2, y_2), \cdots, (x_m, y_m)\}$;

Attribute set $A = \{a_1, a_2, \cdots, a_d\}$.

Process: Function TreeGenerate (D, A)

1: Generate node *tnode*;

2: *if* the samples in D are all belong to the same category C *then*

3: Mark *tnode* as a type C node; *return*

4: *end if*

5: *if* $A = \emptyset$, OR the sample in D takes the same distance on A: *then*;

6: Mark *tnode* as a leaf node, and its category is marked as the class with the largest number of samples in D: *return*

7: *end if*

8: Choose the optimal partition attribute a_* from A;

9: For each value of a_*^v *do*

10: Generate a branch for node; let: D_v means a sample subset of D in which a_* is taken the volue of a_*^v;

11: *if* D_v is empty, *then*

12: Mark the branch node as a leaf node, and its category is marked as the class with the most samples in D; *return*

13: *else*

14: Take TreeGenerate($D_v, A\{a_*\}$) as the branch node

15: *end if*

16: *end for*

Figure 7.2   The basic algorithm flow of the decision tree.

the generated decision tree, and using its parent node or root node as a new leaf node, thus simplifying the decision tree's goal.

The pruning of the decision tree can be achieved by minimizing the loss function or cost function of the decision tree. Suppose there is $|T|$ leaf nodes of the tree T, and t is a leaf node of the tree T. There are N_t samples of this leaf node, of which there are N_{tk} samples of class k, $k = 1, 2, \ldots, K$. $H_t(T)$ is the empirical entropy on the leaf node t, $\alpha \geq 0$ is the parameter; then, the loss function that defines the learning of the decision tree is

$$C_\alpha(T) = \sum_{t=1}^{|T|} N_t H_t(T) + \alpha |T| \tag{7.21}$$

Among them, the experience entropy is

$$H_t(T) = -\sum_k \frac{N_{tk}}{N_t} \log \frac{N_{tk}}{N_t} \tag{7.22}$$

Let

$$C(T) = \sum_{t=1}^{|T|} N_t H_t(T) = -\sum_{t=1}^{|T|} \sum_{k=1}^{K} N_{tk} \log \frac{N_{tk}}{N_t} \tag{7.23}$$

Then there is

$$C_\alpha(T) = C(T) + \alpha|T| \tag{7.24}$$

Among them, $C(T)$ is the degree of fit between the model and the training data, $|T|$ is the complexity of the model, and α is used to control the influence between the two. $\alpha = 0$ represents the case of only considering the degree of fitting of the model to the training data, without considering the complexity of the model.

Pruning is the process of choosing the model with the smallest loss function when α is determined. When α is determined, the larger the subtree, the better the fit between the model and the training data, but the higher the complexity of the model. Conversely, when α is determined, the smaller the subtree, the lower the complexity of the model, but the poorer the fit between the model and the training data. In fact, pruning using the loss function minimization principle is the process of using regularized maximum likelihood estimation for model selection. So the decision tree generation learns the local model, and the pruning of the decision tree learns the overall model.

7.3 Support Vector Machine

7.3.1 *Intervals and support vectors*

Given the training sample set $D = \{(x_1, y_1), (x_2, y_2), \ldots, (x_m, y_m)\}$, the most basic idea of classification learning is to find a dividing hyperplane in the sample space based on the training set D, and separate different types of samples. But there may be many hyperplanes that can separate the training samples, as shown in Figure 7.3.

Among them, the division in the "center" of the two types of training samples is the best, namely the dashed hyperplane in Figure 7.4. The resulting classification results are the most robust and have the strongest generalization ability to unseen samples.

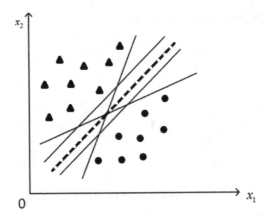

Figure 7.3   The hyperplane separates the two types of training samples.

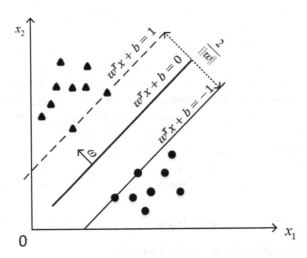

Figure 7.4   Support vector and interval.

In the sample space, the division of the hyperplane can be described by the following linear equation:

$$w^T x + b = 0$$

where $w = (w_1; w_2; \ldots; w_d)$ is the normal vector, which determines the direction of the hyperplane; b is the displacement term, which determines the distance between the hyperplane and the origin. The division of the hyperplane is determined by the normal vector w and the displacement b, and is recorded as (w, b). The distance from any point x in the sample space to the hyperplane (w, b) can be written as

$$r = \frac{|w^T x + b|}{||w||}$$

Assuming that the hyperplane (w, b) can correctly classify the training samples; that is, for $(x_i, y_i) \epsilon D$, if $y_i = +1$, then there is $w^T x_i + b > 0$; if $y_i = -1$, then

$$\begin{cases} w^T x_i + b \geq +1, y_i = +1; \\ w^T x_i + b \leq -1, y_i = -1. \end{cases}$$

As shown in Figure 7.4, the training sample points closest to the hyperplane make the equal sign true, and they are called "support vectors".

$$\gamma = \frac{2}{||w||}$$

where γ is called the "interval" [10].

To find the partition hyperplane with the "maximum interval", that is, to find the parameters w and b that can meet the constraints, so that y is the largest, i.e.,

$$\max_{w,b} \frac{2}{||w||}$$

$$s.t. \ y_i \left(w^T x_i + b \right) \geq 1, i = 1, 2, \ldots, m. \tag{7.25}$$

In order to maximize the interval, it is only necessary to maximize $||w||^{-1}$ which is equivalent to minimizing $||w||^2$, so formula (7.25) can be rewritten as

$$\min_{w,b} \frac{1}{2} ||w||^2$$

$$s.t. \ y_i \left(w^T x_i + b \right) \geq 1, i = 1, 2, \ldots, m. \tag{7.26}$$

This is the basic type of Support Vector Machine (SVM) [35].

7.3.2 *Duality problem*

Solve the basic type of SVM to get the model corresponding to the hyperspace division of the maximum interval

$$f(\boldsymbol{x}) = w^T \boldsymbol{x} + b \tag{7.27}$$

where w and b are model parameters. Equation (7.27) is a convex quadratic programming problem. The Lagrange multiplier method can be used to obtain its "dual problem". For each constraint, the Lagrangian multiplier $\alpha_i \geq 0$ is added. The Granger function can be written as

$$L(w, b, \alpha) = \frac{1}{2}||w||^2 + \sum_{i=1}^{m} \alpha_i \left(1 - y_i \left(w^T x_i + b\right)\right) \qquad (7.28)$$

where $\alpha = (\alpha_1; \alpha_2; \ldots; \alpha_m)$. Let the partial derivative of $L(w, b, \alpha)$ with respect to w and b be zero to obtain

$$w = \sum_{i=1}^{m} \alpha_i y_i x_i, \qquad (7.29)$$

$$0 = \sum_{i=1}^{m} \alpha_i y_i. \qquad (7.30)$$

Substituting Eq. (7.29) into (7.28), the w and b in $L(w, b, \alpha)$ can be eliminated, and then considering the constraints of Eq. (7.30), we get the dual problem as follows:

$$\max_{\alpha} \sum_{i=1}^{m} \alpha_i - \frac{1}{2} \sum_{i=1}^{m} \sum_{j=1}^{m} \alpha_i \alpha_j y_i y_j x_i^T x_j$$

$$s.t. \ \sum_{i=1}^{m} \alpha_i y_i = 0,$$

$$\alpha_i \geq 0, \ i = 1, 2, \ldots, m. \qquad (7.31)$$

After solving for α, find w and b to get the following model:

$$f(x) = w^T x + b = \sum_{i=1}^{m} \alpha_i y_i x_i^T x + b \qquad (7.32)$$

The α_i solved from the dual problem (7.31) is the Lagrange multiplier in Eq. (7.28), which corresponds to the training sample (x_i, y_i). Due to the inequality constraints in Eq. (7.27) the above process needs to meet the KKT (Karush–Kuhn–Tucker) conditions, i.e. requirements,

$$\begin{cases} \alpha_i \geq 0; \\ y_i f(x_i) - 1 \geq 0; \\ \alpha_i(y_i f(x_i) - 1) = 0. \end{cases} \qquad (7.33)$$

For any training sample (x_i, y_i), there is always $\alpha_i = 0$ or $y_i, f(x_i) = 1$. If $\alpha_i = 0$, the sample will not appear in the summation of Eq. (7.32); that is it will not have any effect on $f(x)$; if $\alpha_i > 0$, $y_i f(x_i) = 1$, the corresponding sample point is located on the boundary of the maximum interval, which is a support vector, and shows the importance of support vector machine nature: after the training is completed, most of the training samples do not have to be retained, and the final model is only related to the support vector.

Use SMO (Sequential Minimal Optimization) algorithm [27] to solve Eq. (7.31). The basic idea of the algorithm is to first fix all parameters except α_i and then find the extreme value on α_i. Due to the constraint $\sum_{i=1}^{m} \alpha_i y_i = 0$, if variables other than α_i are fixed, α_i can be derived from other variables. So SMO selects the two variables α_i and α_j each time and fixes other parameters. In this way, after parameter initialization, SMO continuously performs the following two steps until convergence:

(1) Select a pair of variables α_i and α_j to be updated;
(2) Fix parameters other than α_i and α_j and solve Eq. (7.31) to obtain the updated α_i and α_j.

Further, determine the offset term b; note that for any support vector, (x_i, y_i) have $y_s f(x_s) = 1$; namely,

$$y_s \left(\sum_{i \in S} \alpha_i y_i x_i^T x_s + b \right) = 1 \qquad (7.34)$$

where $S = \{i | \alpha_i > 0, i = 1, 2, ..., m\}$ is the subscript set of all support vectors. Choose any support vector and solve Eq. (7.34) to obtain b. In practice, the average value of all support vectors is often used, such as Eq. (7.35), to make the result more robust:

$$b = \frac{1}{|S|} \sum_{s \in S} \left(y_s - \sum_{i \in S} \alpha_i y_i x_i^T x_s \right) \qquad (7.35)$$

7.3.3 *Soft interval and regularization*

In practical problems, the training dataset is often linearly inseparable; that is, noise or singular points appear in the sample. After these singular points are removed, most of the remaining sample points are linearly separable, as shown in Figure 7.5. The support vector machine learning method for linearly separable problems is not applicable to linearly inseparable training data, because at this time the inequality constraints in all the above methods

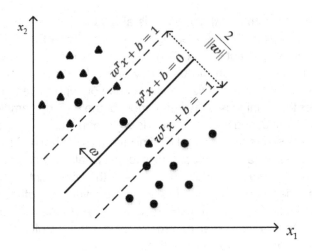

Figure 7.5   Schematic diagram of soft separation.

cannot hold. This requires that the hard interval be modified to maximize the soft interval.

Linear inseparability means that some sample points (x_i, y_i) cannot meet the constraint conditions. In order to solve this problem, a relaxation variable $\varepsilon_i \geq 0$ can be introduced for each sample point (x_i, y_i), and the constraint condition becomes

$$y_i \left(w^T x_i + b \right) \geq 1 - \varepsilon_i \tag{7.36}$$

At the same time, for each relaxation variable ε_i, pay the price, the objective function becomes

$$L(w, b, \alpha) = \frac{1}{2} \|w\|^2 + C \sum_{i=1}^{m} \varepsilon_i + \sum_{i=1}^{m} \alpha_i \left(1 - y_i \left(w^T x_i + b \right) \right) \tag{7.37}$$

$C > 0$ is called the penalty parameter, which is generally determined by the application problem. When the value of C is large, the penalty for misclassification increases. If the C value is small, the penalty for misclassification is reduced. The minimization objective function (7.37) contains two meanings: make $\frac{1}{2} \|w\|^2$ as small as possible; that is, the interval is as large as possible, and the number of misclassified points is as small as possible; C is the Harmonic coefficient of both.

There is another explanation for linear support vector machine learning, which is to minimize the following objective function:

$$\sum_{i=1}^{m} [1 - y_i (w^T x_i + b)]_+ \lambda ||w||^2 \qquad (7.38)$$

The first term of the objective function is the experience loss or experience risk, the function

$$L(y(w^T x + b)) = [1 - y(w^T x + b)]_+ \qquad (7.39)$$

called the hinge loss function, where the subscript "+" indicates the following function that takes a positive value:

$$[z]_+ = \begin{cases} z, z > 0 \\ 0, z \leq 0 \end{cases} \qquad (7.40)$$

When the sample points (x_i, y_i) are correctly classified and the confidence $y_i(w^T x_i + b)$ is greater than 1, the loss is 0; otherwise the loss is $y_i(w^T x_i + b)$. The second term of the objective function is the L_2 norm of w with the coefficient λ, which is the regularization term.

The graph of the hinge loss function is shown with dotted lines in Figure 7.6. The 0–1 loss function is also drawn with a thick black line in the figure. In contrast, the hinge loss function must not only be classified correctly, but also the loss is only 0 when the degree of confidence is high enough. The hinge loss function has higher requirements for learning.

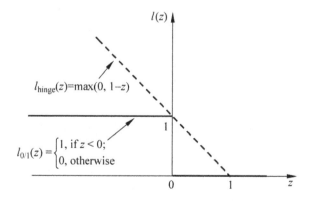

Figure 7.6   Hinge loss function.

With the above ideas, the linear support vector machine learning problem of the linear inseparable time of the training dataset can be considered in the same way as the linear separable time of the training dataset. The linear inseparable linear support vector machine learning problem becomes the following convex quadratic programming problem:

$$\max_{w,b,\varepsilon} \; \frac{1}{2}||w||^2 + C\sum_{i=1}^{m} \varepsilon_i$$

$$s.t. \; y_i\left(w^T x_i + b\right) \geq 1 - \varepsilon_i, \quad i = 1, 2, \dots, m$$

$$\varepsilon_i \geq 0, \quad i = 1, 2, \dots, m \tag{7.41}$$

where w and b are model parameters. Equation (7.41) is a convex quadratic programming problem, which can be obtained by using the Lagrangian multiplier method. For each constraint, add the Lagrangian multiplier $\alpha_i \geq 0$, $\mu_i \geq 0$, then the Lagrange function of this problem can be written as

$$L\left(w, b, \alpha, \mu\right) = \frac{1}{2}||w||^2 + C\sum_{i=1}^{m} \varepsilon_i$$

$$+ \sum_{i=1}^{m} \alpha_i \left(1 - \varepsilon_i - y_i \left(w^T x_i + b\right)\right) - C\sum_{i=1}^{m} \mu_i \varepsilon_i \tag{7.42}$$

where $\alpha = (\alpha_1; \alpha_2; \dots; \alpha_m)$, $\mu = (\mu_1; \mu_2; \dots; \mu_m)$.

Let the partial derivative of $L(w, b, \alpha, \mu)$ for w and b is zero, then get

$$w = \sum_{i=1}^{m} \alpha_i y_i x_i,$$

$$0 = \sum_{i=1}^{m} \alpha_i y_i,$$

$$C = \alpha_i + \mu_i.$$

Substituting Eq. (7.39) into (7.38), we can get the dual problem of Eq. (7.37)

$$\max_{\alpha} \sum_{i=1}^{m} \alpha_i - \frac{1}{2}\sum_{i=1}^{m}\sum_{j=1}^{m} \alpha_i \alpha_j y_i y_j x_i^T x_j$$

$$s.t. \; \sum_{i=1}^{m} \alpha_i y_i = 0,$$

$$0 \leq \alpha_i \leq C, \; i = 1, 2, \dots, m. \tag{7.43}$$

Comparing Eq. (7.42) with the dual problem under hard intervals (7.31), it can be seen that the only difference between the two lies in the constraints on the dual variables: the former is $0 \leq \alpha_i \leq C$ and the latter is $0 \leq \alpha_i$. Therefore, the same algorithm in Section 7.3.2 can be used to solve Eq. (7.42).

7.3.4 *Kernel function*

The classification problem is nonlinear. In this case, you can use a nonlinear support vector machine. This section describes the nonlinear support vector machine; its main feature is the use of kernel tricks [4, 12].

(1) Kernel tricks

First, let's look at a nonlinear classification example: Figure 7.7 is a classification problem.

The triangle in Figure 7.7 represents the positive instance point, and the circle represents the negative instance point. As can be seen from the figure, the positive and negative instances cannot be correctly separated by a straight line (linear model). But they can be separated with an elliptic curve (nonlinear model).

Let the original space be $\chi \epsilon R^2 \, x = (x^{(1)}, x^{(2)})^T \epsilon \chi$, and the new space be $Z \epsilon R^2$, and $z = (z^{(1)}, z^{(2)})^T \epsilon Z$, defines the transformation (mapping) of the original space into the new space

$$z = \phi(x) = ((x^{(1)})^2, (x^{(2)})^2)^T. \tag{7.44}$$

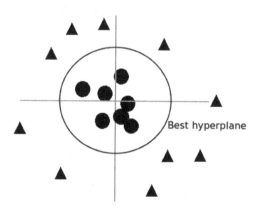

Best hyperplane

Figure 7.7   Schematic diagram of nonlinear classification.

After transforming $z = \phi(x)$, the original space $\chi \epsilon R^2$ is transformed into a new space $Z \epsilon R^2$, and the points in the original space are correspondingly transformed into the points in the new space, and the ellipse in the original space

$$w_1 \left(x^{(1)}\right)^2 + w_2 \left(x^{(2)}\right)^2\right)^T + b = 0. \tag{7.45}$$

is transformed into a line in the new space

$$w_1 z^{(1)} + w_2 z^{(2)} + b = 0. \tag{7.46}$$

In the transformed new space, the straight line $w_1 z^{(1)} + w_2 z^{(2)} + b = 0$ can correctly separate the positive and negative instance points after transformation. In this way, the nonlinear separability problem in the original space becomes a linear separability problem in the new space.

(2) Kernel function

Let $\phi(x)x$ denote the eigenvectors after mapping x, so the hyperplane is divided in the feature space. The corresponding model can be expressed as

$$f(x) = w^T \phi(x) + b \tag{7.47}$$

where w and b are model parameters. Similar to (7.26), there is

$$\min_{w,b} \frac{1}{2} \|w\|^2$$

$$s.t. \ y_i \left(w^T \phi(x_i) + b\right) \geq 1, i = 1, 2, \ldots, m. \tag{7.48}$$

The dual problem is

$$\max_{\alpha} \sum_{i=1}^{m} \alpha_i - \frac{1}{2} \sum_{i=1}^{m} \sum_{j=1}^{m} \alpha_i \alpha_j y_i y_j \phi(x_i)^T \phi(x_j),$$

$$s.t. \ \sum_{i=1}^{m} \alpha_i y_i = 0,$$

$$\alpha_i \geq 0, \ i = 1, 2, \ldots, m. \tag{7.49}$$

Solving Eq. (7.49) involves calculating $\phi(x_i)^T \phi(x_j)$, which is the inner product after the samples x_i and x_j are mapped to the feature space. Since the dimensionality of the feature space may be very high and may even be infinite, directly calculating $\phi(x_i)^T \phi(x_j)$ is usually difficult; imagine the following function:

$$k(x_i, x_j) = \langle \phi(x_i), \phi(x_j) \rangle = \langle \phi(x_i)^T \phi(x_j) \rangle^2 \qquad (7.50)$$

That is, the inner product of x_i and x_j in the feature space is equal to the result calculated by using the function $k(\bullet, \bullet)$ in the original sample space. It is not necessary to directly calculate the inner product in the high-dimensional or even infinite-dimensional feature space, so Eq. (7.50) can be rewritten as

$$\max_{\alpha} \sum_{i=1}^{m} \alpha_i - \frac{1}{2} \sum_{i=1}^{m} \sum_{j=1}^{m} \alpha_i \alpha_j y_i y_j k(x_i, x_j)$$

$$s.t. \ \sum_{i=1}^{m} \alpha_i y_i = 0,$$

$$\alpha_i \geq 0, \ i = 1, 2, \ldots, m. \qquad (7.51)$$

After solving, we can get

$$f(x) = w^T \phi(x) + b$$

$$= \sum_{i=1}^{m} \alpha_i y_i \phi(x_i)^T \phi(x) + b$$

$$= \sum_{i=1}^{m} \alpha_i y_i k(x, x_i) + b \qquad (7.52)$$

The function $k(\bullet, \bullet)$ here is the "kernel function", and the following theorem defines the kernel function [11].

Definition 7.8 (Kernel function). Let χ be the input space, and $k(\bullet, \bullet)$ is the symmetric function that defines $\chi \times \chi$, then k is the kernel function if and only if for any data $D = \{x_1, x_2, \ldots, x_m\}$, the kernel matrix K is always positive semidefinite:

$$K = \begin{bmatrix} k(x_1, x_1) & \cdots & k(x_1, x_m) \\ \vdots & \ddots & \vdots \\ k(x_m, x_1) & \cdots & k(x_m, x_m) \end{bmatrix} \qquad (7.53)$$

The quality of the feature space is crucial to the performance of the support vector machine. It is always expected that the samples are linearly

Table 7.2   Commonly used kernel functions.

Name	Expression
Linear kernel	$k(x_i, x_j) = x_i^T x_j$
Polynomial kernel	$k(x_i, x_j) = (x_i^T x_j)^d$, $d \geq 1$ is the degree of polynomial
Gaussian kernel	$k(x_i, x_j) = \exp\left(-\frac{||x_i - x_j||^2}{2\sigma^2}\right)$, $\sigma > 0$ is the bandwidth of the Gaussian
Laplace kernel	$k(x_i, x_j) = \exp\left(-\frac{||x_i - x_j||}{\sigma}\right)$, $\sigma > 0$
Sigmoid kernel	$k(x_i, x_j) = \tanh(\beta x_i^T x_j + \theta)$, $\beta > 0, \theta > 0$

separable in the feature space. However, when the form of the feature map is not known, it cannot be determined what kind of kernel function is suitable, and the kernel function only implicitly defines this feature space. Therefore, how to choose the correct kernel function is very important. Table 7.2 lists several commonly used kernel functions [33].

In addition, kernel functions can also be obtained through function combinations, for example:

- If k_1 and k_2 are kernel functions, then for any positive numbers γ_1 and γ_2 the linear combination is also a kernel function:

$$\gamma_1 k_1 + \gamma_2 k_2 \tag{7.54}$$

- If k_1 and k_2 are kernel functions, then the direct product of the function is also a kernel function:

$$k_1 \otimes k_2 (x, z) = k_1(x, z)k_2(x, z) \tag{7.55}$$

- If k_1 is a kernel function, then any function $g(x)$ is also a kernel function:

$$k(x, z) = g(x)k_1(x, z)g(z) \tag{7.56}$$

7.4   Integrated Learning

7.4.1   *Random forest*

Bagging in integrated learning is a parallel integrated learning method. It is based on bootstrap sampling and randomly takes a sample from a given dataset containing n samples and puts it into the sampling set, and then puts the sample back to the initial dataset, so that the sample may be selected in the next sampling. After k sub-random sampling operations, you can get a subset that contains k samples. You can repeat doing this m times and get m sample sets each of which contains k samples, and train m base classifiers with each sample set. The final classifier is combined with the base classifiers. This is the basic process of bagging.

"Random forest" [6] refers to an algorithm that uses multiple decision trees to train and predict samples, i.e., an algorithm that contains multiple decision trees. The final output category of the random forest is determined by the mode of the category output by the individual decision tree.

There are two keywords in the name of "random forest": one is "random" and the other is "forest". "Forest" is easy to understand. A decision tree is called a tree, so hundreds of trees can be called a forest. From an intuitive point of view, each decision tree is a classifier. If it is a classification problem, then for an input sample, the k trees will have k classification results. The random forest integrates all the classification voting results, and assigns the category with the most votes as the final output category. This is the simplest bagging idea.

Random forest is an extension of bagging. The construction process of the random forest is roughly as follows:

(1) The bootstrap resampling method randomly samples back k samples from the training set. The sample size of each sample is the same as that of the original training set, and finally k training sets can be obtained.
(2) Next, we will train k decision tree models based on k training sets.
(3) For each decision tree model, randomly select m features from the M features, and select the best feature for splitting each time.
(4) Each tree will continue to split in the same way, and the training examples that have been split until the node belong to the same category. No pruning is required during the splitting of the decision tree.
(5) Finally, multiple decision trees are combined to obtain a random forest. For classification problems, the final classification result will be decided by multiple classifiers. For regression problems, the final prediction result will be determined by the average of multiple prediction values.

A schematic diagram of random forest construction is shown in Figure 7.8.

The key to constructing a random forest is how to choose the optimal m and to solving this problem is mainly to calculate the out-of-bag error rate

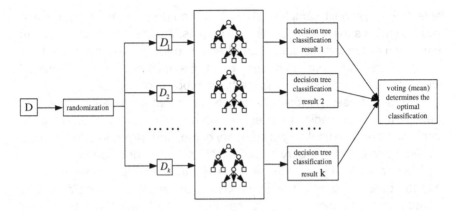

Figure 7.8   Schematic diagram of the random forest.

(oob error rate). When constructing each tree, different bootstraps are used for the training set, so for the first tree, about 1/3 of the training examples did not participate in the generation of the first tree. For such sampling characteristics, oob estimation can be performed. First, for each sample, calculate the classification of the tree as the oob sample (about 1/3 of the tree); then use a simple majority vote as the classification result of the sample; finally, the ratio of the number of misclassifications to the total number of samples is used as the oob misclassification rate of the random forest. The oob error rate is an unbiased estimate of the random forest generalization error, and its result is similar to fold cross-validation that requires a lot of calculations.

Compared with general algorithms, random forest has a great deal of advantages. It can handle a large number of input variables. The training speed is relatively fast, and in the process of training, it can be detected that all features affect each other. For unbalanced datasets, it can balance errors. However, the random forest algorithm also has some shortcomings. Under noisy conditions, overfitting may occur in classification or regression problems [20].

7.4.2   *Adaboost algorithm*

Boosting is an important integrated learning method [30]. Its main idea is the process of promoting "weak learning algorithms" to "strong learning algorithms". Generally speaking, it is relatively easy to find weak learning algorithms. Then, a series of weak classifiers are obtained through repeated learning, and these weak classifiers are combined to obtain a strong classifier, where Adaboost is a typical Boosting algorithm.

Suppose that given a two-class classification training dataset $T = \{(x_1, y_1), (x_2, y_2), \ldots, (x_N, y_N)\}$, each sample point is composed of an instance and a label, and the instance $x_i \in \chi \subseteq R^n$, $y_i = \{-1, +1\}$, mark $y_i = \{-1, +1\}$.

Algorithm:

Input: training dataset $T = \{(x_1, y_1), (x_2, y_2), \ldots, (x_N, y_N)\}$, where $x_i \in \chi \subseteq R^n$, $y_i = \{-1, +1\}$; weak learning algorithm;

Output: final classifier $G(x)$.

(1) Assuming that the training dataset has a uniform weight distribution, i.e., each training sample plays the same role in the learning of the basic classifier, this assumption guarantees that the basic classifier can be learned from the original data at the beginning; value distribution:

$$D_1 = (w_{11}, \ldots, w_{1i}, \ldots, w_{1N}), \quad w_{1i} = \frac{1}{N}, \quad i = 1, 2, \ldots, N \quad (7.57)$$

(2) Learn the basic classifier repeatedly, and perform the following operations sequentially in each round $m = 1, 2, \ldots, M$:

(a) Use the training dataset with weight distribution D_m to learn and get the basic classifier $G_m(x) : \chi \to \{-1, +1\}$.

(b) Calculate the classification error rate of $G_m(x)$ on the training dataset

$$e_m = P(G_m(x_i) \neq y_i) = \sum_{i=1}^{N} w_{mi} I(G_m(x_i) \neq y_i) \quad (7.58)$$

where w_{mi} represents the weight of the i-th instance in round m, $\sum_{i=1}^{N} w_{mi} = 1$, which is the classification of $G_m(x)$ on the weighted training dataset. The error rate is the sum of the weights of samples misclassified by $G_m(x)$.

(c) Calculate the coefficient of $G_m(x)$

$$\alpha_m = \frac{1}{2} \ln \frac{1 - e_m}{e_m} \quad (7.59)$$

(d) Update the weight distribution of the training dataset

$$D_{m+1} = (w_{m+1,1}, \ldots, w_{m+1,i}, \ldots, w_{m+1,N}) \qquad (7.60)$$

$$w_{m+1,i} = \frac{w_{mi}}{Z_m} \exp(-\alpha_m y_i G_m(x_i)), \quad i = 1, 2, \ldots, N \qquad (7.61)$$

Here, Z_m is the normalization factor

$$Z_m = \sum_{i=1}^{N} w_{mi} \exp\left(-\alpha_m y_i G_m(x_i)\right) \qquad (7.62)$$

It makes D_{m+1} a probability distribution.

Adaboost continuously changes the distribution of the weights of the training data without changing the training data, so that the training data plays a different role in the learning of the basic classifier. The weight of the sample misclassified by the basic classifier $G_m(x)$ can be expanded, and the weight of the sample correctly classified can be reduced. Therefore, the misclassified sample plays a greater role in the next round of learning.

(3) Construct a linear combination of basic classifiers to achieve weighted voting of M classifiers:

$$f(x) = \sum_{m=1}^{M} \alpha_m G_m(x) \qquad (7.63)$$

Get the final classifier finally:

$$G(x) = sign(f(x)) = sign(\sum_{m=1}^{M} \alpha_m G_m(x)) \qquad (7.64)$$

The coefficient α_m represents the importance of the basic classifier $G_m(x)$, and the sum of all α_m is not 1. The symbol of $f(x)$ determines the class of instance x, and the absolute value of $f(x)$ indicates the degree of confidence in the classification. The algorithm block diagram is shown in Figure 7.9.

The training data is shown in Table 7.3. Assume that the weak classifier is generated by $x < v$ or $x > v$, and its threshold value v makes the classifier have the lowest classification error rate on the training dataset. Try the Adaboost algorithm to learn a strong classifier.

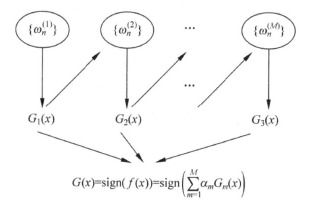

$$G(x)=\text{sign}(f(x))=\text{sign}\left(\sum_{m=1}^{M}\alpha_m G_m(x)\right)$$

Figure 7.9 Adaboost algorithm block diagram.

Table 7.3 Training dataset.

	No.	1	2	3	4	5	6	7	8	9	10
Appendix A.											
Appendix B.	X	(1,5)	(2,2)	(3,1)	(4,6)	(6,8)	(6,5)	(7,9)	(8,7)	(9,8)	(10,2)
Appendix C.	Y	1	1	−1	−1	1	−1	1	1	−1	−1

Solution: The initial data weight points $D_1 = (w_{11}, w_{12}, \dots, w_{110})$, $w_{1i} = 0.1, i = 1, 2, \dots, 10$.

For $m = 1$:

(a) On the training data with weight distribution D_1, the classification error rate is the lowest when the threshold v is 2.5, so the basic classifier is

$$G_1(x) = \begin{cases} 1, & X_1 < 2.5 \\ -1, & X_1 > 2.5 \end{cases}$$

(b) The error rate of $G_1(x)$ on the training dataset $e_1 = 0.3$.
(c) Calculate the coefficient of $G_1(x)$: $\alpha_1 = \frac{1}{2}\ln\frac{1-e_1}{e_1} = 0.4236$.
(d) Update the weight distribution of training data:

$$D_2 = (w_{21}, w_{22}, \dots, w_{210})$$

$$w_{2i} = \frac{w_{1i}}{Z_1}\exp(-\alpha_1 y_i G_1(x_i)), \quad i = 1, 2, \dots, 10$$

$$D_2 = (1/14, 1/14, 1/14, 1/14, 1/6, 1/14, 1/6, 1/6, 1/14, 1/14)$$

$$f_1(x) = 0.4236 G_1(x)$$

The classifier $sign[f_1(x)]$ has three misclassified points on the training dataset.

For $m = 2$:

(a) On the training data whose weight distribution is D_2, the classification error rate is the lowest when the threshold value v is 8.5, so the basic classifier is

$$G_2(x) = \begin{cases} 1, & X_1 < 8.5 \\ -1, & X_1 > 8.5 \end{cases}$$

(b) The error rate of $G_2(x)$ on the training dataset $e_2 = 3/14$.
(c) Calculate $\alpha_2 = 0.6496$.
(d) Update the weight distribution of training data:

$$D_3 = (1/22, 1/22, 1/6, 1/6, 7/66, 1/6, 7/66, 7/66, 1/22, 1/22)$$

$$0.1060, 0.1060, 0.1060, 0.0455)$$

$$f_2(x) = 0.4236G_1(x) + 0.6496G_2(x)$$

The classifier $sign[f_2(x)]$ has three misclassified points on the training dataset.

For $m = 3$:

(a) On the training data with weight distribution D_3, the classification error rate is the lowest when the threshold value v is 5.5, so the basic classifier is

$$G_2(x) = \begin{cases} 1, & X_1 < 5.5 \\ -1, & X_2 > 5.5 \end{cases}$$

(b) The error rate of $G_3(x)$ on the training dataset $e_3 = 3/22$.
(c) Calculate $\alpha_3 = 0.9229$.
(d) Update the weight distribution of training data:

$$D_4 = (1/6, 1/6, 11/114, 11/114, 7/114, 11/114, 7/114,$$

$$7/114, 1/6, 1/38)$$

$$f_2(x) = 0.4236G_1(x) + 0.6496G_2(x) + 0.9229(x)$$

The classifier $sign[f_3(x)]$ has zero misclassification points on the training dataset.

Therefore, the final classifier is

$$G(x) = \text{sign}[f_3(x)] = \text{sign}[0.4236G_1(x)$$
$$+ 0.6496G_2(x) + 0.9229G_3(x)]$$

7.5 Clustering

The clustering task is a kind of "unsupervised learning", the labeling information of the training samples is unknown, and the goal is to reveal the inherent nature and rules of the data through the learning of unlabeled training samples. The task of clustering [38] is to divide the samples in the dataset into several disjoint subsets, and each subset is called a "cluster". The following introduces the most typical k-means algorithm.

7.5.1 *Distance calculation*

The clustering algorithm involves measuring the distance of the samples. First, the distance calculation formula is introduced. Given the samples $x_i = (x_{i1}; x_{i2}; \ldots; x_{in})$ and $x_j = (x_{j1}; x_{j2}; \ldots; x_{jn})$, the most commonly used is "Minkowski distance":

$$\text{dist}_{mk}(x_i, x_j) = \left(\sum_{u=1}^{n} |x_{iu} - x_{ju}|^p \right)^{\frac{1}{p}} \tag{7.65}$$

When $p = 2$, the Minkowski distance is the Euclidean distance

$$\text{dist}_{ed}(x_i, x_j) = ||x_i - x_j||_2 = \sqrt{\sum_{u=1}^{n} |x_{iu} - x_{ju}|^2} \tag{7.66}$$

When $p = 1$, the Minkowski distance is the distance between Mann and Hatton

$$\text{dist}_{man}(x_i, x_j) = ||x_i - x_j||_1 = \sum_{u=1}^{n} |x_{iu} - x_{ju}|) \tag{7.67}$$

7.5.2 *The k-means clustering*

Given a sample set $D = \{x_1, x_2, \ldots, x_m\}$, k-means clustering for the resulting clusters $C = \{C_1, C_2, \ldots, C_k\}$ minimizes the squared error

$$E = \sum_{i=1}^{k} \sum_{x \in C_i} \|x - u_i\|_2^2 \tag{7.68}$$

where $u_i = \frac{1}{|C_i|} \sum_{x \in C_i} x$ is the mean vector of the cluster C_i. The smaller the E, the higher the similarity of the samples in the cluster. To a certain extent, it describes the tightness of the samples in the cluster around the mean vector.

The *k*-means algorithm [26] adopts the greedy strategy to minimize the formula (7.68), and approximates the solution through iterative optimization. The algorithm flow is shown in Figure 7.10.

The k in the algorithm is given in advance, and the selection of this k value is very difficult to estimate. In the k-means clustering algorithm, first an initial partition needs to be determined according to the initial clustering center, and then the initial partition is optimized. The selection of this initial clustering center has a great influence on the clustering results.

7.5.3 *Sample description*

The data object set S is shown in Table 7.4. As a cluster analysis to two-dimensional samples, the number of clusters required $k = 2$.

(1) Select $O_1(0, 2), O_2(0, 0)$ as the initial cluster center, i.e., $M_1 = O_1 = (0, 2)$ $M_2 = O_2 = (0, 0)$.
(2) For each remaining object, according to its distance from the center of each cluster, assign it to the nearest cluster. For O_3:

$$d(M_1, O_3) = \sqrt{(0 - 1.5)^2 + (2 - 0)^2} = 2.5$$

$$d(M_2, O_3) = \sqrt{(0 - 1.5)^2 + (0 - 0)^2} = 1.5$$

Obviously $d(M_2, O_3) \leq d(M_1, O_3)$, so O_3 is assigned to C_2. In the same way, it is calculated that O_4 is assigned to C_2, and O_5 is assigned to C_1. Update, and get the new cluster $C_1 = \{O_1, O_5\}$ and $C_2 = \{O_2, O_3, O_4\}$,

Input: sample set $D = \{x_1, x_2, \dots, x_m\}$, number of clusters k.

Process:

1: Randomly select k samples from D as the initial clustering center $\{u_1, u_2, \dots, u_k\}$

2: *repeat*

3: Let $C_i = \emptyset$ $(1 \leq i \leq k)$

4: *for* $j = 1, 2, \dots, m$

5: Calculate the distance between sample x_j and each cluster center μ_i $(1 \leq i \leq k)$:
$d_{ji} = ||x_j - u_i||_2$;

6: Determine the cluster label of x_j according to the nearest mean vector: $\lambda_j = arg_{min_{i \in \{1,2,\cdots,k\}}} d_{ji}$;

7: Divide the sample x_j into the corresponding cluster $C_{\lambda_j} = C_{\lambda_j} \cup \{x_j\}$;

8: *end for*

9: *for* $i = 1, 2, \dots, k$

10: Calculate the new clustering center: $\mu_i' = \frac{1}{|C_i|} \Sigma_{x \in C_i} x$;

11: *if* $\mu_i' \neq \mu_i$ *then*

12: Update u_i to u_i'

13: *else*

14: Keep μ_i unchanged

15: *end if*

16: *end for*

17: *until* the current cluster center has not been updated

Output: Cluster partition $C = \{C_1, C_2, \dots, C_k\}$

Figure 7.10   The k-means algorithm.

Table 7.4   Data object collection.

O	1	2	3	4	5
x	0	0	1.5	5	5
y	2	0	0	0	0

centered on $M_1 = O_1 = (0, 2)$, $M_2 = O_2 = (0, 0)$.

$$C\_1 = \{O\_1, O\_5\}, C\_2 = \{O\_2, O\_3, O\_4\},$$

$$M\_1 = O\_1 = (0, 2), M\_2 = O\_2 = (0, 0).$$

Calculate the square error criterion

$$E_1 = \left[(0-0)^2 + (2-2)^2\right] + \left[(0-5)^2 + (2-2)^2\right] = 25$$

$$E_2 = 27.25$$

The overall evaluation error is $E = E_1 + E_2 = 25 + 27.25 = 52.25$

(3) Calculate the center of the new cluster

$$M_1 = \left(\frac{0+5}{2}, \frac{2+2}{2}\right) = (2.5, 2)$$

$$M_2 = \left(\frac{0+1.5+5}{3}, \frac{0+0+0}{3}\right) = (2.17, 0)$$

Repeat (2) and (3) to obtain new clusters $C_1 = \{O_1, O_5, C_2 = \{O_2, O_3, O_4\}$, and the center is $M_1 = (2.5, 2)$, $M_2 = (2.17, 0)$.
Repeat (2) and (3) to get new clusters: $C_1 = \{O_1, O_5, C_2 = \{O_2, O_3, O_4\}$, and $M_1 = (2.5, 2)$, $M_2 = (2.17, 0)$.

Calculating the square error criterion: $E = E_1 + E_2 = 12.5 + 13.15 = 25.65$.

That is, after the first iteration, the overall average error value is reduced from 52.25 to 25.65. Since the cluster center remains unchanged in both iterations, the iteration process is stopped and the algorithm is terminated.

7.6 Deep Learning

Deep learning is a sub-problem of machine learning, usually in the form of a multi-layer neural network [16], the purpose of which is to get a better feature representation. Therefore, it is necessary to construct a network model with a certain "depth". The so-called "depth" refers to the number of times of nonlinear feature conversion of the original data. Learning from the original data to get a "deep model", this is deep learning. Deep learning is end-to-end learning, the learning process is not divided into modules, and the overall goal of the task is directly optimized during the training process without human intervention.

7.6.1 *Definition and characteristics of deep learning*

(1) Definition of deep learning

Definition 7.9. Deep learning algorithms are a class of machine learning algorithms based on a biological understanding of the human brain. The working principle of the nerve-central-brain is designed as a continuous iteration and continuous abstraction process. In order to obtain the optimal data feature representation, the algorithm starts with the original signal, and then performs low-level abstraction, and then gradually iterates to high-level abstraction, thereby forming the basic framework of the deep learning algorithm.

(2) General characteristics of deep learning

Generally speaking, deep learning algorithms have the following characteristics:

  (i) Use multiple nonlinear transformations to perform multiple layers of abstraction on the data. This type of algorithm uses multi-layer nonlinear processing units in cascade mode to organize feature extraction and feature conversion. In this cascade model, the data input of the subsequent layer is served by the output data of the previous layer.
 (ii) The goal is to find a more suitable method of conceptual representation. Such algorithms learn data representation methods by building better models. The high-level eigenvalues are derived from the lower-level eigenvalues through deduction, which constitutes a hierarchical structure of data features or abstract concepts. In this hierarchy of eigenvalues, the characteristic data of each layer corresponds to different degrees or levels of abstraction of related overall knowledge or concepts.
(iii) Form a representative feature learning representation method. In the context of large-scale unlabeled data, an observation can be expressed in many ways, such as an image, face recognition data, facial expression data, etc., and some specific representation methods can allow machine learning algorithms to learn. It's easier. Therefore, the research on deep learning algorithms can also be regarded as the study of a wider range of machine learning methods based on concept representation.

7.6.2 *Deep learning model training and optimization*

Deep learning usually uses a deep neural network structure with multiple hidden layers, and its training process is divided into forward propagation of signals and back-propagation of errors.

(1) **Forward propagation:** The input samples are processed layer by layer from the input layer to the output layer. If the actual output of the output layer does not match the expected output, then it goes to the back-propagation phase of the error.

(2) **Back-propagation [31]:** The output is passed back to the input layer, layer by layer, in a certain form, and the error is distributed to all units of each layer. The error signal of each layer unit is obtained as the weight of each unit. The basis of the algorithm flow is as follows:

Step 1: Initial weights and thresholds are small random numbers;
Step 2: Read in the sample set $\{x_0, x_1, \ldots, x_{n-1}\}$ and the expected output $\{t_0, t_1, \ldots, t_{n-1}\}$;
Step 3: For each sample in the training set:

    (a) Forward calculation of the output of each neuron in the hidden layer and the output layer;
    (b) Calculate the loss value of the expected output and network output;
    (c) Reverse calculation and correction of network weights and thresholds;
    (d) If the accuracy requirements or other exit conditions are met, the training is ended, otherwise go to Step (3) to continue.

The optimization of deep learning models can be considered from the following parts: loss function, MBGD (Mini-batch Gradient Descent), exponential smoothing method, adaptive learning rate algorithm, Dropout, Early Stopping, etc.

(1) Loss function

When training neural networks, it is often necessary to determine the objective function, which is the loss function. During training, there are many choices of loss function, the most commonly used is mean-square error (MSE), which is the most basic loss function in regression problems. As shown in Eq. (7.69), for the neural network model with Softmax as the output layer, it is most suitable to use cross-entropy as the loss function. Cross-entropy is more suitable for classification problems. The function form is shown in Eq. (7.71):

$$MSE = \frac{1}{n}\sum_{i}^{N} (\hat{y}_i - y_i)^2 \tag{7.69}$$

$$Loss = -\sum_{i}^{n} y_i \log(\hat{y}_i) \tag{7.70}$$

where $\hat{y}$ is the predicted result, y_i is the true value, and n is the number of samples.

(2) MBGD

When training the neural network model to find the minimum value of the loss function, the gradient descent method [25] is used to solve it step by step in order to obtain the minimum loss function and model parameter values. The three variations of the gradient descent method are BGD (Batch Gradient Descent), SGD (Stochastic Gradient Descent), and MBGD.

At present, MBGD is basically used in deep learning. MBGD trains a small part of the dataset at a time. It is relatively stable when it falls. A set of data in a batch jointly determines the gradient. The direction of falling is not easy to deviate, reducing the randomness. On the other hand, because the number of samples in the batch is much smaller than the entire dataset, the amount of calculations is not very large.

(3) Exponential smoothing

There are many shocks during the gradient descent, as shown in Figure 7.11.

The moving average method is a commonly used method to eliminate fluctuations. The main idea is to use the average value of a set of recent

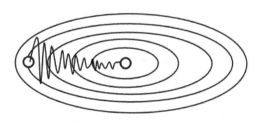

Figure 7.11   Gradient descent oscillation process.

actual data values. To predict future values, exponential smoothing is actually a special weighted moving average method. Its characteristics are listed below:

First, the exponential smoothing method further strengthens the effect of recent observations on the forecast during the observation period. The weights given to observations at different times vary, thus increasing the weight of recent observations, so that the predicted value can quickly reflect actual changes. The weights are reduced by equal series, the first term of this series is the smoothing constant α, and the common ratio is $(1 - \alpha)$;

Second, the exponential smoothing method is flexible for the weights given by the observations, and different α values can be taken to change the rate of change of the weights. If α takes a small value, the weight changes rapidly, and the recent change trend of the observed value is more quickly reflected in the exponential moving average. Therefore, using the exponential smoothing method, you can choose different α values to adjust the smoothness of the trend change. The formula of the exponential smoothing method is shown in Eq. (7.71):

$$y'_{t+1} = \alpha y_t + (1 - \alpha) y'_t, \, y'_0 = 0 \qquad (7.71)$$

where α is a number between 0 and 1, y'_{t+1} is the predicted value at $t + 1$, y'_t is the predicted value at t, and y_t is the true value at time t.

Introducing the exponential smoothing method in the process of gradient descent to smooth the gradient can effectively reduce the gradient shock and speed up the convergence speed. The optimization methods using exponential smoothing are Momentum, RMSprop, and Adam.

(4) Self-applicable learning algorithm

Usually, we use MBGD algorithm for training deep neural networks. However, although this algorithm can bring good training speed, it is not always possible to truly reach the best, but to wander around the best. Another disadvantage is that this algorithm requires us to choose a suitable learning rate. When we use a small learning rate, it will cause the network to converge too slowly during training; when we use a large learning rate, the best may be skipped. All we want is that the network's loss function has a good convergence speed when the network is optimized, and at the same time, it does not cause the swing amplitude to be too large.

(i) The **Momentum Algorithm** can solve the above problem. The basic idea is to calculate the exponentially weighted average of the gradient, and use the gradient to update the weight to make the gradient swing smaller, and at the same time make the network convergence faster. Suppose that in step t of the current iteration step, the iteration formula of the weight of the Momentum algorithm is shown in Eq. (7.72)

$$\nu_{dw} = \beta\nu_{dw} + (1 - \beta)dw$$
$$w = w + \eta\nu_{dw}$$

(7.72)

where ν_{dw} is the gradient momentum accumulated by the loss function during the first t rounds of iteration, initialized to 0, dw is the gradient obtained when the loss function is back-propagated, β is an index of gradient accumulation, and η is the learning rate of the network.

(ii) In order to further solve the problem of excessive swing amplitude and to further accelerate the convergence speed of the function, the RMSProp algorithm performs exponential smoothing on the square of the gradient. It is used to modify the swing amplitude so that the swing amplitude of each dimension is small. Assume that in the t-th iteration process, the weight update formula is as shown in Eq. (7.73):

$$S_{dw} = \beta S_{dw} + (1 - \beta)dw^2$$
$$w = w + \eta\frac{dw}{\sqrt{S_{dw} + \varepsilon}}$$

(7.73)

where S_{dw} is the gradient momentum accumulated by the loss function during the first t rounds of iterations, S_{dw} is initialized to 0, and ε is a small value, usually $\varepsilon = 10^{-8}$, so as to avoid $\sqrt{S_{dw}}$ approaching 0.

(iii) The Adam [23] algorithm is an algorithm that combines the Momentum algorithm and the RMSProp algorithm, using the momentum variable ν_{dw} and the variable S_{dw} in the RMSProp algorithm, assuming training in the t-th round of training. The weight update is shown in Eq. (7.74).

$$\nu_{dw} = \beta_1\nu_{dw} + (1 - \beta_1)dw$$
$$S_{dw} = \beta_2 S_{dw} + (1 - \beta_2)dw^2.$$

(7.74)

To further correct the deviation:

$$\nu_{dw}^{corrected} = \frac{\nu_{dw}}{1 - \beta_1^t}$$
$$S_{dw}^{corrected} = \frac{S_{dw}}{1 - \beta_2^t}.$$

(7.75)

Perform weight update:

$$w = w + \eta \frac{\nu_{dw}^{corrected}}{\sqrt{S_{dw}^{corrected}} + \varepsilon} \qquad (7.76)$$

(5) Dropout

In a deep learning model, if the model has too many parameters and too few training samples, the trained model is prone to overfitting. If the model is overfitted, the resulting model can hardly be used. Dropout can effectively alleviate the occurrence of overfitting and achieve regularization to a certain extent.

Dropout is to randomly "temporarily discard" some neuron nodes with a certain probability during the training of the neural network model. Dropout acts on each small batch of training data. Due to its mechanism of randomly discarding some neurons, it is equivalent to training neural networks of different structures in each iteration, making the model more generalized, and not to rely too much on certain local features. The comparison of the neural network structure before and after applying the Dropout algorithm is shown in Figure 7.12.

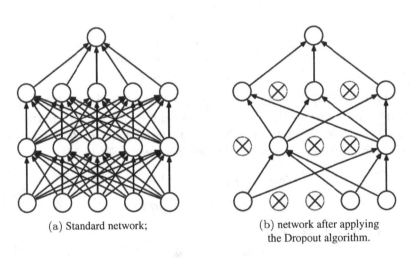

(a) Standard network;   (b) network after applying
                                      the Dropout algorithm.

Figure 7.12   Comparison of network structure.

The processing of Dropout in the training and prediction phases are different:

Training stage: Each neuron is discarded with a probability p, and the output of the i-th neuron is O_i, then

$$O_i = r_i f \left(\sum w_k x_k \right) \tag{7.77}$$

where r_i is a random variable subject to Bernoulli distribution, $P(r_i = 0) = p$.

Prediction phase: Each neuron is retained, no dropout, and each weight is scaled, and multiplied by $(1 - p)$ so that the output of the neurons in the training and test phases have the same expectations.

(6) Early Stopping

When training deep neural networks, it is usually desirable to obtain good generalization performance, i.e., to fit the data well. However, all standard deep neural network structures such as fully connected, multi-layer perceptrons are prone to overfit (overfitting). The generalization ability of the model is usually evaluated by the performance of the model on the test set. The verification set is mainly used for the parameter adjustment of the model to monitor whether the model has overfitting. Early Stopping is a widely used method to solve overfitting. As shown in Figure 7.13, the basic idea is to calculate the model's performance on the verification set during training, and use the verification set error to stop training the neural network early so that the problem of overfitting caused by continued training can be avoided.

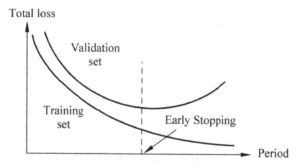

Figure 7.13   Schematic diagram of Early Stopping.

7.6.3 *Applications of deep learning*

Deep learning has gained more and more extensive applications, and has achieved good application results in the fields of pattern recognition, computer vision, speech recognition, natural language processing, etc. [39].

As of 2011, the latest method in feedforward neural network deep learning is to alternately use convolutional layers and max-pooling layers and add a simple classification layer as the top, without introducing the unsupervised training process pre-training. The existing scientific research results show that the deep learning algorithm has almost or already reached a level comparable to humans in some recognition tasks.

In 2012, *The New York Times* introduced a project co-chaired by Andrew Ng and Jeff Dean-Google Brain, which attracted widespread attention. They were well-known experts in the field of international machine learning and large-scale computer systems. This project uses a parallel computing platform composed of 16,000 CPU cores to train a machine learning model called "Deep Neural Networks" [5]. The new model does not artificially set the "abstract concept" boundary like the previous model, but directly puts massive data into the algorithm, allowing the system to automatically learn from the data, so as to "understand" multiple features of things, and speech recognition and image recognition have achieved great success.

In January 2014, the research team of Tang Xiaoou released the DeepID deep learning model with four convolution and pooling layers, and achieved the highest recognition rate at the time of 97.45% on the outdoor face detection database LFW (Labeled Faces in the Wild). In June of the same year, the improved model obtained a recognition rate of 99.15% on the LFW database, which is more accurate than human eye recognition.

In March 2016, AlphaGo's deep learning Go artificial intelligence model, created by Google's artificial intelligence team DeepMind, defeated the international Go champion Li Shishi 4:1, sensationalizing the world.

The Master program created by DeepMind in 2017 once again demonstrated its absolute advantage over human players in the fast chess game. The Master program played 60 games with 60 world champions and domestic champions, and next played the fast chess game every 30 seconds, winning 60:0.

Deep learning has been widely and successfully applied in many fields [24], including smart medical [1, 2], autonomous driving [32], navigation and planning [7, 15, 18, 40], sequence data analysis [8, 13], natural language processing [36], behavior recognition [37], fault diagnosis [22], etc.

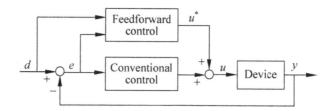

Figure 7.14   General structure of multi-layer neural network control.

In addition, deep reinforcement learning combined with reinforcement learning [3, 21, 34] has also performed well in many fields.

The following gives a three-layer neural network deep neural fuzzy control system to illustrate the specific application of multilayer neural networks [17].

From the knowledge we have learned, the multilayer neural network is basically a feedforward neural network. For example, in the multi-layer neural control system shown in Figure 7.14, there are two control functions, namely, feedforward control and conventional control. The feedforward control is implemented by a feedforward neural network; the training goal of the feedforward part is to minimize the deviation e between the expected output d and the actual device output y. This error is used as input to the feedback controller.

Figure 7.15 shows a three-layer neural network deep neural fuzzy control system. Its goal is to develop a method to realize anthropomorphic control based on fuzzy logic and neural networks. The system contains three types of sub-neural networks: pattern recognition neural network PN, fuzzy inference neural network RN, and control synthesis neural network CN.

The pattern recognition neural network PN realizes the fuzzification of the input signal, and maps the input signal to the membership degree of the fuzzy semantic term through the membership function. In the example in Figure 7.15, there are two input signals, each of which corresponds to three fuzzy semantic items. The fuzzy semantic term describes the signal pattern. The degree of membership of the semantic term is between 0 and 1, which indicates the degree to which the input signal conforms to the description of the semantic term. PN is trained to replace the membership function. After the fuzzification of the input signal is completed, the semantic terms and their memberships are taken as inputs into the fuzzy inference neural network RN, and the rule set in the knowledge base is used for fuzzy inference.

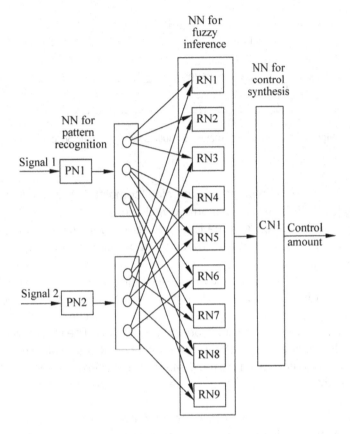

Figure 7.15   Three-layer neural network depth control structure example.

Specifically, the rules satisfying the fuzzy semantic terms of the input signal are used for reasoning, and the coupling strength of each decision rule is calculated. The example in Figure 7.15 has nine if–then decision rules, and each rule corresponds to one RN. For an input signal, the condition of each rule contains only one fuzzy semantic item; hence, for this example, the input of each RN is two fuzzy semantic items, respectively from two different SNs. Each RN is trained to replace the decision rules in the rule set. The RN outputs the regular coupling degree as an input to control the synthetic neural network. Neural network systems use a series of steps and membership functions that control fuzzy semantic terms to output the final control variables; these steps include single rule reasoning, generating fuzzy control variables, and deblurring. These steps are all replaced by the

CN network. After the PN, RN, and CN networks are constructed, they can be connected into a deep fuzzy control network as shown in Figure 7.15. Global training is performed on the basis of the training of the three sub-networks to further optimize the control effect and realize the whole process from collecting the status signals to outputting the control variables.

7.7 Summary

This chapter is divided into six subsections to introduce linear regression, decision tree, support vector machine, integrated learning, clustering, and deep learning:

Section 7.1 introduces linear regression, a statistical analysis method that uses regression analysis to determine the interdependent quantitative relationship between two or more variables. The subsection mainly introduces univariate linear regression and multiple linear regression.

Section 7.2 discusses the decision tree. The decision tree is a predictive model, which represents a mapping relationship between object attributes and object values. In the subsection, the three main steps of the decision tree learning algorithm, namely, feature selection, tree generation and pruning of trees, and tree pruning as well as the commonly used ID3 algorithm and C4.5 algorithm are introduced.

Section 7.3 analyzes the support vector machine SVM, which is a generalized linear classifier that performs binary classification of data by supervised learning. Its decision boundary is the maximum marginal hyperplane that solves the learning samples. Regularize the term to optimize the structural risk, and at the same time, use the kernel method to perform nonlinear classification.

Section 7.4 mainly mentions random forest and Adaboost in integrated learning. Random forest is an algorithm that uses multiple decision trees to train and predict samples. The final output category is determined by the mode of the categories output by individual decision trees, and Adaboost is an iterative algorithm that trains different weak classifiers for the same training set, and then combines these weak classifiers to form a stronger final classifier.

Section 7.5 deals with clustering, an unsupervised learning technique that discovers the inner structure. The subsection mainly introduces K-means clustering. Its core idea is to give a set of data points and the required number of clusters k. The K-means algorithm is based on the following: A certain distance function repeatedly divides the data into k clusters.

Section 7.6 introduces deep learning, which concept is derived from the research of artificial neural networks. It is to learn the internal laws and representation levels of sample data. By combining low-level features to form more abstract high-level representation attribute categories or features, to discover distributed feature representation of data.

References

1. Abdel-Zaher, A.M. and Eldeib, A.M. (2016). Breast cancer classification using deep belief networks, *Expert Systems with Applications, 46*: 139–144.
2. Affonso, C., Rossi, A.L.D., Vieira, F.H.A. and de Carvalho, A.C.P.d.L.F. (2017). Deep learning for biological image classification, *Expert Systems with Applications, 85*: 114–122.
3. Arulkumaran, K., Deisenroth, M.P., Brundage, M. and Bharath, A.A. (2017). A brief survey of deep reinforcement learning, *IEEE Signal Processing Magazine*.
4. Boser, B.E. (1992). A training algorithm for optimal margin classifiers, *Proc. Annu. Workshop Comput. Learning Theory Acm.* (in Pittsburgh, PA).
5. Bottou, L., Curtis, F. and Nocedal, J. (2018). Optimization methods for large-scale machine learning, *SIAM Review, 60*: 223–311.
6. Breiman, L. (2001). Random forests, *Machine Learning, 45*: 5–32.
7. Chen, Y.F., Everett, M., Liu, M. and How, J.P. (2017). Socially aware motion planning with deep reinforcement learning. arXiv:1703.08862v2 [cs.RO] 4 May 2018.
8. Chong, E., Han, C. and Park, F.C. (2017). Deep learning networks for stock market analysis and prediction: Methodology, data representations, and case studies, *Expert Systems with Applications*.
9. Cohen, J., Cohen, P., West, S.G. and Aiken, L.S. (2003). *Applied Multiple Regression/Correlation Analysis for the Behavioral Sciences* (Lawrence Erlbaum Associates, Hillsdale, NJ).
10. Cortes, C. and Vapnik, V. (1995). Support-vector networks, *Machine Learning, 20*: 273–297.
11. Cristianin, N. and Shawe-Taylar, J. (2000). *An Introduction to Support Vector Machines and Other Kernel-Based Learning Methods* (Cambridge University Press, Cambridge).
12. Deng, N.Y. and Tian, Y.J. (2005). *The New Data Mining Methods — Support Vector Machine* (Science Press, Beijing).
13. Dong, Y. and Li, D. (2014). *Automatic Speech Recognition: A Deep Learning Approach* (Springer, London).
14. Draper, N.R. and Smith, H. (1981). *Applied Regression Analysis*, 3rd edn. (Wiley, New York).
15. Gao, W., Hsu, D., Lee, W.S., Shen, S. and Subramanian, K. (2017). Intention-net: Integrating planning and deep learning for goal-directed autonomous navigation. arXiv:1710.05627v2 [cs.AI] 17 Oct 2017

16. Goodfellow, I., Bengio, Y. and Courville, A. (2016). *Deep Learning* (Vol. 1), (MIT Press, Cambridge), pp. 326–366.

17. Gu, J.X., Wang, Z.H., Kuen, J., Ma, L.Y., Shahroudy, A., Shahroudy, A., Shuai, B., Liu, T., Wang, X., Wang, G., Cai, J. and Chen, T. (2018). Recent advances in convolutional neural networks, *Pattern Recognition, 77*: 354–377.

18. Guo, S.Y., Zhang, X.G., Zheng, Y.S. and Du, Y.Q. (2020). An autonomous path planning model for unmanned ships based on deep reinforcement learning, *Sensors, 20*: 426.

19. Hastie, T., Tibshirani, R. and Friedman, J. (2001). *The Elements of Statistical Learning: Data Mining, Inference, and Prediction* (Springer-Verlag, New York).

20. Hastie, T., Tibshirani, R. and Friedman, J. (2009). *The Elements of Statistical Learning: Data Mining, Inference, and Prediction*, Chapter 15 "Random Forests" (Springer-Verlag, New York).

21. Henderson, P., Islam, R., Bachman, P., Pineau, J., Precup, D. and Meger, D. (2017). Deep reinforcement learning that matters, In *Proceedings of the 32*nd *AAAI Conference on Artificial Intelligence* (in USA).

22. Iqbal, R., Maniak, T., Doctor, F. and Karyotis, C. (2019). Fault detection and isolation in industrial processes using deep learning approaches, *IEEE Transactions on Industrial Informatics, 1*.

23. Kingma, D. and Ba, J. (2014). Adam: A method for stochastic optimization, *Computer Science*.

24. Lecun, Y. and Bengio, Y. (1998). *Convolutional Networks for Images, Speech, and Time Series*, (MIT Press, Cambridge).

25. Lecun, Y., Bottou, L., Bengio, Y. and Haffner, P. (1998). Gradient-based learning applied to document recognition, *Proceedings of the IEEE, 86*: 2278–2324.

26. Likas, A., Vlassis, N. and Verbeek, J.J. (2003). The global k-means clustering algorithm, *Pattern Recognition, 36*: 451–461.

27. Platt, J.C. (1999) *Fast Training of Support Vector Machines Using Sequential Minimal Optimization*, (MIT Press, Cambridge).

28. Quinlan, J.R. (1986). Induction on decision tree, *Machine Learning, 1*: 81–106.

29. Quinlan, J.R. (1992) *C4.5: Programs for Machine Learning*, (Morgan Kaufmann Publishers, Ross Quinlan).

30. Rodriguez, J.J. and Maudes, J. (2008). Boosting recombined weak classifiers, *Pattern Recognition Letters, 29*: 1049–1059.

31. Rumelhart, D.E., Hinton, G.E. and Williams, R.J. (1986). Learning representations by back-propagating errors, *Nature, 323*: 533–536.

32. Sallab, A., Abdou, M., Perot, E. and Yogamani, S. (2017). Deep reinforcement learning framework for autonomous driving, *Electronic Imaging, 2017*: 70–76.

33. Sánchez A, V.D. (2003). Advanced support vector machines and kernel methods, *Neurocomputing, 55*: 5–20.

34. Serrano, W. (2019). Deep reinforcement learning algorithms in intelligent infrastructure, *Infrastructures, 4*:52.

35. Stitson, M.O., Weston, J.A.E., Gammerman, A., Vovk, V. and Vapnik, V. (1996). Theory of support vector machines, *University of London, 117*: 188–191.

36. Tom, Y., Devamanyu, H., Soujanya, P. and Erik, C. (2018). Recent trends in deep learning based natural language processing, *IEEE Computational Intelligence Magazine, 13*: 55–75.
37. Wang, J.D., Chen, Y.Q., Hao, S.J. and Peng, X.H. (2019). Deep learning for sensor-based activity recognition: A survey, *Pattern Recognition Letters*, 119, 3–11.
38. Xu, R. and Wunsch, D. (2005). Survey of clustering algorithms, *IEEE Trans. Neural Networks, 16*: 645–678.
39. Zhang, W. (1988). Shift-invariant pattern recognition neural network and its optical architecture, *Proc. JSAP* (in Japanese).
40. Zhu, M.X., Wang, X.S. and Wang, Y.H. (2018). Human-like autonomous car-following model with deep reinforcement learning, *Transportation Research Part C: Emerging Technologies, 97*: 348–368.

PART 3
Application Examples of Artificial Intelligence

Algorithms — The Soul of AI
Computing Power — The Power of AI

Algorithms are accurate and complete descriptions of problem-solving solutions, and are clear instructions for solving a series of problems. They represent the strategy mechanism for describing problem-solving in a systematic way. Algorithms are the soul of artificial intelligence.

Computing power is the mathematical induction and transformation ability of the machine, i.e., the ability to convert abstract complex mathematical expressions or numbers into mathematical formulas that can be understood by mathematical methods. Computing power is the power of artificial intelligence.

The continuous innovation of algorithms and the continuous enhancement of computing power provide effective guarantees for artificial intelligence applications and greatly promote the development of artificial intelligence.

The applications of artificial intelligence discussed in Chapter 8 to Chapter 11 i.e., expert systems, intelligent planning, pattern recognition, speech recognition, and natural language processing all show the successful application of deep learning in solving artificial intelligence problems.

Expert System

8

Expert system is one of the main areas of artificial intelligence research and application, and has been developed and successfully applied for more than 50 years. As Feigenbaum, the pioneer of the expert system, said: "the power of the expert system is generated from the knowledge it deals with, rather than from some formalism and the reference patterns it uses" [25]. This is in line with a famous saying: Knowledge is power. By the 1980s, expert systems were rapidly developed and widely used around the world. Since the beginning of the 21st century, the expert system has been a valuable intelligent decision-making and problem-solving tool as well as a powerful assistant for human experts [10, 36].

8.1 Overview of Expert Systems

This section discusses the definition, characteristics, structure, and construction steps of an expert system. One source of constructing an expert system is an expert related to the problem. What is an expert? Experts are individuals who have a special ability to understand certain issues. Experts develop skills to solve problems effectively and quickly through experience. Our job is to "clone" these experts in the expert system.

8.1.1 *Definition, characteristics, and types of expert systems*

(1) Definition of the expert system

Various definitions exist for expert systems [5, 18, 19, 57].

Definition 8.1. An expert system is an intelligent computer program system that contains a large amount of expert-level knowledge and experience in a certain field. It can use the knowledge of human experts and problem-solving methods to deal with problems in this field. In other words, an expert system is a program system with a large amount of expertise and experience. It uses artificial intelligence and computer technology to make inferences and judgments based on the knowledge and experience provided by one or more experts in a certain field to simulate human expert decision-making process in order to solve the complex problems that need to be handled by human experts; in short, the expert system is a computer program system that simulates human experts to solve domain problems.

In addition to the above, there are other definitions of expert systems. Here is the definition of expert system given by Feigenbaum in 1982 [25].

Definition 8.2. An expert system is an intelligent computer program that uses knowledge and inference procedures to solve those problems that are difficult enough to require significant human expertise for solving them. That is, an expert system is a computer system that emulates the decision-making ability of a human expert. The term "emulate" means that the expert system is intended to act, in all respects, like a human expert [25].

Below is the definition of expert systems given by Weiss and Kulikowski [63].

Definition 8.3. Expert systems use computer models inferred from human experts to deal with complex problems in the real world that require experts to explain and draw the same conclusions as experts.

(2) Characteristics of expert systems

In general, expert systems have some common characteristics and advantages [10, 16].

The expert system has the following six characteristics:

(i) **Heuristic:** Expert systems can use expert knowledge and experience to make inferences, judgments, and decisions.

(ii) **Transparency:** The expert system can explain its own reasoning process and answer the questions raised by the user, so that the user can understand its reasoning process and improve the sense of trust in the expert system.

(iii) **Flexibility:** Expert systems can continuously update and increase knowledge, thus allowing expert systems to have a very wide range of applications.

(iv) **Dealing with uncertainty:** Imperfect knowledge leads to uncertainty; the expert system can process uncertain rules and data, make inferences, and use IF–THEN rules to derive problem solutions from the initial data.

(v) **The representation of knowledge:** Knowledge representation represents a specific problem in a specific way and storage. The best knowledge coding scheme is selected based on the type of knowledge. IF–THEN rules, semantic networks, and frameworks are the most commonly used schemes and are applied to the knowledge graph.

(vi) **Strong interpretability:** The expert system has the ability to reason, and it can be used to achieve internal recommendations in the industry. It mainly uses financial, medical, and other fields that require interpretability.

(3) Types of expert systems

According to the nature of the problem solved by the expert system, it can be roughly divided into the following types:

(i) Expert system for interpretation:

The task of the interpretation expert system is to determine the meaning of known information and data by analyzing and interpreting them [23].

(ii) Expert system for prediction:

The task of the prediction expert system is to infer what might happen in the future by analyzing past and present known conditions [14, 22, 49, 72].

(iii) Expert system for diagnosis:

The task of the diagnosis expert system is to infer the cause of a malfunction of an object based on the observed conditions (data) [17, 38, 45, 56, 70]. Many expert systems have been used in the medicine area [1, 4, 13, 51].

(iv) Expert system for design:

The task of the design expert system is to find the target configuration that meets the constraints of the design problem according to the design requirements [27, 37, 58, 63, 72].

(v) Expert system for planning:

The task of a planning expert system is to find a sequence or step of actions that can achieve a given goal [9, 12, 21].

(vi) Expert system for monitoring:

The task of the monitoring expert system is to continuously observe the behavior of the system, object or process, and compare the observed behavior with the behavior it should have in order to find abnormal conditions and issue alerts [6, 28, 52, 55].

(vii) Expert system for control:

The task of the control expert system is to adaptively manage the comprehensive behavior of a controlled object or object to meet the expected requirements [3, 11, 69].

(viii) Expert system for debugging:

The task of the debugging expert system is to give treatment opinions and methods to the failed object [7, 44, 71].

(ix) Expert system for instruction:

The task of the teaching expert system is to teach and coach students with the most appropriate lesson plans and teaching methods based on their characteristics, weaknesses, and basic knowledge [35, 43, 64, 67].

(x) Expert system for repair:

The task of the repair expert system is to process the faulty object, system, or equipment and restore it to normal operation. The repair expert system has functions for diagnosis, debugging, planning, and execution.

In addition, there are decision expert systems and consulting expert systems [31, 33, 37, 68]. Some expert systems are developed based on the fuzzy technique [15, 20, 35, 50, 53].

8.1.2 *Structure and construction steps of expert systems*

(1) Structure of expert systems

Figure 8.1 shows a simplified block diagram of the expert system. Figure 8.2 shows the structure of the ideal expert system. Since the tasks and characteristics required for each expert systems are different, the system structure is not the same and generally only some modules in the figure are included.

The interface is a medium for information exchange between people and the system, which provides users with an intuitive and convenient means

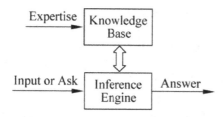

Figure 8.1   Simplified structure of expert systems.

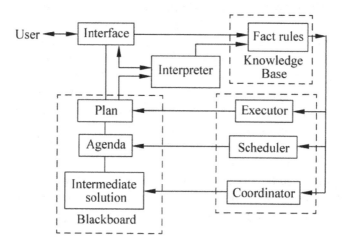

Figure 8.2   Structure of an ideal expert system.

of interaction. The function of the interface is to identify and interpret information such as commands, questions, and data that the user provides to the system, and to translate this information into an internal representation of the system. On the other hand, the interface also provides the user with questions, results, and explanations that are presented to the user in a form that is easy for the user to understand.

The blackboard is a database used to record the control information, intermediate assumptions, and intermediate results used in the system's reasoning process. It includes plans, agendas, and intermediate solutions. The plan records the current processing plan, goals, current status of the problem, and problem background. The agenda records some actions to be performed, most of which are derived from the existing results in the blackboard and the rules in the knowledge base. The intermediate solution area stores the results and candidate hypotheses that have been generated by the current system.

The knowledge base consists of two parts. One is the known data or information related to the current problem; the other is the general knowledge and domain knowledge used in reasoning. Most of this knowledge is expressed in the form of rules, networks, and processes.

The scheduler selects an item from the agenda as the next action to be performed by the system, on the basis of the control knowledge given by the system builder (usually using the priority method). The actuator applies the information recorded in the knowledge base and on the blackboard to perform the actions selected by the scheduler. The main function of the coordinator is to correct the results obtained when new data or new hypotheses are obtained, to maintain consistency before and after the results.

The function of the interpreter is to explain the behavior of the system to the user, including the correctness of the interpretation of the conclusions and the reasons for the system to output other candidate solutions. In order to accomplish this, it is often necessary to take advantage of the intermediate results, intermediate assumptions, and knowledge in the knowledge base recorded on the blackboard.

The expert system usually consists of six parts: knowledge base, comprehensive database, reasoning machine, interpreter, human–machine interface, and knowledge acquisition.

(i) Knowledge base

The knowledge base is used to store the expertise of expert systems in a domain, including facts, feasible operations, and rules. The knowledge in the knowledge base originates from domain experts and is the key to determining the capabilities of the expert system. That is, the quality and quantity of knowledge in the knowledge base determine the quality level of the expert system.

(ii) Global database

A comprehensive database is a collection that reflects the current problem-solving status and is used to store all the information generated during the operation of the system as well as the required raw data, including user input information, intermediate results, reasoning process records, etc.

(iii) Reasoning machine

The reasoning machine (inference engine) is used to memorize the rules and control strategies used, to enable the entire expert system to work in a logical and coordinated manner. The inference engine is able to reason and derive conclusions on the basis of knowledge, rather than simply searching for ready-made answers.

(iv) Interpreter

The interpreter is able to explain to the user the behavior of the expert system, including explaining the correctness of the inference conclusions and the reasons for the system to output other candidate solutions.

(v) Interface

An interface enables the system to talk to the user, enabling the user to enter the necessary data, ask questions, and understand the reasoning process and reasoning results.

(vi) Knowledge acquisition

Responsible for establishing, modifying, and expanding the knowledge base, including knowledge extraction, collection, modeling, and verification.

(2) Construction steps of the expert system

The key to successfully build a system is to start building the system as early as possible, starting with a relatively small system and gradually expanding it into a fairly large and sophisticated test system [18, 26, 29].

The general steps to establish a system are as follows:

(i) Designing the initial knowledge base. The designing of the knowledge base is the most important and arduous task in building an expert system. The designing of the initial knowledge base includes the following steps: the knowledge of the problem, the conceptualization of the knowledge, the formalization of the concepts, the regularization of the forms, and the legalization of the rules, which have been introduced in the section on the knowledge base in Chapter 2 and will not be repeated here.

(ii) Development and testing of prototypes. After selecting the knowledge expression method, we can proceed to build the experimental subset required by the entire system, which includes the typical knowledge of the entire model and only involves sufficiently simple tasks and reasoning processes related to the experiment.

(iii) Improvement and induction of knowledge base. Repeatedly improve the knowledge base and reasoning rules in order to conclude more perfect results. After a considerable amount of effort, the system has reached the level of a human expert within a certain range.

8.2 Rule-based Expert System

This chapter will discuss a rule-based expert system, a framework-based expert system, a model-based expert system, and a web-based expert system one by one according to the working mechanism and structure of expert systems. This section describes a rule-based expert system [8, 63, 66].

8.2.1 *Working model and architecture of a rule-based expert system*

(1) Working model of a rule-based expert system

The idea of a production system is simple but very effective. The production system is the basis of the expert system, and the expert system is developed from the production system. The rule-based expert system is a computer program that processes specific problem information (facts) in the working memory using a set of rules contained in the knowledge base, inferring new information through the reasoning machine. Its working model is shown in Figure 8.3.

As can be seen from Figure 8.3, a rule-based expert system uses the following modules to model the production system:

(i) Knowledge base. Establish a long-term memory model of people with a set of rules.

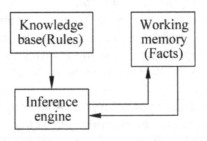

Figure 8.3   Rule-based working model.

(ii) Working memory. Establish a human short-term memory model that stores the facts of the problem and the new facts inferred by the rules.

(iii) Inference engine. By combining the facts of the problems stored in the working memory with the rules stored in the knowledge base, a human reasoning model is established to infer new information. The inference engine acts as a reasoning module for the production system model and compares the facts with the preconditions of the rules (the former) to see which rules can be activated. Through these activation rules, the inference engine adds the conclusions to the working memory and processes them until no other preconditions of the rules match the facts in the working memory.

The rule-based expert system does not require an exact match for human problem-solving, but can provide a reasonable model for solving the problem using a computer.

(2) Structure of a rule-based expert system

The complete structure of a rule-based expert system is shown in Figure 8.4. Among them, the knowledge base, inference engine, and working memory are the core of this expert system. The other components or subsystems are as follows:

(iv) User interface. Through this interface, the user observes the system and talks (interacts) with the system.

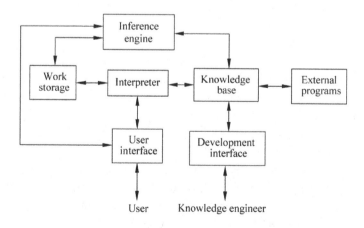

Figure 8.4   Structure of a rule-based expert system.

(v) Development interface. The knowledge engineer develops the expert system through this interface.

(vi) Interpreter. Provides an explanation of the reasoning process of the system.

(vii) External procedures. Such as database, expansion disk, and algorithm, etc., support the work of the expert system. They should be easily accessible and usable by expert systems.

Rule-based expert systems have been in development and application for decades and have been proven to be an effective technology. The flexibility of expert system development tools can greatly reduce the development time for rule-based expert systems. Although expert systems have evolved toward goal-oriented design in the 1990s, rule-based expert systems continue to play an important role. Rule-based expert systems have many advantages and disadvantages. It is important to match development tools to problem solving when designing and developing expert systems.

8.2.2 *Features of a rule-based expert system*

Any expert system has its advantages and disadvantages. Its advantages are the reason for developing such expert systems, and its disadvantages are the reason for improving or creating new expert systems to replace such expert systems.

(1) Advantages of a rule-based expert system

The rule-based expert system has the following advantages.

(i) Natural expression

For many problems, humans use IF–THEN-type sentences to naturally express their knowledge of solving problems. The advantage of this easy-to-capture knowledge in the form of rules makes the rule-based approach more attractive for expert system design.

(ii) Separation of control and knowledge

The rule-based expert system separates the knowledge contained in the knowledge base from the control of the inference engine. This feature is not unique to rule-based expert systems, but is a hallmark of all expert systems. This valuable feature allows the knowledge or control of the expert system to be changed separately.

(iii) Knowledge modularization

Rules are independent blocks of knowledge. A rule logically extracts the facts related to the problem in the THEN part from the facts established in the IF part. Since it is an independent block of knowledge, a rule is easy to check and correct.

(iv) Easy to expand

The separation of expert system knowledge and control can easily add rules that can be reasonably explained by expert system knowledge. As long as you adhere to the grammatical rules of your chosen software to ensure a logical relationship between rules, you can add new rules anywhere in the knowledge base.

(v) Intelligence level increases proportionally

Even a rule can be a valuable piece of knowledge. It can tell the expert system some new information about the problem from the established evidence. As the number of rules increases, the level of intelligence of the expert system for this problem increases similarly.

(vi) Use related knowledge

Expert systems use only rules that are relevant to the problem. Rule-based expert systems may have a large number of rules that raise a lot of issues. But expert systems can decide which rules to use to solve current problems based on what they have discovered.

(vii) Get explanation from strict grammar

Because the problem-solving model matches the various facts in the working memory, it often provides an opportunity to decide how to put information into the working memory. Because information may already be placed by using rules that depend on other facts, the rules used can be tracked to derive information.

(viii) Consistency check

The strict structure of the rules allows expert systems to perform consistency checks to ensure that the same situation does not behave differently. The shells of many expert systems are able to use the strict structure of rules to automatically check the consistency of rules and warn developers that there may be conflicts.

(ix) Use of heuristic knowledge

The typical advantage of human experts is that they are particularly proficient in using the "law of thumb" or inspiring information to help them solve problems efficiently. These heuristics are "trading tricks" that are extracted from experience, and they are more important than the basic principles learned in the classroom. You can write heuristic rules for general situations to draw conclusions or control the search of the knowledge base efficiently.

(x) Use of uncertain knowledge

For many issues, the information available will only establish the level of trust for some issues, rather than asserting it with complete certainty. Rules are easily written in a form that requires uncertain relationships.

(xi) Variables can be shared

Rules can use variables to improve the efficiency of expert systems. These can be limited to many instances in the working memory and pass the rules test. In general, by using variables, you can write general rules that apply to a large number of similar objects.

(2) Disadvantages of rule-based expert systems

The rule-based expert system has the following disadvantages: The rules and facts must match exactly, there is an unclear logical relationship between the rules, the processing is slow, and it may not be applicable to certain areas.

8.3 Model-based Expert System

The rule-based expert system is based on the logical mental model, which is a computer program system that uses rule logic or framework logic and uses logic as a tool to describe heuristic knowledge. Expert systems that integrate various models have stronger functions in terms of knowledge representation, knowledge acquisition, and knowledge application than those based on logical mental models, making it possible to significantly improve the design of expert systems. This section describes a model-based expert system [34, 62, 65].

8.3.1 *Proposal of a model-based expert system*

There are different opinions on the research content of artificial intelligence. There is a view that artificial intelligence is the study of the computational methods of obtaining, expressing, and using various qualitative models (physical, perceptual, cognitive, and social system models). According to this view, the knowledge base in a knowledge system is a combination of various models, which are often qualitative models. Since the establishment of the model is closely related to knowledge, the acquisition, expression, and use of the model naturally include knowledge acquisition, knowledge representation, and knowledge use. The model summarizes qualitative physical models and mental models. Looking at the design of the expert system from this point of view, it can be considered that an expert system is a combination of models with different principles and operating modes.

The advantages of using a variety of qualitative models to design expert systems are obvious. On the one hand, it increases the functionality of the system and improves the performance indicators; on the other hand, it can independently study various models and their related problems and use the obtained results to improve the system design. There is a PESS (Purity Expert System), an expert system development tool that utilizes four models: logic-based mental models, neural network models, qualitative physical models, and visual knowledge models. These four models are not isolated, and PESS allows users to combine these models. Based on these viewpoints, the nuclear reactor fault diagnosis expert system and the TCM medical diagnosis expert system based on neural network have been completed; this provides a solution to overcome the bottleneck problem of knowledge acquisition in expert systems. The qualitative physical model provides a description of deep knowledge and reasoning; this improves the problem solving and interpretation ability of the system. As for the visual knowledge model, it can effectively use visual knowledge, and can use graphics and clustering technique to express human knowledge and object data in the system and complete human–computer interaction tasks [47].

Among many models, artificial neural network models are the most widely used. As early as 1988, some people applied neural networks to expert systems to promote the development of traditional expert systems.

8.3.2 *Expert system based on neural networks*

The neural network model is essentially different from the logic-based mental model in the current expert system from knowledge representation, reasoning mechanism, to control method. Knowledge changes from explicit representation to implicit representation. This knowledge is not converted into rules through human processing, but is automatically obtained through learning algorithms. The reasoning mechanism changes from the retrieval and verification process to the competition of the implicit mode on the network. This kind of competition is parallel and related to specific characteristics, and transforms the abstract concepts in the specific domain input mode into the input data of the neural network, and appropriately interprets the output data of the neural network according to the characteristics of the domain.

How to combine the neural network model with the logic-based mental model is a topic worthy of further study. From the perspective of human problem-solving, knowledge storage and low-level information processing are distributed in parallel, while high-level information processing is sequential. Deduction and induction are indispensable from logical reasoning, and the combination of the two can better express the intelligent behavior of human beings. From the designing of the expert system integrating the two models, the knowledge base is composed of some knowledge elements, which can be a neural network module or a set of rules or framework of logic modules. As long as the input transformation rules and output interpretation rules of the neural network are formally expressed so that they are similar to the external interface and the knowledge expression structure used by the system, the traditional reasoning mechanism and scheduling mechanism can be directly applied to the expert system. The integration of the network and the traditional expert system work together and complement each other. Depending on the focus, there are three modes of integration:

(1) Neural network-supported expert system. It is based on the traditional expert system and supplemented by related technologies of neural networks. For example, knowledge and examples provided by experts are automatically acquired through neural networks. Another example is the use of neural network parallel reasoning techniques to improve the efficiency of reasoning.

(2) Expert system-supported neural networks. Taking the relevant technology of the neural network as the core, the expert system in the corresponding field is established, and the relevant technology of the expert system is used to complete the interpretation and other aspects.

(3) Collaborative neural network expert system. For large complex problems, it is decomposed into several sub-problems. For each

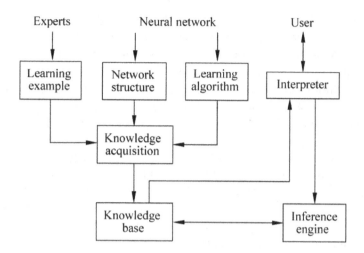

Figure 8.5   Basic structure of neural network expert system.

sub-problem, choose to use a neural network or expert system to realize a coupling relationship between the neural network and the expert system.

Figure 8.5 shows the basic structure of a neural network expert system. Among them, the automatic acquisition module inputs, organizes, and stores the learning examples provided by the experts, selects the structure of the neural network, and invokes the learning algorithm of the neural network to realize knowledge acquisition for the knowledge base. After the new learning instance is input, the knowledge acquisition module automatically obtains a new network weight distribution by learning the new instance, thereby updating the knowledge base.

The neural network expert system possesses the following features:

(1) The knowledge representation of a neural network is an implicit representation that associates several knowledges of a problem domain with each other in a neural network. For a combined expert system, both explicit and implicit representations of knowledge are employed.
(2) A neural network realizes automatic knowledge acquisition through case learning. Domain experts provide learning examples and their expected solutions, and neural network learning algorithms continually modify the weight distribution of the network. The neural network that

achieves stable weight distribution after learning and correcting errors is the knowledge base of the neural network expert system.

(3) The reasoning of a neural network is a forward nonlinear numerical calculation process, and it is also a parallel reasoning mechanism. Since the output of each output node of the neural network is a numerical value, an interpreter is required to interpret the output mode.

(4) A neural network expert system can be represented by a weighted directed graph or by a neighboring weight matrix. Therefore, several independent expert systems in the same knowledge domain can be combined into a larger neural network expert system, as long as each sub-node with connections between systems can be connected. The combined neural network expert system can provide more learning examples, and through learning and training, a more reliable and rich knowledge base can be obtained. In contrast, if several rule-based expert systems are combined into a larger expert system, since the rules in each knowledge base are determined individually, the redundancy and inconsistency of the rules in the combined knowledge base are large; that is to say, the more the rules of each subsystem, the less reliable the combined large system knowledge base.

8.4 Web-based Expert System

With the development of Internet technology, the Web has gradually become the interactive interface of most software users. Software is gradually becoming networked and embodied as a Web service. The development of expert systems is also inseparable from this trend. The user interface of the expert system has gradually moved closer to the Web, and the knowledge base and inference engine of the expert system have gradually interacted with the Web interface. The Web has become a new and important feature of the expert system [42, 60, 61].

8.4.1 *Structure of the Web-based expert system*

The Web-based expert system is a new technology that integrates traditional expert systems and Web data interaction. This combined technology simplifies the application of complex decision analysis methods, delivering solutions to workers through the intranet, or delivering solutions to customers and suppliers via the Web.

The traditional expert system is mainly for people to interact with a single machine, and at the most through the client/server network structure

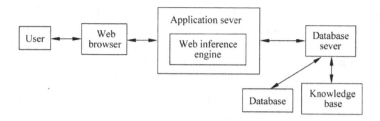

Figure 8.6   Structure of a Web-based expert system.

to interact within the local area network. The Web-based expert system locates human–computer interaction at the Internet level. Experts, knowledge engineers, and ordinary users can access the expert system's application server through the browser, and transfer the problem to the Web inference engine, and then, the Web inference engine, through the background database server, accesses the database and the knowledge base to derive some conclusions and then tells the user the conclusions. The simple structure of the Web-based expert system is shown in Figure 8.6. It is mainly divided into three levels: browser, application logic layer, and database layer. This structure conforms to the three-layer network structure.

Based on this basic Web-based expert system architecture, a wide variety of Web-based expert systems and their tools can be designed. Here is an example of the structure of a Web-based remote diagnosis expert system for aircraft faults.

In the aviation department, the traditional method for diagnosis of aircraft faults is to analyze and judge the faults of the on-site crew according to the fault phenomenon, and then take corresponding measures. For technical problems that cannot be handled on site, it is often necessary to consult relevant technical personnel or relevant experts in the field, and the process of contacting experts not only affects the timely processing of faults, but also causes huge losses to the department. A Web-based expert system for remote diagnosis of aircraft faults provides a new way to solve such problems. The system makes full use of the rich maintenance experience of old maintenance personnel and experts to provide convenient and fast remote fault diagnosis solutions for the maintenance department, and improve the work ability and efficiency of the department.

The remote diagnosis expert system is mainly composed of three parts: a server-side diagnostic expert system based on knowledge base, a diagnostic consulting system based on Web browser, and a maintenance management system for expert knowledge base. The core of the system is an expert system based on knowledge base. It not only has database management and deductive capabilities, but also provides intelligent modules such as expert reasoning and judgment. In order to improve data transmission efficiency and structural flexibility, the system adopts a browser/Web/server three-tier architecture, and the user sends an aircraft failure phenomenon, a consultation request, etc. to the Web server through a browser, and the server-side expert system receives the browser. After requesting the information, the knowledge base is called, the inference module is run to perform the inference and judgment, and finally the generated fault diagnosis result is displayed on the browser to realize the function of remote diagnosis. The core of fault diagnosis is the expert system, and the key to the designing of the expert system is the designing of the knowledge base. Usually, the storage of the knowledge base is in the form of a linked list. The expansion, deletion, and modification operations of the knowledge base are essentially a node for inserting, deleting, and modifying a linked list. Compared with the linked list, the source language DBMS is used to manage the knowledge base. The design of the library structure is simpler and faster, and the operation of the knowledge base is also convenient and reliable. After a comprehensive analysis of many current database products, choose MS SQL Server 2000 as the expert system database management system, since it is not only a high-performance multi-user database system, but it also provides Web support, with data fault tolerance, integrity check and security, and other functions. It can realize interoperation between data in the network environment. The fault diagnosis expert system is mainly composed of knowledge base (rules, facts), inference engine, interpreter and Web interface, as shown in Figure 8.7.

The knowledge base of the expert system consists of a rule base and a fact base. The rule base stores a collection of production rules; the fact base stores a collection of facts, including the facts or intermediate results (facts) entered and some facts from the final reasoning. At present, the combination of expert systems and databases is mainly achieved by system coupling — "strong coupling" and "weak coupling". Strong coupling means that the DBMS manages both the rule base and the fact store; the system design is more complex with this method. Weak coupling combines the expert system and the DBMS as two separate subsystems that manage the rule base and the fact base, respectively.

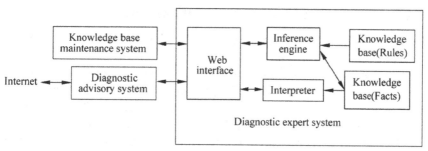

(a) Structure of the remote diagnostic expert system

(b) The process of Web user access server expert system

Figure 8.7   Structure of the Web-based expert system of aircraft fault remote diagnosis.

In order to improve the understandability (comprehensibility), testability, reliability, and maintainability of the system, the expert system is constructed by weakly coupling, and the rule base and the fact base are managed separately.

The inference engine is a program for memorizing the rules used and the operation of the control system, so that the entire expert system can coordinate the work in a logical manner, and the choice of the reasoning method will have a great influence on the performance of the entire expert system.

There are three main methods of reasoning: forward reasoning, reverse reasoning, and forward and reverse mixed reasoning. The system mainly uses forward reasoning, first verifies the correctness of the submitted diagnostic request, and then reads the corresponding rules in the rule base according to the diagnostic request, searches the known fact table in the fact base, and finds the fact that matches the request condition.

The interpreter explains the behavior of the expert system to the user, including explaining the correctness of the reasoning process and the reasons why the system had to output other candidates. The inference engine and interpreter are implemented by the source language ASP technology, and the interface with the knowledge base is realized by ODBC.

8.4.2 Example of a Web-based expert system

As an example, this section introduces a Web-based expert system for the remote diagnosis of aircraft faults.

The design of the Web-based aircraft-fault remote-diagnosis expert system involves more content, including database technology, artificial intelligence technology, Web technology, and also combined with aircraft fault diagnosis technology. It is an interdisciplinary, multi-branch comprehensive information processing system. A prototype system has been established for a certain type of aircraft, which can achieve remote diagnosis of common faults. However, a lot of hard and detailed work is yet to be done, such as updating and improving the knowledge base, further improving intelligence, and speeding up the diagnosis. Only by continuously improving the overall performance of the entire system can the remote diagnosis expert system be more practical and better serve the department.

The function and structure of the Web-based aircraft fault remote diagnosis expert system have been introduced previously. The implementation of this system is discussed below. The first is the implementation of its diagnostic consulting system.

(1) Implementation of the diagnostic consultation system

In order to enable the user to employ the expert diagnosis system conveniently and quickly, the user-oriented application must be based on the browser/server (B/S) mode in the design, so that the user can quickly realize expert consultation through the browser and troubleshoot timely. The user page is designed in HTML format, using dynamic interaction, dynamic generation and ActiveX control technology, and the embedded ASP (Active Server Page) program to achieve connection with the expert system of the remote server.

To achieve the connection between the Web and the expert system, there are many technologies that can be used, such as CGI (Common Gateway Interface), ISAP, Java Applet, ASP, and PHP (Personal Home Page); choose ASP technology to achieve interface programming between Web and expert systems.

ASP is a development environment for Microsoft's Web server. It runs under Microsoft's IIS (Internet Information Server/Windows NT) or PWS (Personal Web Server/Windows 95/98). ASP is built into HTML files. It is written in the JavaScript or VBScript scripting language and provides application objects, session objects, request objects, response objects, server objects, etc., which can be used to receive and send information from the browser and provide data and provide access data components (ADO), file access components, AD conversion components, content connection components, and more. By interacting with the database through the ADO (Active Data Object) component, you can achieve high-performance connectivity to any ODBC compliant database or OLE DB data source. ADO allows web developers to easily connect a database to an "activated" Web page to access and manipulate data. Since the ASP application is running on the server side, and not on the browser, it achieves independence of the ASP from the browser and improves the efficiency of data processing.

(2) Management and maintenance of knowledge base

Because the knowledge base plays a vital role in the entire expert system, its own advantages and disadvantages will directly affect the quality of the diagnosis results, so it is of great significance to the management and maintenance of the knowledge base. The knowledge base system should always maintain consistency of the production rules, and accuracy and completeness of the fact data throughout the operation.

The knowledge base mainly comes from domain experts and past event records. Therefore, it requires a large amount of data collection, analysis, processing, and sorting work, and it is necessary to structure and standardize these data. To this end, various fault phenomena are classified, indexing and creating keywords to facilitate processing and retrieval of data.

Based on the collection, analysis, and arrangement of the original data, according to the data structure design specification, the main table of the database system is established in the SQL Server system, and the relationship between various data is determined at the same time, and a large amount of original data is collected intensively to construct the system basic information base.

8.5   Design of the Expert System

This section takes the rule-based expert system as an example to discuss the general design method of the expert system.

The following is a discussion of the steps or processes by which a knowledge engineer designs and develops a reverse-rule based expert system, and illustrates the design process with a personal investment planning problem as an example. Through the iterative process of system knowledge expansion, testing and refinement, it can be observed how the capabilities of the expert systems designed and developed are gradually improved and upgraded. Among them, some design suggestions are also involved.

When discussing the rule deduction system, it was pointed out that the rule-based system contains two kinds of reasoning methods, namely forward reasoning and backward reasoning (reverse reasoning). Forward reasoning operates from a fact or condition to a goal or action, while backward reasoning operates from a goal or action to a fact or condition.

Before designing any expert system, the designer's first task is to gain a general understanding of the relevant issues, including the need to determine the goals of the system, the main issues considered by the experts, and how the experts can use the information obtained to derive recommendations. Based on this understanding, it is possible to start thinking about the design method of the actual system.

The design of any type of expert system is a highly iterative process. First, get a small amount of knowledge from domain experts, use that knowledge to code the system, and then test the system. The test results are used to identify the deficiencies of the system and becomes the focus of further discussions with domain experts. This cycle runs through the entire increasing process of project knowledge; through evolutionary mode, the capabilities of expert systems are improved and upgraded to expert levels. Figure 8.8 illustrates this loop design process.

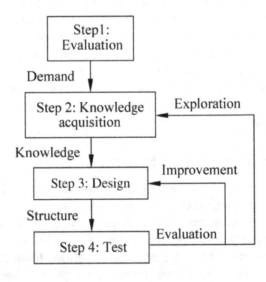

Figure 8.8   Design process based on the rule expert system.

This loop development approach is used to build a backward reasoning system, but this loop processing method is not unique to this type of system. Interestingly, this approach matches the work of the back-inference system. That is, first determine the main goals of the system and the methods that can establish these goals (target rules); then look for ways to obtain information that supports these target rules. This process naturally leads to deep rules that contain more primitive information. As with the operation of the backward reasoning system, this development process gradually moves from abstraction to concrete action.

The development of expert systems for financial advisory services has been very active, and loan application review, business strategy master plan, portfolio selection, etc. are very representative projects. Projects in these areas can attract the developers of expert systems for the following reasons: systems can provide real remuneration, tasks are easy to define, there exist realistic experts, and many expert systems are already available for financial advisory services. Most expert systems for the financial sector use backward reasoning techniques.

The representative tasks of designing and developing a reverse reasoning expert system include the following seven items: defining the problems, defining goals, designing goal rules, expanding systems, improving systems, designing interfaces, and evaluating systems.

However, it must be recognized that these tasks are only part of a highly iterative process of the system. First follow these steps to create a part of the expert system, and then repeat these steps over and over again, so that the system is perfected to the expert performance level.

8.6 Expert Systems Based on Machine Learning

Expert systems with various functions (such as analysis, classification, interpretation, prediction, identification, diagnosis, design, planning, control, teaching, etc.) may no longer be called "expert systems" but may be called intelligent diagnostic instrument, intelligent planner, intelligent control system and xx intelligent system. But in essence it still belongs to the category of expert systems, and it is also technically innovative, even higher than the traditional expert system. This section first introduces the general situation of the development and application of various expert systems based on machine learning, and then illustrates the application of expert systems based on deep learning.

8.6.1 *Introduction to expert systems based on machine learning*

In the past 10 years, many machine learning-based expert systems have been developed and applied. Deep learning uses multi-layer neural networks to represent abstract data to build computational models. For example, the effective application of deep learning algorithms such as convolutional neural networks, recurrent neural networks, and generative adversarial networks has completely changed our understanding of information processing in expert systems.

The fault detection and diagnosis (FDD) expert system is an important area of traditional expert systems. The machine learning-based fault diagnosis expert system is an important development direction of new expert systems. For example, to overcome the shortcomings of traditional expert system rule representation, a machine learning method for training and modifying rules was proposed to make the expert system a self-learning expert system [40]; after the method was applied to the expert system for cattle disease diagnosis, the performance of the expert system was improved. For another example, in order to provide support for the advanced computer expert system for severe accident management, two novel concepts are proposed, namely, first, support for plant state assessment and subsequent decision-making based on advanced machine learning algorithms; second, based on application graph theory and hydraulic technology provide the technical support center staff with practical guidance on the best equipment to implement the selected strategy [48]. In addition, there are glaucoma fundus image diagnosis tools based on convolutional neural network [54], industrial process fault detection and isolation [70], track fault monitoring expert system [30] and deep learning-based power equipment fault diagnosis expert system [41], etc.

Another important aspect of machine learning-based expert systems is data and image analysis. Data science is an interdisciplinary field that involves analyzing data to make useful inferences and deductions. The combination of data science and machine learning is the key to the automation of the data analysis process. It enables the analysis expert system to complete the data analysis work in an automated way, and provides a more effective and faster method for data analysis. Examples of this are stock market analysis and forecasting [22], case-based expert application of the system in data analysis [23], breast cancer image analysis [2], etc. Among them, a study reviewed the main deep learning concepts related to medical image analysis and summarized more than 300 cases in this field, investigating deep learning for medical image classification, object detection, segmentation, registration and other tasks. Based on this, it is pointed out that deep learning algorithms (especially convolutional networks) have become the preferred method of medical image analysis [39].

Over the years, research advances in deep learning have attracted increasing interest from people in how to use deep learning in robotic systems. Deep reinforcement learning will make robotic systems take a step towards establishing autonomous systems with a higher level of understanding of the visual world. Currently, deep learning enables reinforcement learning to be extended to previously difficult problems such as learning robot control strategies directly from camera inputs in the real world. For example, based on the discussion of the applications, benefits, and difficulties of deep learning, research studies explore the practical factors that must be considered when using deep learning and how to apply deep learning to other research in the field of robotics [32]. Another example, inspired by Google DeepMind games and Go presentations, proposed a framework for autonomous driving using deep reinforcement learning; due to strong interaction with the environment (including other vehicles, pedestrians, and road engineering), it is difficult to consider autonomous driving as a supervised learning problem. Ahmed and Abdel-Zaher propose a framework for deep reinforcement learning and incorporates recurrent neural networks for formation integration to enable autonomous vehicles to handle partially observable scenarios. The framework has been tested in an open source 3D racing simulator called TORCS. Simulation results show that autonomous driving can be learned under complex road curvature and simple interaction with other vehicles [3].

Expert systems based on deep learning are also used for stock market prediction, film rate category prediction, tomato leaf disease detection, industrial process fault detection, mobile robot navigation [32], interpretation and certification, social network analysis, forecast interpretation and demonstration, natural language processing, automatic fast and accurate classification [46], medical question answering system [64], information retrieval and recommendation system classification [67], sensor activity recognition [59], and other directions.

8.6.2 *Example of expert systems based on deep learning*

As mentioned earlier, the task of the fault diagnosis expert system is to infer the cause of the malfunction of the diagnosis object based on the observed conditions (data). After inputting the current information of the device, the diagnostic system can call historical data for inference, get the running status information of the detection object, and give an explanation. The following introduces a fault detection and diagnosis expert system for substation power equipment, and proposes a detection algorithm for high-voltage bushings and insulators, as well as the design and implementation of this fault diagnosis expert system [41].

(1) SVM high-voltage bushing detection based on Hu invariant moment

(i) Detection principle and method

Targeting the problem of high-voltage bushing detection, a transformer high-voltage bushing database is used. According to the specific distribution of high-voltage bushings in the substation, a support vector machine (SVM) high-voltage bushing detection method based on Hu invariant moment is proposed and applied to accurate registration of high-voltage bushings. The improved Niblack algorithm combined with morphological closed operation is introduced into the feature extraction step. This removes most of the interference in the image and retains the morphological characteristics of the high-voltage bushing, thereby improving the success rate of high-voltage bushing extraction. After extracting features from the area to be identified, use each area feature as detection data, and use SVM to classify the area to be identified. At the same time, during the SVM training process, the SVM parameters are optimized to obtain the best parameters in the data set to obtain the best detection accuracy.

(ii) Detection algorithm structure

The SVM high-voltage bushing detection method based on Hu invariant moment is optimized for the special environment of the substation and the characteristics of the data set. First, the original image is converted into a grayscale image, and then the improved Niblack method is used to perform threshold segmentation on the image to remove complex background interference. Then, according to the morphological characteristics of the bushing and the interference object, the morphological closed operation is used to expand and corrode the image, eliminate the interference of the cable and the fence, and obtain the area to be identified. After the preprocessing is completed, the invariant region in the image is calculated using Hu invariant moments to obtain the characteristics of the region to be identified. Finally, the SVM is used as a classifier to classify the regions to be identified, and the optimal parameters of the SVM are found during the training process of the SVM to improve the classification accuracy of the samples. A block diagram of the fault detection principle and detection algorithm is shown in Figure 8.9.

The core of this detection algorithm consists of two parts: feature extraction based on Hu invariant moments and SVM classifier classification based on genetic algorithm optimization. The feature extraction part includes image preprocessing and Hu moment invariant feature extraction.

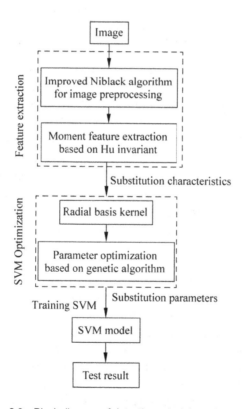

Figure 8.9 Block diagram of detection principle and algorithm.

SVM classification is divided into genetic algorithm-based parameter optimization and SVM training, and the model is used for detection after the model training is completed.

The steps of SVM parameter optimization based on genetic algorithm are divided into the following steps:

(a) encode the SVM parameters and generate an initial population;
(b) decode the chromosomes of all individuals in the population to form an SVM parameter model;
(c) train the parameter model using the training data set to obtain a trained SVM classifier;
(d) use the method of cross-validation to evaluate the performance of the SVM classifier to obtain the fitness of each individual in the population;
(e) determine whether the conditions for stopping the optimization are met (the evolution algebra reaches the upper limit, or an optimal solution is generated). If it is satisfied, save the result and stop searching; if it is not satisfied, select, cross, and mutate the individuals in the population to form a new generation of population, and go to step (b).

The proposed SVM detection algorithm based on Hu invariant moment can effectively detect high-voltage bushing, and improves the reasonable setting of SVM parameters and the classification effect of SVM.

(2) Insulator detection based on multi-scale convolutional neural networks

Aiming at the characteristics of wide distribution and large-scale change of insulators in substations, an insulator detection method based on multi-scale convolutional neural networks was proposed based on insulators in power substations. This algorithm uses the difference in sensitivity of image blocks of different scales to different objects, and designs three CNNs networks of different scales for learning and detection, respectively. Finally, three detection fusion algorithms are designed based on the characteristics of the three networks, and the confidence matrices of the three networks are fused to obtain better detection results. Compared with the traditional convolutional neural network, the algorithm has a stronger anti-interference ability, can adapt to more complex environments, and has a better anti-interference ability for occlusion problems between devices. Experimental results show that compared with the SIFT algorithm and the faster R-CNN algorithm, this method has more accurate identification and more accurate location of insulators.

(3) Expert system for fault diagnosis of power equipment

(i) Fault diagnosis expert system structure

Based on the high-voltage bushing and insulator detection algorithm, a fault diagnosis expert system for power equipment is designed. The system is mainly divided into two parts: the detection subsystem and the diagnostic subsystem. The detection subsystem accurately identifies and locates the equipment, and the diagnostic subsystem detects and diagnoses the thermal state of the equipment. The algorithm of the diagnostic subsystem has a self-learning ability. Knowledge and rules are acquired by training the algorithm model and stored in the algorithm model invisible. No manual extraction is needed; this feature improves the knowledge acquisition ability and self-learning ability of the expert system. The diagnostic subsystem uses the detection results and combines infrared images to locate the heating part of the device through the registration technology of visible light images and infrared images. Subsequently, the equipment heating information is input into the system, and the operating status of the equipment is diagnosed through the knowledge base and inference engine of the diagnosis subsystem, and finally the equipment failure information and maintenance suggestions are obtained.

Compared with the traditional expert system, this system makes full use of the detection algorithm and integrates the detection knowledge base and inference engine into the detection algorithm, which reduces the difficulty of system design and maintenance and increases the adaptability of the system. This system structure is mainly composed of a detection subsystem and a diagnosis subsystem, and each part contains different content and completes different functions. Each part of the system is relatively independent, which is convenient for modification and data addition. The system block diagram is shown in Figure 8.10.

As can be seen from Figure 8.10, the detection subsystem of the system can run independently, and its detection results are used as input data for the diagnostic subsystem. In actual operation, the high-voltage bushing detection subsystem and the insulator detection subsystem of the detection system need to be trained first, and the training model is stored. The detection system calls the visible light database and the trained model to complete the diagnostic function.

(ii) Detection subsystem

The main function of the detection system is to detect and locate the object to be identified, which mainly includes three parts: a detection

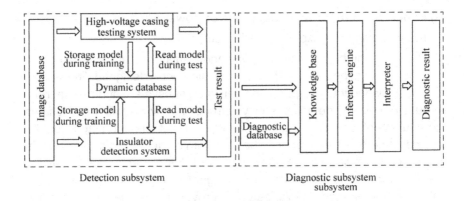

Figure 8.10　Expert system architecture.

database, a high-voltage bushing detection system, and an insulator detection system. The high-voltage bushing inspection system and the insulator inspection system contain the algorithms and models used to perform the inspection independently. The specific detection algorithm is as described above, and the model includes the SVM model and the multi-scale CNNs network model.

(iii) Software structure of the fault diagnosis expert system

This system calls the MATLAB 2014a related interface, can read and adjust various parameters of convolutional neural network through software setting data, train and test SVM and convolutional neural network, and finally output the diagnosis results. The internal structure and running process of this software can intuitively reflect the parameters that need to be adjusted during training and the algorithms that need to be selected. The final results and maintenance suggestions can also be displayed directly. The user does not need to open the algorithm program one by one for debugging, but just click the software related button to set it. Therefore, the software is easy to operate and easy to use, which reduces the training difficulty for operators.

(iv) System implementation

This research designs and implements an expert system for power equipment fault diagnosis based on deep learning based on deep learning and to detect the device; the diagnosis system combines the detection results with the device's infrared information so that the system can obtain the device's heat level and location. Then the system calls the fault knowledge base to get the fault information and maintenance suggestions of the equipment. Finally, the system functions are realized through software, and the expected diagnostic accuracy is achieved.

8.7 Summary

As an important breakthrough in the application of artificial intelligence, expert systems have been increasingly used in many fields, showing its strong vitality.

Section 8.1 first studied the basic problems of the expert system, including the definition, classification, characteristics, structure, and construction steps of the expert system. Then, the expert systems based on different technologies are discussed. Sections 8.2–8.4 discuss rule-based expert systems, model-based expert systems, and web-based expert systems. From the working principles and models of these systems, it can be seen that various technologies and methods of artificial intelligence are well combined and applied in expert systems, providing a good example for the development of artificial intelligence.

Section 8.5 introduces the design of expert systems. First, a rule-based maintenance consulting system is taken as an example to explain the design process of the expert system, and the design is carried out using EXPERT development tools. Then, the general design methods and design tasks based on rule-based expert system are discussed.

Section 8.6 summarizes the research and applications of expert systems based on machine learning, especially deep learning, and provides an example of the design and implementation of a fault diagnosis expert system for power equipment on the basis of deep learning, which shows that machine learning and deep learning have been widely used in expert systems and have extremely wide and good development prospects.

Some new ideas and technologies of computer science have also played an important role in the development of expert systems. The distributed expert systems and collaborative expert systems that have been developed and applied are the result of applying the distributed processing and collaborative working mechanisms in computer science. The widespread application of machine learning in expert systems will surely promote expert systems into a new development period. The expert system is one of the earliest and most effective areas of artificial intelligence application research. People expect it to have new developments and new breakthroughs, and to become a powerful tool for intelligent management and decision-making in the 21st century.

References

1. Abu-Nasser, B.S. (2017). Medical expert systems survey, *International Journal of Engineering and Information Systems*, *1*(7): 218–224.
2. Ahmed, M. and Abdel-Zaher, A.M.E. (2016). Breast cancer classification using deep belief networks, *Expert System with Applications*, *46*: 139–144.
3. Ahmed, M. and Abdel-Zaher, A.M.E. (2017). Deep reinforcement learning framework for autonomous driving, *IS&T International Symposium on Electronic Imaging, Autonomous Vehicles and Machine*, (Society for Imaging Science and Technology). https://doi.org/10.2352/ISSN.2470-1173.2017.19. AVM-023 ©2017.
4. Almurshidi, S.H. and Naser, S.S.A. (2018). *Expert System for Diagnosing Breast Cancer Analysis*, (Al-Azhar University, Gaza, Palestine).
5. Ao, Z.G. (2010). *Artificial Intelligence and Expert System*, (Mechanical Industry Press, Beijing, in Chinese).
6. Ashraf, S.M., Gupta, A. Choudhary, D.K. and Chakrabarti, S. (2017). Voltage stability monitoring of power systems using reduced network and artificial neural network, *International Journal of Electrical Power & Energy Systems*, *87*: 43–51.
7. Batista, L.O., de Silva, G.A. and Araújo, V.S., Araújo, V.J.S., Rezende, T. S., Guimarães, A.J. and Souza, P.V. (2019). Fuzzy neural networks to create an expert system for detecting attacks by sql injection, *International Journal of Forensic Computer Science*, *13*(1): 8–21.
8. Buchanan, B.G. and Shortliffe, E.H. (1984). Rule Based Expert System, the MYCIN Experiments of Stanford Heuristic Programming Project, (Addison Wesley Publishing Company, New York).
9. Cai, Z.X. and Fu, K.S. (1986). Robot planning expert system, *Proc. IEEE Int'l Conf. on Robotics and Automation*, Vol. 3, pp. 1973–1978 (IEEE Computer Society Press, San Francisco).
10. Cai, Z.X., John, D. and Gong, T. (2014). Advanced Expert System: Principles, Design and Application, 2nd Edition, (Science Press, Beijing, in Chinese).
11. Cai, Z.X., Wang, Y.N. and Cai, J.F. (1996). A real-time expert control system, *AI in Engineering*, *10*(4): 317–322.
12. Cai, Z.X. (1988). An expert system for robotic transfer planning, *Computer Science and Technology*, *3*(2): 153–160.
13. Carlos, A., André, L.D.R., Vieira, F.H.A. and de Leon Ferreira de Carvalho, A. C. P. (2017). Deep learning for biological image classification, *Expert Systems with Applications*, *85*: 114–122.
14. Cavalcante, R.C., Brasileiro, R.C., Souza, V.L., *et al.* (2016). Computational intelligence and financial markets: A survey and future directions, *Expert Systems with Applications*, *55*: 194–211.

15. Cui, W. (2014). Research and Implementation of Intelligent Manufacturing Expert System Based on Uncertainty and Fuzzy Reasoning, Tianjin University Master's Degree Thesis.
16. Darrel, R. (2017). Expert Systems: Design, Applications and Technology, (Nova Science Publishers, Inc.)
17. Duan, Y. and Li, H.C. (2009). Research on fault diagnosis expert system based on fault tree, *Science Technology and Engineering*, *8*(7): 1914–1917.
18. Durkin, J. (1994). Expert System Design and Development, (Macmillan Publishing Company, New York).
19. Durkin, J. (2002). History and applications. In: C.T. Leondes (ed.) Expert System, Ch. 1, (Academic Press, San Diego).
20. Duygu, İ. and Süleyman, G. (2019). Design and implementation of the fuzzy expert system in Monte Carlo methods for fuzzy linear regression, *Applied Soft Computing Journal*, *77*, 399–411.
21. Edyta, B., Marek, K., Aneta, N., *et al.* (2017). An expert system for underground coal mine planning, *Gospodarka Surowcami Mineralnymi*, 113–127.
22. Eunsuk, C., Chulwoo, H. and Frank, C.P. (2017). Deep learning networks for stock market analysis and prediction: Methodology, data representations, and case studies, Durham Research Online, (Durham University, UK). ©2017, http://creativecommons.org/licenses/by-nc-nd/4.0/.
23. Ezekiel, T., Ogidan, K.D. and Yoney, K.E. (2018). Machine learning for expert systems in data analysis, 2nd International Symposium on Multidisciplinary Studies and Innovative Technologies, ISMSIT.
24. Feigenbaum, E. and Cohen, P. (1984). The Handbook of Artificial Intelligence, Vol. 3, (William Kaufman, Loa Altos, CA).
25. Feigenbaum, E. (1982). Expert Systems in the 1980s, *Infotech State of the Art Report*, Series 9, No. 3.
26. Giarratano, J. and Riley, G. (1988). Expert Systems: Principles and Programming, (PWS Publishing Company).
27. Guo, X.Q., Hao, X.Y., Mao, H.K., *et al.* (2017). Research status and development of expert system of casting process, *Foundry Technology*, (8): 1793–1795.
28. Hamman, H., Hamman. J., Wessels, A., Scholtz, J. and Steenekamp, J. (2018). Development of multiple-unit pellet system tablets by employing the SeDeM expert diagram system I: Pellets with different sizes, *Pharmaceutical Development and Technology*, *23*(7): 706–714.
29. Hayes, R.F., Waterman, D. and Lenat, D. (eds.) (1983). Building Expert Systems, (Addison Wesley, New York).
30. He, W. and Chang, S. (2019). Design and implementation of track fault monitoring system based on expert system, *Computer Age*, (1): 46–47.
31. He, W. and Chang, S. (2016). Research on intelligent agriculture management platform based on expert system, *Computer Knowledge and Technology*, (31): 52–53.
32. Jahanzaib, S. and Tarique, A. (2018). A survey of deep learning techniques for mobile robot applications, *Journal of Latex Class Files*, *14*(8): 1–10.

33. Kim, H.-S., Sun, C.-G. and Cho, H.-I. (2019). Site-Specific Zonation of Seismic Site Effects by Optimization of the Expert GIS-Based Geotechnical Information System for Western Coastal Urban Areas in South Korea, *International Journal of Disaster Risk Science*, *1*, 117–133.

34. Kitamura, Y., Ikeda, M. and Mizoguchi, R. (2002). A model-based expert system based on domain ontology. In: Leondes, C.T. (ed.), Expert Systems, Chapter 6, (Academic Press, San Diego).

35. Ivanciu, L.-N. and Sipos, E. (2018). Fuzzy logic based expert system for academic staff evaluation and progress monitoring, ResearchGate, 2018, DOI: 10.12783/dtcse/cmee2017/19995.

36. Leondes, C.T. (ed.) (2002). Expert Systems, the Technology of Knowledge Management and Decision Making for the 21st Century, (Academic Press).

37. Li, J.P., Li, F.M. and Lv, Q. (2015). Design and application of coking coal Blending Expert System, *Fuel & Chemical Processes*, (6): 1–3.

38. Li, Z.W. (2002). Design of web-based remote fault diagnosis expert system for aircraft, *Computer Applications and Software*, (12): 64–65.

39. Litjens, G., Thijs, K., Babak, E.B., Setio, A.A.A., Ciompi, F., Ghafoorian, M., van der Laak, J.A., van Ginneken, B. and Sánchez, C.I. (2017). A survey on deep learning in medical image analysis, *Medical Image Analysis*, *42*: 60–88.

40. Liu, L.-J., Wang, Y.-D. and Guo, M.-Z. (2005). The research and application of the self-learning expert system based on BP network, *Proceedings of the Fourth International Conference on Machine Learning and Cybernetics*, pp. 4153–4157, Guangzhou, 2005, 18–21 August.

41. Lu, J. (2017, in Chinese). Fault Diagnosis Expert System of Power Equipment Based on Deep Learning, [D]. Beijing University of Technology Master's Degree Thesis, May 2017.

42. Lu, L., Cai, L.C., Gao, X., *et al.* (2018). Application of intelligent expert system for liquor fermentation based on cloud computing platform, *Brew Science and Technology*, *2018*(12): 88–91.

43. Lu, L., Liu, B. and Zhang, P.H. (2019). Design and implementation of knowledge base for athlete training expert system, *Computer and Digital Engineering*, (2): 314–319.

44. Luis, M.T.-T., Indira, G.E.-S., Bernardo, G.-O., *et al.* (2013). An expert system for setting parameters in machining processes, *Expert Systems with Applications*, *40*(17): 6877–6884.

45. Ma, Z.W., Xu, H.Y. and Qian, W.P. (2013). Intelligent diagnosis and decision support system for blast furnace based on expert system, *Metallurgical Automation*, *37*(6): 7–14 (in Chinese).

46. Marmar, M. and Marc, M. (2015). iClass: Combining Multiple Multi-Label Classification with Expert Knowledge, *IEEE 14th International Conference on Machine Learning and Applications*, 843–848.

47. Martın, deDiego I., Siordia, O.S.A., Fernández-Isabela, A., Condea, C. and Cabelloa, E. (2019). Subjective data arrangement using clustering techniques for training expert systems, *Expert Systems with Applications*, *115*: 1–15.

48. Martin, G. and František, J. (2018). Utilization of expert systems in severe accident management, *IEEE 19th International Scientific Conference on Electric Power Engineering*, Brno, pp. 1–4.

49. Mesran, M., Syahrizal, M. and Suginam, S. (2018). Expert system for disease risk based on lifestyle with fuzzy mamdani, *International Journal of Engineering and Technology, 7(2.3)*: 88–91.

50. Meysam, R.K., Haleh, A., Mojtaba, M. and Haghighi, M.K. (2017). Fuzzy expert system for diagnosing diabetic neuropathy, *World Journal of Diabetes, 2*: 80–88.

51. Mirmozaffari, M. (2019). Developing an expert system for diagnosing liver diseases, *EJERS, 4*(3): 1–5.

52. Mok, K.W., Geoffrey, S. and Chen, L.P. (2014). Design and algorithm development of an expert system for continuous health monitoring of sewer and storm water pipes, *Office Automation*, (s1): 35–38.

53. Pritpal, S. (2018). Indian summer monsoon rainfall (ISMR) forecasting using time series data: A fuzzy-entropy-neuro based expert system, *Geoscience Frontiers, 4*: 1243–1257.

54. Raghavendra, U., Sulatha, V., Bhandary, A.G. and Rajendra, A.U. (2018). Novel expert system for glaucoma identification using non-parametric spatial envelope energy spectrum with fundus images, *Biocybernetics and Biomedical Engineering, 38*(1): 170–180.

55. Saracin, C.G., Popescu, M.O. (2014). Expert diagnose system and real-time monitoring of an electric power installation, *Electrotechnica Electronica Automatica, 62*(3): 54.

56. Tong, Y.T. and Li, Z.H. (2013). Research and improvement of fault diagnosis method based on expert system, *Electronic Design Engineering, 21*(16): 83–87 (in Chinese).

57. Walker, T.C. and Miller, R.K. (1990). Expert systems handbook: An assessment of technology applications, (The Fairmont Press Inc.).

58. Wang, H.L. (2019). Design of fault diagnosis expert system for natural gas engine based on fault tree, *Electronic Technology and Software Engineering*, (2): 29–30.

59. Wang, J., Chen, Y., Hao, S., Peng, S. and Hu, L. (2019). Deep learning for sensor-based activity recognition: A survey, *Pattern Recognition Letters, 119*: 3–11.

60. Wang, M., Wang, H., Xu, D., Wan, K.K. and Vogel, D. (2004). A web service agent-based decision support system for securities exception management, *Expert Systems with Applications, 27*: 439–450.

61. Wang, X.B. and Yang, Z.J. (2015). A new web-based expert system development method, *Computer Technology and Development*, (8): 147–151.

62. Weiss, S.M., Kulikowski, C.A. and Amarel, S.A. (1978). A model-based method for computer-aided medical decision-making, *Artificial Intelligence, 11*(1–2): 145–172.

63. Weiss, S.M. and Kulikowski, C.A. (1984). A practical guide to designing expert systems, (Rowmand and Allenkeld Publishers).

64. Yao, Z. (2019). Development of medical question answering system based on deep learning, *China Medical Equipment, 34*(12): 88–91,141.
65. Yoshinobu, K., Mitsuru, I. and Riichiro, M. (2002). A model-based expert system based on a domain ontology. In: C.T. Leondes (ed.) Expert Systems, Chapter 6, (Academic Press, San Diego).
66. Zhang, B.C., Bu, Q.Y., Zhou, Z.J., *et al.* (2018). Evaluation of the health status of the controller switch based on the expert system of the confidence rule base, *Control and Decision,* (4): 805–812 (in Chinese).
67. Zhang, S., Yao, L., Sun, A.X. and Yi, T. (2018). Deep learning based recommender system: A survey and new perspectives, *ACM Computing Surveys, 1*(1): 1–35.
68. Zhang, T., Lu, J. and Shen, J.J. (2017). Intelligent irrigation expert decision system based on internet of things, *Modern Agricultural Science and Technology, 21*: 176–177 (in Chinese).
69. Zhang, Z.J., Wang, X.H., Zeng, X.F., *et al.* (2018). An intelligent attitude control method of aircraft based on online identification and expert system, *Navigation, Positioning and Timing,* (4): 50–58.
70. Zhao, Z., Xu, G., Ei, Y., *et al.* (2019). Fault detection and isolation in industrial processes using deep learning approaches, *IEEE Transactions on Industrial Informatics, 15*(5), 3077–3084.
71. Zhou, P.F., Qiao, J. and Li, L. (2018). Research on intelligent scheduling expert system for shared cars, *Computer Applications and Software,* (4), 109–111.
72. Zohreh, S.K., Hossein, B. and Isa, E. (2018). An expert system for predicting shear stress distribution in circular open channels using gene expression programming, *Water Science and Engineering, 2*: 167–176.

Intelligent Planning

9

Intelligent planning is an important problem solving technique. Compared with general problem solving, intelligent planning focuses more on the problem solving process than on solving the problem. In addition, the problems to be solved in planning, such as robot world problems, are often real-world problems rather than more abstract mathematical model problems. Due to these characteristics and a wide range of application occasions and application prospects, the intelligent planning systems have attracted a lot of research interest from the artificial intelligence community and achieved many research results [4, 10, 29].

In the study of intelligent planning, robot planning and problem solving are often discussed as typical examples. This is not only because robot planning is one of the most important research objects of intelligent planning, but also because robot planning can be visually and intuitively tested. In view of this, intelligent planning is often referred to as robot planning. The principles, methods, and techniques of robot planning can be applied to other planning objects or systems. Intelligent planning or robot planning is an important application field of artificial intelligence after expert systems and machine learning. It is also an important research field of robotics, and an interesting combination point of artificial intelligence and robotics [21, 30].

The intelligent planning discussed in this chapter is called high-level planning in robot planning, with different planning goals, tasks, and methods than low-level planning.

9.1 Overview of Intelligent Planning

In this section, we first introduce the concepts and definitions of planning, and then discuss the tasks of intelligent planning systems.

9.1.1　*Concept and function of planning*

In intelligent planning research, some focus on the proof machine based on the resolution principle, they apply general heuristic search technology, and represent the desired goal by logic calculus. STRIPS (STanford Research Institute Problem Solver) and ABSTRIPS belong to this type of system. This system represents the world model as an arbitrary set of first-order predicate calculus formulas, uses resolution refutation to solve the problem of the specific model, and uses the means-ends analysis strategy to guide the solution system to meet the required goal. Another planning system uses supervised learning to speed up the planning process and to improve problem solving. PULP-I is a learning system with learning ability, which is based on analogy. The PULP-I system uses a semantic network to represent knowledge, which is a step forward than just using the first-order predicate formula. Since the 1980s, other planning systems have been developed, including nonlinear programming, induction-based planning systems, hierarchical planning systems, and expert planning systems. With growing research on artificial neural networks, multi-agent systems, genetic algorithms, etc., in recent years, research hotspots based on artificial neural networks, multi-agent-based planning, evolutionary planning, and machine learning-based planning have emerged.

(1) Planning concept

Definition 9.1. Starting from a particular problem state, seeking a series of behavioral actions, and establishing a sequence of operations until the goal state is obtained. This solution process is called **planning**.

Definition 9.2. A planning system is a system that involves the steps in the problem solving process. Examples include computer or aircraft design, train or car transportation routes, and financial and military planning issues.

In daily life, planning means determining the course of action before action. The term "planning" refers to the process of calculating a few steps before performing any step. A plan is a description of an action process. It can be an unordered target list like a department store list; but in general, planning has an implied ordering with a certain goal. For example, for most people, wash your face and brush your teeth or rinse your mouth before eating breakfast. In another example, there is a goal of a lunch in a workday plan, but the details, such as where to eat, what to eat, when to eat, etc., are not stated. Detailed planning related to the lunch is a sub-plan of full-time planning. Most plans have a large sub-planning structure, and each goal in the plan can be replaced by a more detailed sub-plan that achieves this goal. Although the resulting plan is a linear or partial ordering of a problem solver, the goals implemented by operators often have a hierarchical structure.

We have discussed various problem representation methods and search solving techniques in Chapters 2 and 3, and introduced some of the more novel search reasoning techniques in subsequent chapters. These methods and techniques can be used for intelligent planning. For example, by applying state space search technology, a planning problem can be represented as a state or a node, and a planning action (or an event) can be represented as an operator or a link symbol; by using a state space search solution, an operator sequence can be obtained, i.e., the action sequence of planning, which is the result of planning. Other methods, such as predicate logic, semantic network, framework, ontology, rule deduction system, expert system, multi-agent system, and genetic algorithm, can also be used for intelligent planning.

(2) The role of planning

For major issues in the national economy and society and for important issues in science and technology, engineering, and people's livelihood, scientific planning and decision-making are required. Then, according to the formulated plan, we gradually achieve the prescribed goals. The strength of the decision will determine the success or failure of the action. Intelligent decision systems and intelligent planning systems are important means of scientific decision making. Together with expert systems, they will become powerful tools for intelligent management, and decision making in the 21st century. Examples include national and regional national economic and social development plans, fiscal budgets, large-scale water conservancy projects, key economic construction projects, and fiscal and financial regulation.

For instance, the national economic and social development plan mainly outlines the national strategic intention, clarifies the government's work priorities, and guides the behavior of market subjects. It is a grand blueprint for national economic and social development and an important basis for the government to perform its duties of economic regulation, market supervision, social management, and public services.

As another example, the fundamental role of urban planning is to serve as the basic basis for building cities and managing cities. It is the premise and basis for ensuring the rational construction of cities and the rational development and utilization of urban land and normal business activities, and is a comprehensive means to achieve urban social and economic development goals.

As can be seen from these examples, planning plays an important guiding role in various undertakings and work. If there is a lack of planning, it may lead to sub-standard problem solving or even the wrong problem solving.

Planning can be used to monitor the problem solving process and to detect errors before they cause a major hazard. The benefits of planning can be summarized as simplifying searches, resolving conflicts, and providing a basis for error compensation.

Numerous positive experiences and negative lessons tell us that scientific planning methods not only contribute to the country and society, but also to personal learning and work. For individuals, the use of personal notebooks (work calendars or calendars, and memos) is very beneficial for work and study. Use your scientific planning ideas and methods to plan your study, work, research, and life; plan your future, prepare you for the future, make decisions more scientifically, act more effectively, achieve better and faster results, and make your future even better! Use scientific planning ideas and methods to plan national events and social issues, plan the future of the country, make social members more prepared for the future, and make the life of the public tomorrow even better!

9.1.2 *Classification of planning*

According to the different planning contents, planning methods, and the essence of planning, planning can be classified as follows:

(1) Classification according to planning content

Planning contents are varied, but the more important and common planning contents include the following: the country's long-term strategic goal planning, major national economic and social issues planning, national economic and social development five-year and annual plans of national and local governments, and the financial budget, the national finance and financial regulation strategy and planning, talent strategy planning, enterprise workshop scheduling, water, land and air traffic operation scheduling, urban and environmental planning, etc.

There are generally several sub-plans for each plan. For example, urban planning includes sub-planning such as central city planning, suburban planning, industrial space layout planning, professional system planning, and key regional planning. As another example, environmental planning involves watershed environmental economic system planning, urban environmental economic system planning, development zone environmental economic system planning, regional land sustainable use planning, and urban solid waste management planning.

(2) Classification according to the planning method

Planning methods are also diverse. The most effective methods include non-hierarchical and hierarchical planning, linear and nonlinear programming, synchronous and asynchronous planning, planning based on scripting, framework, and ontology, planning based on expert system, competition-based planning, planning based on resolution principles, planning based on rule deduction, planning based on induction, planning system with learning ability, planning based on computational intelligence, partial order planning, artificial neural network-based planning, multi-agent-based planning, evolutionary planning, multi-objective programming, and uncertainty and dynamic programming.

In a planning system, two or more methods may be used simultaneously to solve the same problem comprehensively in order to obtain better planning results.

(3) Classification according to the actual nature of the plan

For classification according to the actual nature of the plan, it means to dilute the content of the plan, and only consider the essence of the plan, such as goals, tasks, approaches, costs, etc., to carry out comparative abstract planning. According to its essence, the plan can be divided into the following:

(i) Task planning: Plan the goals and tasks to solve the problem, also known as high-level planning.
(ii) Path planning: Plan the path, routine, cost, etc., of solving the problem, also called middle-level planning.
(iii) Trajectory planning: Plan spatial geometric trajectories for solving problems and their generation, also called low-level planning.

A complete prediction of any aspect of the real world is almost impossible. Therefore, you must be prepared to face the failure of planning. However, if the problem is decomposed into as many independent (or nearly independent) sub-problems as possible during planning, then the failure of a certain planning step has a very local impact on the planning. In this way, it is more reasonable to use the problem decomposition method for problem solving and planning.

9.2　Task Planning

From this section onwards, task planning and path planning will be discussed, respectively. For task planning, planning of the block world, planning based on the principle of refutation, planning system with learning ability, hierarchical planning, and planning based on the expert system are introduced. For path planning, the main methods and development trends of robot path planning are reviewed. The robot path planning based on immune evolution and sample learning, and the robot path planning based on ant colony algorithm are studied.

9.2.1　*Robot planning in the block world*

Problem solving is a process of seeking a certain sequence of actions to achieve a goal. The problem solving of a robot is to seek a sequence of actions (possibly including paths) of a robot. This sequence enables the robot to achieve the desired work goal and complete the specified work tasks [33, 43, 59].

(1) Robot problems in the block world

The development of robotics has opened up new application prospects for solving artificial intelligence problems and formed a new research field — robotics. The concepts of many problem solving systems can be experimentally studied and applied for solving robot problems. Robot problems are both simple and intuitive. In a typical representation of a robot problem, the robot is able to perform a set of actions. For example, imagine a building block world and a robot. The world is a number of marked cubic blocks (assumed to be the same size here); they are either stacked on top of each other or placed on the table; the robot has a movable manipulator that can grab the blocks and move blocks from one place to another. Examples of actions that the robot can perform in this example are as follows:

unstack(*a,b*): Pick up block *a* stacked on block *b*. Before performing this action, the robot's hand (manipulator) is required to be empty, and the top of block *a* must be empty.

stack(*a,b*): Stack block *a* on block *b*. Before the action, the robot has to grasp block *a*, and the top of block *b* must be empty.

pickup(*a*): Pick up block *a* from the table and grab it. The robot is required to be empty handed before the action, and there is nothing on the top of block *a*.

putdown(*a*): Place block *a* on the desktop. The robot should have been grasping block *a* before the action.

Robot planning includes many functions, such as identifying the world around the robot, presenting action plans, and monitoring the execution of these plans. What is to be studied is mainly the action sequence problem of the integrated robot; that is, in a given initial situation, the specified goal is reached after a certain sequence of actions.

A production system that uses state description as a database is one of the simplest problem solving systems. Both the state description and goal description of the robot problem can be composed of predicate logic formulas. In order to specify the actions performed by the robot and the results of performing the actions, the following predicates need to be applied:

ON(*a,b*): The block *a* is above the block *b*.

ONTABLE(*a*): The block *a* is on the desktop.

CLEAR(*a*): There is nothing on top of block *a*.

HOLDING(*a*): The robot is holding block *a*.

HANDEMPTY: The robot is empty.

Figure 9.1(a) shows the robotic problem of the initial layout. This layout can be represented by the conjunction of the following predicate formulas:

CLEAR(*B*): The top of block *B* is empty

CLEAR(*C*): The top of block *C* is empty

ON(*C,A*): Block *C* is piled on block *A*

ONTABLE(*A*): Block *A* is placed on the desktop

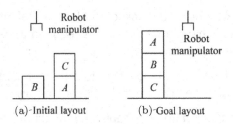

Figure 9.1 Robot problem in the block world.

ONTABLE(*B*): Block *B* is placed on the desktop

HANDEMPTY: The robot is empty

The goal is to build a pile of blocks, in which block *B* is piled on top of block *C*, and block *A* is stacked on top of block *B*, as shown in Figure 9.1(b). You can also use predicate logic to describe this goal as:

$$ON(B,C) \wedge ON(A,B)$$

(2) Solving planning sequences using F rules

The F rule is used to represent the action of the robot. This is a rule called the STRIPS planning system, which consists of three parts. The first part is a prerequisite. In order to enable the F rule to be applied to the state description, this prerequisite formula must be a predicate calculus expression that logically follows the facts in the state description. Before applying the F rules, you must be sure that the prerequisites are true. The second part of the F rule is a predicate called the delete table. When a rule is applied to a state description or database, the contents of the delete table are deleted from the database. The third part of the F rule is called the add table. When a rule is applied to a database, the contents of the add table are added to the database. For the example of stacked wood, the move action can be expressed as follows:

move(*X*,*Y*,*Z*): Moves the object *X* from above the object *Y* onto the object *Z*.

prerequisites: CLEAR(*X*), CLEAR(*Z*), ON(*X*,*Y*)

delete table: ON(*X*,*Z*), CLEAR(*Z*)

add table: ON(*X*,*Z*), CLEAR(*Y*)

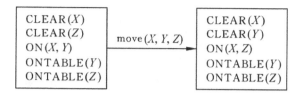

Figure 9.2   Search tree representing move actions.

If move is the only operator or applicable action for this robot, then a search graph or search tree as shown in Figure 9.2 can be generated.

Considering more specifically the example shown in Figure 9.1, the four actions (operators) of the robot can be expressed in STRIPS form as follows:

(i) stack(X,Y)

Prerequisites and deletion table: HOLDING(X)∧CLEAR(Y)

Add table: HANDEMPTY, ON(X, Y)

(ii) unstack(X, Y)

Prerequisites: HANDEMPTY∧ON(X,Y)∧CLEAR(X)

Delete table: ON(X,Y), HANDEMPTY

Add table: HOLDING(X),CLEAR(Y)

(iii) pickup(X)

Prerequisites: ONTABLE(X)∧CLEAR(X)∧HANDEMPTY

Delete table: ONTABLE(X)∧HANDEMPTY

Add Table: HOLDING(X)

(iv) putdown(X)

Prerequisites and deletion form: HOLDING(X)

Add table: ONTABLE(X), HANDEMPTY

Assume that the goal is the state shown in Figure 9.1 (b), i.e., ON(B, C) ∧ ON(A, B). Starting from the initial state description shown in Figure 9.1(a), only the unstack(C,A) and pickup(B) actions can apply the F rule. Figure 9.3 shows the full state space for this problem, with thick lines indicating the solution path from the initial state (marked with $S0$) to the goal state (marked with G). Unlike the traditional state space drawing method, this state space diagram shows the symmetry of the problem without placing the initial node

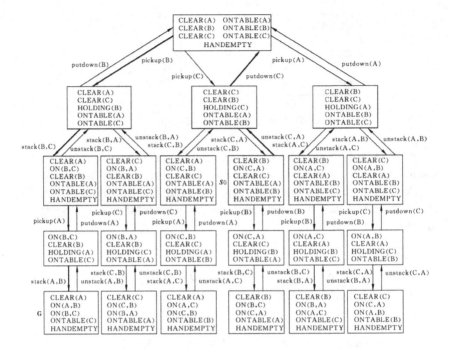

Figure 9.3   State space of the building block robot problem.

*S*0 on the vertices of the graph. Also, note that each rule in this example has an inverse rule.

Following the branch line shown by the thick line, starting from the initial state, the F rule on the connecting arc is sequentially read in the forward direction, and a sequence of actions that can reach the goal state is obtained:

{unstack(*C*, *A*), putdown(*C*), pickup(*B*), stack(*B*, *C*), pickup(*A*), stack(*A*, *B*)}

This sequence of actions is called planning to achieve the goal of the robot problem in this block world.

9.2.2   *Task planning based on the resolution principle*

STRIPS is planning based on the resolution principle, which leads to general conclusions from the solved problems. The previous section has introduced the composition of F rules.

(1) Composition of the STRIPS system

STRIPS was successfully researched by Fikes, Hart, and Nilsson in 1971 and 1972 as part of the Shakey robotic program control system. This robot is a self-propelled cart designed to move around a simple environment and can be operated in simple English commands. Shakey contains the following four main parts:

(i) Wheels and their propulsion systems.
(ii) Sensing system consisting of a TV camera and a contact bar.
(iii) A computer that is not on the vehicle body to perform programming. It analyzes the feedback and input commands from the onboard sensors and sends a signal to the wheels that triggers the system to advance.
(iv) Radio communication systems for the transfer of data between computers and wheels.

STRIPS is the program that decides which instruction to send to the robot. The robot world includes some rooms, doors between rooms, and movable boxes; in more complicated cases, there are lights and windows. For STRIPS, the specific outstanding real world that exists at any time is described by a set of predicate calculus clauses. For example, clause

$$INROOM(ROBOT, R_2)$$

is an assertion in the database and indicates that the robot is in room 2 at that time. As the actual situation changes, the database must be corrected in time. Generally speaking, a database describing the world at any moment is called a world model.

The control program contains a number of subroutines that, when executed, will cause the robot to move through a door, push a box through a door, turn off a light, or perform other actual actions. These programs are complex in nature, but are not directly related to problem solving. For robot problem solving, these programs are a bit like the relationship between walking and picking up objects in human problem solving.

The composition of the entire STRIPS system is as follows:

(i) World model. Calculate formulas for first-order predicates.
(ii) Operator (F rule). Includes prerequisites, delete tables, and add tables.
(iii) Operation method. Apply state space representation and means-end analysis. Here is an example:

States: (*M*, *G*), including the initial state, the intermediate state, and the goal state.

Initial state: $(M_0, (G_0))$
Goal state: Get a world model with no unmet goals left.

(2) Planning process of the STRIPS system

The answer to each STRIPS question is the sequence of operators that implement the goal, and the plan to reach the goal. The following example illustrates the solving process for STRIPS system planning.

Example 9.1. Consider a relatively simple case of the STRIPS system, which requires the robot to go to the neighboring room to retrieve a box. The world model of the initial state and the goal state of the robot is shown in Figure 9.4.

There are two operators, gothru (walk through) and pushthru (push through), which are described below:

OP1: gothru(d, r_1, r_2);

The robot passes through d between the room r_1 and the room r_2, i.e., the robot enters the room r_2 through the door d from the room r_1. Prerequisites: INROOM (ROBOT, r_1) $\wedge$

CONNECTS (d, r_1, r_2); the robot is in room r_1, and door d connects r_1 and r_2.

Delete table: INROOM(ROBOT,*S*); for any *S* value.

Add table: INROOM(ROBOT, r_2).

OP2: pushthru(b,d,r_1,r_2)

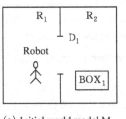
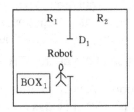

(a) Initial world model M_0 (b) Goal world model G_0

Figure 9.4   A simplified model of STRIPS.

Table 9.1   Difference table.

Difference	Operator	
	gothru	pushthru
Robot and object are not in the same room	×	
Object is not in the goal room		×
Robot is not in the target room	×	
Robot and object are in the same room, but are not in the goal room		×

The robot pushes the object b from the room r_1 through the door d to the room r_2.

Prerequisites: INROOM(b, r_1) ∧ INROOM(ROBOT, r_1) ∧ CONNECTS (d, r_1, r_2)

Delete table: INROOM (ROBOT, S), INROOM (b, S); for any S.

Add table: INROOM (ROBOT, r_2), INROOM (b, r_2).

The difference table for this problem is shown in Table 9.1.

Assume that the initial state M_0 and the goal state G_0 of this problem are as follows:

$$M_0: \begin{cases} \text{INROOM(ROBOT, } R_1) \\ \text{INROOM(BOX}_1, \ R_2) \end{cases}$$

$$\text{CONNECTS}(D_1, R_1, R_2)$$

G_0: INROOM(ROBOT, R_1) ∧ INROOM(BOX$_1$, R_1) ∧ CONNECTS (D_1, R_1, R_2)

Below, the means-end analysis method is used to solve this robot plan step by step.

(1) Do the GPS main loop iteration until M_0 matches G_0.
(2) Begin.
(3) G_0 cannot satisfy M_0; find out the difference between M_0 and G_0. Although this problem cannot be solved immediately, if the initial database contains the statement INROOM(BOX$_1$, R_1), the solution process for this problem can be continued. GPS finds that their difference d1 is INROOM (BOX$_1$, R_1); that is, the box (object) is placed in the goal room R_1.

(4) Select the operator: an operator related to reducing the difference d_1. According to the difference table, the STRIPS selected operator is the following:

OP2: pushthru (BOX_1, d, r_1, R_1)

(5) Eliminate the difference d_1 and set the prerequisite G_1 for OP2 as the following:

G1: INROOM (BOX_1, r_1) $\wedge$ INROOM (ROBOT, r_1) $\wedge$ CONNECTS (d, r_1, R_1)

This prerequisite is set as a sub-goal, and STRIPS attempts to reach G_1 from M_0. Although G_1 is still not satisfied, it is not possible to find a direct answer to this question right away. However, STRIPS found the following:

in case

$$r_1 = R_2 \text{ and } d = D_1$$

The current database contains INROOM (ROBOT, R_2)
Then this process can continue. Now the new sub-goal G_1 is the following:

G_1: INROOM (BOX_1, R_2) $\wedge$ INROOM (ROBOT, R_2) $\wedge$ CONNECTS (D_1, R_2, R_1)

(6) GPS(p); repeat steps 1–4, iterating over the call to solve this problem.

Step 1: The difference d2 between G_1 and M_0 is

INROOM (ROBOT, R_2)

That is, the robot is required to move to the room R_2.

Step 2: According to the difference table, the relevant operator corresponding to d_2 is

OP1: gothru(d, r_1, R_2)

Step 3: The prerequisites for OP1 are

G2: INROOM (ROBOT, R_1) $\wedge$ CONNECTS (d, r_1, R_2)

Step 4: Apply the permutation formulas $r_1 = R_1$ and $d = D_1$, and the STRIPS system can reach G_2 (Choice of path direction).

(7) Apply the operator gothru(D_1, R_1, R_2) to M_0 to find the intermediate state M_1:

Delete table: INROOM (ROBOT, R_1)

Add table: INROOM(ROBOT, R_2)

$$M_1: \begin{cases} \text{INROOM(ROBOT, } R_2) \\ \text{INROOM(BOX}_1, R_2) \end{cases}$$

$$\text{CONNECTS}(D_1, R_1, R_2)$$

Apply the operator pushthru to the intermediate state M_1.

Delete table: INROOM (ROBOT, R_2), INROOM (BOX$_1$, R_2)

Add table: INROOM (ROBOT, R_1), INROOM (BOX$_1$, R_1)
Another intermediate state M_2 is obtained:

$$M_2: \begin{cases} \text{INROOM(ROBOT, } R_1) \\ \text{INROOM(BOX}_1, R_1) \end{cases}$$

$$\text{CONNECTS}(D_1, R_1, R_2)$$

$$M_2 = G_0$$

(8) End.

Since M_2 matches G_0, we solved this robot planning problem through means-end analysis. In the solution process, the STRIPS rules used are the operators OP1 and OP2, i.e.,

$$\text{gothru}(D_1, R_1, R_2), \text{pushthru(BOX}_1, D_1, R_2, R_1)$$

The intermediate state models M_1 and M_2, i.e., the sub-goals G_1 and G_2, are shown in Figure 9.5.

As can be seen from Figure 9.5, M_2 is identical to the goal world model G_0 of Figure 9.4.

Therefore, the final planning obtained is {OP1, OP2}, i.e.

$$\{\text{gothru}(D_1, R_1, R_2), \text{pushthru(BOX}_1, D_1, R_2, R_1)\}$$

The search map for this robot planning problem is shown in Figure 9.6, and the AND/OR tree is shown in Figure 9.7.

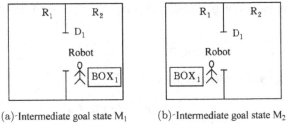

(a)-Intermediate goal state M_1 (b)-Intermediate goal state M_2

Figure 9.5   World model of the intermediate goal state.

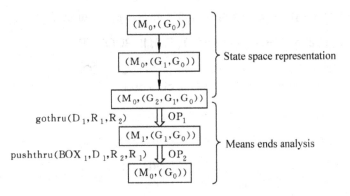

Figure 9.6   Search diagram of a robot planning example.

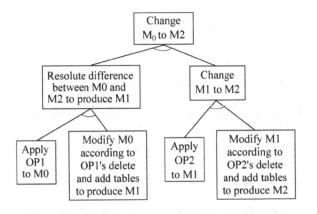

Figure 9.7   AND diagram of a robot planning example.

9.3 Planning System with Learning Ability

The PULP-I robot planning system is a learning system that uses managed learning, and its principle of action is based on an analogy. There is a rule method called the triangulation method, which actually has a certain degree of learning ability [52].

Although STRIPS can solve planning tasks in many different situations, there are also several weaknesses. For example, applying the resolution theorem to prove that the system may produce many irrelevant and redundant clauses, and it takes an unhelpful amount of time to produce these clauses. In addition, planning for a goal involves searching for the appropriate sequence of operators, while composing a longer sequence of control actions requires more searching. This requires an extremely large amount of computer memory and time.

Applying a learning system with learning capabilities can help overcome this shortcoming. Applying a managed (supervised) learning system to robot planning not only speeds up the planning process, but also improves the ability to solve complex tasks. In fact, the basic idea of this planning approach is to apply simulations between existing unplanned tasks and any known similar tasks to reduce the search for answers. There is a learning robotic planning system called PULP-I (Purdue University Learning Program), which was developed by Purdue University's S. Tangwongsan and King-Sun Fu. The PULP-I system is capable of accumulating knowledge through the learning process and can express a plan consisting of a suitable sequence of operators in a world model space, transforming a known initial world model into a model that satisfies a given input command. In addition to speeding up planning, the PULP-I system has two outstanding advantages. First, the input goal statement sent from the operator to the PULP-I can be directly expressed as an English sentence instead of a first-order predicate calculus formula. Second, the application of auxiliary objects in the planning process improves the system's ability to operate on objects, making the operation more flexible.

9.3.1 *Structure and operation modes of the PULP-I system*

(1) Structure of the PULP-I system

The general structure of the PULP-I system is shown in Figure 9.8. The dictionaries, models, and procedures in the diagram are the memory parts

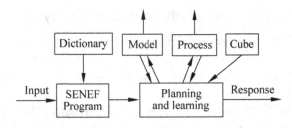

Figure 9.8   The overall structure of the PULP-I system.

of the system, which gather all the information. A "dictionary" is a collection of English words, each of which remains on the LISP's property sheet. The "model" includes facts about the current state of objects in the model world. For example, the information ROOM$_4$ consists of its location, size, neighboring rooms, and the doors that connect these rooms. The model information is not fixed; it may change with the change in the environment. In addition, whenever an operator is applied, the model is fixed at the right time. The "process" concentrates on the prepared process knowledge. This process knowledge is a tabular structure that contains a sequence of instructions. Each instruction may be a task statement that is related to the task's process, a locally defined object, or an operator.

The "Cubes" concentrate LISP procedures, which work together with "planning" to search and correct the "model". Some of the programs within the block are primitive operators of the robot, which correspond to some action programs; executing these programs would cause changes in the state of the objects within the model world.

The input goal statement sent by the operator to PULP-I is directly represented by an English command sentence. This command sentence cannot be processed immediately to develop the simulation. The meaning of the sentence must be extracted and decoded by internal expressions. This process can be seen as the understanding of the input commands. One program called SENEF (SEmantic NEtwork Formation) is a formation program and uses a semantic network to represent knowledge. In fact, the entire PULP-I internal data (knowledge representation) structure is the semantic network, and its program is designed to transform command sentences into semantic network expressions.

(2) Operation mode of the PULP-I system

The PULP-I system has two modes of operation: learning mode and planning mode. In the learning mode, the knowledge entered into the system

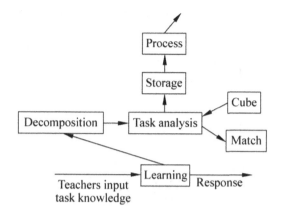

Figure 9.9   Structure of the PULP-I system in learning mode.

is provided by the operator or the so-called "teacher". Figure 9.9 shows the system operation in learning mode. The system first decomposes the given process knowledge into a set of sub-processes. The original process knowledge is decomposed into several knowledge blocks, each of which is a knowledge package. Then, it is tested by the task analysis program, which analyzes the knowledge package and obtains its extracted representation through a semantic matching program.

When a certain command sentence is sent to the system, PULP-I enters the planning mode. Figure 9.10 shows the structure of the PULP-I system in the planning mode.

The primary role of this planning system is to create a plan that transforms the existing world into a world state that satisfies a given command. The generated plan consists of an ordered arrangement of some primitive operators. After obtaining a successful plan, the world model is revised, and the system outputs planning time and planning details to meet the input commands.

9.3.2 *World model and planning results of the PULP-I system*

The PULP-I system is capable of performing a series of planning tasks. Figure 9.11 shows the initial world model for a specific task.

This planning environment consists of six rooms that communicate with each other through the doorway (except for rooms 4 and 6). The environment includes five boxes, two chairs, one table, one ladder, one trolley,

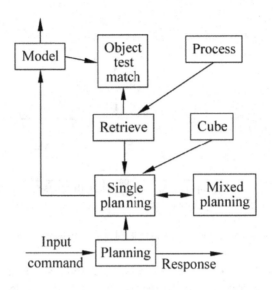

Figure 9.10   Structure of the PULP-I system in planning mode.

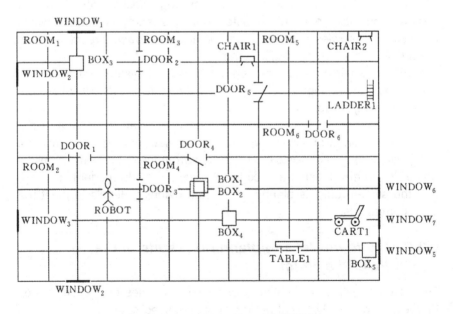

Figure 9.11   Initial world model of PULP-I.

seven windows and a mobile robot. It can be seen that it is more complicated than the STRIPS system.

Compared to the STRIPS and ABSTRIPS systems, the planning time for the PULP-I system can be almost negligible. This shows that the robotic planning system with learning ability can greatly improve the planning speed of the system.

It can be concluded that the learning, problem solving, and planning system PULP-I has successfully demonstrated the improvement of planning performance. This improvement is reflected not only in the speed of planning, but also in the establishment of complex planning capabilities.

9.4 Planning Based on Expert Systems

Planning based on expert systems is mainly used for high-level robot planning. Although a robotic planning system with managed learning capabilities can speed up the planning process and improve problem solving capabilities, it still has some problems. First of all, the semantic network structure of such expression clauses is too complicated, so the design technique is difficult. Second, related to the complex internal data structure of the system, the PULP-I system has many subsystems. And it takes a lot of time to write the program. Again, although the PULP-I system performs question answer or suggestion and explanation much faster than the STRIPS series, it is still not fast enough.

The researchers began with the use of expert system technology for different levels of robot planning and programming. This section will combine the authors' research on the robot planning expert system to introduce robot planning based on expert systems.

9.4.1 *Structure and planning mechanism of the system*

The robot planning expert system is a robot planning system established with the structure and technology of the expert system. Most successful expert systems mimic the human integrated mechanism with a rule-based system. Here, we also use a rule-based expert system to build a robot planning system.

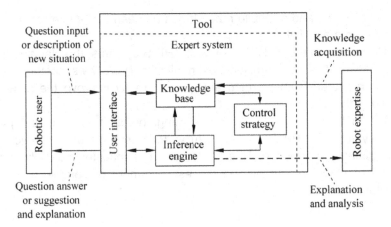

Figure 9.12 Robot planning based on expert systems.

The rule-based robot planning expert system consists of five parts, as shown in Figure 9.12.

(1) Knowledge base. It is used to store expert knowledge and experience in specific areas, including world models of robotic work environments, initial states, object descriptions, and the possible actions or rules.

(2) Control strategy. It contains a comprehensive mechanism to determine what rules the system should apply and how to find them. When using the PROLOG language, its control strategy is search, matching, and backtracking.

(3) Inference engine. It is used to remember the rules and control strategies and reasoning strategies used. Based on the information in the knowledge base, the inference engine enables the entire robot planning system to work logically and in coordination, make decisions, and find the ideal sequence of robot operations.

(4) Knowledge acquisition. First get the expert knowledge of a particular domain. This knowledge is then transformed into a computer program using programming languages. Finally, save them in the knowledge base for use.

(5) Explanation and description. Through the user interface, interactions between the expert system and the user enable the user to input data, ask questions, know the reasoning results, and understand the reasoning process.

In addition, to build an expert system, certain tools are needed, including computer systems or networks, operating systems and programming languages, and other supporting software and hardware. For the robot planning system studied in this section, we have used the DUAL-VAX11/780 computer, the VM/UNIX operating system, and the C-PROLOG programming language.

The total database changes when each rule is adopted or an operation is performed. The goal of a rule-based expert system is to gradually change the state of the total database by executing the rules one by one and its related operations until an acceptable database (called the goal database) is obtained. Combining these related operations in turn forms an operational sequence that gives the operations the robot must follow and the sequence of the operations. For instance, for the robot transfer operation system, the planning sequence gives the process actions required by the handling robot to carry one or more specific parts or artifact from the initial position to the target position.

9.4.2 *ROPES robot planning system*

An example of a robot planning system using an expert system is given below. This is a less complicated example. We built this system using a rule-based system and the C-PROLOG programming language, and it is called the ROPES (RObot Planning Expert Systems) system [7–9, 11, 13, 17–20, 22, 24].

(1) System simplified block diagram

A simplified block diagram of the ROPES system is shown in Figure 9.13.

To build an expert system, you must first acquire expert knowledge carefully and accurately. Expert knowledge of the system includes knowledge from experts and personal experiences, textbooks, manuals, papers, and other references. The acquired expert knowledge is represented by computer programs and statements and stored in the knowledge base. Inference rules are also placed in the knowledge base. These procedures and rules are compiled in the C-PROLOG language. The main control strategies of this system are searching, matching, and backtracking.

The program operator (user) at the system terminal inputs initial data, asks questions, and talks to the inference engine; then, the answer and the inference result, i.e., the planning sequence, are obtained at the terminal from the inference machine.

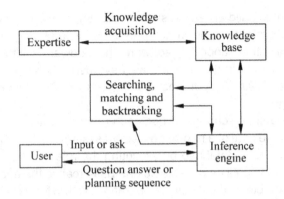

Figure 9.13 Simplified block diagram of the ROPES system.

(2) World models and assumptions

The ROPES system contains several subsystems for task planning, path planning, transfer operation planning, and for finding a collision-free path for the robot. Here, the transfer operation planning system is taken as an example to illustrate some specific problems of the system.

Figure 9.14 shows the world model of the robot assembly line. As can be seen from the figure, the assembly line passes through six working sections (sections 1–6). There are six doorways to connect with each relevant section. Ten assembly robots (robots 1–10) and ten work stations (stations 1–10) are installed beside the assembly line. On the racks on both sides of the shop where the assembly line is located, there are ten parts to be assembled, which have different shapes, sizes, and weights. In addition, there is a mobile handling robot and a transport trolley. This robot can send the required parts from the rack to the designated workbench for assembly robots to assemble. When the size of the parts being transported is large or heavy, the handling robot needs to transport them with a small truck. We call this part "heavy".

In addition to the assembly line model presented in Figure 9.14, we can also use Figure 9.15 to indicate the possible sequence of operations of the handling robot.

In order to express knowledge, describe rules, and understand planning results, some definitions of this system are given as follows:

go(*A,B*): The handling robot moves from position *A* to position *B*, among them

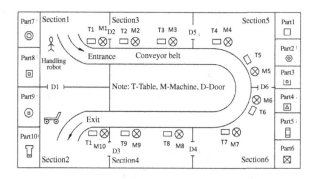

Figure 9.14   Environmental model of the robot assembly line.

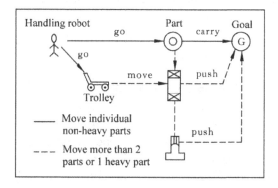

Figure 9.15   Flow chart of handling the robot operation.

$A = (areaA,\ Xa,\ Ya)$: the position $(Xa,\ Ya)$ in section A,

$B = (areaB,\ Xb,\ Yb)$: the position $(Xb,\ Yb)$ in section B,

$Xa,\ Ya$: the horizontal and vertical coordinate meters of the Cartesian coordinates in section A;

$Xb,\ Yb$: The number of coordinate meters in section B.

gothru(A,B): The handling robot moves from position A through a door to position B.

carry($A,\ B$): The handling robot grabs the object from position A to position B.

carrythru($A,\ B$): The handling robot grabs the object from position A through a certain door and arrives at position B.

move(*A*, *B*): The transport robot moves the cart from position *A* to position *B*.

movethru(*A*, *B*): The handling robot moves the car from position *A* through a certain door to position *B*.

push(*A*, *B*): The handling robot pushes the heavy parts from position *A* to position *B* with the trolley.

pushthru(*A*, *B*): The handling robot uses a trolley to push heavy parts from position *A* through a door to position *B*.

loadon(*M*,*N*): The handling robot loads a heavy part *M* onto the trolley *N*.

unload(*M*,*N*): The handling robot removes a heavy part *M* from the cart *N*.

transfer (*M*, cartl, *G*): The handling robot unloads the heavy part *M* from the car (cartl) to the target position *G*.

(3) Planning and implementation results

As mentioned above, the planning system uses a rule-based expert system and the C-PROLOG language to generate a planning sequence. The planning system uses a total of 15 rules, each of which contains two subrules, so in fact 30 rules are used in total. Store these rules in the system's knowledge base. These rules are used in conjunction with C-PROLOG's evaluated predicates to quickly derive inference results. The planning performances of several systems are compared below.

The ROPES system is implemented on the DUAL-VAX11/780 computer and VM/UNIX (4.2BSD) operating system on the Purdue University Computer Network (PECN) at Purdue University using the C-PROLOG language. The PULP-I system was implemented on a CDC-6500 computer explaining the LISP on Purdue University's Purdue Computer Network (PCN). The STRIPS and ABSTRIPS systems were solved on a PDP-10 computer using partially compiled LISP (excluding garbage collection). It is estimated that the actual average operating speed of the CDC-6500 computer is eight times higher than that of the PDP-10. However, due to the PDP-10's ability to partially compile and clean up the junk, its data processing speed is actually slightly lower than that of the CDC-6500. The DUAL-VAX11/780 and VM/UNIX systems are also many times slower than the CDC-6500. However, for comparison purposes, we used the same computation time unit to process the four systems and compare them directly.

Table 9.2   Comparison of world models of planning systems.

System name	System name				
	Room	Door	Box	Others	Total
STRIPS	5	4	3	1	13
ABSTRIPS	7	8	3	0	18
PULP-I	6	6	5	12	27
PULP-24	6	7	5	15	33

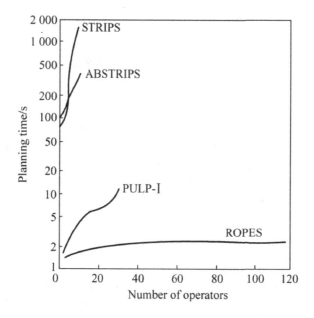

Figure 9.16   Comparison of planning speed and number of operators.

Table 9.2 compares the complexities of these four systems, where the PULP-24 system is used to represent the ROPES system. It is clear from Table 9.2 that the ROPES (PULP-24) system is the most complex, the PULP-I system is the second, and the STRIPS and ABSTRIPS systems are the simplest.

The planning speeds of these four systems are graphically represented by the logarithmic coordinates of Figure 9.16. From the curve, it can be seen that PULP-I plans much faster than STRIPS and ABSTRIPS.

Table 9.3 Comparison of planning time.

Operator number	CPU planning time (seconds)	
	PULP-I	PULP-24
2	1.582	1.571
6	2.615	1.717
10	4.093	1.850
19	6.511	1.967
26	6.266	2.150
34	12.225	$\cdots$
49	$\cdots$	2.767
53	$\cdots$	2.950
62	$\cdots$	3.217
75	$\cdots$	3.233
96	$\cdots$	3.483
117	$\cdots$	3.517

Table 9.3 carefully compares the planning speeds of the two systems, PULP-I and ROPES. As can be seen from Figure 9.18 and Table 9.3, the planning speed of the ROPES (PULP-24) system is much higher than that of the PULP-I system.

9.5 Path Planning

When moving various mobile bodies in complex environments, navigation and control are required, and effective navigation and control require optimized decision making and planning. A mobile intelligent robot is a typical mobile body. The mobile intelligent robot is a kind of robot system that can realize the certain operation function by realizing the autonomous movement of the target in the obstacle environment by sensing the environment and its own state through the sensor.

Navigation technology is the core of mobile robot technology, and path planning is an important link and topic of navigation research. The so-called path planning means that the mobile robot searches for an optimal or suboptimal path from the initial state to the goal state according to a certain performance index (such as distance, time, energy, etc.). The main problems involved in path planning include the following: using the obtained environment information of the mobile robot to establish a more reasonable model and then using an algorithm to find an optimal or near-optimal collision-free path from the initial state to the goal state; dealing with the uncertainties in the model and errors in path tracking to minimize the impact of external objects on the robot; how to use all known information to guide the robot's actions, resulting in relatively better behavioral decisions. How to quickly and effectively complete the navigation task of mobile robots in complex environments is still one of the main directions for future research. How to combine the advantages of various methods to achieve better results is also a problem to be explored. This section will present some of our research on path planning [6, 12].

9.5.1 *Main methods of robot path planning*

There are three main types of mobile robot path planning methods.

(1) Case-based learning planning method

Case-based learning planning methods rely on past experience for learning and problem solving. A new case can be obtained by modifying the old case in the case base that is similar to the current situation. Applying case-based learning to the path planning of a mobile robot can be described as follows: first, an instance library is built using the information used or generated by the path planning, and any instance in the library contains environmental information and path information for each planning. These examples can be obtained through a specific index. Then, the examples generated by the current planning task and environment information are matched with the cases in the case base to find an optimal matching case, and then the case is corrected and used as the final result. Mobile robot navigation requires good adaptability and stability, and a case-based approach can meet this demand.

(2) Planning method based on environment model [16,36,38,58,61]

The planning method based on the environmental model first needs to establish an environmental model about the robot's motion environment. In many cases, due to the uncertainty of the working environment of the mobile robot, including non-structural, dynamic and real-time properties, and reliability, the mobile robot cannot establish a global environment model, but can only establish a local environment model based on sensor information in real time, so the real time and reliability of the local model has become the key to determine whether the mobile robot can move safely, continuously, and smoothly. The methods of environmental modeling can basically be divided into two categories: network/graph modeling methods and grid-based modeling methods. The former mainly includes the free space method, vertex image method, generalized cone method, etc., which can obtain relatively accurate solutions, but the computational cost is quite large, which is not suitable for practical applications. The latter is much simpler to implement, so it is widely used, and its typical representative is the quaternary tree modeling method and its extension algorithm.

The planning method based on the environmental model can be subdivided into a global path planning method with completely known environmental information and a partial path planning method with completely unknown or partially unknown environmental information according to the completeness of the environmental information. Since the environmental model is known, the design criteria for global path planning would be to maximize the effectiveness of the planning as much as possible. There are many mature methods in this field, including the viewable method, tangential method, Voronoi diagram method, topological method, penalty function method, grid method, and so on.

As a hot issue in current planning research, local path planning has been studied intensively. In the case where the environmental information is completely unknown, the robot does not have any prior information, so the plan is to improve the obstacle avoidance ability of the robot, and the effect is second. The methods that have been proposed and applied are the incremental D*Lite algorithm and the rolling window-based planning method. When the environment is partly unknown, the planning methods mainly include the artificial potential field method, fuzzy logic algorithm, genetic algorithm, artificial neural network, simulated annealing algorithm, ant colony optimization algorithm, particle swarm optimization algorithm, and heuristic search method. Heuristic methods include Algorithm A*, incremental graph search algorithm (also known as Dynamic Algorithm A*), Algorithms D*, and focused D*. The United States launched the "Mars Pathfinder" detector in December 1996. The path planning method adopted by the "Sojna" Mars rover is the Algorithm D*, which can independently determine the obstacles on the road ahead and pass the real-time re-planning to make decisions about the actions that follow.

(3) Behavior-based path planning method

The behavior-based approach was developed by Brooks in his well-known inclusive structure, an autonomous robot design technique inspired by biological systems that uses a bottom-up principle of animal evolution, trying to work from simple agents to build a complex system. Using this method to solve the problem of mobile robot path planning is a new development trend. It decomposes the navigation problem into many relatively independent behavior units, such as tracking, collision avoidance, and target guidance. These behavioral units are complete motion control units consisting of sensors and actuators with corresponding navigation functions. Each behavior unit behaves differently; these units work together to complete the navigation task.

Behavior-based methods can be roughly divided into three types: reflective behavior, reactive behavior, and deliberate behavior. The reflective behavior is similar to the frog's knee reflex. It is an instantaneous stress instinct response. It can respond quickly to sudden situations, such as the emergency stop of a mobile robot during exercise, but the method is not intelligent. It is generally used in combination with other methods. The deliberate behavior uses the known global environment model to provide the optimal sequence of actions for the agent system to reach a specific target. It is suitable for planning in complex static environments. The real-time re-planning of mobile robots in motion is a deliberate behavior. There is a reverse action to get out of the danger zone, but since careful planning requires a certain amount of time to execute, it reacts slowly to unpredictable changes in the environment. Reactive behavior and deliberate behavior can be distinguished by sensor data, global knowledge, reaction speed, theoretical power, and computational complexity. Recently, in the development of deliberate behavior, a declarative cognitive behavior similar to human brain memory emerged. The application of such planning depends not only on sensors and existing prior information, but also on the target to be reached. For a target that is far away and temporarily invisible, there may be a behavioral bifurcation point; that is, there are several behaviors to be adopted, and the robot has to choose the optimal choice. This decision making behavior is a declarative cognitive behavior. It is used for path planning that can make mobile robots have higher intelligence, but due to the complexity of decision making, this method is difficult to use in practice, and this area needs further study.

9.5.2 *Development trends of path planning*

With the expansion of the application range of mobile robots, the requirements of mobile robot path planning technology are getting higher and higher. Sometimes a single planning method cannot solve some planning problems well, so the combination of multiple planning methods will be a new development trend.

(1) Combination of reactive behavior-based planning and deliberate behavior-based planning

The planning method based on reactive behavior can achieve good planning results under the premise of establishing a static environment model but is not suitable in the case where there are some non-model obstacles (such as tables, people, etc.) in the environment. To this end, some scholars have proposed a hybrid control structure which combines deliberate behavior with reactive behavior, which can better solve this type of problem.

(2) Combination of global path planning and local path planning

Global planning is generally based on known environmental information, and the scope of adaptation is relatively limited; local planning can be applied in the case where the environment is unknown, but sometimes the response speed is not fast, and the quality of the planning system is high, so if the two are combined, better planning results can be achieved.

(3) Combination of traditional planning methods and new intelligent methods

Some new intelligent technologies have been introduced into path planning in recent years, and have also promoted the integration of various methods, such as the combination of artificial potential field [46], evolutionary computing [5,15,53,65], neural network [25,26], and fuzzy control [60]. In addition, trajectory planning is also combined with machine learning to improve the trajectory planning performance [14,34,44,47].

9.6 Robot Path Planning Based on Ant Colony Algorithm

Many path planning methods, such as path planning algorithms based on evolutionary algorithms and path planning algorithms based on genetic algorithms, have problems such as excessive computational cost and difficulty in solution construction. It is difficult to design evolutionary operator and genetic operator in complex environments. Ant colony optimization algorithms can be introduced to overcome these shortcomings, but there are also some difficulties in using ant colony algorithms to solve path planning problems in complex environments [23]. This section first introduces the ant colony optimization (ACO) algorithm, and then introduces a mobile robot path planning method based on the ant colony algorithm [10, 27, 28].

9.6.1 *Introduction to the ant colony optimization algorithm*

Biologists have found that ant colonies in nature have significant self-organizing behavior characteristics during foraging, such as the following: (1) ants will release a substance called pheromone during movement; (2) the released pheromone will gradually decrease over time; ants can detect whether there are similar pheromone trajectories in a specific range; (3) ants will move along the path with many pheromone trajectories and so on. It is based on these basic characteristics that ants can find a shortest path from the nest to the food source. In addition, the ant colony also has a strong ability to adapt to the environment. As shown in Figure 9.17, when an obstacle suddenly appears on the route that the ant colony passes, the ant colony can quickly find a new optimal path.

This foraging behavior of ant colonies has inspired a large number of scientific workers, resulting in the ant colony optimization algorithm (ACO). Ant colony algorithm is a simulation of the actual ant colony collaboration

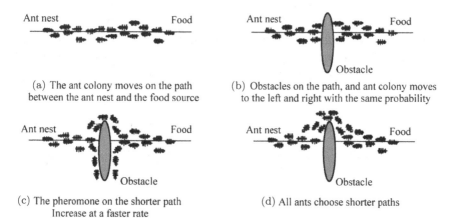

(a) The ant colony moves on the path between the ant nest and the food source

(b) Obstacles on the path, and ant colony moves to the left and right with the same probability

(c) The pheromone on the shorter path Increase at a faster rate

(d) All ants choose shorter paths

Figure 9.17 Adaptive behavior of an ant colony.

process. Each ant independently searches for solutions in the space of candidate solutions and leaves a certain amount of information on the found solutions. The better the performance of the solution, the greater the amount of information left by the ant, and the more likely the solution is to be selected again. In the initial stage of the algorithm, the information amount of all solutions is the same. As the algorithm advances, the information amount of the better solution gradually increases, and the algorithm eventually converges to the optimal solution or the approximate optimal solution. The basic model of the ant colony system is explained by taking the TSP problem of n cities in the plane as an example. The TSP problem for n cities is to find the shortest path through n cities once and finally back to the starting point. Let m be the number of ants in the ant colony, d_{ij} ($i, j = 1, 2, \ldots, n$) represents the distance between city i and city j, and $\tau_{ij}(t)$ represents the information amount remaining on the connected line ij at time t. During the movement, any ant k ($k = 1, 2, \ldots, m$) determines the transfer direction according to the following formula of the probability transfer rule:

$$p_{ij}^k = \begin{cases} \dfrac{\tau_{ij}^n(t)\eta_{ij}^n(t)}{\sum_{s \in allowed_k} \tau_{ij}^n(t)\eta_{ij}^n(t)}, & \text{if } j \in allowed_k \\ 0, & \text{Otherwise} \end{cases} \quad (9.13)$$

where p_{ij}^k represents the probability that ant k is transferred from position i to position j in time t; η_{ij} represents the degree of expectation from city i to city j and is generally taken as $\eta_{ij} = 1/d_{ij}$; $allowed_k = \{0, 1, \ldots, n-1\} - tabu_k$ (where $tabu_k$ is the city set that ants k went before), which represents the city that ants k will choose next. As time goes by, the information left in the past will gradually disappear. The parameter $(1 - \rho)$ is used to indicate the degree of information volatilization. After n times, each ant completes a cycle, and the amount of information on each path is adjusted according to the following formula:

$$\tau_{ij}(t + n) = \rho(t)\tau_{ij}(t) + \Delta\tau_{ij}, \quad \rho \in (0, 1) \quad (9.14)$$

$$\Delta\tau_{ij} = \sum_{k=1}^{m} \Delta\tau_{ij}^k \quad (9.15)$$

wherein $\Delta\tau_{ij}^k$ represents the amount of information that the kth ant left on the path ij in the current cycle, and $\Delta\tau_{ij}$ indicates the increment of the information amount on the path ij in the current cycle.

$$\Delta\tau_{ij}^{k} = \begin{cases} \dfrac{Q}{L_k} & \text{Ant } k \text{ passes through grid } i \text{ along } j \text{ direction} \\ 0 & \text{Otherwise} \end{cases} \quad (9.16)$$

where Q is a constant and L_k represents the length of the path taken by the kth ant in this cycle; at the initial moment, $\tau_{ij}(0) = C$, $\Delta\tau_{ij} = 0$ ($i, j = 0, 1, \ldots, n-1$). The selection of the parameters Q, C, ρ in the basic model of the ant colony system is generally determined by experimental methods.

The stopping condition of the algorithm can take a fixed evolution generation number or stop the calculation when the evolutionary trend is not obvious.

9.6.2 *Path planning based on ant colony algorithm*

The path planning problem of the robot is very similar to the foraging behavior of the ant. The path planning problem of the robot can be regarded as the process of circumventing some obstacles from the ant nest to find food. As long as there are enough ants in the nest, these ants can avoid the obstacle to find the shortest path from the nest to the food. Figure 9.23 is an example of the ant colony bypassing the obstacle to find a path from the nest to the food. Most foreign literature studies focus on simulating ant colony communication and collaboration in multi-robot systems. Some scholars have studied the ACO-based robot path planning problem. In order for the ant to find food (goal point), an odor zone is established near the food, and as long as the ant enters the odor zone, the food is found along the direction of the scent. In the obstacle area, because the obstacle can block the smell of food, the ants are unable to smell the food, and can only choose the walking path according to the heuristic pheromone or randomly. The planned complete robot walking path consists of three parts: the path from the starting position of the robot to the initial position of the ant, the path from the initial position of the ant to the position where the ant enters the odor area, and the path from the position where the ant enters the odor area to the end position.

(1) Environmental modeling

Let the robot walk on the limited motion area (environment map) on a two-dimensional plane, and there are a limited number of convex static obstacles distributed inside. For the sake of simplicity, the robot is modeled as a point robot, and the static obstacles in the walking area are correspondingly "expanded" according to the actual size and safety requirements of the robot, and the obstacle boundary after "expansion" is the safe area, and the obstacles do not intersect with each other, and also the obstacles and the area boundaries do not intersect with each other.

The description of environmental information should consider three important factors: (i) how to store environmental information in the computer; (ii) ease of use; (iii) more efficient problem solving. A two-dimensional Cartesian rectangular grid is used to represent the environment. Each rectangular grid has a probability. A probability of 1 indicates that there is an obstacle. When it is 0, there is no obstacle, and the robot can pass freely. The selection of the grid size directly affects the performance of the algorithm. The smaller the grid selection, the higher the environmental resolution, but the anti-interference ability is weak, the environmental information storage is large, and the decision speed is slow; if the grid selected is large, the anti-interference ability is strong. The amount of environmental information stored is small, the decision speed is fast, but the resolution is degraded, and the ability to find paths in a dense obstacle environment is weakened.

(2) Establishment of neighboring areas

In general, ants move around the nest, there are no obstacles near the nest, and ants can walk freely in this area. In this way, a neighboring area is established in the nest, and after the ants are randomly placed in the area, they are free to cross the obstacle area and feed for food. The neighboring area may be a sector or a triangular area as shown in the shaded areas shown in Figures 9.18(a) and (b). The neighborhood is established by finding the nearest vertical distance d from the starting point toward the end point to the obstacle, as shown in Figure 9.18(c), using this distance as the radius or the height of the triangle to create a sector or triangle.

(3) Establishment of odor zone

Any kind of food has an odor that attracts ants to crawl toward it, thus creating a food odor zone as shown in Figure 9.19. As long as the ants enter the odor zone, the ants will smell the scent and crawl towards the food location. In the non-odor zone, the ant does not smell the odor due to obstacle obstruction, and the feasible path can only be selected according to the

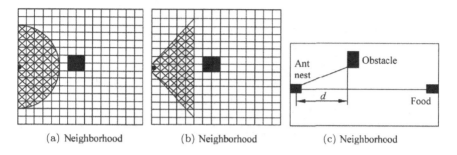

(a) Neighborhood   (b) Neighborhood   (c) Neighborhood

Figure 9.18   Adjacent area.

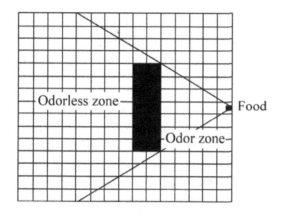

Figure 9.19   Food odor area.

method 6 described below. When the ant enters the scent zone, it moves toward the food and eventually finds food. The odor zone is established by scanning a straight line from the food toward the starting position, and the area before the obstacle is encountered is the odor zone.

(4) Composition of the path

The path consists of three parts: the path from the starting position of the robot to the initial position of the ant, the path from the initial position of the ant to the position where the ant enters the odor area, and the path from the ant entering the odor area to the end position as shown in Figure 9.20, and set to path0, path1, and path2, respectively, so the total path length is
$L_{path} = L_{path0} + L_{path1} + L_{path2}$.

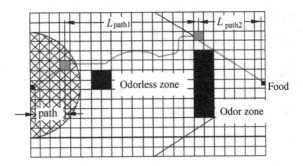

Figure 9.20   Path composition.

(5) Adjustment of path

The path the ant walks through is curved and must be adjusted to a smooth path. The adjustment method is shown in Figure 9.21: start from the starting point S and constantly search until point Q is found, so that the connection line between the next point G of Q and S passes through the obstacle, and the connection line from the point in front of Q (including the point Q) and S does not cross the obstacle, connect Q and S, then the closest point to obstacle in $\overline{SQ}$ is D, then SD is the path that needs to be found. Next, let D be S, and then find D between S and G until the S point coincides with G. The resulting connection is the adjusted path. Obviously, $\overline{SD}$ is the shortest distance from S to D, and $\overline{DG} < \overline{DQ} + \overline{QG}$, so the line segment $\overline{SDG}$ is the shortest path that bypasses the obstacle along the curve. Let the total number of grids be N, and the number of grids from the start point to the end point is M, then the worst time complexity is $O(N^2)$, and the best time complexity is $O(M^2)$.

(6) Choice of path direction

The ants can select three walking grids along the food direction numbered as 0, 1, and 2, respectively, as shown in Figure 9.22. Each ant selects a direction of travel based on the probability of three directions and moves to the next grid.

At time t, the probability $p_{ij}^k(t)$ that ant k moves from grid i along $j(j\{0,1,2\})$ to the next grid is the following:

$$
p_{ij}^k(t) = \begin{cases} \dfrac{[\tau_{ij}(t)]^\alpha \cdot [\eta_{ij}(t)]^\beta}{\sum_{s\in J_k(i)} [\tau_{ij}(t)]^\alpha \cdot [\eta_{ij}(t)]^\beta} & j \in J_k(i) \\ 0 & \text{Otherwise} \end{cases} \tag{9.17}
$$

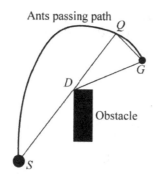

Figure 9.21   Path adjustment method.

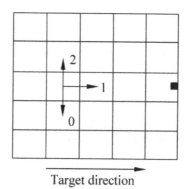

Target direction

Figure 9.22   Path direction selection.

where $J_k(i) = \{0, 1, 2\}$ where tabu_k represents the grid set that ant k next allows to select. The list tabu_k records the grid that ant k has just crossed. α and β indicate the relative importance of pheromones and heuristic factors, respectively. η_{ij} is a heuristic factor that represents the degree to which the ant moves from the grid i along j ($j\{0, 1, 2\}$) to the next. In the ant system (AS), η_{ij} is usually taken the reciprocal of the distance between city i and city j. Since the distance between the grids is equal, you can take 1 and then formula (9.17) becomes

$$p_{ij}^k(t) = \begin{cases} \dfrac{[\tau_{ij}(t)]^\alpha}{\sum_{s \in J_k(i)} [\tau_{ij}(t)]^\alpha} & j \in J_k(i) \\ 0 & \text{Otherwise} \end{cases} \qquad (9.18)$$

Method for ants to choose a direction: if the transition probability of each selectable direction is equal, one direction is randomly selected; otherwise, the direction with the highest probability is selected according to (9.18) as the ant's next walking direction.

(7) Update of pheromone

An ant moves in one of three directions on the grid to the next grid, so three pheromones are placed in each grid, and each pheromone is updated according to the following formula:

$$\tau_{ij}(t + n) = \rho\tau_{ij}(t) + \Delta\tau_{ij} \tag{9.19}$$

$$\Delta\tau_{ij} = \sum_{k=1}^{m} \Delta\tau_{ij}^{k} \tag{9.20}$$

where $\Delta\tau_{ij}$ represents the increment of the pheromone along the j ($j\{0,1,2\}$) direction of this iteration grid i. $\Delta\tau_{ij}^{k}$ indicates the amount of pheromone along the j ($j\{0,1,2\}$) direction of the kth ant in this iteration, and ρ indicates the residual degree after volatilization of the pheromone trajectory on a certain path and is taken as 0.9. If the ant k does not pass the grid i to the next grid in the j direction, then the $\Delta\tau_{ij}^{k}$ value is 0 and is represented as

$$\Delta\tau_{ij}^{k} = \begin{cases} \dfrac{Q}{L_k} & \text{Ant } k \text{ passes through grid } i \text{ along } j \text{ direction} \\ 0 & \text{Otherwise} \end{cases} \tag{9.21}$$

where Q is a normal number and L_k is the length of the kth ant after the path adjustment in this tour.

(8) Algorithm description

The steps of the path planning-based ant colony algorithm (PPACO) are as follows:

Step 1: Environment modeling;

Step 2: Establish a neighboring area of the nest and an odor area produced by the food;

Step 3: Place enough ants in the neighboring area;

Step 4: Each ant selects the next walking grid according to the above-mentioned method 6 (Choice of path direction);

Step 5: If an ant creates an invalid path, delete the ant, otherwise wait until the ant reaches the odor area and finds food along the odor direction;

Step 6: Adjust the effective path that the ant walks and save the optimal path in the adjusted path.

Step 7: According to the above method 7 (Update of pheremone), change the pheromone of the valid path;

Repeat Steps 3–7 until the number of iterations or the running time exceeds the maximum, ending the entire algorithm.

9.7 Intelligent Planning Based on Machine Learning

This section first introduces the progress of research on intelligent planning based on machine learning, and then takes an example to discuss the application of intelligent planning based on machine learning.

9.7.1 *Advances in intelligent planning based on machine learning*

In recent years, machine learning has been used more and more in automatic planning. This subsection briefly introduces research and applications of intelligent planning based on machine learning and then the progress of research on autonomous route planning for unmanned ships.

(1) Overview of intelligent planning applications based on machine learning

Machine learning has been successfully applied in the fields of pattern recognition, speech recognition, expert systems, and automatic planning. Deep reinforcement learning (DRL) can effectively solve the path planning problem of continuous state space and action space. It can directly use raw data as input and the output results as execution, and realize end-to-end learning mode, which greatly improves the efficiency and convergence of the algorithm. In recent years, DRL has been widely used in the fields of planning, control and navigation of robot control, intelligent driving, and traffic control [3].

First, machine learning has been widely used in the planning of various robots and intelligent moving bodies; examples include patrol robot path planning based on HPSO and reinforcement learning [51]; robot path planning in unknown environments based on deep reinforcement learning [56];

robust capture planning for multi-arm robots based on cloud-based 3D networks and related rewards [37]; deep learning-based fog robot method for object recognition and grabbing planning for deburring surfaces by robot [1]; deep reinforcement learning from virtual to reality for continuous control of mobile robots without map navigation [40]; global path planning for novel planetary rover based on learning [57]; autonomous path planning for unmanned ships based on deep reinforcement learning [32]; considering navigation experience rules for intelligent collision avoidance navigation for unmanned ships [49, 50]; obstacle avoidance and path planning for agents based on deep reinforcement learning [54]; and so on.

Secondly, intensity deep learning is more commonly applied to the underlying planning and control of moving bodies (robots); examples include model migration trajectory planning for deep reinforcement learning of intelligent vehicles [56]; a four-rotor aircraft based on deep reinforcement learning low-level control [39]; and so on.

In addition, machine learning is also applied to non-robot planning; examples include social awareness movement planning with deep reinforcement learning [26]; artificial intelligence-assisted planning based on machine learning [35]; integration based on intent network goal-oriented autonomous navigation for planning and deep learning [31]; and so on.

In recent years, reinforcement learning has attracted wide attention. It can realize the mapping of learning from the environment to behavior, and seek the most accurate or optimal action decision through "maximizing value function" and "continuous action space".

(i) Maximizing value function

Mnih *et al.* proposed a deep Q network (DQN) algorithm, which opened up the widespread application of DRL [45]. The DQN algorithm utilizes the powerful fitting capabilities of deep neural networks to avoid the huge storage space of the Q table, and uses experience replay memory and target networks to enhance the stability of the training process. At the same time, DQN implements an end-to-end learning method that uses only raw data as input and the output result as the Q value for each action. The DQN algorithm has achieved great success in discrete action, but it is difficult to achieve high-dimensional continuous action. If the continuously changing movements are split indefinitely, the number of movements will increase exponentially as the degree of freedom increases, which will cause catastrophic latitude problems and may cause great training difficulties. In addition, discretizing actions removes important information about the structure of the action domain. The Actor–Critic (AC) algorithm has the ability to deal with continuous motion problems and is widely used in continuous motion space [2]. The network structure of the AC algorithm includes the Actor network and the Critic network. The Actor network is responsible for outputting the probabilities of the actions, and the Critic network evaluates the output actions. In this way, the network parameters can be continuously optimized and the optimal action strategy can be obtained; however, the random strategy of the AC algorithm makes it difficult for the network to converge. The deep deterministic policy gradient (DDPG) algorithm for solving deep reinforcement learning (DRL) problems in continuous states was developed [41].

(ii) Continuous action space

The DDPG algorithm is a model-free algorithm that combines the advantages of the DQN algorithm with empirical replay memory and the target network. At the same time, the AC algorithm based on deterministic policy gradient (DPG) is used to make the network output result have a certain action value, so as to ensure that DDPG is applied to the field of continuous action space. DDPG can be easily applied to complex problems and larger network structures. A framework for a human-like autonomous vehicle following plans based on DDPG was put forward [62]. Under this framework, the self-driving car learns from the environment through trial and error to obtain the path planning model of the self-driving car, which has shown good experimental results. This research has shown that DDPG can gain insights into driver behavior and help develop human-like autonomous driving algorithms and traffic flow models.

(2) Research progress in autonomous route planning for unmanned ships

Improving the autonomous driving level of ships has become an important guarantee for enhancing the safety and adaptability of ships. Unmanned ships can be further adapted to the complex and volatile environment at sea. This requires unmanned ships to have autonomous path planning and obstacle avoidance capabilities, so as to effectively complete tasks and enhance the ship's comprehensive capabilities.

The research direction of unmanned ships involves autonomous path planning, navigation control, autonomous collision avoidance, and semi-autonomous task execution. As the basis and prerequisite of autonomous navigation, autonomous path planning plays a key role in ship automation and intelligence [42]. In the actual navigation process, ships often meet other ships. This requires a reasonable method to guide ships to avoid other ships and to sail according to targets.

At present, research on autonomous path planning for unmanned ships is carried out at home and abroad. These methods include traditional algorithms, such as APF, speed obstacle method, Algorithm A*, and some intelligent algorithms such as the ant colony optimization algorithm, genetic algorithm, neural network algorithm, and other DRL related algorithms.

In the field of intelligent ships, the application of DRL in unmanned ship control has gradually emerged as a new research area. For example, path learning and maneuvering methods for unmanned cargo ships based on Q learning were developed [25]; as another example, autonomous navigation control of unmanned ships based on the relative value iterative gradient (RVIG) algorithm was developed [55]; based on the Dueling DQN algorithm to automatically avoid collisions of multiple ships, a behavior-based USV local path planning and obstacle avoidance method was proposed [58]. DRL overcomes the shortcomings of the usual intelligent algorithms, which require a certain number of samples and have fewer errors and response times.

Many key autonomous path planning methods have been proposed in the field of unmanned ships. However, these methods have focused on small- and medium-sized USV studies, while relatively few studies have been conducted on unmanned ships. This study has chosen DDPG for unmanned channel planning because it has a strong deep neural network function fitting ability and a good generalized learning ability [25].

9.7.2   *Autonomous path planning based on deep reinforcement learning for unmanned ships*

An example of the application of deep learning in intelligent planning is introduced below, namely, autonomous path planning for unmanned ships based on deep reinforcement learning. Focus on the autonomous route planning model of unmanned ships based on deep reinforcement learning [32].

Reinforcement learning has performed well in solving continuous control problems and is widely used in areas such as path planning. This autonomous path planning proposes a DRL-based model to implement intelligent path planning for unmanned ships in unknown environments. Through continuous interaction with the environment and the use of historical empirical data, the model can use DDPG algorithms to learn the best action strategies in a simulated environment. The navigation rules and the conditions encountered by the ship are converted into navigation restricted areas to achieve the safety of the planned path and ensure the validity and accuracy of the model. The data provided by the ship's automatic identification system (AIS) is used to train this path planning model. An improved DRL is then obtained by combining DDPG with artificial potential fields. Finally, the path planning model is integrated into the electronic chart platform for experiments. Comparative experimental results show that the improved model can realize autonomous path planning with fast convergence and good stability.

(1) DDPG algorithm principle

The following paragraphs introduce an autonomous path planning model for unmanned ships based on DRL.

DRL is an end-to-end learning method that combines DL and RL, and uses both the DL's perception ability and the RL's decision making ability [48], which can effectively solve the disadvantages of traditional drones in the air and promote the progress of continuous motion control. DDPG is an algorithm in DRL that can be used to solve continuous motion space problems. Among them, the depth refers to the deep network structure, and the policy gradient is a policy gradient algorithm, which can randomly select actions in the continuous action space according to the learned strategy (action distribution). The purpose of determinism is to help the policy gradient avoid random selection and output specific operating values.

(i) AC algorithm

DDPG is based on the AC algorithm, and its structure is shown in Figure 9.23.

The network structure of the AC framework includes a policy network and an evaluation network. The policy network is called an actor network and the evaluation network is called a critic network. The actor network is used to select the action corresponding to the DDPG, while the critic network evaluates the advantages and disadvantages of the selected action by calculating a value function. The actor network and the critic network are two independent networks that share state information. The network uses state information to generate operations, while the environment feeds back the resulting operations and outputs rewards. The critic network uses

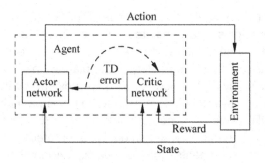

Figure 9.23   Actor–Critic (AC) algorithm structure.

status and rewards to estimate the value of current actions and continuously adjusts its own value function. At the same time, the actor network has updated its action strategy in the direction of increasing action value. In this loop, the critic network evaluates the action strategy through a value function, provides a better gradient estimation for the strategy network, and finally obtains the best action strategy. It is very important to evaluate the action strategy in the critic network, as it is more conducive to the convergence and stability of the current actor network. The above features ensure that the AC algorithm can obtain the best action strategy with gradient estimation in the case of low variance.

(ii) DDPG algorithm structure

The combination of DDPG and DQN under the premise of the AC algorithm further improves its stability and effectiveness of network training, making it more conducive to solving continuous state and action space problems. In addition, DDPG uses DQN's experience replay memory and target network to solve the problem of non-convergence when using neural networks to approximate function values. At the same time, DDPG subdivides the network structure into online networks and target networks. The online network is used to output actions in real time through online training, evaluate actions and update network parameters, and includes the online Actor network and the online Critic network, respectively. The target network includes the target Actor network and the target Critic network, which are used to update the value network system and the Actor network system, but do not perform online training and network parameter update. The target network and the online network have the same neural network structure and initialization parameters.

The flow of DDPG algorithm is shown in Figure 9.24.

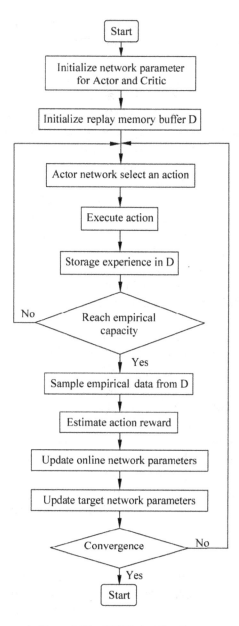

Figure 9.24   DDPG algorithm flow.

(2) Structural design of an autonomous route planning model for unmanned ships based on DDPG algorithm

The DDPG algorithm is a combination of deep learning and reinforcement learning. Based on the algorithm, an autonomous path planning model for unmanned ships is designed. The algorithm structure mainly includes communication algorithms, empirical replay mechanisms, and neural networks. The output actions of this model are gradually made accurate by using the AC algorithm to output and judge the ship's action strategy. By using the empirical replay mechanism, historical algorithms can output and judge the ship's action strategy.

During the experiment, there are many environmental and behavioral states of ships, so it is necessary to use neural networks for fitting and induction. The current state of the unmanned ship obtained in the environment is used as the input of the neural network, and the output is the Q value that the ship can perform Q learning actions in the unmanned environment. By continuously training and adjusting the parameters of the neural network, the model can learn the best action strategy in the current state.

Figure 9.25 shows the structure of the path planning model for unmanned ships based on DDPG algorithm. The model mainly consists of three parts: communication algorithm (AC), environment (ship motion controller and ship navigation information fusion module), and experience replay memory. Among them, the model obtains environmental information and ship status data through the "ship navigation information fusion module" and uses it as the input state of the AC algorithm. By randomly extracting data from the experience buffer pool for repeated training and learning, the optimal ship action strategy is output, which can meet the maximum cumulative return of the ship during the learning process. Finally, the unmanned ships can avoid obstacles and reach their destinations with the help of ship motion controllers.

(3) Model execution process

An unmanned ship path planning model based on the DDPG algorithm is used to abstract a real complex environment, and then it is transformed into a simple virtual environment through the model. At the same time, the model's action strategy is applied to the electronic chart platform environment to obtain the optimal planned trajectory of unmanned ships, and to implement the end-to-end algorithm learning process in the actual environment.

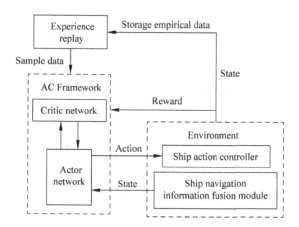

Figure 9.25   Structure of the unmanned ship path planning model based on DDPG algorithm.

The unmanned ship model is executed as follows:

(i) Start the unmanned route planning process, and the system reads the ship data through the ship navigation information fusion module.

(ii) Call the system trajectory planning model, and use the ship data as the input state, and process and calculate the model to obtain the ship's action strategy in the current state.

(iii) The model transforms the action strategy into the actual action that the unmanned ship should take based on the actual movement of the ship.

(iv) The ship motion controller analyzes and obtains the action to be performed, and executes the action.

(v) The model acquires the new status information of the unmanned ship at the next moment after the action is performed, and determines whether the state of the ship after the action is completed is the end state.

(vi) If it is not the final state, the model continues to use the state information of the ship, and then calculates and judges the action that the ship should take at the next moment and cycles through it. If it is in the end state, it means that the unmanned ship has completed the path planning task, and the model has finished the calculation and call.

9.8 Conclusion

For traditional path planning algorithms, historical empirical data cannot be recycled and used for online training and learning, which leads to lower accuracy of the algorithm, and the actual planned path is not smooth. This study proposes an autonomous path planning method for unmanned ships based on the DDPG algorithm. First, ship data is acquired based on an electronic chart platform. Then, the model is designed and trained in combination with ship maneuverability and crew experience, and verified under three classic encounter situations on the electronic chart platform. Experiments show that the unmanned ship has taken the best and reasonable action in an unfamiliar environment, successfully completed the task of autonomous route planning, and achieved unmanned operation. Finally, an autonomous route planning method for unmanned ships based on improved DRL is proposed, and the continuous operation output further verifies the effectiveness and reliability of the method.

The research and experimental results show that the autonomous path planning system for unmanned ships based on deep reinforcement learning has higher convergence speed and planning efficiency, the planned route is more in line with navigation rules, and the autonomous route planning and collision avoidance of unmanned ships are realized.

9.9 Summary

This chapter discusses the intelligent planning problem, i.e., the robot planning problem. First, the concepts, definitions, classifications, and functions of intelligent planning are discussed, and general methods for performing tasks in robot planning systems are explained. Classify intelligent planning from the essence of planning problems, and divide them into task planning, path planning, and trajectory planning. Then, task planning and path planning, respectively are studied in each section.

Task planning starts with robot planning of the block world, and gradually discusses robot planning in depth. The robot planning in question includes the following methods:

(1) Rule deduction. Solve the planning sequence using the F rule.
(2) Logical calculus (resolution principle) and the general search method. The STRIPS and ABSTRIPS systems belong to this method.
(3) Planning systems with learning ability. An example is the PULP-I system, which uses analog technology and semantic network representation.
(4) Planning based on expert systems. An example is the ROPS planning system; it has a faster planning speed, a stronger planning ability and greater adaptability.

In the path planning section, the main methods and development trends of robot path planning are discussed, and the results of our research are introduced, including an ant colony-based algorithm for robot path planning, and path planning based on machine learning. There are many planning methods for path planning based on artificial potential field, robot local path planning based on simulated annealing algorithm, and robot path planning based on immune evolution and example learning. These research examples are all mostly based on computational intelligence.

Machine learning has been successfully applied in the field of automatic planning. Deep reinforcement learning can effectively solve the path planning problem of continuous state space and action space. It can directly use the original data as input and use the output result as the execution action to implement the end-to-end learning mode, which greatly improves the efficiency and convergence of the algorithm. In recent years, deep learning and deep reinforcement learning have been widely used in the fields of robot control, intelligent driving, and traffic control. At the end of this chapter, an overview of intelligent planning based on machine learning is given, and examples of intelligent planning based on deep learning are listed.

The following are worth mentioning: first, intelligent robot planning has developed into a comprehensive application with multiple methods. Second, intelligent robot planning methods and technologies have been applied in image processing, computer vision, operational decision making and command, production process planning and monitoring, and robotics, and will be more widely used. Third, intelligent robot planning still has some further research issues, such as planning in dynamic and uncertain environments, coordinated planning of multiple robots, and real-time planning. In the future, more advanced intelligent robot planning systems and technologies will surely emerge.

References

1. Ajay, K.T., Nitesh, M. and John, K. (2019). A fog robotics approach to deep robot learning: application to object recognition and grasp planning in surface decluttering, *2019 International Conference on Robotics and Automation* (ICRA), Montreal, QC, Canada, pp. 4559–4566.
2. Bahdanau, D., Brakel, P., Xu. K., Goyal, A., Lowe, R., Pineau, J., Courville, A. and Bengio, Y. (2016). Actor–critic algorithm for sequence prediction, arXiv 2016, arXiv:1607.07086.

3. Bu, X.J. (2018). *Research on Robot Path Planning in Unknown Environment Based on Deep Reinforcement Learning*, Master's Degree Thesis, Harbin Institute of Technology (in Chinese). DOI: CNKI:CDMD:2.1018.896554

4. Cai, Z.X., Zou, X.B., Chen, H., *et al.* (2016). *Key Techniques of Navigation Control for Mobile Robots under Unknown Environment*, (Science Press, Beijing, in Chinese).

5. Cai, Z.X. and Peng, Z.H. (2002). Cooperative coevolutionary adaptive genetic algorithm in path planning of cooperative multi-mobile robot system, *Journal of Intelligent and Robotic Systems: Theories and Applications*, *33*(1): 61–71.

6. Cai, Z.X., Li, Y., *et al.* (2020). *Intelligent Vehicle Perception, Mapping and Target Tracking*, (Science Press, Beijing, in Chinese). In publication.

7. Cai, Z.X. and Fu, K.S. (1988). Expert system based robot planning, *Control Theory and Applications*, *5*(2): 30–37 (in Chinese).

8. Cai, Z.X. and Fu, K.S. (1986). Robot planning expert systems, *Proc. IEEE International Conferenece on Robotics and Automation*, *3*, 1973–1978, (IEEE Computer Society Press, San Francisco).

9. Cai, Z.X. and Fu, K.S. (1987). ROPES: A new robot planning system, *Pattern Recognition and Artificial Intelligence*, *1*(1): 77–85 (in Chinese).

10. Cai, Z.X., He, H.G. and Chen, H. (2009). *Theory and Method of Navigation Control for Mobile Robots in Unknown Environment*, (Science Press, Beijing, in Chinese).

11. Cai, Z.X. and Jiang, Z.M. (1991). A multirobotic pathfinding based on expert system, *Preprints of IFAC/IFIP/IMACS Int. Symposium on Robot Control*, pp. 539–543, (Pergamon Press).

12. Cai, Z.X. and Liu, J. (2002). Research progress of evolutionary robots, *Control Theory and Applications*, *19*(4): 493–499 (in Chinese).

13. Cai, Z.X. and Tang, S.A. (1995). Multirobotic planning based on expert system. *High Technology Letters*, *1*(1): 76–81

14. Cai, Z.X., Zheng, J.J. and Zou, X.B. (2006). Radar-based mobile robot real-time obstacle avoidance strategy, *Journal of Central South University* (Natural Science Edition), *37*(2): 324–329 (in Chinese).

15. Cai, Z.X., Zhou, X., Li, M.Y., *et al.* (2000). Evolutionary control architecture of autonomous mobile robots based on function/behavior integration, *Robot*, *22*(3): 169–175 (in Chinese).

16. Cai, Z.X. and Zou, X.B. (2004). Research on environmental cognition theory and technology of mobile robot, *Robot*, *26*(1): 87–91 (in Chinese).

17. Cai, Z.X. (1992). A knowledge based flexible assembly planner, *IFIP Transaction*, *B-1*, 365–371 (North Holland).

18. Cai, Z.X. (1995). An expert system for high-level planning of robots, *High Technology Letters*, *5*(1): 21–24 (in Chinese).

19. Cai, Z.X. (1988). An expert system for robot handling planning, *Chinese Journal of Computers*, *11*(4): 242–250 (in Chinese).

20. Cai, Z.X. (1988). An expert system for robotic transfer planning, *Computer Science and Technology*, *3*(2): 153–160.

21. Cai, Z.X. (1988). *Principles and Applications of Robots*, (Central South University of Technology Press, Changsha, China, in Chinese).
22. Cai, Z.X. (1989). Robot path finding with collision avoidance, *Computer Science and Technology*, 4(3): 229–235.
23. Cai, Z.X. (2015). *Robotics*, 3rd edn., (Tsinghua University Press, Beijing, in Chinese).
24. Cai, Z.X. (1986). Some research works on expert system in AI course at Purdue, *Proc. IEEE Int. Conf. on Robotics and Automation*, Vol. 3, pp. 1980–1985, (IEEE Computer Society Press, San Francisco).
25. Chen. C., Chen, X.Q., Ma, F., Zeng, X.J. and Wang, J. (2019). A knowledge-free path planning approach for smart ships based on reinforcement learning, *Ocean Engineering, 189*, 106299.
26. Chen, Y.F., Michael, E., Liu, M. *et al.* (2017). Socially aware motion planning with deep reinforcement learning, *2017 IEEE/RSJ International Conference on Intelligent Robots and Systems* (IROS), Vancouver, BC, pp. 1343–1350.
27. Dorigo, M. and Stutzle, T., translated by Zhang, J. *et al.* (2007). *Ant Colony Optimization*, (Tsinghua University Press, Beijing, in Chinese).
28. Dorigo, M., Maniezzo, V. and Colorni, A. (1996). Ant system: optimization by a colony of cooperating agent, *IEEE Transactions on Systems, Man and Cybernetics, 26*(1): 1–13.
29. Fu, K.S., Gonzalez, R.C. and Lee, C.S.G. (1987). *Robotics: Control, Sensing, Vision and Intelligence*, (McGraw-Hill, New York).
30. Fu, K.S., Cai, Z.X. and Xu, G.Y. (1987). *Artificial Intelligence and Its Applications*, (Tsinghua University Press, Beijing, in Chinese).
31. Gao, W., David, H.W. and Lee, W.S. (2017). Intention-net: integrating planning and deep learning for goal-directed autonomous navigation, arXiv:1710.05627v2 [cs.AI] October 17, 2017.
32. Guo, S., Zhang, X.G., Zheng, Y.S. and Du, Y.Q. (2020). An autonomous path planning model for unmanned ships based on deep reinforcement learning, *Sensors*, 2020, 20, 426; doi:10.3390/s20020426.
33. Hanheide, M., Göbelbecker, M., Horn, G.S., *et al.* (2015). Robot task planning and explanation in open and uncertain worlds, *Artificial Intelligence, 247*: 119–150.
34. Honig, W., Preiss, J.A., Kumar, T.K.S., Sukhatme, G.S. and Ayanian, N. (2018). Trajectory planning for quadrotor swarms, *IEEE Transactions on Robotics, 34*(4): 856–869.
35. Huang, D.X. (2017). The prospect of artificial intelligence-aided planning based on machine learning, *Urban Development Studies, 24*(5): pp. 50–55.
36. Huang, M.D., Xiao, Xiaoming, M., Cai, Z.X., *et al.* (2007). Application of environmental feature extraction in mobile robot navigation, *Control Engineering, 14*(3): pp. 332–335 (in Chinese).
37. Jeffrey, M., Florian, T., Pokorny, B.H., *et al.* (2016). A cloud-based network of 3D objects for robust grasp planning using a multi-armed bandit model with correlated rewards, *2016 IEEE International Conference on Robotics and Automation* (ICRA), Stockholm, pp. 1957–1964.

38. Ji, J., Khajepour, A., Melek, W. and Huang, Y. (2016). Path planning and tracking for vehicle collision avoidance based on model predictive control with multiconstraints, *IEEE Trans. Vehicle Technology*, 66(2): pp. 952–964. DOI: 10.1109/TVT.2016.2555853.
39. Lambert, N.O., Drewe, D.S., Yaconelli, J., Calandra, R., Levine, S. and Pister, K.S.J. (2019). Low-level control of a quadrotor with deep model-based reinforcement learning, *IEEE Robotics and Automation Letters*, 4(4): pp. 4224–4230.
40. Lei, T., Giuseppe, P. and Liu, M. (2017). Virtual-to-real deep reinforcement learning: continuous control of mobile robots for mapless navigation, arXiv:1703.00420v4 [cs.RO] July 21, 2017.
41. Lillicrap, T.P., Hunt, J.J., Pritzel, A., Heess, N., Erez, T., Tassa, Y., Silver, D. and Wierstra, D. (2015). Continuous control with deep reinforcement learning, *ResearchGate*, arXiv:1509.02971v1 [cs.LG].
42. Liu, Z., Zhang, Y., Yu. X. and Yuan, C. (2016). Unmanned surface vehicles: An overview of developments and challenges, *Annual Review Control*, 41, 71–93.
43. Lynch, K.M. and Park, F.C. (2017). *Modern Robotics: Mechanics, Planning, and Control*, (Cambridge University Press).
44. Mihelj, M., Bajd, T., Ude. A., *et al.* (2019). *Robotics*, Springer, 2019.
45. Mnih, V., Kavukcuoglu, K., Silver, D., *et al.* (2013). Playing atari with deep reinforcement learning, arXiv 2013, arXiv:1312.5602.
46. Orozco-Rosas, U., Montiel, O. and Sepúlveda, R. (2019). Mobile robot path planning using membrane evolutionary artificial potential field, *Applied Soft Computing*, 77: 236–251.
47. Richter, C., Bry, A. and Roy, N. (2013). Polynomial trajectory planning for quadrotor flight, presented at *Robotics: Science and Systems, Workshop on Resource-Efficient Integration of Perception, Control and Navigation for Micro Aerial Vehicles*.
48. Serrano, W. (2019). Deep reinforcement learning algorithms in intelligent infrastructure, *Infrastructures*, 2019, 4(3): 52; https://doi.org/10.3390/infrastructures-4030052.
49. Shen, H.Q., Hashimoto, H., Matsuda, A., *et al.* (2019). Automatic collision avoidance of multiple ships based on deep Q-learning, *Applied Ocean Research*, 86: 268–288.
50. Shen, H.Q., Guo, C., Li, T.S., *et al.* (2018). Intelligent collision avoidance navigation method for unmanned ships considering sailing experience rules, *Journal of Harbin Engineering University*, 39(6): 998–1005.
51. Song, Y. (2019). *Research on Path Planning of Inspection Robot Based on HPSO and Reinforcement Learning*, Master's Degree Thesis, Guangdong University of Technology.
52. Tangwongsan, S. and Fu, K.S. (1979). Application of learning to robotic planning, *International Journal of Computer and Information Science*, 8(4): 303–333.
53. Wang, L-F., Tan, K.C. and Chew, C.M. (2006). *Evolutionary Robotics from Algorithms to Implementations*, (World Scientific, Singapore).

54. Wu, D. (2019). *Research and Application of Agent's Obstacle Avoidance and Path Planning Based on Deep Reinforcement Learning*, Master's Degree Thesis, University of Electronic Science and Technology, Chengdu, China.
55. Yang, J., Liu, L., Zhang, Q. and Liu, C. (2019). Research on autonomous navigation control of unmanned ship based on unity3D, in *Proceedings of the 2019 IEEE International Conference on Control, Automation and Robotics* (ICCAR), Beijing, China, April 19–22, 2019, pp. 2251–2446.
56. Yu, L.L., Shao, X.Y., Long, Z.W., *et al.* (2019). Model migration trajectory planning method for deep reinforcement learning of intelligent vehicles, *Control Theory and Applications*, 36(9): 1409–1422 (in Chinese).
57. Zhang, J., Xia, Y.Q. and Shen, G.H. (2019). A novel learning-based global path planning algorithm for planetary rovers, *Neorocomputing*, 361: 69–76.
58. Zhang, R.B., Tang, P., Su, Y., Li, X., Yang, G. and Shi, C. (2014). An adaptive obstacle avoidance algorithm for unmanned surface vehicle in complicated marine environments, *IEEE CAA Journal of Automatica Sinca*, 1, 385–396.
59. Zhang, Y., Sreedharan, S., Kulkarni, A., *et al.* (2015). Plan explicability and predictability for robot task planning, arXiv:1511.08158 [cs.AI].
60. Zhao, H., Cai, Z.X. and Zou, X.B. (2003). Path planning based on fuzzy ART and Q learning, *Proceedings of the Tenth Annual Conference of the Chinese Society of Artificial Intelligence*, Guangzhou, 2003, pp. 834–838 (in Chinese).
61. Zheng, J.J., Cai, Z.X. and Yu, J.X. (2006). An obstacle avoidance strategy for mobile robots in dynamic environment, *High Technology Letters*, 16(8): 813–819.
62. Zhu, M., Wang, X. and Wang, Y. (2018). Human-like autonomous car-following model with deep reinforcement learning, *Transportation Research Part C Emerging Technologies*, 97: 348–368.

Intelligent Perception 10

After years of research on artificial intelligence, the development of artificial intelligence has been divided into the following three directions: computational intelligence, perceptual intelligence, and cognitive intelligence. Computational intelligence refers to the ability of a computer to quickly calculate and store memory. Perceptual intelligence refers to the ability of the machine to perceive vision, hearing, and touch. Cognitive intelligence refers to the ability of a machine to understand and reason [31]. In recent years, perception intelligence has made good progress in visual recognition and speech recognition, and because of the full use of pattern recognition and deep learning technology, machines have become similar to humans in terms of perceptual intelligence.

This chapter discusses pattern recognition and two important areas of perceptual intelligence: image understanding, which deals with visual intelligence, and speech recognition, which deals with auditory intelligence.

10.1 Introduction to Pattern Recognition

10.1.1 *What is pattern recognition?*

To know what pattern recognition is, you must understand what pattern is first. Although we often use this word, a lot of effort is required to fully explain it.

Define 10.1. *A pattern means a form of subjective rationality used to explain the structure of things.* It is a core knowledge system abstracted and sublimated from production experience and life experience. However, it should be noted that the mode is not the thing itself, but a form of existence.

Define 10.2. *Pattern recognition refers to the processing and analysis of various forms of information that characterize things or phenomena, so as to achieve the purpose of describing, identifying, classifying, and explaining things or phenomena.*

Pattern recognition began in the 1850s and became popular in the 1970s and 1980s. It is an important part of information science and artificial intelligence. It is mainly used in image analysis and processing, speech recognition, voice classification, communication, computer-aided diagnosis, data mining, etc. Although pattern recognition seems to be very large and has been used for a long time, the effect seems to be unsatisfactory.

For example, when humans see something, they usually subconsciously classify it by the following rules: whether it is an animal or a plant, which family it belongs to, whether it is medicinal or not, whether it is poisonous or not, whether it has fruit or not, whether the flower is beautiful or not, and so on. A long list of classifications constitutes people's overall perception of such things. This is the human recognition of pattern. This skill is very simple and almost innate for humans and even some animals.

But in pattern recognition, machines do not seem to be as "smart" as one might expect. The workflow of manually extracting features to the machine and letting the machine judge the attributes of other things is just scratching the surface. According to this method, although it is possible to find a really great horse, it is also possible to retrieve a stinky toad because for the machine, even distinguishing the simplest "0", "O", "o", and "·" will take a lot of effort.

10.1.2 *The difference between pattern recognition and machine learning*

Unlike pattern recognition, in which humans actively describe certain features to machines, machine learning can be understood as follows: the machine itself to find and extract (training/learning) some rules (model) from the known empirical data (samples) through a specific method (algorithm); the extracted rules can be used to judge something unknown (prediction).

In other words, the difference between pattern recognition and machine learning is that the former feeds the machine with various feature descriptions, so that the machine can judge the unknown things, while the latter feeds the machine with a large number of samples of a certain thing, letting the machine find the features by itself through the samples, and finally judge something unknown.

From a technical perspective, machine learning generally analyzes various samples fed by humans in the same way. What we see in black is just three parameters RGB in the computer with the value of 0, and white is these three parameters with 255. Therefore, the distinction between black and white is easy in machines.

Based on a large number of samples of a certain thing, the machine summarizes the general laws of this type of thing. The skills used in the summary process are what we often call "algorithms". When enough samples ensure that the algorithm summarizes a set of proven rules, the machine can use these rules to make decisions and predict events in the real world.

Although technology continues to evolve, without exception, the development of a new technology is always based on the original technology. Every new achievement is achieved by standing on the shoulders of giants.

Although new technology will continue to occupy the trend, this does not mean that the old technology has nothing to do. In the field of artificial intelligence, although pattern recognition has gradually faded, it still plays a unique role. For example, in some simple color recognition fields, the dimensions of parameters are relatively small, and the definition is relatively obvious. If we use big data to model and calculate, it will undoubtedly complicate the task. Different technical algorithms can play their respective roles in different fields.

10.1.3 *Research methods of pattern recognition*

Patterns can also be divided into two types: abstract and concrete. Abstract patterns, such as consciousness, thought, argumentation, etc., belong to the category of recognition, and it is another branch of artificial intelligence. The pattern recognition we are talking about refers to the classification and recognition of specific patterns measured on objects such as speech waveforms, seismic waves, electrocardiograms, electroencephalograms, pictures, photos, text, symbols, and biological sensors.

Pattern recognition research mainly focuses on two aspects: one is researching how the organisms (including humans) perceive objects, which belongs to the category of cognitive science, and the other is how to implement the theory and methods of pattern recognition in computers for a given task. The former is the research content of physiologists, psychologists, biologists, and neurophysiologists, and the latter has achieved systematic research results through the efforts of mathematicians, informatics experts, and computer scientists in recent decades.

Utilizing a computer to identify and classify a set of events or processes, the identified events or processes can be either specific objects such as text, sound, and images, or abstract objects such as states and degrees. These objects are distinguished from information in a digital form and are called pattern information.

In principle, pattern recognition can be divided into two types: statistical and syntactic pattern recognition.

(1) Statistical pattern recognition

Statistical pattern recognition is a method that has been developed earlier and is more mature. The identified object is first digitized and transformed into digital information suitable for computer processing. A pattern is often represented by a large amount of information. Many pattern recognition systems also perform pre-processing tasks after the digitization to remove mixed interference signal information and to reduce certain distortions. This is followed by feature extraction, i.e., a set of features are extracted from the digitized or pre-processed input pattern. The so-called feature is a selected metric, which remains unchanged or almost unchanged for general distortions and contains as little redundant information as possible. The feature extraction process maps the input patterns from object space to feature space. At this time, the pattern can be represented by a point or a feature vector in feature space. This mapping not only compresses the amount of information but is also easy to classify. In decision theory methods, feature extraction plays an important role, but there is no general theoretical guidance, and only analyzing the specific identification objects helps to decide which features to choose. After feature extraction, it can be classified, i.e., it can be re-mapped from feature space to decision space. Then, a discriminant function is introduced and its values corresponding to each category are calculated from the feature vectors, and classification is performed by comparing the discriminant function values.

(2) Syntactic pattern recognition

The syntactic method is also known as the structural method or the linguistic method. The basic idea is to describe a pattern as a combination of simpler sub-patterns. Then a sub-pattern can be described as a combination of much simpler sub-patterns. Finally, a tree-like structure description is obtained. The simplest sub-pattern at the bottom is called pattern primitives. The problem of selecting primitives in the syntactic method is equivalent to the problem of selecting features in the decision theory method. The selected primitives are usually required to provide a compact description of the structural relationship of the pattern, and it must be easy to extract using non-syntactic methods. Obviously, the primitives themselves should not contain important structural information. A pattern is described by a set of primitives and their combination, which is called a pattern description sentence, which is equivalent to the combination of words and phrases in a language, as well as the combination of words and characters. The rules for combining primitives into patterns are specified by the so-called syntax. Once the primitives are identified, the recognition process can be performed by parsing, i.e., analyzing whether a given pattern statement conforms to a specified grammar, and those that meet a certain type of grammar are classified into this class.

The selection of the pattern recognition method depends on the nature of the problem. If the identified object is extremely complex and contains rich structural information, a syntactic approach is generally adopted. If the identified object is not very complex or does not contain obvious structural information, a decision theory approach is usually used. These two methods cannot be separated completely because in the syntactic method, the primitives are extracted using the decision theory method. In the application, these two methods are combined and applied to different levels, and often get better results.

With the continuous progress of artificial intelligence technology, various artificial intelligence technologies, such as fuzzy sets, neural networks, and expert systems have been gradually applied to pattern recognition research and have shown good application and development prospects.

10.2 Image Analysis and Understanding

10.2.1 *Image engineering*

Vision is the most complete perception system of human beings. The image carrier can provide multi-dimensional information. In many cases, it cannot be replaced by any other information form. Letting a computer or machine "see" is quite a great progress. In order to let a machine truly observe the world like a human or an animal, it relies on computer vision and image recognition [13].

Images are obtained by observing the objective world in various forms and means with various observation systems, which can directly or indirectly act on human eyes and then produce visual perception. While image technology is a general term for various image processing technologies, image engineering is an overall framework for the research and application of various image technologies.

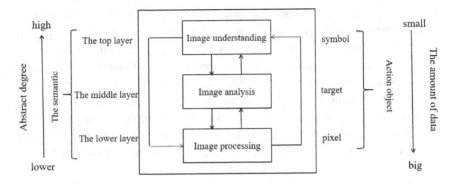

Figure 10.1   Image engineering.

The content of image engineering can be divided into three levels: image processing, image analysis, and image understanding. These three levels are both related and different, as shown in Figure 10.1.

The key point of image processing is the transformation between images. Although people often use image processing to refer to various image technologies, the more narrowly defined image processing is mainly to process images to improve the visual effect of the image and lay the foundation for automatic recognition, or to compress and encode the image to reduce the need for storage.

Image analysis is mainly to detect and measure the objects of interest in the image and obtain their information, so as to establish a description of the image. If image processing is image to image, then image analysis is image to data. The data here can be the measurement results of target features or symbolic representations based on the measurements, which both describe the characteristics and properties of the target.

The focus of image understanding is to further study the nature of the objects in the image and their interconnections based on image analysis, and to understand the meaning of the image content and the interpretation of the original objective scene, so as to guide and plan actions.

If image analysis mainly studies the objective world with the observer's view, image understanding is learning the entire objective world (including things that are not directly observed) with the help of knowledge and experience from an objective view.

Image processing, image analysis, and image understanding are at three different levels of abstraction and data volume. Image processing is a relatively low-level operation. It is mainly processed at the image pixel level, and the amount of data processed is very large. Image analysis is the middle layer. Segmentation and feature extraction transfer the image describing task from pixels into a more concise non-graphical description. Image understanding is a high-level operation, and basically operates on the symbols abstracted from description. The processing process and method have many similarities with human reasoning.

10.2.2 *Image processing and image analysis*

(1) Image function and image acquisition

The information contained in an image first appears as the intensity of light (Intensity), which changes with the spatial coordinates (x, y), the wavelength of the light, and time t, so the image function can be written as

$$I = f(x, y, \lambda, t) \tag{10.1}$$

If only the energy of the light is taken into consideration without its wavelength, there are only black and white differences in visual effects without color changes. At this time, it is called a black and white image or a gray image.

$$I = f(x, y, t) = \int_0^\infty f(x, y, \lambda, t) V_s(\lambda) d\lambda \tag{10.2}$$

where $V_s(\lambda)$ is the relative visual acuity function.

When the color effect of different wavelengths is considered, it is a color image. According to the principle of three primary colors, any one color can be decomposed into the three primary colors of red, green, and blue [10]. So, a color image can be expressed as

$$I = \{f_r(x, y, t), f_g(x, y, t), f_b(x, y, t)\} \tag{10.3}$$

where

$$f_c(x, y, t) = \int_0^\infty f(x, y, \lambda, t) R_c(\lambda) d\lambda, c \in \{r, g, b\},$$

and $R_c(\lambda)$ represents the visual acuity function for the three primary colors of red, green, and blue, respectively.

A digital image is a sample and quantization process to transform an image existing in its natural form into a digital form suitable for computer processing as shown in Figure 10.2. An image is represented inside a computer as a matrix, and each element in the matrix is called a pixel. Image digitization requires specialized equipment. There are various electronic

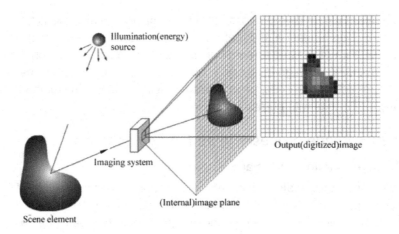

Figure 10.2   Digital image acquisition.

and optical scanning equipment, electromechanical scanning equipment, and manual digitizers. In computers, images can be divided into four basic types: binary image, gray image, index image, and true color RGB image according to the color and grayscale. Most image processing software supports these four types of images.

(2) Image processing

Image processing refers to the theory, methods, and techniques of using a computer to perform noise removal, enhancement, restoration, segmentation, and feature extraction on an image in order to improve the visual effect of the image and make it convenient for users to observe and further analyze it.

(i) Image transformation: Due to the large size of the image array, processing directly in the spatial domain involves a large amount of calculations. Therefore, various image transformation methods, including indirect processing techniques such as Fourier transform, Walsh transform, and discrete cosine transform (DCT), are often used to convert the processing in the spatial domain into the transformed domain. These methods not only can reduce the amount of calculations, but also can obtain more efficient processing (for example, Fourier transform can perform digital filtering in the frequency domain). At present, the wavelet transform in emerging research has good localization characteristics in both time and frequency domains. It has also been widely and effectively applied in image processing.

(ii) Image compression: Image compression technology can reduce the amount of data describing the image (i.e., the number of bits) in order to save the transmission band, processing time, and reduce the amount of memory occupied. Compression can be obtained without distortion, or it can be performed with acceptable distortion. Coding is the most important method in compression technology. It is the earliest and more mature technology in image processing technology.

(iii) Image enhancement and restoration: The purpose of image enhancement and restoration is to improve the quality of the image, such as removing noise and improving the sharpness of the image. Image enhancement does not consider the cause of image degradation, highlighting the part of interest in the image. For example, enhancing the high-frequency components of the image can make the edge of the object clear and the details obvious, while strengthening the low-frequency components can reduce the influence of noise. Image restoration requires a certain understanding of the causes of image degradation. Generally speaking, a "degradation model" should be established according to the degradation process, and then some filtering method should be used to restore or reconstruct the original image.

(iv) Image segmentation: Image segmentation is one of the key technologies in digital image processing. It refers to the extraction of meaningful features in the image. The meaningful features include edges and regions in the image. This is the basis for further image recognition, analysis, and understanding. Although many methods for edge extraction and region segmentation have been developed, there is no effective method that is generally applicable to various images. Therefore, the research on image segmentation is still developing, and it is one of the research hotspots in image processing.

(v) Image description: Image description is a necessary prerequisite for image recognition and understanding. As the simplest binary image, its geometric characteristics can be used to describe the characteristics of the object. The general image description method uses two-dimensional shape description. It has two types of methods: boundary description and area description. For special texture images, two-dimensional texture features can be used. With the further development of image processing research, research on three-dimensional object description has begun, and volume description, surface description, generalized cylinder description, and other methods have been proposed.

(vi) Image classification (recognition): Image classification (recognition) belongs to the category of pattern recognition. Its main content is that after certain preprocessing (enhancement, restoration, compression) of the image, image segmentation and feature extraction are utilized to classify it. Image classification often uses classic pattern recognition methods, including statistical pattern classification and syntactic (structural) pattern classification. Fuzzy pattern recognition and artificial neural network pattern classification, which have been newly developed in recent years, have received increasing attention in image recognition.

The contents of image processing are interrelated. A practical image processing system often combines several image processing techniques to get the target result. As for image processing, an image is still an image after processing. But image analysis extracts some useful metrics, data, or information from the image. The goal is to get some numerical result and not to produce another image.

(3) Image analysis

Extracting some useful metrics, data, or information from an image is called image analysis. The basic step of image analysis is to divide the image into non-overlapping regions, each region is a continuous set of pixels, measure their properties and relationships, and finally compare the obtained image relationship structure with the classification model to determine its type. The basis of recognition or classification tasks is the similarity of the images. A simple similarity can be defined by the distance in the feature space of the region. Another similarity measure based on pixel values is the correlation of image functions. The similarity defined in the last relational structure is called structural similarity.

The content of image analysis overlaps with the fields of pattern recognition and artificial intelligence, but image analysis differs from typical pattern recognition. Image analysis is not limited to classifying specific areas in an image into a fixed number of categories; it is mainly to provide a description of the image being analyzed. To this end, it is necessary to use both pattern recognition technology and the image knowledge base, i.e., the content of knowledge expression in artificial intelligence. Image analysis needs to use the image segmentation method to extract the features of the image, and then describe the image symbolically. This kind of description can not only answer the existence of a specific object in the image, but also make a detailed description of the image content.

Segmentation, description, and identification for the purpose of image analysis and understanding will be used in various automated systems, such as character and graphic recognition, product assembly and inspection with robots, automatic military target recognition and tracking, fingerprint recognition, X-ray photos, and automatic processing of blood samples. In such applications, it is often necessary to comprehensively apply technologies such as pattern recognition and computer vision, and image processing more often appears as pre-processing.

10.2.3 *Image understanding*

(1) The definition of image understanding

Define 10.3. *Image Understanding (IU) is the task-oriented reconstruction and interpretation of a scene by means of images.* It is a science that uses computer systems to interpret images semantically and realizes a system similar to human vision to understand the world.

Image understanding studies the following: what targets are in the image, the relationship between the targets, in what scene the image is, and how to apply the scene. Figure 10.3 is a typical example of image semantic understanding. First, the foreground object of the image is determined, so that it can be clearly known that the description object of the

Figure 10.3   An example of image understanding.

image is a car; then, the background category of the image is sequentially determined including the sky, trees, grass, and road, and the environmental information of the foreground object is obtained for describing the semantic label and geometric structure of the image scene in detail.

In the process of image understanding, the computer not only needs to roughly infer the foreground and background knowledge of the image, but also needs to have the ability to provide accurate pixel-level annotation, accurately divide the pixel area to which each semantic concept belongs, and complete the semantic interpretation of the image content. When understanding the image content, the computer perceives the image based on the bottom visual characteristics, while humans perceive the image through a series of scene information, abstract information, and logical information expressed in the image; that is, human vision directly translates the image content into semantic information. There are significant objective differences between computers and humans in understanding images; that is, there is a "semantic gap" between the visual representation of images and high-level semantic information. How to solve this bottleneck has become a hotspot and difficulty in the research on computer vision and artificial intelligence. This research has far-reaching theoretical value and practical application significance.

With the development of computer vision and artificial intelligence disciplines, related research contents are constantly expanding and crossing each other. Image understanding is not only an extension and expansion of computer vision research, but also an important new research and application field of human intelligence research. It has been widely used in the fields of industrial vision, human–computer interaction, visual navigation, virtual reality, specific image analysis and interpretation, and biological vision research.

(2) Development of image understanding

Early research on image understanding can be traced back to computer vision research. Its input is structured or semi-structured data symbols that describe the characteristics of the image. When these data symbols are processed and analyzed by the computer, the semantic descriptions or behavioral decisions are obtained as output for mimicking of human vision to achieve the purpose of perception and understanding of the objective world. The line drawing representation method is used to describe the object in the image, and the obtained object line is matched with the geometrically transformed object model, which can better realize the recognition of three-dimensional objects, creating a precedent for computers to "understand" the world [25]. However, many complex scenes in the real world are difficult to characterize completely with simple lines. In order to obtain a more comprehensive way of computer vision perception, D. Marr of the Massachusetts Institute of Technology's Artificial Intelligence Lab combined image processing, cognitive psychology, and biological neurology in the process of image understanding to propose the well-known Marr's computational theory of vision. Marr's computational theory of vision is the first complete vision system framework, which has played a vital role in the development of computer vision perception [24].

With the in-depth study of image understanding by scholars, people have found deficiencies in Marr's theory. For example, Marr's theory believes that the process of visual perception is a bottom-up 3D reconstruction process and lacks high-level knowledge feedback, which causes many visual problems to become morbid problems, making it impossible to construct a three-dimensional reconstruction framework [23]. Aiming at the problem of "passive resilience", the theories of purpose vision and active vision [3] have been successively proposed, which makes computer vision understanding and human visual perception processes more consistent in principle, emphasizing the necessity and importance of high-level knowledge feedback in vision algorithms, and the important role of the visual subject and the external environment. However, because there is no uniform standard for the expression and feedback of high-level knowledge, it is difficult to establish an effective calculation model.

With the development of human brain understanding-based intelligence and machine learning, a human visual understanding framework based on machine learning has been constructed. The framework relies on the scene structure consistent with the real image to reasonably inference the process of visual understanding. Based on summarizing the constraint information, it indirectly reveals the abstract pattern of image understanding, and the cognitive mode of human vision is fully considered in the entire computing model. Therefore, visual research based on learning has become an important content in the field of image understanding in recent years, and in particular, computational models based on probabilistic reasoning can deeply solve complex problems in human thinking.

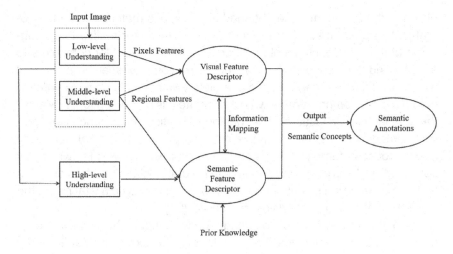

Figure 10.4　Image understanding process.

(3) The level of image understanding

The hierarchical structure of image understanding is shown in Figure 10.4. The low level of image understanding takes the image as input data and outputs visual features in pixels. The output of the middle-level understanding is the descriptor of features about the natural objects. These features are formed on the basis of abstraction and simplified overlapping description. The preliminary integration of semantic information in the descriptor of visual features improves the ability to describe features. High-level understanding is based on feature data from the low level and middle level and uses semantic annotation models and prior knowledge to realize the semantic interpretation of images [36]. Therefore, the entire image understanding process is the process of comprehensively processing visual information and knowledge information and analyzing image content by artificial intelligence methods.

The core of the research on image semantic understanding is to solve or reduce the semantic gap between the visual feature expression and high-level semantic information. The expression of visual features of images is the basis of image understanding. How to extract image features efficiently and quickly is the basic task of image understanding. At the same time, the study of image semantic annotation based on knowledge expression and conceptual reasoning is the key basis of image understanding.

(4) Image features

Image features can be divided into two categories according to their representation content and semantic level: visual features and semantic features. Visual features are the basic characteristics of images with intuitive meanings such as color, texture and shape, which correspond to the information obtained by human vision's intuitive perception such as brightness perception, color perception, and shape perception. Semantic features describe the objects and their spatial relationship in the image, i.e., the description of abstract concepts in the image content.

(i) Visual features of images:

Visual features mainly include features such as color, texture, shape, etc. that describe the visual effects of the image. These features are intuitive attributes that the computer can extract from the image.

Color feature is one of the most convenient and widely used visual features, and it has always attracted the attention of researchers. A color feature is a global feature that describes the surface properties of objects in an image or image area. Generally, color features are pixel-based features. The color histogram can count the number of each color value in the image and is not affected by changes such as image translation and rotation. Therefore, color feature is the most commonly used. When color histograms are used to describe the visual characteristics of images, they are often affected by imaging factors such as lighting and blurring. In addition, there are features such as color sets and color moments [28].

Texture features are a perception of the natural attributes of an object's surface, and this perception is independent of color and brightness. Unlike color features, texture features are not pixel-based features; they require statistical calculations in an area containing multiple pixels. According to different mathematical research models, textures can be divided into three categories: statistical texture features, spectral texture features, and structural texture features [12]. In pattern matching, such regional features have great advantages, and will not fail to match due to local deviations. As a statistical feature, texture features often have rotation invariance and strong robustness to noise. However, texture features also have their disadvantages. When the resolution of an image changes, the calculated texture may have a large deviation. In addition, because it may be affected by lighting and reflection conditions, the texture showed in the 2D image may not be the true texture on the 3D object surface. For example, reflections of water, the effects of mutual reflections on smooth metal surfaces, etc. can cause changes in texture. The texture feature is also a global feature, which describes the surface properties of the scene corresponding to the image or image area. However, because texture is only a characteristic of the surface of an object and cannot fully reflect the essential attributes of the object, it is impossible to obtain high-level image content using only texture features [29].

Shape feature is one of the key information for object recognition in the visual system. It has the invariance of displacement, rotation and scale transformation, and can describe areas with semantic meaning or related objects in the image [30]. Because it is related to the semantic concept of the object, the shape feature belongs to the middle-level feature of the image. In image matching and recognition, the shape features of the image can be used more effectively, but they have some shortcomings, including the following: many shape features only describe the local nature of the target, and a comprehensive description of the target often requires massive computing time and high storage space; the target shape information reflected by many shape features is not completely consistent with human intuitive feeling; that is, the similarity of feature space is different from the similarity felt by the human visual system. In addition, the 3D object represented in the 2D image is actually just the projection of the object on a certain plane in space. The shape reflected from the 2D image is often not the true shape of the 3D object. Due to changes in viewpoint, various distortions may occur.

Image understanding depends to a large extent on the recognition and perception of objects in the image, which is the basis for obtaining image semantic information. In order to correctly recognize the objects in the image, it must involve a solution to the problem of the **semantic segmentation of the image**. From the current research results, it can be seen that the academic community has been committed to solving the problem of image semantic segmentation [21], but due to the semantic richness and cognitive complexity of image content, the existing research methods are not perfect in terms of technology.

(ii) Semantic features of images:

The semantic features of an image are semantic information abstracted from the image based on human visual cognition and they can be used to semantically describe the image content. In the process of understanding images, the human visual system not only utilizes the visual characteristics of images, but also adds some perceptual knowledge of semantic concepts. These semantic perceptions cannot be directly obtained from the visual features; however, they must be inferred and judged in combination with prior knowledge.

(5) Semantic annotation of images

The essence of image semantic annotation is to establish an accurate mapping from its visual features to its semantic features. It uses a set of semantic concepts to describe image content, such as objects or scene categories, by mining the semantic knowledge and objective laws implicit in the image. The study of image semantic annotation has been a hotspot in the field of image understanding in recent years. Statistical methods and machine learning techniques are the main methods for constructing image semantic annotation models. According to the different modeling methods used, the classification of image semantic annotation models is shown in Table 10.1.

Table 10.1   Classification of image semantic annotation models.

Methods and techniques	Category	Main model
Statistical Methods	Generative	Translation Model
		Latent Semantic Analysis Model
		Probabilistic Latent Semantic Analysis Model
		Latent Dirichlet Allocation Model
		Related Model
		Markov Random Field Model
	Discriminative	Support Vector Machine Model
		Bayes Model
		Gaussian Mixture Model
		Conditional Random Field Model
Machine Learning Techniques	Induction	Clustering Algorithms
		Associated Learning
		Example Learning
	Teaching	Relevant Feedback
	Analogy	Network Retrieval

(i) Statistics-based image semantic annotation method

Statistics-based image semantic annotation methods can be divided into two types: generative and discriminative [34].

The generative image semantic annotation method is based on the relationship between the visual and semantic features of the labeled images in the training set, and establishes a joint probability model of the two, and uses this probability model to semantically label the unlabeled images. The translation model belongs to the generative image semantic annotation model. It uses the co-occurrence relationship between visual features and semantic features to find the corresponding semantic vocabulary for the visual features of the image area. The entire image annotation process is equivalent to a translation process from image visual features to semantic vocabulary. Revelation from text classification, and topic models such as Probabilistic Latent Semantic Analysis (PLSA) [14] and Latent Dirichlet Allocation (LDA) [5] have also been applied to the research on image annotation. Using hidden topics, the visual features and semantic features are linked to realize the semantic annotation of images. Unlike translation models, these related models do not need to establish a one-to-one mapping relationship between the image visual features and semantic tagging words but uses a probability statistical model to calculate the joint distribution of semantic tagging words and feature vectors and use the association relationship to annotate the image semantically. The Markov Random Field (MRF) model is an image labeling model based on statistical probability methods. The model can model local contexts. Because the training of generative model parameters is more complicated, the ability of MRF models to use multiple features and label context information is limited.

The discriminative image semantic labeling method treats all semantic features as independent classes, learns the corresponding discriminant model for each class, and uses the discriminant model to predict the semantic labeling. Discriminant image semantic annotation models mainly include the Support Vector Machine (SVM) model, Bayes model, Gaussian Mixture Model (GMM), and Conditional Random Field (CRF) [17] model. SVM has significant advantages in solving small sample, nonlinear, high-dimensional pattern recognition. Because the image has multiple visual features, the number of model parameters is large, and a large amount of training data is needed to learn the model parameters [33]. In this case, you can use the GMM model for image semantic annotation. CRF is a probabilistic image model originally used for annotation of sequence data. Because of its strong context description ability, CRF models have been widely used in image annotation. Compared with the MRF model, due to the overall probabilistic analysis features, the CRF model shows a greater advantage in context description and multi-feature utilization [26].

(ii) Image semantic annotation method based on machine learning

The image semantic annotation process not only uses statistical learning methods, but also incorporates many types of machine learning strategies such as induction, teaching, and analogy. Inductive learning is a learning method that is based on a series of examples of a certain concept and is generally summarized by induction. Clustering is an inductive method of unsupervised learning. Using clustering algorithms, it is possible to implement semantic labeling for each region of an image [19]. The inductive algorithm only considers the similarity of visual features and ignores the semantic features when categorizing regions, so that its labeling accuracy is relatively low. Example learning is a typical inductive learning method. From a large number of examples labeled "positive examples" and "negative examples" in advance, general conceptual descriptions are obtained, and they are well used in image annotation [7].

Learning from instruction is a learning method that acquires information from the external environment and then converts the knowledge into general instructions or suggestions. Relevant feedback is a typical example of the learning from instruction method [6]. Iterative feedback information improves the learning efficiency of the system. In order to improve the role of feedback information, researchers have proposed learning strategies such as single-class learning, motivational learning, and multi-directional learning, and achieved improved learning efficiency through discriminative features and multiple visual features. Learning by analogy is a learning method that consists of knowledge derivation by comparing things with similar knowledge. In the case of a small number of labeled training images, the use of analog learning methods can improve the robustness of the image labeling model with a large amount of network image data [20]. In addition, there are some data-driven image annotation models. In the search results corresponding to visual features and semantically labeled vocabularies, vocabularies with significant descriptive properties are mined [32].

10.3 The Case of Image Understanding Based on Deep Learning: DenseCap

The fundamental task of image understanding based on deep learning is to train deep learning neural networks to enable them to correctly understand the deep non-visual semantic information expressed by the image, including the content, the scene, and the implied logical information in the image. This section uses DenseCap, proposed by Fei-Fei Li's team at Stanford University, as an example to introduce how to apply deep learning to solve image understanding problems and realize dense captioning [16].

Dense captioning is to locate entities in the image and generate a multi-angle, multi-entity, prominent area, modular complex natural language description. The implementation of dense captioning can be divided into two stages. The first stage is to detect the object and describe the object by a single word. The second stage is the semantic stage, which generates a text description for each entity that has been located, i.e., perform a "tagged" process with greater density and complexity.

The DenseCap model includes a convolutional network, a new dense localization layer, and a recurrent neural network language model that generates a sequence of labels. The localization layer receives the feature vector of the original image after a convolutional network processing such as VGG16 and proposes some regions of interest (ROI). Then after several fully connected layers region features are converted to proper size vectors that can be processed by LSTM, and finally statements of the ROI are generated. There are two difficulties. One is how to select qualified proposals for LSTM. In this case, a network method similar to RPN (Region Proposal Network) was used. The other is to map different-sized proposals to the same size window as LSTM only accepts fixed-size inputs. Fei-Fei Li's team use a mapping method called bilinear interpolation to replace the ROI pooling layer.

From the DenseCap, we can see that visual captioning has made tremendous progress with deep learning. Image or visual captioning forms the technical foundation for many important applications, such as semantic visual search, visual intelligence for chat bots, photo and video sharing in social media, and helping the visually impaired people perceive the visual content of the surroundings.

10.4 Basic Principles and Development of Speech Recognition

The task of speech recognition is to convert speech into a sequence of words by using a computer program [15]. The ultimate goal is to enable the machine to understand human speech. Speech recognition technology, also known as automatic speech recognition, refers to the high-tech technique that allows machines to recognize and understand the conversion of speech signals into computer-readable text or commands. Speech recognition involves many disciplines such as pattern recognition, signal information processing, phonetics, linguistics, physiology, psychology, artificial intelligence, computer science, and neurobiology. Speech recognition technology is gradually developing into a key technology in computer information processing technology, becoming an emerging high-tech industry with great competitiveness, widely used in fields such as industry, home appliances, communications, automotive electronics, medical treatment, home services, consumer, electronic products, etc.

10.4.1 *How does speech recognition work?*

The essence of speech recognition is a pattern recognition based on speech feature parameters. That is, through learning, the system can classify the input speech according to a certain pattern, and then find the best matching result according to the judgment criterion. The principle of pattern matching has been applied to most speech recognition systems. Figure 10.5 is a basic block diagram of a speech recognition system based on the principle of pattern matching. General pattern recognition includes basic modules such as preprocessing, feature extraction, and pattern matching.

Figure 10.6 shows the framework of the recognition process of a speech recognition system. First, the input speech is preprocessed, and the speech signal is collected through a microphone, and after sampling and A/D conversion, the analog signal is converted into a digital signal. The pre-emphasis, framing, windowing, endpoint detection, and filtering of the digital signal of the speech are then pre-processed. The pre-processed speech signal will extract the parameters that best represent the characteristics of the speech signal according to a specific feature extraction method.

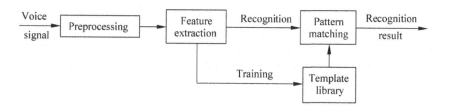

Figure 10.5   Schematic diagram of the speech recognition system.

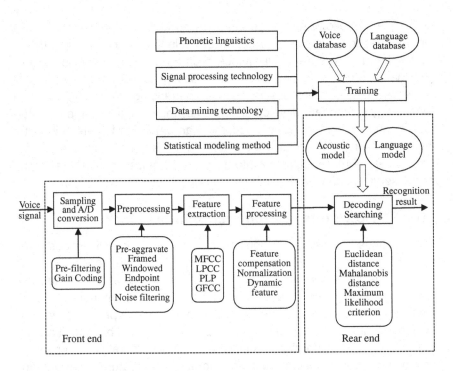

Figure 10.6   Framework of the speech recognition system.

These feature parameters form a characteristic sequence of the speech signal in time series. Commonly used characteristic parameters include pitch period, formant, short-term average energy or amplitude, linear prediction coefficient, perceptual weighted prediction coefficient, short-term average zero-crossing rate, linear prediction cepstrum coefficient, autocorrelation function, Mel cepstrum coefficient, wavelet transform coefficients, empirical mode decomposition coefficients, gamma pass filter coefficients, etc. During the training process, the feature parameters are obtained by different training methods to obtain an acoustic (speech) model and a language model, and then stored in a template library (decoding module). In the decoding process, after the newly acquired speech signal is processed to obtain the feature parameters, the model is matched with the model in the template library and combined with some expert knowledge to obtain the recognition result output.

10.4.2 *Development of speech recognition*

Scientists have been exploring the development of speech recognition technology in the process of developing computers. After nearly half a century of development, millions of people are able to routinely interact with computers in cars, smartphones, cell phones, chat bots, and computers in customer service call centers.

In 1952, AT&T Bell Institute's Davis and others developed Audry, the world's first experimental system that can recognize the pronunciation of ten English digits. In 1960, Denes and others at London College in the UK developed the first computer speech recognition system. Large-scale speech recognition research started in the 1970s and has made substantial progress in the recognition of small vocabularies and isolated words. After the 1980s, the focus of speech recognition research gradually turned to large vocabulary and non-specific continuous speech recognition. At the same time, major changes have also taken place in the research on speech recognition. From the traditional technical ideas based on standard template matching to the statistical ideas based on statistical models, the statistical models are based on HMM methods. The method gradually dominates speech recognition research. HMM can well describe the short-term stationary characteristics of speech signals, and integrates acoustics, linguistics, syntax, and other knowledge into a unified framework. Since then, the research and application of HMM has gradually been the mainstream. For example, the first "unspecified person continuous speech recognition system" is the SPHINX system [18], which was developed by Kai-Fu Lee, who was still pursuing a doctorate at Carnegie Mellon University. The core framework was the GMM–HMM framework, of which the GMM (Gaussian mixture model) is used to model the observation probability of speech, while HMM is used to model the timing of speech. In the late 1980s, artificial neural networks also became a direction for speech recognition research. But this kind of shallow neural network has a general effect on speech recognition tasks, and its performance is not as good as the GMM–HMM model. Speech recognition has entered the first booming period of research and industrial applications, mainly due to the proposed discriminative training criteria and model adaptive methods based on the GMM–HMM acoustic model. The HTK open source toolkit released by Cambridge during this period significantly reduced the threshold for speech recognition research [22]. In the past 10 years, the progress of speech recognition research has been relatively limited. The overall effect of the speech recognition system based on the GMM–HMM framework is far from the practical level, and research and application of speech recognition have created a bottleneck.

After entering the 1990s, speech recognition technology began to be applied to the global market. Many well-known Internet companies have invested heavily in the development and research of speech recognition technology. In the 21st century, the focus of speech recognition technology research has shifted to improvised spoken and natural dialogue and multi-lingual simultaneous translation. In the past few years, some major breakthroughs have been made in the research on impromptu spoken and natural dialogue and simultaneous translation of multiple languages. New speech recognition products have emerged endlessly, and the accuracy has been increasing. It has entered the practical stage.

In 2006, Hinton proposed the use of a RBM to initialize the nodes of a neural network, i.e., a deep belief network (DBN). DBN solves the problem that it is easy to fall into a local optimum during the training of deep neural networks, and the tide of deep learning has officially opened since then. In 2009, Hinton and his student Mohamed applied DBN to speech recognition acoustic modeling and succeeded on a small vocabulary continuous speech recognition database [1]. In 2011, DNN succeeded in continuous speech recognition with a large vocabulary, and achieved the biggest breakthrough in speech recognition in nearly 10 years [9]. Since then, the deep neural network-based modeling method has replaced GMM-HMM and become the mainstream modeling method for speech recognition [8].

Because the recurrent neural network has stronger long-term modeling capabilities, RNN has gradually replaced DNN as the mainstream modeling solution for speech recognition. China University of Science and Technology's Xunfei has combined the characteristics of the traditional DNN framework and RNN to develop a new framework called the feed-forward sequential memory network (FSMN) [35], which adopts a non-cyclic feed-forward structure to achieve the same effect as BLSTM-RNN (Bidirectional Long Short-term Memory Recurrent Neural Network).

Nowadays, speech recognition is the most popular application on mobile terminals, such as voice dialogue robots, voice assistants, interactive tools, and more. Many Internet companies have invested human, material, and financial resources to carry out research and applications in this area. Convenience mode quickly occupied the customer base.

Famous artificial intelligence companies around the world are scrambling to develop voice recognition products and put them on the market. Among the more influential companies and products are Apple's Siri, Google's Google Now and GoogleHome, Microsoft's Cortana, Amazon's Echo and Polly, Facebook's Jibbigo, IBM's ViaVoice, Alibaba's ALIME, iFLY-TEK's MIGU Lingxi and Easytrans, Baidu's Raven H, Tencent's Ding Dang speaker, AISPEECH's Talkinggenie, and a variety of different chat robot products.

10.5   Key Technologies of Speech Recognition

Recognizing speech through the machine needs to respond to different voices, different speaking speeds, different contents, and different environments of different people. Speech signals are characterized by variability, dynamics, instantaneity, and continuity. These factors are all constraints in the development of speech recognition. The following introduces the key technologies of speech recognition in terms of acoustic feature extraction, acoustic model, language model, search algorithm in speech recognition, and performance evaluation.

10.5.1   *Acoustic feature extraction*

After the simulated speech signal is sampled, the waveform data is sent to the feature extraction module, and the appropriate acoustic feature parameters are extracted for subsequent acoustic model training. Good acoustic characteristics should consider the following three aspects. First there should be better distinguishing characteristics. The modeling unit with different acoustic models can be conveniently and accurately modeled. Secondly, feature extraction can also be considered as the compression coding process of voice information. It needs to eliminate the channel and speaker factors, retain the information related to the content, and use the lowest possible parameter dimensions without losing too much useful information for efficient and accurate model training. Finally, robustness, i.e., the ability to resist interference with ambient noise, needs to be considered.

Commonly used acoustic features are Linear Prediction Coefficients (LPCs), Cepstral Coefficients (CEPs), Mel-frequency (Mel), and Mel-Frequency Cepstral Coefficients (MFCCs).

The LPC analysis starts from the human vocalization mechanism. Through the study of the short tube cascade model of the channel, the signal at time *n* can be estimated by the linear combination of the signals at previous times. The LPC can be obtained by achieving the least mean square (LMS) error between the actual speech sample value and the linear prediction sample value. LPC calculation methods include autocorrelation method (Durbin method), covariance method, lattice method, and so on. The fast and effective calculation guarantees the widespread use of this acoustic feature. Acoustic features similar to the predictive parameter model of LPCs include line spectrum versus LSPs, reflection coefficients, and so on.

The homomorphic processing method is used to obtain the logarithm of the discrete Fourier transform (DFT) of the speech signal, and then the cepstrum coefficient can be obtained by using the inverse transform of DFT (IDFT). Therefore, the cepstrum can be understood as the log compression of the autocorrelation sequence. For LPC cepstrum (LPCCEP), after obtaining the linear prediction coefficient of the filter, it can be calculated using a recursive formula. Experiments have shown that using cepstrum can improve the stability of characteristic parameters.

Figure 10.7 shows one frame of data, logarithmic power spectrum, autocorrelation sequence, and cepstrum of the original speech signal. The peak in the cepstrum corresponds to a peak in the autocorrelation sequence, but it is clearer. The position of this peak is at the position of 58th sample, and the corresponding pitch frequency is $(16000/58) = 275\,\text{Hz}$ (the signal sampling rate is $16\,\text{kHz}$). This is a fairly high pitch rate, since the original speech signal was obtained from a female speaker. Because of the strong peak of cepstrum, it is often used for pitch detection.

People are better at identifying small changes in pitch at low frequencies than at high ones. The Mel scale is a nonlinear frequency scale based on the human ear's sensory judgment of equidistant pitch changes. Mel scales associate the perceived frequency or pitch of a pure tone with its actual measured frequency. The relationship between the Mel scale *m* and the frequency *f* is as follows:

$$m = 2595 \log_{10}(1 + f/700) \qquad (10.4)$$

Unlike the acoustic characteristics obtained through the study of human sound mechanism by LPCs, etc., the Mel coefficient is an acoustic characteristic derived from the research results of the human auditory system. This feature is closer to what humans hear.

As the name suggests, MFCCs feature extraction involves two key steps: conversion to Mel frequency and then cepstrum analysis. First transform

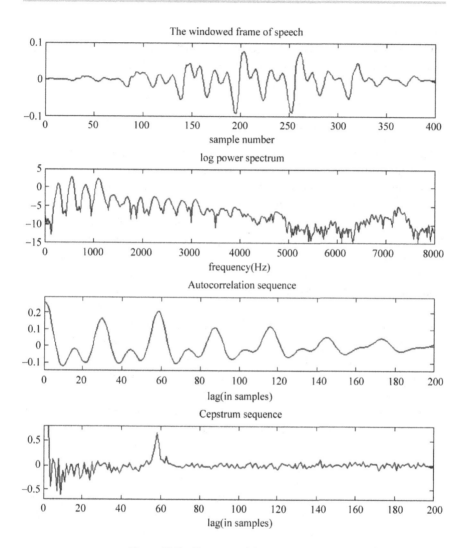

Figure 10.7   Cepstrum of the speech signal.

the time-domain signal into the frequency domain with fast Fourier transform (FFT), then convolve its logarithmic energy spectrum with a triangular filter bank according to the Mel scale distribution, and finally perform a DCT on the vector formed by the output of each filter and use the first N coefficients in DCT transformation. PLP still uses the Durbin method to calculate LPC parameters, but it also uses the method of performing DCT on the logarithmic energy spectrum of auditory excitation when calculating the autocorrelation parameters. Since its introduction by Davis and Mermelstein in 1980, MFCCs have been the most widely used feature in automatic speech and speaker recognition.

10.5.2 *Acoustic model*

The model of a speech recognition system usually consists of an acoustic model and a language model, which correspond to the calculation of speech-to-syllable probability and the calculation of syllable-to-word probability, respectively. Today's mainstream speech recognition systems use the Hidden Markov Model (HMM) as an acoustic model because HMM has many excellent features. The state jump model of the HMM is very suitable for the short-term stationary characteristics of human speech and can conveniently perform statistical modeling on the continuously generated observations (speech signals). HMM has a wide range of applications, and HMM can be modeled for discrete or continuous distribution by selecting different probability densities. HMM and its related technologies are at the heart of speech recognition systems. Since the introduction of HMM theory by Baum and Eagon in 1967, the application of HMM in speech signal processing and related fields has become more and more extensive, playing a key role in the field of speech recognition.

The concept of Markov model is a discrete-time domain finite state automa. HMM means that the internal state of this Markov model is not visible to the outside world, and the outside world can only see the output values at various times. For speech recognition systems, the output value is usually an acoustic feature calculated from each frame. There are two assumptions required to characterize the speech signal using HMM. One is that the internal state transition is only related to the previous state, and the other is that the output value is only related to the current state (or the current state transition). These two assumptions greatly reduce the model's complexity. The corresponding algorithms for scoring, decoding, and training of HMM are forward algorithm, Viterbi algorithm, and forward backward algorithm.

The use of HMM in speech recognition usually involves a one-way left-to-right, self-looping, and spanning topology to model the recognition primitives. A phoneme contains three to five HMM states, and a word is serially formed HMMs by multi-phoneme HMMs, and the entire model of continuous speech recognition is the HMM combining words and silence.

In addition, the phenomenon of cooperative pronunciation of speech indicates that the acoustic model also needs to consider the long-term correlation between speech frames. Co-pronunciation refers to the change of a sound by the influence of adjacent sounds. From the perspective of the sounding mechanism, when the sound of a human vocal organ changes from one to another, it can only change smoothly, so that the spectrum of the latter sound can be different from the spectra under other conditions. The context-dependent modeling method takes this effect into consideration, so that the model can describe speech more accurately. Bi-Phone means we are only considering the effect of the previous tone, and Tri-Phone means that we take both the previous and the next tone effects into consideration at the same time.

In recent years, with the rise of deep learning, the HMM acoustic model with nearly 30 years of usage history has been gradually replaced by the DNN, and the accuracy of the model has also changed dramatically. On the whole, acoustic modeling technology has obvious changes from three dimensions: modeling unit, model structure, and modeling process, as shown in Figure 10.8 [35]. The tremendous feature learning capability of deep neural networks greatly simplifies the process of feature extraction and reduces the dependence of modeling on expert experience. Therefore, the modeling process has gradually shifted from the previous complicated and multi-step process to simple end-to-end modeling. The impact of this process is that the modeling unit gradually evolves from states, three-phoneme models to larger units such as syllables and words, and the model structure changes from classic GMM-HMM

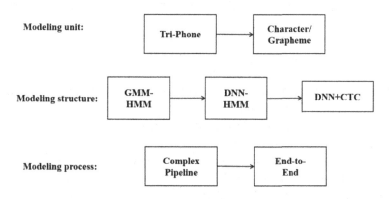

Figure 10.8 Evolution of acoustic modeling.

to DNN + CTC. The intermediate state in the evolution is a hybrid model structure called DNN-HMM. CTC (Connectionist Temporal Classification) is a kind of loss function proposed by Alex Graves *et al.* in 2006 for training RNNs to label unsegmented sequences directly [11].

10.5.3 *Language model*

The purpose of the language model in speech recognition is to give the text sequence with the highest probability based on the output of the acoustic model. Language models are mainly divided into two types: rule models and statistical models.

A rule-based language model is based on the classification of linguistic vocabulary systems according to grammatical semantics, and determines the lexical, syntactic, and semantic relationships of natural language in order to achieve a wide range of basic unique identification of homophones. Its characteristics are suitable for processing closed corpora, which can reflect the long-distance constraint relationship and recursion phenomenon of the language, but this method is not robust; it is not suitable for processing open corpora, and the consistency of knowledge expression is not good.

A statistical language model is based on a large-scale corpus. This method is suitable for processing large-scale real corpus, and the consistency of data preparation is good. Its robustness is strong. However, because its realization is limited by the space and time of the system, it can only reflect the immediate constraints of the language and cannot be processed as long-distance recursion of language. Statistical language models use probabilistic statistics to reveal the inherent statistical laws of language units. Among them, N-Gram is a simple and effective model, and is widely used.

The N-Gram model is based on the assumption that the occurrence of the N-th word is only related to the former $N - 1$ words and is not related to any other words. The probability of the entire sentence is the product of the probability of occurrence of each word. These probabilities can be obtained directly by counting the number of simultaneous occurrences of the N-th words from the corpus. Commonly used techniques are binary Bi-Gram and ternary Tri-Gram.

The performance of a language model is usually measured in terms of cross entropy and complexity. With cross entropy we can know the difficulty of text recognition with the model, or how many bits are needed to encode each word from the compression view. Complexity is the average number of branches of this text represented by the model, and its reciprocal can be regarded as the average probability of each word. Smoothing refers to assigning a probability value to an N-gram combination that is not observed to ensure that the word sequence can always obtain a probability value through the language model. The commonly used smoothing techniques are Turing estimation, deletion interpolation smoothing, Katz smoothing, and Kneser-Ney smoothing.

10.5.4 *Search algorithms in speech recognition*

The search in continuous speech recognition is to find a word model sequence to describe the input speech signal, so as to obtain the word decoded sequence. The search is based on scoring the acoustic model and the language model in the formula. In actual use, it is often necessary to add a high weight to the language model based on experience and set a long word penalty score. The most commonly used search algorithms are Viterbi algorithm, N-best search, and forward–backward search algorithm.

Based on the dynamic programming of the Viterbi algorithm at each time point, calculate the posterior probability of the decoded state sequence to the observation sequence, keep the path with the highest probability, and record the corresponding state information at each node for the final acquisition word decoding sequence. The Viterbi algorithm solves the non-linear time alignment of the HMM model state sequence and the acoustic observation sequence in continuous speech recognition, word boundary detection and word recognition without losing the optimal solution, thus turning this speech recognition algorithm into the basic search strategy.

In order to use various knowledge sources in the search, multi-pass searches are usually performed. For the first time, low-cost knowledge source is used to generate a candidate list or a word candidate grid. Based on this, the second-pass search with expensive knowledge source is performed to get the best path. The previously introduced knowledge sources are acoustic models, language models, and phonetic dictionaries, which can be used for the first search. In order to achieve more advanced speech recognition or spoken language understanding, it is often necessary to use some more expensive knowledge sources to rescore, such as 4th or 5th order N-Gram, 4th or higher context-related models, inter-word correlation model, segmentation model or grammar analysis. Many of the latest real-time large vocabulary continuous speech recognition systems use this multi-pass search strategy.

The N-best search is a multi-pass search method. It generates a candidate list. If it keeps the N best paths at each node, it will increase the computational complexity by N times. A simplified approach is to keep only a few word candidates for each node, but sub-optimal candidates may be lost. A compromise solution is to consider only two word-length paths and keep k paths. The word candidate grid can give multiple candidates in a more compact way, and the algorithm for generating candidate grids can be obtained by making corresponding changes to the N-best search algorithm.

The forward–backward search algorithm is an example of applying the multi-pass search. When a forward Viterbi search is performed using a simple knowledge source, the forward probability obtained in the search process can be used to calculate the objective function of the backward search. Therefore, a heuristic A* algorithm can be used to search out N candidates economically.

10.5.5 *Performance evaluation*

After the speech recognition system is built, a test database is needed to verify the effect of the system, i.e., whether it has reached the predetermined goal. In general, we will evaluate and illustrate the performance of the system through the following parameters.

(1) Word error rate (WER)

We have a raw text and a recognized text with length N. Recognizing word strings is unavoidable due to misinterpretation of word insertion, replacement, and deletion. Let I be the number of inserted words, D the number of deleted words, and S the number of words replaced. Then the word error rate is defined as $WER = (I + D + S)/N$. The word error rate is generally expressed as a percentage.

(2) Accuracy

It is mostly similar to the word error rate, but it does not count the number of words inserted. It is defined as Accuracy $= (N - D - S)/N$. For most tasks, accuracy is actually a poor measurement index because the impact of the insertion is also important for the recognition result. But for some tasks, accuracy is also a reasonable index for evaluating decoder performance.

(3) Speed

Speed is used to evaluate the speed of recognition. Assuming that the audio file is 2 hours and the decoding takes 6 hours, the system recognizes it as $3 \times RT \cdot (3 \times Speed)$.

(4) ROC curve

For a detection task, there will be two cases of false positives and true positive in the detection. The ROC curve is used to evaluate the detection performance. The ROC curve describes the proportion of false positives and true positive. You can use the ROC curve to find the best advantage. At this point, the false positive is the smallest, and the true positive is the largest, which is close to 100%.

10.5.6 *Outlook of speech recognition technology*

In view of the problems in the development of speech recognition technology, the following views are proposed on the development of speech recognition technology.

(1) Improve language models and core algorithms

The language model currently used is only a probability model, and no grammatical model based on linguistics has been used. To make computers understand human language, we must make progress on this point, which is a rather difficult task. In addition, with the continuous development of hardware resources, some core algorithms, such as feature extraction, search algorithms, or adaptive algorithms, will likely be further improved.

(2) Enhance the adaptive ability of speech recognition

Speech recognition technology must be further improved in terms of adaptation so that it is not affected by specific people, accents, or dialects. There are many types of users in the real world. In terms of sound characteristics, there are differences between male voices, female voices, and child voices. In addition, the pronunciation of many people is far from the standard pronunciation. This involves the accent or dialect. If speech recognition can automatically adapt to the voice characteristics of most people, this may be more important than improving the recognition rate by one or two percentage points.

(3) Breaking in robustness of speech recognition

Speech recognition technology needs to be able to eliminate out the effects of various environmental factors. At present, the biggest impact on speech recognition is environmental noise or noise. To achieve effective speech recognition on certain channels with extremely narrow bandwidths, as well as in underwater acoustic communications, underground communications, and strategic and confidential voice communications, it is necessary to deal with the special characteristics of sound signals. For further application of speech recognition technology, a major breakthrough must be made in the robustness of speech recognition.

(4) Realize multi-language hybrid recognition and infinite vocabulary recognition

Simply put, the acoustic models and speech models currently used are too limited, so that users can only use specific speech to recognize specific words. This is due to the limitations of the model on the one hand and the hardware resources on the other. With the advancement of both technologies, future speech and acoustic models may be able to incorporate multiple languages, so users do not have to switch back and forth between languages.

(5) Application of multilingual communication systems

If speech recognition technology has indeed made breakthroughs in the above-mentioned aspects, then the emergence of multilingual communication systems is a logical matter. This will be a perfect combination of speech recognition technology, machine translation technology, and speech synthesis technology. In the end, the multilingual free communication system will give us a new living space.

Bill Gates once said: "Voice technology will make computers drop the mouse and keyboard." Some scientists have also said, "The next generation of computer revolution is from graphical interface to voice user interface." This shows that the development of speech recognition technology has undoubtedly changed people's lives.

In recent years, with the rapid development of the Internet and the widespread application of smart mobile terminals such as mobile phones, a large number of text or speech corpora can be obtained from multiple channels, which has enriched the training of language models and acoustic models in speech recognition. Resources make it possible to build universal large-scale language models and acoustic models.

It can be predicted that the application of speech recognition systems will be more widespread in the next 5–10 years. A variety of speech recognition system products will appear on the market. People will also adjust the way they speak to a variety of recognition systems.

10.6 Case of Speech Recognition Based on Deep Learning: Deep Speech

In this section, we will use the *Deep Speech* system as an example to introduce the application of speech recognition in deep learning. A paper on Deep Speech was published by Andrew Ng's team of the Baidu AI Lab in 2014 [4]. The authors abandoned the traditional speech recognition model framework and turned to an end-to-end speech recognition model framework based on deep learning.

For end-to-end speech recognition, the input of the model is the speech features and the output is the recognized text. The entire model has only one deep neural network model, and the model loss uses CTC loss. The network structure of the acoustic model consists of five hidden layers. The first three layers are fully connected layers. The fourth layer is a bi-directional recurrent RNN layer. The fifth layer of the network is a non-RNN layer. It mainly uses the sum of the forward RNN and the reverse RNN in the fourth layer as the output of the hidden unit. Lastly, the sixth layer is the softmax layer, which predicts the probability of recognizing the speech of each period as each letter within each period.

Compared with traditional speech systems, the Deep Speech speech recognition system has a simple structure and better performance. You can model background noise, reverberation, or speaker changes directly without manually designing components, and you can directly learn the features that are robust to such effects. Based on this, Baidu has developed a new generation of Deep Speech speech recognition systems, Deep Speech 2 [2]. Currently, its recognition accuracy can reach 97%.

10.7 Summary

This chapter briefly introduces the most important application technology of artificial intelligence, namely intelligent perception, which includes pattern recognition, image analysis and understanding, and speech recognition. Two specific cases illustrate the application of deep learning in visual perception and speech perception.

This chapter is divided into seven subsections.

Section 10.1 introduces the definition of pattern recognition and the differences between pattern recognition and machine learning. There are two types of pattern recognition: statistical pattern recognition and syntactic pattern recognition.

Section 10.2 studies image engineering from image processing, image analysis, to image understanding. Image processing mainly refers to performing various processing procedures on the image to improve the visual effect. Image analysis is mainly to detect and measure the objects of interest in the image and obtain their information, so as to establish a description of the image. Image understanding is to further study the nature and meaning of the image.

Section 10.3 uses DenseCap, proposed by Fei-Fei Li's team at Stanford University, as an example to introduce how to apply deep learning to solve image understanding problems.

Section 10.4 discusses how speech recognition works and was developed.

Section 10.5 introduces the key technologies of speech recognition, including acoustic feature extraction, acoustic model, language model, search algorithms, and performance evaluation.

Section 10.6 explores the Deep Speech system, which is a classic example of end-to-end speech recognition systems realized by deep learning.

Due to space limitations, the range of topics covered in this chapter may not be comprehensive, but it can help readers gain a preliminary understanding of intelligent perception.

References

1. Abdel-Rahman, M., George, D., *et al.* (2009). Deep belief networks for phone recognition. NIPS Workshop on Deep Learning for Speech Recognition and Related Applications.
2. Amodei, D., Anubhai, R., *et al.* (2015). Deep speech 2: End-to-end speech recognition in English and Mandarin, ArXiv preprint, ArXiv:1512.02595v1.
3. Aloimonos, J., Weiss, I., *et al.* (1988). Active vision, *International Journal of Computer Vision*, 1(4): 333–356.
4. Awni, Hannun, Case, C., *et al.* (2014). Deep speech: Scaling up end-to-end speech recognition, ArXiv preprint, ArXiv:1412.5567v2.
5. Blei, D.M., Ng, A.Y., *et al.* (2003). Latent Dirichlet allocation, *Journal of Machine Learning Research*, 3: 993–1022.

6. Calumby, R.T., da Silva Torres, R., *et al.* (2014). Multimodal retrieval with relevance feedback based on genetic programming, *Multimedia Tools and Applications*, *69*(3): 991–1019.

7. Chen, Y. and Wang, J.Z. (2004). Image categorization by learning and reasoning with regions, *The Journal of Machine Learning Research*, *5*: 913–939.

8. Dong, Y. and Li, D. (2014). *Automatic Speech Recognition: A Deep Learning Approach*. Springer Publishing Company, Incorporated, ISBN 1447157788, 9781447157786.

9. Geoffrey, E., Hinton, Li, Deng, *et al.* (2012). Deep neural networks for acoustic modeling in speech recognition: The shared views of four research groups, *IEEE Signal Processing Magazine*, *29*(6): 82–97.

10. Gevers, T. and Smeulders, A.W.M. (1999). Content-based image retrieval by viewpoint-invariant color indexing, *Image and Vision Computing*, *17*(7): 475–488.

11. Graves, A., Santiago, F., *et al.* (2006). Connectionist temporal classification: Labelling unsegmented sequence data with recurrent neural networks. ICML 2006, pp. 369–376 (in USA).

12. Haralick, R., Shanmugam, K., *et al.* (1973). Textual features for image classification, *IEEE Transactions on Systems Man and Cybernetics*, SMC-*3*(6): 610–621.

13. Hartley, R. and Zisserman, A. (2003). *Multiple View Geometry in Computer Vision*. Cambridge University Press.

14. Hofmann, T. (1999). Probabilistic latent semantic analysis, *Proceedings of the Fifteenth Conference on Uncertainty in Artificial Intelligence*, Morgan Kaufmann Publishers Inc., pp. 289–296.

15. Huang, X. and Deng, L. (2010). An overview of modern speech recognition. In *Handbook of Natural Language Processing*, 2nd ed. London, UK: Chapman & Hall/CRC Press, pp. 339–366.

16. Johnson, J., Karpathy, A., *et al.* (2016). DenseCap: Fully convolutional localization networks for dense captioning. IEEE Conference on Computer Vision and Pattern Recognition.

17. Lafferty, J., McCallum, A., *et al.* (2001). Conditional random fields: Probabilistic models for segmenting and labeling sequence data, *Proceedings of the International Conference on Machine Learning*, pp. 282–289.

18. Lee, K.-F.. (1989). *Automatic Speech Recognition: The Development of the SPHINX System*. Springer US.

19. Li, Z.X., Shi, Z.P., *et al.* (2008). A survey of semantic mapping in image retrieval, *Journal of Computer-Aided Design & Computer Graphics*, *20*(8): 1085–1096.

20. Li, L.J. and Fei-Fei, L. (2010). OPTIMOL: automatic online picture collection via incremental model learning, *International Journal of Computer Vision*, *88*(2): 147–168.

21. Liu, Y., Liu, J., *et al.* (2013). Weakly-supervised dual clustering for image semantic segmentation, *Proceedings of the IEEE Conference on Computer Vision and Pattern Recognition (CVPR)*, 2075–2082.

22. Mark, G. and Woodland, P. (2006). Recent advances in large vocabulary continuous speech recognition: An HTK perspective. International Conference on Acoustics, Speech, and Signal Processing, ICASSP.
23. Marr, D. and Nishihara, H.K. (1978). Representation and recognition of the spatial organization of three-dimensional shapes, *Proceedings of the Royal Society of London B: Biological Sciences, 200*(1140): 269–294.
24. Marr, D. (1982). *Vision: A Computational Investigation into the Human Representation and Processing of Visual Information.* New York: W. H. Freeman and Company.
25. Roberts, L. (1963). *Machine Perception of Three-Dimensional Solids.* New York: Garland Publishing.
26. Russell, C., Kohli, P., *et al.* (2009). Associative hierarchical CRFs for object class image segmentation, *Proceedings of the IEEE International Conference on Computer Vision*, pp. 739–746.
27. Simon, H.A. (1983). Why should machines learn? In *Machine Learning I* (eds. R. S. Michalski, J. G. Carbonell & T. M.Mitchell), pp. 25-–37. Morgan Kaufmann, Los Altos, CA, USA.
28. Swain, M.J. and Ballard, D.H. (1991). Color indexing, *International Journal of Computer Vision, 7*(1):11–32.
29. Tamura, H., Mori, S., *et al.* (1978). Textural features corresponding to visual perception, *IEEE Transactions on Systems, Man and Cybernetics, 8*(6): 460–473.
30. Tan, K.L., Ooi, B.C., *et al.* (2000). Indexing shapes in image databases using the centroid-radii model, *Data and Knowledge Engineering, 32*(3): 271–289.
31. Wang, Y.Q. (1998). *Principles and Methods of Artificial Intelligence.* Xi'an: Xi'an Jiaotong University Press.
32. Wang, X.J., Zhang, L., *et al.* (2008). Annotating images by mining image search results, *IEEE Transactions on Pattern Analysis and Machine Intelligence, 30*(11):1919–1932.
33. Wang, Y., Sun, S., *et al.* (2015). A self-adaptive weighted affinity propagation clustering for key frames extraction on human action recognition, *Journal of Visual Communication and Image Representation, 33*: 193–202.
34. Zhang, S., Huang, J., *et al.* (2012). Automatic image annotation and retrieval using group sparsity, *IEEE Transactions on Systems Man & Cybernetics, Part B Cybernetics, A Publication of the IEEE Systems Man & Cybernetics Society, 42*(3): 838–849.
35. Zhang, S., Liu, C., *et al.* (2015). Feedforward sequential memory networks: A new structure to learn long-term dependency, arXiv:1512.08301v2.
36. Zhao, J. (2016). Research on Some Key Techniques of Image Semantic Understanding, PhD Thesis. Taiyuan: Taiyuan University of Technology.

Natural Language Understanding

11

Language is an important sign that humans are different from other animals. A natural language is a spoken (voice) and written (text) language of interpersonal communication that is different from a formal language or an artificial language (such as a logical language and a programming language). A natural language, as the most basic and direct tool for human expression and exchange of ideas, exists everywhere in human social activities. The baby's first cry is to express (announce) his/her advent to the world in words (voice).

This chapter will first discuss the concept of natural language processing (NLP), with a brief history of the development, research significance, and system composition and model; next, it will study the grammar analysis, semantic analysis, and context analysis of natural language one by one; then, it will explore important issues such as machine translation; finally, examples of natural language understanding system based on deep learning are given.

11.1 Overview of Natural Language Understanding

Ever since the first machine translation system was introduced in 1954, after more than half a century of hard work, computer scientists, linguists, and psychologists have achieved many important research results and more and more widely used applications in the study of restricted language understanding and domain-oriented language understanding. In particular, in the past two decades, we have achieved fruitful results and great progress. However, it is still a long way to go for making natural language understanding research finally achieve the goal of the machine truly understanding human language.

What is language and language understanding? How is natural language understanding related to human intelligence? How did natural language understanding research develop? How are computer systems that understand natural language composed and what are their models? These questions are of interest when studying natural language understanding.

11.1.1 *Language and language understanding*

Language is the natural medium for human communication. It includes spoken and written languages as well as body language (such as mute and semaphore). A more formal formulation is that language is a collection of representations, conventions, and rules used to convey information. Language consists of statements, each consisting of words; when constructing statements and languages, certain grammatical and semantic rules should be followed. Language consists of speech, vocabulary, and grammar. Speech and text are the two basic attributes that make up a language [10,43]. Without a variety of spoken and written languages, such as English, Chinese, French, and German, full and effective communication between humans is hard to imagine. Language evolves with the development of human society and humanity itself. Modern language allows anyone with normal language skills to exchange thoughts, feelings, and technology with others.

To perform a study of natural language understanding, we must first have a basic understanding of the composition of natural language [22,63,73,75].

Language is a vocabulary and grammatical system that combines sound and meaning, and is a material form that realizes thinking activities. Language is a symbolic system, but it is different from other symbol systems [11].

Language is based on words, and vocabulary is subject to grammar to form meaningful and understandable sentences. Sentences form sections and chapters in a certain form. Vocabulary can be divided into words and phrases. Phrases are a fixed combination of words, such as idioms in Chinese. Words are composed of morphemes. For example, in English, "teachers" is composed of two morphemes: "teaching" and "master". Also in English, "teacher" is also composed of two morphemes: "teach" and "-er". Morphemes are the smallest meaningful units that make up a word. The word "teaching" itself has the meaning of education and guidance, while the word "teacher" has the meaning of "human". Similarly, "-er" in English is also a suffix that means "person".

Grammar is the law of language organization. Grammatical rules restrict how morphemes constitute words and how words form phrases and sentences. Language is formed in this tightly constrained relationship [21, 39]. The rule that uses morphemes to form words is called the rules of word formation, such as teach + er → teacher. A word has different forms: singular, plural, negative, positive, and so on. This rule for constructing a word form is called a configuration method, such as teacher + s → teachers. Here "s" is just a morpheme with plural meaning after the original word, which does not become a new word, but a plural form of the same word. The structuring method and the word formation method are called lexical methods. Another aspect of the lexical method is the syntax. Syntax can be divided into two parts: the phrase construction method and the sentence construction method. The phrase construction method is a rule for collocation of words into phrases, such as red + pencil → red pencil. Here "red" is an adjective that modifies a pencil and combines it with the noun "pencil" to form a new noun. The rules for making sentences are the rules for making sentences with words or phrases. For example, "I am a student of the Department of Computer Science" is a sentence constructed in accordance with the rules of the English sentence. Figure 11.1 is a complete illustration of the above construction.

On the other hand, language is a combination of sound and meaning, and each word has its own form of speech. The pronunciation of a

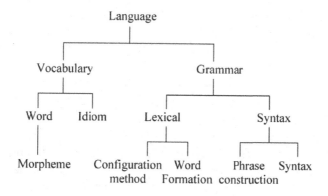

Figure 11.1   Composition of the language.

word is composed of one or more syllables, and syllables are composed of phonemes, and phonemes are divided into vowel phonemes and consonant phonemes. There are not many phonemes involved in a natural language, and a language usually has only a few dozen phonemes. The smallest unit of speech consisting of a pronunciation action is the phoneme.

Natural language understanding is an interdisciplinary subject that was developed by the development and integration of related disciplines such as linguistics, logic, physiology, psychology, computer science, and mathematics; it can study spoken or written language. A language exchange is a knowledge-based communication.

11.1.2 *Concept and definitions of natural language processing*

We use the written and spoken languages that humans have used for thousands of years, such as Chinese, English, French, and Spanish, which are called natural languages to distinguish them from artificial languages, such as the computer programming languages BASIC, C, LISP, PROLOG, Java, and Python. According to statistics, knowledge recorded in the form of linguistic characters in human history accounts for about 80% of the total knowledge. Language information processing technology has become an important sign of the level of modernization in a country.

Natural language processing, also known as computing linguistics, is a discipline that understands and produces human language content and is a subfield of computer science and machine learning. Natural language processing is a technique that uses computers to process and apply humans' verbal and written natural languages. It is a multidisciplinary and interdisciplinary subject involving linguistics, mathematics, computer science, cybernetics, etc. It is an important branch of the artificial intelligence discipline, and one of the early and active research fields of artificial intelligence.

Natural language processing includes two aspects: natural language understanding and natural language generation. Natural language understanding systems transform natural language into a form that is easier for computer programs to process and understand. The natural language generation system converts computer data related to natural language into natural language. Natural language understanding is also called computing linguistics. However, the research contents of natural language processing and natural language understanding are generally roughly equivalent. Natural language understanding and natural language processing are often intertwined. Natural language generation is often equivalent to machine translation, involving text translation and speech translation. Among them, synchronous speech translation is a dream that people have long pursued.

There is no uniform definition of natural language processing and natural language understanding in the world. Here are a few representative but different definitions.

Definition 11.1. Natural language processing (NLP) could be defined as the discipline that studies the linguistic aspects of human–human and human–machine communication, develops models of linguistic competence and performance, employs computational frameworks to implement processes incorporating such models, identifies methodologies for iterative refinement of such processes and models, and investigates techniques for evaluating the result systems [47].

Definition 11.2. Natural language processing is the use of computer tools to perform various types of processing of human-specific written and spoken forms of language [24].

Definition 11.3. Natural language processing is the use of computers to process and manipulate linguistic information such as sounds, shapes, meanings, etc., including the input, output, recognition, conversion, compression, storage, retrieval, analysis, understanding and generation of letters, words, phrases, sentences, and chapters. It is a marginal discipline formed on the basis of related disciplines such as linguistics, computer science, cybernetics, artificial intelligence, cognitive psychology, and mathematics [9].

In addition, there are more definitions of natural language processing and natural language understanding. Each definition should have merit due to differences in the focus or professional background.

11.1.3 *Research areas and significance of natural language processing*

(1) Research fields and directions of natural language understanding

Natural language processing has a very wide range of research fields and research directions. In the following, some research directions are given according to the different application fields.

(i) Optical character recognition (OCR):

Optical character recognition (text recognition) automatically recognizes printed or handwritten text by means of a computer system and converts them into electronic text that can be processed by a computer. For character recognition, image recognition of characters is mainly studied, but for high-performance character recognition systems, it is often necessary to study language understanding and technical problems at the same time [45, 50, 52].

(ii) Speech recognition:

Speech recognition, also known as Automatic Speech Recognition (ASR), aims to convert vocabulary content in human speech into a computer-readable written representation. The applications of speech recognition technology include voice dialing, voice navigation, indoor device control, voice document retrieval, simple dictation data entry, and others [56].

(iii) Machine translation:

Machine translation research uses computer programs to automatically translate words or speech from one natural language into another. In simple terms, machine translation is transforming a natural language word into another natural language word. We can use corpus technology to conduct more complex translations automatically [14, 16].

(iv) Automatic digest or automatic abstracting:

Automatic abstraction is the process of applying a computer to summarize a specified article, that is, automatically summarizing the main content and meaning of the original document, refining and forming an abstract or abbreviation. Commonly used automatic abstracts include mechanical abstracts. Based on the external features of the article, some of the original sentences that express the central meaning of the article are extracted and composed into a coherent abstract.

(v) Syntax parsing:

Syntax parsing is also known as parsing in natural language. It uses the syntax of natural language and other relevant knowledge to determine the functions that make up the components of the input sentence to establish a data structure and to acquire the meaning of the input sentence [22].

(vi) Text categorization/document classification:

Text classification is also called document classification. It is a process of automatically classifying texts by using a computer to automatically classify texts based on text content under a given classification system and classification standards, including two processes: learning and classification. The learning system learns a function (classifier) from the labeled data. The classification system uses the learned classifier to classify the newly given text.

(vii) Information retrieval:

Information retrieval is a query method or query process that uses a computer system to find relevant documents required by users from a large number of documents. In short, information retrieval is the science of searching for information, such as searching for metadata of documents, files, and description files in massive files or searching in databases [62].

(viii) Information extraction:

Information extraction mainly refers to the use of computers to automatically extract a specific type of information (such as events and facts) from a large number of structured or semi-structured texts, and to form structured data, and fill in the database for users to query the use of the process. Its broad goal is to allow the calculation of unstructured data.

(ix) Information filtering:

Information filtering refers to using the computer system for automatically identifying and filtering document information that meets certain conditions. It generally refers to the automatic identification and filtering of harmful information on the network, and is mainly used for information security and protection. That is to say, information filtering is the process of filtering or deleting certain sensitive information on the Internet according to certain specific requirements.

(x) Natural language generation:

Natural language generation refers to the process of transforming the internal representation of syntactic or semantic information into a symbol string composed of natural language symbols. A transformation technique from deep structure to surface structure is the inverse process of natural language understanding. From the results of the generation, there are forms such as statement generation, segment generation, and chapter generation. Among them, the generation of statements is more basic and important.

(xi) Speech synthesis:

Speech synthesis, also known as text-to-speech conversion, automatically converts written text into corresponding speech representations.

(xii) Question answering system:

The question answering system is using the computer system to understand the questions people ask, through automatic reasoning and other methods, then automatically find the answers from the relevant knowledge resources, and respond to the questions. Sometimes, the answering technology and speech technology, the multi-modal input/output technology, and the human–computer interaction technology combine to form a human–machine dialogue system.

In addition, there are more research directions of nature language processing, such as language teaching, parts-of-speech tagging, automatic proofreading, speaker recognition/identification/verification, etc. [66].

(2) The significance of natural language understanding research

As a high-level important direction of language information processing, natural language understanding has always been one of the core issues of the artificial intelligence community. Nowadays, natural language understanding is another important and dynamic application research field of artificial intelligence after expert systems and machine learning. If computers can truly understand natural language, the exchange of information between humans and computers can be carried out in the natural language that people are familiar with, which will have a major impact on human social progress, economic development, and improvement of people's lives, greatly facilitating human production activities and daily life, with incalculable social and economic value.

Significant advances in the study and application of natural language understanding will also cause a major breakthrough in artificial intelligence, and will make a special contribution to other areas of science and technology, promote the further development of other disciplines and departments, and have a profound impact on human beings' lives. After machine translation, information retrieval, text categorization, text comprehension, automatic summarization, automatic proofreading, automatic dictionary editing, and automatic text recognition all require that computers should have the capability to automatically analyze, understand, and generate natural language. In particular, with the rapid expansion of the Internet and the Internet of Things, the information resources on the Internet are accelerating growth. In the face of massive amounts of information, people eagerly hope that computers can have knowledge of natural language and can help people accurately obtain the online information they need.

Language is the carrier of thinking and the tool of interpersonal communication. The technical level of language information processing and the amount of information processed each year have become one of the important indicators for measuring the level of modernization in a country.

11.1.4 *Basic methods and advances in research on natural language understanding*

(1) Basic methods of natural language understanding research

There are two different types of research methods in natural language processing: rationalist and empiricist.

The main belief of rationalism is that a large part of human language knowledge is innate and genetically determined. Its representative is the American linguist N. Chomsky whose "Inner Language Function" theory holds that children learn so much complicated matter at such a small age despite receiving a very limited amount of information. This is hard to explain about language comprehension. Therefore, the rationalist approach attempts to circumvent these difficult problems by assuming that humans' language ability is an innate and inherent instinct.

Technically, rationalism advocates the establishment of a symbolic processing system by manually writing an initial language representation system generally represented by rules, constructing a corresponding reasoning program; then the system interprets the natural language as a symbolic structure according to rules and procedures. Thus, in the natural language processing system, the words of the input sentence are first parsed by the lexical analyzer according to the well-written lexical rules; then, according to the designed lexical rules, the lexical analyzer analyzes the grammatical structure of the input sentence; finally, the grammatical structure is mapped to semantic symbols expressed in logical formulas, semantic networks, intermediate languages, etc. according to the transformation rules.

The main theory of empiricism is the following: it is known that the human brain has some cognitive abilities, but the human brain does not have some specific treatment principles and treatment methods for specific language components at the beginning; however, the child's brain even at the beginning has treatment processing abilities such as association, pattern recognition, and induction that enable children to take full advantage of sensory input to master specific natural language structures.

Technically, empiricism advocates the establishment of specific mathematical models to learn complex and extensive linguistic structures, and then applies methods such as statistics, machine learning, and pattern recognition to train model parameters to expand the use of language. The empirical natural language processing method is based on statistical methods, and thus the empirical method is also called the statistical natural language processing method. Statistical natural language processing requires the collection of some text as the basis for building statistical models called corpus. A database of large quantities of corpus that has been screened, processed, and annotated is called a corpus base. Statistical processing methods are generally based on large-scale corpora, and are therefore also called corpus-based natural language processing methods.

(2) The history and development situation of natural language understanding

Research on natural language processing dates back to the 1920s. However, it is generally believed that research on natural language processing began with the study of machine translation systems. The emergence of electronic computers made natural language understanding and processing possible. Since the computer is capable of symbol processing, it is possible to apply a computer to process and understand language. With the development of computer technology and the overall technology of artificial intelligence, natural language understanding has made continuous progress.

The development process of natural language processing can be roughly divided into the following: the beginning period, the period of recovery development, and the period of prosperity and development represented by large-scale real text processing.

(i) Sprout period (from 1940s to mid-1960s):

During this period, the empirical approach to natural language processing was dominant. Machine translation is the earliest research field of natural language understanding. In the late 1940s, people tried to use computers to translate the fast growing scientific and technical materials. In 1949, the United States and the Soviet Union began a machine translation study of Russian–English and English–Russian scripts. Due to the limitations of theory and technology in the early research, the technical level of the developed machine translation system was low and could not meet the requirements of practical applications. In 1954, the University of Georgetown in the United States worked with IBM to translate Russian texts into English on the IBM 701 computer for the first machine translation experiment. It showed the feasibility of machine translation for the first time.

In 1956, N. Chomsky proposed the theory of formal language and transformational generative grammar, placing natural language and programming language on the same level, using unified mathematical methods to define and explain them. His transformational generative grammar TG has enabled linguistic research to enter the quantitative research phase and has also contributed to the development of programming languages. The grammatical system established by Chomsky is still the grammatical system that grammatical analysis must rely on in the study of natural language understanding.

Machine translation, as the core research field of natural language processing, experienced an uneven development path during this period. The rough design of the first generation machine translation system led to poor translation quality. As the research progressed, what people saw was not the success of machine translation, but some limitations that could not be overcome. In November 1966, the Language Automated Processing Advisory Committee of the American Academy of Sciences submitted a consultation report on machine translation to the National Foundation. The report came to a negative conclusion on machine translation.

For some time thereafter, the study of machine translation fell to a low point. During this period, researchers began to reflect on the reasons for the failure of machine translation, which also led to a deeper concern about the nature of natural language understanding.

(ii) Recovery development period (from late 1960s to 1980s).

During this period, research in the field of natural language processing was controlled by rationalist methods. People were more concerned with the science of thinking and simulated intelligent behavior by building many small systems. During this period, the theory of computational linguistics made great progress and matured. The development of the natural language understanding system in this period can be divided into two stages:

the stage of keyword matching technology in the 1960s and the stage of syntactic–semantic analysis technology in the 1970s.

In 1968, MIT successfully developed ELIZA, a Semantic Information Retrieval (SIR) system. It can remember the facts that users tell it in English, then it will interpret these facts, and answer users' questions. The ELIZA system can simulate a conversation between a psychologist (machine) and a patient (user).

During this period, many important theoretical research results were obtained, including constraint jurisdiction theory, extended transfer network, lexical functional grammar, functional unity grammar, generalized phrase structure grammar, and syntactic analysis algorithm. These results laid a good theoretical foundation for the automatic syntactic analysis of natural language. In terms of semantic analysis, lattice grammar, semantic network, preferred semantics and Montague grammar were proposed. Among them, Montague grammar put forward the idea of using mathematical logic to study the grammatical structure and semantic relationship of natural language, which opened up a new avenue for natural language processing research.

The great progress in the study of natural language comprehension in syntactic and semantic analysis is also reflected in the establishment of some influential natural language processing systems, which have made great progress in the depth and difficulty of language analysis. For example, the LUNAR human–machine interface designed by Woods allows conversation with the database in plain English to assist geologists in finding, comparing, and evaluating chemical analysis data for lunar specimens brought back by the Apollo 11 spacecraft. As another example, the SHRDLU language understanding dialogue system developed by Winogand is a limited human–machine dialogue system, which combines syntax, semantics, reasoning, context, and background knowledge into one, and successfully realizes man–machine dialogue, and is used to command the robot's building block classification and stacking test. The robotic system is capable of accepting human natural language instructions, stacking blocks, and answering or asking simple questions.

After entering the 1980s, research on the applications of natural language understanding was further developed, machine learning research was also very active, and many practical systems with high levels appeared. Among them, the famous ones are METAL and LOGOS in the United States, PIVOT and HICAT in Japan, ARIANE in France and SUSY in Germany. These systems are important achievements in the study of natural language understanding, indicating that natural language understanding has achieved great progress in theory and applications.

The research results obtained during this period laid a solid theoretical foundation not only for the further development of natural language understanding, but also for the development of human language competence and the promotion of related disciplines such as cognitive science, linguistics, psychology, and artificial intelligence that have important theoretical and practical significance.

(iii) Prosperous development period (from 1990s to the present):

Since the 1990s, natural language processing researchers have been increasingly examining practical and engineering solutions. The empirical methods have been re-recognized and rapidly developed, resulting in a number of commercial natural language human–machine interfaces. Machine translation systems have entered the international market, e.g., the English human–machine interface system Intellect produced by American Artificial Intelligence Company (AIC), the computer translation system SYSTRAN developed by the European Community in Georgetown University, USA, and the statistical machine translation model based on the noise channel model of IBM and its implementation translation system, etc.

The prominent mark of natural language processing research in this period is the use of corpus statistical methods for natural language processing, and this puts forward corpus linguistics that plays an important role. Because corpus linguistics acquires linguistic knowledge from large-scale real corpus, the understanding of natural language laws is more objective and accurate, and thus, more and more researchers are interested. With the rapid development and wide application of computer networks, the acquisition of corpus is more convenient, the corpus is larger, and the quality is higher, so the rise of corpus linguistics in turn promotes the rapid development of other related technologies of natural language processing. A series of natural language processing systems based on statistical models were developed. In the past decade, the statistical machine learning method based on large-scale corpus and its application in natural language processing has begun to receive much attention and research. The corpus-based machine translation method has been fully developed, and the rule-based machine translation system has also ended its single situation in the world. For example, a research team led by Leech of the United Kingdom designed the CLAWS system using a corpus LOB with a word-like tag.

In addition, the successful application of statistical methods, such as hidden Markov model in speech recognition has also played an important role in promoting the development of natural language processing.

Deep learning architectures and algorithms have gained increasing use in NLP research. In the past decade, neural networks have achieved excellent results on various NLPs based on dense vector representation. This trend is due to the successful application of embedded words and deep learning methods. Deep learning enables multi-level automatic learning. In contrast, traditional machine learning-based NLP systems rely heavily on hand-crafted functionality; this hand-crafted functionality is time consuming and often incomplete. Early analysis of a sentence by NLP research can take up to 7 minutes, and now natural language documents of millions of Web pages can be processed in less than a second. Many complex algorithms based on deep learning have been proposed to deal with difficult NLP problems, such as recurrent neural networks (RNNs), convolutional neural networks (CNNs), memory enhancement strategies, attention mechanisms, unsupervised models, reinforcement learning methods, deep generative language models, etc. Advances in deep learning research will lead to further substantial or even breakthrough progress in NLP.

Interestingly, while the various schools of artificial intelligence debated their different viewpoints, the two sides rational language and empiricism in the field of natural language processing in the late 1980s and early 1990s were also arguing. It was not until the last decade that people calmed down from the vague debate and began to realize that neither idealism nor empiricism could solve the complex problem of natural language processing alone. Only when the two are combined can a solution be found. Even the establishment of new integrated theoretical methods is the road to natural language processing research. The two methods have gone from antagonism to mutual integration and common development, bringing natural language processing research into an unprecedented period of prosperity.

The research on intelligent computers proposed and carried out since the 1980s also puts new demands on natural language understanding. In the past decade, research on multimedia computers has been proposed. New intelligent computers and multimedia computers require a more user-friendly interface to allow natural language, text, images, and sound signals to be directly input into the computer. Requiring computers to communicate with humans in natural language requires the computers to have natural language skills, especially oral comprehension and generative capabilities.

The study of oral comprehension promotes the practical use of the human–machine dialogue system. Natural language is the most direct way of expressing knowledge. Therefore, the study of natural language understanding also provides a new way for the knowledge acquisition of expert systems. In addition, research in natural language understanding has promoted the development of computer-aided language instruction (CALI) and computer language design (CLD). It can be seen that the study of natural language understanding in the 21st century will make new breakthroughs and become more widely used than ever before.

(3) The development trend of natural language understanding research

Based on the above discussion of the development of natural language, we summarize below some of the trends in international natural language processing research.

(i) The rationalist approach based on syntactic–semantic rules and the empiricism approach based on models and statistics "take turns", and the period in which each controls the situation of natural language processing research has ended. From antagonism to mutual integration and common development of the two methods, researchers have begun to join hands and complement each other. Researchers have begun to pay attention to both shallow and deep processing, pay equal attention to statistics and rules, form a hybrid system, and find solutions for integration. In order to establish a new integrated theoretical approach, natural language processing research has entered an unprecedented period of prosperity and development.

(ii) Corpus linguistics can acquire linguistic knowledge from large-scale real corpus, making the understanding of natural language laws more objective and accurate, and making the processing of large-scale real texts the main strategic goal of natural language processing. The rise of corpus linguistics has in turn promoted the rapid development of other related technologies in natural language processing, and a series of natural language processing systems based on statistical models have been developed.

(iii) Empiricism advocates the establishment of specific mathematical models to learn complex and extensive linguistic structures, and then applies statistical, machine learning, and pattern recognition methods to train model parameters to expand the scale of language use. It is based on statistical methods, so statistical mathematical methods are receiving increasing attention. In natural language processing, machine automatic learning methods are increasingly used, especially deep learning methods to acquire language knowledge and perform natural language processing.

(iv) The role of vocabulary is becoming more and more important in natural language processing, and there is a strong tendency of "lexicalism". After the corpus, the construction of the vocabulary knowledge base has become a new research issue of general concern.

(v) Create a spoken dialogue system and a voice conversion engine. Early text-based conversations have now expanded to include voice conversations in mobile devices for information access and task-based applications.

(vi) Mining social media to provide information about health or finance, and to identify people's emotions and provide emotional products and services.

Speech processing has made breakthrough progress and is widely used in all walks of life to promote industrial development and benefit hundreds of millions of people.

11.1.5 *Levels of the natural language understanding process*

Although a language is expressed as a series of text symbols or a stream of sounds, the internal structure is actually a hierarchical structure. This level can be clearly seen from the composition of language. A sentence expressed as words is composed of **morphemes → words or word form → phrases or sentences**, while sentences expressed as sounds are composed of **phonemes → syllables → phonetic words → phonetic sentences**, and each level is grammatically constrained by the rules. Therefore, the process of language analysis and understanding should also be a hierarchical process. Many modern linguists divide this process into five levels: speech analysis, lexical analysis, syntactic analysis, semantic analysis, and pragmatic analysis. Although these levels are not completely isolated, this hierarchical division does help to better embody the composition of the language itself.

(1) Speech analysis

In a voice language, the smallest independent sound unit is a phoneme, and a phoneme is a sound or a group of sounds that distinguishes it from other phonemes. For example, pin and bin have two different phonemes, /p/ and /b/, respectively, but the phonemes /p/ in pin, spin, and tip are the same phoneme, which corresponds to a set of slightly different tones. Speech analysis is based on the phoneme rules, which distinguishes individual phonemes from the voice stream, and then finds a syllable and its corresponding morpheme or word according to the phoneme morphological rule [7, 74].

(2) Lexical analysis

The main purpose of lexical analysis is to find out the morphemes of words and obtain linguistic information. For example, the word unchangeable is composed of un-change-able. In such languages as English, it is easy to find each word in a sentence because words are separated by spaces. But finding each morpheme is much more complicated for words such as importable, which can be im-port-able or import-able. This is because im, port and import are all morphemes. In contrast, finding a morpheme in Chinese is an easy task because each word in Chinese is a morpheme; but it is far from easy to separate the words [40].

(3) Syntactic analysis

Syntactic analysis is the analysis of the structure of sentences and phrases. In the study of automatic language processing, the study of syntactic analysis is the most concentrated, which is inseparable from the contribution of Chomsky. There are many methods for automatic parsing, such as phrase structure grammar, lattice grammar, extended transfer network, functional grammar, and so on. The largest unit of syntactic analysis is a sentence. The purpose of the analysis is to find out the relationship between words, phrases, etc. and their respective roles in the sentence, and to express them in a hierarchical structure. This hierarchical structure can reflect the affiliation, direct component relationships, or grammatical functional relationships.

(4) Semantic analysis

For the real words in a language, each word is used to refer to things and to express concepts. A sentence is composed of words. The meaning of a sentence is directly related to the meaning of the words it contains, but it is not simply the sum of the meaning of the words. The words of "I beat him" and "He beat me" are exactly the same, but the meanings of the expressions are completely opposite. Therefore, the structural meaning of a sentence should also be considered. For the English phrase "a red table", its structural meaning is that the adjective that modifies the noun is before the noun, but in French it is different; in "one table rouge", the adjective is placed after the modified noun. Semantic analysis is to find out the true meaning or concept expressed by language by analyzing the meaning of the word, the meaning of the structure and the meaning of its combination. In the automatic understanding of language, semantics as well as context and semantics have become important research objects [35, 41, 68].

(5) Pragmatic analysis

Pragmatics, also known as linguistic pragmatism, is a branch of semiotics and a theory for studying the relationship between linguistic symbols and users. Specifically, pragmatics studies the influence of the external environment on language users, the environmental knowledge of the language, and the relationship between language and language users in a given locale. The natural language processing system that focuses on pragmatic information focuses more on the speaker/observer model setting than on the structural information embedded in a given discourse. Some linguistic environment computing models have been proposed to describe the speakers and their communication purposes, the listeners and how they reorganize the speaker information. The difficulty in constructing these models is finding how to combine all aspects of natural language processing and various uncertain physiological, psychological, social, cultural (such as language skills, emotional behavior, community or linguistic areas, educational background) and other factors into a complete model.

11.2 Lexical Analysis

Lexical analysis is part of the compiler that constructs and analyzes words in the source program, such as constants, identifiers, operators, and reserved words, and transforms the words in the source program into internal representations, and then the internal representation is passed to the rest of the compiler. Lexical analysis is the basis for understanding words. Its main purpose is to segment words from sentences, find out each morpheme of words, obtain linguistic information of words, and determine the meaning of words. For example, misunderstanding is composed of mis-understanding, and its meaning consists of these three parts. Different languages have different requirements for lexical analysis. For example, there is a big gap between English and Chinese. Every word in Chinese is a factor morpheme, so it is quite easy to find out each morpheme, but it is very difficult to separate the words.

Words in English and other languages are naturally separated by spaces, and it is easy to distinguish a word, which is convenient for finding each word of the sentence. However, English words have changes in parts of speech, number, tense, derivation, and deformation. Therefore, it is much more complicated to find out each morpheme, and it is necessary to analyze the suffix or the prefix. For example, uncomfortable can be un-comfort-able or uncomfort-able, because un, comfort, and able are all morphemes.

In general, lexical analysis can obtain a lot of useful linguistic information from morphemes. As mentioned earlier, the morpheme "s" that constitutes the ending of a word in English usually means a plural noun, or a third person singular verb, while "ly" is a suffix of an adverb, and "ed" is a past or past participle of a verb. This information is very useful for syntactic analysis. In addition, a word can have many derivatives and variants, e.g., program, which can be changed to programs, programmed, programmer, programming, and programmable. If you put these words into the dictionary, it will become very large, but these have only one root. Electronic dictionaries in natural language understanding systems generally only place roots to support morpheme analysis, which greatly reduces the size of electronic dictionaries.

An algorithm for English lexical analysis is given below:

repeat

    look for study in dictionary

    if not found

    then modify the study

until study is found or no further modification is possible

It can analyze English words that change according to English grammar rules, where "study" is a variable and the initial value is the current word.

For example, for words "matches" and "studies", you can do the following analysis:

matches for studies cannot be found in dictionary

match studie modification 1: remove "-s"

    match studi modification 2: rem ove "-e"

   study modification 3: turn i into y

In this way, you can find the match "studi" after modification 2, and you can find the match "study" after modification 3.

The word meaning judgment is a difficult point in English lexical analysis. Words often have multiple explanations, and it is often impossible to judge using a dictionary. To judge the meaning of the word it can only be analyzed using other related words and phrases in the sentence. For example, there are three explanations for the word "diamond": diamonds, baseball fields, and diamond. Please consider the sentence below:

John saw Steve's diamond shimmering from across the room.

Here, it can be seen that the word "diamond" must be a diamond, because only a diamond can shine, and diamonds and baseball fields will not shine.

11.3   Syntactic Analysis

The previous two sections described the various levels of the linguistic analysis process and lexical analysis. In the beginning of this section, we will discuss issues such as syntactic analysis, semantic analysis, and pragmatic analysis.

Syntactic analysis has two main functions: (1) analyzing the structure of a sentence or phrase, determining the words that make up a sentence, the relationship between the phrases, and their respective roles in the sentence, and expressing these relationships as a hierarchy. (2) Standardize the syntactic structure. In the process of analyzing sentences, the derivation process of analyzing the relationship between the components of the sentence is expressed in a tree graph, so that the graph becomes a parse tree. Syntactic analysis is performed by a specially designed parser whose analysis process is the process of constructing a syntactic tree, transforming each input legal statement into a parse tree.

As described in Section 11.1.4, the analysis of natural language processing is divided into a rule-based approach (rationalist) and a statistical-based approach (empiricist). The various methods based on rules are described below.

11.3.1   *Phrase structure grammar*

In the rule-based approach, phrase structure grammar and Chomsky grammar are two powerful formal tools for describing natural languages and programming languages, which can formally describe and analyze the analyzed sentences.

Definition 11.4. A phrase structure syntax G consists of four parts, T, N, P, and S:

T is the set of terminators, and the terminator is the word (or symbol) of the language being defined.

N is a set of nonterminal symbols that cannot be used in the resulting sentence and are specifically used to describe the grammar. Obviously, T and N do not intersect, and both of them together form the symbol set V, so there are

$$V = T \cup N, T \cap N = \emptyset$$

P is a production rule set with a form of $a \to b$, where $a \in V^+$, $b \in V^*$, $a \neq b$. V^* denotes a set of all symbol strings composed of symbols in V, and V^+ denotes a set of other symbol strings other than the empty string (empty set) $\emptyset$ in V^*.

S is the start character and is a member of the set N.

The phrase structure grammar G can be described as the following quad form:

$$G = (T, N, S, P)$$

As long as these four parts are given, a specific formal language can be defined.

The basic operation of phrase structure syntax is to rewrite one symbol string into another. If $P: a \to b$ is a production rule, then a symbol string containing the subsymbol string a can be overwritten by b, and the process is denoted as "$\Rightarrow$". If $u, v \in V^*$, and $uav \Rightarrow ubv$, then uav directly generates ubv, or ubv is derived directly from uav. If the production rules are used in a different order, then many different symbol strings can be generated from the same symbol. The language $L(G)$ defined by a phrase structure grammar is a set of symbol strings W derived from the start character S. That is, for a symbol string to belong to $L(G)$ it must meet the following two conditions:

(1) The symbol string contains only the terminator T.
(2) The symbol string can be derived from the start character S according to the syntax G.

As can be seen from the above definition, a language defined by phrase structure grammar is composed of a series of production rules. A simple phrase structure syntax is given below.

Example 11.1. $G = (T, N, S, P)$
    $T = \{\text{the, man, killed, a, deer, likes}\}$
    $N = \{S, NP, VP, N, ART, V, Prep, PP\}$
    $S = S$
    P: (1) S → NP + VP
        (2) NP → N
        (3) NP → ART + N
        (4) VP → V
        (5) VP → V + NP
        (6) ART → the | a
        (7) N → man | deer
        (8) V → killed | likes

11.3.2 *Chomsky's formal grammar*

Chomsky took the idea of Shannon's finite state Markov process, used finite automata as a tool to describe the grammar of the language, and defined the finite state language as a language with finite state grammar, and established a finite state model of language in 1956. He used the axiomatic method in mathematics to study natural language. Algebra and set theory are used to define formal language as a sequence of symbols. According to the rule set used in formal grammar, four types of grammar are defined: (1) unconstrained phrase structure grammar, also known as type 0 grammar; (2) context-dependent grammar, also known as type 1 grammar; (3) context-free grammar, also known as type 2 grammar; (4) regular grammar, i.e., finite state grammar, also known as type 3 grammar.

The higher the model, the more constraints it has, the weaker the generation ability, the smaller the language set that can be generated, and the weaker the description ability.

(1) Unconstrained phrase structure grammar

Unconstrained phrase structure grammar is one of the most powerful forms of grammar in Chomsky's formal grammar. It does not impose more restrictions on the two sides of the production rule of the phrase structure grammar. It only requires that x contains at least one non-terminal character, i.e.,

$$x \rightarrow y(x \in V^+, y \in V^*)$$

The type 0 grammar is a non-recursive grammar; that is, it is impossible to determine whether the string is a sentence in a language defined by the grammar after reading a symbol string. Therefore, type 0 syntax is rarely used for natural language processing.

(2) Context-related grammar

Context-related grammar is a phrase structure grammar that satisfies the following constraints:

$$x \rightarrow y$$

is a production rule, the length of y (i.e., the number of symbols in the symbol string) is always greater than or equal to the length of x, and x, $y \in V^*$. For example,

$$AB \rightarrow CDE$$

is a valid production rule in the context of the grammar, but not

$$ABC \rightarrow DE$$

This constraint ensures that context-related grammar is recursive; that is, if you write a program, you can finally determine whether a string is a sentence in a language defined by this grammar after reading a symbol.

Natural language is a context-dependent language, and context-dependent languages need to be described by a type 1 grammar. Grammar rules allow it to have multiple symbols on the left (including at least one non-terminal) to indicate context correlation; that is, when replacing a non-terminal, you need to consider the context in which the symbol is located. However, the number of right symbols of the rule is required to be no less than that of the left to ensure the recursion of the language. Consider the following production:

$aAb \rightarrow ayb$ ($A \in N, y \neq \emptyset$, a and b cannot be $\emptyset$ at the same time)

When using replacement A, it can only be done when the contexts are a and b.

However, in practice, since the syntactic analysis of context-free languages is far more effective than that of context-dependent languages, it is hoped that the automatic understanding of natural languages can be realized on the basis of enhancing the syntactic analysis of context-free languages. The extended transfer network that will be introduced later is based on a natural language syntax analysis technique realized by this kind of thinking.

(3) Context-free grammar

Each rule of context-free grammar takes the following form:

$$A \rightarrow x$$

In this formula, $A \in N$, $x \in V^+$; that is, the left side of each production rule must be an alone non-terminal character. In this system, rules are applied without relying on the context in which symbol A is located, and are therefore referred to as context-free grammars.

(4) Regular grammar

Regular syntax can only generate very simple sentences. It has two forms: left linear syntax and right linear syntax. In a left linear grammar, all rules must take the form

$$A \rightarrow Bt \quad \text{or} \quad A \rightarrow t$$

Among them, A, $B \in N$, $t \in T$; that is, A and B are alone non-terminal characters, and t is a separate terminator. In a right linear grammar, all rules must be written as follows:

$$A \rightarrow tB \quad \text{or} \quad A \rightarrow t$$

11.3.3 *Transition network*

Syntactic analysis can be performed using the transition network (TN). The transfer network is used to represent grammar in automata theory. The TN in syntactic analysis consists of nodes and arcs, with nodes representing states, and arcs corresponding to symbols, and they transition from one given state to another state through the symbol. The corresponding TN is shown in Figure 11.2. In the figure, q_0, q_1,..., q_T are states, q_0 is the initial state, and q_T is the final state. The conditions of the state transition and the direction of the transition are given on the arc. This network can be used to analyze sentences as well as to generate sentences.

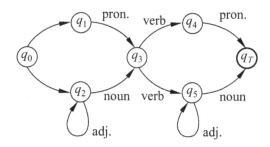

Figure 11.2 The transfer network (TN).

Table 11.1 Sentence recognition process.

Word	Current state	Arc	New state
The	A	a $\xrightarrow{\text{det}}$ b	b
Little	B	b $\xrightarrow{\text{adj.}}$ b	b
orange	B	b $\xrightarrow{\text{adj.}}$ b	b
Ducks	B	b $\xrightarrow{\text{noun}}$ c	c
Swallow	C	c $\xrightarrow{\text{verb}}$ e	e
Flies	E	e $\xrightarrow{\text{noun}}$ f	f (recognition)

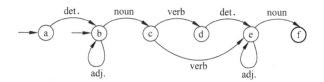

Figure 11.3 Example of a transition network.

For example, the process of identifying the sentence "The little orange ducks swallow flies" using TN is shown in Table 11.1 (the lexical analysis is omitted here, and the network is shown in Figure 11.3).

The recognition process reached the f state (final state), so the sentence was successfully recognized. The results of the analysis are shown in Figure 11.4. As can be seen from the above process, this sentence can also take other arcs in the network, such as the word ducks can also

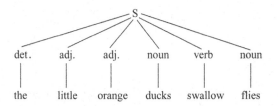

Figure 11.4   TN analysis tree.

go through arc c $\xrightarrow{\text{verb}}$ d ($c \rightarrow d$), but the next swallow cannot find a suitable arc. At this point corresponding to this path, the sentence is rejected.

It can be seen that in the process of network identification, various possible paths should be found, so the algorithm should adopt either a parallel or backtracking mechanism.

(1) Parallel algorithm: The key idea is to select all arcs that can reach the next state in any state and perform experiment at the same time.
(2) Backtracking algorithm is to select one of the arcs that can pass, and keep other possibilities of paths, so that you can choose to return if necessary. This approach requires a stack structure.

11.3.4 *Lexical functional grammar*

The lexical function grammar (LFG) was proposed by Kaplan and Bresnan in 1982. It is a functional grammar that emphasizes the role of vocabulary. LFG uses a structure to express the order of features, functions, vocabulary, and composition. Both the ATN syntax and the conversion syntax are directional. The conditions and operations of the ATN syntax require that the use of the syntax be directional because the registers are only accessible after they have been set. An important part of LFG work is to eliminate this ordering restriction through a multi-layered description that is not contradictory.

LFG description of sentences is divided into two parts: constituent structure (C-structure) and functional structure (F-structure). C-structure is the result of surface analysis generated by context-free grammar. On this basis, a series of algebraic transformations are used to generate the F-structure. The LFG uses two rules: context-free grammar rules that add subscripts and lexical rules. Table 11.2 shows the rules and terms of some lexical functional grammars, where ↑ denotes the direct component of the previous level of the current component, such as ↑ in the rule NP is S, ↑ in the

Table 11.2   LFG syntax and dictionary.

Grammar rules:

S → NPVP

(↑ Subject) =↓ ↑=↓

NP → Determiner Noun

VP → Verb NP NP

↑=↓ (↑ Object) =↓ (↑ Object − 2) =↓

Lexical entries:

A Determiner   (↑ Definiteness) = Indefinite

(↑ Number) = Singular

baby Noun   (↑ Number) = Singular

(↑ Predicate) = 'Baby'

girl Noun   (↑ Number) = Singular

(↑ Predicate) = 'Girl'

handed Verb   (↑ Tense) = Past

(↑ Predicate) = Hand < (↑ Subject), (↑ Object),

(↑ Object □ 2) >

the Determiner (↑ Definiteness) = Definite

toys Noun   (↑ Number) = Plural

(↑ Predicate) = 'Toy'

VP is also S; ↓ represents the current component. Therefore, (↑ Subject) =↓ means that the subject of S is the current NP. The expression "<>" is the syntax pattern, 'Hand = <(↑ Subject), (↑ Object), (↑ Object − 2) >, which means that the predicate verb "hand" has a subject, a direct object, and an indirect object.

The process of analyzing sentences by using the LFG syntax is as follows:

(1) Obtaining a C-structure using context-free grammar analysis, regardless of the subscript in the grammar; the C-structure is a direct component tree;

(2) Defining each non-leaf node as a variable, and establishing a functional description (a set of equations) according to the subscripts in the lexical rules and grammar rules;
(3) The algebraic transformation is performed on the opposite equation, and each variable is obtained to get a functional structure F-structure.

If the above process can get more than one set of solutions, then the sentence is identifiable and more than one analysis result is obtained. Analysis of multiple solutions indicates that there is ambiguity in the original sentence, and no solution indicates that it cannot be identified.

LFG can also be used for sentence generation. The difference between analysis and generation is only in the first step. The analysis is from sentence to C-structure, while the generation is directly generated C-structure and sentences by context-free grammar. Similarly, if there is more than one solution, the sentence is correct.

11.4 Semantic Analysis

Establishing a syntactic structure is only one step in the language understanding model, and further requires semantic analysis to obtain the meaning expressed by the language. The first step is to determine the meaning of each word in the sentence, which involves considering ambiguity in the meaning of the word and the structure of the sentence; for example, the English word "go" can have more than 50 meanings. Even if a word has a lot of meanings, in a certain context, in a phrase, its meaning is usually unique. This is due to the constraints. This kind of constraint relationship can be used to obtain the meaning of words and sentences through semantic analysis. The second step is more complicated: to determine the semantics based on existing background knowledge, further reasoning is required to get the correct results. If it is known that "Manager Zhang drove to the store", then to answer the question "Is Manager Zhang sitting in the car?" you must first derive the words "driving" and "sitting in the car" from the meaning of "driving the car". The relationship between concepts is the only way to answer this question correctly.

Semantic analysis generally uses two methods: semantic network representation and logical representation. In Sections 2.4 and 2.7, we introduced semantic network representations and predicate logic representations, and discussed the semantics of predicate logic and the semantics of semantic networks. You can return to review these sections before you read this section. As an example, the following paragraph first introduces the semantic logic analysis method, and then introduces semantic and grid grammars.

(1) Semantic logic analysis

A logical form expression is a framework structure that expresses a specific form of case and a series of additional facts, such as "Jack kissed Jill", which can be expressed in the following logical form:

(PAST S1 KISS – ACTION [AGENT (NAME j1

PERSON "Jack")][THEME ENAME (NAME j2 PERSON "Jill")])

It expresses a past case S1. PAST is an operator that indicates that the type of structure is in the past, S1 is the name of the case, KISS-ACTION is the form of the case, and AGENT and THEME are descriptions of the object, with the agent and the theme.

The logical structure of the corresponding syntactic structure can be different, but the meaning of the expression should be constant. In "The arrival of George at the station" and "George arrived at the station", syntactically one is a noun phrase, and the other is a sentence, but their logical form is the same.

(DEF/SING a1 ARRIVE – EVENT (AGENT a1

(NAME g1 PERSON "George")) (TO – LOC a1(DEF S4 STATION)))

(PAST a2 ARRIVE – EVENT [AGENT a1(NAME g1 PERSON "George")]

[TO – LOC a1 (NAME S4 STATION)])

Based on the definition of syntactic structure and logical form, semantic parsing rules can be applied, so that the final logical form can effectively constrain ambiguity. The parsing rule is also a mapping transformation of a pattern.

(S SUBJ + animate

MAIN – V + action – verb)

This pattern can match any sentence that has an action and a living subject. The form of the mapping rule is the following:

(S SUBJ + animate MAIN – V + action – verb)

(?* T(MAIN – V)) [AGENT V (SUBJ)]

where? indicates that there is no temporal information about the event, and * represents a new instance. If there is a syntactic structure:

(S MAIN – V ran

SUBJ (NP TDE the HEAD man)

TENSE past)

Use the above mapping (assuming that the NP mapping is done with other rules):

(? r1 RUN1 [AGENT (DEF/SING m1 MAN)])

Temporal information can use another mapping rule:

(S TENSE past) (PAST??)

Combine the above mappings to finally get a logical form representation:

(PAST r1 RUN1 [AGENT(DEF/SING m1 MAN)])

This is just a simple example. In the application of rules, there are still many analytical strategies.

(2) Semantic analysis grammar

A variety of semantic analysis grammars have been developed, such as semantic grammar and grid grammar. Semantic grammar is a grammar rule set that combines grammar knowledge and semantic knowledge and defines it in a unified way. It is context-free and morphologically the same grammar as natural language grammar. It uses symbols that represent semantic types, rather than NP, VP, PP, etc., which represent non-terminators of syntactic components, thus defining grammar rules that contain semantic information. Semantic grammar can exclude meaningless sentences, has higher efficiency, and can skip syntax problems that have no effect on semantics. The disadvantage is that a large number of grammar rules are required for its application and therefore it can only apply to areas that are severely restricted.

The grid grammar method allows the analytic results to be constructed around the verb. Although its grammar rules only describe the syntax, the structure produced by the analysis results in a semantic relationship rather than a strict syntactic relationship. In this representation, the noun phrase and the prepositional phrase contained in a statement are represented by their relationship with the verb in the sentence, which is called a grid/lattice, and the representation structure is called a grid grammar. The lattice in the traditional grammar only indicates the function of a word or phrase in the sentence, such as the main character, the object, and so on, and only reflects the change rule of the ending, and thus is called the surface lattice. In the lattice grammar method, the lattice represents the semantic relationship, which reflects the thoughts and concepts contained in the sentence, and is therefore called the deep lattice. Compared with the phrase structure grammar, the lattice grammar method has a better description of the deep semantics of the sentence; no matter how the form of the sentence changes, such as the statement becomes a question, the affirmative sentence becomes a negative sentence, and the active voice becomes a passive voice. The semantic relationship between the underlying layer and the lattice relationship represented by each noun will not change accordingly. The combination of lattice grammar and type hierarchy can explain ANT semantically.

11.5 Automatic Understanding of Sentences

Sentences are generally divided into simple sentences and compound sentences. The understanding of simple sentences is easier than compound sentences, and it is the basis for understanding compound sentences. Therefore, we first discuss the understanding of simple sentences and then discuss the understanding of compound sentences.

11.5.1 *Understanding of simple sentences*

Since a simple sentence can exist independently, in order to understand a simple sentence, i.e., to establish an in-machine expression corresponding to the simple sentence, the following two aspects are required:

(1) Understand each word in the statement.
(2) Based on these words, form a structure that can express the meaning of the whole sentence.

The first job seems to be easy; it seems that just looking up the dictionary can solve it. In fact, because many words in English have more than one meaning, the exact meaning of a word in a sentence cannot always be determined using the word itself. It can only be determined through grammatical analysis and contextual relations. For example, the word diamond has three meanings: "diamond", "baseball field", and "diamond". In the following sentence:

I'll meet you at the diamond.

In the middle, since "at" requires a time or place noun as its object, it is obvious that "diamond" here has the meaning of "baseball field" and cannot have other meanings.

The second item is also a relatively difficult job. Because you want to unite words to form a structure that represents the meaning of a sentence, you need to rely on a variety of sources of information, including knowledge of the language used, knowledge of the domain in which the statement relates, and knowledge about the idioms that the language user should follow.

(1) Keyword matching method

The simplest method of natural language understanding, perhaps a keyword matching method, is effective in some specific situations. The method is simply summarized as follows: two types of samples, matching and action are specified in the program. Then create a mapping from matching samples to action samples. When the input statement matches the matching sample, the action specified by the corresponding sample is executed, so that it seems that the machine actually realizes the purpose of understanding the user's question.

This method of keyword matching is particularly effective as a natural language interface in a similar database consulting system, although it does not have any sense of understanding.

(2) Syntactic analysis tree

Although the keyword matching method is simple, it ignores a lot of information in the statement. To ensure that the details of the meaning of the statement are not ignored, the details of the structure of the statement must be determined. This means to perform grammar analysis. To do this, you must first give a grammar that describes the structure of the symbol string in that particular language in order to produce a structure called a grammar parse tree for each statement that conforms to the grammar rules.

A simple grammar for the English subset is given below:

S → NP VP

NP → the NP1

NP → NP1

ADJS → ∈ |ADJ ADJS

VP → V

VP → V NP

N → Joe|boy|ball

ADJ → little|dig

V → hit|ran

Among them, uppercase is a non-terminal character, while lowercase is a terminal character, and ∈ represents an empty string.

Figure 11.5 is a grammar parse tree constructed using the grammar to syntactically analyze the statement "Joe hit the ball".

Using the given grammar to analyze the input statement in order to find a grammar analysis tree can be seen as a search process. To implement this process, you can use a top-down approach, which is somewhat similar to forward reasoning. It starts with the start character and then applies the rules in P to generate the branches of the tree layer by layer until a complete sentence structure is generated. If the structure matches the input statement, it ends successfully; otherwise, it restarts from the top level and generates other sentence structures until the end. You can also use a bottom-up approach, which is somewhat similar to reverse reasoning. It is based on the words of the input statement; first look for rules from P, try to merge the words into larger structural components, such as phrases or sub-category sentences, etc., then further combine these components, and generate a grammar parse tree in reverse until the root node of the tree is the start character.

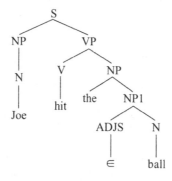

Figure 11.5 Example grammar parse tree.

(3) Semantic analysis

Just analyzing a sentence grammar structure based on the parts of speech information cannot guarantee its correctness. This is because the grammatical structure of some sentences needs to be determined by means of word meaning information; that is, semantic analysis is required. We have discussed semantic analysis in Section 11.4.

An easy way to perform semantic analysis is to use semantic grammar. The so-called semantic grammar is based on the traditional phrase structure grammar, and the concept of grammatical categories such as N (noun) and V (verb) is replaced by the special category of the field in question.

11.5.2 *Understanding of complex sentences*

As described above, the understanding of a simple sentence does not involve the relationship between sentences. Its understanding process is to first assign a word to a meaning, and then assign a structure to the entire statement. The understanding of a set of sentences, whether it is an article selection or a conversation excerpt, requires the discovery of the interrelationship between sentences. In a particular article, the discovery of these relationships plays a very important role in understanding.

This relationship includes the following: the same thing, part of the things, things related to action, part of the action, causal relationship, and planning order.

To understand these complex relationships, you must have a wide range of knowledge, i.e., rely on a large knowledge base, and the organization of the knowledge base plays an important role in understanding these relationships correctly.

If the knowledge base has a large capacity, then one thing is more important, namely, how to focus the problem on the relevant part of the knowledge base. Some of the knowledge representation methods introduced in Chapter 2, such as semantic networks and knowledge graph, will help in doing this.

For example, let's take a look at the following article fragment:

"Then, the pump is fixed to the workbench. The bolts are placed in small plastic bags".

The bolts in the second sentence should be understood as the bolts used to fix the pump. Therefore, if the bolts to be used are placed in "focus" when understanding the whole sentence, the understanding of the whole

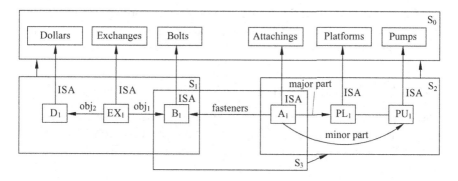

Figure 11.6 Example of a partitioned semantic network.

sentence is not a problem. To do this, we need to express knowledge about "fixed" so that it can be easily extracted when it comes to "fixed".

Figure 11.6 shows a partitioned semantic network associated with a fixed pump with four partitions: the S_0 partition contains some general concepts such as dollars, exchanges, and bolts; the S_1 partition contains special entities associated with the purchase of bolts; the S_2 partition that contains the water pump is fixed on the workbench as a special entity for this operation; the S_3 partition contains special entities related to the same fixed operation. Using the partitioned semantic network and using the association of its partitions at certain levels can better deal with the problem of centralized focus. When a partition is in focus, the elements in a high-level partition become observable. For the above example, when the second sentence is understood, because it is about the event of "fixing the pump on the workbench", the example focus of the Figure 11.6 partition semantic network is in the S_2 partition. Since the level of the S_0 partition is higher than that of the S_2 partition, the S_0 partition is observable. When understanding the second sentence, it is obvious that the "bolt" cannot match any element of the S_2 partition, so the focus area is changed from S_2 to the lower level S_3 partition. Since the "bolt" matches B_1, the result of the matching means that the "bolt" in the second sentence must be the bolt used for fixing in the first sentence, so that the two sentences before and after become a coherent piece of the article.

When the input article segment describes the plot of the behavior of the person or thing, the target structure can be used to help understand.

For such a plot, figuring out the character's goals and how to achieve them is the focus of understanding. For ease of understanding, for the various goals that often arise, you can write the appropriate plans and call them whenever you need them, so that when some information in the story is omitted, you can also derive them from these plans.

11.6 Corpus Linguistics

The corpus is a database for storing linguistic materials, and corpus linguistics is a discipline based on corpus for linguistic research. The basis of corpus linguistics research is a large-scale real corpus [38, 39].

(1) The development, definition, and research content of corpus linguistics

As a branch of natural language processing, the corpus based on statistical methods mainly involves the collection, storage, retrieval, statistics, parts of speech and lexical tagging, syntactic and semantic analysis of machine-readable natural language texts, and applications of corpus in the fields of language quantitative analysis, dictionary editing, machine translation, etc.

The earliest corpus began in the late 1950s to early 1960s. In 1961, Franeis and KuCera of Brown University in the United States built the Brown Corpus and received 1 million words.

Since corpus-based machine translation has achieved certain success, in the 1980s corpus research showed a trend of rapid development and unprecedented prosperity and a large number of corpora were built. The LOB corpus, which is the size of the Brown corpus, was built in 1983. Both the Brown corpus and the LOB corpus are automatically annotated with parts of speech, the former using the rule method and the latter using the statistical method. Both the Brown Corpus and the LOB Corpus are classics of corpus construction. During this period, the size of the corpus was gradually expanded, and the COBUILD corpus of about 20 million words was built by the Collins Press and the University of Birmingham in the United Kingdom. In 1987, Collins Press, with the support of the COBUILD corpus, compiled and published the Collins COBUILD English Language Dictionary, which is a typical example of the application of corpus in lexicography.

In the 1990s, the size of the corpus continued to expand. Tens of millions of word-level corpora and hundreds of millions of word-level corpora such as the French corpus "Tresor de la Langue Francaise" appeared one after another. The depth of processing also expanded from part-of-speech tagging to syntactic and semantic annotation. For example, PTB (Penn Tree Bank) at the University of Pennsylvania is a syntactically annotated corpus.

The 13th International Conference on Computer Linguistics, held in 1990, proposed that dealing with large-scale real texts would be a strategic goal for a long period of time to come. This research method based on large-scale real text processing has brought natural language processing research to a new stage.

Some definitions have been given for corpus linguistics.

Definition 11.5. The study of language based on textual material is called corpus linguistics [1].

Definition 11.6. Language research based on real-life language application examples are called corpus linguistics [49].

Definition 11.7. The method of using corpora as a starting point for linguistic description or verifying linguistic hypotheses with corpora is called corpus linguistics [17].

Through the analysis and processing of a large number of real texts, it is possible to obtain a range of knowledge required to understand natural language, establish a corresponding knowledge base, and realize a knowledge-based intelligent natural language understanding system. Through the processing of the corpus, the corpus is changed from raw corpus to valuable mature corpus.

With the wide application of statistical methods in natural language processing, corpus linguistics has become a remarkable research direction in recent years, and even developed into the mainstream of language research, which has an increasingly important influence on many fields of language research.

Corpus linguistics has a wide range of research contents, which can be summarized into three aspects, namely, the construction and compilation of corpora, the processing and management of corpora, and the application of corpora.

(2) Characteristics of corpus linguistics

Corpus linguistics (hereinafter referred to as the present method or system) is based on large-scale real text processing. Compared with the previous syntax–semantic analysis method (hereinafter referred to as the previous method or system), it has the following characteristics:

(i) Different theoretical basis: The previous method was based on the syntactic–semantic analysis method, which belongs to the category of rationalist methods; whereas the present method is based on the method of large-scale real text processing, which belongs to the category of empirical methods.

(ii) Different processing methods: In the previous method, the system mainly relied on the theory and method of linguistics, which is a rule-based method. The present system is a corpus processing system based on statistical methods, and relies on the statistical nature analysis of a large number of texts.

(iii) Different test scales: In the past, the system used a small number of carefully selected examples for testing, whereas the present system needs to process millions of real texts collected from various publications.

(iv) Different grammar analysis requirements: The previous system was relatively simple to perform complete grammar analysis; whereas due to the complexity of the real text, it is almost impossible for the present system to perform complete grammatical analysis on all sentences, and just the necessary parts are analyzed.

(v) Processing documents involves different fields: The previous systems generally involved only a narrow domain, whereas the present system is able to target a wider field, even domain-free; that is, the system does not need to use specific domain knowledge when running.

(vi) Different text formats: The text processed by the previous system was only some plain text, whereas the present system is oriented to real text. Most of the real texts are texts that contain typesetting information after being processed by word processing software, and their processing techniques are worthy of attention.

(vii) Different application objects: The previous system was only suitable for the processing of "story" texts, whereas the present system is based on large-scale real corpus, and it is necessary to deal with a large amount of real news corpus.

(viii) Different evaluation methods: In the previous, the system used only a small number of artificial design examples to evaluate, whereas the present system needs to apply a large number of real texts for a large-scale objective and quantitative evaluation, and must pay attention to both the system quality and the system processing speed.

(3) Types of corpora

According to different classification standards, corpora can be divided into multiple types. For example, monolingual and multilingual corpora (by language), single-media corpus and multimedia corpus (by documented media), national and international corpora (by geographical distinction), general corpora and specialized corpora (by field of use), balanced corpus and parallel corpus (by distribution), synchronic corpus and diachronic corpus (by corpus time period), raw corpus and annotation (matured) corpus (by corpus processing or not), etc.

The more influential typical corpora include the Penn Tree Bank (PTB) and the LDC Chinese Tree Bank (CTB), the European Union's dictionary and corpus for spoken translation technology (Lexica and Speech-to-Speech Translation Technologies, LC-STAR), the Prague Dependency Treebank (PDT), the Peking University Corpus, and the Academia Sinica Corpus in China.

An in-depth discussion of corpus types, typical corpora, corpus modeling, and Chinese corpus is beyond the scope and space of this book. For those who need to learn more about related content, please refer to monographs and textbooks on natural language processing or natural language understanding.

11.7 Main Models of Natural Language Understanding Systems

Language communication is a kind of knowledge-based communication processing. Both the speaker and the listener are processing some information. To be exact, the human brain has not yet revealed the mystery of the human brain's processing and understanding of language. To use the computer's symbol processing and reasoning functions to realize language understanding, we must first have some basic processing capabilities. The models for language understanding are discussed below [8, 51].

(1) Basic model

The speaker has a clear purpose of speaking, such as expressing an opinion, conveying a certain message, or instructing the other party to do something, and then processing to generate a string of text or sound for

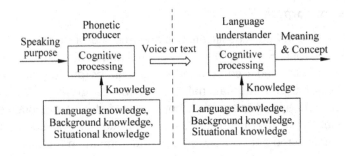

Figure 11.7   Basic model of language understanding.

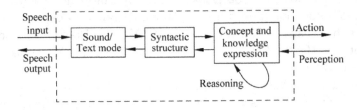

Figure 11.8   Unilateral model of language understanding.

the receiver to process. The speaker chooses the words, sentence struc-ture,stress, intonation, and so on. It must also incorporate the knowledge accumulated in the previous or last conversations. Figure 11.7 shows the basic model of natural language understanding.

(2) Unilateral model

From the perspective of language generation or reception unilaterally, the cognitive processing is shown in Figure 11.8.

For language input, the first is speech or text recognition, then the syn-tactic analysis of the language, establishing the syntactic structure, and finally the expression and reasoning of semantic concepts.

(3) Hierarchical model

The composition of language is hierarchical, and the processing of lan-guage should also be a hierarchical process. Layering can decompose a very complex process into modular, independent, step-by-step processes between modules, as shown in Figure 11.9. Going down from the top of the diagram it is a process of language understanding, while going bottom-up it is a process of language generation.

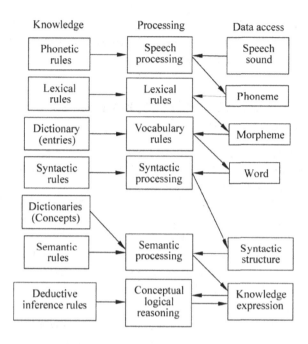

Knowledge	Processing	Data access
Phonetic rules	Speech processing	Speech sound
Lexical rules	Lexical rules	Phoneme
Dictionary (entries)	Vocabulary rules	Morpheme
Syntactic rules	Syntactic processing	Word
Dictionaries (Concepts)		
Semantic rules	Semantic processing	Syntactic structure
Deductive inference rules	Conceptual logical reasoning	Knowledge expression

Figure 11.9   Hierarchical model of language understanding.

The knowledge on the left is stored for a long time, while the data on the right is stored for a short time. The above layered model provides a process of sequential layer-by-layer processing, but as already mentioned above, in fact, the processing of language by humans does not exactly follow such a layered model. People often have to understand the syntactic structure from the perspective of semantics, and analyze the parts of speech from the perspective of syntactic structure; otherwise they cannot understand. Some words may depart from traditional grammar, but can still be understood by people. Therefore, if the system works strictly in this layer-by-layer manner, it is very unreliable. As long as there is a slight problem at the bottom level, the entire understanding process will completely collapse. For example, as long as there is a word misspelled in the text when typing, the entire sentence becomes incomprehensible. In fact, people are fully equipped with this kind of fault tolerance.

A more comprehensive model can be established by retaining the above-mentioned layered model but breaking the boundaries of the hierarchy, and typically it can be carried out in a "blackboard" system. In the above layered model, all data accesses are placed on the "blackboard", which can be accessed by all processing layers, and the processing results are written into the "blackboard". In this way, each processor is not limited to using only one level of results, but can use all levels of information.

11.8 Natural Language Processing Based on Deep Learning

With the continuous development of mobile communication and machine learning, the dream of realizing automatic dialogue between humans and machines is gradually becoming a reality. Automatic speech processing mainly includes three technologies: speech coding, speech synthesis, and speech recognition. Automatic speech recognition technology is mainly to complete the conversion from speech to text for non-specific person speech recognition. The main methods of speech recognition include feature parameter matching method, hidden Markov model method, and neural network method. Before 2006, people tried to use superficial neural network learning to train supervised deep feedforward neural networks with little effect. Until Hinton *et al.* proposed in 2006 a layer-by-layer greedy unsupervised pre-trained deep neural network, deep learning theory was successfully applied in machine learning, and then research hotspots in the field of machine learning began to turn to deep learning. Microsoft successfully applied deep learning to the speech recognition system, reducing the word error rate by about 30%, and achieved a major breakthrough in speech recognition. Then, Microsoft's research results on large vocabulary speech recognition based on the context-dependent deep neural network–hidden Markov model completely changed the original technical framework of the speech recognition system. Deep learning uses multiple layers of nonlinear structures to transform low-level features into more abstract high-level features, and transforms input features in a supervised or unsupervised way, thereby improving the accuracy of classification or prediction [14, 26, 57]. The wide demand of mobile communication for speech recognition has made speech mobile terminal applications enter the daily life of the general public. A new wave of speech research and application is emerging at home and abroad. Deep learning models have more layers of nonlinear transformations than traditional shallow models, have more powerful expression and modeling capabilities, and have greater advantages for complex signal processing.

11.8.1 *Overview of deep learning-based natural language processing technologies*

In the past 10 years, breakthroughs have been made in deep learning research. In 2009, deep learning was successfully used for speech recognition for the first time. Since then, acoustic models based on deep neural networks have gradually replaced the Gaussian mixture model (GMM) as the mainstream model for acoustic modeling of speech recognition, which has greatly promoted the development of speech recognition technology and made speech recognition technology practical [32, 48].

The overall structure of the speech recognition process is shown in Figure 11.10. The input training speech signal is preprocessed and feature extracted to obtain the feature vector sequence of the speech signal, and the acoustic model is trained to obtain the "acoustic model score". The language model estimates the possibility of hypothetical word sequences by learning the correlation between words or sentences from the training corpus, and obtains the "language model score". The feature vector sequence is obtained after pre-processing and feature extraction of the tested speech and the acoustic model score and language model score calculated from several hypothetical word sequences. After decoding and searching, the word sequence with the overall output score is finally obtained. The word sequence is used as the recognition result.

Beginning in 2010, deep neural networks began to have an important impact on speech recognition. A new type of deep neural network learning for speech recognition and related applications was discussed at the

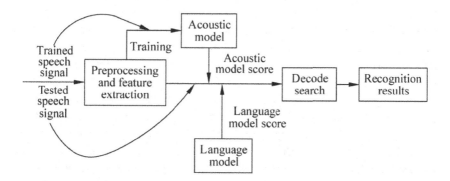

Figure 11.10   Overall structure of the speech recognition process.

2013 International Conference on Acoustics, Speech and Signal Processing (ICASSP). The learning structure, representation, and optimization of audio, speech, and visual information processing were communicated and discussed at the International Conference on Machine Learning (ICML) in 2011 and 2013. By now, deep learning theory has been successfully applied for isolated word recognition, phoneme recognition, initials recognition, and large vocabulary continuous speech recognition. It is mainly used to extract high-level features of speech data with stronger representation capabilities and to construct HMM acoustic models.

(1) Automatic speech processing based on deep learning

Deep learning has conducted in-depth research on automatic speech recognition, speech synthesis, speech coding, natural language question answering, speech enhancement, semantic matching, etc., and has obtained rich results and been widely used. The following paragraphs describe the progress of related technologies in these aspects [28].

(i) Automatic speech recognition

(a) Acoustic modeling:

In recent years, deep learning has achieved good results in language models, such as the RBM language model. Unlike N-gram language models, these neural network-based language models can map word sequences to continuous space to evaluate the probability of a word appearing to solve the problem of data sparseness. Some scholars use RNNs to construct language models, hoping to make full use of all context information to predict the next word in a recursive way, and then effectively deal with long-distance language constraints. Based on a recurrent neural network–restricted Boltzmann machine (RNN-RBM), the long distance information can be captured. In addition, the dynamic adjustment of language models based on the characteristics of sentences in language is also discussed. The experimental results show that the performance of continuous speech recognition for a large vocabulary using the RNN-RBM language model has been greatly improved. Some studies summarize the current status of deep learning-based speech recognition technology, and review recent years of research progress on deep learning-based speech recognition, including acoustic model training guidelines, deep learning-based acoustic model structure, and deep learning-based acoustic model training efficiency optimization, and deep learning-based acoustic model speaker adaptation and deep learning-based end-to-end speech recognition [2, 15, 18]. Recently, machine learning-based voice activity detection (VAD) has shown advantages over traditional VAD on multi-feature fusion tasks [60]. Through joint learning of front-end speech signal processing and back-end acoustic modeling, an integrated end-to-end automatic speech recognition (ASR) paradigm is proposed; a unified deep neural network (DNN) framework for remote speech processing is used to achieve high-quality enhanced speech and high-precision ASR [19, 22, 67]. In addition, CNNs are used for speech recognition for people who have difficulty swallowing [41], the research and applications of power dispatching speech recognition based on DNNs [21], and so on.

(b) Speech detection:

The advantage of incorporating multiple acoustic features is critical to the robustness of voice activity detection. A method for detecting pathological speech based on deep learning is proposed. Based on five-fold cross-validation, the performance of three machine learning algorithms of DNN, support vector machine, and GMM is evaluated. The experience shows that the accuracy of the neural networks reaches 99.32%, which is superior to the GMM and the support vector machine [23]. VAD is an important subject in audio signal processing. Contextual information is essential to improve VAD performance at low signal-to-noise ratios and explore contextual information through three levels of machine learning. Among them, in the middle layer, a DNN generates multiple base predictions in different contexts of a single frame, and then aggregates the base predictions to better predict the frame, which is different from the enhancement method with computationally expensive training of a classifier set for multiple base predictions [78]. A joint framework for speech enhancement combining noise classification and DNN is also proposed. The type of noise of contaminated speech is determined by VAD-DNN and NC-DNN, and then the corresponding SE-DNN model to enhance speech [64].

(c) Speech separation:

Based on deep learning for speech separation technology research, a deep learning-based reverberation speech separation model is proposed to learn inverse reverberation and denoising by learning the spectral mapping between "polluted" speech and pure speech. By extracting a series of spectral characteristics, the temporal dynamic information of adjacent frames is fused, and the DNN transform is used to encode the frequency spectrum to recover the pure speech spectrum. Finally, the time-domain signal is reconstructed and the feature classification capability of the DNN is established to complete the separation of the two-tone reverberation speech [80].

(d) Speech synthesis:

Speech synthesis based on deep learning has become a hot research area. Some studies have introduced speech recognition, speech synthesis, speech enhancement, and other directions in the field of speech signal and information processing. In the direction of speech synthesis, several speech synthesis methods based on deep learning models were introduced [19]. An auxiliary classification framework for training speech synthesis systems using DNN and RNN was proposed. The ANN uses a regression model that includes several hidden layers and an affine transformation layer to transform context features into a set of speech synthesis parameters. The research methods of speech synthesis were explored, including traditional speech synthesis methods and deep learning-based methods, and experiments combining image recognition and speech synthesis have been implemented [12]. The Mongolian unit stitching speech synthesis method is discussed, and the Mongolian speech synthesis is studied based on deep learning using a combination of hard stitching and soft stitching [27]. The HMM-RBM and HMM-DBN speech synthesis methods are proposed, and the decision tree state clustering is performed according to the spectral parameters. The spectral envelope data corresponding to each state are used to train the corresponding RBM or DBN, respectively; the synthesis phase uses the RBM or DBN salient layer probability density function model to replace the Gaussian mean. Through the powerful modeling capabilities of the RBM/DBN model, the distribution characteristics of the spectral envelope can be better fitted, and the over-smoothing of the synthesized speech is weakened [42]. A DNN-based speech synthesis method was proposed. In the training phase, DNN is used to replace the traditional decision tree and the GMM model based on the HMM parameter synthesis method to establish the mapping relationship between linguistic features and acoustic features. In the synthesis stage, it is directly replaced with the predicted value of DNN. The Gaussian mean of the traditional method and the corresponding training data variance replace the variance of the Gaussian model in the traditional method for parameter generation [29, 79]. A speech synthesis method based on DBN was proposed, and a multi-distribution deep belief network (MD-DBN) was proposed. With the help of different types of RBM in MD-DBN, the spectrum/fundamental frequency characteristics and unvoiced information can be modeled simultaneously, and the joint probability distribution of syllables and acoustics features can be estimated [34].

There is also research in the following area: a new text-to-speech conversion algorithm based on the full convolution mechanism of attention, and a statistical model for the learning of the speech synthesis process can turn some text into speech [30]. A multi-speaker speech synthesis method based on speaker embedding was proposed. Its model is based on the Tacotron network, but the post-processing network of the model is modified by the extended convolutional layer used in the Wavenet architecture to make it more suitable for speech; a multi-speaker speech can be generated by using only one neural network model [43]. A method for data selection and expansion is proposed and analyzed. Its framework uses DNN-based statistical parameters to implement speech synthesis [59]. An auxiliary classification framework for training speech synthesis systems using DNNs and RNNs was proposed. The artificial neural network used is a regression model that includes several hidden layers and an affine transformation layer to transform context features into a set of speech synthesis parameters.

(e) Speech coding:

Speech research based on deep learning is also more active. The development of a speech coding quantization algorithm based on a neural network framework was considered in the context of a scalable real-time audio/speech encoder based on a perceptual adaptive matching pursuit algorithm. The architecture of the quantization part of the coding algorithm based on the deep auto encoder (DAE) neural network is given, and its structure and learning function are described [3]. A classification and recognition method of ship radiated noise based on deep self-encoding network was proposed. Welch power spectrum estimation method is used to obtain the power spectrum characteristics of ship radiated noise, and then the structure of the original training sample set is optimized to obtain a new training sample set, and the training is constructed. A deep self-encoding network to realize classification and recognition of ship-radiated noise was proposed [71]. A new reference-free speech quality evaluation method based on Stacked Auto Encoder (SAE) was proposed, which was implemented by a DNN composed of BP neural network and SAE; the essential features of speech are extracted by the stacked auto encoder, and then features are mapped to subjective MOS scores via BP neural networks [72].

In order to improve the speech quality after speech enhancement, a comprehensive feature based on self-encoding features is proposed. First, the autoencoder is used to extract the self-encoding features, and then the Group Lasso algorithm is used to verify the complementarity and redundancy of the self-encoding features and the auditory features. Finally, the features are recombined to obtain comprehensive features as the input features of the speech enhancement system for speech enhancement [77]. A new method of speech classification based on the stack auto encoder was proposed. This method was implemented by a DNN composed of a stack auto encoder and a Softmax classifier. The classification accuracy of the algorithm is better than traditional algorithms under different background noise and different signal-to-noise ratios [46].

(2) Automatic text processing based on deep learning

The research on automatic text processing based on deep learning has achieved relatively rich results. Based on deep learning a comprehensive study summarizes the research background and development history of machine reading comprehension technology; the research progress of the three key technologies of word vector, attention mechanism, and answer prediction are introduced, the current machine reading comprehension research is also analyzed, and an outlook of the future development trend of machine reading comprehension technology is provided [40]. Text classification technology based on deep learning is the research background. The text classification process, the distributed representation of text, and the text classification model based on deep learning neural network were introduced. Several typical model structures were performed with sentiment analysis and topic classification as tasks, and experiment and analysis were conducted [44]. The Chinese word segmentation method based on the dilated CNN model was proposed. Adding the Chinese character root information and using the CNN to extract features are done to enrich the input features; using the dilated CNN model and adding the residual structure for training can give a better understanding of semantic information and increase the calculation speed [65]. After systematically reviewing the application of deep learning in natural language processing in the clinical field, a quantitative analysis of the literature/text was performed to assess the current research methods, scope, and background of deep learning in natural language processing in the clinical field [69]. A new generative auto-summarization solution was proposed, which includes an improved word vector generation technology and a generative auto-summary model.

Attention mechanism, gated recurrent unit structure, bidirectional RNN, and multilayer RNN were introduced. Network and cluster search have improved the accuracy and sentence fluency of generative summaries [20, 76].

Emotional understanding is an active direction in the research on automatic text processing based on deep learning [33, 35, 55, 58]. Some studies have proposed a novel deep learning-based method to detect the three emotions in text dialogues—happiness, sadness, and anger. The essence is to combine semantic and emotional-based representations to achieve more accurate emotion detection [13]. Another research report introduces a corpus of 40,000 tagged Arabic tweets covering several topics, proposes three deep learning models (CNN, LSTM, and RCNN) for Arabic sentiment analysis, and verifies the word embedding performance of the three models on the proposed corpus [53]. Design a model that can extract both features and classifications. The model includes a CNN for feature extraction and a DNN that performs sentiment classification. A CNN consists of three convolutional layers that filter the input spectrogram in the time and frequency dimensions and two dense layers, forming the deep part of the model [61]. A research study introduces the deep learning technology used in sentiment analysis, and points out that deep learning technology has become the latest hotspot in current natural language processing and predictive emotions; this survey focuses on various uses in different applications of sentiment analysis at the sentence level and the target level styles of deep learning methods [55]. In order to improve the accuracy of the intelligent speech emotion recognition system, a speech emotion recognition model based on CNN feature representation was proposed. The convolution model is based on the Lenet-5 model, adding a layer of convolution layer and pooling layer, and changing the two-dimensional convolution kernel to a one-dimensional convolution kernel. In the model, the feature transformation is characterized, and finally the SoftMax classifier is used to realize the emotion classification. Simulation results verify the effectiveness of the network model [31].

(3) Other natural language processing technologies based on deep learning

In addition to automatic speech recognition and automatic text processing, other deep learning-based speech processing technologies also involve speech enhancement, natural language question answering, and semantic matching.

(i) Speech enhancement:

Use deep learning to enhance the sound spectrum [54]. Becerra *et al.* proposed two new variants of frame-level cost functions for training DNNs to achieve lower word error rates in speech recognition [7]. Xu *et al.* propose a speech enhancement algorithm based on automatic coding generative adversarial network. It adopts a comprehensive learning framework that combines automatic encoder (AE) and generative adversarial network (GAN) to perform end-to-end processing at the level of speech waveform and automatically extracts speech features, supervised learning of the nonlinear relationship between noisy speech and pure speech, and modeling of speech as a combination of labels and latent attributes in a probability model [70]. An improved speech recognition method using adaptive MFCC and deep learning was proposed to improve the speech recognition rate [4].

(ii) Deep language-based natural language Q&A

How automatic speech recognition in dialog systems has evolved from the traditional GMM-HMM (Gaussian Hybrid Model–hidden Markov model) architecture to the most recent nonlinear deep DNN-HMM) scheme is discussed; through DNN acoustic modeling, the results show that speech recognition performance has reasonable accuracy [6].

(iii) Semantic matching

A semantic matching model based on convolutional deep neural networks was proposed for document-based automatic question and answer (Q&A) tasks in order to extract features for each pair of questions and documents, and calculate their scores accordingly [25].

Deep learning research in automatic speech recognition, speech synthesis, speech coding, natural language question answering, speech enhancement, semantic matching, etc., has been implemented through experiments or applications, showing that its performance is superior to traditional technology [36].

11.8.2 *Natural language processing example based on deep learning*

As an example, this subsection introduces a deep learning-based speech recognition model and its application in smart homes [5]. The developers of the speech recognition model propose a deep learning speech recognition model based on a noise reduction auto encoder. The model parses out phrase control instructions to control household equipment. The speech recognition model mainly includes two parts: first, unsupervised learning pre-training is performed, and some network nodes are randomly set to 0 before pre-training to artificially simulate noise data. Then it uses the weight matrix of restricted Boltzmann machine to train each hidden layer in turn, modify the weights by comparing the deviation of the input data and the output data, and optimize the parameters. Then, supervised fine-tuning is performed, and the trained parameters are used as the initial values of the entire network. The error back-propagation algorithm is used to adjust the parameters of the entire network model.

The speech recognition process mainly includes the preprocessing, feature extraction, and pattern matching of speech signals. The proposed speech recognition model for smart homes is continuous low vocabulary recognition for non-specific people. The speech recognition process is shown in Figure 11.11. First, the speech signal is pre-processed to eliminate the effects of human vocal organs and speech acquisition devices on the speech signal. Then, the speech recognition acoustic model is established based on the extracted speech features and pattern matching is performed. Speech recognition decision outputs recognition results. The speech recognition model is more sensitive to the characteristics of speech control instructions for smart homes, and can parse home control instructions when the sound information is complex or in the presence of noise interference.

In order to effectively extract the representation of the original data in the hidden layer and enhance the learning ability, a deep auto encoder with multiple hidden layers is used. In a deep auto encoder, RBM is used to encode and decode the input data of each layer, and compare the original input data with a convergence calculation to obtain the optimal parameter adjustments for each layer, and complete the feature training of one layer, and the output data after layer coding is used as the input data for the next

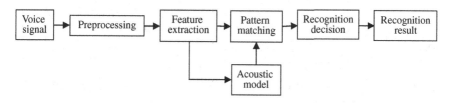

Figure 11.11   Speech recognition process.

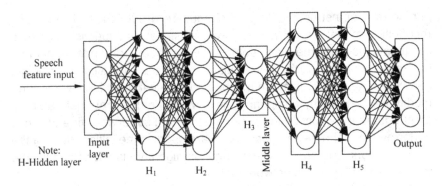

Figure 11.12   Model of a deep noise reduction auto encoder.

layer. Data processing is performed on each layer in the same way, and feature training for all layers is completed.

In deep learning, a neural network with enough levels will have a strong learning ability, but too many levels are prone to gradient disappearance or gradient burst problems. After repeated model tests, the noise reduction auto encoder is used in this speech recognition system, as shown in Figure 11.12. It consists of one input layer, five hidden layers, and one output layer. The number of nodes in each layer is $390 \times 680 \times 680 \times 50 \times 680 \times 680 \times 390$.

In Figure 11.12, the input layer contains 390 nodes, corresponding to the voice input features. The number of nodes of the two hidden layers H_1 and H_2 connected to the input layer is 680. Two high-dimensional hidden layer feature spaces are constructed in turn; the hidden layer H_3 with 50 intermediate nodes is the encoding output; the two hidden layers H_4, H_5, and the output layer jointly complete the decoding work. In the selection of network node types, the input layer, the intermediate coding layer, and the output layer use Gaussian linear excitation nodes, and other hidden layers use Sigmoid nonlinear excitation Bernoulli nodes.

The convergence calculation takes the mean square error of the original input and decoded data as the objective function, and adjusts the parameters, and the loss function of the noise reduction auto encoder is the following:

$$J(w, b) = \left[\frac{1}{m}\sum_{i=1}^{m} J(w, b; x^{(i)}, y^{(i)})\right] + \frac{1}{2}\sum_{l-1}^{n_l-1}\sum_{i-1}^{s_i}\sum_{j=1}^{s_j+1}(w_{ji}^{(l)})^2 + \sum_{xls} L(x, g(f(x)))$$

(11.1)

Among them, $g(f(x))$ represents the noise data simulated in the input data. The first term of formula (11.1) represents the average reconstruction error; the second term represents the weight constraint term to prevent overfitting; the third term represents the constraint expression of noise reduction.

11.9 Summary

The natural language comprehension/natural language processing discussed in this chapter is an early research area of artificial intelligence research. It is receiving unprecedented attention and has made some important progress.

Natural language understanding is a difficult and challenging research task. It requires a large and extensive knowledge base, including linguistic and phonetic knowledge such as morphology, grammar, semantics, and phonetics, as well as related background knowledge. When studying natural language understanding, multiple knowledge representation and reasoning methods may be used. This is fully reflected in this chapter.

When discussing "language" and its "understanding", language is defined as the medium through which humans communicate, and understanding was viewed as a mapping from natural sentences to machine representations and the machine's function of performing human language. Then, natural language understanding is divided into lexical analysis, phonetic analysis, grammatical analysis, syntactic segmentation, and semantic analysis. Subsequent content is mainly developed around these levels. These levels influence and restrict each other, and ultimately solve the problem of language understanding as a whole.

Lexical analysis constructs and analyzes the words in the source program, transforms the words in the source program into internal representations, and then passes the internal representations to the rest of the compiler. Lexical analysis is the basis of understanding words. Its main purpose is to segment words from sentences, find out the morphemes of words, obtain linguistic information of words, and determine the meaning of words.

The main function of syntactic analysis is to analyze sentence or phrase structure and normalize syntactic structure. Syntactic analysis methods include phrase structure grammar, Chomsky formal grammar, transfer network, extended transfer network, and lexical functional grammar (LFG).

These analyses establish the syntactic structure and lay an important foundation for understanding language.

Establishing the syntactic structure is only one step in the language understanding model, and further semantic analysis is needed to obtain the meaning expressed by the language. Semantic analysis generally uses two methods: semantic network representation and logical representation. Semantic analysis determines the meaning of each word in the sentence. Based on the definition of the syntactic structure and the logical form, the semantic form is used to effectively restrict the ambiguity of the logical form in order to obtain a correct understanding.

The understanding of simple sentences and the comprehension of complex sentences are discussed. The understanding of simple sentences includes the understanding of each word in a sentence and the structure that makes up the meaning of the sentence. The simple sentence understanding methods used include keyword matching, syntactic parse trees, and semantics. Understanding compound sentences requires finding relationships between the sentences. Understanding complex relationships between sentences requires a large knowledge base. In order to establish such a knowledge base, some suitable knowledge representation methods need to be adopted; partitioned semantic network is one such feasible representation method.

A corpus is a database that stores linguistic materials, and corpus linguistics is a linguistic research discipline based on a corpus, and is a language research based on real-life language application examples. Corpus linguistics is based on large-scale real corpora. The section on Corpus Linguistics introduces the development, definition, research content, and characteristics of corpus linguistics, as well as corpus types and typical corpora.

Language communication is a kind of knowledge-based communication processing. Both the speaker and the listener are processing some information. The speaker has a clear speaking purpose, choice of words, sentence structure, stress, intonation, and so on. It must also incorporate the knowledge accumulated in the previous or last conversation, etc. This requires the establishment of models for natural language understanding, including basic models, unilateral models, and hierarchical models.

The last section of this chapter discusses natural language processing based on deep learning, and uses speech recognition as a representative to illustrate the application of deep learning in natural language processing. With the continuous development of mobile communication and machine learning, the realization of human–machine automatic dialogue is gradually becoming a reality. Acoustic models based on DNNs have gradually replaced the GMM as the mainstream model for speech recognition acoustic modeling, which has greatly promoted the development of speech recognition technology and has made speech recognition technology practical. Deep learning has conducted in-depth research in areas such as automatic speech recognition, speech synthesis, speech coding, natural language question answering, speech enhancement, and semantic matching, and has achieved rich results and been widely used. The final section summarizes the application of deep learning in natural language processing, introduces a speech recognition model based on deep learning and its application in smart homes, and proposes a deep learning speech recognition model based on noise reduction automatic encoder. Parse out phrase control instructions to achieve control of home appliances.

Creating spoken dialogue systems and speech conversion engines is a new research direction of natural language processing. Text-based conversations have been expanded to include voice conversations on mobile devices for information access and task-based applications. Mining social media to provide information about health or finance, and to identify people's emotions and provide emotional products and services, has become an important development and application area of natural language.

Deep learning architectures and algorithms have been increasingly used in NLP research. Many complex algorithms based on deep learning such as RNNs, CNNs, and memory enhancement strategies and reinforcement learning methods have been proposed to deal with difficult NLP problems. The progress of deep learning research will lead to further substantial and even breakthrough progress in NLP.

References

1. Aijmer, K. and Altenberg, B. (1991). *English Corpus Linguistics: Studies in Honour of Jan Swartvik*. London: Longman.
2. Amodei, D., Anubhai, R., Battenberg, E., *et al.* (2015). Deep speech 2: End-to-end speech recognition in English and Mandarin. https://arxiv.org/abs/1512.02595, 2015.
3. Avramov, V., Herasimovich, V., Petrovsky, A., *et al.* (2018). Sound signal invariant DAE neural network-based quantizer architecture of audio/speech coder using the matching pursuit algorithm. Advances in Neural Networks — ISNN 2018, Lecture Notes in Computer Science, Vol. 10878, 511–520.
4. Bae, H.S., Lee, H.J. and Lee, S.G. (2016). Voice recognition based on adaptive MFCC and deep learning, *Proceedings of the 2016 IEEE 11th Conference on*

Industrial Electronics and Applications, Hefei, China, June, 2016, pp. 1542–1546.

5. Bao, X.A., Xu, H., Zhang, N., *et al.* (2019). Speech recognition model based on deep learning and its application in smart home, *Journal of Zhejiang University of Technology* China, *41*(2): 217–223.

6. Becerra, A. de la Rosa, J. and Gonzalez, E. (2018). Speech recognition in a dialog system: from conventional to deep processing. *Multimedia Tools and Applications*, *77*(12), 5875–15911, DOI: 10.1007/s11042-017-5160-5.

7. Becerra, A., de la Rosa, J.I., Gonzalez, E., *et al.* (2017). Speech recognition using deep neural networks trained with non-uniform frame-level cost functions, *2017 IEEE International Autumn Meeting on Power, Electronics and Computing* (ROPEC), Ixtapa, Mexico, Nov 8–10, 2017.

8. Bengio, Y., Ducharme, R., Vincent, P. and Jauvin, C. (2003). A neural probabilistic language model, *Journal of Machine Learning Research*, *3*(Feb): 1137–1155.

9. Cai, Z.X. and Chen, A.B. (2008). *Dictionary of Artificial Intelligence*, (Chemical Industry Press, Beijing, in Chinese).

10. Cai, Z.X. and Xu, G.Y. (2010). *Artificial Intelligence and Its Applications*, Fourth Edition, (Tsinghua University Press, Beijing, in Chinese).

11. Cambria, E. and White, B. (2014). Jumping NLP curves: A review of natural language processing research, *IEEE Computational Intelligence Magazine*, *9*(2): 48–57.

12. Chao, L.W. (2018). Research on image-based speech synthesis, *Electronic Production*, July, pp. 32–33, (in Chinese).

13. Chatterjee, A., Gupta, U., Chinnakotla, M.K., *et al.* (2019). Understanding emotions in text using deep learning and big data, *Computers in Human Behavior*, *93*:309–317, DOI: 10.1016/j.chb.2018.12.029.

14. Chen, M.X., Firat, B.A., *et al.* (2018). The best of both worlds: Combining recent advances in neural machine translation, arXiv preprint arXiv:1804.09849, 2018.

15. Chen, Z.H., Jain, M., Wang, Y.Q., *et al.* (2019). End-to-end contextual speech recognition using class language models and a token passing decoder, *IEEE International Conference on Acoustics, Speech and Signal Processing* (ICASSP), Brighton, UK, May 2019, pp. 6186–6190.

16. Collobert, R., Weston, J., Bottou, L., *et al.* (2011). Natural language processing (almost) from scratch, *Journal of Machine Learning Research*, *12*(Aug): 2493–2537.

17. Crystal, D. (1991). Stylistic Profiling. *English Corpus Linguistics: Studies in Honour of Jan Swartvik*. London: Longman. pp. 221–238.

18. Dai, L.R., Zhang, S.L. and Huang, Z.Y. (2017). Status and prospect of speech recognition technology based on deep learning, *Data Collection and Processing*, *32*(2): pp. 221–231.

19. Dai, L.R. and Zhang, S.L. (2014). Deep speech signal and information processing: Research progress and prospects, *Data Acquisition and Processing*, *29*(2): 171–179.

20. Devlin, J., Chang, M.W., Lee, K. and Toutanova, K. (2018). BERT: Pre-training of deep bidirectional transformers for language understanding, arXiv preprint arXiv:1810.04805. 2018.
21. Dou, J.Z., Luo, S.Z., Jin, Y., *et al.* (2019). Research and application of power dispatching speech recognition based on deep neural network, *Hubei Electric Power, 43*(3): 16–22 (in Chinese).
22. Elman, J.L. (1991). Distributed representations, simple recurrent networks, and grammatical structure, *Machine Learning, 7*(2–3): 195–225.
23. Fang, S.H., Tsao, Y., Hsiao, M.J., *et al.* (2018). Detection of pathological voice using cepstrum vectors: A deep learning approach, *Journal of Voice, 33*(5): 634–641, DOI: 10.1016/j.jvoice.2018.02.003.
24. Feng, Z.W. (1996). *Computer Processing of Natural Language*, (Shanghai Foreign Language Education Press, Shanghai, in Chinese).
25. Fu, J. (2019). Application and improvement of convolutional deep neural network in document-based automatic question and answer tasks, *Computer Applications and Software, 36*(8): 177–180.
26. Goldberg, Y. (2016). A primer on neural network models for natural language processing, *Journal of Artificial Intelligence Research, 57*: 345–420.
27. Guo, S.N. (2019). Discussion on Mongolian unit splicing speech synthesis method, *Science and Informatization* June 2019, 131, 133.
28. Huang, X., Acero, A., Hon, H.W. and Reddy, R. (2001). *Spoken Language Processing*, (Prentice Hall, New York).
29. Huang, X.D. (2018). Big data for speech and language processing, *2018 IEEE International Conference on Big Data*, Seattle, WA, USA, 2018, p. 2.
30. Jayawardhana, P., Aponso, A. and Rathnayake, A. (2019). An intelligent approach of text-to-speech synthesizers for English and Sinhala languages, *Proceedings of 2nd IEEE International Conference on Information and Computer Technologies* (ICICT), pp. 229–234.
31. Jiang, P.G., Fu, H.L., Tao, H.W., *et al.* (2019). Feature characterization based on convolution neural networks for speech emotion recognition, *Chinese Journal of Electron Devices, 42*(4): 998–1001.
32. Jurafsky, D. and Martin, J.H., translated by Feng, Z.W, *et al.* (2005). *Comprehensive Review of Natural Language Processing*, (Electronic Industry Press, Beijing, in Chinese).
33. Kang, H., Yoo, S.J. and Han, D. (2012). Senti-lexicon and improved Naïve Bayes algorithms for sentiment analysis of restaurant reviews, *Expert System with Applications, 39*: 6000–6010.
34. Kang, S., Qian, X. and Meng, H . (2013). Multi-distribution deep belief network for speech synthesis, *ICASSP*, IEEE, Columbia, USA, pp. 8012–8016.
35. Keshavarz, H. and Abadeh, M.S. (2017). ALGA: Adaptive lexicon learning using genetic algorithm for sentiment analysis of microblogs, *Knowledge-Based Systems, 122*(15) April, 1–16.
36. Kumar, A., Irsoy, O., *et al.* (2015). Ask me anything: dynamic memory networks for natural language processing, arXiv preprint arXiv:1506.07285.2015.
37. Lee, J., Song, K-S., Noh, K.J., Park, T-J. and Chang, J-H. (2019). DNN based multi-speaker speech synthesis with temporal auxiliary speaker ID embedding.

Proceedings of IEEE International Conference on Electronics Information and Emergency Communication (ICEIC), 2019: 1–4.

38. Leech, G., Garside, R. and Bryan, M. (1994). CLAWS4: The tagging of the British national corpus, *Proc. of the 15th International Conference on Computational Linguistics.* Kyoto, Japan, pp. 622–628.

39. Leech, G. (1992). Corpora and theories of linguistic performance, In: Svarvik(ed.) *Directions in Corpus Linguistics,* (Mouton de Gruyter, Berlin), pp. 105–122.

40. Li, Z.J. and Wang, C.B. (2019). A review of machine reading comprehension based on deep learning, *Computer Science, 46*(7): 7–12.

41. Lin, B.Y., Huang, H.S., Sheu, R.K., *et al.* (2018). Speech recognition for people with dysphasia using convolutional neural network, *Proceedings of IEEE International Conference on Systems Man and Cybernetics Conference,* Miyazaki, Japan, Oct 7–10, 2018, pp. 2164–2169,

42. Ling, Z., Deng, L. and Yu, D. (2013). Modeling spectral envelopes using restricted Bohzmann machines and deep belief networks for statistical parametric speech synthesis, *IEEE Transactions on Audio, Speech, and Language Processing, 21*(10): 2129–2139.

43. Liu, K.Y. and Guo, B.Y. (1991). *Natural Language Processing,* (Science and Technology Press, Beijing, in Chinese).

44. Liu, T.T., Zhu, W.D. and Liu, G.Y. (2018). Research progress of text classification based on deep learning, *Electric Power Information and Communication Technology 16*(3): 1–7.

45. Liu, X.D. (2007). Overview of natural language understanding, *Statistics and Information Forum, 22*(2): 5–12.

46. Ma, H.F., Zhao, Y.J., Liu, K., *et al.* (2007). A speech classification algorithm using a stack automatic encoder, *Journal of Xidian University* (Natural Science Edition), *44* (5) : 13–17 (in Chinese).

47. Manaris, B. (1999). Natural language processing: A human-computer interaction perspective, *Advance in Computer, 47*(1): 1–16.

48. Manning, C.D., Surdeanu, M., Bauer, J., *et al.* (2014). The Stanford Core NLP natural language processing toolkit, *Proceedings of the 52nd Annual Meeting of the Association for Computational Linguistics, System Demonstrations* (Association for Computational Linguistics, Stroudsburg, PA, 2014), pp. 55–60.

49. McEnery, T. and Lilson, A. (1996). *Corpus Linguistics.* Edinburph University Press.

50. Mikolov, T., Chen, K., Corrado, G. and Dean, J. (2013). Efficient estimation of word representations in vector space, arXiv preprint arXiv:1301.3781, 2013.

51. Mikolov, T., Karafi, M. and Burget, L., *et al.* (2010). Recurrent neural network based language model, *Interspeech, 2*(2010): 3.

52. Mikolov, T., Sutskever, I., Chen, K., *et al.* (2013). Distributed representations of words and phrases and their compositionality, *Advances in Neural Information Processing Systems, 2013*: 3111–3119.

53. Mohammed, A. and Kora, R. (2019). Deep learning approaches for Arabic sentiment analysis, *Social Network Analysis and Mining, 9*(1): DOI:10.1007/s13278-019-0596-4.

54. Nanzaka, R., Kitamura, T., Adachi, Y., *et al.* (2018). Spectrum enhancement of singing voice using deep learning, *IEEE International Symposium on Multimedia*-ISM, pp. 167–170, DOI:10.1109/ISM.2018.00-18.
55. Prabha, M.I.O. and Srikanth, G.U. (2019). Survey of sentiment analysis using deep learning techniques, *International Conference on Innovation in Information Communication and Technology* (ICIICT,2019), Chennai, India, April 25–26, 2019.
56. Shengsheng, L. (2019). Speech recognition technology, *Peak Data Science*, (4): 182–183.
57. Socher, R., Lin, C., Manning, C.C. and Ng, A.Y. (2011). Parsing natural scenes and natural language with recursive neural network, *Proceedings of the 28th international conference on machine learning* (ICML-11), pp. 129–136.
58. Socher, R., Perelygin, A., Wu, J.Y., *et al.* (2013). Recursive deep models for semantic compositionality over a sentiment Treebank, *Proceedings of the conference on empirical methods in natural language processing* (EMNLP), *1631*: 1642.
59. Toman, M., Meltzner, G.S. and Patel, R. (2018). Data requirements, selection and augmentation for DNN-based speech synthesis from crowd sourced data, *19th Annual Conference of the International Speech Communication Association*, Hyderabad, India, August 02–September 06, 2018.
60. Vecchiotti, P., Principi, E., Squartini, S., *et al.* (2018). Neural networks for joint voice activity detection and speaker localization, *Proceedings of European Signal Processing Conference* (EUSIPCO), Rome, Italy, September 3–7, 2018, pp. 1567–1571.
61. Vrebcevic, N., Mijic, I. and Petrinovic, D. (2019). Emotion classification based on convolutional neural network using speech data, *Proceedings of the 42nd International Convention on Information and Communication Technology, Electronics, and Microelectronics* (MIPRO), Opatija, Croatia, May 20–24, 2019, pp. 1007–1012.
62. Wang, C.H., Zhang, M. and Ma, S.P. (2007). Overview of the application of natural language processing in information retrieval, *Journal of Chinese Information Processing, 21*(2): 35–45 (in Chinese).
63. Wang, G. (1988). *Basics of General Linguistics*, (Hunan Education Press, Changsha, China, in Chinese).
64. Wang, W.B., Liu, H.G., Yang, J.H., *et al.* (2019). Speech enhancement based on noise classification and deep neural network, *Modern Physics Letters B, 33*(17): DOI: 10.1142/S0217984919501884.
65. Wang, X., Li, C. and Chen, J. (2019). Chinese word segmentation method based on dilated convolutional neural network model, *Journal of Chinese Information Processing, 33*(9): 24–30.
66. Weston, J., Bengio, S. and Usunier, N. (2011). Wsabie: Scaling up to large vocabulary image annotation, in *IJCAI, 11*: 2764–2770.
67. Wu, B., Li, K.H. and Ge, F.P. (2017). An end-to-end deep learning approach to simultaneous speech dereverberation and acoustic modeling for robust speech recognition, *IEEE Journal of Selected Topics in Signal Processing, 11*(8): 1289–1300, DOI: 10.1109/JSTSP.2017.2756439.

68. Wu, Q.G. (1995). *Introduction to Semantics*, Second Edition, (Hunan Education Press, Changsha, China, in Chinese).
69. Wu, S., Roberts, K., Datta, S., *et al.* (2019). Deep learning in clinical natural language processing: a methodical review, *Journal of the American Medical Informatics Association, 27*(3): 457–470. DOI:10.1093/jamia/ocz200.
70. Xu, C.D., Xu, R.L. and Zhou, J. (2019). Speech enhancement algorithm based on automatic coding to generate adversarial networks, *Computer Engineering and Design, 40*(9): 2578–2583.
71. Yan, S.G., Kang, C.Y., Xia, Z.J., *et al.* (2019). Classification and recognition of ship radiated noise based on deep self-coding network, *Ship Science and Technology, 41*(2): 124–130.
72. Yang, M.J. and Zhang, G.S. (2018). Voice quality evaluation method based on stack automatic encoder, *Small Microcomputer System, 39*(10): 2134–2137 (in Chinese).
73. Yao, T.S., Zhu, J.B., Zhang, H., *et al.* (2002). *Natural Language Comprehension*—a study that makes machines understand human language, (Tsinghua University Press, Beijing, in Chinese).
74. Yoshioka, T., Chen, Z., Dimitriadis, D., *et al.* (2019). Meeting transcription using virtual microphone arrays, arXiv preprint arXiv:1905.02545.
75. Yu, Z.B. (2005). *Research on Natural Language Understanding*, Master Degree Thesis of East China Normal University.
76. Zhang, K.J., Li, W.N., Qian, R., *et al.* (2019). Automatic text summarization scheme based on deep learning, *Computer Application, 39*(2): 311–315.
77. Zhang, T., Ren, X.Y., Liu, Y. and Geng, Y.Z. (2019). Speech enhancement acoustic feature extraction based on self-coding features, *Computer Science and Exploration, 13*(8):1341–1350.
78. Zhang, X.L. and Wang, D.L. (2016). Boosting contextual information for deep neural network based voice activity detection, *IEEE-ACM Transactions on Audio Speech and Language Processing, 24*(2): 252–264, DOI: 10.1109/TASLP.2015.2505415.
79. Zen, H., Senior, A. and Schuster, M. (2013). Statistical parametric speech synthesis using deep neural networks, *IEEE IC-ASSP*, British Columbia, pp. 7962–7966.
80. Zhou, Y., Zhao, H.M., Chen, J. and Pan, X.Y. (2019). Research on speech separation technology based on deep learning, *Cluster Computing-the Journal of Networks Software Tools and Applications, 22*(S4): S8887–S8897 DOI: 10.1007/s10586-018-2013-6.

Prospects of Artificial Intelligence

12

The growth of any new thing does not proceed smoothly. In science, whenever a new science invention or new discipline is born or a new idea comes out, it is often subject to many kinds of criticism and opposition and even to persecution.

Artificial intelligence is no exception. Since the birth of artificial intelligence in human society, artificial intelligence has caused some controversy. Since coming out into the world in 1956, artificial intelligence has struggled and grown in a very difficult environment. On the one hand, some people in society have doubts about the science of artificial intelligence or are afraid of the development of artificial intelligence. In some countries, artificial intelligence is even regarded as anti-scientific heresy and is opposed and criticized. On the other hand, in the scientific community, some people have expressed doubts about artificial intelligence and have expressed disbelief or rejected artificial intelligence research.

In recent years, the unprecedented rapid development and universal application of artificial intelligence has brought about well-being and joy to human beings, but also caused some concerns and controversy. For example, people are worrying that further development of intelligent robots will lead to human unemployment, and that the realization of the ultimate goal of artificial intelligence may only cause humans to become slaves to intelligent machines.

True science, like any other truth, can never be suppressed, nor can it run counter to the service and benefit of mankind. Artificial intelligence research is bound to eliminate all kinds of danger and all kinds of interference. It is like a rolling river, the back wave pushes the front wave, and each wave moves forward higher than the other.

This chapter will briefly discuss the impact of artificial intelligence on humans and the safety issues of artificial intelligence, analyze the integration of artificial intelligence technologies, and look forward to the development of artificial intelligence industrialization.

12.1 The Impact of Artificial Intelligence on Humans

The development of artificial intelligence has had a profound impact on humankind and its future. These impacts involve human economic interests, social functions, and cultural life. Artificial intelligence also brings some challenges and security issues to human society [12,13,30]. They are discussed below one by one.

12.1.1 *Great benefits of artificial intelligence*

Artificial intelligence uses intelligent machines to replace humans in mental and physical labor, and brings great benefits to humans. These benefits include the following:

(1) Economic benefits

Artificial intelligence provides unprecedented good development opportunities for companies and businesses around the world. It can improve almost all commercial business processes, promote the transformation and upgrading of industries and the national economy, increase industrial productivity, and increase enterprise productivity and economic benefits greatly [6].

Artificial intelligence promotes economic transformation and upgrading. For example, on the one hand, intelligent manufacturing requires the application of key technologies such as distributed systems, intelligent networks, intelligent control, intelligent reasoning, and intelligent decision-making to build intelligent machines and human–machine fusion systems to achieve flexibility, integration, and automation, information and intellectualization of manufacturing. Artificial intelligence provides various intelligent technologies for intelligent manufacturing, which is an important foundation and key technical guarantee for the transformation and upgrading of intelligent manufacturing. On the other hand, intelligent manufacturing is an important cross-cutting application area of artificial intelligence, involving intelligent robots, distributed intelligent systems, intelligent reasoning, intelligent control, intelligent management, and intelligent decision-making.

(2) Social benefits

Artificial intelligence can replace humans' difficult and dangerous labor positions, create new jobs, and promote changes in social structure and thinking concepts [8]; we can apply artificial intelligence to fight extreme poverty and improve the quality of life of people in remote and poor areas [4]; the development of artificial intelligence can also be used to assist in the search for world peace [29].

(3) Scientific and technological benefits

Artificial intelligence research has made, and will continue to make, a significant impact on the various fields of science and technology, including computer technology. The development and application of artificial intelligence has promoted the development of data science, network technology, algorithm technology, parallel processing, automatic programming and dedicated intelligent chip hardware, and other technologies. In turn, this has promoted the development of artificial intelligence science and technology, which has created greater benefits to humanity.

(4) Educational benefits

The rapid development of artificial intelligence technology has brought innovative educational opportunities and experience to all levels and types of education [31]. Artificial intelligence technology has been applied to create personalized intelligent learning platforms and intelligent education systems such as teaching assistants. Chat robots and teaching robots are widely used to promote the cross-integration of artificial intelligence and education.

(5) Ecological benefits

We can apply artificial intelligence perception and identification technology to detect a wide range of ecological data, and provide real-time and accurate basis for environmental governance and ecological civilization construction; we can develop artificial intelligence unmanned systems to replace human beings to perform dangerous, monotonous, and difficult tasks that are harmful to physical health.

(6) Health benefits

We can develop and apply various artificial intelligence medical systems and devices, including various medical detection, diagnosis, surgery, and rehabilitation robots, etc.; we can apply artificial intelligence technology to develop various new drugs, and quickly and accurately find and treat various infectious diseases, difficult and dangerous diseases, and provide services for health care, saving lives, and improving health [7].

(7) Cultural benefits

The development of artificial intelligence has opened many new windows for human culture. Artificial intelligence can improve humans' knowledge and cultural life. For example, intelligent speech recognition and smart phones have enriched the cultural and entertainment life of humans; machine vision and virtual reality technology have made a profound impact on image art; and smart tourism provides tourists with efficient, cheap, and safer travel solutions.

(8) Governance benefits

The application of artificial intelligence technology, combined with the Internet, big data, block chain, and other technologies, can promote economic, political, cultural, social, and ecological governance. Development and governance of artificial intelligence applications such as smart cities, intelligent transportation, intelligent driving, smart healthcare, smart agriculture, intelligent finance, intelligent education, intelligent security, intelligent justice, intelligent management, intelligent command, social intelligence, intelligent military affairs, and intelligent economy, all have a place in uses of artificial intelligence. Artificial intelligence technology is also an important means to ensure the safety of artificial intelligence itself.

In summary, it can be seen that artificial intelligence technology has made a huge impact on human social progress, economic development, and cultural improvement. As time progresses and technology advances, this effect will become increasingly apparent. There are also some effects that may be difficult for us to predict now. It is certain that artificial intelligence will have an increasingly greater impact on the material and spiritual civilization of humanity.

12.1.2 *Security issues of artificial intelligence*

Many major inventions and important technologies in history have brought some negative effects besides bringing benefits to human beings, and have made some people worried or upset. These examples show that any "high-tech" has two sides, and may become a double-edged sword. Artificial intelligence is also a double-edged sword. While it brings great benefits to human beings, there are also some negative issues, especially security issues.

(1) Psychological security

The rapid development of artificial intelligence has made its capabilities increasingly powerful, and the magical power of intelligent robots has become increasingly greater. This exposes some people in society to psychological threats, or mental threats. They are worried that if intelligent machines have the same thinking ability, emotions, and creativity as humans, then once the intelligence of these intelligent machines surpasses human intelligence, they will "share the world with humans", and even dominate humans and become the rulers of society, and human beings will become slaves of artificial intelligence. If this fear of artificial intelligence is not channelized, it may develop into a type of mental panic disorder [22, 25, 36]. In addition, the widespread use of artificial intelligence and robots gives people more opportunities and time to work with intelligent machines, which will increase the loneliness of related personnel, making them feel lonely, isolated, and disturbed [5, 23].

(2) Social security

In the past few decades, the structure of human society has been undergoing changes quietly and daily [11]. In the past, people dealt directly with machines, but now they have to deal with traditional machines with the help of intelligent machines. That is to say, the traditional social structure of "human–machine" has gradually been replaced by the new social structure of "human–intelligent machine–machine". People have felt and will see more; artificial intelligence "doctor", "secretary", "reporter", "editor", etc. and robot "nurse", "waiter", "traffic police", "operation workers ", "cleaners ", "nanny", etc. will all be performed by intelligent systems or intelligent robots. In this way, humans must learn to live in harmony with artificial intelligence and intelligent robots in order to adapt to this new social structure [8, 12].

Another social problem caused by artificial intelligence is the potential for massive unemployment. Intelligent machines can replace humans in many tasks, especially with mental and physical strength, and will cause some people to be laid off. A research report from the University of Oxford in the United Kingdom stated that more than 700 occupations will be replaced by intelligent machines, of which the sales, administration, and service industries will be the first to bear [12].

It has been proposed that an artificial intelligence will surpass humans in many tasks over the years as shown in Table 12.1 [30].

Table 12.1   Tasks in which artificial intelligence will exceed humans over time.

Task	Language translation	Writing an essay	Driving a truck	Retail job	Writing a bestseller	Autonomous surgery
Year	2024	2026	2027	2031	2049	2053

(3) Political security

The increasing use of artificial intelligence for political advocacy has created geopolitical inequality and imbalances. In some Western countries, information dissemination before the elections was mainly carried out through leaflets and posters. Today, this type of information is mainly disseminated in digital form, including the use of advanced technologies such as artificial intelligence to influence voters' opinions. For example, with the wealth of data provided by Facebook, the characteristics of potential voters and even the emotions they experience can be determined. Two examples of this manipulation supported by Facebook's huge data are the 2016 Brexit referendum and the US presidential election of the same year [24].

(4) Ethical security

Ethical issues of artificial intelligence have attracted the attention of society, and the advancement of artificial intelligence technology may bring significant risk to human society. For example, in the field of service robots, the risks and ethical concerns are mainly related to the care of children and the elderly and the development of autonomous robotic weapons. Companion robots can provide children with a pleasant experience and stimulate their curiosity. However, the child must be taken care of by an adult, and the companion robot is not qualified to be the child's caregiver. If a child spends too much time with a companion robot, it will cause the child to lack social ability and cause the child to be socially isolated to varying degrees.

Applying military robots also raises some ethical issues. For instance, ground-armed robots are used or missiles are fired by drones and unmanned vehicles during the battle, causing casualties to the opposing soldiers and even innocent people. Weapons are generally lethal strikes under human control; however, military robots can autonomously lock down and attack targets and destroy their lives.

The use of artificial intelligence media and the Internet to expose personal privacy and violate the privacy and personality rights enjoyed by natural persons is another type of ethical issue that cannot be ignored. The Internet and artificial intelligence platforms for "human flesh search" often cause victims to commit suicide [21].

(5) Legal security

The development and application of intelligent machines has brought many unprecedented legal problems, and traditional laws are facing severe challenges. What new legal issues have arisen? Please see the examples below.

Who is responsible for the accident in a driverless car? Traffic regulations may be fundamentally rewritten. For another example, does it violate international conventions when robots shoot and kill people on the battlefield? With the improvement of intelligent machines' thinking ability, they may put forward opinions on society and life, and even political opinions. These problems can be dangerous and disturbing to human society.

A "Robot Judge" can automatically generate an optimal judgment result by analyzing the existing data. The jobs that will face the same unemployment threats by judges include teachers, lawyers, and artists. Many works today can be created by intelligent machines, and even press releases can be written by reporter robots. Intelligent software systems can also compose and draw. Existing laws related to the protection of intellectual property rights may be subverted. In the age of artificial intelligence, law will also reshape the requirements for occupations, and legal concepts will be rebuilt. Soon, "Robots must not harm humans" will be written into labor protection laws at the same time as "Humans must not abuse robots."

In addition, in the medical field, there are safety problems in the responsibility of medical accidents caused by the use of medical robots, and in the field of law enforcement that robot police perform police functions. How should these issues be considered and addressed? Therefore, several related legal issues need to be resolved. Several liability issues and security issues of artificial intelligence products in the legal field need to be taken seriously and dealt with as early as possible. Robot developers must bear legal responsibility for their smart products [28].

(6) Military security

With the continuous development of artificial intelligence and intelligent machines, research institutions and military organizations in some countries have tried to use artificial intelligence technology (unmanned systems) for military purposes, and research and development and use of intelligent weapons, which has caused tremendous harm to human society and world peace.

For example, during the wars in Iraq and Afghanistan, the United States deployed more than 5,000 remote-controlled robots and some heavily armed robots for reconnaissance, demining, and direct operations. Ground-armed robots and intelligent armed drones not only killed many enemy soldiers, but also caused many casualties among innocent civilians.

People have expressed great concern and resolute opposition to the development and use of intelligent weapons. In August 2017, Elongation Musk gathered with 116 CEOs and artificial intelligence researchers from 26 countries to sign an open letter requesting the United Nations to ban the use of artificial intelligence weapons [20]. The open letter contains an important narrative: "Once deadly autonomous weapons are developed, they will make the scale of the armed conflict more than ever before, and the timetable will be faster than humans can understand. Once this Pandora's Box is destroyed it is difficult to turn it on. Therefore, we urge States parties to the United Nations to find a way to protect us all from these dangers."

A similar open letter was issued by Professor Toby Walsh of the University of New South Wales, Australia, admonishing countries to oppose a military-based artificial intelligence arms race. The open letter has been signed by 3,150 researchers in the field of robotics and artificial intelligence, along with 17,701 others.

In order to prevent the application of intelligent weapons, Max Tegmark, founder of the Future Life Institute, urged everyone to participate in "safety engineering", ban the use of lethal autonomous weapons, and ensure the peaceful use of artificial intelligence by humans [1].

(7) Cognitive security

The comprehensive development of artificial intelligence and its deep integration with the real economy, so that artificial intelligence will promote all walks of life and enter millions of households, will change people's traditional ideas and thinking modes, and even reduce their cognitive ability. For example, in the Go game between AlphaGo and international Go players, artificial intelligence and human thinking are fundamentally different, which has changed the nature of the Go game and the traditional thinking paradigm of the human Go game [27]. As another example, students and adults who rely too much on computers will significantly reduce their active computing and independent thinking skills.

In the past, traditional knowledge printed on books, newspapers, or magazines was fixed, but the knowledge in the knowledge base of artificial intelligence systems can be constantly modified and updated. Once the users of the intelligent system overly believe in the recommendations of the artificial intelligence system, they may be reluctant to use their brains and will trust the intelligent system, which will reduce their cognitive abilities. They may even gradually lose their initiative in solving problems and their sense of responsibility for tasks. The in-depth application of artificial intelligence may also make relevant scientific and technical personnel lose the opportunity to intervene in problem solving and information processing, and may change their thinking and working methods in a subtle way.

(8) Technical security

History fully proves that if any high-tech technique is not well controlled or goes out of control, it will bring great danger to humankind. As is well known, the achievements of chemical science are used to make chemical weapons; the achievements of biology are used to make biological weapons; major advances in nuclear physics research have led to the threat of nuclear weapons. Now some people worry that intelligent machines will one day force their creators — humans to accept their enslavement, threatening human safety [2].

More dangerous than biochemical and nuclear technology, artificial intelligence technology is an information technology that can be transmitted and copied extremely quickly. Therefore, there is greater risk than "explosion" technology; that is, if artificial intelligence technology falls into the hands of extremists and the like, then they will use artificial intelligence technology for criminal activities against humanity and society [13, 15].

12.2 Deep Fusion of Artificial Intelligence Technology

Knowledge is the source of artificial intelligence, data is the basis of artificial intelligence, and algorithms are the soul of artificial intelligence. In the development process of artificial intelligence, they have become the core elements of artificial intelligence alone or together, and have played an important role in the development of artificial intelligence. With the further development and widespread application of artificial intelligence, it is difficult for a single artificial intelligence technology to meet high target requirements, and the integration (fusion) of different artificial intelligence technologies has become inevitable for the historical development of artificial intelligence. This section lists several examples to illustrate the deep integration of artificial intelligence technology.

12.2.1 *Fusion of artificial intelligence technology in machine learning*

Machine learning is an important area for the integration of artificial intelligence technologies. Although this book divides machine learning into "knowledge-based artificial intelligence" and "data-based artificial intelligence" for discussion, many artificial intelligence research studies still show the integration of knowledge, data, and algorithms, i.e., technology fusion. Among them, Knowledge Discovery in Database (KDD), referred to as "knowledge discovery" for short, is a typical example.

Knowledge acquisition is a bottleneck of intelligent information processing. With the development and widespread application of database technology and computer network technology, knowledge acquisition faces new opportunities and challenges. The amount of data stored in databases and computer networks around the world, which can be called massive data, is extremely large and growing. Although the database system provides management and general processing of these data, and can carry out certain scientific research and commercial analysis on these data, it is difficult to effectively process and apply such huge data by manual processing. People need to adopt new ideas and technologies to carry out advanced processing of data to find and discover certain rules and patterns in order to better find useful information and help companies, scientific communities, and government departments to make correct decisions. Database knowledge discovery can extract the knowledge hidden in massive data by analyzing the data and its relationship.

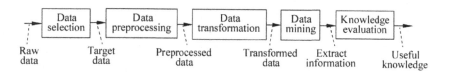

Figure 12.1 Knowledge discovery process.

Definition 12.1. KDD is the nontrivial process of identifying valid, novel, potentially useful, and ultimately understandable patterns in data.

In short, knowledge discovery is a process of identifying new knowledge through a large amount of data, and a process of deep fusion of data and knowledge.

Figure 12.1 shows the knowledge discovery process given by Fayyad in 1996 [19].

This process is to identify useful knowledge through a large amount of data in the database.

12.2.2 Fusion of AI technology in deep reinforcement learning

As discussed in the previous chapters of this book, reinforcement learning is a knowledge-based machine learning method that has decision-making capabilities but is helpless with perceptual problems; deep learning is a data-based machine learning method with strong perception, but lacks decision-making ability. Deep reinforcement learning is a machine learning method based on the fusion of knowledge and data. It combines the perceptual ability of deep learning with the decision-making ability of reinforcement learning. It can be controlled directly based on the input image. The intelligent method provides a new solution for the perception and decision-making of complex systems.

(1) Principle framework of the deep reinforcement learning system

Deep reinforcement learning (DRL) is an end-to-end perception and control system, which has strong generality. The learning process is shown in Figure 12.2. It can be described as follows:

(i) At each moment, the learning system interacts with the environment to obtain a high-dimensional observation, and uses the DL method to perceive this observation to obtain specific state feature representations, such as context feature representations.

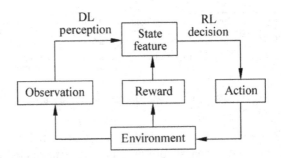

Figure 12.2   Block diagram of deep reinforcement learning.

(ii) Evaluate the value function of each action based on the expected return, and map the current state characteristics to the corresponding action through some RL decision strategy.

(iii) The environment reacts to this action and gets the next new observation. By continuously cycling the above process, the optimal strategy can be finally obtained to achieve the goals.

It can be seen from the structure of the deep reinforcement learning system that deep reinforcement learning has both the perceptual ability of deep learning and the decision-making ability of reinforcement learning, which reflects the fusion of data-based learning and knowledge-based learning.

(2) Deep reinforcement learning based on convolutional neural networks

Deep reinforcement learning based on convolutional neural networks is a type of deep reinforcement learning that is widely used. Because convolutional neural networks have natural advantages for image processing, the combination of data-based convolutional neural networks and knowledge-based reinforcement learning to process image data's perceptual decision-making tasks is a typical example of the integration of different machine learning technologies and has become a subject of research focus.

(3) Deep reinforcement learning based on recurrent neural networks

Deep reinforcement learning based on recurrent neural networks is another type of widely used deep reinforcement learning. The problems faced by deep reinforcement learning often have strong time dependence, and recurrent neural networks are suitable for dealing with problems related to time series. Reinforcement learning and recurrent neural networks complement each other's advantages, and deep integration has become the main form of deep reinforcement learning.

12.2.3 Fusion of deep learning and traditional artificial intelligence technology

Not only is there a fusion of many different artificial intelligence technologies in machine learning, but also there is a common fusion of knowledge-based artificial intelligence and data-based artificial intelligence in other areas of artificial intelligence, such as natural language processing, expert systems, automatic planning, and database optimization.

(1) Natural language processing

At the same time as different views were being debated in various fields of artificial intelligence, from the late 1980s to the early 1990s the natural language processing academia was based on syntactic–semantic rules (knowledge) rationalism and based on models and statistics (data) empiricism; the two perspectives were opposing each other and were endlessly debated. It was not until the last 10 years or so that they calmed down from the vague debate and started to realize that irrespective of whether it is rationalism or empiricism, it is impossible to solve the complex problem of natural language processing alone; the establishment of a new integrated theoretical method is the main route of natural language processing research. Gone are the days when the rationalist and the empirical "rule in turn" controlled the situation of natural language processing research.

(2) Expert system

An expert system is a traditional field of knowledge-based artificial intelligence. For more than 10 years, machine learning methods based on the fusion of data and knowledge have been widely used in the development of expert systems. The use of multi-layer neural networks such as convolutional neural networks, recurrent neural networks, and generative adversarial networks to represent abstract data to build computing models has completely changed the face of expert system information processing. Many expert systems based on machine learning, especially deep reinforcement learning, have played an important role in fault detection and diagnosis, data and image analysis, robot control systems, market prediction, social network analysis and prediction, medical question answering systems, information retrieval, and recommendation system classification. Natural language is the most direct way to represent knowledge; therefore, expert systems have also evolved from the integration of natural language processing to provide a new way to acquire knowledge.

(3) Automatic planning

Deep reinforcement learning can effectively solve the path planning problem of continuous state space and action space. It can directly use the original data as input and use the output result as the execution function to achieve the end-to-end learning mode, which greatly improves the efficiency and convergence of the planning algorithm. In recent years, DRL has also been widely used in the planning, control, and navigation of robot control, intelligent driving, and traffic control. Deep reinforcement learning is also widely applied to the underlying planning and control of moving bodies (robots). Robot path planning based on deep reinforcement learning in unknown environments, autonomous path planning for unmanned ships based on deep reinforcement learning, agent obstacle avoidance and path planning based on deep reinforcement learning, intelligent vehicle model migration trajectory planning based on deep reinforcement learning, four-rotor aircraft low-level control based on deep reinforcement learning, etc., are all representative successful applications.

12.3 Industrialization of Artificial Intelligence

This section first reviews the historical development stages of international artificial intelligence industrialization, discusses the main areas of current artificial intelligence industrialization, summarizes the current status of artificial intelligence industrialization, and finally analyzes the development trend of artificial intelligence industrialization, with the aim of giving a more comprehensive understanding of artificial intelligence industrialization.

12.3.1 *Current status of AI industrialization*

After analyzing and summarizing the published report data and various perspectives, the status and characteristics of artificial intelligence development in the world's major economically developed countries are summarized [9, 14, 33–35].

(1) Foundation of industrialization and significant increase in number of enterprises

In recent years, the number of international artificial intelligence companies has grown rapidly, with the United States leading the way, and China and the European Union faring equally. As of 2017, global artificial intelligence companies were concentrated in the United States (2,905, accounting for 48.11%), China (670, accounting for 11.10%), and the European Union (657, accounting for 10.8%). The total of the three accounts for 70.01%. By March 2019, the number of Chinese and American companies changed significantly, with the United States falling to 40.3% and China rising to 22.1%. From the end of 2017 to the first quarter of 2019, the gap between the two narrowed from 37.0% to 18.2% in the past two years.

(2) The investment and financing environment is unprecedentedly promising

In terms of financing scale, the artificial intelligence industry is also the largest in the United States, followed by Europe and China. Artificial intelligence has become one of the most popular investment fields in 2017. The United States has the most (US$4.54 billion), accounting for 42%, followed by Europe (US$2.02 billion) and China (US$1.83 billion), accounting for 18.7% and 16.9%, respectively, which together account for approximately 78%. By March 2019, the proportion of Sino-US investment and financing had changed greatly: the United States had dropped to 36.5%, and China had increased to 23.5%. From the end of 2017 to the first quarter of 2019, the gap between the two narrowed from 25.1% to 13.0% in the past two years.

(3) Country policies promote industrial development opportunities

In the development of new generation artificial intelligence, various advanced science and technology powers compete to introduce national development strategies, which have provided unprecedented opportunities and fierce competition for the development of artificial intelligence in various countries and the world.

Among these artificial intelligence development strategies, the representative ones include the National Artificial Intelligence Research and Development Strategic Plan of the United States in 2016, the New Generation Artificial Intelligence Development Plan of China in 2017, and the European Union Artificial Intelligence of the European Union in 2018.

(4) Higher starting point of industrialization technology

The combination of artificial intelligence and big data, Internet, life science, and other technologies has promoted increasingly advanced and mature artificial intelligence technology, and increased the level of intelligence. The artificial intelligence industry can obtain more powerful and comprehensive technical support. Perceived intelligence and cognitive intelligence have begun to integrate organically, and the artificial intelligence industry is developing from "perceived intelligence" to "cognitive intelligence". Perceived intelligence involves technologies such as intelligent speech, pattern recognition, and natural language understanding, and already has a fairly mature scale of application foundation; however, cognitive intelligence requires anthropomorphic intelligence such as "artificial emotion" and "machine thinking", which is in further development and exploration; there is still a long way to go in terms of practical applications.

(5) Shortage of artificial intelligence talents

Artificial intelligence talents in countries around the world, including the United States, are in short supply, and the competition for high-end artificial intelligence talents in the world is fierce. It is estimated that the annual salary of high-end artificial intelligence talents is about 3 million US dollars. China lacks talents in artificial intelligence, there must be at least one million artificial intelligence talents to meet the needs of China's comprehensive artificial intelligence development gap.

There is a need to ensure the sustainable development of the new generation of artificial intelligence industry internationally, and ensure that the new generation of artificial intelligence industry has a high starting point, large scale, high quality, and stable, rapid, and comprehensive development.

12.3.2 *Development trend of AI industrialization*

The driving force for the upgrading of the artificial intelligence industry stems from a comprehensive breakthrough in the core elements of artificial intelligence. The joint development of knowledge, data, algorithms, and computing power has made artificial intelligence more powerful and jointly promoted a new wave of artificial intelligence. After synthesizing and analyzing various viewpoints, we can obtain the following development trend of artificial intelligence industrialization [3, 16, 17, 26].

(1) Breakthrough in AI core technology promotes strong industrial development

The business model dividends formed by the development of information technology are gradually disappearing, calling for a new generation of innovative technologies to drive the full upgrade of business models. As an innovative technology, artificial intelligence will be applied to all walks of life, and promote the rapid development of traditional industries, and realize the transformation, upgrading, and reshaping of the entire industry. The accelerated breakthroughs in various core technologies of artificial intelligence have promoted the strong development of the artificial intelligence industry.

(2) Diversified development in the artificial intelligence industry

Most of the current applications of the artificial intelligence industry belong to specialized fields, such as human face recognition, voice recognition, video surveillance, etc., which are used to perform specific tasks. Their level of industrialization is relatively low and needs to be further improved. With the rise of industries such as intelligent manufacturing, intelligent robots, intelligent driving, machine learning, intelligent medical treatment, intelligent control, intelligent transportation, intelligent networks, and intelligent society, the artificial intelligence industry will face more complex environments and handle more complex technical issues. It is necessary to improve production efficiency more effectively and better improve people's quality of life; in other words, the application of artificial intelligence industrialization must develop from a single to a pluralistic one.

(3) The process of deep fusion of AI and the real economy has further accelerated

Traditional industries rely on the basic technology of artificial intelligence and data resources of various industries to implement the innovation and deep integration of artificial intelligence and the real economy, which has become another trend in the development of artificial intelligence. This integration will effectively promote fee reduction and transformation and upgrading in industries such as machinery manufacturing, transportation, healthcare, online shopping and retail, financial insurance, and home appliances. For example, in the field of intelligent manufacturing, in addition to mechanical manufacturing and electronic and electrical manufacturing, iron and steel metallurgy is also an important new field of intelligent manufacturing; new products and services for intelligent steel manufacturing will accelerate the cultivation of new kinetic energy for steel and metallurgy, and create new growth points of the steel industry, which in turn will promote structural optimization and industry upgrade of the steel industry [10].

(4) Intelligent service mode appears to seamlessly combine online and offline

The widespread application of distributed computing platforms of artificial intelligence has expanded the scope of online services. At the same time, the strong development of artificial intelligence industrialization has provided new ways and new communication modes for intelligent services, thereby accelerating the integration process of offline services and online services and promoting the transformation and upgrading of more industries to intellectualization.

(5) Gradually realize the layout of the entire industry chain

The growth in economic strength of various countries and the advancement of basic technology of artificial intelligence can ensure the realization of the entire artificial intelligence industry, chain layout, including the basic artificial intelligence industry, technology industry, and application industry, and lay a solid foundation for the comprehensive realization of artificial intelligence development goals and the construction of a strong intelligent country basis.

(6) Speed up the training of AI talents at all levels

High-quality artificial intelligence talents at all levels are the first resource for artificial intelligence foundation and industrial development. There is a serious shortage of artificial intelligence talent in countries around the world, and China is no exception. For example, in 2005, a discipline named intelligent science and technology (very close to AI) was started at Peking University, and in 2020 there were 183 universities in the country that had set up the discipline; 215 universities have also developed the discipline of artificial intelligence. In total, 386 universities have AI and Intelligent science and technology disciplines in China. It is predicted that this number will be more than 500 at the end of 2021. Thousands of doctoral and master's degrees and tens of thousands of undergraduates in the field of artificial intelligence have been trained nationwide so far, becoming the backbone of China's development of artificial intelligence. Artificial intelligence colleges and artificial intelligence training bases are also emerging in large numbers. The training of high-quality artificial intelligence talents has been accelerated through multiple modes and multiple channels; there should be few high-level talents at the top level, solid and strong talents at the middle level, and many strong talents at the bottom level. It is necessary to make full use of big data and Internet technologies, develop and improve artificial intelligence online teaching platforms, and provide online education services for artificial intelligence teaching at all levels.

(7) Focus on the development of AI sharing platforms

In the process of developing artificial intelligence, major developed countries in the world attach great importance to the construction of artificial intelligence development platforms [18, 37]. This development platform should be highly open and fully shared, and open to various fields of artificial intelligence research, development, and application, so that artificial intelligence technology personnel around the world can realize artificial intelligence resource sharing. This artificial intelligence platform should also be comprehensive and extensive, with the most authoritative, complete, and advanced artificial intelligence system connotation, capable of providing technical support and information consultation in various areas of artificial intelligence. However, building such an advanced artificial intelligence sharing platform will require the cooperation of various countries and longer time.

(8) Step up the research and construction of artificial intelligence law [12, 32]

Faced with the legal, moral, and ethical issues caused by the development of artificial intelligence, the artificial intelligence technology community, the legal community, and the legislative and law enforcement agencies have already begun to pay attention to artificial intelligence legislation, and some countries or regions have also formulated relevant laws. For example, the state of Nevada in the United States has regulations for driverless vehicles, and many countries have legislation prohibiting the development of anthropomorphic robots or clones. Some countries, including China, are studying artificial intelligence legislative issues and ethical issues, and planning to control issues as much as possible in the research and development and design stages, especially in the software development and algorithm debugging stages. Never allow artificial intelligence itself or people with ulterior motives to use artificial intelligence technology to endanger human interests and security. We must do everything possible to ensure human trust and security in artificial intelligence technology.

The new era of artificial intelligence industrialization has obvious characteristics and great advantages such as high starting point, large scale, and excellent quality, which can ensure the stable, rapid, and comprehensive development of the new generation of artificial intelligence industrialization. The domestic and foreign artificial intelligence industry is developing steadily in the direction of strengthening, diversification, globalization, deep integration with the real economy, and seamless integration between offline and online. It will serve the country, benefit the people, and create huge social and economic benefits. We must seize the opportunities, give full play to potential advantages, vigorously cultivate artificial intelligence talents, and continue to develop the artificial intelligence industry, to make positive contributions to basic research on artificial intelligence, scientific and technological progress, and industrial development, and to develop the national economy and improve people's lives.

References

1. Anthony, A. and Max, T. (2017). Machines taking control doesn't have to be a bad thing, *The Guardian*, September 16, 2017.
2. Surging News. (2019). Artificial Intelligence vs. Software and hardware security issues, (in Chinese), September 12, 2019, http://www.elecfans.com/d/1070447.html.
3. AVIC Love Maker (2018). Data uncovering: current situation and development trend of artificial intelligence industry, October 7, 2018, https://baijiahao.baidu.com/s?id=1613631463295530028&wfr=spider&for=pc.
4. Bacchi, U. (2016). Artificial intelligence could now help us end poverty, *Huffington Post*, August 19, 2016, https://www.huffingtonpost.com/entry/artificial-intelligence-satellite-images-locate-povery-researchers_us_57b71211e4b0b51733a2dd20.
5. BBC. (2017). Psychologists claim social media, increases loneliness, March 06, 2017, http://www.bbc.com.uk/newsbeat/article/39176828/us-psychlogists-claim-social-media-increases-loneliness.
6. Beijing Internet of Things Intelligent Technology Application Association (2018). How does artificial intelligence promote the transformation and upgrading of traditional enterprises? March 12, 2018, https://www.sohu.com/a/225339445_487612.
7. Cai, Z.X., Liu, L.J., Cai, J.F. and Chen, B.F. (2020). *Artificial Intelligence and Its Applications*, 6th Edition, (Tsinghua University Press, Beijing, in Chinese).
8. Cai, Z.X. and Xu Guangyou. (2004). *Artificial Intelligence and Its Applications*, 3rd Edition, Postgraduate Books, Chapter 12, (Tsinghua University Press, Beijing, in Chinese).
9. Cai, Z.X. (2016). 40 years of artificial intelligence in China, *Science & Technology Review*, 34(15): 12–32; doi: 10.3981/j.issn.1000-7857.2016.15.001, (in Chinese).

10. Cai, Z.X. (2015). Application of artificial intelligence in metallurgical automation, *Metallurgical Automation*, *39*(1): 1–5, (in Chinese).
11. Cai, Z.X. (1987). Quiet Chang, *China Youth Daily*, July 4, 1987, (in Chinese).
12. Cai, Z.X. (2017). Social issues of artificial intelligence, *Unity*, (6): 20–27, (in Chinese).
13. Cai, Z.X. (1995). The profound influence of artificial intelligence on human being, *High Technology Letters*, *5*(6): 55–57, (in Chinese).
14. China Finance and Economics (2018). Artificial intelligence expands new industry space, http://finance.china.com.cn/industry/20181112/4806283. shtml, (in Chinese).
15. China Information Security Editorial Department. (2015). Artificial intelligence, angel or devil?, *China Information Security*, (9): 50–53, (in Chinese).
16. China Science and Technology Policy Research Center, Tsinghua University. (2018). China Economic Report: Current Status and Future of Artificial Intelligence in China, October 11, 2018, http://www.sohu.com/a/258848488_ 468723, (in Chinese).
17. CIC Investment Consulting Network. Analysis of the development status and prospects of China's artificial intelligence industry (2018), http://www.ocn.com. cn/touzi/chanye/201807/zmslu26085929.shtml, (in Chinese).
18. Curiosity Institute (2015). Google opened its own artificial intelligence platform, what can it do? November 11, 2015, http://www.qdaily.com/articles/17361. html.
19. Fayyad, U.M., Piatetsky-Shapiro, G. and Smyth, P. *et al.* (eds). (1996). *Advances in Knowledge Discovery and Data Mining*. Cambridge, MA: AAAI/MIT Press.
20. Future of Life Institute. An open letter to the United Nations Convention on Certain Conventional Weapons, (2017). *LA Times*, August 21, 2017, https:// futureoflife.org/autonomous-weapons-open-letter-2017.
21. Future of Life Institute (2017). Asilmar AI Principles, https://futureoflife.org/ ai-principles.
22. Future Think Tanks (2018). Inexplicable fear of artificial intelligence, July 5, 2018, https://www.7428.cn/vipzj21113/.
23. Gershgorn, D. (2017). The Quartz guide to artificial intelligence: What is it, why is it important, and should we be afraid?, *Quartz*, September 10, 2017, https://qz.com/1046350/the-quartz-guide-to-artificial-intelligence-ce-what-is-it-why-is-it-important-and-should-we-be-afraid.
24. Guimon, P. (2018). Brexit wouldn't have happened without Cambridge Analytica, *El Pais*, March 27, 2018, https://elpais.com/elpais/2018/03/27/inenglish/ 1522142310_757589.html.
25. Hawking, S. (2013). Artificial intelligence may make humans extinct, *Going to the World*, (1): 13. https://www.theguardian.com/technology/2017/sep/16/ ai-will-superintelligent-computer-replace-us-robots-max-tegmark-life-3-0.
26. Jingxiong AI Frontier. (2018). 2018 In-depth Analysis Report on the Development of the World Artificial Intelligence Industry Blue Book, http://www.sohu. com/a/282485963_100143859.
27. Lei, J.P. (2016). End of man–machine war: AlphaGo defeats Li Shishi 4:1, *Tencent Technology*, March 15, 2016, http://tech.qq.com/a/20160315/049899. htm.

28. Liu, J.Y. and Liu, H. (2019) Legal Issues Facing the Era of Artificial Intelligence, Not Alone on the Road to Law Exam. https://mp.weixin.qq.com/s?src=11&timestamp=1573111511&ver=1959&signature=z9T9dUK4nz SEic*x8bBHBN*X-esXHTReKRQttiK64t1wSwc2xQwPRO3JvpMpqP8WCgsw uq1X40iiin9VVwW9iOsV409dZrVCGu-9w2RGx094zYmukyNjBEnh6P0fM0-o&new=1.

29. Nurminen, N. (2017). Could artificial intelligence lead to world peace? May 30, 2017, http://www.aljazeera.com/indepth/features/2017/05/scientist-race-build-peace-machine-170509112307430.html.

30. Rouhiainen, L. (2019). *Artificial Intelligence: 101 Things You Must Know Today about Our Future* (CreateSpace Independent Publishing Platform).

31. Rouhianen, L. (2016). The future of higher education: How emerging technologies will change education forever, *Amazon*, October 10, 2016, https://www.amazon.com/future-higher-education-emerging-technologies/dp/15394 50139.

32. Situ, M.Q. and Liu, Z.F. (2017). Artificial intelligence and ethics, *Chinese Information Technology Education*, 17: 55–59, (in Chinese).

33. Sohu. (2018). Analysis of the development status of the artificial intelligence industry, technological breakthroughs and application demonstrations are accelerating, http://www.sohu.com/a/241938808_473133.

34. Sohu. (2018). Artificial intelligence health: What is the development of the artificial intelligence industry? http://www.sohu.com/a/242209867_297710.

35. Sohu. (2018). Prospective economist. Analysis of the development status of the global artificial intelligence industry in 2018. http://www.sohu.com/a/242596348_100014972.

36. Xiang. (2018). Encyclopedia users, Editorial of Need for Chinese clothing. Fear of artificial intelligence, Sogou Encyclopedia, https://www.sogou.com/tx?query=%E4%BA%BA%E5%B7%A5%E6%99%BA%E8%83%BD%E6%81%90%E6%83%A7&hdq=sogou-site-706608cfdbcc1886&ekv=3&ie=utf8&.

37. Xinhua Net. (2015). Li Yanhong: Hope to build the world's largest artificial intelligence development platform, http://news.xinhuanet.com/politics/2015lh/2015-03/11/c_134057584.htm.

Epilogue

In the process of writing this book, in addition to discussing artificial intelligence technology issues, as authors, we also bluntly published many other opinions about artificial intelligence. We focused on artificial intelligence especially in this last chapter. Whether it involves the discussion of the future impact of artificial intelligence on human society, economy, and culture, or the analysis of deep integration of artificial intelligence technology, artificial intelligence industrialization, and artificial intelligence security, we do not shy away from expressing our views. While inadequacies are inevitable, I hope to stimulate discussion and correct any erroneous views.

We are optimistic about the development prospects of artificial intelligence and believe that artificial intelligence will have a better tomorrow. Although that day may be far away, many large and small problems need to be solved to overcome the numerous difficulties and obstacles. The arrival of this day requires hard work and expensive costs as well as generations of artificial intelligence people who continue to struggle.

With the joint effort of the four authors, the preparation of our new book on artificial intelligence has been completed. The Goose Mountain that my study faces is not only a blessed place of natural beauty from the past, but has developed into the small and famous E'yang Mountain Park Natural Scenic Area. The Moon Island, which is separated by the Xiangjiang River from the Goose Mountain, has changed from a deserted island into an artificial intelligence bliss world, namely, a smart amusement park featuring sports and entertainment, attracting tourists from all over the world.

Readers and friends are welcome to visit E'yang Mountain and Moon Island to enjoy the happiness of the natural scenery and the entertainment world.

Index

neural network (NN), 6, 12, 178
   artificial neural networks, 11
   deep neural network, 12, 14, 144
   depth, 286
   dropout, 292
   feedforward neural network, 15
   layered neural networks, 15
   multi-scale convolutional neural
     networks, 330
   multilayer neural network, 12, 286
   recurrent neural network, 15
   synthetic neural network, 296
neuron, 9, 183
   biological neurons, 15
neuron model, 183
Newell, Allen, 6, 7
Newton, 177
Ng, Andrew, 144, 429
Nilsson, N. J., 349
node, 38, 39, 56, 70
   AND nodes, 44
   goal node, 110
   leaf nodes, 108
   matching sub-goal literal node,
     113
   most promising nodes, 92
   node extension, 90
   OR nodes, 44
   parent node, 38, 43, 110
   root node, 264
   situation node, 59
   successor node, 44, 91
nonlinear model, 273
nonlinear mapping, 181
nonlinear transformations, 287
numbers, 5

objective function, 270
   minimization objective function,
     270
objective function value, 218
observation
   high-dimensional observation,
     503
observation statement, 152

odor zone, 374
offspring, 217
ontology, 21, 35, 48, 51, 52, 55, 63, 68
   automated ontology, 68
   common sense ontology, 52
   domain ontology, 53
   extension-level ontology, 54
   knowledge representation
     ontology, 52
   middle-level ontology, 54
   ontology concepts, 54
   ontology construction, 68
   ontology description language, 55
   ontology engineering, 53
   ontology model, 53
   ontology modeling process, 54
   ontology of linguistics, 53
   ontology prototypes, 53
   ontology technology, 56
   task ontology, 53
   top-level ontology, 54
operations
   symbolic operations, 11
operator, 36, 39, 450
   reducing redundant cluster
     operator, 231, 249
   repair operator, 212
optima
   "known" optima, 222
   global optima, 220
optimal path, 371
optimization, 17
   ant colony optimization, 370
   constrained optimization, 214
   database optimization, 505
   multi-objective optimization, 215,
     217
optimization problem, 207
   constrained optimization
     problems, 207, 213, 249
   discrete optimization problem,
     241
   multi-objective optimization
     problems, 207, 223, 249

Printed in the United States
by Baker & Taylor Publisher Services